MW00527007

"One of the ways of demonstrating t.. _____
to understand the conversations and debates from which they emerged. John Fesko has done precisely this. Digging around each plant in the Westminster garden, Fesko exposes the rich soil that still nourishes our faith and practice. I picked up this book expecting to find a resource to be consulted, but found myself reading the whole work through with rapt attention. There is gold in these hills!"

Michael Horton, J. Gresham Machen Professor of Systematic Theology and Apologetics, Westminster Seminary California; author, *Calvin on the Christian Life*

"Finally we have a solid analysis and an expert portrayal of the theology of the Westminster Standards in which the time of its writing and its direct influence are also described. John Fesko has gathered an enormous amount of information that makes this book a sourcebook par excellence. He does the church and its theology a great favor with this overview, helping us to understand the Westminster Confession and catechisms not only in their theological context, but also in their relevance for today."

Herman Selderhuis, Professor of Church History, Theological University of Apeldoorn; Director, Refo500, The Netherlands

"Drawing upon a significant body of recent research, John Fesko has written an admirably clear and accessible study of the teaching of the Westminster Confession. By situating the successive chapters in their original seventeenth-century setting, he provides an informed exposition of their content and significance. This study will be immensely useful not only for theological students, but for all who require a better understanding of the most important Reformed confession in the English-speaking world."

David Fergusson, Professor of Divinity and Principal, New College, University of Edinburgh

"Seldom has an exposition of the Westminster Standards been as useful as John Fesko's *Theology of the Westminster Standards*. Dr. Fesko understands the necessity of placing these monumental documents in their proper contexts. He has uncovered a massive amount of contemporary literature and expertly explains the theological statements of the Standards in the light of these works. For everyone interested in confessionalism, this is an essential volume. It will be a standard work for decades to come."

James M. Renihan, Dean and Professor of Historical Theology, Institute of Reformed Baptist Studies

"Fesko's volume is an outstanding and very welcome addition to the growing field of literature on the Westminster Confession of Faith. In these pages Fesko goes straight to the primary sources, skillfully mining relevant sixteenth- and seventeenth-century texts in order to explain the historical and theological developments leading up to the assembly. Moreover, he provides fresh and insightful analysis of the theology of the Confession itself. Do you want to grow in your knowledge and understanding of the Reformed faith in general, and the theology of the Westminster Confession in particular? If the answer is yes, then pick up and read this marvelous book. I heartily commend it!"

Jon D. Payne, Presbyterian Church in America church planter, Charleston, South Carolina; Visiting Lecturer, Reformed Theological Seminary; Series Editor, *Lectio Continua* Expository Commentary on the New Testament

The Theology of the Westminster Standards

The

THEOLOGY

of the

WESTMINSTER

STANDARDS

HISTORICAL CONTEXT AND
THEOLOGICAL INSIGHTS

J. V. FESKO

CROSSWAY

WHEATON, ILLINOIS

Published by Crossway
        1300 Crescent Street
        Wheaton, Illinois 60187

Cover design: Dual Identity, inc.

Cover images: The Bridgeman Art Library

First printing 2014

Printed in the United States of America

Trade paperback ISBN: 978-1-4335-3311-2
PDF ISBN: 978-1-4335-3312-9
Mobipocket ISBN: 978-1-4335-3313-6
ePub ISBN: 978-1-4335-3314-3

Library of Congress Cataloging-in-Publication Data
Fesko, J. V., 1970–
  The theology of the Westminster standards : historical
context and theological insights / J. V. Fesko.
    pages cm
  Includes bibliographical references and index.
  ISBN 978-1-4335-3311-2 (tp)
  1. Westminster Confession of Faith. 2. Reformed
Church—Doctrines. I. Title.
BX9183.F47   2014
238'.5—dc23   2013041373

Crossway is a publishing ministry of Good News Publishers.

VP		24	23	22	21	20	19	18	17	16	15	14
15	14	13	12	11	10	9	8	7	6	5	4	3	2	1

To W. Robert Godfrey,
defensor fidei reformata

Contents

Preface

Ever since I first heard about the Westminster Standards—the Confession and the Larger and Shorter Catechisms—I began to study and read them with great interest and appreciation. During my days in seminary, when I found myself having to defend what was for me the newly discovered Reformed faith, I found the Confession to be immensely helpful in its explanation of the various doctrines of the Bible. The more I read, the more I realized that there was much to be learned from these documents. After further academic preparation in graduate school, I set out to write a line-by-line commentary on the Confession, a task I soon discovered was like trying to scale Mount Everest without the proper equipment. Not only was each line of the Confession loaded with dense theological significance, but also I routinely found myself running into dead ends because I was unable to consult numerous primary sources that were nestled in footnotes. I realized that writing the type of commentary I wanted would require a lot of financial resources, either to purchase seventeenth-century works or at least to travel to libraries around the world to gain access to them. I eventually decided that my goal, for the time being, was unattainable, and so I set the project aside for another day.

Nearly a decade would pass before I saw the light of opportunity dawn when I noticed several technological developments. The first was the discovery of Early English Books Online, which afforded me access to an abundant number of sixteenth- and seventeenth-century theological works. The second were the libraries around the world, in addition to Google's project of scanning old books, that opened a new window of opportunity; this was especially true when the Post-

Reformation Digital Library (www.prdl.org) was launched. The PRDL is a tremendous resource that gave me access to virtually every conceivable work I could desire, and what was even better, I could now download these works to my computer or iPad and read and study numerous early modern theological works. I have to admit that I do miss sitting in a special-collections room, carefully turning the pages of an ancient tome, and walking away knowing that I have actually touched a piece of the seventeenth-century. However, what would once have cost tens of thousands of dollars in travel and expenditures for purchasing antiquarian books was now virtually free of charge.

I initially prepared my research for this book as the source material for a course that I teach at Westminster Seminary California on the Westminster Standards. The course was once an elective but is now required for all graduating seniors. I wanted to expose students to not only the theology of these documents but also their history, brilliance, and precision. At the same time, any honest exploration of history will quickly expose the weaknesses of those who wrote documents such as the Westminster Standards. I want to disabuse contemporary readers of the Westminster Standards of a saccharine view of history, one in which these documents were written in a golden age of piety and theology. History is messy, and the times are often complex. The more I study the historical context of the Westminster Standards, the more I am struck by the complexity and messiness of it all.

I am also impressed, however, by the truth of a medieval maxim, namely, that God draws straight lines with crooked sticks. In other words, as messy and complex as the seventeenth century was, the Westminster Standards are an amazing set of confessional documents. A testimony of their abiding worth is that many Reformed denominations still, hundreds of years later, profess and confess the Reformed faith as it is codified in the Westminster Standards.

Still, in my own ministry in the Orthodox Presbyterian Church, I have found that many in the church are unfamiliar with the rich history surrounding these documents, as well as the subtlety, beauty, and precision that mark them. I have sat on the floor of meetings of presbytery or general assembly and listened to ministers and elders appeal to these documents in an imprecise way. I have been guilty of this myself, which is one of the reasons I wanted to undertake a more deliberate and historically sensitive study of these documents—so that I could learn, study, and appreciate what my theological fore-bearers preserved for the church. The Westminster divines wrote their confession of faith and catechisms chiefly for the glory of God and the edification of the church. I have sought to study and document my research in this book toward the same two goals: *soli Deo gloria* and the edification of the church.

My hope and prayer is that people will benefit from this book in a number of ways. First, that ministers, elders, teachers, candidates for the ministry, and seminarians would have a resource where they can learn more about the Westminster Standards. These documents are rich and deep, and at times, given the passage of time, clouded in a certain degree of obscurity. Second, my desire would be that inter-ested laymen within the church would also be able to benefit from this book. Granted, those with theological training will have an easier time digesting its contents. I nevertheless believe that a patient reading of this book will profit anyone who is willing to invest the effort.

Third, I see this book not as an ending but as a beginning. Anyone who has carefully studied the Westminster Standards and the assem-bly that wrote them knows that there is a mountain of information, one that will occupy generations to come. In this regard, then, I see this book as an introduction to the subject, and one that is not exhaus-tive but illustrative of the theology of the early modern Reformed tra-dition. For this reason I have included a select annotated bibliography to encourage others to dive into the primary and secondary sources and do their own research.

Fourth, given that the Westminster Standards form the core of the Savoy Declaration (1658) and the Second London Confession (1689), the Congregational and Reformed Baptist versions of the Confession, I hope that this work proves useful and edifying for those beyond the various Presbyterian churches that employ the Confession and cat-echisms as their doctrinal standards. In the end, I have written this book for the church, that it might better understand the faith once delivered to the saints.

Readers should note several things about this book before they wade into it:

1. I cite the original 1646–1647 edition of the Confession, catechisms, and Directory for Public Worship published in a facsimile, *The Westminster Standards* (Audubon, NJ: Old Paths Publications, 1997). All references, unless otherwise noted, come from this edition.

2. The original edition of the catechisms did not number the questions. I have employed common numbering found in later editions for ease of reference.

3. Unless otherwise noted, all quoted confessions and catechisms are taken from Jaroslav Pelikan and Valerie Hotchkiss, *Creeds and Confessions of Faith in the Christian Tradition*, vol. 2 (New Haven, CT: Yale University Press, 2003).

4. For some, the repeated inclusion of life spans following theologians' names may seem tedious, but I believe it is vital to know when a theologian lived. The inclusion of these dates shows that numerous theologians between 1560 and 1640 were formative upon the expressions of the Standards. So in each chapter I provide the life span, birth, death, baptism date, or period in which each theologian flourished. I have obtained these dates from a number of sources, including Google and the *Dictionary of National Biography*, but chiefly through the PRDL. I have obtained the dates of a number of the Westminster divines from volume 1 of the *Minutes and Papers of the Westminster Assembly*, edited by Chad Van Dixhoorn, 5 vols. (Oxford: OUP, 2012).

5. Throughout this study I employ the term *divine* as shorthand for a member of the Westminster Assembly, even though this word was a common seventeenth-century term that simply meant "theologian."

6. All scriptural quotations are rendered as they appear in the sources I quote or are taken from the King James Bible. I have chosen to use the King James Version because it was the Bible commonly in use when the Westminster Standards were created.

7. Though early modernity covers 1500–1800, in this study I use the term primarily to cover the sixteenth and seventeenth centuries, and hence I refer to early modern Reformed theology.

8. The bulk of the references and citations from primary sources have been obtained directly from them. If I was alerted to an impor-

tant work by a secondary source, I place that secondary source in the footnote after the primary-source reference, which means I have consulted the primary source directly. All other references obtained from secondary sources are clearly marked by the phrase "as quoted in," or similar wording.

9. All foreign-language translations, unless otherwise indicated, are my own; the original-language quotation or phrase typically appears in the footnote.

10. Titles of works and publishers' names in early modern sources sometimes vary among citations or editions of the same work. I have not tried to reconcile all such instances or the diverse spellings of terms in quotations (including *then* for *than*), a common occurrence prior to the standardization of English spelling. Nor have I modernized spellings or supplied omitted apostrophes.

In the end, I hope that you, the reader, find this material as interesting, fascinating, and inspiring as I have. *Tolle et lege!* Take up and read!

Acknowledgments

A project of this magnitude and depth is not created in a vacuum and usually relies upon the kindness and long-suffering of colleagues and friends who read over drafts to ensure clarity, accuracy, and competency. This book is no exception to this rule, and therefore there are a number of people I want to thank for reading through early drafts: Ryan McGraw, Brent Ferry, John Muether, Nic Lazzereschi, Mike Horton, Jon Payne, Herman Selderhuis, Jim Renihan, David Fergusson, John Stovall, Brian Hecker, and Wally King. I am especially grateful to Dave VanDrunen for reading over the whole manuscript and making careful editorial and substantive suggestions. I have greatly benefited from the help of these friends and colleagues, but I alone bear the responsibility for any shortcomings or errors.

Thank you to my wife, Anneke, my lads, Val and Rob, and Carmen Penelope, whom my wife presently carries (and whom I hope to convince to like Princess Leia and a blaster rather than Barbie and her pink Corvette—that's at least what this scruffy nerf herder can hope for). I am thankful for your love, encouragement, prayers, and support. I hope that you, my children, will come to love and embrace the Reformed faith and that you will learn much from the Westminster Standards.

The first time I came across Bob Godfrey was at a Ligonier conference during the controversy surrounding Evangelicals and Catholics Together. As someone who was relatively new to the Reformed faith, I found Bob's lecture on Luther, the Reformation, and the doctrine of justification inspiring. I admired his gifts and, quite frankly, his moxie to herald boldly the scriptural teaching on *sola fide*. But this was not the first time Bob engaged challenges to the Reformed faith. During the days of the Shepherd controversy at Westminster Theological Seminary in Philadelphia, Bob spent some time in one of his classes addressing the doctrine of justification and concluded, "It seems to me much wiser to stay with the presentation of the doctrine as found in the Standards. And of course I argue that because I am convinced that the doctrines found in the Standards faithfully reflect the Scripture." Later in his ministry, in 1993, Bob was appointed as the third president of Westminster Seminary California, and in his inaugural address he told the gathered audience of the seminary's continued commitment to the Reformed confessions, not merely as historical artifacts and relics of tradition, but as vital and vibrant testimonies of the summarized teachings of Scripture.

Whether in the Shepherd controversy, Evangelicals and Catholics Together, or his role in the formation of the United Reformed Churches of North America, Bob has been a stouthearted defender of the Reformed faith. I am reminded of what King Leonidas and his vastly outnumbered Spartans told King Xerxes at the outset of the Battle of Thermopylae when ordered to surrender their weapons to the Persian armies: *molōn labe* ("come and take them"). What so many willingly surrender, Bob has firmly held in his grasp and let no one take. But at the same time, he has willingly and freely given away the Reformed faith to anyone who would ask. He has defended the Reformed faith from its critics, detractors, and wandering disciples, and has freely given it away to students and people in the church, to anyone willing to listen throughout his nearly forty-year ministry. Bob has done this because he not only loves the Reformed faith, but also loves Christ's bride, the church. So I can think of no other person to whom I would rather dedicate this book on the Westminster Standards. Thank you, Bob, for being a *defensor fidei reformata*, a defender of the Reformed faith.

Abbreviations

§ (*pl.* §§)	section, paragraph, or article
ACW	Ancient Christian Writers
ANF	*Ante-Nicene Fathers*
aphor.	aphorism
art.	article
Annotations	Westminster divines, *Annotations upon All the Books of the Old and New Testament* (London: Evan Tyler, 1657)
b.	born
bap.	baptized
BCP	Book of Common Prayer
BRJ	*British Reformed Journal*
ca.	*circa*
col(s).	column(s)
comm.	commenting on
CNTC	*Calvin's New Testament Commentaries*
CO	*Calvini Opera*
CR	*Corpus Reformatorum*
CTJ	*Calvin Theological Journal*
CUP	Cambridge University Press
d.	died

DLGTT	Richard A. Muller, *Dictionary of Latin and Greek Theological Terms* (Grand Rapids: Baker, 1986)
DPW	Directory for Public Worship
Dutch Annotations	Theodore Haak, ed., *The Dutch Annotations upon the Whole Bible* (London: John Rothwell, Joshua Kirton, and Richard Tomlins, 1657)
EEBO	Early English Books Online
epist.	epistle, letter
EQ	*Evangelical Quarterly*
fl.	flourished
fol(s).	folio(s)
HTR	*Harvard Theological Review*
IAOC	imputed active obedience of Christ
JEH	*Journal of Ecclesiastical History*
LC	Larger Catechism
LCC	Library of Christian Classics
LD	Lord's Day
loc.	*locus*
LW	*Luther's Works*, American Edition, ed. Jaroslav Pelikan and Helmut T. Lehmann, 55 vols. (Philadelphia: Muehlenberg and Fortress; St. Louis: Concordia, 1955–1986)
MAJT	*Mid-America Journal of Theology*
MP	member of Parliament
MPWA	Chad Van Dixhoorn, ed., *Minutes and Papers of the Westminster Assembly*, 5 vols. (Oxford: OUP, 2012)
MQR	*Mennonite Quarterly Review*
NPNF [1]	*Nicene Post-Nicene Fathers*, First Series

NPNF [2]	*Nicene Post-Nicene Fathers*, Second Series
obj.	objection
OUP	Oxford University Press
p. (*pl.* pp.)	page
PRDL	Post-Reformation Digital Library (www.prdl.org)
PRRD	Richard A. Muller, *Post-Reformation Reformed Dogmatics*, 4 vols. (Grand Rapids: Baker, 2003)
rep.	reply
RPW	regulative principle of worship
RTR	*Reformed Theological Review*
SBET	*Scottish Bulletin of Evangelical Theology*
SC	Shorter Catechism
SCJ	*Sixteenth Century Journal*
serm.	sermon
sess.	session
SJT	*Scottish Journal of Theology*
s.v.	*sub verbo* (under the term)
vol(s).	volume(s)
WCF	Westminster Confession of Faith
Werke	Martin Luther, *D. Martin Luthers Werke* (Berlin: Weimar, 1883–1929)
WJK	Westminster John Knox Press
WTJ	*Westminster Theological Journal*

1

Introduction

The Westminster Standards (1646–1647) are loved by many and employed as the confessional standards by numerous Presbyterian denominations around the world. The Confession and catechisms of the
Westminster Assembly have been praised by theologians, both in the
seventeenth century and in our own day, as being the high-water mark
of Reformed theology in the early modern period (ca. 1500–1800).
Given that the Westminster Standards are admired and confessed, it
is only natural that over the years theologians would write a number
of books that explained the doctrine of the Standards. Such works appeared quite quickly following the creation of the Standards. Most notable, for example, is David Dickson's (1583–1663) *Truths Victory over
Error*, or Thomas Watson's (ca. 1620–1686) *Body of Divinity*, which
was a series of sermons upon the Shorter Catechism.[1] Other notable
works include, but are not limited to, those by Thomas Boston (1676–
1732), A. A. Hodge (1823–1886), and Edward Morris (1825–1915).[2]
Theologians immediately saw a need to explain and comment upon
the Confession and catechisms. Other commentaries were written,
and the practice continues unabated in our own day, not only with the

---

[1] David Dickson, *Truths Victory over Error* (Edinburgh: John Reed, 1684); Thomas Watson, *A Body of Practical Divinity* (London: Thomas Parkhurst, 1692).
[2] Thomas Boston, *Body of Divinity*, vols. 1–2 in *Complete Works of Thomas Boston* (1853; Stoke-on-Trent: Tentmaker, 2002); A. A. Hodge, *The Confession of Faith: A Handbook of Christian Doctrine Expounding the Westminster Confession* (Edinburgh: Banner of Truth, 1958); Edward D. Morris, *Theology of the Westminster Standards: A Commentary Historical, Doctrinal, Practical on the Confession of Faith and Catechisms and the Related Formularies of the Presbyterian Churches* (Columbus, OH: n.p., 1900).

contribution of new commentaries but also with the republication of older volumes, as well as studies on specific sections of the Standards.[3]

But characteristic of the older commentaries, in contrast to their contemporary counterparts, is a better connection to the history, events, and theology of the seventeenth century. Dickson was alive during the creation of the Westminster Standards, interacted with theologians who were present, and was one of the theologians who wrote *The Summe of Saving Knowledge*, which was a summary of the Westminster Standards appended to the documents by the Scottish Kirk. Dickson, by virtue of being alive during the period, was intimately familiar with the context of the Standards. Present-day commentators, on the other hand, stand at a significant disadvantage. Not only are they separated from the assembly by hundreds of years, but also they often have different theological questions pressing them and at times different philosophical assumptions, given that they live after, rather than prior to, the Enlightenment.

For example, one commentary on the Larger Catechism discusses the theology of neoorthodoxy, especially the thought of Karl Barth (1886–1968) and Emil Brunner (1889–1966), in its treatment of the catechism's doctrine of Scripture.[4] As necessary as it is to bring the historic teaching of the Reformed faith to bear upon present-day theological challenges, it is important first to establish historically what the Standards have taught before its theology can be pressed into service. Another challenge to a proper understanding of the Standards is when contemporary historians and commentators read the Standards through the grid of later theological developments.[5]

---

[3] See, e.g., G. I. Williamson, *The Westminster Confession of Faith for Study Classes* (Phillipsburg, NJ: P&R, 1964); Williamson, *The Westminster Shorter Catechism for Study Classes* (Phillipsburg, NJ: P&R, 2003); Rowland S. Ward, *The Westminster Confession of Faith: A Study Guide* (Wantirna, Australia: New Melbourne, 1996); John H. Gerstner et al., *The Westminster Confession of Faith: A Guide, Commentary* (Signal Mountain, TN: Summertown Texts, 1992); Robert Shaw, *An Exposition of the Westminster Confession of Faith* (Fearn: Christian Focus, 1998); Francis R. Beattie, *The Presbyterian Standards* (Greenville, SC: Southern Presbyterian Press, 1997); J. Ligon Duncan, ed., *The Westminster Confession into the 21st Century*, 3 vols. (Fearn: Christian Focus, 2003–2009); R. C. Sproul, *Truths We Confess: A Layman's Guide to the Westminster Confession of Faith*, 3 vols. (Phillipsburg, NJ: P&R, 2006–2007); Robert Letham, *The Westminster Assembly: Reading Its Theology in Historical Context* (Phillipsburg, NJ: P&R, 2009); Richard A. Muller and Rowland S. Ward, *Scripture and Worship: Biblical Interpretation and the Directory for Public Worship* (Phillipsburg, NJ: P&R, 2007); Johannes G. Vos, *The Westminster Larger Catechism: A Commentary*, ed. G. I. Williamson (Phillipsburg, NJ: P&R, 2002).

[4] Vos, *Larger Catechism*, 443.

[5] See, e.g., Ralph Cunnington, "Definitive Sanctification: A Response to John Fesko," *EQ* 84, no. 3 (2012): 234–52, esp. 240–45; Williamson, *Westminster Confession*, 23.

Recently promising steps have been made to situate properly the Westminster Standards within the doctrinal and historical context of the seventeenth century.[6] However, given the massive amount of primary-source literature and the scope of the Standards, there is much more that can be done to unearth the original context of the assembly. Much of this work has been greatly assisted by the publication of the extant minutes of the assembly, which provide the contemporary reader with a window into the inner workings, debates, and concerns of the assembly.[7] But the theology of the Standards does not lie exclusively in the minutes, as important as they are. Rather, the Westminster Assembly was part of a broader ongoing conversation with Patristic, medieval, Reformation, and contemporary seventeenth-century theologians. Anyone who wants to understand the thought and ethos of the Standards must enmesh themselves, as much as possible, in the literature of the period. What theological works, for example, were the Westminster divines reading? What were their theological interests, concerns, fears, and passions? What were the historical events of the day, and how did they shape seventeenth-century English life?

The Importance of the Original Historical Context

It is often said that the three most important rules to purchasing real estate are location, location, location. A similar maxim is true for good historical theology—context, context, context. The best explanations of the doctrine of the Standards must rest upon the testimony of the time.[8] Such a contextual reading of the Standards will undoubtedly produce several important results. By enmeshing the Standards in their original context, the reader is forced to look for cognitive dissonances, that is, things that do not quite fit the contemporary way of stating or understanding things. True, many people still profess the Reformed faith as found in the Westminster Standards, but much has changed over the last 350-plus years. Think for a moment about what was happening in our own country twenty-five, fifty, or one hundred

---

[6] See, e.g., Letham, *Westminster Assembly*, passim; Muller and Ward, *Scripture and Worship*, passim.
[7] Chad Van Dixhoorn, ed., *The Minutes and Papers of the Westminster Assembly 1643–62*, 5 vols. (Oxford: OUP, 2012). Hereafter abbreviated as *MPWA*.
[8] Quentin Skinner, "Meaning and Understanding in the History of Ideas," *History and Theory* 8, no. 1 (1969): 3–53.

years ago; things were quite different. The seventeenth century was a period that was marked, for example, by different general beliefs about the world. The seventeenth century was a period when most Protestant theologians, with little dissenting opinion, believed that the pope was the antichrist; this was a virtually unquestioned fact. It was also a period when people believed in ghosts and spirits. In one such account, the supposed testimony of the ghost of an old woman played a role in the execution of a bishop, John Atherton (1598–1640).[9] What has this ghost's tale to do with the Westminster Standards?

This slice of early modern English history is but one small example of how differently things functioned during the time of the Westminster Assembly. One might certainly debate the existence of ghosts in our own day, but to say with a serious face that a message from a ghost would play a part in the arrest, conviction, and execution of a church official must surely be the stuff of fiction, not history. Yet, this is precisely what happened in the case of Bishop Atherton's execution.[10] When the layers of this bizarre case are pulled away, they reveal that Bishop Atherton was opposed to Laud's imposition of high-church Arminian and Papist practices upon the Church of England, and that the rumors surrounding Mother Leakey's ghost, as well as the false charge of buggery, were quite possibly an elaborate conspiracy to discredit and remove Atherton and replace him with a bishop more congenial to Laud's policies.[11] Adding to the complexity of the politics and religion of the time, a number of Presbyterians, including Westminster divine Robert Baillie (1602–1662), saw the conviction of Bishop Atherton as further reason to reject and remove Episcopacy "root and branch," given its corruption.[12] This whole event is but one illustration of the differences between the seventeenth century and the present day.

Theologically speaking, the Standards contain curious turns of phrase, oblique rejections of doctrines without persons or responsible parties named, and peculiar terms—such things that often pass un-

---

[9] Peter Marshall, *Mother Leakey and the Bishop: A Ghost's Story* (Oxford: OUP, 2007); cf. Nicolas Barnard, *The Penitent Death of a Woefull Sinner; or, the Penitent Death of John Atherton, Late Bishop of Waterford in Ireland* (London: W. Bladen, 1642).
[10] Marshall, *Mother Leakey*, 116.
[11] Ibid., 89–108.
[12] Ibid., 104.

noticed by contemporary readers but were well known to theologians of the period. What, for example, does the term *general equity* mean (19.4) and what is the difference between the moral law as a *covenant* and as a *rule* (19.5)? Why does the Confession say that the kingdom of Christ is the visible church (25.2), whereas *God*, not Christ, is the "Supream Lord and King of all the world" (23.1)? When the Confession states that God has ordained "whatsoever comes to pass," but at the same time his decree has not taken away "liberty or contingency of second Causes" but rather has established them (3.1), how can the divines affirm both a sovereign decree and contingency? Why do the Standards never employ the word *atonement* (or its variants) when such a word is commonplace in contemporary Reformed theology, especially with regard to popular terms such as *limited atonement*? All of these are questions that we need to ask when reading the Standards, and they can only be answered by investigating the Standards in their original context. Early modern Reformed theologians had a slightly different outlook on life and theology than we do today, and despite whatever similarities in doctrine and conviction are shared with theologians in the twenty-first century, the differences can be significant.

Learning to Read a Confession of Faith

A benefit of reading the Standards within their original historical and theological context is that the contemporary reader learns how to read a confession of faith. In the present day those who employ confessions of faith often fail to understand that confessions can be highly nuanced documents. The running joke in Presbyterian circles is, "Put three Presbyterians in one room and you'll get five different opinions." This humorous observation is equally true of Reformed theology in the early modern period. Confessions of faith were typically written to define truth and fence off heterodoxy and heresy while allowing a degree of doctrinal latitude within the boundaries of the confession. The Confession, for example, explicitly rejects certain doctrines, such as predestination based upon foreknowledge (3.2), justification based upon the worthiness of one's faith (11.1), or transubstantiation (29.6). However, the Westminster Confession is equally silent about a number of other teachings, which typically were viewed as issues of doctrinal liberty—issues upon which theologians could disagree but still be within the bounds of confessional orthodoxy. In the debates over God's decree, for example, and the composition of the Confession's third chapter, one of the divines, George Gillespie (1613–1648), wanted the assembly to compose certain phrases in such a manner that "every one may injoy his owne sence."[13]

In other words, at many points the Confession is very specific in terms of what it rejects or teaches, but at other points it is brilliantly ambiguous or vague, thus allowing various theologians to assent to the document even though it might not advocate each theologian's precise view on a particular subject. Such deliberate ambiguity or vagueness can only be discovered by reading the Confession and catechisms in tandem with the minutes of the assembly and works of the period. For example, one of the more complex issues in theology, whether in the present day or in the seventeenth century, is the relationship of the Mosaic covenant to the other covenants in Scripture; or alternatively stated, what is the Christian's relationship to the Mosaic law? Today many might not realize that at least five different views were held by various commissioners to the assembly. The Confession states the basics of what was the most common view, but when it came to its rejection of other views, it singled out only one position, namely, that of Tobias Crisp (1600–1643). Crisp advocated that there were two covenants of grace, something the Confession explicitly rejects (7.6). It is silent with regard to the other views held.

The Methodology of the Present Study

Given the importance of reading the Standards in their original context, in this study I have opted to place emphasis upon primary over secondary sources. There are numerous commentaries on the Standards that make theological and historical judgments about their doctrinal content, but do so devoid of primary-source analysis. Instead, while I have read much secondary-source analysis of the Standards

---

[13] *MPWA*, sess. 520, October 20, 1645 (3:690).

over the years, I have chosen only to employ what is, in my judgment, essential or necessary secondary literature; I have given preference to primary-source literature, or literature that was within a generation or so of the Westminster Assembly. Moreover, I have chosen to use works not of my own liking, but rather those that primary sources have identified as important or noteworthy.

In this respect it is interesting to follow the bread crumb trail that many of the primary sources have left. In our own day many Reformed theologians would never positively cite Patristic, medieval, Lutheran, or pagan sources, but this is precisely what numerous early modern Reformed theologians did. Hence, for many contemporary readers the sources I have chosen to illustrate certain doctrinal points may seem counterintuitive, but for the early modern Reformed theologian they were perfectly natural, desirable, and necessary. Unlike our own day, when Reformed theologians are content to labor for their entire ministries in theologically sectarian-like settings where orthodoxy is measured by a very narrow set of criteria, the Westminster divines had a different index by which they measured orthodoxy. The divines considered themselves *reformed* Catholics and therefore did not want to isolate themselves from the rest of the church, but saw their broader engagement with other periods of history and other theological traditions as evidence of their catholicity.[14]

In my effort to return the reader to the seventeenth century, I have chosen to cite an original edition of the Westminster Standards with its archaic spelling and punctuation. This has a number of benefits. First, it causes the contemporary reader to slow down and reread each tenet rather than sailing over familiar words. The archaic spelling, punctuation, and capitalization give the contemporary reader a sense of what it would have been like for a seventeenth-century theologian to sit down and read this document for the first time. Second, contemporary readers might not be aware of this, but the original edition of the Confession and catechisms are different at key places in compari-

---

[14] See, e.g., William Perkins, *A Reformed Catholike; or, A Declaration Shewing How Neere We May Come to the Present Church of Rome in Sundrie Points of Religion; and Wherein We Must for Ever Depart from Them with an Advertisement to All Favorers of the Romane Religion, Shewing That the Said Religion Is against the Catholike Principles and Grounds of the Catechisme* (Cambridge: John Legat, 1598); Anthony Wotton, *A Defence of M. Perkins Booke, Called a Reformed Catholike against the Cavils of a Popish Writer* (London: Cuthbert Burby, 1606).

son with modern editions. Scripture proof texts have been changed, and punctuation, at least in one place where it affects the meaning of the statement about the active obedience of Christ, has also been changed. Such changes, while perhaps benefiting the contemporary reader's ability to move from the present day to the past, cloud the original meaning of the text.

The Plan of the Present Study

In setting forth the plan of this study, I should explain, first, what this study is not. It is not a line-by-line exhaustive commentary on the Standards. Such a work would undoubtedly be massive and encyclopedic. The Standards are exhaustive, and as such a line-by-line approach to them would need to be equally exhaustive. Therefore, I do not treat every single doctrinal issue raised within the Standards. There is still much work to be done in helping us to understand better the theology and history of the Westminster Standards. Nevertheless, I have sought to explore key subjects of the Standards in an illustrative fashion. Each chapter of the Confession, for example, could warrant a book-length study, but in order to keep this book to a manageable size, I have treated what, in my mind, are key elements within the Standards, and have *illustrated* these points as much as possible from primary sources.

Second, the study begins with an overview of the historical, religious, and political context in which the Westminster Standards originated. Many of the doctrinal assumptions and beliefs are connected to this all-important context. The study then proceeds with Scripture, God and the decree, covenant and creation, the person and work of Christ, justification, sanctification, the law and the Christian life, the church, worship, and eschatology. I do not doubt that some will pick up this book and be disappointed that I have not treated some subjects, such as church polity, divorce, or the Larger Catechism's exposition of the Decalogue. My hope is that this work will spur others to do historically sensitive studies of these and numerous other subjects that appear within the Standards. In this respect, this study is an introduction to the theology, history, and issues that appear in the Westminster Standards and therefore is not intended to be exhaustive.

Conclusion

The aim of this study is to set the Standards in their original historical setting and explore the world of the seventeenth century. Like a deep-sea diver who plunges into the miry depths and must soon come up to his own world, my hope is that this brief exploration of the marvelous world of seventeenth-century Reformed theology will be interesting, instructive, and edifying for saints living in the twenty-first century and beyond.

2

The Historical and
Theological Context

Politics, divorce, adultery, war, espionage, treason, violence, assassination, torture, and the end of the world are ideas seldom associated with the Westminster Standards. But history tells a different story, as such events and activities were part of the world surrounding the creation of the assembly. Such ideas were not only familiar to the assembly but, in many ways, part of its very formation. People in church pews who take up the Confession and begin to read it likely do not realize they are stepping into a period of history when the authors sometimes heard cannon fire in the background as they debated doctrine; they were writing their confession and catechisms in the midst of a civil war. The historical context is vital, therefore, to our having a fuller understanding of the Standards. Another important dimension of the Standards, one that adds significant texture and depth, is recognizing that the divines who wrote these documents were not one-dimensional Calvinists. Often in popular and academic literature authors apply the term *Calvinism* to the theology of the Standards, which creates the impression that its authors were overly indebted to the theology of John Calvin (1509–1564) or that they somehow departed from the norms that the Genevan Reformer established—in other words, Calvin is the garden of Eden and the Westminster Standards are the fall. The assembly's own interaction with sources from the period easily demonstrates that such ideas are mythological rather than historical.

Hence, this chapter surveys the antecedent historical and theological context that led to the formation of the assembly and the creation of the Westminster Standards. It first explores politics and religion and the birth of the English Reformation. We then move to the subject of "wars and rumors of wars," which deals with a number of key conflicts that were shaped and driven by different theologies—Protestantism versus Catholicism. Events such as the defeat of the Spanish Armada in 1588 and the notorious Gunpowder Plot of 1605 hardly register in the minds of contemporary readers of the Standards, but they were both prominent in the thought of a number of the divines. This chapter will then examine events on the Continent, including the Thirty Years War, which set part of the backdrop for the birth of the civil war between the king and Parliament and the creation of the Westminster Standards. The last two sections briefly explore the immediate theological context of the assembly, the theological chaos of the time, and multiple streams of influence that fed the theological interest and appetite of the assembly's participants. Given this background the reader will be equipped with key principles that will enable a better understanding of the Westminster Standards.

Politics and Religion

At the regal level the Reformation in England was not initially theologically motivated, as it was on the Continent with Martin Luther's (1483–1546) initial grievances against the Roman Catholic Church.[1] As many know, Henry VIII (1491–1547) challenged Luther's efforts at reforming the church and was subsequently awarded the title of *defensor fide* ("defender of the faith") by the pope.[2] However, other things were going on in Henry's life, particularly the quest for a male heir. Henry's first wife, Catherine of Aragon (1485–1536), was unable to give Henry a son to succeed him on the throne of England.

---

[1] Henry VIII, *A Proclamation for Resysting and Withstandying of Most Damynable Heresyes Sowen within This Realme, by the Disciples of Luther and Other Heretykes, Perverters of Christes Religion* (London: Robert Pynson, 1529).

[2] For what follows, see G. W. Bernard, *The King's Reformation: Henry VIII and the Remaking of the English Church* (New Haven, CT: Yale University Press, 2005), 1–72.

Henry had married Catherine in 1509, soon after his ascension to the throne, but as early as 1510 he was reported to have been unfaithful to her. However, a young woman by the name of Anne Boleyn (ca. 1501–1536) caught Henry's eye, but Anne refused to consent to the king's sexual advances and told him she would settle for nothing less than being his wife. The challenge of a young, ambitious woman contributed to a chain of events that eventually led to Henry's divorce from Catherine, England's break from the Roman Catholic Church, and the creation of the Church of England with Henry as its new royal head.[3]

Henry's case for his divorce was supported by the likes of Thomas Cranmer (1489–1556), who, among others, was interested in reform and who made the legal and theological case for the legitimacy of the king's divorce.[4] Henry, notorious for his numerous wives in the quest for a male heir, would eventually die, and his son, Edward VI (1537–1553), born by Henry's third wife, Jane Seymour (ca. 1508–1537), would ascend the throne. Under Edward's reign the reformation of England flourished. The reformation of the Church of England proceeded far beyond Henry's nominal reforms, largely owing to the theological advisors that surrounded Edward, who, at the time of ascension, was only nine years old. Under Edward's reign Continental Reformers such as Martin Bucer (1491–1551) and Peter Martyr Vermigli (1499–1562) were invited to teach at the universities of Oxford and Cambridge. Another Continental Reformer, Johannes à Lasco (1499–1560), a Polish theologian, was given charge over the London's Strangers' Church, which was allowed to set up its own form of church discipline and worship. All three theologians, Bucer, Vermigli, and à Lasco, spent a great deal of time with Cranmer in his home, and it was through the influence of these three that Cranmer's views on the Lord's Supper shifted and took on a decidedly Reformed cast.[5] Another influential Continental theologian who carried on significant epistolary friendships and offered sage counsel to English Reformers was

[3] Peter Marshall, *Reformation England 1480–1642* (London: Bloomsbury, 2003), 27.
[4] See, e.g., Diarmaid MacCulloch, *Thomas Cranmer: A Life* (New Haven, CT: Yale University Press, 1996), 41–78; Carl Trueman, *Luther's Legacy: Salvation and English Reformers 1525–1556* (Oxford: OUP, 1994).
[5] Philip Benedict, *Christ's Churches Purely Reformed: A Social History of Calvinism* (New Haven, CT: Yale University Press, 2002), 235–37.

Heinrich Bullinger (1504–1575).[6] The capstones to the reforms under Edward's reign appeared in 1552 and 1553 with the composition and publication of the Book of Common Prayer and the Forty-Two Articles, largely written by Cranmer.[7]

But during the drama of Henry's divorce, Mary I (1516–1558), his daughter by Catherine, carefully observed her mother's mistreatment.[8] Mary was naturally against the divorce and was very dedicated to her mother's Roman Catholic faith. The seeds of resentment sown during the divorce proceedings would later flower in the persecution of Protestants throughout England. In Mary's mind, Protestants had unjustly treated her mother, and she was determined to restore the Roman Catholic faith to England. Upon Edward's death, Mary, also known as "Bloody Mary" because of her persecution of Protestants, led England back toward Rome. This return was evidence that though the Church of England was officially Reformed under Edward's reign, the Reformation had taken hold only among a small segment of the population.

Shortly after Mary's ascension in 1553, the imperial ambassador from Spain noted how Londoners had obediently taken Easter Communion according to Roman Catholic custom. But among the Protestants, there were many who were resolutely dedicated to the Reformed faith, and more than 280 were martyred, including Cranmer, John Hooper (ca. 1495–1555), Hugh Latimer (ca. 1487–1555), and Nicholas Ridley (ca. 1500–1555).[9] In the wake of the Marian persecutions more than eight hundred Englishmen, gentry, ministers, and those preparing for the ministry went into exile in various Reformed European cities, such as Emden, Strasbourg, Zurich, Basel, and other cantons of Switzerland. But when many of these exiles eventually returned to the British Isles, including theologians such as John Knox (ca. 1514–1572), they brought many theological ideas and plans for reformation with them.[10] In many respects, Mary's persecution had the opposite effect upon the English Reformation than she intended—it made it stronger.[11]

---

[6] Marshall, *Reformation England*, 128.
[7] Benedict, *Christ's Churches*, 238.
[8] Marshall, *Reformation England*, 103.
[9] Benedict, *Christ's Churches*, 241.
[10] Ibid., 242.
[11] Marshall, *Reformation England*, 109.

After Mary's short-lived but nevertheless violent reign, she was succeeded by Elizabeth I (1533–1603). The daughter of Anne Boleyn, Henry's second wife, Elizabeth was raised in the home of Catherine Parr (1512–1548), Henry's sixth bride. Catherine Parr was Protestant by conviction, and her influence upon Elizabeth was significant. Moreover, if Elizabeth rejected the Protestant faith, then it would ultimately entail the acknowledgment of the illegitimacy of her parents' marriage, and hence her claim to the throne would be nullified.[12] Under Elizabeth's reign Reformed theology once again flourished, and more than half of the initial set of Elizabethan bishops came from among those who had sought exile under the Marian persecutions. The first post-Marian archbishop of Canterbury, for example, was Matthew Parker (1504–1575), the executor of Martin Bucer's will; and his successor, Edmund Grindal (1519–1583), was a pallbearer at Bucer's funeral. In Elizabeth's England, John Jewel's (1522–1571) *Apology of the Church of England* (1564), the Geneva Bible—which contained theological notes in the margins written by Continental Reformers—and John Foxe's (1516–1587) *Acts and Monuments* were all published. These were highly influential and further inculcated a new generation in the Reformed faith. They also steeled the nation's resolve regarding its chief place in the apocalyptic battle between the church of Christ and the Roman Catholic Church, the antichrist.[13]

In this history antecedent to the Westminster Assembly two chief things should be noted. First, politics and religion were intertwined. The popular notion that the Reformation was strictly a religious movement, inspired by preaching alone, is closer to mythology than history. As noted earlier, history is typically messy, and such is the case with the English Reformation. While Henry likely pursued reformation for personal benefit and his overactive libido, others such as Cranmer undoubtedly had better motivations. Second, the success and progress of the Reformed faith in the sixteenth century were largely dependent upon the ascension or demise of monarchs. In other words, in England, the Reformation largely flowed from the top to the bottom; it was not a popular democratic movement but rather a movement driven by an

---

[12] Benedict, *Christ's Churches*, 244.
[13] Ibid., 244–45.

oligarchy. This dynamic did not vanish like the morning mist once England crossed the threshold into the seventeenth century. On the contrary, this same relationship between church and state colored the reign of James I of England (1566–1625) and especially that of his son, Charles I of England (1600–1649). The tensions between church and state would eventually give birth both to the Westminster Assembly and to regicide, with the beheading of Charles. More will be said about these events below.

Wars and Rumors of Wars

For contemporary readers of the Westminster Standards, the original historical context is at some distance, not simply in terms of the number of centuries that have passed, but also in terms of the theological culture of early modernity. In the present, people associate religious violence with radicals, extremists, or those religions committed to spreading their beliefs by such means, such as Islam. But in the early modern period, a consequence of the irrefragable bond between politics and religion was that religion and war were also inextricably linked. A microcosm of this reality appears in the life of one of the Reformation's first-generation leaders, Ulrich Zwingli (1484–1531). In the early days of the Reformation a number of Swiss cities embraced the embryonic reform movement, and Zwingli encouraged them to form a political alliance, the Christian Civic Union (1529). Zwingli's intent was not only to strengthen the bonds among the various Swiss cantons that had embraced the Reformed faith but also to reach other cities and add them to the alliance to advance the Reformation. A number of Zwingli's allies warned him about such a move because they feared reprisal by those cities still under Roman Catholic control. Zwingli and the Reformed cities fought a brief war in the summer of 1529, which was followed by the Peace of Kappel; he was somewhat successful and able to expand the influence of the Reformation among other Swiss communities.

Zwingli and the leaders in Zurich became overconfident and overextended themselves by imposing an economic blockade against the Catholic Inner States of Switzerland. In response, the Roman Catholic cantons raised an army and marched on Zurich, routing the Protestant army. Zwingli, wearing a full suit of armor, was with the Protestant army and was killed in battle.[14] Some have claimed that he was merely a chaplain who accompanied the army into battle; however, if he were merely a chaplain, then why would he dress in armor, wear a helmet, and carry a sword and a battle axe?[15] The tragedy of Zwingli's death is accented by its brutality. He was hunched over a dying man, consoling him, when a soldier wielding a stone struck him in the head; Zwingli picked himself up off the ground but was hit again multiple times until he was run through with a lance.

After the battle Catholic soldiers scoured the field looking for wounded Protestants, and upon finding them, finished them off. These soldiers eventually stumbled upon Zwingli, "that vile heretic . . . rascal, that traitor," under a tree and in the throes of death; they drew a sword and cut his throat. The Catholic soldiers wanted to dismember Zwingli and send pieces of him to each of the five cantons allied with the Reformation. However, some objected, and instead he was tried, he was quartered for treason, and then his body was burned for heresy. When his remains were burned, the ashes of pigs were mixed with Zwingli's dismembered body and then the mixture was cast into the air by the mob that had gathered to watch the proceedings.[16]

Was Zwingli a minister or a soldier? Was the Reformation a theological or a political movement? Was the Reformation a theological or a military phenomenon? The answer to these questions is yes. The Reformation was all of these things, and Zwingli's death is but one example of how interconnected and messy the events of early modernity were. As military strategist Carl von Clausewitz (1780–1831) has argued, stripped to its essence, war is simply the exercise of force in order to bring about a political goal—it is merely the implementation of political policy.[17] In this case, given the symbiotic relationship between church and state, war was a natural instrument for advancing or defending theological causes. And this principle generally colored Protestant and Roman Catholic interaction during early modernity.

---

[14] Diarmaid MacCulloch, *Reformation: Europe's House Divided 1490–1700* (London: Penguin, 2003), 175–76.
[15] J. H. D'Aubigne, *History of the Reformation of the Sixteenth Century*, vol. 4 (New York: Robert Carter & Brothers, 1872), 450.
[16] Ibid., 451–54.
[17] Carl von Clausewitz, *On War* (New York: Alfred A. Knopf, 1993), 1.1.24 (p. 99).

As has been noted above, under the Marian persecutions nearly three hundred martyrs died for their faith. However, this is not to say that Protestants were innocent of bloodshed. Roman Catholics suffered under Protestant rule, which was an accelerant to the already burning fires of conflict between the two parties.

The animus between the Reformed and Roman Catholics was fueled by regular armed conflict, such as the St. Bartholomew's Day Massacre (1572). Tensions between the Reformed and Roman Catholics were running high in France. Over the years the Reformed faith had spread quickly; between 1555 and 1570 approximately 1,240 churches were planted in France, and about 10 percent of the French population vowed its allegiance to the Reformed faith.[18] With the untimely death of the French king Henry II (1519–1559), power passed to his widow, Catherine de' Medici (1519–1589). Political unrest marked Catherine's reign, and, coupled with religious strife between the Reformed and Roman Catholics, a number of brief wars broke out.

The first war, occurring between 1562 and 1563, was instigated by the massacre of unarmed Huguenots, adherents to the Reformed faith. An attempt by Protestants in 1567–1568 to seize power failed, leading to another conflict between Huguenots and Roman Catholics, in which the Huguenots were unsuccessful. Catherine and her son, Charles IX (1550–1574), who had ascended the throne at age ten, were convinced that one way to end the strife was to carry out a series of assassinations against Huguenot leaders. At 4:00 a.m. on Sunday, August 23, 1572, Roman Catholics in and around Paris began breaking into Huguenot homes and killing anyone found inside. The massacre went on for two days, and at least three thousand were killed in Paris; approximately another three thousand were killed in the surrounding provinces in the following weeks. The St. Bartholomew's Day massacre, the Marian persecution of Protestants in England, and the Spanish Inquisition (1480–1834) would be recalled, recounted, and seared into the collective memories of Protestants across Europe for generations to come and, as such, set the broader context for Reformed–Roman

---

[18] Benedict, *Christ's Churches*, 134; Meic Pearse, *The Age of Reason: From the Wars of Religion to the French Revolution 1570–1789*, The Baker History of the Church 5 (Grand Rapids: Baker, 2006), 44.

Catholic conflict in England, which played a part in creating the Westminster Assembly.[19]

Collective memories are much shorter in the contemporary period than they were in early modernity. For many today the Second World War (1939–1945) or even the terrorist attacks on the United States of September 11, 2001, are but a distant memory. But such amnesia was not the case for the English Reformed. In a sermon preached on July 18, 1644, before both houses of Parliament, Scottish divine Alexander Henderson (ca. 1583–1646) invoked the "deliverances from the Armada" and "the powder treason" to remind his audience of how God had delivered England from the machinations of their Roman Catholic foes.[20] Henderson was referring to England's victory over the Spanish Armada in 1588 and the infamous Gunpowder Plot of 1605, events that were fifty-six and thirty-nine years before but, in the minds of many, ever-present realities and reminders of the continuing threat of Romanism and the need for Reformation in England. Remember: theology, politics, war, and matters of national security were inseparably entangled.

The conflict between Spain, a Roman Catholic nation, and England, a Protestant nation under Queen Elizabeth, was ultimately rooted in King Henry's convoluted line of successors to his throne. Under Mary's rule, Spain and England had good relations, given her commitment to Roman Catholicism, her persecution of Protestants, and the Spanish blood that coursed through her veins. As mentioned above, Mary's mother was Catherine of Aragon, the daughter of King Ferdinand II (1452–1516) and Queen Isabella of Spain (1451–1504), who was famous for underwriting Christopher Columbus's journey to the new world. When Mary died and Elizabeth ascended the throne, many in England were eager to roll back the influence of Catholicism as well as curtail Spanish political power and influence on English soil.

Elizabeth diligently balked at the marital advances of King Philip II of Spain (1527–1598) when he suggested that Elizabeth replace her half-sister in his marriage bed; he had been married to "bloody" Mary

---

[19] Pearse, *Age of Reason*, 43–47.
[20] Alexander Henderson, "Sermon on Matthew 14:31," in *Sermons Preached before the English Houses of Parliament by the Scottish Commissioners to the Westminster Assembly of Divines 1643–45*, ed. Chris Coldwell (Dallas: Naphtali, 2011), 116.

in an attempt to solidify the political and theological alliance between England and Spain. But it soon became evident that Elizabeth had no intention of marrying Philip, and so she came to represent everything that he detested—a Protestant bastard queen who was repressing Roman Catholics under her rule, encouraging piracy against Spanish shipping, and assisting Protestant rebels against Philip's war in the Netherlands.[21]

By contrast, Philip represented everything that English Protestants feared and loathed. He was waging war against the Reformed faith throughout Europe, oppressing the Reformed in the Netherlands, sowing seeds of treason through espionage and subterfuge in England, and sponsoring Irish Roman Catholics to rebel against Elizabeth's authority. Moreover, Spain was but a short distance from England and was an ideal location from which to launch an invasion of the Protestant island. All signs pointed to war, and the respective monarchs each carried a theological banner, the Reformed or Roman Catholic faith. Elizabeth was also without an heir, and her nearest relative was Mary Queen of Scots (1542–1587), who also happened to be a devoted Roman Catholic. Under the right circumstances, Spain might be able to invade England, remove or kill Elizabeth, and place Mary Queen of Scots upon the throne. More gasoline was poured onto the fires of brewing conflict when Elizabeth pursued a failed attempt to bring Mary to trial and when Pope Pius V (1504–1572) issued the papal bull *Regnans in Excelsis* (1570), which declared that Elizabeth was deposed and excommunicated, and that her subjects were no longer bound to their vows of loyalty. Various plots were also hatched to assassinate Elizabeth, some of which were reported to involve Mary Queen of Scots. Elizabeth eventually caved in to the pressure from her advisors and signed Mary's execution order. Mary's execution then gave Philip of Spain warrant to invade England.[22]

At this point in history, the greatest naval power in the world was Spain.[23] The Spanish fleet consisted of roughly 130 ships, 7,000 sailors, and 17,000 soldiers for the invasion of England. In addition

---

[21] Pearse, *Age of Reason*, 65.

[22] Ibid., 65–67.

[23] J. H. Elliott, *Imperial Spain: 1469–1716* (New York: St. Martin's, 1963), esp. 237–44. My thanks to John Stovall for alerting me to this source.

to this the fleet was supposed to pick up another 17,000 soldiers from the Netherlands to join the invasion force. Yet this enormous strength and superiority was put under the command of the Duke of Medina-Sidonia, Alonso Pérez de Guzmán (1550–1615), who was selected not because of his naval prowess but because of his pedigree. Indeed the duke knew very little about naval combat. Another problem for the Spanish fleet was that it was more like a convoy of vessels than an effective combat unit. The duke brought these shortcomings to the attention of the king, but Philip was confident that he was God's instrument to punish England for its heresy and restore the one true faith to its shores; in fact, Philip received a papal blessing from Sixtus V (1521–1590), which in his mind all but guaranteed a Spanish victory.[24] As can be imagined, the English were just as certain that God would grant them victory.

Philip had planned for the Spanish fleet, after an initial skirmish, to harbor in the Dutch port of Flushing to pick up additional soldiers for the invasion, but Dutch Protestant forces captured the port, thus forcing Philip to harbor in Calais, France. The English navy located the fleet at Calais, sent fire ships—older vessels loaded with flammable materials and set ablaze—and flushed out the Spanish fleet where it was, cutting it to pieces by superior English naval gunfire. The Spanish fleet retreated and sailed north to Scotland with plans to sail around it and down the western coast of Ireland, but along the way the fleet ran into a violent storm, called the "Protestant wind," which battered and destroyed much of the armada. In the end, half of the 130 ships were sunk, and between 5,000 and 15,000 Spanish sailors and soldiers perished. Naturally, this event was interpreted as a vindication of the Reformed cause, and in terms of the grand narrative set forth by Foxe in his *Acts and Monuments*, England was an elect nation chosen by God and was engaged in a battle of apocalyptic proportions against the pope, the antichrist.[25] But just because England won the battle, that did not mean the war was over.

---

[24] Robert Bucholz and Newton Key, *Early Modern England 1485–1714: A Narrative History*, 2nd ed. (Oxford: Wiley-Blackwell, 2009), 140.

[25] Bucholz and Key, *Early Modern England*, 141–43; cf. John Foxe, *Actes and Monuments of Matters Most Speicial and Memorable* (London: Company of Stationers, 1610). For an extended treatment of the battle, see Neil Hanson, *The Confident Hope of a Miracle: The True History of the Spanish Armada* (New York: Knopf, 2005).

On the heels of Elizabeth's death Roman Catholics once again saw a window of opportunity to install a monarch who would return the nation to the one true faith. At the time, many Catholics believed that the martyrdom of Mary Queen of Scots acquired merits that would win them the grace of God and the conversion of the new king, James I, to Catholicism.[26] Roman Catholics desired this theological change because they had suffered under Elizabeth's rule. If Catholic priests were discovered performing the mass or in possession of vestments, they were typically thrown in prison, or even executed for treason. Such executions, however, were long, tortuous affairs. Priests convicted of treason were hung and drawn, and while they were still alive, were disemboweled, were emasculated, had their hearts cut out, and then were quartered.[27] Treason might seem like a strange crime for a priest, but in this context, and especially given the ongoing conflict between England and Spain and the failed invasion, priests were suspected of being foreign spies. These spies reported either to the pope, who had encouraged sedition against Elizabeth through his papal bull, or to the likes of the king of Spain.[28] By the time James ascended the throne in 1603, three women and fifty-eight men had been put to death under Elizabeth's reign.[29]

Eager to restore Roman Catholicism to England, Guy Fawkes (1570–1606), a native of England who fought with Spanish forces in the Netherlands in an effort to raise sympathy and military support for English Roman Catholics, took matters into his own hands when it became clear that Spain would not act to invade England or assassinate King James.[30] Fawkes and other conspirators devised a plot to blow up Parliament in its opening session. This would eliminate not only England's ruling body but also its monarch, King James, and would then clear the way to install a Roman Catholic monarch on England's throne. Fawkes and twelve others planned their assassination and moved thirty-six barrels of gunpowder into the "cellar" of Westminster. Estimated at between one and five tons of explosives, such a quantity would have literally

---

[26] Antonia Fraser, *Faith and Treason: The Story of the Gunpowder Plot* (New York: Anchor, 1996), xxix.
[27] Ibid., 20.
[28] Ibid., 24.
[29] Ibid., 29.
[30] Ibid., xxx.

blown the roof off Westminster.[31] Someone loosely associated with the conspiracy had a twinge of conscience and wrote an anonymous letter to the authorities alerting them to the plot. In the wee hours of November 5, Fawkes was discovered lurking about Westminster's cellar, guarding the explosives. He was arrested and then interrogated.[32]

Authorities tortured Fawkes in an effort to get him to reveal the names of others involved in the plot to assassinate the king along with Parliament. They put him on the rack, even though such practice was contrary to English common law employed under Henry VIII's reign.[33] Under torture Fawkes folded and gave up his fellow conspirators, some of whom were hunted down and killed, while others were imprisoned, tried, and eventually executed by hanging, then drawn and quartered. One of the conspirators, Everard Digby (ca. 1578–1606), was hung from the halter for a short time and then cut down, which meant he was fully conscious when he was drawn and quartered. When the executioner tore out Digby's heart, he lifted it up, showed it to the crowd, as was the custom, and said, "Here is the heart of a traitor."[34] But such brutality did not mean that all in the crowd were unsympathetic to those being executed, as during some executions people cried for the executioner to allow the condemned to hang until he was dead so that the subsequent drawing and quartering would be done upon a corpse rather than a conscious person.[35]

The execution of the Roman Catholic conspirators was not the end of the infamous Gunpowder Plot, as the effects would echo into the immediate and distant future. The plot was firmly etched into English culture, given its daring and potentially earth-shattering proportions. As in our own day, such events quickly seep into the imagination, and art imitates life. William Shakespeare's (1564–1616) *Macbeth*, first performed in 1606 and written on the heels of the failed plot, involves the assassination of a king; and *King Lear*, also performed in 1606, contains the words, "Friendships fall off, brothers divide . . . in countries, discord; in palaces treason."[36] The political and religious

[31] Ibid., 120–21.
[32] Ibid., 168.
[33] Ibid., 176–77.
[34] Ibid., 231.
[35] Ibid., 266.
[36] Ibid., 143 (quoting *King Lear*, act 1, scene 2), 280.

consequences were significant; in the wake of the failed plot Roman Catholics were not allowed to practice law, serve in the army or navy, act as executors of wills, be guardians to minors, possess weapons, receive university degrees, or vote in an election. These prohibitions would not be lifted until 1797, when Catholics were allowed to vote in local elections, and 1829, with the Catholic Emancipation. And in 1613 a bill was introduced in Parliament to require Roman Catholics to wear red hats, as was required of Jews in Rome, so they could be easily identified and ridiculed, but the measure was defeated.[37]

The events of the failed Spanish invasion and the Gunpowder Plot also echoed in the theological literature of the period and weighed heavily on the minds of a number of the Westminster divines. Bishop Godfrey Goodman (1582–1656) published his memoirs about forty years after the failed plot, right about the time when the assembly was meeting, and in them he recounted the events and essentially cast a shadow over Roman Catholics, implying that any Catholic might be a terrorist.[38] Moreover, sermons were typically preached in remembrance of both events. Such sermons were preached by Westminster divines Cornelius Burgess (ca. 1589–1665), Thomas Gataker (1574–1654), and William Strong (d. 1654).[39] Not only were these events seared into the collective memory of Reformed English Protestants, but they were also regularly mentioned in theological works of the period.[40] To say the least, Roman Catholicism was not merely an ideology or something to be debated over coffee, but a threat both to the church

---

[37] Ibid., 283.

[38] Godfrey Goodman, *The Court of King James the First*, 2 vols. (London: Richard Bentley, 1839), 2:110–18; Fraser, *Faith and Treason*, 284.

[39] Cornelius Burgess, *Another Sermon Preached to the Honorable House of Commons Now Assembled in Parliament, November Fifth, 1641* (London: P. Stephens and C. Meredith, 1641); Thomas Gataker, *An Anniversarie Memoriall of Englands Delivery from Spanish Invasion* (London: Philemon Stephens and Christopher Meredith, 1626); William Strong, *The Commemoration and Exaltation of Mercy. Delivered in a Sermon Preached to the Honorable, the House of Commons, at Margarets Westminster, November 5, 1646. Being the Day of Their Publike Thanksgiving, for That Eminent and Ancient Mercy, the Deliverance of Them, and the Whole Kingdome in Them, from the Popish and Hellish Conspiracy of the Powder Treason* (London: Francis Tyton, 1646).

[40] See, e.g., Thomas Cartwright, *A Confutation of the Rhemists Translation, Glosses and Annotations on the New Testament* (Leiden: William Brewster, 1618), comm. Rev. 22:20 (p. 761); John Mayer, *A Commentary upon All the Prophets Both Great and Small* (London: Abraham Miller and Ellen Cotes, 1652), dedicatory epist. (fol. A4r); Richard Baxter, *The Unreasonableness of Infidelity*, in *The Practical Works of the Rev. Richard Baxter*, vol. 20 (1655; London: James Duncan, 1830), 105, 309; Thomas Watson, *A Body of Practical Divinity* (London: Thomas Parkhurst, 1692), 259; John Downame, *The Christian Warfare against the Devil World and Flesh* (London: William Stansby, 1634), 2.34.7 (p. 1003); William Twisse, *A Discovery of D. Jackson's Vanitie* (Amsterdam, 1631), 317; Thomas Adams, *A Commentary or, Exposition upon the Divine Second Epistle General Written by the Blessed Apostle St. Peter* (London: Jacob Bloome, 1633), 18, 552.

and to national security, according to many Reformed theologians of the period.

Encroaching Threats and the Formation of the Assembly

The immediate historical context of the assembly carried much of the Reformed–Roman Catholic baggage with it; just because a number of years had passed since the failed Spanish invasion and foiled Gunpowder Plot, that did not mean all was quiet. For a number of years before the assembly met—as well as during the assembly's most productive years, 1643–1647, when it produced the Confession and catechisms—the Thirty Years War (1618–1648) raged on the Continent. Like most conflicts of the period, this war was driven by, among other things, theology. The two sides were the Protestant Union and the Catholic League.[41] The trigger for the war was the takeover of Bohemia. Because of the earlier reforms of John Huss (ca. 1369–1415), the Roman Catholic Church had lost its monopoly over Bohemia's two million residents; the Bohemian Protestants were tolerated under the reign of Rudolf II (1552–1612), the Holy Roman emperor. Rudolf's successor was supposed to be the Archduke Ferdinand of Styria (1578–1637), a devout Roman Catholic. Bohemian Protestants naturally feared their freedom would be curtailed under this new king.[42]

The Protestant citizens of Bohemia decided to make their opposition known to Ferdinand through a celebration of the "Defenestration of Prague," which originally occurred in 1418 when Hussites tossed church officials out a large castle window, from which they plummeted to their deaths. On the bicentennial of this event, Protestants seized two leading Catholic nobles and another bystander, and reenacted the event, though to a lesser end; the victims landed in a pile of dung and emerged unharmed. Still, this event brought repercussions. Riled by the defenestration celebration, the Bohemians raised an army of sixteen thousand men and invaded and captured the Catholic city of Pilsen. Naturally, King Philip III of Spain (1578–1621) sent reinforcements, and others sympathetic to their cause joined the Bohemian

---

[41] Pearse, *Age of Reason*, 152.
[42] Ibid., 153. Styria is in modern-day Austria.

Protestants.[43] The Protestants were ultimately unsuccessful, Bohemia was re-Catholicized, more than a hundred thousand Protestants were exiled, and the University of Prague was given over to the control of Jesuit theologians.[44] This conflict would eventually spread, engulf thousands, and as is usually the case, involved butchery, cruelty, and savage atrocities committed by both sides.

An example of the brutality of the conflict comes from Sweden and King Gustavus Adolphus (1594–1632), a committed Lutheran. Adolphus and his German allies unsuccessfully engaged Roman Catholic forces, which laid siege to and sacked the city of Magdeburg in 1631. When the Catholic forces approached the outskirts of the city, citizens loyal to the Holy Roman emperor ran out to greet their liberators, only to be slaughtered. Fearful citizens fled to the safe haven of churches, but Roman Catholic soldiers locked the doors and burned them down though they were full of women and children. Protestant clergy were dragged out of their homes and burned with their libraries, and women were singled out, dragged behind horses, and raped. It was also reported that Croat and Walloon soldiers spiked children on their lances and then threw them into bonfires. In the end roughly twenty thousand of the city's thirty thousand inhabitants were slaughtered.[45] The Thirty Years War brought the forcible imposition of the Roman Catholic faith, which Bohemia, Hungary, and significant portions of Austria suffered, and only armed resistance prevented the same from happening in the northern Palatinate, Bavaria, and southern Germany. The Westminster divines, therefore, lived under the long shadow and threat of Roman Catholicism.[46] In early modernity, theology was no ivory tower endeavor—theology often wrote checks that were cashed in blood.

The Westminster divines, however, not only had reason to fear Roman Catholicism abroad, especially with the Thirty Years War raging on the Continent, but also had homegrown reasons to be concerned. King James I was generally sympathetic to Reformed theology

---

[43] Ibid., 153–54.
[44] Ibid., 156–57.
[45] Ibid., 159–60. For a broader treatment of the Thirty Years War, see Cicely Veronica Wedgwood, *The Thirty Years War* (1938; New York: New York Review Book, 2005).
[46] Pearse, *Age of Reason*, 162.

and allowed it to flourish under his reign. One of the most notable examples was the fact that he sent a delegation to the Synod of Dort (1618–1619).[47] However, James's son, Charles, was not so inclined. With the sound of "Remember, remember, the fifth of November" echoing in their minds reminding them of the failed Gunpowder Plot, many Englishmen were leery of their new king because of his perceived Roman Catholic sympathies. Under his reign Charles promoted William Laud (1573–1645), who became bishop of London in 1628 and, later, archbishop of Canterbury in 1633.

Under Laud's leadership far more Arminian ministers were promoted to key posts in the Church of England, whereas formerly under James, ministers who held to Reformed theology were regularly promoted.[48] Laud ordered that all Communion tables be moved back to the eastern ends of churches, their location when the Church of England was still under papal authority. He also required ministers to wear vestments, bow at the utterance of the name of Christ, and strictly follow the Book of Common Prayer, which involved kneeling at the Lord's Supper, a practice that looked very similar to the Roman Catholic veneration of the host; and he banned unlicensed preachers—Congregationalists who were, usually, of Reformed conviction. Laudians believed they were restoring beauty to the church, but their detractors thought all of this was a thinly veiled return of Roman Catholic practices.[49]

Another cause for alarm arose with respect to the king's choice of a bride. In 1625 Charles married the daughter of Henry IV of France (1553–1610), Henrietta Maria (1609–1669). Henrietta was a Roman Catholic, and among the stipulations for this royal union was that she would be allowed to worship according to her convictions. This meant that the king had to staff a chapel with Roman Catholic clergy, which in many ways was a symbolic eyesore to many Reformed ministers; they, after all, had a den of theological iniquity nestled within the very court of the king. But of equal concern was the question of offspring and in whose faith they would be raised. This was not an unfounded

---

[47] M. W. Dewar, "The British Delegation at the Synod of Dort—1618–19," *EQ* 46, no. 2 (1974): 103–16.
[48] Bucholz and Key, *Early Modern England*, 236–37.
[49] Ibid., 237.

fear because the pope allowed Henrietta to marry this heretic king with a secret proviso given specifically to Henrietta that she raise the children as Roman Catholics. Given all of these factors, his appointment of Laud, the persecution of Reformed ministers, his marriage to Henrietta, who would corrupt the king's theology, and his toleration of Papists in the heart of his court, many believed that Charles was a crypto-Roman Catholic.[50]

The straw that broke the proverbial camel's back and started a chain reaction that would eventually lead to civil war and the formation of the Westminster Assembly was the effort of Charles and Laud to impose Anglican worship practices upon Presbyterian Scotland. The Scottish Kirk did not have a formal liturgy like that prescribed in the Book of Common Prayer, and so the imposition of a perceived Arminian high-church liturgy caused many Scotsmen to believe that they were being forcibly led back to Rome. This action created a firestorm of resistance not only among the politicians and church leaders but also among the Scottish population.

On July 23, 1637, the ill-fated day when the new liturgy was supposed to be performed, the dean of Edinburgh arrived at St. Giles Cathedral to carry out his task. As he began to read from the Book of Common Prayer, an old woman, Jenny Geddes, stood up and cried out, "Villain, dost thou say mass at my lug," and she took her stool in hand and threw it at the dean's head. Others quickly followed her lead and bedlam ensued. The dean threw off his vestment and took off running, and so the bishop of Edinburgh mounted the pulpit to try to restore order, which drew a cascade of sticks and stones and shouts from the congregation, "A Pope, a Pope, Antichrist." To say the least, the Laudian priests gave up on trying to impose the liturgy upon Scotland.[51]

The imposition of Laud's liturgy was formally rejected when representatives of nearly every key constituency of Scotland, excluding Roman Catholics, signed the National Covenant (1638) in the Greyfriars' churchyard in Edinburgh. The document states that the Scots rejected "all kind of Papistry" and that Roman Catholics were

---

[50] Ibid., 238–39.
[51] Roy Middleton, "Historical Introduction," in George Gillespie, *A Dispute against the English Popish Ceremonies*, ed. Chris Coldwell (Dallas: Naphtali, 2013), xxv.

"damned and confuted by the word of God and Kirk of Scotland." But the signatories especially detested and refused the "usurped authority of that Roman Antichrist upon the scriptures of God, upon the kirk, the civil magistrate, the consciences of men." The National Covenant then enumerates the various points that the Scots perceived as the corruption of doctrine, and these largely anticipate many, if not all, of the subjects that the divines would later reject in the Westminster Standards. For example:

> His corrupted doctrine concerning original sin . . . our justifica-
> tion by faith only, our imperfect sanctification and obedience to
> the law; the nature, number, and use of the holy sacraments; his
> five bastard sacraments . . . his blasphemous opinion of transub-
> stantiation . . . his dispensations with solemn oaths, perjuries, and
> degrees of marriage forbidden in the world . . . his devilish mass
> . . . blasphemous priesthood; his profane sacrifice for the sins of
> the dead . . . calling upon angels or saints departed, worshipping of
> imagery, relicks, and crosses . . . his general and doubtsome faith;
> his satisfaction of men for their sins; his justification by works . . .
> works of supererogation, merits, pardons . . . his erroneous and
> bloody decrees made at Trent.[52]

The National Covenant bound its signatories to propagate and defend the Reformed faith "all the days of our life." In many respects the National Covenant was a declaration of theological war against the attempted invasion of Charles and Laud.

But as was the case in early modernity, declarations of theological war were tantamount to declarations of war *simpliciter*—there was no separation of church and state. For the church to reject the authority of the state in theological matters was tantamount to treason, and naturally Charles perceived the National Covenant in precisely this manner.[53] So he called upon his noblemen and lords to raise an army and march on Scotland, and the Scots responded in kind by raising an army of their own. The Scots were motivated by theology and love of country, and were well trained because they had many veterans of

---

[52] All quotations of the National Covenant come from *The Westminster Confession* (1646; Glasgow: Free Presbyterian Publications, 1995), 347–54.
[53] Marshall, *Reformation England*, 211–15.

Continental wars. Charles counted on the English hatred of the Scots to motivate his army, but many of those who were conscripted were reluctant to leave their homes and invade Scotland to fight fellow Protestants. Many of the Englishmen may have disliked the Scots, but they had greater contempt for Laud.

Rather than engage in battle, Charles opted for a truce, the Treaty of Berwick, in June 1639. But by 1640 the king was nearly bankrupt, had a hostile Scottish army to the north, and consequently had to call Parliament, which had not met for some eleven years. Parliament was not inclined to meet the king's request for money to fund his war with the Scots until the king heard their grievances. Charles was unwilling to work with Parliament and quickly dissolved it. He nevertheless plunged headlong into battle against the Scots and was roundly defeated. The Scots defeated the king's army, occupied Durham and Northumberland Counties, and forced Charles to sign the Treaty of Ripon, which required him to pay £850 per day until a permanent agreement could be reached. The biggest problem, however, was that there was now no English army between Scotland and London, and so Charles had to call Parliament once again.[54]

What has now come to be called the Long Parliament, which was officially in session from 1640 to 1660 and consisted largely of Protestants of Reformed conviction, sought to restrict the king's power so that he could not impose Roman Catholic worship upon England as he had done under Laud's leadership in the 1630s.[55] During the initial meetings of Parliament Charles and the MPs negotiated back and forth, with both sides reluctant to give in to the other's demands. Meanwhile, in the fall of 1641 the Roman Catholics of Ireland arose and took up the sword against their Protestant countrymen; and approximately three thousand to four thousand Protestants were killed in this uprising. However, by the time word of this rebellion reached Parliament, the number killed had been exaggerated to two hundred thousand, which only stoked Protestant fears and confirmed, in the minds of many, the need to spread the Reformed faith throughout the kingdoms of England, Scotland, and Ireland. Many Protestants feared

---

[54] Bucholz and Key, *Early Modern England*, 243–44.
[55] Ibid., 245.

that the Irish would invade England and try to impose Catholicism upon them.[56] These events finally and irretrievably fractured whatever spirit of cooperation existed between Charles and Parliament, and civil war ensued.

The king departed London with 236 royalist MPs in his wake, which left 302 members of Parliament in the capital.[57] At the outset of the civil war, royalist forces were successful, gaining a number of victories, and even captured the port of Bristol. The occupation of Bristol was crucial because its strategic port allowed Charles to shuttle troops and supplies from Ireland; Charles made an alliance with the Roman Catholics of Ireland in order to bolster the size of his army. Parliament sought outside assistance as well and reached out to the Scots in the North, who had one of the most effective armies in the British Isles. In so doing, Parliament signed the Solemn League and Covenant (1643) with Scotland.[58] To be clear, the messiness of the situation is best captured by Robert Baillie's (1602–1662) famous characterization of this alliance: "The English were for a civill Leage, we for a religious Covenant."[59] In other words, Baillie and other Scots were well aware that the English wanted and needed the Scottish armies to defeat Charles; on the other hand, the Scots were not so much concerned about Charles as interested in seeing Presbyterianism and the Reformed faith take hold in England.

The Solemn League and Covenant was written to promote and bind its signatories to the reformation and defense of religion in the three kingdoms of Scotland, England, and Ireland. Many of the same concerns voiced in the National Covenant of 1638 were repeated in the Solemn League and Covenant. However, the covenant specifically states:

> We shall sincerely, really, and constantly, through the grace of God, endeavour, in our several places and callings, the preservation of the reformed religion in the Church of Scotland, in doctrine, worship, discipline, and government, against our common enemies;

---

[56] Ibid., 248.
[57] Ibid., 250–51.
[58] Ibid., 255.
[59] Robert Baillie, "Letter to Mr. W. Spang, 26 July 1643," in *The Letters and Journals of Robert Baillie*, vol. 2, ed. David Laing (Edinburgh: Robert Ogle, 1841), 90.

the reformation of religion in the kingdoms of England and Ireland, in doctrine, worship, discipline, and government, according to the word of God, and the example of the best reformed Churches; and shall endeavour to bring the Churches of God in the three kingdoms to the nearest conjunction and uniformity in religion, confession of faith, form of church-government, directory for worship and catechizing; that we, and our posterity after us, may, as brethren, live in faith and love, and the Lord may delight to dwell in the midst of us.[60]

This covenant and the pursuit of reformation in the three kingdoms laid the blueprint for the Westminster Standards and its attending documents, such as the Form of Government and Directory for Public Worship. To that end, Parliament called the Westminster Assembly, which at first was tasked with revising the Thirty-Nine Articles, but was later given the responsibility to write a new confession of faith, catechisms, and attending documents. To ensure that the assembly would stay on course, the Scots sent six representatives to serve as advisors to the assembly. The differences and interests of the parties surfaced in the origins of each set of representatives— the English divines were called and authorized by Parliament; the Scottish divines were commissioned and authorized by the Kirk of Scotland.[61]

Theological Chaos

It would be a mistake to think that the only perceived theological threat against the Reformed faith in England was the Roman Catholic Church. Rome was certainly the antichrist in the minds of many Reformed ministers in seventeenth-century England, and therefore it was one of the chief foci of theological polemic. However, theology did not exist on a continuum with Roman Catholicism on the left and Reformed theology on the right. Rather, early modern England, especially London, was a hotbed of religious pluralism that included but

---

[60] All quotations from the Solemn League and Covenant come from *The Westminster Confession* (1646; Glasgow: Free Presbyterian Publications, 1995), 358–60.
[61] S. W. Carruthers, *The Everyday Work of the Westminster Assembly*, ed. J. Ligon Duncan (Greenville, SC: Reformed Academic Press, 1994), 45.

was not limited to Arminians, Anabaptists, antinomians, enthusiasts, Erastians, Familists, Brownists, Papists, Quakers, Socinians, and the like. One work that documented the various sects and theological groups was that of heresiographer Thomas Edwards (1599–1647), *Gangraena*, which was a catalog of errors, heresies, and blasphemies extant in London between 1642 and 1646.[62] In this three-part work Edwards provides a list of errors and relevant passages from the person or group advocating the doctrinal error.

For example, in the third part of his work, Edwards discusses the error of the anthropomorphites, those who believed that God had a physical body, as well as those who believed that the narrative of Adam's fall was merely an allegory.[63] Westminster divine and Scottish advisor Samuel Rutherford (1600–1661) wrote a similar work, entitled *A Survey of the Spiritual Antichrist*. In it he explains and refutes Familism, a sixteenth-century antinomian sect, as well as the teaching of other antinomians of the period, including John Saltmarsh (d. 1647), William Dell (d. 1664), Tobias Crisp (1600–1643), and John Eaton (1575–1630).[64] To say the least, English religious culture was fragmented, and the divines of the Westminster Assembly sought to bring theological uniformity in doctrine and practice.

The Work and Influences of the Assembly

A parallel to the doctrinal pluralism of early modern England was the plurality of streams of theological influence that flowed into the Westminster Assembly. One of the repeated mantras of the present day is the idea that John Calvin is the normative theologian of the Reformed tradition. What Martin Luther is for Lutheranism, Calvin is for Calvinism. This notion appears on a number of levels but is likely fueled by the use of the term *Calvinism*, whether in popular or academic literature. While historians and theologians will acknowledge that there were many other Reformers and theologians who contributed to the

---

[62] Thomas Edwards, *The First and Second Part of Gangraena; or, A Catalogue and Discovery of Many of the Errors, Heresies, Blasphemies and Pernicious Practices of the Sectaries of This Time*, 3rd ed. (London: Ralph Smith, 1646); Edwards, *The Third Part of Gangraena; or, A New and Higher Discovery of the Errors, Heresies, Blasphemies, and Insolent Proceedings of the Sectaries of These Times* (London: Ralph Smith, 1646).

[63] Edwards, *The Third Part of Gangraena*, 2, 6.

[64] Samuel Rutherford, *A Survey of the Spiritual Antichrist* (London: Andrew Crooke, 1648).

work of the Reformation, the term nevertheless persists.[65] However, in the early modern period *Calvinism* (as well as its variants) originally was used as a term of derision to marginalize Reformed theologians as sectarians.[66] Calvin, though influential, was but one among a host of theological contributors in the early modern period. His relative influence can be measured by the number of times his name was invoked or cited in the minutes of the Westminster Assembly.[67]

Of the more than six hundred names cited in the assembly's minutes we find the following selected names, among others:

Names Cited	Times Cited
Ainsworth, Henry (1569–1622)	3
Ambrose (337–397)	4
Ames, William (1576–1633)	6
Amyraut, Moïse (1596–1664)	2
Aquinas, Thomas (ca. 1225–1274)	3
Aretius, Benedictus (ca. 1522–1574)	2
Aristotle (384–322 BC)	7
Arminius, Jacob (1560–1609)	1
Augustine (354–430)	25
Bellarmine, Robert (1542–1621)	5
Beza, Theodore (1516–1605)	29
Bucanus, Gulielmus (d. 1603)	1
Bucer, Martin (1491–1551)	8
Bullinger, Heinrich (1504–1575)	1
Calvin, John (1509–1564)	25
Cameron, John (ca. 1579–1625)	11

---

[65] See, e.g., Benedict, *Christ's Churches*, with its subtitle, *A Social History of Calvinism*; Dewey D. Wallace Jr., *Shapers of English Calvinism, 1660–1714: Variety, Persistence, and Transformation* (Oxford: OUP, 2011).

[66] Richard Muller, *Calvin and the Reformed Tradition: On the Work of Christ and the Order of Salvation* (Grand Rapids: Baker, 2012), 51–69; Muller, "Reception and Response: Referencing and Understanding Calvin in Seventeenth-Century Calvinism," in *Calvin and His Influence, 1509–2009*, ed. Irena Backus and Philip Benedict (Oxford: OUP, 2011), 182–202.

[67] "Register of Citations," in *MPWA*, 1:148–61.

Names Cited	Times Cited
Cartwright, Thomas (1534–1603)	12
Chamier, Daniel (1565–1621)	8
Chrysostom, John (347–407)	16
Cotton, John (1585–1652)	11
Cyprian (d. 258)	12
Davenant, John (bap. 1572, d. 1641)	4
De Dieu, Louis (1590–1642)	2
Dort, Synod of (1618–1619)	2
Downame, John (1571–1652)	1
Du Moulin, Pierre (1568–1658)	3
Gerhard, Johann (1582–1637)	3
Gomarus, Franciscus (1563–1641)	4
Junius, Franciscus (1545–1602)	6
Knox, John (ca. 1514–1572)	1
Lasco, Johannes à (1499–1560)	1
Luther, Martin (1483–1546)	12
Melanchthon, Philip (1497–1560)	3
Musculus, Wolfgang (1497–1563)	2
Olevianus, Caspar (1536–1587)	1
Piscator, Johannes (1546–1625)	12
Scotus, John Duns (ca. 1265–1308)	3
Second Helvetic Confession (1566)	1
Tertullian (ca. 160–220)	10
Tilenus, Daniel (1563–1633)	5
Ursinus, Zacharias (1534–1583)	1
Ussher, James (1581–1656)	1
Vermigli, Peter (1499–1562)	2
Voetius, Gisbert (1589–1676)	2

Names Cited	Times Cited
Ward, Samuel (1572–1643)	2
Whitaker, William (1547–1595)	11
Zanchi, Girolamo (1516–1590)	4
Zepper, Wilhelm (1550–1607)	3

Immediately evident in this sampling of the six-hundred-plus citations is the broad variety of cited authorities, which includes philosophers such as Aristotle, Patristic theologians (Augustine, Cyprian, Tertullian), sixteenth-century Reformers (Beza, Bucer, Bullinger, Calvin, Ursinus), Lutheran theologians (Gerhard, Luther, Melanchthon), contemporaries of the divines (e.g., Cameron, Cotton, de Dieu, Voetius), other confessional documents (Second Helvetic Confession, Synod of Dort), and other theologians who fall into the "dark age" of Reformed theology.

The "dark age" is from 1560 to 1640, a period corresponding roughly to the time of Calvin's death until the start of the Westminster Assembly. This is a dark age not because of a lack of learning, skill, knowledge, or theological acumen, but due to the lack of awareness on the part of contemporary readers of this period. A popular pattern in the analysis of Reformed theology is to explain and define the Reformed tradition in terms of Calvin's *Institutes*, then hop to the Westminster Standards (1646–1647), and then leap into the present day.[68] Little to no effort is expended to examine, whether positively or negatively, the sources that the Westminster divines themselves were using. The above-cited list of names illustrates the point that the theological conversation was broad and was carried across a number of historical, theological, geographical, and generational boundaries. This is not to say that the divines engaged all of these sources in a positive manner; sometimes they were cited critically, and other times positively. What the list does show is the need to illuminate the Westminster Standards by the surrounding theological sources and conversation partners of the period.

One such example comes from Edward Leigh (1602–1671), a lay

---

[68] See, e.g., Richard B. Gaffin, "Biblical Theology and the Westminster Standards," *WTJ* 65 (2003): 165–79; cf. Muller, *Calvin and the Reformed Tradition*, 39.

theologian who also wrote on numerous other subjects, including law and history. He was a colonel in the parliamentary army and was a member of Parliament during the composition of the Westminster Standards. He was elected an MP for Stafford in place of a member who was no longer physically able to carry out his duties.[69] Leigh was educated at Oxford under the tutelage of William Pemble (1591–1623).[70] Among the many works that Leigh authored was his *Systeme or Body of Divinity*, published in 1654, with a second edition issued in 1662.[71] The subtitle of this work gives a hint as to its breadth and depth in covering the theological issues of his day:

> Wherein the Fundamentals and main Grounds of Religion are Opened: The Contrary Errours Refuted: Most of the Controversies Between Us the Papists, Arminians and Socinians Discussed and handled. Several Scriptures Explained and vindicated from corrupt Glosses: A Work seasonable for these times, wherein so many Articles of our Faith are questioned, and so many gross Errours daily published.

In Leigh's work a quick glance at the marginal notes and citations immediately disabuses the reader of the notion that Calvin was the normative theologian of the period. For example, on one page from his treatment of the doctrine of Scripture Leigh cites John Rainolds (1549–1607), Francis Junius, Tertullian, John Lightfoot (1602–1675), Cicero (106–43 BC), Daniel Chamier, Wolfgang Musculus, Josephus (37–ca. 100), Origen (184–253), Sixtus Sinensis (1520–1569), Robert Bellarmine, and Eusebius (263–339).[72] Such citation patterns are common throughout Leigh's work and provide a window into the theology of a person who was present, interacted with the divines, and to a certain extent participated in the process of creating the Westminster Standards.[73]

---

[69] *Notitia Parliamentaria: Concerning an Account of the First Returns and Incorporations of the Cities, Towns, and Boroughs, in England and Wales, That Send Members to Parliament . . . and . . . A Series or Lists of the Representatives in the Several Parliaments Held from the Reformation 1541, to the Restoration 1660* (London: Browne Willis, 1750), 249.
[70] "Edward Leigh," in *Dictionary of National Biography*, vol. 32, ed. Sidney Lee (New York: Macmillan, 1892), 432–33.
[71] Edward Leigh, *A Systeme or Body of Divinity: Consisting of Ten Books* (London: William Lee, 1654).
[72] Leigh, *Body of Divinity*, 1.5 (p. 55).
[73] Though the *Dictionary of National Biography* states that Leigh's theological reputation "procured him a seat in the Assembly of divines," his name does not appear in the minutes of the assembly.

Further evidence that the divines were committed to the principles enunciated in the Solemn League and Covenant, that they would reform the churches of the three kingdoms according to the best examples of the Reformed churches, comes in their correspondence with other ecclesiastical bodies. Not only did the divines regularly communicate with the Kirk of Scotland; they also wrote letters to the churches of Bremen, Switzerland (Geneva, Berne, Zurich, Basel, Schafhausen), Holland (Zealand, Holland, East-Holland, Gelderland, Over Ysell, Utrecht, Frizeland, Groningen), France, Poland, Germany (Hesse, Anhalt, Hanau), and Transylvania (modern-day Romania).[74]

Another theological stream is the influence of James Ussher and the Irish Articles (1615). Ussher was the archbishop of Armagh, Ireland, and one of the more influential theologians of his day. He was also chiefly responsible for overseeing the creation and composition of the Irish Articles; he was initially nominated to serve in the assembly but declined, given his support of Charles.[75] In 1648 the House of Lords again considered adding Ussher to the assembly, but there is no record that he ever joined it.[76] Ussher may have been absent in body but not in spirit, as the divines referred to the Irish Articles in their creation of the Westminster Standards; at times, they borrowed significant sections, albeit slightly reworded, from the Irish Articles.[77] The divines neither wrote their documents *ex nihilo* nor cribbed the work of one theologian, such as Calvin. They used a wide variety of sources.

Another stream of influence is the education of the Westminster divines. A cursory survey of the curriculum in place at Cambridge University in the early seventeenth century, the time when a number of divines matriculated, reveals the many subjects that future divines learned. The study of ethics at Cambridge, for example, meant intense

---

Hence as a member of Parliament, he was undoubtedly involved in the broader process but likely did not participate in the actual debates and composition of the Standards as a formally called and elected divine.

[74] *MPWA*, sess. 190, April 2, 1644 (2:659); see also 5:41–43, 73, 179.

[75] Alan Ford, *James Ussher: Theology, History, and Politics in Early-Modern Ireland and England* (Oxford: OUP, 2007), 85–103; Charles Richard Elrington, *Life of Archbishop Ussher*, in James Ussher, *The Whole Works of the Most Rev. James Ussher*, 17 vols. (Dublin: Hodges and Smith, 1847–1864), 1:43–44.

[76] *MPWA*, 1:141.

[77] B. B. Warfield, "The Westminster Doctrine of Holy Scripture," in *The Works of Benjamin B. Warfield*, ed. E. D. Warfield et al., 10 vols. (1931; Grand Rapids: Baker, 1981), 6:169–90.

use of Aristotle alongside Protestant authors such as Lutheran theologian Philip Melanchthon and Remonstrant Hugo Grotius (1583–1645).[78] Students would have also studied Aristotelian metaphysics.[79] The theological curriculum involved weekly theological disputations between students, which were observed not only by students but also by scholars.[80] In these disputations it should come as no surprise that the questions posed usually dealt with subjects hotly debated between Protestants and Roman Catholics.

In one random sampling of seven manuscripts there were fifty-one questions, out of which thirty-six were distinctly Protestant, and fifteen were over commonly held Protestant and Roman Catholic beliefs. There were twenty-one questions on grace, justification, and free will, four on the nature of ministry, four on the papacy, four on the Lord's Supper, three on the intermediate state, two on the use of images, six on ethics, and seven miscellaneous questions. That twenty-one out of fifty-one questions covered grace and justification, with the pronouncements of the Council of Trent as the chief foil, should come as no surprise, given that this was one of the main issues dividing Protestants and Roman Catholics.[81] Students were also catechized through catechisms written by John Preston (1587–1628) and Anthony Tuckney (1599–1670), among other documents; Tuckney would eventually serve as one of the divines to the assembly.[82]

Beyond immediate influences, such as disputations and catechetical activities, students at Cambridge were exposed to a broad swath of theological thinking, as notebooks from the period are peppered with references to Thomas Aquinas, Bonaventure (1221–1274), Duns Scotus, and Peter Lombard (ca. 1096–1164). In addition to this students were encouraged to read a host of other church fathers and medieval theologians.[83] Over at Oxford University there was a similar educational pattern, and the earlier presence and influence of two

---

[78] E.g., Philip Melanchthon, *Enarratio Aliquot Librorum Ethicorum Aristotelis* (Vitebergae, 1545); Melanchthon, *Ethicae Doctrinae Elementa, et Enarratio Libri quinti Ehicorum* (Wittenberg: Hans Lufft, 1578); William T. Costello, *The Scholastic Curriculum at Early Seventeenth-Century Cambridge* (Cambridge: Harvard University Press, 1958), 64.
[79] Costello, *Scholastic Curriculum*, 70–83.
[80] Ibid., 110.
[81] Ibid., 113.
[82] Ibid., 111.
[83] Ibid., 121–22.

Continental Reformed theologians, Martin Bucer and Peter Martyr Vermigli, left an indelible impression upon this institution.[84] Other Continental influences upon English Reformed theology include Zacharias Ursinus and the Heidelberg Catechism. The catechism was originally written in 1563, largely under the guidance and leadership of Ursinus, and it was first translated and published in English in 1572.[85] The Heidelberg Catechism was required reading along with other key theological documents and works, including Alexander Nowell's (ca. 1507–1602) *Catechism*, Calvin's catechism, likely the *Geneva Catechism* of 1541, and Andreas Hyperius's (1511–1564) *Elements of the Christian Religion*. Students were encouraged to supplement their required reading, if they desired, with Heinrich Bullinger's *Catechism*, Calvin's *Institutes*, John Jewel's *Apology of the Church of England*, and the Thirty-Nine Articles.[86]

Westminster divines such as Thomas Goodwin (1600–1680) recalled using the Heidelberg Catechism as young men; Goodwin writes: "I received the sacrament at Easter, when I was fourteen years old, and for that prepared myself as I was able. I set myself to examine whether I had grace or not; and by all the signs in Ursin's Catechism, which was in use among the Puritans at the College, I found them all, as I thought, in me."[87] But Goodwin also reports that he attended the lectures of Richard Sibbes (ca. 1577–1635), "whose lectures the Puritans frequented," and that he read Calvin's *Institutes*.[88] Hence, though the assembly was a decidedly English event, it was by no means a theological island. The assembly had numerous streams of influence that must be taken into account: its broader reading habits, connec-

---

[84] C. M. Dent, *Protestant Reformers in Elizabethan Oxford* (Oxford: OUP, 1983), 4–16.

[85] See, e.g., *The Catechisme, or Manner How to Instruct and Teach Children and Others in the Christian Faith Appointed to Bee Read in All the Lands and Dominions of the Late Right and Mightie Prince, Frederike, Countie Palatine of the Rhein, One of the Electors of the Holy Empire, and Duke in Bauier / newly translated out of Latin and Dutch into Englishe* (London: Henrie Middleton, 1578); R. Scott Clark and Joel R. Beeke, "Ursinus, Oxford, and the Westminster Divines," in *The Westminster Confession into the 21st Century*, ed. J. Ligon Duncan, 3 vols. (Fearn: Christian Focus, 2003–2009), 2:9.

[86] Alexander Nowell, *A Catechism Written in Latin*, ed. Goerge Elwes Corrie, trans. Thomas Norton (Cambridge: CUP, 1853); Andreas Hyperius, *Elementa Christianae Religionis* (Erlangen: George Böhme, 1901); Heinrich Bullinger, *Caechesis pro Adultiorbius Scripta* (Tiguri: Frosch, 1563); John Jewel, *An Apology of the Church of England* (London: R. B. Seeley and W. Burnside, 1839); Dent, *Protestant Reformers*, 88.

[87] Thomas Goodwin, *Memoir of Thomas Goodwin, D.D.*, in *The Works of Thomas Goodwin*, 12 vols. (1861–1866; Eureka: Tanski, 1996), 2:lii; Clark and Beeke, "Ursinus, Oxford, and the Westminster Divines," 10.

[88] Goodwin, *Memoir*, lii.

tion to other Reformed churches on the Continent, interaction with other Reformed confessions and catechisms, as well as the education of a number of its members at Cambridge and Oxford. Any attempt to skip over this all-important theological and historical context or to anchor the assembly's theology to one source, such as Calvin, is likely to distort the meaning of the Standards.

Conclusion

Early modern England was far from simple; as with present-day events, complexity marked the history surrounding the formation of the assembly. Out of the tangled web of politics, war, theology, and passion the assembly produced a Confession and two catechisms. Against this backdrop, modern readers can have a greater understanding of what often lurks beneath the surface in some of the Confession's cryptic statements, such as its identification of the pope as the antichrist. And at the same time, readers can have a greater appreciation of the Confession's sobriety at many points; the divines were not swayed by the winds of antinomianism, on the one hand, or neonomianism, on the other. The Confession and catechisms are marked by a great deal of circumspection. But against the intellectual and theological backdrop, hopefully contemporary readers will have the bearings to be able to appreciate the acumen, depth, and clarity of the Standards. They represent the very best of the doctrine, government, and worship of the Reformed churches. Equipped with this historical and theological context, then, we are now prepared to begin to explore the theology of the Westminster Standards and its doctrine of Scripture.

3

The Doctrine of Scripture

The opening chapter of the Confession reveals the commitment to what has been called the formal cause of the Reformation, namely, the centrality of the doctrine of Scripture. From the earliest days of the Reformation and the writings of Ulrich Zwingli (1484–1531), such as his "Of the Clarity and Certainty or Power of the Word of God" (1522), the Reformed tradition has affirmed that the Word of God is clear and that people can understand it without human direction if they have the assistance of the Holy Spirit.[1] This was a direct challenge to the teaching of the Roman Catholic Church, which believed that only the church, the magisterium, had the authority and ability to interpret Scripture. In his famous and widely cited *Disputations on Holy Scripture*, Cambridge theologian William Whitaker (1548–1595) argued that "all doctrine is to be judged by the scriptures" and that the "apostles preached nothing which could not be established by the scriptures of the prophets, and did perfectly agree with them."[2] This

---

[1] Ulrich Zwingli, "Of the Clarity and Certainty or Power of the Word of God," in *Zwingli and Bullinger*, ed. G. W. Bromiley, LCC (Philadelphia: Westminster, 1953), 59–95; Zwingli, "Von Klarheit und Gewißheit des Wortes Gottes," in *Zwingli's Werke*, vol. 1, *CR* 88:338ff.; cf. W. P. Stephens, *Theology of Huldrych Zwingli* (Oxford: Clarendon, 1986), 51–57.

[2] William Whitaker, *A Disputation on Holy Scripture against the Papists Especially Bellarmine and Stapleton*, trans. William Fitzgerald (1849; Orlando, FL: Soli Deo Gloria, 2005), 5.8 (p. 457); Whitaker, *Disputatio de Sacra Scriptura contra Huius Temporis Papistas, Inprimis Robertum Bellarminium Jesuitam, Pontoficium in Collegio Roman, et Thomam Stapletonum* (Cambridge, 1588), 342; cf. Wayne R. Spear, "The Westminster Confession of Faith and Holy Scripture," in *To Glorify God and Enjoy God*, ed. John L. Carson and David W. Hall (Edinburgh: Banner of Truth, 1994), 88, 99; Frits G. M. Broeyer, "Traces of the Rise of Reformed Scholasticism in the Polemical Theologian William Whitaker (1548–95)," in *Reformation and Scholasticism: An Ecumenical Enterprise*, ed. Willem J. Van Asselt and Eef Dekker (Grand Rapids: Baker, 2001), 158–59; see similar comments in Amandus Polanus, *Syntagma Theologiae Christianae* (Hanoviae, 1609), 1.14 (cols. 95–96); Johannes

is the pulse that throbs through the Westminster Standards and finds its source in this first chapter.[3]

The opening chapter on Scripture is not unique; it reflects a number of theological works of its day, which begin with the doctrines of Scripture and God.[4] In fact, B. B. Warfield (1851–1921) has explained that one could make a case that any number of early modern works could probably be identified as the source material for the Confession's chapter on Scripture, and he mentions writings by John Ball (1585–1640), Gulielmus Bucanus (d. 1603), Thomas Cartwright (1534–1603), and John Calvin (1509–1564) as possible candidates.[5] The Confession also follows the approach of catechisms of the period. In his brief catechism, Westminster divine William Gouge (1575–1653) begins with two questions. First, "What is everyone most bound to know? Answ. Everyone is bound to have knowledge of God and of himself." This first question likely echoes the opening pages of Calvin's *Institutes* where Calvin discusses the twofold knowledge of God. The second question, however, asks something that Calvin does not immediately treat: "Where is this knowledge to be had? A. In the holy Scriptures, contained in the old and new testament." A third question asks, "Who is the author of the Scripture? A. The holy spirit of God who inspired holy men, to write them."[6] In another catechism of the period Ezekiel Rogers (1584–1661) similarly explains where sinful man is able to discover the knowledge of salvation, what the Scriptures are, and what they teach.[7] James Ussher (1581–1656) opens his catechism with the following question and answer: "What sure grounds have we to build our religion upon? Ans. The word of God contained in the Scriptures."[8]

Polyander, André Rivet, Antoninus Walaeus, and Antonius Thysius, *Synopsis Purioris Theologiae*, ed. Herman Bavinck (Leiden: Didericum Donner, 1881), 2.1.1 (p. 7).
[3] B. B. Warfield, "The Westminster Doctrine of Holy Scripture," in *The Works of Benjamin B. Warfield*, ed. E. D. Warfield et al., 10 vols. (1931; Grand Rapids: Baker, 1981), 6:155.
[4] See, e.g., Polanus, *Syntagma*, 1.11–47 (cols. 72–832); James Ussher, *A Body of Divinitie; or, The Summe and Substance of Christian Religion* (London: Thomas Downes and George Badger, 1645), 6ff.; Edward Leigh, *A Systeme or Body of Divinity: Consisting of Ten Books* (London: William Lee, 1654), 1.1–9 (pp. 1–120).
[5] Warfield, "Doctrine of Holy Scripture," 161.
[6] William Gouge, *A Short Catechisme, Wherein Are Briefly Laid Down the Fundamental Principles of Christian Religion* (London: John Beale, 1615), n.p.
[7] Ezekiel Rogers, *The Chiefe Grounds of Christian Religion, Set Down by Way of Catechizing. Gathered Long Since for the Use of an Honourable Family* (London: J. R., 1642), n.p.
[8] James Ussher, *The Principles of Christian Religion: Summarily Set Down according to the Word of God: Together with a Brief Epitome of the Bodie of Divinitie* (London: P. B., 1647), 1.

Samuel Rutherford (1600–1661), one of the Scottish advisors to the assembly, writes in his catechism that people learn about the doctrine of faith "in God's wisdom (1 Cor. 2:6) in the Old and New Testament, containing all things to make us wise to salvation."[9] One of the most immediate influences upon the Confession, however, was the Irish Articles (1615), which begins with the following statement: "The ground of our religion and the rule of faith and all saving truth is the word of God, contained in the Holy Scripture" (§ 1).[10] Given the Confession's place in history at the threshold of high orthodoxy (1640–1700), as well as the theological traffic between England and the rest of the European continent, Westminster's doctrine of Scripture therefore represents a summary of the early modern Reformed doctrine of Scripture given in confessional form.[11]

The Broader Historical Context

When we approach the Confession to evaluate its doctrine of Scripture, attention should be given to the broader context of earlier Reformed symbols. Confessions were not written in a vacuum or in isolation from other confessional documents. Antecedents were compared and consulted, or at least a general knowledge of them would have been familiar to the divines. For example, the First and Second Helvetic Confessions (1536 and 1566) were widely distributed; there is also the *Harmony of Reformed Confessions*, assembled under the editorial supervision of Theodore Beza (1519–1605) in Geneva.[12] Edward Leigh believed that the *Harmony* demonstrated that Reformed churches were united in their beliefs.[13] The corpus of Reformed symbols, therefore, is crucial to historical contextualization. For the *Harmony*, this corpus included the Augsburg, Sueveland, Basel, First Helvetic, Saxony, Wirtemburg, Gallican, Second Helvetic, Belgic, Bohemia, and

---

[9] Samuel Rutherford, *The Soume of Christian Religion*, § 1, in *Catechisms of the Second Reformation*, ed. Alexander F. Mitchell (London: James Nisbet, 1886), 161.
[10] Warfield, "Doctrine of Holy Scripture," 169.
[11] *PRRD*, 2:92; Warfield, "Doctrine of Scripture," 161.
[12] *Harmonia Confessionum Fidei* (Geneva, 1581); Beza, *An Harmony of the Confessions of the Faith of the Christian and Reformed Churches, Which Purely Profess the Holy Doctrine of the Gospel, in All the Chief Kingdoms, Nations, and Provinces of Europe* (Cambridge: Thomas Thomas, 1586).
[13] Edward Leigh, *Treatise of Religion and Learning and of Religious and Learned Men* (London, 1656), § 13 (p. 169).

Scots Confessions, as well as the Thirty-Nine Articles. The Irish Articles should also not be forgotten.

Against this backdrop it is noteworthy to observe that some Reformed confessions, the First and Second Helvetic, and the *Harmony*, as well as the Irish Articles, begin with the doctrine of Scripture. Other confessions, such as the Gallican and Belgic Confessions, begin with the general knowledge of God and then segue to the doctrine of Scripture.[14] Some might think that this represents a significant difference between the Westminster Confession and other documents, since Westminster begins with Scripture and the Belgic, for example, begins with God. Hence, the argument goes, the Belgic begins with natural theology, and Westminster with supernatural theology, rendering the Belgic indebted to rationalism rather than Scripture. Others, such as Arthur Cochrane, have leveled the opposite charge: that even though the Confession begins with Scripture, the Standards nevertheless represent a devolution from earlier Reformation expressions, and as such, they represent a fall into the abyss of rationalism, among other fatal flaws.[15]

Such claims, however, fail to account for what the two documents actually state. The Belgic Confession begins with God and the means by which we know him—creation and the Word (§§ 1–2). The Westminster Confession similarly states,

> Although the light of Nature and the works of Creation and Providence do so far manifest the Goodnesse, Wisdome, and Power of God, as to leave men inexcusable yet are they not sufficient to give that knowledge of God and of his Will, which is necessary unto salvation. Therefore it pleased the Lord, at sundry times, and in divers maners, to reveale himself, and to declare that his Will unto his Church . . . [and] to commit the same wholly unto writing: which maketh the Holy Scripture to be most necessary. (1.1)

God and Scripture, or Scripture and God, both come inextricably intertwined in the opening of a number of Reformed confessions, and

---

[14] Richard A. Muller, "'The Only Way of Man's Salvation': Scripture in the Westminster Confession," in *Calvin Studies VIII: Presented at the Colloquium on Calvin Studies, Held January 26–27, 1996, at Davidson College and the Davidson College Presbyterian Church*, ed. John Leith (Davidson, NC: Davidson College, 1996), 22n36.

[15] Arthur C. Cochrane, *Reformed Confessions of the 16th Century* (Philadelphia: Westminster, 1966), 30.

slight variations in the order of presentation do not reveal a commitment to rationalism over and against Scripture.[16] William Ames (1576–1633), for example, treats the doctrine of Scripture under the locus of the church, but this does not mean his doctrine is committed to rationalism or that it is not fundamental to his theology.[17] A confession should be evaluated by what it states about Scripture and its role in salvation rather than where the subject of Scripture falls within the order of presented doctrines. This is not to slight the importance of the order of a confession, but is simply an effort to highlight the importance of evaluating the Confession's order in light of its affirmation about Scripture.

Revelation

The Confession begins, then, with the doctrine of revelation. It makes reference to the "light of Nature," which is manifest in the works of creation and providence. Such a statement echoes a number of other confessional sentiments to the same effect. The Canons of Dort (1618–1619) similarly state, "There is, to be sure, a certain light of nature remaining in man after the fall, by virtue of which he retains some notions about God, natural things, and the difference between what is moral and immoral, and demonstrates a certain eagerness for virtue and for good outward behavior."[18] The light of nature reveals God's goodness, wisdom, and power, but this knowledge is insufficient for salvation (1.1). This affirmation is not earth-shattering, as the divines cite a number of *sedes doctrinae* (chair passages) that deal with the natural knowledge of God.[19] The assembly's *Annotations* upon Romans explain that God partly reveals himself by the light of nature to man's conscience by virtue of man's creation in the image of God and through the creation, whereby the divine attributes are reflected. The Second

---

[16] Karl Barth, *Church Dogmatics*, ed. G. W. Bromiley and T. F. Torrance, 14 vols. (1956; Edinburgh: T&T Clark, 1998), I.2:522–23; cf. *PRRD*, 2:98; Richard A. Muller, "*Duplex cognitio dei*' in the Theology of Early Reformed Orthodoxy," *SCJ* 10, no. 2 (1979): 57.

[17] William Ames, *The Marrow of Theology*, trans. John Dykstra Eusden (1968; Grand Rapids: Baker, 1997), 1.34 (pp. 185–89).

[18] Canons of Dort, third and fourth main points, art. 4.

[19] Ps. 19:1–3; Rom. 1:19–20, 32; 2:14–15; cf. Rom. 2:1; contra Rogers and McKim who argue that the light of nature reflects a "Platonic-Augustinian" view of revelation (Jack B. Rogers and Donald K. McKim, *The Authority and Interpretation of the Bible: An Historical Approach* [1979; Eugene: Wipf & Stock, 1999], 203). Karl Barth makes the same claim (Karl Barth, *The Theology of the Reformed Confessions*, trans. Darrell L. Guder and Judith J. Guder [1923; Louisville: WJK, 2002], 45–46).

Helvetic Confession (1566), has a similar assertion when it states that the law "was at one time written in the hearts of men by the finger of God, and is called the law of nature" (12.1). Works of the period, such as that of Pierre Du Moulin (1568–1658), *A Treatise on the Knowledge of God*, set out the extent to which fallen man can know God by natural means.[20] Regardless of this knowledge, man is without excuse "before the righteous judgment of God."[21]

The assembly's comments on Psalm 19 explain that God reveals himself both naturally and supernaturally. The natural means are common to all people and focus upon God's works; in this case, the heavens appear to all and hence are available to all. They afford natural revelation, "due consideration whereof might well incite a natural man to praise the author of so great a work, and benefit." Supernatural revelation, on the other hand, was "not common at that time, but of a special grace and favor, indulged unto the seed of Abraham, the nation of the Hebrews."[22] The natural revelation of God is clearly, therefore, non-salvific. But this does not mean that the light of nature has no other function than to render fallen man incapable of denying God's existence.

There is, in a limited sense, a natural theology within the Westminster Standards.[23] The phrase "light of Nature" appears five times in the Confession. The light of nature gives fallen man a general knowledge of God (1.1), which "showeth that there is a God, who hath Lordship and Soveraignty over all, is good, and doth good unto all, and is therefore to bee feared, loved, praised, called upon, trusted in, and served, with all the heart, and with all the soule, and with all the might" (21.1). The church employs the light of nature to regulate some aspects of worship and determine certain matters related to polity that are common to all people (1.6). The light of nature plays a role in determining the proper limits of Christian liberty, in that a person is not supposed to publish any opinions that are contrary to the light of nature or to the "known Principles of Christianity" (20.4).

---

[20] Pierre Du Moulin, *A Treatise on the Knowledge of God*, trans. Robert Codrington (London: William Sheares, 1634), 1–3; Muller, "*Duplex cognitio dei*," 58–59.
[21] *Annotations*, comm. Rom. 1:19–20.
[22] *Annotations*, comm. Ps. 19:1–3.
[23] Muller, "Scripture in the Westminster Confession," 23.

The light of nature also guides the unregenerate so that they may morally "frame their lives" (10.4).

When the Confession turns to special revelation, it reflects the common Reformed understanding of the twofold knowledge of God (*duplex cognitio Dei*).[24] The twofold knowledge of God was present in the works of Reformed theologians such as Pierre Viret (1511–1571), but the doctrine was likely popularized by Calvin in the final, 1559 edition of his *Institutes* and echoed in the theology of Reformed orthodoxy; it served as a firewall against the elevation of natural knowledge of God. God is known by all people as Creator but is known only to the elect as Redeemer, and this saving knowledge of God comes exclusively through the Scriptures.[25] As Calvin writes, "Since God is first manifested, both in the structure of the world and in the general tenor of Scripture, simply as the Creator, and afterwards reveals himself in the person of Christ as redeemer, hence arises a twofold knowledge of him."[26] Or as John Downame (1571–1652) explains, "Divinity is a doctrine of glorifying God, whereof there be two parts: One, that concerns God: that other, concerning *Emanuel*, God with us."[27] According to the Confession, then, and in accordance with common formulations of the period, the saving knowledge of God comes exclusively through Scripture.

Unlike contemporary doctrinal works, early modern works discuss what Scripture is, how it is to be received and understood, and what Scripture as a whole means. This last element, the meaning of the whole of Scripture, was defined as the foundation (*fundamentum*) and the focus or center (*scopus*) of Scripture. The *scope* of Scripture can also indicate the doctrinal focus. In early modern Reformed works, Christ or the gospel is usually identified as the scope of Scripture. An example of this pattern occurs in the First Helvetic Confession when it states, "The entire biblical Scripture [*scopus Scripturae*] is solely concerned that man understand that God is kind and gracious to him

---

[24] Muller, "*Duplex cognitio dei*," 54; *PRRD*, 1:288–93; cf. Jan Rohls, *Reformed Confessions: Theology from Zurich to Barmen* (Louisville: WJK, 1997), 30.

[25] *DLGTT*, s.v. *duplex cognitio Dei*, 97; Pierre Viret, *A Verie Familiare and Fruitful Exposition of the Christian Faith Contaeined in the Common Crede, Called the Apostles Crede* (London: n.d.), fol. Bi; Muller, "*Duplex cognitio dei*," 55–56.

[26] John Calvin, *Institutes of the Christian Religion*, trans. John Allen (Grand Rapids: Eerdmans, 1949), 1.2.1; Calvin, *Institutio Christianae Religionis* (Geneva: Robert Stephanus, 1559).

[27] John Downame, *The Summe of Sacred Divinitie Briefly and Methodically Propounded* (London: William Barret, 1620), 1.1; Muller, "*Duplex cognitio dei*," 60.

and that he has publicly exhibited and demonstrated this his kindness to the whole human race through Christ his Son" (§ 5).[28] This statement shows that Christ rests at the doctrinal center of the Bible, and hence at the center of a Reformed soteriology. This is not to say that Christ is the touchstone of every doctrine but that all doctrine points, in one way or another, to the person and work of Christ.[29] As Thomas Watson (ca. 1620–1686) explains: "What is the main scope and end of Scripture? Answ. To chalk out a way to salvation: It makes a clear discovery of Christ."[30]

These principles, special revelation in Scripture and Christ as its scope, appear in the latter half of the opening paragraph of the Confession:

> Therefore it pleased the Lord, at sundry times, and in divers maners, to reveale himself, and to declare that his Will unto his Church; and afterwards, for the better preserving and propagating of the Truth, and for the more sure establishment and comfort of the Church against the corruption of the flesh, and the malice of Satan and of the World; to commit the same wholly unto writing. (1.1)

The Confession traces its arguments along the lines of Hebrews 1:1, which is cited as a proof text, as is evident in the phrase "sundry times and in divers maners." The assembly's *Annotations*, for example, explain that the "doctrine of the gospel was revealed unto the fathers; that it was not at once altogether revealed, but a little and a little," and that now God has revealed himself through "his natural Son, coessential, or of the same essence with the Father."[31] In other words, the gospel is revealed and terminates in the zenith of God's revelation, which is in the Son, Jesus Christ.

But embedded in this opening paragraph is a crucial element that distinguishes Reformed belief from Roman Catholic convictions and serves as a leitmotif throughout this first chapter on Scripture. Going back to the writings of Heinrich Bullinger (1504–1575) and earlier, Reformed theologians explained the nature of the Word in terms of the

---

[28] *PRRD*, 2:82.
[29] Ibid., 2:212.
[30] Thomas Watson, *A Body of Practical Divinity* (London: Thomas Parkhurst, 1692), 15.
[31] *Annotations*, comm. Heb. 1:1.

verbum agraphon et engraphon, the "unwritten and written word."[32] This was an important distinction, one that emphasized that God's spoken Word took precedence over his written Word. It might not be immediately apparent, but giving priority to the unwritten (or spoken) Word of God meant that the Word of God existed first, prior to the church. By contrast, Roman Catholics argued that the church existed first and then created the Word. If the church existed first, then its authority was equal to that of Scripture; but if the Word existed first, then the church, naturally, was the product of the Word and hence subject to its authority.

Bullinger, for example, writes, "Their doctrine, first of all taught by a lively expressed voice, and after that set down in writing with pen and ink, is the doctrine of God and the very true word of God."[33] The Word of God begins not with what is written, which would naturally raise questions related to the Canon, but with what is spoken. The unwritten Word of God gives rise to the written Word of God. This type of distinction appears in the works of those such as Wolfgang Musculus (1497–1563), Bucanus, and Leigh.[34] It was also confessed quite early in the Reformation in the Ten Theses of Bern (1528), which state, "The holy catholic church, whose sole head is Christ, has been begotten from the Word of God, in which also it continues, nor does it listen to the voice of any stranger" (§ 1). In other words, the divines do not advocate that the Bible itself is a dead letter, a book containing dusty propositions to be affirmed or denied. Rather, the written Word is a vehicle or instrument for the Word of God by which he continually speaks to the church. As Bullinger writes in the Second Helvetic Confession, "God himself spoke to the fathers, prophets, apostles, and still speaks to us through the Holy Scriptures" (1.1). And likewise, the divines affirm that the supreme authority in the church by which all controversies of religion are adjudicated is "no other but the Holy Spirit speaking in the Scripture" (1.10).[35]

---

[32] *DLGTT*, s.v. *verbum Dei*, 324; contra Rohls, *Reformed Confessions*, 33–35.

[33] Heinrich Bullinger, *The Decades of Henry Bullinger*, ed. Thomas Harding, 4 vols. (1849–1852; Grand Rapids: Reformation Heritage, 2004), serm. 1, 1:54.

[34] Wolfgang Musculus, *Common Places of Christian Religion*, trans. John Man (London, 1578), 350–51; Gulielmus Bucanus, *A Body of Divinity; or, Institutions of Christian Religion* (London: Daniel Pakeman, Abel Roper, and Richard Tomlins, 1659), loc. 4 (p. 49); Leigh, *Body of Divinity*, 1.8.

[35] *PRRD*, 2:81, 182, 184–85, 191, 201.

The point here is that the Word produces the church; the church does not produce the Word. Edward Leigh explains that the written Word is conditional, whereas the unwritten Word is necessary:

> It is not then absolutely and simply necessary, that the word of God should be delivered to us in writing, but only conditionally, and upon supposition. God for a long time, for the space of 2400 years, unto the time of Moses, did instruct his Church with an immediate living voice and had he pleased still to go on in that way, there had been no necessity of Scripture now, more then in that age; there was a continual presence of God with them, but now there is a perpetual absence in that way; and the word of God was written.[36]

Without the Word of God there would be no church, and therefore, the Roman Catholic Church cannot claim that it created the Word and thus has the authority to define the Canon or claim that church traditions are as authoritative as Scripture.

Leigh's claim differs from the view of Johann Eck (1486–1543), the famous Roman Catholic theologian who once debated Martin Luther (1483–1546): "The church is older than Scripture, for when the apostles began to preach, there was no written gospel, no letter of Paul, and yet there was the church dedicated by Christ's blood."[37] Calvin, on the other hand, writes: "If the Christian Church has been from the beginning founded on the writings of the prophets and the preaching of the apostles, wherever that doctrine is found, the approbation of it has certainly preceded the formation of the Church; since without it the Church itself had never existed."[38] Johannes Scharpius (1572–1648) very concisely states, "Scripture, or the word of God, is the foundation of the church." The Word of God is the seed from which the church grows; the seed is older than its progeny.[39] From the earliest days of the Reformation, this was a key principle for the Protestant understanding of the relationship between God's revelation and the

---

[36] Leigh, *Body of Divinity*, 1.7 (p. 84); similarly Watson, *Body of Practical Divinity*, 15.

[37] Johann Eck, *Enchiridion of Commonplaces against Luther and Other Enemies of the Church*, trans. Ford Lewis Battles (Grand Rapids: Baker, 1979), 1.4 (pp. 11–13); Eck, *Enchiridion Locurm Communium adversus Lutheranos* (Ingolstadij, 1529).

[38] Calvin, *Institutes*, 1.7.2.

[39] Johannes Scharpius, *Cursus Theologicus* (Geneva: Petrum et Iacobum Chouët, 1620), cols. 63–64: "Scriptura enim seu verubum Dei, est Ecclesiae fundamentum: Eph. 2.20. . . . At semon sobloe illa, cuius est semon, antiquius est."

church. As Luther writes, "Scripture is the womb from which arises divine truth and the Church."[40]

Inspiration

The Confession does not give a specific theory of inspiration but simply states that the Scriptures "are given by inspiration of God, to be the rule of faith and life" (1.2). This approach stands in contrast to other expressions of the day, such as those from Calvin or Leigh. Calvin once stated that the Holy Spirit "dictated" the Scriptures, though he did not always maintain this conviction unreservedly, arguing also that the apostles wrote "in a certain manner" (*quodammodo*), "under the guidance and dictation of the Spirit of Christ."[41] Leigh, on the other hand, believed that the efficient and original cause of the Scriptures is "God the Father dictating" the Word.[42] The Hungarian Confession (1562) states that God "dictated" the canonical books of Scripture.[43] And likewise, Trent also held that God is the author of both Old and New Testaments "as either directly spoken by Christ or dictated by the Holy Spirit."[44]

Even though a number of theologians opted to express the doctrine of inspiration in terms of dictation, that did not mean this opinion was uniform throughout church history. In the Middle Ages, Thomas Aquinas (1225–1274) did not speak in terms of dictation but instead argued that the Holy Spirit influenced the authors of Scripture to use their judgment in employing certain terms over others.[45] And the *Leiden Synopsis*, written by four Reformed theologians who also served as delegates to the Synod of Dort, also tiptoes around the issue and maintains that the authors of Scripture were not passive but "energetic" and applied their own memories, skills, and styles, resulting in a diversity of styles and vocabulary among the various books of the Bible. Yet the Holy Spirit preserved them from "every error of mind, memory, language."[46]

---

[40] Martin Luther, *First Lectures on the Psalms I*, in *LW*, 10:397 (*Werke* 3:454).

[41] John Calvin, *2 Corinthians and Timothy, Titus, & Philemon*, in *CNTC* (1964; Grand Rapids: Eerdmans, 1994), comm. 2 Tim. 3:16, p. 330 (*CO* 51:383); Calvin, *Institutes*, 4.8.8; cf. *PRRD*, 2:237.

[42] Leigh, *Body of Divinity*, 1.8 (p. 81).

[43] Hungarian Confession 4.22, in *Die Bekenntnisschriften reformierten Kirche*, ed. E. F. Karl Müller (Leipzig: A. Deichertsche Verlagsbuchhandlung Nachf., 1903), 405.

[44] Council of Trent, sess. 4, April 8, 1546, first decree.

[45] Aquinas, *Summa Theologica*, IIIa, q. 60, art. 5, ad 1; *PRRD*, 2:42.

[46] *Synopsis Purioris*, 3.7 (p. 18): "Non enim semper mere *pathetikos*, passive, sed et *energetikos*, effective se habuerent, ut qui et ingenium, menisque agitationem et discursum, et memoriam,

But where the issue of inspiration leaves its mark is in the Confession's exclusion of the apocryphal books. Following its list of the canonical books, the Confession states, "The Books commonly called Apocrypha, not being of Divine inspiration, are no part of the Canon of the Scripture; and therefore are of no authority in the Church of God, nor to be any otherwise approved, or made use of, than other human Writings" (1.3). In its typically oblique fashion, the Confession does not explicitly identify the Roman Catholic Church as the institution with which it disagrees, but this statement directly conflicts with the declarations of the Council of Trent, which includes the Apocrypha in its list of canonical books of the Bible. Trent also anathematizes anyone who does not accept "as sacred and canonical these entire books and all their parts."[47] Robert Bellarmine (1542–1621) contended that the inclusion of the Apocrypha was necessitated by testimony of the apostolic church and that the apostles themselves declared them canonical.[48]

Reformed opinions, however, were the polar opposite. In his *Disputations on Holy Scripture*, one of the definitive Reformed responses to Roman Catholic claims about Scripture, Whitaker elaborates upon a number of reasons why the apocryphal books are rejected. He bases his arguments largely upon the fact that the Old Testament was written by the prophets, but the Apocrypha does not bear the same authoritative imprimatur found in the prophets. The writers of Ecclesiasticus and Maccabees, for example, lived long after the last prophet of the Old Testament, Malachi. Whitaker also appeals to Augustine (354–430), who recognized that not even the Jews themselves esteemed Maccabees as highly as the Old Testament. In other words, Israel, the Old Testament church, never accepted these books as part of their Canon.[49]

---

dispositionem et ordinem stylumque suum (unde scriptionum in iis diversitas) adhibuerunt . . . praesidente tame perpetuo Spiritu S., qui ita eos egit et rexit, u tab omni error mentis, mororiae, linguae et calami, ubique praeservarentur." Similar statements appear in John White, *A Way to the Tree of Life Discovered in Sundry Directions for the Profitable Reading of the Scriptures* (London: R. Royston, 1647), § 4 (pp. 57–63); Muller, "Scripture in the Westminster Confession," 25; *PRRD*, 2:226, 236–37.

[47] *Dogmatic Decrees of Trent*, sess. 4, first decree.

[48] Robert Bellarmine, *De Verbo Dei Scripto et Nonscripto*, 1.10, in *Disputationes Roberti Bellarmini Politiani, Soietatis Jesu, de Controversiis Christianae Fidei, adversus Huius Temporis Haereticos*, vol. 1 (Ingolstatdt: D. Sartorius, 1587), 1.6–15; Whitaker, *Disputations*, 1.5 (p. 53).

[49] Whitaker, *Disputations*, 1.5 (pp. 50–52).

Authority

Related to the overall commitments to the doctrine of revelation, the Confession rests the authority of Scripture not upon the testimony of man or the church, as in Roman Catholic theology, but "wholly upon God (who is Truth it selfe) the Author thereof" (1.4). The nature of this statement can be understood against the backdrop of Augustine's famous statement, "For my part, I should not believe the gospel except as moved by the authority of the Catholic Church."[50] Augustine's statement was the locus of a pitched battle between Protestants and Catholics.[51] In fact, Leigh comments that these words were "so well known to the Papists that one can hardly exchange three words with them, but they will produce them."[52] Leigh then explains that Augustine made the statement when he was a pagan and that it was the authority of the church that first impressed him, not that he believed that the Scriptures required the authentication of the church to establish their authority. Leigh cites the arguments of Musculus, Calvin, Vermigli, and Whitaker as supporting witnesses of this interpretation.[53]

Central to the Confession's doctrine of Scripture is the belief that authority lies with the source; as Leigh writes, "From the divine flows the canonical authority of the Scripture."[54] Whitaker offers one of the more common ways Reformed theologians would argue this point: "Scripture has for its author God himself; from whom it first proceeded and came forth. Therefore the authority of scripture may be proved from the author himself, since the authority of God himself shines forth in it. 2 Tim. 3.16, the whole scripture is called *theopneustos*."[55] For Reformed theologians, inspiration and authority were inextricably combined. Going back to Bullinger, for example, the themes of inspiration and authority go hand in hand with the idea that the Bible is the very Word of God: "Let us therefore in all things believe the word of God delivered to us by the scriptures. Let us think

---

[50] Augustine, *Against the Epistle of Manichaeus*, § 5, in *NPNF*[1] 4:131.
[51] See, e.g., Martin Luther, *That the Doctrines of Men Are to Be Rejected*, in *Works of Martin Luther*, vol. 2 (Philadelphia: Castle, 1915), 451–53; Calvin, *Institutes*, 1.7.3.
[52] Leigh, *Body of Divinity*, 1.2 (p. 18).
[53] Ibid.
[54] Ibid., 1.3 (p. 28).
[55] Whitaker, *Disputations*, 3.3 (p. 289).

that the Lord himself, which is the very living and eternal God, does speak to us by the scriptures."[56] Similar statements appear in Calvin and Musculus.[57]

Key, however, to the affirmation of the authority of the Scriptures is the necessity of the inward illumination of the Holy Spirit. The assembly's advocacy of the necessary illumination of the Spirit certainly refutes the claim that early modern Reformed theologians were indebted or committed to rationalism. Whitaker again offers a common formulation when he writes, "With respect to us, therefore, the authority of the scripture depends upon, and is made clear by, the internal witness of the Holy Spirit; without which, though you were to hear a thousand times that this is the word of God, yet you could never believe in such a manner as to acquiesce with an entire assent."[58] The power of raw or unregenerate reason does not convince the reader of Scripture's authority; only the internal witness of the Holy Spirit—the Spirit's work of effectual calling.

Proof of Divinity

Reformed theology was insistent upon the necessity of the Spirit's work to convince a person of Scripture's truth, but this did not preclude consideration of external evidences or proof of the divinity of the Scriptures—the divines were not mystics. The Confession lists a number of things that might move a person to esteem and revere the Scriptures, including the testimony of the church (a likely nod to Augustine's earlier statement about the authority of the church inducing him to accept the Scriptures), the heavenliness of its contents, the effectiveness of its doctrine, the beauty of its style, its internal consistency, the overall scope of Scripture (which was to glorify God), its doctrine of salvation, and many other excellent features. The Confession states that all of these things "are Arguments whereby it doth abundantly evidence itself to be the Word of God" (1.5).

Some have argued that this list of proofs for the divinity of the Word represents a turn toward rationalism, a departure from the simple

---

[56] Bullinger, *Decades*, 1:56–57.
[57] Calvin, *Institutes*, 1.7.1; Musculus, *Common Places*, 387–88.
[58] Whitaker, *Disputations*, 3.3 (p. 290).

faith of the earlier Reformation.[59] But such a characterization fails to consider three key points. First, one must consider the Confession's insistence upon the necessary and prerequisite work of the Spirit: "Yet notwithstanding, our full persuasion and assurance of the infallible truth, and Divine authority thereof, is from the inward work of the Holy Spirit bearing witnesse by and with the Word, in our hearts" (1.5). The Confession rests the belief in the Scriptures not upon reason but upon the internal witness of the Spirit. Second, the Confession's affirmations of these external and internal proofs of divinity echo numerous statements from earlier Reformed works; the divines did not somehow depart from or corrupt the supposed "pristine" theology of the Reformation.

Calvin, for example, devotes a chapter in his *Institutes* to "rational proofs to establish belief of the Scripture."[60] Bucanus answers the question as to how a person might know that God has inspired the Scriptures: "Partly by testimonies, partly by reason. And by testimonies, partly inward, partly outward. The internal witness is one alone: namely, of the holy Ghost inwardly speaking to our heart, and persuading us that those writings are inspired by God, and sealing them up in our hearts." But Bucanus also lists the "outward testimonies," which include thirteen different characteristics that prove the inspiration of the Scriptures.[61]

Reflective of this broader Reformed consensus, Whitaker lists eight different proofs of divinity in his *Disputations on Scripture*:

1. Majesty of the doctrine.
2. Simplicity, purity, and divinity of the style.
3. Antiquity of the books.
4. The oracles themselves self-evidently manifest their authority.
5. Miracles prove their authority.
6. Enemies of God have unsuccessfully tried to destroy the Scriptures.
7. Testimony of the martyrs.

---

[59] See comments by T. F. Torrance, *Scottish Theology: From John Knox to John McLeod Campbell* (Edinburgh: T&T Clark, 1996), 127; also Rogers and McKim, *Authority and Interpretation*, 220–21; cf. *PRRD*, 2:256, 264–65.
[60] Calvin, *Institutes*, 1.8.1.
[61] Bucanus, *Institutions*, 45–49.

8. Many of the authors' inability to write such sublime truth apart from the gift of the Holy Spirit.

Yet, like the Westminster Confession after him, Whitaker nevertheless stipulates, "These topics may prove that these books are divine, yet will never be sufficient to bring conviction to our souls so as to make us assent, unless the testimony of the Holy Spirit be added." He goes on to write, "Those previous arguments may indeed urge and constrain us; but this (I mean the internal testimony of the Holy Spirit) is the only argument which can persuade us."[62] These arguments and others like them appear in Leigh as well, who deliberates over the internal and external proofs and mentions that theologians have given nearly forty arguments to prove that the Scriptures are inspired by God.[63]

A third key element that proves that the divines safeguarded against rationalism was their bitter opposition to Socinianism, which they believed was the seventeenth-century rebirth of Pelagianism.[64] Leigh, for example, wrote:

The inspiration of the Spirit is considered as an efficient cause, which disposes our faculties to believe the truth, and not as an argument of the truth. The Pelagians say, the faculties of the soul are well enough disposed to understand and believe the things of God without the inward inspiration and illumination of the Spirit.

Leigh believed that Socinianism's exclusive reliance upon raw, unaided reason had repercussions upon one's soteriology and the need for the work of the Spirit: "Socinians will have nothing but reason, no infused habits, and so they destroy the testimony of the Spirit."[65]

Confirmation of Leigh's fear comes from the Racovian Catechism (1602), the first Socinian confessional document, which rehearses many of the above-mentioned proofs for the divinity of Scripture, but makes no recourse whatsoever to the necessary work of the Holy Spirit to convince a person of the inspiration of the Scriptures.[66] By contrast,

---

[62] Whitaker, *Disputations*, 3.3 (pp. 294–95).
[63] Leigh, *Body of Divinity*, 1.2 (p. 7).
[64] See David Dickson, *Truths Victory over Error* (Edinburgh: John Reed, 1684), 1.1 (pp. 1–2).
[65] Leigh, *Body of Divinity*, 1.2 (p. 16).
[66] *The Racovian Catechism*, trans. Thomas Rees (London: Longman, Hurst, Rees, Orme, and Brown, 1818), 1.1 (pp. 1–10).

the Confession states, "We acknowledge the inward illumination of the Spirit of God to be necessary for the saving understanding of such things as are revealed in the Word" (1.6).[67] Failure to read the Confession in its historical context, such as against the backdrop of Socinian claims, might lead historians to conclude that the Westminster Confession is rationalistic, but one has to ignore several key statements in the Confession to reach such a conclusion. However, in comparison with the Racovian Catechism, and in light of the documented fears of theologians such as Leigh, one cannot responsibly level the charge of rationalism against the Confession.

Sufficiency

Given Scripture's divine origin, the Standards argue for the sufficiency of the Scriptures, but this sufficiency is narrowly focused upon two specific ends. The Shorter Catechism (q. 3) says:

Q. What do the Scriptures principally teach?
A. The Scriptures principally teach, What man is to believe concerning God, and what duty God requires of man.

This echoes expressions found in earlier works, such as that of William Ames, who argued that the Scriptures are the "rule of faith and morals."[68] The Confession states that the whole counsel of God embraces "things necessary for his own Glory, mans salvation, Faith, and Life" (1.6). But what do they mean by this limited purpose of belief and duty?

First, the sufficiency and limited purpose of the Scriptures mirror what was by then a standard theological distinction in Reformed dogma between archetypal and ectypal theology.[69] The use of the distinction has been traced to Francis Junius (1545–1602) and the development of theological prolegomena, a subject largely left untreated by the Reformers.[70] According to Junius archetypal theology deals with matters pertaining to the wisdom of God, and this wisdom is some-

---

[67] Muller, "Scripture in the Westminster Confession," 27.
[68] Ames, *Marrow of Theology*, 1.34.10 (p. 187).
[69] *PRRD*, 1:225–37.
[70] Willem J. Van Asselt, "The Fundamental Meaning of Theology: Archetypal and Ectypal Theology in Seventeenth-Century Reformed Thought," *WTJ* 64 (2002): 321.

thing that we worship but cannot investigate.[71] Archetypal theology is something proper to God and cannot be communicated to the creature, a limitation due to the finitude, not the fallen state, of the creature.[72] Ectypal theology, however, is the divine wisdom concerning the things of God, which flows from the archetype but is suited to the creature and is communicated by God's grace for his glory.[73] In short, archetypal theology is God's knowledge of himself, and ectypal theology is the true, finite, revealed knowledge of God suited to humanity's capacities and for their salvation.[74]

Though Junius may have been the first to employ the distinction, it was quickly adopted and used by numerous Continental Reformed theologians, including Amandus Polanus (1561–1610), Petrus van Mastricht (1630–1706), Francis Turretin (1623–1687), and Johannes Cocceius (1603–1669).[75] But as was the trend in early modern Europe, theological dialogue moved back and forth between the Continent and the British Isles. Hence it should be no surprise to find the distinction in English theologians such as Edward Leigh. He explains these two terms very succinctly in the following manner: "Archetypal, or divinity in God, of God himself," is that "by which God by one individual and immutable act knows himself in himself, and all other things out of himself, by himself." On the other hand, "ectypal and communicated" theology is "expressed in us by divine revelation after the pattern and idea which is in God, and this is called *theologia de Deo*, divinity concerning God."[76]

John Owen (1616–1683) addresses what lies at the core of the limited function of the Scriptures in terms of the archetypal-ectypal distinction when he writes: "It is necessary to the unlimited self-sufficiency of God that he himself alone may know himself perfectly (Psa. 147:5). His understanding is perfect and has no limits. . . . This attribute . . . may not improperly be called 'archetypal theology.'" By contrast, God has made known his will through the Scriptures "to

---

[71] Francis Junius, *De Vera Theologia*, in *Opuscula Theological Selecta*, ed. Abraham Kuyper (Amsterdam: Frederic Muller, 1882), chap. 4 (p. 51).
[72] Ibid., chap. 4 (p. 52).
[73] Ibid., chap. 5 (p. 53).
[74] *DLGTT*, s.v. *theologia archetypa*, *theologia ectypa*, 299–301.
[75] Van Asselt, "Fundamental Meaning of Theology," 323.
[76] Leigh, *Body of Divinity*, 1.1 (p. 2).

which all of our thoughts and doctrine, our worship of him and our obedience to him, ought always to be conformed; and so, indeed should all of our theology."[77] Ectypal theology is limited, vis-à-vis the infinite archetype, but it is nonetheless sufficient for man that he might know what he must believe concerning God and his duties toward him. In other words, the fact that revelation is limited in its function does not mean it is insufficient for its purposes. In this respect, Leigh argues that Scripture is a perfect rule of faith and obedience and is sufficient to instruct Christians in all points of faith and doctrine. "Whatsoever is needful to believe or to do to please God," writes Leigh, "and save our souls, is to be found here; whatsoever is not here found, is not needful to believe and practice for felicity."[78]

The implication of the sufficiency of Scripture is that the Confession opposes the Roman Catholic teaching that the church is the only body authorized to interpret the Scriptures. From the earliest days of the conflict between Rome and the Reformers, this was a point of contention. Roman Catholic theologian Johann Eck objected to the "Lutheran" belief that the Scriptures were clear, or perspicacious, and concluded, "Therefore laymen and crazy old women treat them in a domineering manner." Eck cites 2 Peter 3:15–16 and the apostle's words that there are some things in the Scriptures that are difficult to understand and unsound people consequently twisted them. Eck writes, "Note the difficulty of those Scriptures, and how (when Paul was living) they were distorted, just as the Lutherans do today."[79] This is one of the reasons why the Roman Catholic Church opposed the translation of the Scriptures into the vernacular.[80]

Even though the Confession speaks of the overall clarity, or perspicacity, of the Scriptures, it at the same time admits that some portions are difficult to understand:

> All things in Scripture are not alike plain in themselves, nor alike
> clear unto all: yet those things which are necessary to be known,

---

[77] John Owen, *Biblical Theology*, trans. Stephen P. Westcott (1661; Morgan, PA: Soli Deo Gloria, 1996), 1.3 (p. 15); cf. Carl R. Trueman, *The Claims of Truth: John Owen's Trinitarian Theology* (Carlisle: Paternoster, 1998), 54–56, 61–62; Sebastian Rehnman, *Divine Discourse: The Theological Methodology of John Owen* (Grand Rapids: Baker, 2002), 57–71.

[78] Leigh, *Body of Divinity*, 1.7 (pp. 82–83).

[79] Eck, *Enchiridion*, § 4 (p. 47).

[80] Bellarmine, *De Verbo Dei*, 2.15 (pp. 174–84).

believed, and observed for salvation, are so clearly propounded, and opened in some place of Scripture or other, that not only the learned, but the unlearned, in a due use of the ordinary means, may attain unto a sufficient understanding of them. (1.7)

The way Leigh explains this doctrinal point is that the Scriptures are clear in the fundamentals, such as the Decalogue, the teachings of the Apostles' Creed, the Lord's Prayer, and the like.[81] Moreover, there are many things in the Scriptures that are clear in terms of what the Word itself teaches, but not in terms of the mysteries it reveals. The doctrine of the Trinity is a mystery and cannot be comprehended, but if we look to the affirmations of the Word, we can know that there is one God in three persons: "The words are plain and easy: every man understands them, but the mystery contained in those words passes the reach of man; we may well discern these things to be so, though we cannot fully conceive how these things should be so."[82]

The Confession acknowledges that there are places in the Scriptures that are difficult to understand but that "the infallible Rule of Interpretation of Scripture is the Scripture it selfe" (1.9). An interpreter can take a difficult passage and compare it with other passages that speak more clearly to the same subject. The *analogiae Scripturae* (the analogy of Scripture) is a bedrock teaching of the Reformed tradition and goes back to the earliest days of the sixteenth century. Bullinger, for example, writes, "First of all you must understand, that some things in the scriptures, or word of God, are so plainly set forth, that they have need of no interpretation, neither will admit any exposition." The Scriptures are as clear as the sun, and attempting to clarify some passages would be like trying to brighten the sun's light with a torch.[83] But Bullinger also explains that unclear scriptural passages can be illuminated from other brighter portions of the Bible: "There is also, beside these, another manner of interpreting the word of God; that is, by conferring together the places which are like or unlike, and by expounding the darker by the more evident, and the few by the more in number."[84]

---

[81] Leigh, *Body of Divinity*, 1.7 (p. 100).
[82] Ibid., 1.7 (p. 99).
[83] Bullinger, *Decades*, 1:75.
[84] Ibid., 1:78.

Bullinger's method of interpretation was eventually codified in his Second Helvetic Confession, lending evidence of the widespread belief of this interpretive principle:

> We hold that interpretation of the Scriptures to be orthodox and genuine which is gleaned from the Scriptures themselves (from the nature of the language in which they were written, likewise according to the circumstances in which they were set down, and expounded in the light of like and unlike passages and of many clearer passages) and which agrees with the rule of faith and love, and contributes much to the glory of God and man's salvation. (2.1)

Bullinger was not unique in this interpretive principle, as others, such as Bucanus, argued that the Scriptures were to be interpreted according to their constant and perpetual sense, as in the manifest places of Scripture agreeable to the Apostles' Creed, Decalogue, the Lord's Prayer, and the general principles and axioms of every point of divinity.[85]

Central to the Reformed exposition of Scripture, and hence its insistence upon the Bible's clarity, is the principle that there is one sense to Scripture, not four, as medieval exegetes had long maintained.[86] According to earlier medieval exegesis, such as the method advocated by Aquinas, there is the literal (or historical) sense, the spiritual, the allegorical, and the anagogical. Aquinas explains that the other three senses rest upon the literal sense, which is the only source for theological argumentation, and that nothing necessary for faith is contained in the spiritual sense that is not elsewhere given in the literal sense. Other medieval theologians argued for the historical, allegorical, and tropological senses of Scripture.[87] However, the fourfold approach to interpretation originated not in the Middle Ages but in the Patristic era. According to Augustine the historical sense tells the reader what happened, the aetiological gives the reason or cause as to why something was written, the analogical shows the harmony between the

---

[85] Bucanus, *Institutions*, 51.
[86] On the quadriga see Robert M. Grant with David Tracy, *A Short History of the Interpretation of the Bible* (1963; Philadelphia: Fortress, 1984), 83–91; Richard A. Muller, "Biblical Interpretation in the Era of the Reformation: The View from the Middle Ages," in *Biblical Interpretation in the Era of the Reformation*, ed. Richard A. Muller and John Thompson (Grand Rapids: Eerdmans, 1996), 30–20; *PRRD*, 2:449.
[87] Aquinas, *Summa Theologica*, Ia, q. 1, art. 10.

two testaments, and the allegorical sense provides what should be figuratively understood.[88]

In contrast to earlier views, the divines, along with the Reformed tradition, affirm that there is only one sense in Scripture, the literal or grammatical, whether the interpretation arises from the words taken in a strict or a figurative sense. The divines acknowledge that many things in the Old Testament are revealed in terms of types and ordinances that fore-signify Christ's coming (7.5). Whitaker and Leigh recognize the importance and legitimacy of typology, or what some theologians of the period termed the "mystical sense of Scripture."[89] But Whitaker and Leigh do not concede the legitimacy of the quadriga. Rather, the mystical sense is part of the text's singular meaning. As Leigh explains:

> The mystical or spiritual sense is that in which the thing expressed in the literal sense signifies another thing in a mystery, for the shadowing out of which it was used by God. The waters of the flood, with which the ark was upheld, signified baptism, by which the church is saved under the new covenant, as the apostle teaches (1 Pet. 3:21), that history (Exo. 12), *it is a Passover unto the Lord*, is spoken figuratively, the other words properly. The mystical sense is, the bones of Christ were no more broken then of the Paschal Lamb, which did signify Christ.[90]

There are not, therefore, multiple senses of Scripture, according to Reformed theologians; rather, as Whitaker argues, the literal sense contains a sign (a type) that points to the thing signified (the antitype). To recognize the relationship between type and antitype does not introduce a new sense but only draws out what was originally concealed in the sign.[91]

Good and Necessary Consequence

The divines were not biblicists who confined their doctrine to a bald reading of the Scriptures. Given that they employed the analogy of

---

[88] Augustine, *The Profit of Believing*, § 5, in *NPNF*[1] 3:349.
[89] Whitaker, *Disputations*, 5.2 (p. 406); Leigh, *Body of Divinity*, 1.9 (p. 105); Daniel Chamier, *De Interpretatione Scripturae*, in *Panstratiae Catholicae sive Controversiarum de Religione adversus Pontificos Corpus*, 2nd ed., vol. 1 (n.p., 1629), 15.1–3 (pp. 261–65).
[90] Leigh, *Body of Divinity*, 1.9 (p. 105).
[91] Whitaker, *Disputations*, 5.2 (p. 407).

Scripture, comparing various passages together, they also engaged in arguments from the implicit statements of the Bible. The Confession explains, "The whole Councel of God concerning all things necessary for his own Glory, mans salvation, Faith, and Life, is either expressly set down in Scripture, or by good and necessary consequence may be deduced from Scripture" (1.6). This statement finds antecedents from the earliest days of the Reformation in such documents as the Tetrapolitan Confession (1530), which states that preachers were to draw their sermons from teaching that is "contained in the Holy Scriptures or has sure ground therein" (§ 1).[92] Leigh, for example, explains that the Scriptures explicitly deliver all doctrines that are necessary for salvation, as it pertains to both faith and good works, but other teachings, such as infant baptism or the consubstantiality of the Father and the Son, are expressed implicitly and must be determined by good and necessary consequence.

Leigh notes that some Roman Catholic theologians thought doctrine should be limited to the express statements of Scripture.[93] Richard Hooker (1554–1600) was also critical of the use of good and necessary consequences in theological argumentation. Hooker objected to the idea that "contained in the Scriptures" meant expressly stated. He understood that certain teachings were not expressly stated, such as the Trinity, the co-eternity of the Father and Son, the procession of the Spirit, and infant baptism. But he was nonetheless dubious as to how far a good and necessary consequence could be carried. In particular, Hooker doubted that "reformed church-discipline" could be necessarily deduced from Scripture.[94]

One of the Scottish divines, George Gillespie (1613–1648), directly responded to Hooker's objections in his own treatment of the subject. There he notes that Arminians, Arians, antitrinitarians, Socinians, and Papists reject the interpretive principle.[95] In his explanation he draws upon the works of John Cameron (ca. 1579–1625), Lutheran theologian Johann Gerhard (1582–1637), and Aquinas to prove his

---

[92] PRRD, 2:82.
[93] Leigh, Body of Divinity, 1.7 (p. 87).
[94] Richard Hooker, Of the Laws of Ecclesiastical Polity, 2 vols. (1907; London: J. M. Dent & Sons, 1954), 1.14.2 (p. 216); cf. C. J. Williams, "Good and Necessary Consequence in the Westminster Confession," in The Faith Once Delivered, ed. Anthony T. Selvaggio (Phillipsburg, NJ: P&R, 2007), 173.
[95] Also Dickson, Truths Victory over Error, 1.9 (pp. 12–13); PRRD, 2:497.

point. First, he argues that although arguments and consequences are drawn by deductive reason, the resulting consequent is not believed by the power of reason but because it is "the truth and will of God."[96] According to his citation from Cameron, Gillespie argues that reason is an instrument in this process, not the foundation of the argument.[97]

Citing Lutheran theologian Gerhard, he also draws a distinction between corrupt and regenerate reason, the latter of which judges divine things not by human reason but by divine rules, and stands on scriptural principles, which are opposed to the wisdom of the flesh.[98] Gillespie then cites Aquinas on the legitimacy of two different types of consequences: sufficient and necessary (or certain).[99] The Scottish theologian maintains that there are two such consequences in Scripture: those things that are necessary and those that are suitable, or in harmony, with Scripture.[100] Gillespie appeals to Scripture to support his argument and draws upon Christ's proof for the resurrection, where Jesus proves that God is the God of the living, not the dead, based upon the tense of a verb (Matt. 22:31, 33; Luke 20:37–38); Gillespie also cites Paul's argument from a consequence in Scripture regarding Christ's resurrection (Acts 13:33–34).[101]

Gillespie explains at length how important good and necessary consequences are for a proper understanding of Scripture:

> Diverse other great absurdities must follow, if this truth be not admitted. How can it be proved that women may partake of the Sacrament of the Lord's supper, unless we prove it by necessary consequence from Scripture? How can it be proved that this or that Church, is a true Church, and the ministry thereof, a true ministry, and the baptism ministered therein true baptism? Sure no express Scripture will prove it, but necessary consequence will. How shall this or that individual believer, collect from Scripture, that to him,

---

[96] George Gillespie, *A Treatise of Miscellany Questions Wherein Many Useful Questions and Cases of Conscience Are Discussed and Resolved* (Edinburgh: Gedeon Lithgow, 1649), § 20 (p. 239).

[97] John Cameron, *Praelectionum in Selectiora Quaedam Novi Testamenti Loca, Salmurii Habitarum*, 3 vols. (Saumur: Girard & Dan. Lerpinière, 1632), 1:364.

[98] Gillespie, *Treatise of Miscellany Questions*, § 20 (p. 239); cf. Johann Gerhard, *Theological Commonplaces*, vol. 25, *On the Church*, trans. Richard J. Dinda, ed. Benjamin T. G. Mayes (St. Louis: Concordia, 2010), 25.11.8, § 252 (p. 550); Muller, "Scripture in the Westminster Confession," 30.

[99] Aquinas, *Summa Theologica*, Ia, q. 32, art. 1.

[100] Gillespie, *Miscellany Questions*, § 20 (p. 239).

[101] Ibid., § 20 (p. 240).

even to him the covenant of grace and promises thereof belong? Will Scripture prove this otherwise, than by necessary consequence?[102]

As one can well imagine, Gillespie was not alone in his opinions. Other divines, such as Leigh, Rutherford, and Robert Baillie (1602–1662), made similar arguments concerning the resurrection of Christ and infant baptism.[103] Leigh also cited the works of two other Reformed theologians on this principle, Nicolaus Vedel (1596–1642) and Jean Daillé (1594–1670), as further evidence of the widespread use of good and necessary consequence as an interpretive principle in early modern Reformed theology.[104]

The question that naturally surfaces is whether the divines were simply applying raw reason and building doctrinal conclusions upon logic rather than Scripture. Some have drawn this conclusion, but others, such as Warfield, have demonstrated that good and necessary consequences are the application of the analogy of Scripture, or Scripture interpreting Scripture. Echoing sentiments expounded above, Warfield explains:

> We must depend upon our human faculties to ascertain what Scripture *says*; we cannot suddenly abnegate them and refuse their guidance in determining what Scripture *means*. This is not, of course, to make reason the ground of the authority of inferred doctrines and duties, whether "expressly set down in Scripture" or "by good and necessary consequence deduced from Scripture": but their authority, when once discovered, is derived from God, who reveals and prescribes Scripture, either by literal assertion or by necessary implication.[105]

In this respect, it is important to understand what the divines, and later Warfield, argue; namely, the issue of a good and necessary

---

[102] Ibid., § 20 (pp. 243–44); cf. "Williams, "Good and Necessary Consequence," 176–77.

[103] Leigh, *Body of Divinity*, 1.8 (p. 87); Samuel Rutherford, *Christ Dying and Drawing Sinners to Himself* (Edinburgh: T. Lumisden, 1727), 321; Robert Baillie, *Anabaptism, the True Fountaine of Independency, Antinomy, Brownisme, Familisme* (London: Samuel Gellibrand, 1647), 37; cf. Williams, "Good and Necessary Consequence," 177.

[104] Leigh, *Body of Divinity*, 1.8 (p. 87); Jean Daillé, *La foi fondée sur les Saintes Escritures, contre les nouveaux méthodistes*, 2nd ed. (1661), 47–51; Nicolaus Vedel, *Rationale Theologicum seu de Necessitate et Vero Usu Principiorum Rationis ac Philosophiae in Controversiis Theologicis Libri Tres* (Geneva: Jacobum Chouët, 1628), 1.3 (pp. 22–27), 1.5 (pp. 37–49), 2.5 (pp. 183–90).

[105] Warfield, "Doctrine of Holy Scripture," 226.

consequence is not a matter of placing Scripture and reason in the balance and producing a conclusion.[106] Instead, the principle involves collating and comparing various passages of Scripture, which is evident in Gillepsie's language of *collecting* teachings from Scripture, and explaining how they all fit together.[107] At this point the Confession's doctrine of good and necessary consequence distinguishes it from the Roman Catholic view, which bases doctrine upon tradition; and it is also different from the approaches of Anabaptists and Quakers, who claim new revelation.[108] To this end, the Confession asserts that divine revelation has ceased (1.1).[109]

The Importance of Original Languages

Given all that we have seen the Confession to argue thus far, it should be no surprise that the divines insist upon the authority of the original languages of Scripture for correct doctrine. The Confession affirms the necessity of Hebrew and Greek as "authentic," and therefore the church must make final appeal to original languages in all controversies of religion. But making final appeal to the original languages does not mean that the Scriptures should not also be translated into the vernacular languages. The Confession states, "But, because these Original Tongues are not known to all the people of God, who have right unto, and interest in the Scriptures, and are commanded, in the fear of God, to read and search them, therefore, they are to be translated into the vulgar Language of every Nation unto which they come" (1.8). Once again, though the Confession makes no mention of it, its opinion directly conflicts with the doctrine of the Roman Catholic Church. The Council of Trent officially endorsed the use of the "old Latin Vulgate edition" and placed anyone who rejected it under anathema.[110] A corollary of the use of the Vulgate was the celebration

---

[106] Cf. Torrance, *Scottish Theology*, 129.

[107] *PRRD*, 2:499.

[108] Williams, "Good and Necessary Consequence," 179; cf. George Fox, *Something in Answer to That Book Called the Church-Faith Set Forth by Independents and Others; Agreed upon by Divine Messengers, Meeting at the Savoy in London. And Also, to that Book, Intitled, the Confession of Faith, Approved on by the Church of Scotland* (London: Robert Wilson, 1660); W. Parker, *The Late Assembly of Divines Confession of Faith Examined* (London, 1651).

[109] Dickson, *Truths Victory over Error*, 1.3, 5 (pp. 1–2, 7–8). See also Garnet Howard Milne, *The Westminster Confession of Faith and the Cessation of Special Revelation: The Majority Puritan Viewpoint on Whether Extra-Biblical Prophecy Is Still Possible* (Milton Keynes: Paternoster, 2007).

[110] Council of Trent, sess. 4, April 8, 1546, first decree.

of the mass in Latin rather than in the vernacular languages of the various countries wherever people worshipped.[111]

The Confession simply echoes principles long established in Reformed churches concerning both the significance of the original languages and the necessity to translate them into the vernacular. In his *Disputations*, for example, Whitaker gives five chief arguments for the necessity of translating the Scriptures:

1. It is commanded by God (Deut. 31:11–12, 27:19–20).
2. People should not be deprived of their principal weapon against Satan.
3. The Scriptures are to be read publically so that people may benefit from them (1 Cor. 14:6–7, 19).
4. The Lord commands and requires that the church be instructed in the mysteries of salvation.
5. Christ taught the people in their native language; the apostles also did likewise on the day of Pentecost.[112]

In these arguments, which are generally echoed by the Confession, Whitaker propounds points that were affirmed not only among the Reformed, but also by Patristic theologians, such as Jerome (ca. 347–420) and Chrysostom (ca. 347–407), and Lutherans, such as Martin Chemnitz (1522–1586), whom Whitaker cites. Chrysostom, for example, exhorts his listeners to obtain "at least the New Testament, the apostolic epistles, the Acts, the Gospels" as their constant teachers and "dive into them as into a chest of medicines."[113] Whitaker draws his fifth argument, that Christ taught in the vernacular, from Chemnitz, thus showing that the necessity of the Scriptures in the vernacular was not an isolated Reformed belief but one that was shared by other Protestants.[114]

In terms of the exegetical process as it incorporated the original languages, Leigh offers an illustrative window into early modern Re-

---

[111] Ibid., sess. 22, September 17, 1562, § 8.

[112] Whitaker, *Disputations*, 2.15 (pp. 235–49).

[113] Chrysostom, *Homilies on Colossians*, 9, in *NPNF*[1] 13:300–301; cf. Whitaker, *Disputations*, 2.15 (pp. 239–40).

[114] Martin Chemnitz, *Examination of the Council of Trent*, trans. Fred Kramer, vol. 1, pt. 1, of *Chemnitz's Works* (1971; St. Louis: Concordia, 2007), 1.7.3 (pp. 198–99); cf. Whitaker, *Disputations*, 2.15 (p. 242).

formed exegesis, namely, the exegetical methodology common among the Westminster divines. He gives six basic guidelines for the proper interpretation of a text:

1. Consider the text exactly in itself, the grammar of it, the rhetoric, and its logic.
2. Compare parallel places, the obscure with the clear.
3. Make use of paraphrases and versions, such as Chaldean, the Septuagint, Syriac, and Arabic.
4. For the knowledge of any particular phrase, go through the same steps above.
5. Ensure that all exposition agrees with the analogy of faith, which is comprehended in the Apostles' Creed.
6. Consult with Jewish expositors, the church fathers, and other interpreters, both popish and Protestant, that are useful for a right understanding, so long as they are read critically.[115]

Leigh then goes on to list various Jewish commentators worthy of consultation: David Kimchi (1160–1235), Abraham Ibn Ezra (1089–1164), and Maimonides (1135–1204). He also mentions the Talmud, a chief text of rabbinic Judaism.[116]

Leigh lists those whom he regards as the best commentators on the various books of the Bible; the list is expansive and includes Augustine, Chrysostom, Gregory of Nazianzus (ca. 329–390), and Tertullian (ca. 160–225) among the Patristics, and Aquinas and Bernard of Clairvaux (1090–1153) among medieval exegetes. From the Reformation Leigh includes Calvin, Musculus, Vermigli, Martin Bucer (1491–1551), and Martin Luther. From early orthodoxy he mentions Johannes Piscator (1546–1625), Theodore Beza, Francis Junius, Girolamo Zanchi (1516–1590), David Pareus (1548–1622), Robert Rollock (1555–1599), and Andrew Willet (ca. 1561–1621). And from among his contemporaries he lists André Rivet (1572–1651), Daniel Featley (1582–1645), and Gisbert Voetius (1589–1676).[117] This list of exegetes and theologians shows that the divines were not myopic in their exegetical and theological labors; they consulted a wide spectrum

---

[115] Leigh, *Body of Divinity*, 1.9 (p. 111).
[116] Ibid., 1.9 (p. 112).
[117] Ibid., 1.9 (pp. 112–20).

of sources in the construction of their theological convictions. Leigh's broad cross-section of consulted works and authors was by no means unique, as this was the standard *modus operandi* for Reformed theologians.[118] In other words, Reformed theologians did not completely eliminate all reference to tradition; rather, they engaged with and employed it critically in the construction of their theology.[119] Moreover, neither were the divines indebted to one theologian, such as Calvin. They were learned men of letters with a broad knowledge base that they regularly employed in the exegesis and exposition of Scripture.

Conclusion

The Confession's opening chapter identifies the well from which all doctrine is drawn, and this reflects one of the chief tenets of the Reformation's principle of *sola Scriptura*. Scripture alone is the sole arbiter of Christian faith and practice in the church. Read in its historical context, the first chapter of the Confession appears fairly conventional, affirming numerous points articulated by a host of English and European early modern Reformed theologians. However, it also succinctly summarizes the early modern Reformed doctrine of Scripture, codifying key doctrinal principles such as the analogy of Scripture, the limits of the canon of Scripture, the sufficiency of Scripture, and the vital importance of good and necessary consequences. Yet, when compared with the beliefs and practices of the Confession's dialogue partners, such as the Roman Catholic Church, the quiet doctrinal affirmations of the first chapter stand in stark contrast to the anathemas of the Council of Trent. In the next chapter, we turn to the subject of God and the decree.

---

[118] *PRRD*, 2:341, 348.
[119] See Heiko A. Oberman, "Introduction: Scripture and Tradition," in *Forerunners of the Reformation: The Shape of Late Medieval Thought* (Cambridge: James Clarke, 1967), 53–66; Irena Backus, "The Fathers in Calvinist Orthodoxy: Patristic Scholarship," in *The Reception of the Church Fathers in the West: From the Carolingians to the Maurists*, ed. Irena Backus, 2 vols. (Leiden: Brill, 2001), 2:867–88.

4

God and the Decree

A common assumption about the Reformation is that it swept away everything to do with the Roman Catholic Church and started with a blank slate. But many fail to realize that the Reformation was a *reform* movement; the Reformers did not start from scratch but reformed erroneous areas of doctrine and practice. While perhaps it is an overgeneralization, the Reformation was largely focused upon issues related to soteriology. The doctrine of God was not an area of significant theological debate, but Reformed theologians sharply disagreed with their Roman Catholic opponents where the doctrine of God intersects with soteriology; in areas related to the doctrine of predestination, a renewed Augustinianism, and Paulinism, moved front and center in the debate arena.

This chapter, therefore, surveys the doctrines of God and the decree in order to explore several things. First, how does the doctrine of God relate to the decree? Second, what are the various components of the decree? There are several key issues subsumed under the doctrine of the decree: not merely matters related to the doctrine of election, God's sovereign choice of who is elected in Christ unto eternal life, but also the relationship between divine sovereignty and human responsibility. But before we can survey God and the decree, it is helpful to note how the doctrine of the decree has been received in recent literature. Such an analysis provides a context in which misperceptions of the nature of God's sovereignty can be judged correctly—not by caricature but by a contextually sensitive examination of the theology of the Standards on these two doctrines.

Perceptions of the Decree

The opening paragraph of the Confession's third chapter contains what is arguably one of the most cherished and at the same time vilified statements in the history of theology. The divines write, "God, from all eternity, did, by the most wise and holy Counsel of his own Will, freely, and unchangeably ordain whatsoever comes to passe" (3.1). Much has been made about the fact that the divines in a sense begin their Confession with the doctrine of the decree. True, the Confession has two antecedent chapters, one on Scripture and the other on the triune God, but God's first interaction with his creatures comes not in terms of the grace of the gospel but in terms of the dreaded decree.

J. B. Torrance, for example, explains that the Confession is more indebted to the later Calvinism of Theodore Beza (1519–1605) and William Perkins (1558–1602), inasmuch as predestination was the major premise of their understanding of the nature of creation and redemption. Torrance claims instead that earlier Reformation documents and theologians, such as the 1560 Scots Confession or John Calvin (1509–1564) and his *Institutes*, treat election under christology and soteriology respectively.[1] Torrance has elsewhere argued that the decree (and hence predestination) became central for the later Reformed theology, whereas Christ was central for Calvin.[2]

Torrance's analysis echoes the earlier claims of Basil Hall, who popularized the Calvin-versus-the-Calvinists thesis. One of Hall's chief claims was that Reformed theologians moved the doctrine of predestination into a direct relationship with the doctrine of God, where medieval theologians had discussed it, rather than treating it in the context of soteriology, where Calvin discussed the subject. This shift,

---

[1] J. B. Torrance, "Strengths and Weaknesses of Westminster Theology," in *The Westminster Confession in the Church Today: Papers Prepared for the Church of Scotland Panel on Doctrine*, ed. Alasdair I. C. Heron (Edinburgh: St. Andrews, 1982), 46.
[2] J. B. Torrance, "The Concept of Federal Theology—Was Calvin a Federal Theologian?," in *Calvinus Sacrae Scripturae Professor: Calvin as Confessor of Holy Scripture*, ed. Wilhelm H. Neuser (Grand Rapids: Eerdmans, 1994), 20.

argued Hall, "re-opened the road to speculative determinism which Calvin had attempted to close."[3]

More recently, Jan Rohls argues that in those confessions where election is imported into the doctrine of God, the point of departure for soteriology is no longer historical action in terms of the believer's justification and sanctification but God's pre-temporal decree, and the decrees are expounded in their most logical form, whereby election is conceived in a supralapsarian model.[4] Though Rohls does not state his point in precisely these terms, he implies that when election is treated under the doctrine of God, it becomes extreme and connected to logic rather than to God's saving action in Christ.

One has to wonder whether this perception of the nature of the decree has been caused by reading the Confession in the light of later developments in Reformed theology rather than in its own histori-cal-theological context. A factor contributing to the misreading of the Confession is the theology of Jonathan Edwards (1703–1758), who denied the idea of contingency, something the Confession affirms. Edwards instead taught the idea of *philosophical necessity*, which he defined as "nothing else than the full and fix'd Connection between the Things signified by the Subject & Predicate of a Proposition, which affirms Something to be true. When there is such a Connection, then the Thing affirmed in the Proposition is necessary, in a Philosophical Sense."[5] Nothing, according to Edwards, can occur without a cause, and there is a "fixed connection" between cause and effect. For Edwards, if everything has a cause, there can be no contingency in the world. For him, contingency means that something has no cause. Therefore, Edwards writes:

> If Things may be without Causes, all this necessary Connection and Dependence is dissolved, and so all Means of our Knowledge is

---

[3] Basil Hall, "Calvin and the Calvinists," in *John Calvin*, Courtenay Studies in Reformation Theology 1 (Appleford: The Sutton Courtenay Press, 1966), 25–27; cf. similar comments by Thomas F. Torrance, *Scottish Theology: From John Knox to John McLeod Campbell* (Edinburgh: T&T Clark, 1996), 105.

[4] Jan Rohls, *Reformed Confessions: Theology from Zurich to Barmen* (Louisville: WJK, 1998), 150–51; cf. similar comments in Karl Barth, *The Theology of the Reformed Confessions*, trans. Darrell L. Guder and Judith J. Guder (Louisville: WJK, 2002), 136.

[5] Jonathan Edwards, *A Careful and Strict Enquiry into The Modern Prevailing Notions of That Freedom of Will, Which Is Supposed to Be Essential to Moral Agency, Vertue and Vice, Reward and Punishment, Praise and Blame* (Boston: S. Kneeland, 1754), 1.3 (p. 16).

gone. If there be no Absurdity or Difficulty in supposing one Thing
to start out of Non-Existence, into Being, of itself without a Cause;
then there is no Absurdity or Difficulty in supposing the same of
Millions and Millions.[6]

Edwards's advocacy of philosophical necessity did not go unnoticed.
William Cunningham (1805–1861) argued that Edwards's views were
compatible with the teaching of the Reformers and the Westminster
Standards.[7] Cunningham argued that there is nothing in the Standards that precludes philosophical necessity, but at the same time the
Standards do not require ministers to hold the teaching.[8] Cunningham
came to Edwards's defense because a number of Church of Scotland
ministers held to the doctrine of philosophical necessity and because
fellow Scottish minister William Hamilton (1788–1856) accused Edwards, and those who held to his doctrine, of heresy. Hamilton writes:

> The Scottish Church asserts with equal emphasis, the doctrine of
> the Absolute Decrees of God, and the doctrine of the Moral Liberty
> of Man. The theory of Jonathan Edwards, touching the Bondage
> of the Will, is, on the Calvinistic standards of the Westminster
> Confession, not only heterodox but heretical; and yet, we have seen
> the scheme of Absolute necessity urged, by imposing authority, and
> even apparently received with general acquiescence, as that exclu-
> sively conformable to the recognized tenets of our Ecclesiastical
> Establishment![9]

Hamilton was not alone in his criticism of Edwards, but his contention is important for the following reason: Edwards denies contingency
whereas the Confession teaches it.[10] Hamilton's critique and Cunning-

---

[6] Ibid., 2.3 (p. 45); cf. Richard A. Muller, "Jonathan Edwards and the Absence of Free Choice: A
Parting of the Ways in the Reformed Tradition," *Jonathan Edwards Studies* 1, no. 1 (2011): 12.
[7] William Cunningham, *Historical Theology: A Review of the Principal Doctrinal Discussions in the
Christian Church since the Apostolic Age*, 2 vols. (1862; Edinburgh: Banner of Truth, 1969), 1:581;
Cunningham, "Calvinism and Philosophical Necessity," in *The Reformers and the Theology of the
Reformation, Collected Works of the Rev. William Cunningham*, vol. 1 (Edinburgh: T&T Clark, 1862),
471–525.
[8] Cunningham, "Philosophical Necessity," 483; Muller, "Edwards and the Absence of Free Choice," 18.
[9] William Hamilton, in *The Collected Works of Dugald Stewart*, ed. William Hamilton, vol. 6 (Edinburgh: T&T Clark, 1877), 402; Muller, "Edwards and the Absence of Free Choice," 16.
[10] Muller, "Edwards and the Absence of Free Choice," 18; cf. Sean Michael Lucas, "'He Cuts Up Ed-
wardism by the Roots': Robert Lewis Dabney and the Edwardsian Legacy in the Nineteenth-Century
South," in *The Legacy of Jonathan Edwards*, ed. D. G. Hart, Sean Michael Lucas, and Stephen J.
Nichols (Grand Rapids: Baker, 2003), 200–16.

ham's defense of Edwards's views raise the question vis-à-vis criticisms raised by Torrance and Hall. Does the Confession teach determinism? Is the Confession rightly read through the later developments of Edwardsianism and those who embraced philosophical necessity?

The short answer to these questions is that the Confession does not teach philosophical determinism (or necessity) and does affirm contingency. The Confession specifically states:

> God, from all eternity, did, by the most wise and holy Counsel of his own Will, freely, and unchangeably ordain whatsoever comes to passe: yet so, as thereby neither is God the Author of sin, nor is violence offered to the will of Creatures; nor is the Liberty or *contingencie of second Causes* taken away, but rather established. (3.1, emphasis added)

What do the divines mean by this statement? What do they mean by *contingency*, and how does that relate to God having unchangeably ordained "whatsoever comes to passe"? How do the decree and contingency relate to predestination unto eternal life? And how do all of these things relate to God's freedom and humanity's freedom? Answers to these questions require that we briefly investigate the doctrinal backdrop to the decree and examine a series of theological terms that delineate how God relates to his creation.

Doctrinal Backdrop: God and the Created Order

By its very nature the Confession has a rather simple list of divine attributes: "There is but one only, living, and true God, who is infinite in Being and Perfection, a most pure Spirit, invisible, without body, parts, or passions; immutable, immense, eternal, incomprehensible, almighty, most wise, most holy, most free, most absolute" (2.1). In addition to these attributes, the Confession also states that God is all-sufficient, "not standing in need of any creatures he hath made," and that his knowledge, which is infinite and infallible, is independent of the creature, and nothing is contingent or uncertain to him (2.2). On the whole, these attributes largely deal with God as he is absolutely, or as he is in and of himself. The Confession also lists a series of attributes that show how God relates to his creation. God is "most loving, gracious, merciful, long-suffering, abundant in goodnesse and truth, forgiving iniquity, transgression, and sin; the rewarder of them that diligently seek him; and with all, most just, and terrible in his judgments, hating all sin, and who will by no means clear the guilty" (2.1).

This division of attributes, though listed together in chapter 2, relies upon a standard way of explaining God's person and work, namely, his *opera ad intra* (internal work) and *opera ad extra* (external work). In other words, God can be considered either absolutely, separately from his creation, or relatively, as he is related to his creation. As Johannes Wollebius (1589–1629) notes, "Both essential and personal works include those affecting God alone [*ad intra*] and those whose effects are felt outside of God [*ad extra*]."[11] Likewise he states, "Those works of God which have their object outside of him are either immanent and internal, or outgoing and external."[12]

The distinction between God's internal and external work rests upon another key distinction covered in the previous chapter, *archetypal* and *ectypal theology*—God's knowledge of himself, which is perfect, infinite, and known only to him, and the revealed copy or shadow, which is perfect and true but finite and suited for humanity.[13] With these two terms God's knowledge is considered absolutely and as it relates to humans, who are part of God's created order. A series of technical doctrinal terms follow this internal-external pattern: God's hidden will (*voluntas arcana*) and his revealed will (*voluntas revelata*); God's will within the deliberations among the Trinity (*voluntas immanens*) and vis-à-vis the created order (*voluntas transiens*); God's necessary knowledge (*scientia necessaria*) and his knowledge that relates to created things (*scientia voluntaria*); God's righteousness relative to his being and attributes (*iustitia absoluta et in se*) and his righteousness in relation to his creatures, whether in judgment or mercy (*iustitia relata*); God's own power as it is considered absolutely (*potentia absoluta*) and as it relates to creation and the natural order (*potentia ordinata*).

---

[11] Johannes Wollebius, *Compendium Theologiae Christianae*, 1.3.1, in *Reformed Dogmatics*, ed. and trans. John W. Beardslee III (New York: OUP, 1965), 45.
[12] Ibid., 1.3.2 (p. 46).
[13] Richard A. Muller, "God as Absolute and Relative, Necessary, Free, and Contingent: The *Ad Intra–Ad Extra* Movement of Seventeenth-Century Reformed Language about God," in *Always Reformed: Essays in Honor of W. Robert Godfrey*, ed. R. Scott Clark and Joel E. Kim (Escondido, CA: Westminster Seminary California, 2010), 57–58.

In each of these terms the first deals with an absolute attribute of God, and the latter with that same attribute as it relates to the creation.[14]

The division of attributes and works shown in table 1 is not precise, in that the divines did not intend their Confession to be an academic discussion, but it nevertheless illustrates the absolute-relative nature of God as he is in himself and as he relates to his creation.

Table 1. God as absolute in himself and as relative to creation

Absolute	Relative
• infinite • immutable • immense • eternal • incomprehensible • most free • most absolute • all-sufficient • knowledge . . . independent upon the creature • nothing . . . contingent	• loving, gracious, merciful, long-suffering [toward creatures] • manifesting his glory . . . upon them [creatures] • fountain of all being • sovereign dominion • all things open and manifest

Understanding God's attributes, considered both absolutely and relatively, is key to the proper understanding of how the divines explain the nature of the decree. This absolute-relative distinction (*opera ad intra–ad extra*) highlights the independence and freedom of God in contrast to the created order. God is free, for example, to create and not to create; the creation is not part of God, neither is it an emanation from him, but rather it is radically contingent—it does not exist necessarily but is created *ex nihilo*.[15]

The Decree
Necessary and Contingent
When we look at the decree in general, the absolute-relative distinction immediately strikes the reader because God "freely, and unchangeably" ordains "whatsoever comes to passe" (3.1). God's freedom lies at the core of the decree; he is under no obligation, whether external or

[14] Muller, "God as Absolute and Relative," 58–59.
[15] Ibid., 59.

internal, to create anything. Edward Leigh (1602–1671) spells this out when he explains that there are two works of God, internal (or immanent) and external (or transient). The internal work of God is his will from eternity, called the decree, by which God determined in eternity what he would do in time. The external work of God is the manifestation of the decree in the works of creation and providence. Leigh then explains at length how the decree is absolute: "God's Absolute Decree, is that whereby the Lord, according to the Counsell of his own Will, hath determined with himself what he will do, command, or forbid; permit, or hinder, together with the circumstances of the same, Acts 2.23, and 4.28. Luke 22.22. John 7.30."[16] In the marginal note, Leigh cites William Ames (1576–1633) and his definition of the decree, which is "the firm decision by which he performs all things through his almighty power according to his counsel."[17] Ames notes the differences between man and God when it comes to knowledge. Man must first consider information outside himself in order to make a decision about something, whereas God knows all things from himself, even before they exist, because they are possibilities only in the divine mind.[18] Hence, the decree is free and absolute because it depends solely on God and not in any way upon the creation. Wollebius succinctly states this same point: "A decree of God is an internal act of the divine will, by which he determines, from eternity, freely, with absolute certainty, those matters which shall happen in time."[19]

God ordains whatsoever comes to pass, but then the Confession stipulates, "Yet so as thereby neither is God the Author of sin, nor is violence offered to the will of the Creatures, nor is the Liberty or contingencie of second Causes taken away, but rather established" (3.1). God ordains the occurrence of all things but in such a way that human beings are responsible for their actions. With this qualification the divines affirm both necessity and contingency; whatever God

---

[16] Edward Leigh, *A Systeme or Body of Divinity: Consisting of Ten Books* (London: William Lee, 1654), 3.1 (pp. 216–17). See the nearly identical explanation in Wollebius, *Compendium Theologiae Christianae*, 1.3.2 (pp. 46–47).

[17] William Ames, *The Marrow of Theology*, trans. John Eusden Dykstra (1968; Grand Rapids: Baker, 1997), 1.7.2 (p. 94).

[18] Ibid., 1.7.13–15 (p. 95). See a very similar explanation in Francis Turretin, *Institutes of Elenctic Theology*, ed. James T. Dennison Jr., trans. George Musgrave Giger (Phillipsburg, NJ: P&R, 1992–1997), 4.1.14–15.

[19] Wollebius, *Compendium Theologiae Christianae*, 1.3.3 (p. 47); cf. Ames, *Marrow of Theology*, 1.7.36 (p. 97).

ordains necessarily comes to pass, but it can and will come to pass contingently. What do they mean, however, by *contingency*? Contingency does not mean that something does not have a cause, as Jonathan Edwards argued. Rather, it means that something could be otherwise. God's decree, for example, is contingent in the sense that he was under no external or internal necessity to decree anything—he was free to decree and free not to decree. Hence, the decree is contingent in its genesis. But once God decrees it, there is no longer contingency from the divine perspective, as the divines assert: "In his sight all things are open and manifest; his knowledge is infinite, infallible, and independent upon the creature, so as nothing is to him contingent, or uncertain" (2.2). As it pertains to creatures, however, the divines state that the decree, far from taking away freedom and contingency, establishes it. Without God decreeing to create creatures that have the freedom to choose among various options, there would be no freedom whatsoever because free creatures would not exist.

William Twisse (1578–1646), the first moderator of the Westminster Assembly, explains the nature of contingency and its medieval theological roots, drawing attention to Thomas Aquinas (1225–1274) and John Duns Scotus (ca. 1266–1308).[20] Twisse believes that for Aquinas the root of contingency lies in the will of God as the *efficacious* agent, whereas Scotus places it in the will of God as a *free* agent.

---

[20] There is debate in the secondary literature over two issues: (1) whether Reformed orthodoxy taught contingency; and (2) to what degree the Reformed were influenced by Duns Scotus. Paul Helm has criticized the idea of contingency as it has been explained and offered by several European scholars. See Paul Helm, "Synchronic Contingency in Reformed Scholasticism: A Note of Caution," *Nederlands Theologisch Tijdschrift* 57 (2003): 207–22; A. J. Beck and A. Vos, "Conceptual Patterns Related to Reformed Scholasticism," *Nederlands Theologisch Tijdschrift* 57 (2003): 223–32; Paul Helm, "Synchronic Contingency Again," *Nederlands Theologisch Tijdschrift* 57 (2003): 234–38; Willem J. van Asselt, J. Martin Bac, and Roelf T. te Velde, eds., *Reformed Thought on Freedom: The Concept of Free Choice in Early Modern Reformed Theology* (Grand Rapids: Baker, 2010), 1–49. For the first issue, it seems that Helm denies the very type of contingency that Reformed theologians advocated. Helm writes: "Of course to a man the Reformed scholastics held that God decrees whatever comes to pass. So in their understanding, given that God decrees A, then A will occur. So that even if we leave to one side the issue of the metaphysical character of the universe or of human action within it, as these matters might be considered in isolation, for the Reformed scholastics the very fact of God decreeing some action imposes a necessity upon it" (Helm, "Synchronic Contingency in Reformed Scholasticism," 216; cf. Brian Hecker, "Resembling the Divine: Divine and Human Freedom in the Theology of William Twisse [c. 1577–1646]," [MA thesis, Westminster Seminary California, 2010], 91–92). But as will be seen below, Twisse specifically states that God's decree does not impose necessity upon creatures. For the second issue, the influence of Duns Scotus on contingency seems to be a bit overstated, as Twisse, for example, appeals both to Aquinas and to Duns Scotus on matters of contingency. As others have argued, the Reformed were quite eclectic in their use and appropriation of philosophical ideas (Richard A. Muller, "Reformation, Orthodoxy, 'Christian Aristotelianism,' and the Eclecticism of Early Modern Philosophy," *Nederlands Archeif voor Kerkgeschiedenis* 81, no. 3 [2001]: 306–25).

Twisse elaborates upon these two points by noting that God, as an efficacious agent, can ordain to bring something to pass either necessarily or contingently, "producing necessary things necessarily, and agents rationall for the producing of contingent things, contingently and freely."[21] Twisse illustrates this point by noting that God preordained that Josiah would burn the bones of the prophets upon the altar (2 Kings 23:16) and Cyrus would proclaim liberty to the Jewish exiles so they could return to Israel (Ezra 1:1–2), but then he asks rhetorically, "What sober Divine hath made doubt whether *Josias* and *Cyrus* did not herein, that which they did freely?" Twisse cites a second example in God's decree that none of Christ's bones should be broken, and then writes, "Yet what sober man should make question, whether the Souldiers did non [sic] as freely abstaine from breaking Christs bones?"[22]

At first glance, Twisse's arguments may seem novel, at least to post-Enlightenment eyes that only know of efficient causality (that is, only one agent can act at one time), but to the early modern mind, the affirmation of multiple agents acting with differing motives and ends upon the same event was not at all troubling. Twisse, for example, cites Irish Articles 11, which also affirms contingency: "God from all eternity did by his unchangeable Counsell ordaine, whatsoever in time should come to passe: yet so as thereby no violence is offered to the wills of the reasonable creatures, and neither the liberty nor contingency of second causes is taken away, but established rather."[23] Readers should note that this is the immediate source of the Confession's statement on the same point.

Beyond the affirmations of contingency from the Confession and the Irish Articles, both documents touch upon a long-held doctrinal conviction among Reformed theologians. John Calvin employs the illustration of a merchant who wanders into a bad part of town, falls among robbers, and is murdered. Calvin argues that the merchant's death was not only foreseen by God but also decreed by him.[24] Ac-

---

[21] William Twisse, *The Riches of God's Love unto the Vessells of Mercy, Consistent with His Absolute Hatred or Reprobation of the Vessells of Wrath*, 2 vols. (Oxford: Tho Robinson, 1653), 1:95.
[22] Ibid.
[23] Ibid.
[24] John Calvin, *Institutes of the Christian Religion*, trans. John Allen (Grand Rapids: Eerdmans, 1949), 1.16.9.

cording to a post-Enlightenment understanding of causality, there is ultimately only one actor in this scenario, God, because the trail of toppled dominoes leads back to God's decree. But in an early modern understanding of causality, one that accounts for contingency, the decree does not cause the domino to fall by necessity; rather, the domino would fall over by its own free choice. In Calvin's description of "future contingencies" he notes, "What God decrees, must necessarily come to pass; yet it is not by absolute or natural necessity."

To illustrate his point, Calvin appeals, like Twisse, to the unbroken bones of Christ. Since Christ was a human being like any other, his bones were capable of breaking, but by virtue of God's decree it was impossible that they could be broken.[25] Calvin writes:

> Here we perceive that the distinctions of relative and absolute necessity, as well as necessity of consequent and of consequence, were not without reason invented in the schools; since God made the bones of his Son capable of being broken, which, however, he had exempted from being actually broken, and thus prevented, by the necessity of his purpose, what might naturally have come to pass.[26]

Calvin's appeal to this medieval distinction employed by Thomas Aquinas, *necessity of the consequence* and *necessity of the consequent*, is a key piece of data in understanding the relationship between the decree and the free actions of creatures.[27]

Necessity of the consequent is something that cannot be otherwise; it is something that is absolutely necessary.[28] If I enter a room full of chairs and sit in one of them, then by the necessity of the consequent, it is impossible that I am sitting in any of the other chairs. By contrast, the necessity of the consequence (which is also called a hypothetical necessity), is a necessity that eventuates due to a certain set of circumstances.[29] If I enter a room and sit in one of several available chairs, then my eventual choice is a hypothetical necessity, given my coming to the room, my intention to sit, the availability of seating, and fac-

[25] Ibid.
[26] Ibid.
[27] Aquinas, *Summa Theologica*, Ia, q. 19, art. 3.
[28] *DLGTT*, s.v. *necessitas consequentis*, 200.
[29] Ibid.

tors influencing my choice. Hypothetical necessities (necessities of the consequence) are part of the world God has created. But God is still free with respect to these hypothetical necessities; he is not obligated to them. God is free to ordain things however he sees fit, but once he decrees that something will happen, then he is bound to his own will, and hence his decree brings about a necessity of the consequent (I'm sitting in *this* chair and none other).[30] In terms of Calvin's appeal to the frangibility of Christ's bones, it was a hypothetical necessity that Christ's bones could break, given the incarnation. But given the decree, it was an absolute necessity that they would not break. Or as William Ames explains the same point:

> The will of God does not imply a necessity in all future things, but only a certainty in regard to the event. Thus the event was certain that Christ's bones should not be broken, because God willed that they should not be. But there was no necessity imposed upon the soldiers, their spears, and other secondary causes then present.[31]

As complex as these things might be, Reformed theologians have long maintained the seemingly contradictory teachings of divine sovereignty and human responsibility. This is no mere isolated phenomenon in the Reformed tradition but appears in numerous works of early modern Reformed theologians. Petrus van Mastricht (1630–1706), for example, argues that semi-Pelagians, Jesuits, Remonstrants, Lutherans, and Anabaptists deny contingency, and Stoics embrace fate. By contrast, the Reformed embrace both necessity and contingency.[32] As Calvin did before him, Christoph Pezel (1539–1604) relates hypothetical and absolute necessity in order to reject Stoicism (or fatalism), in a section from his polemical work entitled "Of Necessity, Fate and Contingency, against the Stoics and Libertines."[33] He argues that contingency depends upon the immutability of divine providence.[34]

---

[30] Ibid.

[31] Ames, *Marrow of Theology*, 1.7.49 (p. 99); cf. Willem J. van Asselt et al., *Introduction to Reformed Scholasticism*, trans. Albert Gootjes (Grand Rapids: Reformation Heritage, 2011), 198–200.

[32] Petrus van Mastricht, *Theoretico-Practica Theologia*, vol. 1 (Utrecht: W. van de Water, 1724), 3.10.30 (pp. 396–97); cf. Johannes Heidegger, *Corpus Theologiae Christianae* (Tiguri, 1732), 7.49 (p. 263); cf. Heinrich Heppe, *Reformed Dogmatics: Set Out and Illustrated from the Sources*, ed. Ernst Bizer, trans. G. T. Thomson (London: George & Unwin, 1950), 265–69.

[33] Christoph Pezel, *Argumenta et Obiectiones: De Praecipuis Captibus Doctrinae Christianae* (Harnisch, 1581), 165.

[34] Ibid., 191–92.

In other words, apart from God's decree and the ordination of the existence of creatures, there would be no freedom or contingency in the world; one must account for both primary and secondary causes in any one event.[35]

Zacharias Ursinus (1534–1583), the author of the Heidelberg Catechism, has an extended section in his commentary on the catechism where he treats issues related to liberty and contingency. He answers the objection raised in the following syllogistic argument concerning the decree and contingency:

> MAJOR PREMISE: If something is determined by the immutable decree of God, then it cannot be done freely or contingently.
> MINOR PREMISE: Many things are done freely and contingently.
> CONCLUSION: Many things are not done by the immutable decree of God or else liberty and contingency are eliminated.[36]

The syllogism posits the incompatibility of the decree and contingency. But Ursinus contends that the decree and contingency are indeed compatible: as pertains to the first cause, or the immutable decree, an event cannot be done contingently, because if God wills something to occur, it will necessarily come to pass; but as pertains to the second cause, or the human agent, events occur contingently and freely. Ursinus writes:

> For contingency is the order between a changeable cause and its effect: just as necessity is the order between a necessary cause and its effect. Hence the cause must be of the same character as the effect. But the same effect may proceed from a changeable and necessary cause in different respects, as is the case with all things which God does through his creatures; of which both God and his creatures are the cause. Thus in respect to God there is an unchangeable order between cause and effect; but in respect to creatures, there is a changeable order between the cause and the same effect. Hence in regard to God it is necessary, but in regard to the creature it is contingent in the same effect. Therefore it is

---

[35] Ibid., 192.
[36] Zacharias Ursinus, *The Commentary of Dr. Zacharias Ursinus on the Heidelberg Catechism*, trans. G. W. Williard (1852; Phillipsburg, NJ: P&R, n.d.), 161.

not absurd that the same effect should be said to be necessary and contingent in respect to different causes, that is, in respect to an unchangeable first cause acting necessarily, and in respect to a changeable second cause acting contingently.[37]

The point, as complex as it might appear, is very simple: God is sovereign and human beings are responsible.

William Ames explains that God determines all things, great and small—the contingent, necessary, and free. He helpfully offers examples of each of these categories of things decreed by God. God necessarily decreed the glorification of Christ and that the church should be saved through him. He also decreed that Pharaoh would overthrow the people of Israel, but "Pharaoh and Israel worked freely." Likewise, God determined the selling of Joseph into slavery, but the evil hearts of men also freely willed and carried out these events. Hence the accidental killing of another, the cast lot, sparrows falling to the ground, the number of hairs upon the head, or all things in the created realm come about necessarily, freely, and contingently.[38]

According to the Confession God does ordain whatsoever comes to pass, but he does so in such a way that he is not the author of sin, nor is violence offered to the will of the creature, and contingency and freedom are established. All too often people do not carefully read the Confession's statement about the decree. Critics, for example, fail to coordinate the Confession's doctrine of the decree with its affirmations about providence, free will, and contingency. Note how the Confession succinctly states the same points as the above-cited argument by Ursinus: "Although, in relation to the fore-knowledge and decree of God, the first Cause, all things come to passe immutably, and infallibly: yet, by the same Providence, he ordereth them to fall out, according to the nature of second causes, either necessarily, freely, or contingently" (5.2).[39] Likewise, in its chapter on human free will, the

---

[37] Ibid., 161–62.

[38] Ames, *Marrow of Theology*, 1.7.45 (pp. 98–99).

[39] The Leiden Synopsis uses very similar language, namely, that divine providence does not destroy human freedom but establishes it (Johannes Polyander, André Rivet, Antonius Walaeus, and Antonius Thysius, *Synopsis Purioris Theologiae*, ed. Herman Bavinck [Lugduni Batavorum: Didericum Donner, 1881], 11.11 [p. 90]). In context the *Synopsis* refers to Augustine who makes a similar point: "Therefore he governs all things in such a manner as to allow them to perform and exercise their own proper movements. For although they can be nothing without him, they are not what he is" (Augustine, *City of God*, 7.30, in *NPNF*[1] 2:140).

Confession states, "God hath indued the Will of man with that natural liberty, that is neither forced, nor by any absolute necessity of nature determined to good or evil" (9.1). Adam was not forced to sin; he did so freely.

On this issue, Twisse explains that the decree "brings no necessity at all of sinning upon man." He insists, "The necessity following upon this will of God, is nothing prejudiciall to the liberty or contingency of second agents in their severall operations."[40] Concerning Acts 4:28 Twisse argues that God ordained that the events of the crucifixion should occur: Judas would betray Christ, Herod would mock him, Pilate would condemn him, the people would cry out for his crucifixion, the soldiers would crucify him—all of these things were decreed. But Twisse stipulates:

> But how came it to passe? Not necessarily, but contingently, that is in this Authours phrase evitably and avoidably, in as much as it was joined with an absolute possibility to come to passe otherwise; Nor with a possibility only but with a free power in the agents to have forborne all these contumelious carriages of theirs towards the Son of God. For both *Judas* had free will to abstain from betraying him, and *Herod* with his *Herodians* could have abstained from their contumelious handling of him, and *Pilate* from condemning him, and the Priests and people from conspiring against him; and the Souldiers from crucifying him, only they had no power to abstain from all or any of these vile actions in an holy manner, as no man else hath power to abstaine from any evil in a gracious manner, without grace.[41]

In context, Twisse appeals to both Aquinas and Augustine (354–430). In particular, Twisse cites Aquinas to show that necessity and contingency are both wrapped up in the decree.[42] In other words, in a certain sense, Twisse's affirmation of necessity and contingency, and the Confession's for that matter, is not new but has ancient pedigree in the Patristic and medieval periods.

Some might question the need for such scholastic hairsplitting

---

[40] Twisse, *Riches of God's Love*, 1:28.
[41] Ibid., 2:64.
[42] See Aquinas, *Summa Theologica*, Ia, q. 19, art. 8.

and seemingly speculative theology as it pertains to the divine decree. But buried beneath all of these distinctions, and stated quite simply and succinctly in the Confession, are the principles of divine sovereignty and human responsibility. God, despite the decree of Adam's fall, is not the author of sin. God does not force anyone to do anything. In fact, the Confession—unlike Calvin—for example, argues that God *permitted* the fall; permission is a category that Calvin largely rejected. The Confession states, "This their sin, God was pleased, according to his wise and holy counsell to permit, having purposed to order it to his own glory" (6.1).[43] Judas could have refrained from betraying Christ, but instead freely chose to do so, and he freely chose suicide over repentance.

This point cannot be stressed enough: the divines believed that if human actions were not contingent (that is, freely chosen), then God could in no way hold sinners accountable for their sin. Conversely, if human acts were not truly contingent and free, then there would be no need for the response of faith to the preaching of the gospel. Another important element to consider is that Reformed theologians believed that God is free, and in an analogous fashion so are his creatures. The Confession states that God is "most free" (2.1) and that man, male and female, was created "after his own Image" with the "Law of God written in their hearts, and power to fulfill it: and yet, under a possibility of transgressing, being left to the liberty of their own will, which was subject unto change" (4.2).[44] The Confession affirms freedom of the will, but there are some important qualifiers regarding the nature of humanity's freedom.

Free Choice

Regarding humanity's free choice (*liberum arbitrium*), the divines set forth their abilities under the fourfold estate, as St. Augustine did long before them (WCF 9.2–5):

---

[43] Cf. Calvin, *Institutes*, 1.18.2; Thomas Watson, *A Body of Practical Divinity* (London: Thomas Parkhurst, 1692), 39; William Perkins, *A Golden Chaine; or, The Description of Theologie, Containing the Order of Causes of Salvation and Damnation, according to God's Word* (London: Edward Alde, 1592), § 6.
[44] Hecker, "Resembling the Divine," 24–25.

- *Innocency.* "Freedom, and power, to will, and to do that which was good."
- *Sin.* "Hath wholly lost all ability of Will to any spiritual good."
- *Grace.* "By [God's] grace alone, inables him freely to will, and to do that which is spiritual good . . . but doth also will that which is evil."
- *Glory.* "Immutably free to good alone, in the state of Glory only."[45]

In the garden Adam was free to sin and not to sin, but once he sinned, he plunged himself and all of his progeny into bondage. The nature of the bondage, however, is important to note; while fallen humanity is unable to do any spiritual good, this does not mean people have lost freedom of choice. The Reformers make a common distinction between what Martin Luther (1483–1546) famously called the bondage of the *will* (*voluntas*) and free choice (*liberum arbitrium*).[46]

The human will is bound to sin, but our choices are free and not forced upon us. Even though God decrees whatsoever comes to pass, people freely make their own choices. God is not the author of sin and offers no violence to the will of creatures—they freely choose sin. Only through the grace of the gospel does fallen humanity freely choose what is spiritually good, though we are still hampered by the abiding presence of sin. When sinners are converted and ultimately glorified, they are completely freed from sin and immutably able freely to choose good. The question naturally arises, whom does God free from the bondage of sin?

The Decree and Predestination

The Confession states, "By the Decree of God, for the manifestation of his Glory, some men and Angels are predestinated unto everlasting life, and others fore-ordained to everlasting death" (3.3). Quite simply, only those whom God elects unto eternal life are freed from the bondage of sin. The surrounding context of this statement brings a number of important qualifications. The first is a rejection of the

---

[45] Augustine, *The Problem of Free Choice: De Libero Arbitrio*, ACW, trans. Dom Mark Pontifex (New York: Newman, 1955), 2.37.14 (p. 118); Leigh, *Body of Divinity*, 4.1 (p. 303); Perkins, *Golden Chaine*, § 9. Some, however, argue for a threefold state of man, but it differs very little from the more common fourfold state (James Ussher, *A Body of Divinitie; or, The Summe and Substance of Christian Religion* [London: Thomas Downes and George Badger, 1645], 8 [p. 123]).
[46] Martin Luther, *Bondage of the Will*, in *LW*, 33:3–296.

position most commonly associated with Jacob Arminius (1560–1609) on predestination. In the previous paragraph the divines reject the idea that God decrees something based upon his foreknowledge. The Confession states, "Although God knows whatsoever may, or can come to passe upon all supposed conditions, yet hath he not decreed any thing because he foresaw it as future, or as that which would come to passe upon such conditions" (3.2). As is their practice, the divines obliquely reject two views: predestination by middle knowledge and by foreknowledge, both of which were advocated by Arminius, as well as Roman Catholic and Lutheran theologians.[47]

The divines acknowledge that God "knows whatsoever may, or can come to passe upon all supposed conditions" (3.2). Without specifically identifying their topic as such, they address the question of middle knowledge (*scientia media*). What is middle knowledge? Recall from the above-cited set of terms related to God's knowledge: God's necessary knowledge (*scientia necessaria*) and his voluntary knowledge (*scientia voluntaria*), which relates to created things.[48] God's necessary knowledge is proper to himself and is logically prior to his decree; it rests solely upon God alone. By contrast, God's voluntary knowledge is related to the execution of his decree. God's voluntary knowledge, so called because it is the result of God's will, his *voluntas*, is also called free knowledge or the knowledge of vision (*scientia libera seu visionis*) because God knows everything about his creation. According to some, between God's necessary and voluntary knowledge is his middle knowledge, which is God's knowledge of future contingents based upon their occurrence.[49] In other words, God knows that if he approaches a person on Tuesday, when he is tired and grumpy, the sinner will reject the gospel; but if God approaches the same person on Wednesday, when he is happy and rested, the sinner will accept the gospel.[50]

The point of employing middle knowledge was to carve out a patch of supposedly genuinely free human choice, one not hindered by the

---

[47] Cf. David Dickson, *Truths Victory over Error* (Edinburgh: John Reed, 1684), 3.2 (p. 33); Formula of Concord, 11; The Arminian Articles (1610), 1–4.
[48] Ames, *Marrow of Theology*, 1.6.24–27 (p. 96); cf. Watson, *Body of Practical Divinity*, 30–33.
[49] *DLGTT*, s.v. *scientia Dei*, 274–75.
[50] Ames, *Marrow of Theology*, 1.6.28 (p. 96).

decree of God.[51] This divine consideration would allow God to elect people based upon their foreseen free choice of the gospel.[52] In his ordering of the divine decrees as it pertains to predestination, Arminius has four decrees:

1. God decrees to appoint Christ as the Redeemer.
2. God decrees absolutely to appoint those who repent and believe in Christ unto salvation and to damn the impenitent.
3. God decrees "to administer in a sufficient and efficacious manner the means which were necessary for repentance and faith."
4. God decrees to save and damn specific people based upon his foreknowledge of their decisions for or against the gospel.[53]

In the fourth decree Arminius clearly advocates predestination by God's foreknowledge, but in the third decree he creates room for human choices based in God's middle knowledge.[54] In the third decree God works in an "efficacious manner" and decrees to use "the means which were necessary for repentance and faith." Note that this third decree is not absolute as it is for the Westminster divines and the Reformed tradition. For Arminius, the first decree is absolute, but God has in mind not specific individuals but only types of people, namely, the repentant and unrepentant—they are categories, not specific individuals predestined to eternal life.

In a sense, the divines acknowledge that the category of middle knowledge exists, though they simply place this attribute under God's necessary knowledge. Evidence of this appears in a scriptural proof text from Matthew 11:21, 23. In this text Christ tells Bethsaida and Chorazin that *if* the mighty works Jesus had performed before these two cities had been done in Tyre and Sidon, these Gentile cities would have repented in sackcloth and ashes. The point is that Christ did not perform miraculous works in Tyre and Sidon but neverthe-

---

[51] On the likely origins of this idea see Luis de Molina (1535–1600), *On Divine Knowledge: Part IV of the Concordia*, trans. Alfred J. Freddoso (Ithaca: Cornell University Press, 1988), disp. 52.1–9 (pp. 164–68).

[52] *DLGTT*, 275.

[53] Jacob Arminius, *Declaration of Sentiments*, in *The Works of James Arminius*, ed. and trans. James Nichols and William Nichols, 3 vols. (1828–1875; Grand Rapids: Baker, 1996), 1:653–54; also Arminius, *Certain Articles*, 15.1–4, in *Works*, 2:719.

[54] Richard A. Muller, *God, Creation, and Providence in the Thought of Jacob Arminius* (Grand Rapids: Baker, 1991), 150–51.

less knew what would have happened if he had. So, yes, "although God knows whatsoever may, or can come to passe upon all supposed conditions, yet hath he not decreed any thing because he foresaw it as future, or as that which would come to passe upon such conditions" (3.2).

The divines reject predestination based upon middle knowledge or foreseen faith and insist upon the absolute nature of the decree:

> Those of man-kinde that are predestinated unto Life, God, before the foundation of the world was laid, according to his eternall and immutable purpose, and the secret Counsell and good pleasure of his Will, hath chosen, in Christ, unto everlasting glory, out of his meer free grace and love, without any fore-sight of Faith, or Good-works, or perseverance in either of them, or any other thing in the creature, as conditions, or causes moving him thereunto. (3.5)[55]

As a proof text for this paragraph the divines cite Ephesians 1:4, 9, which states that God chose the elect in Christ according to his own purpose.

The divines also reject election based upon middle knowledge because they believe that such a view rests upon an ontological absurdity.[56] According to Arminius, God decreed to elect those whom he foresaw believing in Christ, and this choice to believe was not something that God decreed but arose strictly and solely from the fallen sinner. God, therefore, would providentially support the existence of the sinner but not decree anything specific to the sinner's choice. Arminius believed that the decree and contingency were contradictory.[57]

On the contrary, Pierre Du Moulin (1568–1658) explains that God must concur by his providence with the actions of people, but not in such a way that he is the cause of their evil works. In any one action both God and the creature are concurrent causes to bring about one

---

[55] One of the first works to reject middle knowledge was William Twisse, *Dissertatio de Scientia Media Tribus Libris Absoluta, Quorum Prior Gabr. Penottum ad Partes Vocat in Suo Libertatis Humanae Propugnaculo, Posteriores Duo Fra. Suaresio Oppositi Sunt, Duosque Libros Ejus de Scientia Dei Inscriptos Refellendos Suscipiunt* (Arnhem, 1639).

[56] Richard A. Muller, "Grace, Election, and Contingent Choice: Arminius's Gambit and the Reformed Response," in *The Grace of God, the Bondage of the Will*, ed. Thomas R. Schreiner and Bruce A. Ware, vol. 2 (Grand Rapids: Baker, 1995), 267.

[57] Arminius, *Conference with Junius*, prop. 6, in *Works*, 3:81–82.

effect.[58] Du Moulin's point is that human free choice can exist only if God decrees it. As the Confession states, God ordains whatsoever comes to pass and thereby establishes contingency and secondary causes (3.1). Or as Francis Turretin (1623–1687) explains:

> There was nothing from eternity which could be the cause of the determination of a thing indifferent to either part except the will of God; not his essence or knowledge, for neither can operate *ad extra* separated from the will. Therefore, as no effect can be understood as future (whether absolutely or hypothetically) without the divine decree (because no creature can be in the world without the divine causality), so no future conditional thing can be knowable before the decree.[59]

In simpler terms, Turretin's point is this: How can someone decide to choose to believe in the gospel if he does not yet exist? How can God watch the actions of people who do not yet exist except in his mind unless he decrees their existence and the choices they make? The only way a person can exist and consequently make choices is if God first decrees his existence and decisions. As Ames explains:

> A middle knowledge by which God is imagined by some to know by hypothesis before the decree of his will that certain things will be, if such and such free causes meet such and such conditions— knowledge of this kind cannot stand with the absolute perfection of God. For it both supposes that events will happen independently of the will of God and also makes some knowledge of God depend on the object.[60]

Apart from the decree nothing will happen; hence, the Confession, along with the Reformed tradition, rejects predestination based upon middle knowledge and foreseen faith.[61] Edward Leigh, citing Ames, Gisbert Voetius (1589–1676), and John Prideaux (1578–1650), argues, "That *scientia media* which the Jesuits glory of as a new Light, is but the very old error of natural man, which looks upon things contingent,

---

[58] Pierre Du Moulin, *Anatomy of Arminianisme* (London: Nathaniel Newbery, 1620), 3.15 (pp. 15–16); Muller, "Grace, Election, and Contingent Choice," 267.
[59] Turretin, *Institutes*, 3.13.10.
[60] Ames, *Marrow of Theology*, 1.7.28 (p. 96).
[61] Muller, "Grace, Election, and Contingent Choice," 266.

as not decreed and determined by the will of God."[62] Again, the divine decree establishes liberty, contingency, and second causes.

The Object of Predestination

The divines did not want to write an academic theological treatise, but they nevertheless engaged in a number of technical debates in the course of writing the Standards. One such issue was the question of the object of predestination. In other words, when God elects people unto salvation, does he take sin into account? Does God predestine people apart from any consideration of sin and the fall, or does he choose people that are already considered as fallen and thus in need of redemption? And if God does account for the fall, how does he do so? The Confession does not explicitly address this particular question, but it does lean in the direction of infralapsarianism. Briefly, infralapsarians argue that in the decree the object of predestination is created and fallen man. Supralapsarians, on the other hand, argue that in the decree the object of predestination is man as creatable and liable to fall.[63]

In the past, some confessional documents left the issue completely undefined, such as William Whitaker's Lambeth Articles (1595), which state, "God from eternity has predestined some men to life, and reprobated some to death" (§ 1). However, the Synod of Dort (1618–1619)

---

[62] Leigh, *Body of Divinity*, 3.1 (p. 220); cf. William Ames, *Rescriptio Scholastica & Brevis ad Nic. Grevinchovii Responsum Illud Prolixum, Quod Opposuit Dissertationi de Redemptione Generali, & Electione ex Fide Praevisa* (Harderwijk: Nicolai à Wieringen, 1645); Gisbert Voetius, "De Scientia Dei," in *Selectarum Disputationum Theologicarum*, vol. 1 (Utrecht: Johannem à Waesberge, 1648), 246–64, esp. 254, 256–57, 264; John Prideaux, *Viginti-Duae Lectiones de Totidem Religionis Capitibus* (Oxford: Hen. Hall, 1648), 15–31.

[63] *DLGTT*, s.v. *praedestinatio*, 234–35. One should note that the two chief terms *infra-* and *supralaparianism* are the most basic designations and a number of variants have been ignored in recent literature. Turretin identifies three different opinions: those who ascend above the fall (*supra lapsum*), and hence are *supralapsarians*; those who descend below the fall (*infra lapsum*), and others who stop in the fall (*in lapsu*) (*Institutes*, 4.9.3). In his *Conference with Junius*, Arminius identifies three positions: two supras, man as to be created or man as created but unfallen, and one infra, man as created and fallen (Jacob Arminius, *Friendly Conference of James Arminius with Francis Junius*, prop. 2, in *Works*, 3:24). Edward Leigh confirms Arminius's taxonomy and offers the same: *homo condendus* (man to be made), man already made, but not fallen, and man made and fallen (Leigh, *Body of Divinity*, 3.1 [p. 220]). Baxter also offers the same taxonomy (Richard Baxter, *Catholick Theologie: Plain, Pure, Peaceable* [London: Nevill Simmons, 1675], 1.1.15 [p. 57]). If these theologians are accurate, then according to the compiled taxonomies, there are at least two kinds of infras and two kinds of supras. However, establishing a paradigm is further complicated when one adds the question of whether there is a double or single decree. For an analysis of the various positions, see Richard A. Muller, "Revising the Predestination Paradigm: An Alternative to Supralapsarianism, Infralapsarianism, and Hypothetical Universalism" (Mid-America Fall Lecture Series, Dyer, Indiana, Fall 2008).

expressly decided in favor of infralapsarianism, though it makes no mention of supralapsarianism: "Before the foundation of the world, by sheer grace, according to the free good pleasure of his will, he chose in Christ to salvation a definite number of particular people out of the entire human race, which had fallen by its own fault from its original innocence into sin and ruin."[64]

The Confession takes a similar path: "As God hath appointed the Elect unto glory; so hath he, by the eternal and most free purpose of his Will, fore-ordained all the means thereunto. Wherefore they who are elected, *being fallen in Adam*, are redeemed by Christ" (3.6, emphasis added). The divines could have simply written: "they who are elected are redeemed by Christ." In the assembly's *Annotations*, for example, we find the following explanation of Romans 9:21, reflecting the infralapsarian view with its mention of election from the corrupt mass of humanity: "By this metaphor," namely, the potter's lump of clay, "is intimated the originall of all mankind out of one bloud, Act. 17.26. out of this corrupt masse, it is in Gods power of his free will to appoint some to everlasting glory, and others to everlasting shame and ignominie."[65] The divines, therefore, specifically chose to indicate that God predestined fallen man to eternal life. But like the Synod of Dort before them, the divines make no mention of supralapsarianism.

Questions arise as to whether supralapsarianism was slighted or viewed as heterodox. In other words, how can someone who was a supralapsarian subscribe to a document that expresses itself in an infralapsarian direction? There are two things to consider. First, a number of theologians of the period viewed the question of the object of predestination as an intramural debate. True, sometimes this debate was quite heated; Baxter notes, "There is no part of this Controversie more contentiously and I fear presumptuously and too audaciously handled."[66] Others, such as Francis Junius (1545–1602), Twisse, Turretin, and Leigh argue that there were no significant differences

---

[64] Synod of Dort, First Main Point, art. 7; cf. J. V. Fesko, "Lapsarian Diversity at the Synod of Dort," in *Drawn into Controversie: Reformed Theological Diversity and Debates within Seventeenth-Century British Puritanism*, ed. Michael A. G. Haykin and Mark Jones (Göttingen: Vandenhoeck & Ruprecht, 2011), 99–123.
[65] *Annotations*, comm. Rom. 9:21. The *Dutch Annotations* (comm. Rom. 9:21) have virtually the same comment, even with appeal to Acts 17:26.
[66] Baxter, *Catholick Theologie*, 1.1.15 (p. 57).

among the proponents of the different positions. Junius, for example, told Arminius that the different opinions were "seemingly opposed, but not really contrary."[67] Turretin likewise remarks:

> We must take notice that whatever the disagreement of theologians may be on this subject, yet the foundation of faith remains secure on both sides and that they are equally opposed to the deadly error of Pelagians and semi-Pelagians. Both they who ascend higher in this matter and include the creation or the fall of man in the decree of predestination, and they who suppose both all agree in this: that men were considered by God as equal (not unequal) and such that their choice depended upon God alone (from which foundation all heretics depart).[68]

Twisse also comments a number of times not only that the Synod of Dort allowed supralapsarianism, but also that the issue of disagreement was not enough to cause a breach between the different parties. Twisse believes that the disagreement was over a matter of "mere logick."[69]

Second, confessions are not exhaustive documents but only state the basic position of the church as a whole. The Confession's statement that predestined man was considered fallen in Adam does not, therefore, automatically preclude a supralapsarian position. After all, theologians of the period expressed their views in variegated ways. The well-known supralapsarian Johannes Maccovius (1588–1644), one of the delegates to the Synod of Dort, outlines the object of predestination as follows:

> Regarding the goal, with respect to the intention, the human object of predestination is creatable man [*homo creabilis*]. Regarding the goal with respect to execution, the human object of predestination is man to be created and created, man being permitted to fall and fallen [*homo condendus, conditus, permittendus in lapsum, lapsus*].[70]

---

[67] Arminius, *Conference with Junius*, prop. 2, in *Works*, 3:24.

[68] Turretin, *Institutes*, 4.9.4; cf. Leigh, *Body of Divinity*, 3.1 (p. 220).

[69] Twisse, *Riches of God's Love*, 1:32, 35.

[70] Johannes Maccovius, *Scholastic Distinctions: Johannes Maccovius (1588–1644) on Theological and Philosophical Distinctions and Rules*, ed. and trans. Willem J. van Asselt, Michael D. Bell, Gert van den Brink, Rein Ferwerda (Apeldoorn: Instituut voor Reformationderzoek, 2009), 7.4 (pp. 156–57).

In other words, even a supralapsarian such as Maccovius understood the object of predestination in some sense to be created and fallen man. Edward Leigh offers a similar dissection of the issue: "Man simply considered is the object of Predestination, in respect of the preordination of the end; but man corrupted, if we respect the ordination of the means which tend to that end; or man absolutely, in respect of the supreme or last end, not in respect of this, or that subordinate end."[71] In other words, theologians might look at the object of predestination absolutely or relatively, and depending upon each one's vantage point, give different answers to the question of who was the object of election.

The Destiny of the Non-Elect

Despite the general unanimity among Reformed theologians on the doctrine of predestination, there are a number of variants regarding how theologians account for the non-elect, or the *reprobate*, those who have been rejected by God. Some theologians, such as Calvin, posit a double decree: one decree of election and another decree of reprobation.[72] The elect and the reprobate are the subject of separate decrees. Other Reformed theologians argue for a single decree of election and maintain that God "passes by" the non-elect. This view dates back to Augustine, who explains reprobation in terms of preterition, and it was held by Pierre Du Moulin, Heinrich Bullinger (1504–1575), and others.[73]

The Confession leans toward Augustine and away from Calvin:

> The rest of man-kinde God was pleased, according to the unsearchable counsel of his own Will, whereby he extendeth, or with-holdeth mercy, as he pleaseth, for the glory of his Soveraign Power over his creatures, to passe by; and, to ordain them to dishonor and wrath, for their sin, to the praise of his glorious justice. (3.7)[74]

---

[71] Leigh, *Body of Divinity*, 3.1 (p. 220).

[72] Calvin, *Institutes*, 3.21.5; Amandus Polanus, *The Substance of Christian Religion, Soundly Set Forth in Two Books* (London: John Oxenbridge, 1595), 16–17; Johannes Maccovius, *Scholastic Distinctions*, 7.2 (p. 155).

[73] Augustine, *To Simplician—On Various Questions*, 1.20 (p. 402), in *Augustine: Earlier Writings*, ed. John Baillie et al., trans. John H. S. Burleigh, LCC (London: SCM, 1953); Augustine, *On Nature and Grace*, § 5, in *NPNF*[1] 5:123; Augustine, *Enchiridion*, § 98, in *NPNF*[1] 3:268; cf. *Anatomy of Arminianisme*, 12.13 (p. 91); Second Helvetic Confession, § 10; cf. Cornelis P. Venema, *Heinrich Bullinger and the Doctrine of Predestination: Author of 'the Other Reformed Tradition'?* (Grand Rapids: Baker, 2002), 95–97.

[74] Rohls, *Reformed Confessions*, 152.

The point the divines implicitly make with such a distinction, namely, the predestination of the elect and the preterition of the non-elect, is that God does not treat both groups in the same way. God positively and actively brings about the salvation of the elect, but he does not positively and actively bring about the reprobation of the non-elect. To do this would make God the author of sin, something the Confession 3.1 explicitly denies.

One of the Westminster divines, John Arrowsmith (1602–1659), explains a number of issues related to preterition ("passing by") that provide contextual information as to why the Confession employs this language. Arrowsmith writes, "Preterition or negative Reprobation is an eternal decree of God purposing within himself to deny unto the Non-elect that peculiar love of his, wherewith election is accompanied, as also that special grace which infallibly bringeth to glory."[75] Arrowsmith defends the propriety of the term *preterition*, commenting that "some bold writers have jeered it" because it was used by Prosper of Aquitaine (ca. 390–ca. 455), who noted that it was a Pelagian tenet, "That of all mankinde the Grace of Christ *passeth by none* [*praetereat*]."[76] Prosper also employs the term in his book *The Call of the Nations*: "We indeed see it happen that the grace of the Saviour passes by some men and that the prayers of the Church in their favour are not heard."[77]

Despite ridicule from some opponents, Arrowsmith clings to the viability of the term and argues that God has chosen the elect before the foundation of the world but has not written the names of the non-elect in the book of life (cf. Eph. 1:4; Rev. 17:8). Therefore, *preterition* is the best term to account for God's actions toward the non-elect.[78] And despite the differences in nomenclature—*preterition* versus *a decree of reprobation*—Arrowsmith identifies the similarities of his explanation with Calvin's views on reprobation.[79] Central to Arrowsmith's view is that both election and preterition originate with God; sinful humanity

---

[75] John Arrowsmith, *Armilla Catechetica: A Chain of Principles* (Cambridge: John Field, 1659), 5.2.1 (pp. 310–11).
[76] Ibid., 5.2.1 (pp. 311–12).
[77] Prosper of Aquitaine, *The Call of All Nations*, trans. P. de Letter, S. J., ACW (Westminster: New Press, 1952), 1.13 (p. 53); Arrowsmith, *Armilla Catechetica*, 5.2.1 (p. 312).
[78] Arrowsmith, *Armilla Catechetica*, 5.2.2 (p. 312).
[79] Ibid., 5.2.2 (p. 313); cf. Calvin, *Institutes*, 3.22.3–6.

in no way can lay claim upon God. Arrowsmith has nothing but words of praise for Peter Lombard (ca. 1096–1164), for example, and quotes him regarding the fact that humanity cannot lay any claim upon God: "But, it seems to me, this word 'ought' is poisoned. For it bears a manifold and complex meaning. Nor does it properly apply to God, who is not our debtor, except perhaps from his own promise; but we are his debtors from what we have done."[80]

Yet Arrowsmith is keen to highlight what preterition entails; he specifically states that the *consequents*, not the *effects*, of preterition are: permission to sin (specifically by unbelief), determination in sin, and condemnation for sin. In other words, there is not a strict cause and effect relationship between preterition and sin. Maccovius, for example, states that reprobation is "a necessary antecedent of condemnation and sins," and not the cause; he specifically reproves Johannes Piscator (1546–1625), who "errs enormously" for stating that "sins are the effects of reprobation."[81] The last element, condemnation, is what Arrowsmith identifies as *positive reprobation*. Negative reprobation is the absolute decree of God's sovereign will, without consideration of the creature, and positive reprobation is an act of punitive justice for sins committed by the creature.[82] Though election and preterition are both decrees of God, they function differently. Arrowsmith cites Aquinas to argue his case:

> Reprobation differs in its causality from predestination. This latter is the cause both of what is expected in the future life by the predestined—namely, glory—and of what is received in this life—namely, grace. Reprobation, however, is not the cause of what is in the present—namely, sin; but it is the cause of abandonment by God. It is the cause, however, of what is assigned in the future—namely, eternal punishment. But guilt proceeds from the free-will of the person who is reprobated and deserted by grace.[83]

---

[80] Peter Lombard, *The Sentences*, trans. Giulio Silano (Toronto: PIMS, 2007–2010), 1.43.3; Arrowsmith, *Armilla Catechetica*, 5.2.3 (p. 315).

[81] Maccovius, *Scholastic Distinctions*, 7.21 (p. 165); cf. Johannes Piscator, *Disputatio Theologica de Praedestinatione Opposita Disputationi Andreae Schaafmanni* (Herborn: Christopher Corvinus, 1595).

[82] Arrowsmith, *Armilla Catechetica*, 5.2.3 (pp. 315–16).

[83] Aquinas, *Summa Theologica*, Ia, q. 23, art. 3, ad. 2; Arrowsmith, *Armilla Catechetica*, 5.2.3 (pp. 316–17).

Arrowsmith, therefore, finds both scriptural and historical warrant for his understanding and use of preterition.[84]

Arrowsmith builds upon Aquinas and offers his own explanation of the causal relationship between preterition and damnation. He writes, "Whereas negative reprobation is no proper cause, either of damnation itself, or the sin that bringeth it, but an antecedent onely; wherefore the Non-elect are indeed said to be fitted to that destruction which their sins in the conclusion bring upon them, but not by God."[85] In support of his claim, Arrowsmith cites John Davenant (1572–1641), the bishop of Salisbury, who writes:

> It is true that the Elect are severally created to the end & intent that they may be glorified together with their Head Christ Jesus: But for the Non-elect we cannot truly say that they are created to the end that they may be tormented with the devil and his angels. For we may then say, God maketh such a thing for such an end, when he giveth the thing a nature and qualities fitted for such an end. Now no man is created by God with a nature and quality fitting him to damnation. Nay, take every man as he is created by God, and he is a capable and fitted subject for salvation: But, when he was at his best, so fitted, that he might runne himself into the pit of perdition. But neither in the state of his Innocency, nor in the state of the fall and his corruption doth he receive any thing from God which is a proper and fit means to bring him to his damnation. And therefore damnation is not the end of any mans creation.[86]

Though none of the specific nomenclature of necessity and contingency appears in this quote, the principles are certainly present. For Arrowsmith, Davenant, and the Confession, preterition was an absolute decree to pass by the non-elect; but considered relatively, or contingently, damnation was the result of the person's freely chosen path of sin.

---

[84] Edward Leigh offers the same distinctions as Arrowsmith, negative and positive reprobation, which he also draws from Davenant, who obtains the distinctions from Junius's conference with Arminius (cf. Leigh, *Body of Divinity*, 3.1 [p. 222]; John Davenant, *Dissertationes Duae: Prima de Morte Christi . . . Altera de Praedestinatione & Reprobatione* [Cambridge: Roger Daniels, 1650], 7 [pp. 172–74, esp. 173]; Arminius, *Conference with Junius*, prop. 6, in *Works*, 3:56). Maccovius also employs the same positive-negative distinction regarding reprobation (Maccovius, *Scholastic Distinctions*, 7.8–9 [p. 159]).

[85] Arrowsmith, *Armilla Catechetica*, 5.3.3 (pp. 335–36).

[86] John Davenant, *Animadversions: God's Love to Mankinde* (London: John Partridge, 1641), 70. Note, Arrowsmith incorrectly identifies the page for the citation (p. 89) and omits a sentence from the quotation (*Armilla Catechetica*, 5.3.3 [pp. 336–37]).

Conclusion

Despite the criticisms offered by contemporary historians and theologians, the Confession's chapter on the decree represents some of the most highly nuanced discussions about divine sovereignty and human responsibility in early modern Reformed theology. There is a twofold problem with much of the contemporary criticism of the Standards. First, critics read the chapter on the decree through the lens of the Enlightenment, one that has jettisoned numerous theological distinctions that allowed the divines to affirm seemingly contradictory ideas. Subsequent Reformed theologians who have read the document in a similar fashion, such as through Edwards's affirmation of philosophical necessity and rejection of contingency, have arguably fostered such a misinformed reading.

Second, many of the critics have held the Confession up to an artificial standard by comparing it to the formulations of Calvin. Yet, even then, such facile comparisons have only juxtaposed Calvin and the Confession concerning the order of topics, failing to analyze their differences in genre (a theological manual versus a confession of faith) and doctrinal refinements over a number of decades (1559 versus 1647), and ignoring what Calvin actually says about the decree and his employment of a number of scholastic technical distinctions, such as the necessity of consequence versus a consequent thing. This is to say nothing of the false presupposition that Calvin is the normative theologian of the tradition and that later generations were obligated to follow his formulations. In fact, a number of the divines, such as Twisse or Arrowsmith, or others such as Leigh, saw their own views as having roots not only in the Reformation but also in the Patristic and medieval periods. They were rather eclectic in the sources upon which they drew, but, at the same time, they were nonetheless Reformed theologians, not *Calvinists*.

Though many of the issues related to the decree, election, preterition, and human freedom are complex, the Confession breathes the air of a streamlined simplicity. In one sense, the ease with which the Confession states these issues is but the tip of the iceberg; many complex matters lie beneath the dark surface of the waters. Nevertheless, such is the nature of a confession of faith—it pins down key affirmations, denies false teachings, and does so in such a way that allows room for disagreement on some of the particular points of doctrine. These traits appear not only in the Confession's third chapter but also in its treatment of the doctrine of the covenants, which will be treated in the next chapter.

5

Covenant and Creation

"It was the best of doctrines, it was the worst of doctrines" could describe the doctrine of the covenants in the Westminster Standards, given its positive and negative reception. B. B. Warfield (1851–1921) characterizes the Confession as the embodiment of Reformed doctrine, gleaned from a broad cross-section of theologians, including Robert Rollock (1555–1598), Thomas Cartwright (ca. 1535–1603), John Preston (1587–1628), William Perkins (1558–1602), William Ames (1576–1633), John Ball (1585–1640), Edward Fisher (fl. 1627–1655), and David Dickson (1583–1663). The architectonic principle of the Confession appears in the schematized federal theology, the covenants of works and grace.[1]

Recent critics, however, have blamed the doctrine of the covenants for all that is wrong with the Confession. One writer claims that "Calvin knew nothing" of the dual-covenant structure of works and grace and that "these theological innovations" were the work of Calvin's successors.[2] Holmes Rolston believes that the Confession bases man's dealings with God upon law rather than grace, which supposedly inverts Calvin's understanding.[3] Other writers, such as J. B. Torrance, have argued that the covenants of works and grace were unknown to Calvin and the Reformers, and Calvin would never have taught such a concept. According to Torrance, God's dealings with man are always,

---

[1] B. B. Warfield, "The Westminster Assembly and Its Work," in *The Works of Benjamin B. Warfield*, ed. E. D. Warfield et al., 10 vols. (1931; Grand Rapids: Baker, 1981), 6:56–57.
[2] Holmes Rolston III, *John Calvin versus the Westminster Confession* (Richmond: John Knox, 1972), 23.
[3] Holmes Rolston III, "Responsible Man in Reformed Theology: Calvin versus the Westminster Confession," *SJT* 23, no. 2 (1970): 129, 142–43.

even pre-fall, on the basis of grace, whereas in a covenantal structure theologians construed the relationship between God and man contractually, legally.[4] Torrance echoes the earlier objections raised by Karl Barth (1886–1968), that covenant theology distorted Calvin.[5] Though both Rolston and Torrance offered their criticisms nearly forty years ago, and those criticisms have been ably refuted, they have continued to be repeated by others in recent years.[6]

There have been others who, while generally sympathetic to the overall theology of the covenants, have nevertheless leveled criticisms against chief elements of it. John Murray (1898–1975) rejected the concept of the covenant of works, as well as the idea that the covenant of works was in some sense repeated at Sinai.[7] Murray's rejection of the covenant of works was based upon the idea that "Scripture always uses the term covenant, when applied to God's administration to men, in reference to a provision that is redemptive or closely related to redemptive design."[8] Hence, according to Murray, Adam was not in covenant with God. Concerning the republication of the covenant of works at Sinai, Murray writes, "The view that in the Mosaic covenant there was a repetition of the so-called covenant of works, current among covenant theologians, is a grave misconception and involves an erroneous construction of the Mosaic covenant, as well as fails to assess the uniqueness of the Adamic administration."[9] Murray contends:

> In connection with the promise of life it does not appear justifiable to appeal, as frequently has been done, to the principle enunciated in certain texts (cf. Lev. 18:5; Rom. 10:5; Gal. 3:12), "This do and thou shalt live." The principle asserted in these texts is the principle of equity, that righteousness is always followed by the corresponding award.[10]

---

[4] J. B. Torrance, "Covenant or Contract? A Study of the Theological Background of Worship in Seventeenth-Century Scotland," *SJT* 23, no. 1 (1970): 62.

[5] See Karl Barth, *Church Dogmatics*, 14 vols. (Edinburgh: T&T Clark, 1936–1968), VI.2:54–66.

[6] T. F. Torrance, *Scottish Theology: From John Knox to John McLeod Campbell* (Edinburgh: T&T Clark, 1996), 62; Douglas A. Campbell, *The Deliverance of God: An Apocalyptic Rereading of Justification in Paul* (Grand Rapids: Eerdmans, 2009), 14–15, 940n11; cf. Richard A. Muller, *After Calvin: Studies in the Development of a Theological Tradition* (Oxford: OUP, 2003), 63–104, 175–90.

[7] John Murray, "Adamic Administration," in *Collected Writings of John Murray*, vol. 2, *Select Lectures in Systematic Theology* (Edinburgh: Banner of Truth, 1977), 47–59.

[8] Ibid., 49.

[9] Ibid., 50.

[10] Ibid., 55–56.

Whether or not his claims are true biblically, Murray stands at odds historically with how the Westminster divines and theologians of the period, reflected in the Confession and catechisms, understood these texts and their bearing upon the covenant of works.

More recent criticisms, especially those of Torrance and Rolston, have typically been interested in proving dogmatic claims rather than trying to understand the Confession's doctrine of the covenants in its own right. Rolston and Torrance equate Reformed theology with the views of Calvin; if people would only bypass the bastardization of Calvin's thought by his irresponsible successors and reach back to the pure uncorrupted procrustean bed of Geneva, then all would be well.

Contrary to these claims, and more in line with Warfield's assessment, the Confession embodies the teaching of the Reformers, though in a more nuanced and developed form. Moreover, Calvin was not the only theologian contributing to the development of the Reformed tradition. Additionally, Reformed theologians reached back beyond their own time to the Patristic era to construct their theology. The Reformers were not the first to write of God's covenant with Adam. It might surprise some that even Roman Catholic theologians wrote of God's covenant with Adam before this idea was embraced by the Reformed tradition on a wide scale.

Hence, this chapter will briefly survey the historical background to the doctrine of the covenants. We will then examine key elements of the covenants of works and grace and explore related doctrines such as creation and the role of the law before and after the fall, as well as the relationship between the covenants of works and grace and the Mosaic covenant. Lastly, we will explore the question of whether the covenant of redemption (*pactum salutis*) is in any way present within the Confession.

Historical Background

The doctrine of the covenant finds its origins not in the minds of theologians but in the biblical text. It would be odd for a theologian not to speak of a doctrine of the covenants, given the prevalence of the concept in Scripture. It should be no surprise, then, that theologians speak of God's covenants with humanity in a number of different contexts.

Bible translations were one of the first ways that the doctrine of the covenant entered theological discussions. For example, in his Latin translation of the Scriptures, Jerome (ca. 347–420) rendered Hosea 6:7, "But they like Adam transgressed the covenant" (*ispsi autem sicut Adam transgressi sunt pactum*). Roman Catholic theologian Cornelius à Lapide (1567–1637) glosses Hosea 6:7 as "the first parents in paradise violated the covenant with God." Lapide cites a number of Patristic and medieval exegetes who argue the same conclusion, including Jerome, Cyril (ca. 376–444), Rupert of Deutz (ca. 1075–1129), Hugh of St. Victor (ca. 1096–1141), and Nicholas of Lyra (ca. 1270–1349). Lapide was not blindly following tradition but noted that the Septuagint rendered the verse as a common reference to humanity: "Like men they transgressed the covenant."[11]

In addition to Jerome, a number of other Patristic writers refer to the doctrine of the covenant. Irenaeus (130–200), for example, was well aware of the term and in *Against Heresies* explained that God is the author of both the old and new covenants.[12] Early church historians such as Eusebius (ca. 260–340) observed the covenantal continuity between Judaism and Christianity; he argued that they were not two antithetical religions but rather one and the same. Lactantius noted the parallel between the Old Testament practice of circumcision and the New Testament practice of baptism.[13] Augustine (354–430) also mentioned the covenant in his writings. Specifically, in his *City of God*, he argued that infants, though they have not committed actual sin, are still considered guilty of original sin because of Adam's initial covenantal relationship with God.[14]

The covenant concept continued to be employed by theologians in the Middle Ages to varying degrees, but arguably it flowered fully in the early days of the Reformation in the writings of Ulrich Zwingli (1484–1531). Zwingli's first clear statement about the doctrine of the covenant came in November 1525.[15] In a polemical work Zwingli ar-

---

[11] Cornelius à Lapide, *R. P. Cornelii A Lapide e Societate Jesu, Sacrae Scripturae Olim Lovanni, Postea Romae Porfessoris, Commentaria in Duodecim Prophetas Minores* (ex Typographia Balleoniana, 1761), on Hos. 6:7 (p. 111); *PRRD*, 2:437.
[12] Irenaeus, *Against Heresies*, 4.9.1, in *ANF* 2:472.
[13] Eusebius, *The Church History of Eusebius*, 1.4.5–11, in *NPNF²* 1:87–88.
[14] Augustine, *City of God*, 16.29, in *NPNF¹* 2:326.
[15] W. P. Stephens, *The Theology of Huldrych Zwingli* (Oxford: Clarendon, 1986), 186.

gued against the Anabaptists for the legitimacy of infant baptism because it was a sign of the covenant. He expressed his belief that there was one covenant of grace under which all saints, Old Testament and New, were saved. Zwingli was not the only theologian to use the concept. His successor in Zurich, Heinrich Bullinger (1504–1575), published a work specifically on the covenant.

In 1534 Bullinger published *A Brief Exposition of the One and Eternal Testament or Covenant of God*.[16] In this work Bullinger also argues against Anabaptists, who believed that the Old Testament was no longer binding for New Testament Christians. Bullinger, as Zwingli did before him, argues for the unity of the Testaments. Bullinger begins his work by defining *testament* using the relevant Hebrew, Greek, and Latin terms. He concludes that the "very God who has graciously deigned to call this mystery of the unity and fellowship with the divine by a human expression has at the same time followed human custom, on account of the weakness of our nature, in making the covenant or instituting the testament."[17] In other words, God does not come to us in his divine transcendence; rather, he graciously condescends to humanity's level and speaks to people in terms they will understand. God "cuts a deal with man."

Bullinger asserts that the covenant of God is gracious; God grants his mercy to us in the covenant. For example, Bullinger affirms in his *Decades*, a series of doctrinal sermons published in 1549, that "God's mind was to declare the favour and good-will that he bare to mankind, and to make us men partakers wholly of himself and his goodness, by pouring himself out upon us, to our great good and profit, it pleased him to make a league or covenant with mankind."[18] Hence Bullinger emphasizes the divinely initiated nature of the covenant of salvation. But he does not simply argue that God provided salvation and that people are free to act and do as they please. He also emphasizes the mutual responsibilities of the covenant. He writes in his 1534 work on the covenant that it

---

[16] Heinrich Bullinger, *A Brief Exposition of the One and Eternal Testament or Covenant of God (1534)*, ed. and trans. Charles McCoy and J. Wayne Baker, in *Fountainhead of Federalism: Heinrich Bullinger and the Covenantal Tradition* (Louisville: Westminster/John Knox, 1991).

[17] Ibid., 103.

[18] Heinrich Bullinger, *The Decades of Henry Bullinger*, ed. Thomas Harding, 4 vols. (1849–1852; Grand Rapids: Reformation Heritage, 2004), 3.6 (2:169).

is our duty to adhere firmly by faith to the one God, inasmuch as he is the one and only author of all good things, and to walk in innocence of life for his pleasure. For anyone who has neglected these things and has sought false gods, who has lived shamefully or impiously, and who has worshipped God more with ceremonies or external things than with true holiness of life, will be excluded, disinherited, and rejected from the covenant.[19]

Bullinger is not contradicting himself by asserting that salvation is synergistic. On the contrary, he simply ensures that antinomianism does not take root in the hearts of his readers.

Though the covenant concept was first mentioned by Zwingli and later expounded by Bullinger, it did not stay confined to the city limits of Zurich. Rather, the concept spread all over Europe on the winds of the Reformation. In England, various works of the Reformers were translated and published in English, and during the Marian exile, many students and theologians sought refuge in cities such as Bullinger's Zurich.[20] Through these means the covenant concept spread to English theologians such as William Tyndale (1494–1536). Tyndale writes in his prologue to the Gospel of Matthew that the "general covenant, wherein all other are comprehended and included, is this: If we meek ourselves to God, to keep all his laws, after the example of Christ, then God hath bound himself unto us, to keep and make good all the mercies promised in Christ throughout all the scripture."[21] Moreover, Tyndale also sees the covenant as the central means for comprehending Scripture: "The right way, yea, and the only way, to understand the scripture unto salvation, is that we earnestly and above all things search for the profession of our baptism, or covenants made between God and us."[22] Tyndale makes the covenant the hermeneutical principle for the proper understanding of how salvation comes to man: it comes by way of covenant.

With the passage of time the covenant concept continued to spread,

---

[19] Bullinger, *A Brief Exposition*, 111.
[20] Michael McGiffert, "Grace and Works: The Rise and Division of Covenant Divinity in Elizabethan Puritanism," *HTR* 75, no. 4 (1982): 472; Jens Møller, "The Beginnings of Puritan Covenant Theology," *JEH* 14 (1963): 56.
[21] William Tyndale, *Doctrinal Treatises and Introductions to Different Portions of the Holy Scriptures*, The Parker Society, ed. Henry Walter (Cambridge: CUP, 1848), 470.
[22] Ibid., 469.

and inevitably second-generation Reformers also advocated the doctrine of the covenant. John Calvin (1509–1564), a second-generation Reformer, expounded on the covenant in his writings. Like Zwingli, Bullinger, and Tyndale, Calvin affirmed that salvation in the Old Testament is the same as in the New Testament. While acknowledging differences in the way the covenant of grace is administered, he noted that the differences are merely accidental. For example, Calvin writes that the differences between the two Testaments "are such as pertain rather to the mode of administration, than to the substance. In this view, they will not prevent the promises of the Old and New Testament from remaining the same, and the promises of both Testaments from having in Christ the same foundation."[23]

During the Reformation theologians developed and articulated a parallel covenant to the covenant of grace: a covenant of nature. Three theologians played a role in propagating this second covenant: Wolfgang Musculus (1497–1563), Zacharias Ursinus (1534–1583), and Caspar Olevianus (1536–1587).[24] The concept of the covenant of nature was published in Musculus's *Common Places of Christian Religion*,[25] where he writes:

> I find that the covenant of God is of two sortes. The one is generall, an other is special and everlasting. The general covenant is that, which he made with his whole frame of the earth and all that dwelleth therein, as well beastes as men, with the day also and the night, winter and sommer, cold and heate, seed time and harvest.[26]

Musculus connects the general covenant with the creation, as well as God's dealings with humanity on the heels of the flood; he cites Genesis 9 and Jeremiah 33 in support of his explanation. By contrast, "The speciall and everlasting covenant, is the same which he hath vouchsavyd to make with his elect and believing." Musculus identifies

---

[23] John Calvin, *Institutes of the Christian Religion*, trans. John Allen (Grand Rapids: Eerdmans, 1949), 2.11.1.

[24] Richard A. Muller, "The Covenant of Works and the Stability of Divine Law in Seventeenth-Century Reformed Orthodoxy: A Study in the Theology of Herman Witsius and Wilhelmus à Brakel," *CTJ* 29 (1994): 87; Lyle D. Bierma, "Covenant or Covenants in the Theology of Olevianus," *CTJ* 22 (1987): 235–42.

[25] For an overview of Musculus's doctrine of the covenant, see Jordan J. Ballor, *Covenant, Causality, and Law: A Study in the Theology of Wolfgang Musculus* (Göttingen: Vandenhoeck & Ruprecht, 2012), 43–110.

[26] Wolfgang Musculus, *Common Places of Christian Religion* (London, 1613), fol. 121.

the special covenant with God's renaming of Abraham in Genesis 17, though he also invokes Romans 9 and Galatians 3.[27] Thus Musculus bifurcates the covenant: a general covenant with the created order and a special covenant that is strictly for the elect of God.

Ursinus and Olevianus, two famous Heidelberg theologians, also speak of a covenant of nature.[28] Ursinus, for example, associates a covenant of creation with the law of God:

> Q. What does the divine law, or Decalogue teach?
> A. It teaches the kind of covenant that God established with man-kind in creation, how he managed in keeping it, and what God requires of him after establishing a new covenant of grace with him—that is, what kind of person God created, for what pur-pose, into what state he has fallen, and how he ought to conduct his life after being reconciled to God.[29]

By the law of God humanity first learned how we should act; it also showed what God desired from us after the covenant of grace had been initiated. Important to note, however, is that Ursinus associated the covenant of creation not directly with Adam but instead with the broader creation.[30] He writes:

> Q. What is the difference between the law and the gospel?
> A. The law contains the natural covenant, established by God with humanity in creation, that is, it is known by humanity by na-ture, it requires our perfect obedience to God, and it promises eternal life to those who keep it and threatens eternal punish-ment to those who do not. The gospel, however, contains the covenant of grace, that is, although it exists, it is not known at all by nature; it shows us the fulfillment in Christ of the righ-

---

[27] Ibid.

[28] See Lyle D. Bierma, "Law and Grace in Ursinus' Doctrine of the Natural Covenant: A Reappraisal," in *Protestant Scholasticism: Essays in Reassessment*, ed. Carl R. Trueman and R. Scott Clark (Carlisle: Paternoster, 1999), 96–110.

[29] Zacharias Ursinus, Larger Catechism, q. 10, in *An Introduction to the Heidelberg Catechism: Sources, History and Theology*, ed. Lyle D. Bierma et al. (Grand Rapids: Baker, 2005), 164.

[30] David Weir, *The Origins of the Federal Theology in Sixteenth-Century Reformation Thought* (Oxford: OUP, 1990), 105. There is debate about the role Ursinus plays in the development of the covenant of creation. Weir argues that Ursinus was the first theologian to speak of a covenant of creation (ibid., 22). Cf. Robert Letham, "The *Foedus Operum*: Some Factors Accounting for Its Development," *SCJ* 14, no. 4 (1983): 457–67; Peter Alan Lillback, "Ursinus' Development of the Covenant of Creation: A Debt to Melanchthon or Calvin?," *WTJ* 43 (1981): 247. Contra Weir, Lillback, and Letham, cf. Derk Visser, "The Covenant in Zacharias Ursinus," *SCJ* 18, no. 4 (1987): 531–44.

teousness by Christ's Spirit; and it promises eternal life freely because of Christ to those who believe in him.[31]

Ursinus does not speak of a covenant with Adam, but of a covenant that is engrained and embedded in the creation, with the law written upon the human heart, or natural law.

Olevianus also speaks of a covenant of creation throughout his various works. However, he does not only speak of a covenant of grace and a covenant of creation. He uses the covenant concept in many different ways, including a pre-temporal covenant between the Father and the Son to save fallen man; he also mentions briefly a covenant of creation. There is also a covenant between man and the Devil when man rebelled against God, a legal covenant between God and the Israelites when the law was delivered at Sinai, and a covenant between God and his creatures in which he promised providentially to sustain them.[32] Hence, through the writings of Musculus, Ursinus, and Olevianus, the covenant concept is expanded, and the idea of a covenant of creation begins to emerge within Reformed theology. The covenant of creation, however, receives a new name and content from the pens of subsequent theologians, namely, the covenant of works.

With the publication of Musculus's *Common Places* in 1563 and through the work of Ursinus and Olevianus, it does not take long for the concept of a twofold covenant to spread. One of the first explicit uses of the term *covenant of works* appears in Dudley Fenner's (1558–1587) *Sacra Theologia*, published in 1585.[33] Fenner asserts that there are two covenants, "the covenant of works" and "the covenant of the free promise."[34] He then defines the two: "The covenant of works is the covenant where the condition of perfect obedience is

---

[31] Ursinus, Larger Catechism, q. 36.

[32] Lyle D. Bierma, *German Calvinism in the Confessional Age: The Covenant Theology of Caspar Olevianus* (Grand Rapids: Baker, 1996), 107–39.

[33] Weir, *Origins of the Federal Theology*, 119; Michael McGiffert, "Grace and Works: The Rise and Division of Covenant Divinity in Elizabethan Puritanism," *HTR* 75, no. 4 (1982): 492; Trinterud, "Origins of Puritanism," *Church History* 20, no. 1 (1951): 48–49; Visser, "Covenant in Zacharias Ursinus," 534. Circumstantial evidence points to the possibility that Fenner gleaned the covenant of works from Thomas Cartwright. Cartwright, it is argued, obtained the concept from Ursinus during his studies at Heidelberg (Weir, *Origins of the Federal Theology*, 118–19; McGiffert, "Grace and Works," 494–95; Visser, "Covenant in Zacharias Ursinus," 535; and Letham, "The *Foedus Operum*," 464).

[34] Dudley Fenner, *Sacra Theologia sive Veritas Quae Est Secundum Pietatem* (Eustathium Vignon, 1589), 4.1 (p. 39): "*Foedus duplex est: Operum foedus / Gratuitae promissionis foedus.*" He cites Gen. 4:7; Jer. 31:3; Rom. 10:5; Gal. 3:8–10; and Eph. 2:12.

annexed. . . . The covenant of the free promise is the covenant, (a) concerning Christ and blessing given forth in him, which is freely given, and (b) where the condition is: if a person receives Christ."[35] Fenner also connects the covenant of works with the Mosaic covenant. He explains that the covenant with the Jews was a covenant of works, one in which they had to obey all of the things written in the book of the law.[36]

Though Fenner's work was published in 1585, the covenant of works must have been in the theological atmosphere of the times because by 1590 the twofold covenant scheme was employed by theologians such as William Perkins (1558–1602) of Cambridge and Amandus Polanus (1561–1610) of Basel. Perkins writes in *A Golden Chaine* that "Gods covenant, is his contract with man, concerning life eternal, upon certain conditions." The first of God's covenants is the covenant of works, which "is Gods covenant, made with condition of perfect obedience, & is expressed in the morall Law."[37] The second is the covenant of grace, which "is that, whereby God freely promising Christ, and his benefites, exacteth againe of man, that he would by faith receive Christ, and repent him of his sinnes."[38] Like Ursinus before him, Perkins identifies the covenant of works with the moral law, a rule that requires perfect obedience; Perkins appeals to Romans 10:5, among other texts. He also identifies the Decalogue, or Ten Commandments, "as an abridgement of the whole Lawe, and the covenant of workes."[39]

Polanus, on the Continent, similarly writes, "The covenant of workes is a bargain of God made with men concerning eternall life, to which is both a condition of perfect obedience adioyned, to be performed by man, & also a threatening of eternall death if he shal not

---

[35] Fenner, *Sacra Theologia*, 4.3 (p. 39): "*Operum foedus*, est *foedus* ubi conditio annexa est perfecta obedientia. . . . *Foedus* gratuitae promissionis, est *foedus* (a) de *Christo* & *eulogia* in ipso extante, gratuito promissionis, (b) ubi conditio est, si recepiatur *Christus*." He cites the following: (a) Gen. 3:15; 11:35; Deut. 31:15–16; Pss. 74:20; 106:45, 47; 111:5–9; Isa. 44:17; 59:21; 61:8; Jer. 32:43–44; Ezek. 16:6, 60; 34:24–25; 36:26–27; 39:29; 43:9; Hos. 2:18; Zech. 9:11; Mal. 3:1; Gal. 3:12–14; and (b) John 1:11–12; Rom. 5:17; Eph. 2:5, 6, 13.
[36] Fenner, *Sacra Theologia*, 8.1 (p. 123): "Foedus cum Iudaeis ictum, est foedus operum, quo Deus stipulatur Iudaeos fore ipsi peculium prae omnibus populis, si permanserint in omnibus quae scripta sunt in libro legis" (Ex. 19:5; 24:3, 24).
[37] William Perkins, *A Golden Chaine; or, The Description of Theology, Containing the Order of Causes of Salvation and Damnation, according to God's Word* (London: Edward Alde, 1592), § 19.
[38] Ibid., § 31.
[39] Ibid., § 19. Perkins cites Ex. 34:27; 1 Kings 8:9; and Matt. 22:40.

performe perfect obedience (Gen. 2:17)." On the second covenant he writes, "The covenant of grace is the reconciling of the elect with God, by the death of the only mediatour."[40] Like Perkins, Polanus draws the connection between the Decalogue, the moral law, and the covenant of works. Polanus writes, "The repetition of the covenant of workes is made by God, Exod. 19.5. Deut. 5.2. 1 King 8.21. Heb. 8.9."[41] Through the work of Perkins and Polanus the twofold covenant scheme spread throughout England and Continental Europe and was repeated in the works of other theologians such as Johannes Wollebius (1589–1629) and Jacob Arminius (1560–1609).[42]

But just two years after Fenner published his work, Robert Rollock (1555–1599), principal of the University of Edinburgh, became the first Scottish theologian to employ the twofold covenant scheme.[43] In his 1597 *Treatise of God's Effectual Calling*, Rollock echoes the same hermeneutical principle as Tyndale: "For God speaks nothing to man without the covenant. For which cause all the Scripture, both old and new, wherein all God's word is contained, bears the name of God's covenant or testament."[44] Rollock describes the covenant of works using many of the concepts found in Musculus and Ursinus, yet he still defines it along the lines of Perkins and Polanus: "The covenant of works, which may also be called a legal or natural covenant, is founded in nature, which by creation was pure and holy, and in the law of God, which in the first creation was engraven in man's heart."[45] Regarding the covenant of grace Rollock writes:

> In the free Covenant of Grace, or of the gospel, the first ground is
> our Mediator Jesus Christ, crucified also, and dead; or, which is

---

[40] Amandus Polanus, *The Substance of Christian Religion, Soundly Set Forth in Two Books*, trans. Elijah Wilcocks (London: John Oxenbridge, 1595), 88–89; he cites Rom. 8:30; 2 Cor. 5:17–21; and Heb. 9:15.

[41] Ibid., 88.

[42] Johannes Wollebius, *Compendium Theologiae Christianae*, 8.1, in *Reformed Dogmatics*, ed. and trans. John W. Beardslee III (New York: OUP, 1965), 64; Jacob Arminius, *Private Disputation*, 29, in *The Works of James Arminius*, ed. and trans. James Nichols and William Nichols, 3 vols. (1825–1875; Grand Rapids: Baker, 1986), 2:369–71.

[43] G. D. Henderson, "The Idea of the Covenant in Scotland," *EQ* 27, no. 1 (1955): 9.

[44] Robert Rollock, *A Treatise of Our Effectual Calling*, in *The Select Works of Robert Rollock*, ed. William M. Gunn, 2 vols. (Edinburgh: Woodrow Society, 1849), 1:33–34.

[45] Ibid., 34. What is interesting to note is the connection that Rollock has with Heidelberg theology. Henry Charteris, Rollock's biographer, notes how he taught his students: "He diligently trained them in the Catechism of the Palatinate" (Rollock, preface, in *Works*, 1:lxvi; Letham, "The *Foedus Operum*," 464).

the same in effect, the blood of the Mediator, the virtue whereof is twofold. The first serves to satisfy the justice and wrath of God for our sins, for the breach of that covenant of works. The second is, to purchase and merit a new grace and mercy of God for us.[46]

What is important to note in these statements is that they are more developed expressions in comparison to the earlier tradition, but nevertheless exhibit a continuity with it.

Another Scottish theologian, Johannes Scharpius (1572–1648), also wrote of the two covenants, works and grace. The covenant of works is the covenant that God makes on the basis of man's perfect obedience and gives the reward of eternal life, which is captured in the biblical statement "Do this and live" (Lev. 18:5). The covenant of grace, on the other hand, is the covenant based upon the merit of Christ, for those who believe in Christ receive eternal life; and this covenant is captured in the biblical ideas "I am your God, you are mine," and "believe and live."[47] Scharpius argues that the two covenants agree in that they are both covenants, they are entered by two parties, both covenants produce a people of God, both have a mediator—Moses for the former and Christ for the latter—both contain words of promise, and both have the glory of God as their goal. The covenants differ in terms of their respective forms. The covenant of works is "Do this and live" versus "Believe and you will be saved" for the covenant of grace. God is the author of both, but the former is a legal covenant, while the latter is marked by grace.

In terms of the dignity of the mediator, the former has Moses, a servant in God's house, whereas the latter has Jesus, who is the foundation of the covenant. And, lastly, there is the dignity of the respective promises. For the covenant of works, the goal for man is impossible to attain, and the law is not at fault; the defect lies in sinful humanity. By contrast the promises of the covenant of grace are more than sufficient to save sinners. Scharpius lists other differences between the two covenants: The legal covenant is a minister of death; the covenant

---

[46] Rollock, *A Treatise of Our Effectual Calling*, 36.

[47] Johannes Scharpius, *Cursus Theologicus, in Quo Controversiae Omnes de Fidei Dogmatibus, Hoc Seculo Exagitatae, Nominatim inter Nos et Pontificios, Pertractantur; et ad Bellarmini Argumenta Respondetur* (Geneva: Franciscum Nicolaum, 1628), 336.

of grace is a minister of life. The covenant of works is inscribed on tablets of stone; the covenant of grace is written upon hearts of flesh. The legal covenant is veiled, whereas the covenant of grace is openly disclosed. And the covenant of works is temporary, whereas the covenant of grace is eternal.[48] And like Ursinus, Perkins, and Polanus, Scharpius connects the Mosaic covenant with the covenant of works, as he believes that the moral law is simply a repetition of the law of nature.[49]

This brief survey of the development of covenant theology illustrates a number of key points that should be noted in any examination of the Confession's doctrine of the covenants. First, the idea of a prelapsarian covenant between God and humanity has the earliest and oldest pedigree, one that stretches back to the Patristic era and is affirmed later by medieval theologians. This fact is especially evident in the Vulgate's translation of Hosea 6:7 and in the many theologians who embraced Jerome's translation. Second, a bi-covenantal structure to redemptive history finds its origins in the earliest days of the Reformation with Musculus, Ursinus, and Olevianus, who argue for covenants of creation and grace. In particular, there is a close association of the law of nature with this initial covenant, one written upon the heart of humanity and later repeated in the Decalogue at Sinai in the Mosaic covenant. By the time of the Confession, the divines do not create doctrinal categories but merely codify doctrines that have already been in the theological air for quite some time. This is not to say that the Confession's covenant of works and Musculus's general covenant are identical, or that the Confession's covenant of works is the same as medieval or Patristic acknowledgments of God's covenant with Adam. But one cannot help but see the similarities of the concepts and recognize that the more time marches on, the more doctrinal formulation becomes more precise. Third, the development of the doctrine of the covenants is not restricted to one location. The theological discourse and sharing of ideas crosses all sorts of geographical, historical, and, arguably, theological boundaries. The twofold covenant structure cannot be said to be unique to the Confession.

---

[48] Ibid., 336–37.
[49] Ibid., 336, 296.

The Covenant of Works

The opening paragraph of the Confession's chapter on the covenant sets forth a principle that establishes the relationship between Creator and creature. The Confession states:

> The distance between God and the Creature is so great, that although reasonable Creatures do owe obedience unto him as their Creator, yet they could never have any fruition of him as their Blessednesse and Reward, but by some voluntary condescension on Gods part, which he hath been pleased to expresse by way of Covenant. (7.1)

Echoing the distinction between archetypal and ectypal theology— God's knowledge of himself and humanity's knowledge of God—the divines explain that humanity has no natural claim upon God. God is "most absolute" (2.1) "and is alone in, and unto himself all-sufficient, not standing in need of any creatures which he hath made" (2.2). Hence the distance between God and the creature is so great that man cannot approach God as his equal. Rather, God must voluntarily condescend to humanity and does so by means of covenant. In the past, some commentators have been quick to identify these statements as indicating that God's act of creation is not only covenantal but also one of grace.[50] However, such comments should be qualified and illustrated by contextual primary sources.

Theologians have been accustomed of speaking of God's grace in all things, and this grace is typically associated with *saving* grace. Hodge, for example, claims regarding the covenant of works, "This covenant was also in its essence a covenant of grace, in that it graciously promised life in the society of God as the freely-granted reward of an obedience already unconditionally due."[51] However, while early modern Reformed theologians are accustomed to speaking of the covenant of works as bringing God's grace to humanity, the nature and definition of the term *grace* should not be shaped by more recent discussions. In his oft-cited work on covenant theology, John Ball (1585–1640) explains the nature of God's condescension in covenant with humanity.

---

[50] A. A. Hodge, *The Confession of Faith: A Handbook of Christian Doctrine Expounding the Westminster Confession* (Edinburgh: Banner of Truth, 1958), 121.
[51] Ibid., 122.

There is no equality of power and authority between God and the creature, but humanity must accept whatever God offers and commands. Ball writes:

> The covenant is of God, and that of his free grace and love: for although in some Covenant the good covenanted be promised in justice, and given in justice for our workes: yet it was of grace that God was pleased to bind himselfe to his creature, and above the desert of the creature: and though the reward be of justice, it is also of favor.[52]

Ball's explanation reveals that the "grace" is not redemptive but rather expressive of God's condescension to the creature. This conclusion is evident because he talks about "justice for workes."

When Ball elaborates upon the nature of the covenant of works, he provides several rudiments showing that justice, not mercy, marks this covenant: "This Covenant God made in Justice; yet so as it was of Grace likewise to make such a free promise, and to bestow so great things upon man for his obedience."[53] Once again the accent of grace is placed upon the fact that God liberally and freely, apart from necessity or obligation, promised eternal life upon the condition of willing obedience from the creature.[54] Note how Ball emphasizes man's required obedience:

> God did in strict justice require obedience, promise a reward, and threaten punishment: but yet as bountifull and gratious unto his creature, intire and perfect, if he should continue. God did in justice proportion the reward and the worke, the weight of the blessing promised, and the work of obedience required: but yet I cannot thinke it had been injustice in God to have given lesse, or not to have continued so great things to man, so long as he continued his obedience: No, God was pleased to manifest his goodnesse to man continuing in obedience, no lesse then his justice, as formerly in creation he had shewed himselfe exceeding gratious to man, above other visible and corporall creatures.[55]

---

[52] John Ball, *A Treatise of the Covenant of Grace* (London: Edward Brewster, 1645), 2 (p. 7).
[53] Ibid., 2 (p. 9).
[54] Ibid., 2 (p. 6).
[55] Ibid., 2 (p. 9).

Ball highlights several other elements in the covenant of works to prove that it does not offer redemptive grace.

First, the covenant of works is summarized in the scriptural aphorism "Do this and live" (Lev. 18:5). Ball comments that Adam's requirement was "the exact and rigid exaction of perfect obedience in his own person, without the least spot or failing for matter or manner." Had Adam persevered, his obedience would have been rewarded in justice, but not according to merit. Ball believes that no creature could merit anything from God; in the end, all creatures are debtors to God.[56] Second, the covenant of works was one of friendship, not of reconciliation. Once the covenant was breached, there was no way it could be repaired. Ball states, "It promised no mercy or pardon, admitted no repentance, accepted no obedience, but what was perfect and compleat."[57]

One of the Westminster divines, Anthony Burgess (d. 1664), argues similarly concerning God's condescension and the covenant of works. Burgess explains that when God made a covenant with man, it was a "compact of mutuall fidelity," but Adam and God were not equals in this covenant—there was an "inequality of the Covenanters."[58] Burgess makes the same point as Ball regarding the nature of Adam's obedience and what it could have secured. Adam was not told, *"Believe and have life eternall*; but *Obey*, even perfect and entire obedience."[59] However, Adam would not have obtained his reward by merit because the nature of the reward far exceeded the worthiness of his obedience. "It's an infinite good," writes Burgess, "and all that is done by us is finite." Burgess believes that Adam was not capable of obeying without the assistance of God. He acknowledges, however, "Though some will not call it grace, because they suppose that onely cometh by Christ; yet all they that are orthodox do acknowledge a necessity of Gods enabling *Adam* to that which was good, else he would have failed."[60] Another divine, Samuel Rutherford (1600–1661), explains in what way grace attends the covenant of works: "In all pactions between the Lord and

---

[56] Ibid., 2 (p. 10).
[57] Ibid., 2 (p. 11).
[58] Anthony Burgess, *Vindiciae Legis; or, A Vindication of the Morall Law and the Covenants* (London: Thomas Underhill, 1647), 13 (p. 127).
[59] Ibid., 13 (p. 128).
[60] Ibid., 13 (p. 129); cf. Willem J. van Asselt, *The Federal Theology of Johannes Cocceius (1603–69)* (Leiden: Brill, 2001), 265–66.

man, even in a Law-Covenant there is some out-breakings of Grace. Its true, there was no Gospel-Grace, that is a fruit of Christs merite in this Covenant. But yet if grace be taken for undeserved goodnesse."[61]

Wrapped in these statements are a number of fundamentals that appear in the Confession's articulation of the covenant of works. The Confession says, "The first Covenant made with Man, was a Covenant of Works, wherein Life was promised to Adam, and in him to his posterity, upon condition of perfect and personall obedience" (7.2). Within this paragraph are four parts: (1) the existence of the covenant of works, (2) the promise of eternal life as the goal of the covenant, (3) that Adam was a federal representative for "his posterity," and (4) that this covenant required perfect and personal obedience.

First, the divines cite Galatians 3:12, a text that some might not immediately associate with a pre-fall covenant with Adam. Nevertheless, the text says, "And the law is not of faith: but, The man that doeth them shall live in them." As readers likely know, Paul quotes Leviticus 18:5 in the latter half of this verse. So the question arises, how do Galatians 3:12 and Leviticus 18:5, serve as exegetical evidence of the covenant of works? The assembly's annotations explain: "The Law promiseth life to all that keep it, and therefore if it be kept it justifieth and giveth life."[62] In short, the divines lock onto the principle that one *does* the law and *believes* the gospel.[63] The assembly's annotations on Leviticus 18:5 also note that this Old Testament verse shows "how perfect our condition was before the fall."[64] A number of Reformed writers understood Leviticus 18:5 in this manner, namely, that it shows how the law functions—if a person obeys, then he is given life.[65] In Adam's

---

[61] Samuel Rutherford, *The Covenant of Life Opened; or, A Treatise on the Covenant of Grace* (Edinburgh: Robert Brown, 1654), 1.7 (p. 35).

[62] *Annotations*, comm. Gal. 3:12.

[63] See, e.g., comments to this effect by William Perkins, *A Commentarie or Exposition, upon the Five First Chapters of the Epistle to the Galatians* (Cambridge: John Legat, 1604), 292.

[64] *Annotations*, comm. Lev. 18:5.

[65] So, e.g., Ball, *Covenant of Grace*, 2 (pp. 9–10); Thomas Watson, *A Body of Practical Divinity* (London: Thomas Parkhurst, 1692), 74–75; Johannes Maccovius, *Scholastic Discourse: Johannes Maccovius (1588–1644) on Theological and Philosophical Distinctions and Rules*, ed. Willem J. van Asselt et al. (Apeldoorn: Instituut voor Reformatieonderzoek, 2009), 12.4 (p. 225); James Ussher, *A Body of Divinitie; or, The Summe and Substance of Christian Religion* (London: Thomas Downes and George Badger, 1645), 124–25; Rutherford, *Covenant of Life Opened*, 1.7 (p. 35); Peter Bulkeley, *The Gospel-Covenant; or, The Covenant of Grace Opened* (London: Matthew Simmons, 1651), 1.7 (p. 55); Jeremias Bastingius, *An Exposition or Commentarie upon the Catechisme of Christian Religion* (Cambridge: John Legat, 1595), fol. 122; Francis Turretin, *Institutes of Elenctic Theology*, ed. James T. Dennison Jr., trans. George Musgrave Giger (Phillipsburg, NJ: P&R, 1992–1997), 16.2.2.

state in the garden, then, he was given the law, was told to obey, and would have secured eternal life for himself and his posterity had he successfully obeyed God's command.

A popular work from the period, *The Marrow of Modern Divinity*, one commended by Westminster divine Joseph Caryl (1602–1673), explains how these elements cohere:

> The law of Works is as much to say as the covenant of Works, for it is manifest (saith *Musculus*) that the word which signifieth Covenant or Bargain, is put for law, the which covenant or bargain the Lord made with all mankind in *Adam* before his fall, the summe whereof was, *do this, and thou shalt live, and if thou do it not, thou shalt die the death.*[66]

In addition to Galatians 3:12 and Leviticus 18:5 the divines also cite Romans 10:5 and 5:12–20, to support the claim that eternal life was promised to both Adam and his posterity. The assembly's *Annotations* explain that once again Paul cites Leviticus 18:5, and that the apostle states how the law functions: if a person performs the law, then he will live, but if he does not perform it, then he will suffer the curse of the law (Deut. 27:26). That eternal life was in view is confirmed by the assembly's appeal to Luke 10:25–28 in its explanation of Romans 10:5: "To which our Saviours answer to the young man in the Gospel, who demanded of him what he should do to obtain eternall life, agreeth, saying, Keep the commandments: Doe this and thou shalt live."[67]

---

[66] Edward Fisher, *The Marrow of Modern Divinity: Touching Both the Covenant of Works, and the Covenant of Grace* (London: G. Calvert, 1645), 6–7; cf. Musculus, *Common Places*, fols. 118–19.

[67] *Annotations*, comm. Rom. 10:5. Reformed theologians have not always agreed on this; some believed that eternal life was in view; others, that an earthly temporal blessing was in view. The former position was held by Turretin and Polanus, and the latter was held by Westminster divine Thomas Goodwin (cf. Turretin, *Institutes*, 8.6.3; Polanus, *Substance of Christian Religion*, 53; Thomas Goodwin, *Of Creatures, and the Condition of Their State by Creation*, 2.7, in The *Works of Thomas Goodwin*, 12 vols. [Edinburgh: James Nichol, 1861–1866], 7:57; Mark A. Herzer, "Adam's Reward: Heaven or Earth?," in *Drawn into Controversie: Reformed Theological Diversity and Debates within Seventeenth-Century British Puritanism*, ed. Michael A. G. Haykin and Mark Jones [Göttingen: Vandenhoeck & Ruprecht, 2011], 162–82). Herzer identifies adherents to each position and includes Richard Baxter, Francis Junius, Andreas Rijssen, Edward Leigh, and Thomas Watson among those who held that heaven is the reward; he lists Moïse Amyraut, John Cameron, James Ussher, John Downame, and Jeremiah Burroughs as those who argued for an earthly reward (Herzer, "Adam's Reward," 176–77). Even though the assembly's annotations state that heaven is the reward, the Confession and catechisms are not written in such a way as to exclude or prejudice the opposing view; the Confession states that "Life was promised to Adam" (7.2), and the Larger Catechism (q. 20) states that God entered into a "Covenant of Life with" Adam "of which the Tree of Life was a pledge," and the Shorter Catechism (q. 12) says the same. The Larger cites Gen. 2:9; Rom. 10:5; and Gal. 3:12; and the Shorter cites Gen. 2:17 and Gal. 3:12. Cf. Van Asselt, *Federal Theology*, 254–65.

But with the citation of Romans 5:12–20, the divines draw upon the covenantal actions of the two respective heads of fallen and redeemed humanity, Adam and Christ. According to the assembly's *Annotations*, Adam was the "head and root by nature of all mankinde." Adam's sin was imputed to all of his offspring. The *Annotations* state, "Adam and Christ were like two roots or stocks, the one whereof, to wit, Adam, conveyed to his branches, sinne and death; the Christ, to all that are engrafted in him, righteousness and life."[68] The Confession makes these points clear: "They," that is, Adam and Eve, "being the root of all man-kinde, the guilt of this sin was imputed, and the same death in sin and corrupted nature, conveied to all their posterity descending from them by ordinary generation" (6.3). The Confession touches upon a key point of Reformed theology, namely, the covenantal or federal relationship between Adam and his progeny.

John Preston (1587–1628) explains that the righteousness of Christ comes the same way in which people have received the unrighteousness of Adam:

> First, as *Adam* was one man, yet the common roote of all man-kinde, of whom all that are guilty of death, and shall be damned, must be borne: so *Christ*, the second *Adam*, stands as a public person, and the Root of all that shall be ingrafted into, and borne of him. Secondly, as *Adams* first unrighteousness, the first sin he committed, is communicated to men, and made theirs by imputation; and not so only, but by inherency also; (for it hath bred in them original sin) After the same manner, and by the same equity, the righteousness that *Christ* wrought, is made ours by imputation, and this imputative righteousness of *Christ* worketh a righteousness.[69]

Adam was a public person—he acted not on his own behalf but on behalf of all his posterity. Preston's comments also illustrate how closely linked the covenant of works and the doctrine of justification

---

[68] *Annotations*, comm. Rom. 5:12–20.
[69] John Preston, *The Breast-Plate of Faith and Love: A Treatise, Wherein the Ground and Exercise of Faith and Love, as They Are Set upon Christ Their Object, and as They Are Expressed in Good Works, Is Explained* (London: Nicolas Bourne, 1630), serm. 1, Rom. 1:17 (p. 5).

are. Preston is not alone in this construction, as it is common to many and a touchstone of Reformed theology.[70]

Bound with the covenant of works is the moral law, which creates a web of interconnected texts and doctrines in need of exploration. In his *Body of Divinitie* James Ussher (1581–1656) explains this series of conjoined ideas. He identifies the two covenants, works and grace, and then asks which of the two came first. Ussher argues that the law was given first. He then asks how the law was given to Adam if it was supposedly first given to Moses at Sinai. He responds that the written law was first given by Moses, engraved upon the tablets of stone by the finger of God, but that the law was actually first given to Adam and was written upon his heart, and for this reason it is called the "Law of nature" (Rom. 2:14). Ussher expands upon this idea, saying: "It was chiefly written in his heart at his creation, and partly also uttered in his eare in Paradise." Since the fall, however, the moral law has been given in the Decalogue and is the "summe" of the law.[71]

The connection between natural law, the moral law, the Decalogue, and the covenant of works appears in the Confession's chapter on the law, echoing the same points that appear in Ussher's explanation, though the same links can also be found in other theologians.[72] Fisher's statement is brief but representative of these connections: "*Adam* heard as much in the garden, as *Israel* did at *Sinai*, but onely in fewer words, and without thunder."[73] Ursinus offers a similar analysis:

---

[70] Fisher, *Marrow of Modern Divinity*, 14; Thomas Goodwin, *The Triumph of Faith*, in *The Works of Thomas Goodwin*, 12 vols. (Edinburgh: James Nichol, 1861–1866), 4:31–32; Rutherford, *Covenant of Life Opened*, 2.2 (p. 234). John Davenant, *Dissertation on the Death of Christ*, 6, in *An Exposition of the Epistle of St. Paul to the Colossians* (London: Hamilton, Adams, and Co., 1831), 486. Thomas Cartwright, *A Confutation of the Rhemists Translation, Glosses and Annotations on the New Testament* (Leiden: William Brewster, 1618), 343; Pierre Du Moulin, *The Anatomy of Arminianisme* (London: Nathaniel Newbery, 1620), 9.1–2 (pp. 57–58). Edward Leigh cites a number of theologians in support of the federal nature of Adam's office, including Augustine, Theodore Beza, John Calvin, Johannes Piscator, Hilary, Ambrose, and Chrysostom (Leigh, *Body of Divinity*, 4.1 [p. 307]).
[71] Ussher, *Body of Divinitie*, 124.
[72] See, e.g., Perkins, *Golden Chaine*, § 19; Fisher, *Marrow of Modern Divinity*, 7–9; Wilhelmus à Brakel, *The Christian's Reasonable Service*, trans. Bartel Elshout (Morgan, PA: Soli Deo Gloria, 1992), § 12 (1:359); Herman Witsius, *Economy of the Covenants between God and Man*, trans. William Crookshank (1822; Phillipsburg, NJ: P&R, 1990), 1.3.7; Richard A. Muller, "Covenant of Works," 93; Muller, "Divine Covenants, Absolute and Conditional: John Cameron and the Early Orthodox Development of Reformed Covenant Theology," *MAJT* 17 (2006): 21, 24, 26. Other theologians characterize the fall as a violation of the covenant of works, viz. natural law (Wollebius, *Compendium Theologiae Christianae*, 1.13.1 [pp. 75–76]; Johannes Polyander, André Rivet, Antonius Walaeus, and Antonius Thysius, *Synopsis Purioris Theologiae*, ed. Herman Bavinck [Luguni Batavorum: Didericum Donner, 1881], 14.7–8 [pp. 116–17]).
[73] Fisher, *Marrow of Modern Divinity*, 9.

The *moral law* is a doctrine harmonizing with the eternal and unchangeable wisdom and justice of God, distinguishing right from
wrong, known by nature, engraven upon the hearts of creatures
endowed with reason in their creation, and afterwards often repeated and declared by the voice of God through his servants, the
prophets; teaching what God is and what he requires, binding all
intelligent creatures to perfect obedience and conformity to the law,
internal and external, promising the favor of God and eternal life
to all those who render perfect obedience, and at the same time
denouncing the wrath of God and everlasting punishment upon all
those who do not render this obedience, unless remission of sins
and reconciliation with God be secured for the sake of Christ the
mediator.[74]

The Confession likewise states: "God gave to Adam a Law, as a Covenant of Works, by which he bound him, and all his posterity to personall, entire, exact, and perpetual obedience; promised life upon the
fulfilling, and threatened death upon the breach of it" (19.1). Important
to note are the series of proofs the divines offer in support of this statement: Genesis 1:26–27; 2:17; Romans 2:14–15; 10:5; 5:12, 19; Galatians
3:10, 12; Ecclesiastes 7:29; and Job 28:28. One should note the inter-
weaving of texts that deal with both natural law and the covenant of
works; the proof texts are, at a minimum, closely identified, if not out-
right synonymous. Romans 2:14–15 was a text commonly understood
as a reference to natural law. Calvin for example explains, "Paul contrasts nature with the written law, meaning that the Gentiles had the
natural light of righteousness, which supplied the place of the law by
which the Jews are taught, so that they were *a law unto themselves*."[75]
Calvin's explanation is identical to Ussher's, cited above.

The Confession then proceeds to situate the moral law in subsequent redemptive history: "This Law," referring to the law given

---

[74]Zacharias Ursinus, *The Commentary of Dr. Zacharias Ursinus on the Heidelberg Catechism*, trans.
G. W. Williard (1852; Phillipsburg, NJ: P&R, n.d.), 490–91.
[75]John Calvin, *Romans and Thessalonians*, in *CNTC* (1960; Grand Rapids: Eerdmans, 1996), on
Rom. 2:14–15 (p. 48). Similar comments appear in other commentators, such as Philip Melanchthon,
Commentary on Romans, trans. Fred Kramer (St. Louis: Concordia, 1992), comm. Rom. 2:14–15
(pp. 89–90); Giovanni Diodati, *Pious and Learned Annotations upon the Holy Bible* (London: Nicolas
Fussell, 1651), comm. Rom. 2:14; Andrew Willett, *Hexapla: That Is, a Six-Fold Commentarie upon
the Most Divine Epistle of the Holy Apostle S. Paul to the Romanes* (Cambridge: Leonard Greene,
1620), comm. Rom. 2:14–15 (pp. 115–25); Rom. 13:8 (p. 620).

to Adam "as a Covenant of Works," "after his fall, continued to be a perfect rule of righteousnesse, and, as such, was delivered by God upon Mount Sinai, in ten Commandments, and written in two Tables" (19.2). The divines also acknowledge that "this Law," that which was delivered to Adam and subsequently to Israel, is "commonly called Moral" (19.3). In his *Marrow of Modern Divinity*, Fisher has his legalist dialogue partner state the following:

> But, Sir, you said that the Morall Law may in some sence be said to be the Law of workes, and you have also said, that the Law of workes, and the Covenant of works, are all one, by which it should seem, that the Morall Law may in some sence be said to be this covenant of workes, made with all mankinde before *Adams* fall.[76]

Fisher accedes to this statement and cites George Downame (ca. 1563–1634) in support of the identification of the moral law with the covenant of works.

Downame contends that the law can be understood in a number of different senses: it can mean the *Torah*, which can mean the whole teaching of the Old Testament, but it can also refer simply to the covenant of works:

> More strictly and properly the Law signifieth the covenant of workes, which is also called the Law of workes, Rom. 3.27. which upon condition of perfect and perpetuall obedience promiseth justification and salvation to the observers thereof, Rom 10.5. Gal. 3.12. Lev. 18.5. Ezek. 20.11. Acts 13.38. Rom. 3.20, 28.[77]

Downame further elaborates upon these points as he highlights the differences between the law and the gospel. In opposition to Roman Catholic theologian Robert Bellarmine (1542–1621), Downame writes:

> For the first: he cavilleth with *Calvin* and *Chemnitius* and others, as though they understood simply by the Law of workes, that which requireth workes, and by the Law of faith, which requireth faith: as if the Law of faith did not also require workes, and the Law of workes did not also require faith: whereas our writers distinguish

---

[76] See, e.g., Fisher, *Marrow of Modern Divinity*, 7.
[77] George Downame, *A Treatise of Justification* (London: Nicolas Bourne, 1633), 7.4.4 (p. 465).

the two covenants of God, that is, the Law and the Gospell, whereof
one is the covenant of workes, the other, the covenant of grace:
doe teach, that the Law of workes is that, which to justification
requireth works, as the condition thereof: the Law of faith that,
which to justification requireth faith, as the condition thereof. The
former saith, doe this, and thou shalt live, *Rom.* 10.5, *Gal.* 3.12.
Mat. 19.17. the latter believe in Christ, and thou shalt be saved,
John 3.16. *Act* 16.31.[78]

One should note the overlap between the Confession's proof texts and
those offered by Downame, as well as Fisher's explanation. Moreover,
one can conclude that, at a certain level, the Confession represents
the common opinion on the connection and association of the moral
law, the covenant of works, and the Decalogue given in the Mosaic
covenant.

A matter of significant debate, however, was the precise relationship between the covenant of works and the Mosaic covenant. One
of the divines, Samuel Bolton (1606–1654), acknowledges that there
were a number of different positions on this matter (table 2).

Table 2. Bolton's summary of covenantal views

Threefold: Mixed	Threefold: Covenant of Works Repeated	Threefold: Subservient	Twofold
1. Covenant of nature	1. Covenant of nature	1. Covenant of nature	1. Covenant of works
2. Covenant of grace	2. Covenant of promise (or grace)	2. Covenant of grace	2. Covenant of grace*
3. Sinai is mixed: nature and grace.	3. Sinai is a covenant of works.	3. Sinai is subservient, of neither the covenant of works nor the covenant of grace.	

*Samuel Bolton, *The True Bounds of Christian Freedome; or, A Treatise Wherein the Rights of the Law Are Vindicated, the Liberties of Grace Maintained* (London: Austin Rice, 1656), 128–29.

Bolton explains that the mixed view saw three different covenants
in Scripture: a covenant of nature with Adam, the covenant of grace,

---

[78] Ibid., 7.2.6 (p. 443).

and the Mosaic covenant, which was a mixed covenant of nature and grace. A second view held that there were covenants of nature and grace, but that the Mosaic covenant was a repetition of the covenant of works. A third view held to the covenants of nature and grace, but regarded the Mosaic covenant as part of neither the covenant of nature nor the covenant of grace, but a *tertium quid* (a third alternative). Bolton notes that the most common scheme was a twofold view: covenants of works and grace.

Westminster divine Edmund Calamy (1600–1666) offers another layer of views that differs slightly from Bolton's arrangement (table 3).

Table 3. Calamy's summary of covenantal views

Fourfold (Simpson)	Threefold (Burroughs)	Twofold (Pope)	Threefold (Burgess)	Twofold (Calamy)
1. Covenant of works (Adam) 2. Covenant of grace (Abraham) 3. Covenant of works (Israel) 4. Covenant of grace (new covenant)	1. Covenant of works with Adam 2. Covenant of works with Israel 3. Covenant of grace through Jesus	1. Covenant of works with Israel, with no prior covenant, i.e., no covenant with Adam 2. Covenant of grace	1. Covenant of works 2. Covenant of grace with Israel 3. A second covenant of grace	1. Covenant of works 2. Covenant of grace*

*Edmund Calamy, *Two Solomne Covenants Made between God and Man: viz. The Covenant of Workes, and the Covenant of Grace* (London: Thomas Banks, 1646), 1–2; Mark Jones, "The 'Old' Covenant," in *Drawn into Controversie: Reformed Theological Diversity and Debates within Seventeenth-Century British Puritanism*, ed. Michael A. G. Haykin and Mark Jones (Göttingen: Vandenhoeck & Ruprecht, 2011), 187.

Calamy identifies the fourfold scheme with "M. Sympson," a likely reference to Sydrach Simpson (ca. 1600–1655), one of the divines. Simpson's view entailed four covenants: a covenant of works with Adam, a covenant of grace with Abraham, a covenant of works with Israel, and another covenant of grace, which was the new covenant. Calamy connects a second position with Jeremiah Burroughs (ca. 1600–1646), another Westminster divine. According to Calamy, Burroughs held a threefold scheme involving a covenant of works with Adam, another covenant of works with Israel, and a covenant of grace through Christ. Calamy identifies a third position with James Pope (fl. 1675) as its chief advocate.[79] According to Calamy, Pope believed that there were only two covenants: a covenant of works with Israel (with no previous covenant with Adam) and a covenant of grace. The fourth position Calamy associates with Westminster divine Anthony Burgess, who supposedly held a threefold view. In this view there was a covenant of works with Adam, a covenant of grace with Israel, and a second covenant of grace beyond that made with Israel. The fifth and last position Calamy claims as his own, which was the more common twofold view: covenants of works and grace. These taxonomies are very important as they represent historically contextual analyses, not those of modern historians, of the various views present among the members of the assembly and beyond.

Several things need to be said about these taxonomies, especially Calamy's. Upon closer examination there is some imprecision in the reported views. Calamy states that he heard the first two views in person, one reported before a committee of the assembly and the other given in a sermon. He has gathered the other views from written works. So Calamy has possibly misunderstood a person's views. This is likely given what he reports about his fellow divines Burroughs and Burgess. Recent analysis of Burroughs's view has recognized it as similar to the position of John Cameron (1580–1625), one that Bolton identifies as the threefold (subservient) scheme.[80] Burroughs writes:

> The administration of the Law to them it was under another notion, it was to bring them to Christ, and that they might come to see their inability of keeping of that Covenant, and come to understand Christ so much the more, and to be driven unto Christ by having the Law presented to them, God did never intend by giving of the Law to the people of the Jews that it should be a Covenant of eternal life to them; indeed there was this in the administration of it somewhat different from us, some special Covenant about their living in *Canaan*, and about mercies in that promised Land, beyond that that [*sic*] we have in the Law, as we find in the new Testament, they (I say) had this annexed to it.[81]

---

[79] See James Pope, *The Unveiling of Antichrist; or, Antichrist Stript Naked out of All His Scripture-Attyre, by Which He Hath Deceived the Christian World* (London: Henry Overton, 1646).
[80] Jones, "The 'Old' Covenant," 187.
[81] Jeremiah Burroughs, *Gospel Conversation* (London: Peter Cole, 1653), 47; Jones, "The 'Old' Covenant," 187.

Burroughs contends that the administration of the Law, the Mosaic covenant, had different elements "annexed" to the covenant that New Testament believers no longer live under. He makes this point clearer as he propounds the nature of the Mosaic covenant:

> The Law that was first given unto *Adam* and written in his heart, afterwards even obliterated, then it was transcribed by the same hand in tables of stone and given unto them chiefly to shew them their misery, and their need of Christ; to be a preparation for Christs coming into the world; and with this one addition beyond what we have in the new Testament, that there was a temporal covenant annexed unto it, that concern'd their living prosperously in the Land of *Canaan*, (& so far we are delivered even from the Law as it was given by *Moses*, that is, from the connexion of the Covenant that was added unto the delivering of the Law) concerning their happy and comfortable condition in the Land of *Canaan* upon the keeping of their Law.[82]

This is the element that echoes Cameron's own formulation: the Mosaic covenant was neither of works nor of grace, but a third covenant, subservient to the covenant of grace; this view, incidentally, was also Bolton's.[83]

Confirmation that Bolton held to the subservient view comes from the fact that he published Cameron's *Theses on the Threefold Covenant of God with Man* in an English translation as an appendix to his *True Bounds of Christian Freedome*, which, incidentally, is not included with the modern edition of Bolton's work.[84] Other theologians who have been identified with the threefold (subservient) view include Westminster divines Thomas Goodwin (1600–1680) and Obadiah Sedgwick (ca. 1600–1658), as well as John Owen (1616–1683), Samuel Petto (1624–1711), and Edward Fisher.[85]

---

[82] Burroughs, *Gospel Conversation*, 47.

[83] Samuel Bolton, *The True Bounds of Christian Freedome; or, A Treatise Wherein the Rights of the Law Are Vindicated, the Liberties of Grace Maintained* (London: Austin Rice, 1656), 130–31.

[84] Note that the subtitle of Bolton's work continues, *Whereunto Is Annexed a Discourse of the Learned John Camerons, Touching the Three-Fold Covenant of God with Man, Faithfully Translated*; cf. John Cameron, *De Triplici Dei cum Homine Foedere Theses* (Heidelberg, 1608). The appendix appears in Bolton, *True Bounds*, 351–401; cf. Bolton, *The True Bounds of Christian Freedom* (Edinburgh: Banner of Truth, 2001).

[85] Obadiah Sedgwick, *The Bowels of Tender Mercy Sealed in the Everlasting Covenant* (London: Edward Mottershed, 1661), 1.1–2 (pp. 1–7); Muller, "Divine Covenants," 52; Jones, "The 'Old' Cov-

Another weakness in Calamy's taxonomy is reflected in how he reports the views of fellow divine Anthony Burgess. Burgess does not posit two covenants of grace, as Calamy claims. Burgess rattles through the various views: "Some (as you have heard) make it [the Mosaic covenant] a Covenant of workes, others a mixt Covenant, some a subservient Covenant; but I am perswaded to goe with those who hold it to be a Covenant of grace."[86] But Burgess's view is somewhat nuanced and does not fall strictly into a twofold scheme, namely, that there are only two covenants, one of works and the other of grace. He writes:

> The Law (as to this purpose) may be considered more largely, as that whole doctrine delivered on Mount Sinai, with the preface and promises adjoined, and all things that may be reduced to it; or more strictly, as it is an abstracted rule of righteousnesse, holding forth life upon no termes, but perfect obedience. Now take it in the former sense, it was a Covenant of grace; take it in the later sense, as abstracted from *Moses* his administration of it, and so it was not of grace, but workes.[87]

So, Burgess places the Mosaic covenant in the covenant of grace within the broader spectrum of everything propounded at Sinai; but in the narrower view, taken out of the context of its administration, it is a covenant of works.

As reflected in Bolton's taxonomy, there were other views for which Calamy does not account. Bolton identifies a threefold scheme that presents the Mosaic covenant as a mixed covenant, one that has elements of both the covenants of works and of grace. George Walker (1581–1651), one of the Westminster divines, held this view: "For the first part of the Covenant which God made with Israel at Horeb, was nothing else but a renewing of the old Covenant of works which God made with *Adam* in Paradise."[88] But Walker also believed that there

---

enant," 186, 194–202; Michael Brown, *Christ and the Condition: The Covenant Theology of Samuel Petto (1624–1711)* (Grand Rapids: Reformation Heritage, 2012), 87–104; Fisher, *Marrow of Modern Divinity*, 28–29. Baxter seems to lend his qualified approval of this view as well (Richard Baxter, *Aphorismes of Justification* [London: Francis Tyton, 1649], thesis 29 [pp. 144–46]).

[86] Burgess, *Vindiciae Legis*, lect. 24 (p. 232).

[87] Ibid., lect. 24 (p. 233).

[88] George Walker, *The Manifold Wisedom of God in the Divers Dispensation of Grace by Jesus Christ, in the Old New Testament. In the Covenant of Faith. Workes. Their Agreement and Difference* (London: John Bartlet, 1640), 15 (p. 128).

was a second part of the Mosaic covenant, which was more obscurely given in the Levitical laws, the tabernacle, and the ark, which were types of Christ. This dimension of the Mosaic covenant was more clearly set forth in the Deuteronomic version of the covenant and "was nothing else but a renewing of the Covenant of grace which he [God] had before made with their Fathers, *Adam, Abraham, Isaac,* and *Iacob.*"[89]

Other theologians of the period, such as Peter Bulkeley (1583–1659), made distinctions similar to Walker's. Bulkeley believed that the "Covenant of workes was then revealed and made knowne to the children of Israel, as being before almost obliterated and blotted out of mans heart, and therefore God renewed the knowledge of the Covenant of worke to them."[90] Key to Bulkeley's statement is that the covenant of works was *revealed*, not that it was readministered. He also employs the wide-narrow distinction vis-à-vis the covenants of works and of grace as they both relate to the Mosaic covenant: "The Law is to be considered two wayes: First, absolutely, and by it selfe, as containing a covenant of works; Secondly, dependently, and with respect to the covenant of grace."[91]

Even though at least four of the divines, Burroughs, Bolton, Sedgwick, and Goodwin, held to the threefold (subservient) view, and others such as Walker held the mixed view, the more common position was a twofold scheme (works and grace), which was also the more generally held view in the broader Reformed tradition.[92] John Ball, for example, writes, "Most Divines hold the old and new Covenant to be one in substance and kind, to differ only in degrees."[93] Westminster divines such as Samuel Rutherford also polemicized against views such as Cameron's threefold (subservient) scheme.[94] One of the reasons Rutherford argued against this view was that he believed the Mosaic covenant was not a covenant of works; he based his argument upon a number of different texts from Scripture. One such text was Deuteronomy 30:6 and the promise of a circumcised heart.[95]

---

[89] Ibid., 15 (pp. 128–29).
[90] Bulkeley, *The Gospel Covenant*, 1.7 (p. 62).
[91] Ibid., 1.7 (p. 63).
[92] See Turretin, *Institutes*, 12.8.6.
[93] Ball, *Covenant of Grace*, 7 (p. 95).
[94] Rutherford, *Covenant of Life Opened*, 1.11 (pp. 57–58).
[95] Ibid., 1.11 (p. 61).

However, it is important to note the different nuances that a theologian might employ in untangling this challenging issue. In a work commended by Calamy, Thomas Blake (ca. 1597–1657) states his agreement with John Ball and Anthony Burgess that the Mosaic covenant was part of the covenant of grace.[96] But as did Bulkeley and Walker, Blake also acknowledges the broad-narrow distinction when dealing with the Mosaic covenant:

> There are those phrases in Moses, which are ordinarily quoted, as holding out a covenant of Works, and in a rigid interpretation are no other; yet in a qualified sense, in a Gospel-sense, and according to Scripture-use of the phrase, they hold out a covenant of Grace, and the termes and conditions of it.[97]

If it is not already evident, all of the aforementioned views defy a neat and tidy taxonomy. And it is no wonder that Burgess commented, "I do not find in any point of Divinity, learned men so confused and perplexed (being like *Abrahams* Ram, hung in a bush of briars and brambles by the head) as here."[98]

So, then, given the complexity of this issue and the varied opinions, what did the assembly conclude? What does the Confession say on this matter? As previously noted, the Confession affirms the connection between the moral law, natural law, and the Decalogue as the summary of the moral law. The Shorter Catechism confirms this conclusion with two questions regarding the moral law (qq. 40–41):

> Q. What did God at first reveal to man for the rule of his Obedience?
> A. The rule God at first revealed to man for his Obedience, was, the Moral Law (Rom. 2:14–15, 10:5).

> Q. Where is the Moral Law summarily comprehended?
> A. The Moral Law is summarily comprehended in the Ten Commandments (Deut. 10:4).

---

[96] Thomas Blake, *Vindiciae Foederis; or, A Treatise of the Covenant of God Entered with Man-Kinde*, 2nd ed. (London: Abel Roper, 1658), 33 (pp. 210–11).
[97] Ibid., 33 (pp. 215–16).
[98] Burgess, *Vindiciae Legis*, 24 (p. 229).

Beyond this the Confession addresses matters related to the relationship between the covenant of works and the Mosaic covenant, though only briefly. The divines recognize that in the Old Testament the covenant of grace was "differently administered" in comparison to the "time of the Gospel" (7.5). The divines employ a common Aristotelian distinction of *substance* and *accidents* to explain how Christ and the gospel are administered under both periods of redemptive history. They identify Christ as the "substance" of the covenant of grace, revealed in various promises, prophecies, sacrifices, circumcision, and the like, all fore-signifying Christ to come (7.5–6). Though they do not employ the term *accidents* to describe the different elements that attended the covenant of grace in the Old Testament, it is implied. During the New Testament, the earlier sacrifices, circumcision, types, and ordinances gave way to a simpler and clearer revelation of Christ, manifest in the "Preaching of the Word, and the Administration of the Sacraments of Baptisme, and the Lords Supper" (7.6).

That the accidentals of the Old Testament administration of the covenant of grace were stripped away is evident in what the Confession states about the other elements of the Law. Using the common threefold distinction of the moral, ceremonial, and civil law, the Confession states:

> Beside this Law, commonly called Moral, God was pleased to give to the people of Israel, as a Church under age, Ceremoniall Laws containing several typicall Ordinances, partly of worship, prefiguring Christ, his graces, actions, sufferings, and benefits, and partly holding forth divers instructions of moral duties. All which Ceremonial Laws are now abrogated, under the new Testament. (19.3)

> To them also, as a Body Politique, he gave sundry Judicial Laws, which expired together with the State of that people; not obliging any other now, further than the general equity thereof may require. (19.4)[99]

These accidental elements of the administration of the covenant of grace were removed once Christ, the "substance," had arrived. They were no longer necessary.

---

[99] The threefold division of the law (moral, civil, and ceremonial) goes back at least to Aquinas; see *Summa Theologica*, IaIIae, q. 99, art. 4.

Beyond these statements, the divines explicitly exclude only one position regarding the relationship between the covenants of works and grace: "There are not therefore Two Covenants of Grace, differing in substance, but one and the same, under various dispensations" (19.6). Once again the divines offer an oblique rejection of a theological position without identifying the person or institution that holds the view. In this case, the divines reject the view of reputed antinomian Tobias Crisp (1600–1643). Crisp readily accepts the basic twofold covenantal scheme, a covenant of works and a covenant of grace, but as could be expected, given the complexity of the matter, he offers a unique formulation regarding the Mosaic covenant. Crisp believes that Christ is completely absent from the covenant of works because at its core it is "Do this and live," which implies life upon the offering of perfect obedience and curse upon disobedience. On the other hand, Christ stands at the center of the covenant of grace, a covenant that in no way admits the works of the believer in any sense by which the sinner can somehow satisfy the demands of the law. Christ fulfills all of the necessary conditions of the covenant of grace.[100]

Crisp believes, however, that the Mosaic covenant was unique. He does not believe that the Mosaic covenant was in any sense the covenant of works. The covenant of works, for example, demands perfect obedience and has no provision for the forgiveness of sins. But the Mosaic covenant offers the forgiveness of sins (Num. 15:28).[101] Moreover, the Mosaic covenant had priests, who mediated sacrifice, atonement, and the forgiveness of sins; but the Aaronic priesthood paled in comparison to the greater priestly ministry of Christ, a Priest according to the order of Melchizedek.

Crisp offers these comments in his sermon on Hebrews 8:6, which speaks of the superiority of Christ's ministry over the old priestly order.[102] Crisp explains the relationship between the two priestly orders in terms of two different covenants of grace:

> The whole Administration of that Covenant which the Priests had
> to manage, was wholly and only [a] matter of Grace: And though

---

[100] Tobias Crisp, *Christ Alone Exalted: Being the Compleat Works of Tobias Crisp, D.D. Containing XLII Sermons*, 2 vols. (London: William Marshall, 1690), vol. 2, serm. 2 (pp. 246–47).
[101] Ibid., vol. 2, serm. 2 (p. 247).
[102] Ibid., vol. 2, serm. 2 (pp. 246–47).

it were a Covenant of Grace, yet it is opposed to that Covenant
which Christ in his own Person did mediate. Therefore the opposition which stands here, is not between the Covenant of Works, and
the Covenant of Grace, but it is between the Covenant of Grace
weak, imperfect, unprofitable, disannulled; and another Covenant
of Grace that is *perfect, established*, and makes the comers thereunto perfect.[103]

Elsewhere, based upon his exegesis of Jeremiah 31:31, Crisp succinctly states, "Here are two Covenants, a *New Covenant*, and the
Covenant he made with their Fathers."[104]

The question naturally arises, why did the divines specifically zero
in on this view and exclude it? From one vantage point there appears
to be little indication that Crisp's view differs from the cornucopia of
variations that existed at that time on the relationship between the
Mosaic covenant and the covenants of works and grace. Crisp's view
seems as reasonable as some of the other views. What difference is
there, for example, between saying that there is one covenant of grace
with legal accidents that fall away at the advent of Christ, who is the
substance, and saying there are two covenants of grace? Crisp, after
all, indicates that Christ is typified and foreshadowed in the weaker
covenant of grace.[105] The most likely answer is that Crisp's view on the
relationship between the covenants of works and grace and the moral
law struck and severed a nerve that the divines believed was vital to
an orthodox soteriology.

Most Reformed theologians, whether holding a threefold or a twofold covenantal scheme in their several variants, maintained the perpetual necessity and binding nature of the moral law. Crisp, however,
rejected the idea that the moral law was still binding upon believers.
He also denied the connection between the moral law and the Mosaic
covenant:

You see the Apostle from *Jeremiah* brings a direct distinction of
two Covenants, *I will make a new Covenant, not according to the
Covenant I made with their Fathers*. Here are two Covenants, a

103 Ibid., vol. 2, serm. 2 (p. 247).
104 Ibid., vol. 2, serm 2 (p. 250).
105 Ibid., vol. 2, serm. 2 (p. 248).

New Covenant, and the *Covenant made with their Fathers*. Some
may think it was the Covenant of Works at the Promulgation of
the Moral Law: But mark well that Expression of *Jeremiah*, and
you shall see it was the Covenant of Grace. . . . *For* (saith he), *not
according to the Covenant I made with their Fathers, although I
was an Husband unto them.* How can God be considered as *Husband* to a People under the Covenant of Works, which was broken
by Man in Innocency, and so became disannulled or impossible by
the break of it? The Covenant of Works runs thus: *Cursed is every
one that continueth not in all things that are written in the Book
of the Law*; and, *in the day that thou sinnest thou shalt die the
death.* Man had sinned before God took him by the hand to lead
him out of the Land of *Egypt*, and Sin had separated Man from
God; how then can God be called an *Husband* in the Covenant of
Works? The Covenant therefore was not a Covenant of Works,
but such a Covenant as the Lord became a *Husband* in, and that
must be a Covenant of Grace: And yet saith the Lord, *I will make
a new Covenant, not according to the Covenant I made with their
Fathers, &tc.*[106]

For Crisp, the Mosaic covenant was a covenant of grace, but not the
promulgation of the moral law. Moreover, when the Mosaic covenant
was swept away with the advent of the second covenant of grace, the
implication was that the moral law was no longer binding upon the
believer. According to Crisp, the stronger covenant of grace had no
conditions whatsoever; God supplied everything and man was entirely
passive. Conditions were part of the covenant of works, not part of the
stronger covenant of grace.[107]

In his *Vindiciae Legis*, Westminster divine Anthony Burgess specifically engages Crisp on this point. Citing Crisp, Burgess writes,
"Therefore it is a very wilde comparison of one* [in the margin, *Crisp],
that a man under grace hath no more to doe with the Law, then an
English-man hath with the lawes of Spain or Turkie."[108] The divines
understood that the moral law "doth for ever binde all, as well justified

---

[106] Ibid., vol. 2, serm. 2 (p. 250).
[107] Cf. Francis Roberts, *Mysterium et Medulla Bibliorum. The Mysterie and Marrow of the Bible* (London: George Calvert, 1657), 2.2.5 corollary 4 (pp. 111–32).
[108] Burgess, *Vindiciae Legis*, lect. 1 (p. 15); for the engagement of Crisp's views by another Westmin-ster divine, see Rutherford, *Covenant of Life Opened*, 2.10 (pp. 344–48).

persons as others, to the obedience thereof." They believed, "Neither doth Christ, in the Gospel, any way dissolve, but much strengthen this obligation" (19.5). But they were also quick to point out, "Although true Beleevers be not under the Law as a Covenant of Works, to be thereby justified or condemned, yet, is it of great use to them, as well as to others; in that, as a Rule of life informing them of the will of God, and their duty, it directs, and binds them to walk accordingly" (19.6). The divines perceived the threat to the perpetual binding nature of the moral law spread across the various covenants and therefore excluded Crisp's view.

The Confession therefore precludes only one view, but this is not to say that the divines endorsed other views; rather, the Confession does not rule them out. There were certainly many heated debates over these matters. In the Formula Consensus Helvetica (1675) Francis Turretin (1623–1687), for example, explicitly rejects the threefold (subservient) covenantal scheme held by Cameron and Westminster divines Goodwin, Sedgwick, Bolton, and Burroughs:

> We disapprove therefore of the doctrine of those who fabricate for us three Covenants, the Natural, the Legal, and the Gospel Covenant, different in their whole nature and pith; and in explaining these and assigning their differences, so intricately entangle themselves that they obscure not a little, or even impair, the nucleus of solid truth and piety; nor do they hesitate at all, with regard to the necessity, under the Old Testament dispensation, of knowledge of Christ and faith in Him and His satisfaction and in the whole sacred Trinity, to theologize much too loosely and not without danger.[109]

There is nothing that comes close to this type of statement in the Confession. The Formula Consensus Helvetica was never widely adopted as a confession of faith; it quickly evaporated from the theological scene, perhaps because it was too strict on matters that were deemed genuine areas of disagreement between different parties who were considered orthodox.

---

[109] Formula Consensus Helvetica, canon 25, in A. A. Hodge, *Outlines of Theology* (1860; Edinburgh: Banner of Truth, 1991), 663.

The Covenant of Grace

In the Confession's transition from the covenant of works to the covenant of grace the divines make a statement that reveals that Christ lies at the heart of the covenant: "This Covenant of Grace is frequently set forth in Scripture by the name of a Testament, in reference to the death of Jesus Christ the Testator, and to the everlasting inheritance, with all things belonging to it, therein bequeathed" (7.4). This statement identifies Christ as the Testator of the covenant of grace. But what does this mean and why do the divines introduce the concept of testament at this point in their treatment of the covenant of grace? Theological dictionaries from the period, for example, define a testament as follows: "That which we commonly call a mans wil [sic], and appointment for the bestowing of his goodes amongst his Children, or Kindred and Friends. Gal. 3.15. *Though it be but a Mans Testament. Heb. 9.16, 17.*"[110] In his theological dictionary, Robert Cawdry (ca. 1538–1604) defines a testament as a "last will."[111]

One of the chief factors behind this doctrinal position is the English translation of the Greek term *diathēkē*. English Bibles at the time, depending on the context, rendered this Greek word as "testament." In all of the cited proof texts for this paragraph, Hebrews 9:15–17; 7:22; Luke 22:20; and 1 Corinthians 11:25, *diathēkē* is translated as "testament" in the Geneva and King James Bibles as well as in Tyndale's and Wycliffe's translations.[112] To understand the concept, however, and what was connoted by the term *testament* vis-à-vis the work of Christ as Testator, one must delve into several key texts, most notably Hebrews 7:22 and 9:15–17. Westminster divine William Gouge (1575–1653) explains Hebrews 7:22 in terms of Christ's role as the *surety* of the testament. As surety, says Gouge, Christ "ingageth himself for man to God, and for God to man. For man to God, *Jesus* undertaketh

---

[110] Thomas Wilson, *A Christian Dictionarie: Opening the Signification of the Chiefe Wordes Dispersed Generally through Holie Scriptures of the Old and New Testament* (London: W. Iaggard, 1612), s.v. *testament* (p. 483).
[111] Robert Cawdry, *Table Alphabeticall, Contayining and Teaching the True Writing and Understanding Hard Usuall English Wordes, Borrowed from the Hebrew, Greeke, Latine, or French, etc.* (London: Edmund Weaver, 1609), s.v. *testament*.
[112] *The Bible: That Is the Holy Scriptures Conteined in the Old and New Testament* (London: Christopher Barker, 1615); *Holy Bible, Containing the Old and New Testaments with the Apocryphal Books*, trans. John Wycliffe, 4 vols. (Oxford: OUP, 1851); *The First New Testament Printed in the English Language*, trans. William Tyndale (1525; Bristol: The Editor, 1862).

for what can be required of man. For God to man, he undertaketh for what can be desired for God."[113] Whatever is required of sinful man to repair the breach, make satisfaction for sin, and render obedience to the law, Christ as surety undertakes these responsibilities on behalf of the elect.

But Gouge then offers extended exegesis and philological analysis as to why *diathēkē* should be translated as *testament* rather than *covenant*. He notes, like the Confession, that the Greek word is "oft put for a testament, as *Matt.* 26.28. *Gal.* 3.15. *Heb.* 9.16, 17."[114] Gouge contends that the verb *diatithemai*

> signifieth, among other acceptions, to *dispose of a thing by will*. But that Greek verb doth also signifie *to make a covenant*, and from that signification the Greek noun here used, may be translated *a covenant*, and so it is most usually taken in the New Testament, *Luk.* 1.72. *Act.* 3.25. and 7.8. *Rom.* 11.27. *Heb.* 8.6.

Gouge also notes that the Hebrew term *berith* is translated by the term *diathēkē* in the Septuagint, and refers to the concept of covenant.[115] Seemingly torn between the two choices, *testament* and *covenant*, Gouge nevertheless opts for the former on the following grounds:

> In this place the word, *covenant*, seems to be the more proper: for the office of a surety hath a more fit relation to a covenant, then to a testament. Yet I will not deny, but that which is a covenant in matter, and in the manner of making it, may in regard of the confirmation thereof by death, be a *testament*. Thus that which in the Old Testament was a *covenant*, by the death of Christ, may in the New Testament be stiled a *testament*.[116]

According to Gouge, while Hebrews 7:22 might properly use the term *covenant*—i.e., Christ is the surety of the *covenant*—he instead argues that the term *testament* is better suited since a testament deals with the death, or last will, of the testator.

To make his point clearer, Gouge highlights the differences be-

---

[113] William Gouge, *A Learned and Very Useful Commentary on the Whole Epistle to the Hebrewes* (London: T. W. and S. G. for Joshua Kirton, 1655), § 93 (pp. 193–94).
[114] Ibid., § 94 (p. 194).
[115] Ibid.
[116] Ibid., § 94 (p. 195).

tween a covenant and a testament to show why the latter is the preferable translation:

1. A covenant is an agreement between at least two parties, whereas a testament is the declaration of one party.
2. Both parties who make a covenant must be living. A testament, on the other hand, is enacted by the death of the one who made it.
3. A covenant is ratified by the mutual consent of both parties, whereas a testament is ratified only by the one person who made it.
4. A covenant uses conditions on both sides, and a testament consists purely of the favor and grace of the testator.[117]

Given these four factors, Gouge illustrates why he translates *diathēkē* here in Hebrews 7:22 as a *testament*. The covenant of grace is the execution of the will of Christ, the Testator, who not only fulfills the requirements of the law and offers satisfaction for sins, but also bequeaths the inheritance upon his children. This is the essence of Gouge's argument and subsequent explanation of Hebrews 9:15–17. He writes concerning this passage:

> These two verses [vv. 16–17] are added as proof of the necessity of Christs manner of confirming the New Testament as he did, namely by his death. . . . The argument is taken from the common use and equity of confirming Testaments, which is by the death of the Testator. The argument may be thus framed. The new Testament was to be ratified as other Testaments used to be. But other Testaments are ratified by the death of the Testator, &tc. By Testament is here meant that which we commonly call the last will of a man. Whereby he disposeth what belongeth unto him, to be ordered according to his will after his death.[118]

Gouge stresses the superiority of a testament to a covenant, in that Christ's testament is unlike Adam's covenant. Adam's covenant had conditions; if he failed, the blessings of the covenant were forfeited. By contrast, Christ's testament bequeaths legacies to the recipients

---
[117] Ibid.
[118] Ibid., § 93 (p. 369).

without condition, but out of free mercy. True, the reception of the gospel requires faith and repentance, but they are not conditions strictly speaking, such as Adam's conditions in the covenant of works, but are instead the means by which sinners receive and partake of the blessings of the inheritance.[119]

Paragraph 7.4 in the Confession highlights the features of the covenant of grace in contradistinction to the covenant of works, a comparison described in the preceding paragraph:

> Man, by his Fall having made himself uncapable of Life by that Covenant, the Lord was pleased to make a Second, commonly called the Covenant of Grace; Wherein he freely offereth unto sinners Life and Salvation by Jesus Christ, requiring of them Faith in Him that they may be saved, and promising to give unto all those that are ordained unto Life, his holy Spirit, to make them willing, and able to believe. (7.3)

What this paragraph and the following convey is that the covenants of works and grace are mutually exclusive.

In his *Body of Divinitie*, Ussher explains the differences and similarities between the two covenants. He argues that they have two chief things in common: God is the author of both, and they also both declare one kind of righteousness. The two covenants differ, however, as shown in table 4.

The differences between the two covenants are significant and highlight not only the antithesis between the broader categories of law and gospel but also the nature of the covenantal administration of each. The former relies upon man and his own obedience and is known largely by nature, and the latter relies upon Christ and his obedience and is received by faith; the covenant of grace also repairs the breach created by the broken covenant of works, but only for those who are united to Christ. The doctrine of the covenants sets the stage for everything else that follows in the Confession, but especially the work of Christ and the Spirit, or the application of redemption; it also impacts the doctrine of the church, especially as it relates to the administration of the sacraments, which are signs and seals of the

---

[119] Ibid., § 95 (p. 371).

covenant of grace (WCF 27). In many ways the Confession's doctrine of the covenants, especially the covenant of grace, illustrates why the soteriology of the Westminster Standards can be summarized as a redemption that comes through Christ and covenant.

Table 4. Ussher on differences between law and gospel covenants

Covenant of Works (Law)	Covenant of Grace (Gospel)
May be conceived by reason	In all points is beyond reason
Commands to do good but gives no strength	Enables us to do good and the Holy Spirit writes the law upon our hearts (Jer. 31:33)
Only promises life	Promises life and righteousness
Requires perfect obedience	Requires the righteousness of faith (Rom. 3:21–22)
Reveals sin and rebukes us for it	Reveals the remission of sins and frees us from punishment
Is a ministry of wrath, condemnation, and death	Is a ministry of grace, justification, and life
Is grounded in man's own righteousness and requires perfect obedience (Deut. 27:26), and upon default requires satisfaction and everlasting punishment (Ezek. 18:14 [perh. 18:4 or 18:13]; Gal. 3:10, 12)	Is grounded on the righteousness of Christ, admitting payment and performance by another on behalf of as many as receive it (Gal. 3:13–14)*

*Ussher, *Body of Divinitie*, 159. For similar comparisons of the covenants of works and grace, see Ball, *Covenant of Grace*, 3 (pp. 24–25); Bulkeley, *Gospel Covenant*, 1.7 (pp. 54–61); Blake, *Vindiciae Foederis*, 14–16 (pp. 86–93).

The Question of the Covenant of Redemption

One place where the doctrine of the covenant touches upon the person and work of Christ is in chapter 8, though the connection is not immediately apparent. The Confession states:

It pleased God, in His eternall purpose, to choose and ordain the Lord Jesus, His only begotten Son, to be the Mediatour between God and Man; the Prophet, Priest, and King, the Head, and Saviour of his church, the Heir of all things, and Judge of the World: Unto whom He did from all eternity give a People, to be his Seed, and to be by him in time Redeemed, Called, Justified, Sanctified, and Glorified. (8.1)[120]

When we compare this statement from the Confession with the Larger Catechism, we find that the divines introduce the covenant concept to frame the relationship between Christ as Mediator and the elect. The Larger Catechism explains that on the heels of the fall, God entered into the covenant of grace with the elect:

> God doth not leave all mankinde to perish in the estate of sin and misery into which they fell by the breach of the first Covenant, commonly called the Covenant of Works; but, of his meer love and mercy, delivereth his elect out of it, and bringeth them into an estate of salvation by the second Covenant, commonly called the Covenant of Grace. (q. 30)

But the divines push the origins of the covenant of grace further back than its historical manifestation after the fall. The Larger Catechism asks, "With whom was the covenant of Grace made?" It then answers, "The Covenant of Grace was made with Christ, as the second Adam, and, in him, with all the elect, as his seed" (q. 31). Though the covenant of grace was first historically introduced upon the heels of the fall, it was first enacted in eternity past with Christ as the second Adam.

Historically, the dynamic between the covenant made with Adam and the elect has been explained in two ways.[121] In his commentary on the Shorter Catechism, Thomas Watson (ca. 1620–1686) places emphasis upon the covenant of grace made with the elect rather than with Christ as the second Adam. The Shorter Catechism states, for example, that God "did enter into a covenant of grace to deliver them," namely, the elect (q. 20). Watson contends that there is a "Compact and Agreement made between God and fallen Man, wherein the Lord undertakes to be our God, and to make us his People."[122] Watson does not bypass Christ whatsoever, but he does place emphasis upon the

---

[120] Cf. Ursinus, *Commentary*, 96.
[121] On the history and development of the *pactum salutis*, see Richard A. Muller, "Toward the *Pactum Salutis*: Locating the Origins of a Concept," *MAJT* 18 (2007): 11–65; Carol A. Williams, "The Decree of Redemption Is in Effect a Covenant: David Dickson and the Covenant of Redemption" (PhD diss., Calvin Theological Seminary, 2005).
[122] Watson, *Body of Practical Divinity*, 89.

covenant of grace made with believers: "For who is this Covenant made with? Is it not with Believers? And have not they Coalition and Union with Christ; Christ is the head, they are the Body, *Eph.* 1.23."[123] For Watson, there is no other Mediator of the covenant than Christ.[124] But Watson does not touch on God's making a covenant with Christ as the second Adam. A similar structure appears, for example, in Perkins, who writes: "Christ as Mediatour, is first of all elected, and we in him."[125]

On the other hand, other Westminster divines understood God's covenant with Christ, the second Adam, as the covenant of redemption (*pactum salutis*). Scottish divine Samuel Rutherford believed that the covenant made with Christ as the second Adam and the covenant made with the elect were inseparably linked but nonetheless distinct. Christ was engaged as covenant surety, and the two chief parties of the covenant were God the Father as the representative of all three members of the Godhead and God the Son as the second person of the Trinity, who would undertake the work of redemption. The covenant of grace, on the other hand, was that agreement with the triune God, on the one side, and fallen humanity, on the other; God, out of free love and mercy, decided to repair the broken covenant of works and redeem the elect. The former, the covenant of redemption, was the cause of the latter, the covenant of grace.[126]

From the earliest days of the reception and interpretation of the Confession, the covenant of redemption was viewed as compatible with it. *The Summe of Saving Knowledge*, written by David Dickson (ca. 1583–1662), and appended to the Westminster Standards by the Scottish church, states the following:

The summe of the Covenant of Redemption is this, God having freely chosen unto life, a certain number of lost mankind, for the glory of his rich grace, did give them before the world began, unto God the Son appointed Redeemer .... But by vertue of the foresaid bargain made before the World began, he is in all ages, since the

123 Ibid., 92.
124 Ibid., 93.
125 Perkins, *Galatians*, Gal. 3:16 (p. 210); Muller, "Toward the *Pactum Salutis*," 43.
126 Samuel Rutherford, *The Covenant of Life Opened*, 2.8 (pp. 308–9).

166 The Theology of the Westminster Standards

fall of *Adam*, still upon the work of applying actually the purchased benefits unto the elect; and that he doth by way of entertaining a Covenant of free grace and reconciliation with them, through Faith in himself, by which Covenant he makes over to every believer a right and interest in himself, and to all his blessings.[127]

Theologians of the period, therefore, as well as Westminster divines such as Rutherford, or others like Thomas Goodwin, Obadiah Sedgwick, Edward Leigh, and Anthony Burgess, believed that the Westminster Standards and covenant of redemption were more than compatible.[128] The covenant of redemption is another example of a doctrinal teaching that was not addressed directly by the Standards but left as an orthodox extra-confessional matter, like the differing views on the relationship between the covenant of works and the Mosaic covenant.

Conclusion

This treatment of the doctrine of the covenant and related matters demonstrates some important points. First, the Standards embody the broad strokes of the Reformed tradition. The covenants of works and grace were not late developments but have roots that go back to the Patristic era. Reformed theologians simply refined the presentation of these doctrines and connected natural law with the moral law and the administration of that law to Adam and Israel. The divines acknowledged what early Reformers such as Tyndale, and later Rollock, contended, namely, that God did not speak to man apart from covenant, whether Adam in the garden, Israel at Sinai, or the new

---

[127] *The Summe of Saving Knowledge with the Practical Use Thereof* (Glasgow: Robert Sanders, 1669), Head 2, in *The Confession of Faith and the Larger and Shorter Catechisms. First Agreed upon by the Assembly of Divines at Westminster. And Now Appointed by the General Assembly of the Kirk of Scotland* (Glasgow: Robert Sanders, 1669); cf. Muller, "Toward the *Pactum Salutis*," 16. For other places where Dickson treats the covenant of redemption, see David Dickson, *An Exposition of All St. Pauls Epistles, Together with an Explanation of Those Other Epistles of the Apostles, St. James, Peter, John, & Jude* (London: Francis Eglesfield, 1659), comm. Eph. 1:3 (p. 107); 1:6 (p. 113).

[128] Anthony Burgess, *The True Doctrine of Justification Asserted and Vindicated*, 2nd ed. (London: Thomas Underhill, 1654), serm. 37 (pp. 375–76); Thomas Goodwin, *Christ the Mediator*, 1.8–9, in *The Works of Thomas Goodwin*, 12 vols. (Edinburgh: James Nichol, 1861–1866), 5:24–30. Note that in the 1654 edition Leigh does not treat the covenant of redemption but does so in the 1662 edition (Edward Leigh, *A Systeme or Body of Divinity: Consisting of Ten Books* [London: William Lee, 1662], 5.2 [pp. 546–48]); Sedgwick, *Bowels of Tender Mercy*, 1.1 (pp. 3–5). Cf. Carl R. Trueman, "The Harvest of Reformation Mythology? Patrick Gillespie and the Covenant of Redemption," in *Scholasticism Reformed: Essays in Honour of Willem J. van Asselt*, ed. Maarten Wisse, Marcel Sarot, and Willemien Otten (Leiden: Brill, 2010), 199n10.

covenant in Christ. The Westminster doctrine of the covenants also highlights the respective work of the two Adams, their representative disobedience and obedience, which plays a significant role in the Confession's understanding of soteriology, especially the doctrine of justification. If it is not already evident, the covenant of works and justification are joined at the hip and cannot be severed.

This chapter's survey also illustrates the need to understand the Standards in their historical setting. Too many critics approach the documents without a thorough understanding of the doctrine of the covenants, related doctrines, and supporting exegesis. They either tilt at windmills or cut out vital elements of the historic doctrines. The Confession's doctrine of the covenants also shows how a confession of faith functioned in the early modern period. The divines never formally addressed the matter of subscription (the manner and degree to which ministers and elders were required to adhere to the Standards), but at two points—the republication of the covenant of works and the covenant of redemption—a principled diversity of views that existed behind the scenes. This plurality of views confirms that the divines never intended the Confession to be a doctrinal straightjacket but instead a corporate confession for the church, not the manifesto of one particular party. To be sure, some teachings were deemed beyond the line of orthodoxy, such as Crisp's two covenants of grace. But as much as the Confession excludes this one view, its silence speaks volumes regarding the permissibility of other views held among the members of the assembly.

The next chapter will cover matters related to the doctrine of Christ, but does not leave the doctrine of the covenants behind. All that follows in the Confession and catechisms is blanketed under the doctrine of the covenants. As Warfield observed, federal theology is the architectonic principle of the Confession. Hence, whatever the Confession says about the person and work of Christ, it does so under the rubric of Christ, the federal head, the second Adam, the surety of the covenant of grace.

6

The Doctrine of Christ

The doctrine of Christ was central to a number of theological discussions and debates in the post-Reformation period. One of the chief criticisms against the Reformation was that it was a schismatic movement, not a genuine reform of the church. Reformers were therefore keen on demonstrating their continuity with the theological past, particularly the ecumenical councils of the Patristic era that defined the doctrines of the Trinity and Christ for all of Western Christendom. The connections to the Councils of Nicaea (325), Constantinople (381), and Chalcedon (451) were crucial historical anchors for the Reformed tradition, anchors that staved off the criticism of doctrinal novelty and schism. Illustrative of this point, for example, is how Heinrich Bullinger (1504–1575) begins his series of doctrinal sermons, his *Decades*, with a chapter on the four general synods or councils: Nicaea, Constantinople, Ephesus, and Chalcedon. He does this with the express purpose of showing that the Reformation was in accord with the teaching of the early church and was in no way heretical.[1]

In addition to the person of Christ, the Confession sets forth what had become the threefold office (*munus triplex*) of Christ: Prophet, Priest, and King. In terms of the person and work of Christ, there was little debate with the Roman Catholic Church, though there was

---

[1] Heinrich Bullinger, *The Decades of Henry Bullinger*, ed. Thomas Harding, 4 vols. (1849–1852; Grand Rapids: Reformation Heritage, 2004), 1:12–35; cf. Bullinger, *Sermonum Decades Quinque de Potissimis Christianae Religionis Captibus* (Tiguri: Christoph. Froschoverus, 1557).

certainly fierce theological warfare between Reformed theologians and antitrinitarian theologians and churches. In the early days of the Reformation the Reformers dealt with individual antitrinitarian theologians, but over time, ideas spread and antitrinitarian churches arose. The Westminster divines perceived this antitrinitarian heresy as a grave threat to the church.

The other area that witnessed significant theological debate pertaining to the doctrine of Christ concerns the extent of Christ's satisfaction. In other words, for whom did Christ die? Did Christ in some sense die for all people, or did he die only for the elect? From one vantage point this is an easy question to answer if one compares Reformed and Remonstrant answers; Christ died only for the elect according to the Reformed, and he died for all according to Remonstrant theology. But this pat answer fails to address the nuanced discussions that occurred among Reformed theologians and the question of *hypothetical universalism*, namely, that in some sense Christ's satisfaction was sufficient for all people. While hypothetical universalists may be scarce in twenty-first-century Reformed theology, they were common in the early modern period.

Hence, this chapter will treat the person and work of Christ, as well as the extent of his satisfaction. It will show that the Standards are committed to the historic doctrine of Christ enunciated by the ecumenical councils; that Christ holds a threefold office of Prophet, Priest, and King; and that the Confession was written in such a way as to accommodate and allow hypothetical universalism while at the same time denying Remonstrant views on the extent of Christ's satisfaction.

The Person of Christ

In the Confession's elaboration of the person of Christ we find a number of statements that link it to the earlier ecumenical councils of Nicaea, Constantinople, and Chalcedon. The Confession refers to Christ as "the Son of God, the second Person of the Trinity, being very and eternall God, of one Substance, and equall with the Father" (8.2). This statement clearly explains the full deity of Jesus, the second person of the Trinity. Within the immediate context of seventeenth-century

England, one of the most immediate threats to the doctrine of Christ was Socinianism and its denial of the divinity of Christ. John Biddle (1615–1662), an English antitrinitarian who was accused of heresy in 1644, wrote a number of works denying the doctrine of the Trinity, as well as the deity of Christ.[2] In his *Confession of Faith*, for example, Biddle argues that the Father alone is God, and Biddle rejects the common appeal to Genesis 1:26, "Let us make man in our image," as evidence of the Trinity.[3] He deems this verse to indicate that "there was some other person with God, whom he employed in the Creation, as of other things, so of man."[4] Biddle also contends that "the Son is not equal to the Father."[5] Biddle's views are very similar to those advocated by Socinians, though he apparently had no prior knowledge of Polish antitrinitarian theology.[6]

The Racovian Catechism (1609), for example, offers the following question and answer to deny the deity of Christ: "Do you not acknowledge in Christ a divine, as well as a human nature or substance?" The catechism responds:

> If by the terms divine nature or substance I am to understand the very essence of God, I do not acknowledge such a divine nature in Christ; for this were repugnant both to right reason and to the Holy Scriptures. But if, on the other hand, you intend by a divine nature the Holy Spirit which dwelt in Christ, united, by an indissoluble bond, to his human nature and displayed in him the wonderful effects of its extraordinary presence; or if you understand the words in the sense in which Peter employs them (2 Peter i.4), when he asserts that "we are partakers of a divine nature," that is, endued by the favor of God with divinity, or divine properties—I certainly

---

[2] *PRRD*, 4:94–95.

[3] Cf., e.g., *Annotations*, comm. Gen. 1:26; *Dutch Annotations*, comm. Gen. 1:26; Edward Leigh, *A Systeme or Body of Divinity: Consisting of Ten Books* (London: William Lee, 1654), 2.16 (p. 207); Andrew Willet, *Hexapla in Genesin, That Is, A Sixfold Commentary upon Genesis* (London: Thomas Creede, 1608), comm. Gen. 1:26 (p. 14); James Ussher, *A Body of Divinitie; or, The Summe and Substance of Christian Religion* (London: Thomas Downes and George Badger, 1645), 76; Nicolas Estwick, *Pneumatología; or, A Treatise of the Holy Ghost. In Which, the God-Head of the Third Person of the Trinitie Is Strongly Asserted by Scripture-Arguments. And Defended against the Sophistical Subtleties of John Bidle* (London: Ralph Smith, 1648), 2; Thomas Goodwin, *A Discourse of Election*, 2.7, in *The Works of Thomas Goodwin*, 12 vols. (Edinburgh: James Nichol, 1861–1866), 9:131; Thomas Watson, *A Body of Practical Divinity* (London: Thomas Parkhurst, 1692), 66.

[4] John Biddle, *A Confession of Faith Touching the Holy Trinity, According to the Scripture* (London, 1648), § 1 (pp. 4–6).

[5] Ibid., § 2 (pp. 10–11).

[6] *PRRD*, 4:94.

do so far acknowledge such a nature in Christ as to believe that
next after God it belonged to no one in a higher degree.[7]

The Racovian Catechism speaks of Christ in utterly human terms
and claims that if there is anything divine about him, it is merely the
indwelling of the Holy Spirit. In other words, the Racovian Catechism
characterizes Christ in terms typically associated with soteriology and
union with God, not in terms of divinity and full equality with the Father. That is, the Racovian Catechism speaks of Christ as if he were
an ordinary man merely indwelled by the Holy Spirit rather than
being fully divine.

In contrast, the Confession both affirms the co-equality of Christ
with God the Father and embraces the classic formulation of the doctrine of the Trinity: "In the Unity of the God-head there be Three Persons, of one substance, power, and eternity; God the Father, God the
Son, and God the Holy Ghost" (2.3). Such a statement not only stands
contrary to Biddle and the Racovian Catechism, but equally opposes
the ancient christological heresy of Arianism, which taught that Jesus
was the highest of created beings and was thereby entitled to be called
god but not *God*. With Nicaea and Chalcedon, the Confession affirms
the co-substantiality of the Son and Father, namely, the Father and
Son share the same divine essence or substance.

Despite this general agreement with Nicaea, historically there has
been some question as to the degree to which the Westminster divines
embraced a Nicene christology. Recently one analyst, Robert Reymond, has claimed that Nicaea's affirmation of the eternal generation
of the Son is unbiblical and speculative.[8] Reymond claims that John
Calvin (1509–1564) rejected Nicaea's formulations and that the subsequent Reformed tradition embraced his arguments.[9] Reymond poses
the question of whether Westminster's Trinitarianism was Nicene or
Reformed. Though Reymond hedges his arguments, he nevertheless
concludes that while the Confession echoes the Trinitarian formulations of Nicaea, including the language about the eternal generation

---

[7] *The Racovian Catechism*, trans. Thomas Rees (London: Longman, Hurst, Rees, Orme, and Brown, 1818), 4.1 (pp. 55–56).
[8] Robert Reymond, *A New Systematic Theology of the Christian Faith* (Nashville: Thomas Nelson, 1998), 325–26.
[9] Ibid., 327–30.

of the Son, the divines were likely aware of Calvin's "better" formulations and would have wanted the Confession to be shorn from Nicaea's "speculation" and more closely aligned with Calvin's insights.[10]

Reymond's claims are erroneous but at the same time do touch upon issues that the assembly debated concerning the eternal generation of the Son.[11] With the recent transcription and publication of the complete set of minutes of the Westminster Assembly, evidence has surfaced that the eternal generation of the Son was debated; it was debated vis-à-vis the assembly's initial task of revising the eighth article of the Thirty-Nine Articles (1571): "The three creeds, Nicene Creed, Athanasius's Creed, and that which is commonly called the Apostles' Creed, ought thoroughly to be received and believed; for they may be proved by most certain warrants of Holy Scripture." Debate originated in the assembly from the objections of Daniel Featley (1582–1645), who shared Calvin's concern to assert the aseity, or full divinity, of Christ, and Featley's concerns initially placed him at odds with the Nicene Creed.[12]

Featley was concerned that his opposition to Nicaea not be perceived as chronological snobbery, namely, that the present is inherently superior to the past.[13] Nevertheless, he objected to the phrase "God of God" in one sense. Though he believed that "the Sonne is of the Father, and therefore the Father and Sonne being God, it must needs follow, that Christ is God of God," he added, "neither will it hence follow, that the Deitie of the Sonne is of the Deity of the Father."[14] Featley then drew upon Calvin to make his point: "But *Calvin* saith, Christ is *autotheos*, God of himselfe . . . Christ is God of himselfe, *ratione essentiae*, but God of God, *ratione personae*."[15] In other words, Calvin had argued that one can speak of the eternal generation of the Son as it pertains to his *person* but not his *essence*. Featley's point was that just because the Son derived his personhood from the Father, that did

---

[10] Ibid., 340.

[11] After strong criticism of his book, Reymond issued a second edition where he withdrew his claims about a Reformed versus Nicene Trinitarianism. Cf. Robert Reymond, *A New Systematic Theology of the Christian Faith*, 2nd ed. (Nashville: Thomas Nelson, 1998), 323–42; Reymond, *New Systematic Theology* (1st ed.), 324–41; Robert Letham, "Review of Robert L. Reymond: *A New Systematic Theology of the Christian Faith*," *WTJ* 62 (2000): 314–20.

[12] Chad Van Dixhoorn, "Reforming the Reformation: Theological Debate at the Westminster Assembly 1643–52," 7 vols. (PhD diss., Cambridge University, 2004), 1:245.

[13] Daniel Featley, *Sacra Nemesis, The Levites Scourge* (Oxford: Lenard Lichfield, 1644), 13.

[14] Ibid., 15.

[15] Ibid.

not mean he derived his essence from the Father as well.[16] Featley's position echoed not only Calvin's earlier arguments but also the view of the Irish Articles (1615): "The essence of the Father doth not beget the essence of the Son; but the person of the Father beggetteth the person of the Son, by communicating his whole essence to the person begotten from eternity" (§ 9).[17]

Featley offered a second speech in support of his views in which he called the phrase "God of God," a "rock of offence."[18] In one sense, Featley did not object to the phrase because he believed it could easily be proved that Christ was God of God. But Featley was concerned with the possible objection that if Christ was God of God, then he must have his essence communicated to him by the Father; thus Featley feared the misunderstanding of this phrase. He enlisted Theodore Beza (1519–1605) and William Whitaker (1548–1595) to buttress his position. According to Featley, Beza believed that "the Son is from the Father by an unspeakable communication of his whole essence from eternity."[19] Beza's point is that Son's essence is not eternally generated.[20] But for Featley to cite Beza seems to conflict with Calvin's argument that the Son was *autotheos*, of himself God. If the Father communicates his whole essence to the Son, then how can the Son be of himself God? How can Featley speak of a communication of essence if the Son is fully God? To respond to this potential problem Featley drew upon John 5:26: "For as the Father hath life in himself; so hath he given to the Son to have life in himself." It is here that Featley also drew upon Whitaker's claim, "If he be not God of himself, he is not God at all."[21]

What we do not know is how the debate was finally resolved and to what degree these speeches impacted the wording of the Standards.[22] However, there is evidence to conclude that the Standards do not back away from a Nicene Trinitarianism. There are several points to consider in support of this conclusion.

First, recent writers, such as Reymond, have exaggerated Cal-

---

[16] Van Dixhoorn, "Reforming the Reformation," 1:245.
[17] Ibid., 1:246–47.
[18] Featley, *Sacra Nemesis*, 17.
[19] Ibid.
[20] Van Dixhoorn, "Reforming the Reformation," 1:247.
[21] Featley, *Sacra Nemesis*, 17–18.
[22] Van Dixhoorn, "Reforming the Reformation," 1:249.

vin's objections to Nicaea. True enough, the early Reformers, such as Philip Melanchthon (1497–1560), were opposed to the inclusion of traditional creeds in their doctrinal works and catechisms because they were eager to demonstrate that their doctrine arose from Scripture and not church tradition. But as nascent antitrinitarianism began to arise, the Reformers changed their minds. One need only compare Melanchthon's 1521 and 1543 editions of his *Loci Communes* to see the omission and later inclusion of the doctrine of the Trinity.[23]

A similar type of polemical development appears in Calvin's 1536 and 1559 editions of the *Institutes*.[24] Whatever reservations Calvin may have had about the language of the "eternal generation of the Son," he nevertheless taught the concept, understood as the generation of the person and not the essence.[25] Calvin writes, for example:

> It is not right to be silent on the distinction which we find expressed in the Scriptures; which is this—that to the Father is attributed the principle of action, the fountain and source of all things; to the Son, wisdom, counsel, and the arrangement of all operations; and the power and efficacy of the action is assigned to the Spirit. Moreover, though eternity belongs to the Father, and to the Son and Spirit also, since God can never have been destitute of his wisdom or his power, and in eternity we must not inquire after any thing prior or posterior—yet the observation of order is not vain or superfluous, while the Father is mentioned as first; in the next place the Son, as from him; and then the Spirit, as from both. For the mind of every man naturally inclines to the consideration, first, of God; secondly, of the wisdom emanating from him; and lastly, of the power by which he executes the decrees of his wisdom. For this reason the Son is said to be from the Father, and the Spirit from both the Father and the son.[26]

[23] *PRRD*, 4:65; cf. Philip Melanchthon, *Loci Communes (1521)*, in *Melanchthon and Bucer*, ed. Wilhelm Pauck, LCC (Philadelphia: Westminster, 1969); cf. Melanchthon, *Loci Communes (1543)*, trans. J. A. O. Preus (St. Louis: Concordia, 1992).
[24] Cf. John Calvin, *Institutes of the Christian Religion: 1536 Edition*, trans. Ford Lewis Battles (Grand Rapids: Eerdmans, 1975); Calvin, *Institutes of the Christian Religion*, trans. John Allen (Grand Rapids: Eerdmans, 1949).
[25] Calvin, *Institutes*, 1.13.4, 7, 23, 24; Mark Jones, *Why Heaven Kissed Earth: The Christology of the Puritan Reformed Orthodox Theologian, Thomas Goodwin (1600–80)* (Göttingen: Vandenhoeck & Ruprecht, 2010), 113; Brannon Ellis, *Calvin, Classical Trinitarianism, and the Aseity of the Son* (Oxford: OUP, 2012).
[26] Calvin, *Institutes*, 1.13.18.

This statement, combined with Calvin's belief that according to his essence Christ is fully God but that his person originates from the Father, aligns with Nicene formulations wherein "God of God" is governed by the idea that Christ is *homoousias*, of the same substance with the Father.[27] As Warfield helpfully points out, Calvin's objections were not against the Nicene Creed but rather against the formulations of the Nicene fathers; William Whitaker offered the same explanation many years before Warfield.[28]

Second, Featley's objections arose during the revisions of the Thirty-Nine Articles, not during the composition of the Confession and then, later, the catechisms. In the Larger Catechism, a series of questions (8–11) offers a traditional doctrine of the Trinity and employs Nicene language of the eternal generation of the Son:

Q. Are there more Gods then one?

A. There is but one onely, the living and true God.

Q. How many Persons are there in the Godhead?

A. There be three Persons in the Godhead, the Father, the Son, and the Holy Ghost, and these three are one true, eternall God, the same in substance, equall in power and glory; although distinguished by their Peronsall Properties.

Q. What are the Personal Properties of the three Persons in the Godhead?

A. It is proper to the Father to beget the Son, and the Son to be begotten of the Father, and to the Holy Ghost to proceed from the Father and the Son, from all eternity.

Q. How doth it appear that the Son and the Holy Ghost are God, equall with the Father?

---

[27] Ibid., 1.13.6–9; Letham, "Review of Reymond," 317; cf. Calvin, *Institutes*, 1.13.29; B. B. Warfield, "Calvin's Doctrine of the Trinity," in *The Works of Benjamin B. Warfield*, ed. E. D. Warfield et al., 10 vols. (1931; Grand Rapids: Baker, 1981), 5:242–50; Paul Helm, *John Calvin's Ideas* (Oxford: OUP, 2004), 41–45.

[28] Warfield, "Calvin's Doctrine of the Trinity," 250; cf. William Whitaker, *An Answere to the Ten Reasons of Edmund Campian* (London: Felix Kyngston, 1606), 201. Some Reformed theologians argued that the Nicene fathers were not to be taken literally, but metaphorically, when they wrote of the Father's begetting the Son from his essence. See Amandus Polanus, *Syntagma Theologiae Christianae* (Hanoviae: Johannis Aubrii, 1615), 3.4 (p. 203); Heinrich Heppe, *Reformed Dogmatics: Set Out and Illustrated from the Sources*, ed. Ernst Bizer, trans. G. T. Thomson (London: Unwin, 1950), 121–22.

A. The Scriptures manifest that the Son, and the Holy Ghost are God equall with the Father, ascribing unto them such Names, attributes, works, and worship, as are proper to God onely.[29]

These questions affirm the standard "one in substance and three in person" Trinitarian formulation, and they also embrace the ideas of the eternal generation of the Son and procession of the Spirit. Notably, these statements are unlike the formulas of the Irish Articles that echo Calvin's concern about the eternal generation of Christ's person, not his essence.[30] Moreover, there is virtually no divergence between these statements and other confessional documents of the period. The Gallican Confession (1559) speaks of

> the Son begotten from eternity by the Father, the Holy Spirit proceeding eternally from them both; the three persons not confused, but distinct, and yet not separate, but of the same essence, equal in eternity and power. And in this we confess that which has been established by the ancient councils. (§ 6)

The Belgic Confession (1561) likewise states, "We believe that Jesus Christ, according to his divine nature, is the only Son of God—eternally begotten, not made nor created, for then he would be a creature" (§ 10). And the Second Helvetic Confession (1566) also affirms, "The Father has begotten the Son from eternity, the Son is begotten by an ineffable generation, and the Holy Spirit truly proceeds from them both, and the same from eternity" (3.3).

Third, the works of Westminster divines and of theologians of the period confirm the Nicene eternal generation of the Son. Thomas Goodwin (1600–1680) holds that the Godhead is one but that each person of the Godhead is fully God; each person shares in the same nature and is fully divine.[31] However, given a number of statements in Scripture (Ps. 2:7; John 1:14, 18; 3:16; Heb. 1:5; 1 John 4:9), Goodwin nevertheless identifies the Son as the Only Begotten of the Father, which necessitates his eternal generation: "That a generation, or begetting him, is

---

[29] Jones, *Why Heaven Kissed Earth*, 110–11.

[30] *PRRD*, 4:103–4.

[31] Thomas Goodwin, *The Knowledge of God the Father, and His Son Jesus Christ*, 1.1, in *The Works of Thomas Goodwin*, 12 vols. (Edinburgh: James Nichol, 1861–1866), 4:350; Jones, *Why Heaven Kissed Earth*, 114.

the fonndation [*sic*] of his sonship."[32] The begotten Son is the natural Son of God, but not simply by union with him, but by an identity, "or oneness of one and the same essence of the Godhead."[33]

How does Goodwin relate the deity of Christ to his eternal generation? He writes, "The Father communicates all and the whole of himself unto the Son, giving him, by his eternal generation of him, the fullness of the Deity." This statement comes in the context of Goodwin's explanation of John 17, Christ's high priestly prayer, and, in particular, the phrases "All mine are thine," (v. 10), "as we are one," (vv. 11, 21), and "Thou in me" (vv. 22–23). By these statements Goodwin applies the following interpretation: "*All mine*, that is, whatever essential glory or perfection, whatever blessedness, &tc., is in thee is in me, for we are one and co-equal in respect of essence, and of all the same divine perfections of the Godhead."[34] For Goodwin, the Son

> hath all and the whole Godhead communicated to him in the fullness of it, for *essentiae communicatio facit omina communia*, the Godhead being communicated by the Father, all things of the Godhead, or that that can be attributed thereunto, are communicated to all three, only the distinction of persons excepted.[35]

Scottish theologian David Dickson (1583–1663), author of *The Summe of Saving Knowledge*, a summation of the theology of the Standards appended to them by the Scottish Kirk, argues, "The *Greek* word is *hypostasis*, *subsistence*, or *Person*, whereby is understood, the Person of the Father as distinct from the Son, and subsists of himself, and in himself, and is, as the Original of the Person of the Son, by an *eternal and ineffable generation*."[36] Thomas Watson (1620–1686) affirms a similar expression when he writes that the second person of the Trinity is "begotten of the Father before all Time," and that the "Scripture declares the Eternal generation of the Son of God."[37] In his *Male Audis*, Scottish divine George Gillespie (1613–1648) specifically embraces the Nicene creed and its language of the eternal generation

---

[32] Goodwin, *Knowledge of God the Father*, 2.4, in *Works*, 4:427.
[33] Ibid., 2.4, in *Works*, 4:428.
[34] Ibid., 2.7, in *Works*, 9:139–40.
[35] Ibid., 2.7, in *Works*, 9:140; Jones, *Why Heaven Kissed Earth*, 115.
[36] David Dickson, *Truths Victory over Error* (Edinburgh: John Reed, 1684), 2.4 (p. 24).
[37] Watson, *A Body of Practical Divinity*, 63.

of the Son in his defense of Christ's "double Kingdom," his reign as the
eternal Son of God and as Mediator. Gillespie explains that the Nicene
creed specifically identifies Christ and his eternal generation as God
of God and Light of Light.[38]

Some of the more illuminating comments come from Edward Leigh
(1602–1671), who acknowledges the debate over the question of the
eternal generation of the Son. Leigh recognizes both sides of the issue.
On the one hand are "some of our Divines" who argue "Christ is begotten of the Father by a communication of the Divine Essence." But if
this is so, then there is question about the integrity of the full divinity
of Christ: his essence is then derived from the Father and not proper
to the Son; Christ is not *a se*, or from himself divine. Leigh identifies Anthony Wotton (ca. 1561–1626) as a proponent of this criticism
and concern.[39] In his treatment, Wotton offers a defense of Calvin's
position, something, interestingly enough, that Leigh does not mention.[40] Leigh simply writes, "Wotton on Joh. I. goes this way, and some
others."[41] Nevertheless Leigh, perhaps reflecting the opinion of the
majority within the assembly, counterargues, "That Christ hath his
God-head from the Father, makes not against his God-head but for it,
if he hath the same God-head which the Father hath though from the
Father, then he is the same God with the Father."[42] Leigh's promotion
of the eternal generation of the Son is not without qualification. He
notes that the Son's generation is a profound mystery, and to wade
into its waters is dangerous unless a person has clear license from
Scripture. To this end he contently affirms the eternal generation of
the Son as well as the unity of Christ with the Father based upon appeal to Proverbs 8:23, 26; John 1:3; 10:30; 17:5; and Philippians 2:6.[43]

There are several distinct views of this particular issue that explain why it surfaced as a matter of debate at the assembly. Not all

---

[38] George Gillespie, *Male Audis; or, An Answer to Mr. Coleman and His Male Dicis* (London: Robert Bostocke, 1646), 33.

[39] Leigh, *Body of Divinity*, 2.16 (p. 210); cf. Anthony Wotton, *Sermons upon a Part of the First Chap. of the Gospell of S. Iohn* (London: Samuel Macham, 1609), serm. 2 (pp. 56–77).

[40] Wotton, *Sermons*, serm. 2 (pp. 56ff.).

[41] Leigh, *Body of Divinity*, 2.16 (p. 210); cf. Bartholomew Keckerman, *Systema S. S. Theologiae, Tribus Libris Adornatum* (Hanau: Guilielmum Anontinum, 1602), 1.4 (pp. 62–63); Polanus, *Syntagma*, 3.5 (p. 205); Heppe, *Reformed Dogmatics*, 122–23; Johannes Maccovius, *Scholastic Discourse: Johannes Maccovius (1588–1644) on Theological and Philosophical Distinctions and Rules*, trans. Willem J. van Asselt et al. (Apeldoorn: Instituut voor Reformatieonderzoek, 2009), 5.2 (p. 127).

[42] Leigh, *Body of Divinity*, 2.16 (p. 210).

[43] Ibid.

early modern Reformed theologians shared Calvin's concerns.[44] Zacharias Ursinus (1534–1583) unfolded the relationship between Father and Son as a communication of the Father's divine essence: "The eternal Father hath by eternal generation communicated to the Son his essence, but not his person—that is, he begot not the Father, but the Son; neither is the Father the Son, or the Son the Father, although each is very God."[45] In his commentary on the Heidelberg Catechism, Jeremias Bastingius (1551–1595) offers the same view:

> Now why hee is called *Onely begotten*, this reason is brought, because the Father begat him alone of his substance, and that from everlasting, and therefore Christ is the onely coeternall and naturall Sonne of the Father, light of light, very God of very God, as we reade in the *Nicene Creede*: whereby the eternitie of the Sonne of God and his substance all one with the Father is manifest.[46]

James Ussher (1581–1656) offers a similar opinion and contends that the Son has "the foundation of personall subsistence from the Father alone, of whom by communication of his essence he is begotten from all eternity."[47] Likewise, Thomas Cartwright (ca. 1535–1603) succinctly answers the question "What is the Son?" in the following manner: "The second person in Trinity, from all eternity begotten of the Father by communication of his Essence, who is also called the Word."[48]

But a theologian's speaking of the communication of the divine essence does not mean he is opposed to the Son's aseity. Note how William Perkins (1558–1602) holds eternal begottenness and aseity together:

> Although the Sonne be begotten of his Father, yet neverthelesse he is of and by himself very God: for he must be considered either according to his essence, or according to his filiation or Sonneship. In regard of his essence, he is *autotheos* that is, of and by him-

---

[44] *PRRD*, 4:326.

[45] Zacharias Ursinus, *The Commentary of Dr. Zacharias Ursinus on the Heidelberg Catechism*, trans. G. I. Williard (1852; Phillipsburg, NJ: P&R, n.d.), 131; *PRRD*, 4:326.

[46] Jeremias Bastingius, *An Exposition or Commentarie upon the Catechisme of Christian Religion* (London: John Legat, 1595), q. 33 (fol. 63).

[47] James Ussher, *A Body of Divinitie; or, The Summe and Substance of Christian Religion* (London: Thomas Downes and George Badger; 1645), 80.

[48] Thomas Cartwright, *A Treatise of Christian Religion: Substantially, Methodicallie, Plainlie, and Profitablie Treatised* (London: Thomas Man, 1611), 10.

selfe very God: for the Deitie which is common to all the three persons, is not begotten. But as he is a person, and the sonne of the Father, he is not of himselfe, but from an other: for he is the eternall Sonne of his Father. And thus he is truly said to be *very God of very God*.[49]

The same type of arrangement occurs in Francis Turretin (1623–1687), who argues:

> The Son is from the Father, nevertheless he may be called God-of-himself (*autotheos*), not with respect to his person, but essence; not relatively as Son (for thus he is from the Father), but absolutely as God inasmuch as he has the divine essence existing from itself and not divided or produced from another essence (but not as having that essence from himself).[50]

Gisbert Voetius (1589–1676) adds another variant: "The essence may therefore be said to be communicated, given, by the Father, and received, and had, by the Son from that communication or gift. Briefly, the Person of the Father begets the Person of the Son by the communication of the essence."[51] In other words, Voetius argues that the person is communicated by the essence.

These varied expressions should be interpreted not as contradictory but rather as indicating broad agreement in affirming two chief points: (1) the full deity of the Son, and (2) the unity of the Trinity. Though Reformed theologians might differ in how they express these points—e.g., Calvin's eternal communication of sonship or Ursinus's eternal communication of essence—they agree that the Son is *autotheos*, that he is God of himself. And as Warfield has astutely observed: "Despite the influence of Calvin, the great body of the Reformed teachers remained good Nicenists. But they were none the less, as they were fully entitled to be, good 'Autotheanites' also."[52] This description fits

---

[49] William Perkins, *A Golden Chaine*, § 5, in *The Works of That Famous and Worthie Minister of Christ, in the Universitie of Cambridge, M. W. Perkins* (Cambridge: Iohn Legat, 1603), 5; *PRRD*, 4:327; cf. William Perkins, *Exposition of the Symbole or Creed of the Apostles*, in *The Workes of That Famous and Worthy Minister of Christ* (London: John Legat, 1616), 269.
[50] Francis Turretin, *Institutes of Elenctic Theology*, ed. James T. Dennison Jr., trans. George Musgrave Giger (Phillipsburg, NJ: P&R, 1992–1997), 3.29.40; Jones, *Why Heaven Kissed Earth*, 114.
[51] As quoted in Warfield, "Calvin's Doctrine of the Trinity," 275n132; cf. Gisbert Voetius, *Selectarum Disputationum Theologicarum*, vol. 1 (Utrecht: Johannem à Waesberge, 1648), 465.
[52] Warfield, "Calvin's Doctrine of the Trinity," 275.

the Westminster Standards quite well. It should also be noted that none of the aforementioned theologians, contrary to the accusations of "scholastic speculation," attempt to explain the mystery surrounding the manner by which the Son is eternally begotten.[53] Ussher's statement perhaps illustrates the common opinion:

> We find it not revealed touching the manner, and therefore our ignorance herein is better than all their curiosity, that have enterprized arrogantly the search hereof; for if our own generation and frame in our mothers womb be above our capacity, *Ps.* 139.14, 15, it is no marvell if the mystery of the eternall generation of the Son of God cannot be comprehended.[54]

Despite the widespread agreement regarding the aseity of the Son, there was one holdout that originated from within the early modern Reformed tradition, Jacob Arminius (1560–1609).[55] Arminius rejected the common distinction between the Son's essence and person vis-à-vis eternal generation. Arminius reasoned, "Where order is established, it is necessary that a beginning be made from some first person or thing." For Arminius, the Father was of none, the Son originated from the Father, and the Spirit originated from both Father and Son.[56] Correlatively, Arminius rejected the idea that Christ was *autotheos*:

> But it [*autotheos*] may be received in a two-fold signification, according to the etymon of the word; and may mean either *one who is truly and in himself God*, or *one who is God from himself*. In the former signification, I said, the word might be tolerated; but in the latter, it was in opposition to the Scriptures and to orthodox antiquity.[57]

---

[53] So Reymond, *New Systematic Theology* (1st ed.), 325n10.

[54] Ussher, *Body of Divinitie*, 80. Cartwright offers verbatim the same explanation and illustration (Cartwright, *Christian Religion*, 10).

[55] On the widespread acceptance of the aseity of the Son, Gisbert Voetius (1589–1676) lists a large number of Reformed theologians who held to this doctrine, including William Perkins, Bartholomew Keckerman, Lucas Trelcatius, Amandus Polanus, Johannes Wollebius, Girolamo Zanchi, Daniel Chamier, André Rivet, Francis Junius, and William Ames, among many others (Gisbert Voetius, *Selectarum Disputationum Theologicarum*, vol. 1 [Utrecht: Johannem à Waesberge, 1648], 460; Warfield, "Calvin's Doctrine of the Trinity," 274n127).

[56] Jacob Arminius, *Letter to Hippolytus a Collibus*, in *The Works of James Arminius*, ed. and trans. James Nichols and William Nichols, 3 vols. (1825–1875; Grand Rapids: Baker, 1996), 2:693.

[57] Jacob Arminius, *Apology against Thirty-One Theological Articles*, § 21, in *Works*, 2:30; Arminius, *Private Disputations*, 34, corollary, in *Works*, 2:380.

With this statement Arminius rejected the common opinion of the Reformed. Arminius was accused, therefore, of teaching the ontological subordination of the Son because he rejected the application of *autotheos* to the Son.[58]

Aside from the question of the eternal generation of the Son, further confirmation of the Standards' agreement with the three chief ecumenical councils appears in the following statements about the person of Christ:

> The Son of God . . . when the fullnesse of time was come, take upon Him mans nature, with all the Essentiall properties, and common infirmities thereof, yet, without sin: being conceived by the Power of the Holy Ghost, in the womb of the Virgin Mary, of her substance. So that, two whole, perfect, and distinct Natures, the Godhead and the Manhood, were inseparably joyned together in one Person, without Conversion, Composition, or Confusion. Which person is very God, and very Man, yet one Christ, the only Mediator between God and Man. (8.2)

This paragraph embraces the chief points of the ecumenical councils concerning both the full deity and the full humanity of Christ, as is evident in table 5.

The language is not repeated verbatim but the parallels are nonetheless evident, as the Standards affirm the chief points of the ecumenical councils: Christ is fully divine; he is very God. Christ is fully human, very man; he is one person with two natures, of his mother's substance, and both natures are inseparably joined without confusion, change, or division.[59] Like Bullinger, who opened his *Decades* with the texts of the four ecumenical creeds, the divines embraced the teachings of these creeds to demonstrate their catholicity.

---

[58] Richard A. Muller, "The Christological Problem in the Thought of Jacobus Arminius," *Nederlands Archief voor Kerkgeschiedenis* 68 (1986): 151; Arminius, *Private Disputations*, 33.9, in *Works*, 2:379; *PRRD*, 4:329.

[59] On the history of the ecumenical creeds, see Jaroslav Pelikan, *The Christian Tradition*, 5 vols. (Chicago: University of Chicago Press, 1971), 1:172–277; J. N. D. Kelly, *Early Christian Doctrines* (1960; New York: HarperSanFrancisco, 1978), 223–343; Frances M. Young, *From Nicaea to Chalcedon: A Guide to the Literature and Its Background*, 2nd ed. (1983; Grand Rapids: Baker, 2010); Robert Letham, *The Holy Trinity: In Scripture, History, Theology, and Worship* (Phillipsburg, NJ: P&R, 2004), 89–183.

Table 5. Ecumenical councils and the Standards
on the deity and humanity of Christ

Council	Statement	Standards	Heresy Refuted
Nicaea (325)	"Only-begotten begotten from the Father, that is from the substance of the Father, God from God, light from light, true God from true God, begotten not made, consubstantial with the Father"	Larger Catechism qq. 8–11	Arianism, modalism
Constantinople (381)	"Incarnate from the Holy Spirit and the Virgin Mary"	"Being conceived by the Power of the Holy Ghost, in the womb of the Virgin Mary, of her substance" (WCF 8.2).	Nestorianism, Docetism
Ephesus (431)	"We confess the Holy Virgin to be the Mother of God because God the Word took flesh and became man and from his very conception united to himself the temple he took from her."	"Being conceived by the Power of the Holy Ghost, in the womb of the Virgin Mary, of her substance" (WCF 8.2).	Nestorianism, Docetism
Chalcedon (451)	"The same perfect in divinity and perfect humanity, the same truly God and truly man, or a rational soul and a body; consubstantial with the Father as regards his divinity, and the same consubstantial with us as regards his humanity; like us in all respects except for sin . . . one and the same Christ, Son, Lord, Only-begotten, acknowledged in two natures which undergo no confusion, no change, no division, no separation."	"So that, two whole, perfect, and distinct Natures, the Godhead and the Manhood, were inseparably joyned together in one Person, without Conversion, Composition, or Confusion. Which person is very God, and very Man, yet one Christ, the only Mediator between God and Man" (WCF 8.2).	Apollinarianism, Monophysitism, Eutychianism, Nestorianism

The Work of Christ

The Confession places the work of Christ under the rubric of the threefold office (*munus triplex*) of Prophet, Priest, and King. Though popularly attributed to Calvin, the threefold office had been spoken of in the earliest days of the church, appears in Patristic authors such as Eusebius of Caesarea (ca. 263–339) and medieval authors such as Thomas Aquinas (1226–1274), and was anticipated by Johannes à Lasco (1499–1560) before Calvin.[60] The divines situate the work of Christ upon the plain of redemptive history by distinguishing the Son in terms of his ontological equality with God from the incarnation and execution of his office as Mediator: "The Lord Jesus, in his humane nature thus united to the divine, was sanctified and anointed with the holy Spirit, above measure, having in him all the treasures of wisdom and knowledge" (8.3). As noted in the previous chapter, the divines also link the work of Christ with his role as covenant surety (8.3). Christ was ordained and appointed by God through the divine decree to be the only Mediator between God and man (8.1).

As surety, Christ was the one who would not only execute the office and meet the obligations of the broken covenant of works but also fulfill the promises of the covenant of grace. To this end the Confession explains that Christ willingly undertook the office of Mediator and was "made under the Law, and did perfectly fulfill it," but also suffered "grievous torments" in his body and soul, was crucified, died, and was buried, yet arose from the dead on the third day "with the same body in which he suffered, with which also he ascended into Heaven," where he now sits at the right hand of the Father, ruling over his kingdom (8.4). Christ's kingdom, as we will see in a subsequent chapter, is the visible church (25.1).

Though the work in this portion of the Confession is simple and cogent, there are antecedents in the earlier tradition that follow the same pattern of thought. Perkins's *Golden Chaine* offers a similar succinct presentation:

---

[60] Richard A. Muller, "Demoting Calvin: The Issue of Calvin and the Reformed Tradition," in *John Calvin, Myth and Reality: Images and Impact of Geneva's Reformer*, ed. Amy Nelson Burnett (Eugene, OR: Cascade, 2011), 14; cf. Eusebius, *Ecclesiastical History*, 1.3.9, 19, in *NPNF²* 1:86–87; Aquinas, *Summa Theologica*, IIIa, q. 7, art. 8; q. 22, art. 1, ad 3; Johannes à Lasco, "London Confession (1551)," in *Reformed Confession of the 16th and 17th Centuries in English Translation*, ed. James T. Dennison Jr., 3 vols. (Grand Rapids: Reformation Heritage, 2008–2012), 1:563–68; Calvin, *Institutes*, 2.15.1.

In regard of his office, the which being imposed on him by his Father, he did willingly undergoe, and of his own accord. Christ doeth exercise this office according to both natures united in one person, and according to each nature distinct one from the other. . . . This office is appropriate to Christ, that neither in whole, or in part can it be translated to any other. . . . Therefore Christ, as he is God hath under him, Emperours, Kings, Princes, to be his Vicegerents; who therefore are called Gods. Psal. 82.1 But as he is Mediatour, that is, a Priest, a Prophet, and King of the Church, he hath no Vicegerent, Vicar, or Lieutenant, who, in his either Kingly or Priestly office, in both, or but one, can be in his stead. Christs office is threefold, Priestly, Propheticall, Regall, Psal. 110.1, 2, 3, 4, Esai, 42.1.[61]

Perkins mentions that Christ executes his office "according to each nature," which is a point the Confession also raises: "Christ, in the work of Mediation, acteth according to both Natures, by each Nature doing that which is proper to it self" (8.7). The Confession thus echoes Perkins, but why do Perkins and the Confession raise this issue?

Leigh explains that this was a controversy between the Reformed and Roman Catholic churches. According to Leigh, Robert Bellarmine (1542–1621) and Aquinas both argued that Christ was Mediator only according to his human nature. Aquinas, for example, argues that a mediator is a *means* as well as one who unites others together. As a *means* a mediator communicates something from one person to another, but he can only do this if he is distant from each party, according to Aquinas. Thomas therefore concludes that as God, Christ does not differ from the Father and the Holy Spirit in either his nature or his power, nor do the Father and Spirit possess anything that the Son does not. However, both of these mediatory functions can be applied to Christ as a man. As human, Christ is distant from God by both nature and glory. And it belongs to Christ, as man, to unite people to God by communicating to them precepts and gifts, and by rendering unto the Father satisfaction for sin and intercessory prayers on behalf of men. One of the chief texts upon which the Roman Catholics base their argument is 1 Timothy 2:5: "For there is one God, and one mediator between God and men, the man Christ Jesus."[62]

---

[61] Perkins, *Golden Chaine*, § 18, in *Works*, 20.
[62] Aquinas, *Summa Theologica*, IIIa, q. 26, art. 2.

Leigh responds to these arguments by first appealing to the idea presented in 8.7, that Christ is Mediator and "acteth according to both Natures," though Leigh does so simply by invoking the term *God-man*. He also points out that Christ is sometimes called the "son of man" and other times the "Son of God," but this does not mean that Christ is not Mediator according to both natures. Quoting Roman Catholic theologian Cornelius á Lapide (1567–1637), Leigh writes: "In Christ God alone is not Mediator, nor in man alone, but in the God-man. The God-head concurred with the manhood in all the acts of Mediatorship, and that place *1 Tim.* 2.9 [*sic*, likely means 2:5] proves that Christ *qui fuit homo* which was a man is our Mediator, but not *qua homo* as man." In other words, 1 Timothy 2:5 proves that Christ was made man, was incarnate, not that he was a Mediator only according to his human nature.

Notably, in the margin Leigh directs the reader to Perkins's *Golden Chaine*, chapter 18, which was quoted above.[63] Aside from the matter of grounding the work of redemption in both natures of Christ, Leigh argues for the importance of the mediatorial work of the God-man over and against Roman Catholic claims. For Rome, if Christ mediates only according to his human nature, then other humans, such as the saints, may also mediate on behalf of sinners. This, according to Leigh and the Reformed, is unacceptable, as the God-man is the only Mediator between God and man.[64]

The Extent of Christ's Satisfaction

The Confession bases the mediatorial work of Christ upon both natures, and in his earthly ministry Christ "fully satisfied the Justice of his Father; and purchased, not only reconciliation, but an everlasting inheritance in the Kingdom of Heaven, for all those whom the Father hath given unto him" (8.5). In his priestly work Christ made both satisfaction and intercession on behalf of the elect. He made satisfaction through his suffering throughout his life, though the pinnacle came in the garden of Gethsemane and the crucifixion. In his satisfaction he suffered for the sins of the elect. But as Leigh maintains, Christ not

---

[63] Leigh, *Body of Divinity*, 5.4 (pp. 410–11).
[64] Ibid., 5.4 (p. 411).

only suffered for the sins of the elect but also performed perfect righteousness, and the combination of both suffering for sin and perfect obedience to the law secured eternal life for the elect.[65] In this respect, "the Covenant of Grace is laid upon the satisfaction of Christ."[66]

The Standards invoke the term *satisfaction*, but this does not imply the Anselmian satisfaction theory of the atonement. Anselm (1033–1109) advanced the dilemma of *aut satisfactio aut poena*. God would accept either satisfaction or punishment as an answer to humanity's fallen condition: "Either the honor which has been taken away should be repaid, or punishment should follow. Otherwise, either God will not be just to himself, or he will be without the power to enforce either of the two options."[67] By choosing satisfaction over punishment, Anselm eliminated the idea of substitutionary punishment. He therefore located Christ's satisfaction outside the context of punishment and placed it exclusively under the rubric of merit. By his merit Christ repays the debt of honor that the sinner owes, both in terms of what he owes God and as recompense for the failure to give him honor. Christ restores man through his satisfaction and merit.[68]

By way of contrast, an early modern Reformed understanding of satisfaction differs from the Anselmian version because it offers *satisfactio poenalis*, or satisfaction through punishment. It eliminates the false dichotomy of satisfaction *or* punishment and posits a both–and—satisfaction *and* punishment.[69] Few Reformed theologians in the early modern period would dissent from these conclusions, but there are a number of variant views that pertain to the extent of Christ's satisfaction. For whom, and in what sense, did Christ die? Christ most certainly died for the elect—this is undisputed among a host of Reformed and non-Reformed theologians. But in what sense, if any, did Christ die for all?[70]

Presently this question is typically filtered through the grid of

---

[65] Ibid., 5.4 (p. 414).

[66] Ibid., 5.4 (p. 416).

[67] Anselm, *Why God Became Man*, 1.13, in *The Major Works*, ed. Brian Davies and G. R. Evans (Oxford: OUP, 1998), 287; Anselm, *Cur Deus Homo: Libri Duo* (London: David Nat, 1903), 37.

[68] Anselm, *Why God Became Man*, 1.11–12 (pp. 282–86); cf. Dániel Deme, *The Christology of Anselm of Canterbury* (Aldershot: Ashgate, 2004), 91–98.

[69] Willem van Asselt, "Christ's Atonement: A Multi-Dimensional Approach," *CTJ* 38 (2003): 60–61.

[70] For an overview of the various forms of hypothetical universalism, see Richard A. Muller, "Revising the Predestination Paradigm: An Alternative to Supralapsarianism, Infralapsarianism, and Hypothetical Universalism" (Mid-America Fall Lecture Series, Dyer, Indiana, Fall 2008).

"five-point Calvinism" and the famous TULIP acronym: Total deprav-
ity, Unconditional election, Limited atonement, Irresistible grace, and
Perseverance of the saints. According to this modern acronym, Christ
died only for the elect, and all other positions fall under the category of
"four-point Calvinism." As pedagogically useful as the acronym might
be, it is historically problematic for at least three reasons. First, no
early modern Reformed theologian ever uses the acronym, for it originated well after the seventeenth century. Second, no early modern
Reformed theologian uses the term *limited atonement*. One factor contributing to the absence of the term in early modern Reformed theology
is that *atonement* is an English word, and the lion's share of theology
was written in Latin. The common term of the period was *satisfactio*,
hence the English term *satisfaction*. This is why the term *atonement*
does not appear in the Standards, but *satisfaction* appears nine times.[71]

Third, few early modern Reformed theologians saw themselves as
the disciples of Calvin or as Calvinists. The term *Calvinist* was originally created as a term of derision in an effort by the opponents of the
Reformed churches to isolate and brand them as sectarian.[72] Hence,
if read through the alien grid of the TULIP, early modern views are
distorted, and fine nuances that were once carefully argued are lost
with the ham-fisted separation between five-point and four-point Calvinism, as if Calvin were the standard and taught a strict doctrine
of limited atonement, and all other views fall under the category of
universal atonement. Consequently, it is necessary, first, to briefly set
out the various views on the extent of the satisfaction of Christ and
then, second, to determine to what extent the Standards accommodate
these views, if at all.

From within the early modern period authors identify several
major positions on the extent of Christ's satisfaction. John Ball (1585–
1640) acknowledges only two chief positions, covering Remonstrant
and Reformed views; the Remonstrants hold that Christ "died for all
and every man with a purpose to save," and the latter "distinguish the
sufficiency and efficiency of Christs death."[73] Francis Turretin first ac-

---

[71] WCF 11.1, 3; 15.3; LC qq. 70, 71, 194.
[72] Richard A. Muller, *Calvin and the Reformed Tradition: Studies on the Work of Christ and the Order of Salvation* (Grand Rapids: Baker, 2012), 75.
[73] John Ball, *A Treatise of the Covenant of Grace* (London: Edward Brewster, 1645), 2.2 (pp. 204–5).

knowledges, "Though all agree that Christ died for each and every one, still they do not explain their meaning in the same way."[74] He then delineates three different major classes, those who argue that Christ conditionally died for all and absolutely died only for the elect, those who claim that Christ died absolutely for all, and the "common opinion of the Reformed" that Christ died only for the elect.[75] In this three-fold classification Turretin has in mind the views of John Cameron (ca. 1579–1625) and Moïse Amyraut (1596–1664) for the first view, the Remonstrants for the second, and the Reformed for the third. John Davenant (1572–1641), in his treatise on the death of Christ, notes that the church fathers and theologians of the Middle Ages contended that Christ died sufficiently for all, but efficiently, or effectually, for only the elect. Davenant points out that the doctors of the Reformed church from the beginning of the Reformation embraced this common sufficient-efficient theological distinction.[76]

Davenant points to several Reformed theologians to illustrate this claim, including Bullinger, Aretius, Musculus, and Zanchi. Heinrich Bullinger states quite simply: "The Lord died for all: but all are not partakers of this redemption, through their own fault. Otherwise the Lord excludes no one but him who excludes himself by his own unbelief and faithlessness."[77] Benedict Aretius (1505–1574) says, "Christ died for all, yet notwithstanding all do not embrace the benefit of his death, because by their own wickedness, and the corruption of their nature, they despise the offered grace."[78] Wolfgang Musculus (1497–1563) like-wise offers, "We know that all be not partakers of this redemption, but yet the losse of them which be not saved, doth hinder nothing at all, why it shoulde not be called an universal redemption, whiche is ap-pointed not for one nation, but for all the whole world."[79] And Girolamo Zanchi (1516–1590) also holds to the universality of the satisfaction of Christ: "That it is not false that Christ died for all men as it regards

[74] Turretin, *Institutes*, 14.14.7.
[75] Ibid., 14.14.7–8.
[76] John Davenant, *A Dissertation on the Death of Christ*, in *An Exposition of the Epistle of St. Paul to the Colossians*, trans. Josiah Allport, vol. 1 (London: Hamilton, Adams, and Co., 1831), 336.
[77] Ibid., 337–38; cf. Heinrich Bullinger, *A Hundred Sermons upon the Apocalips of Jesu Christe* (n.p.: n.p., 1561), serm. 28 (p. 173).
[78] Davenant, *Dissertation on the Death of Christ*, 338; cf. Benedict Aretius, *Commentarii in Epistolas D. Pauli ad Timoth. Ad Titum, & ad Philemonem* (Bern: Le Preux, 1580), 48–49.
[79] Wolfgang Musculus, *Common Places of the Christian Religion* (London, 1563), fol. 129; Davenant, *Dissertation on the Death of Christ*, 338.

his conditional will, that is, if they are willing to become partakers of his death through faith. For the death of Christ is set before all in the Gospel, and no one is excluded from it, but he who excludes himself."[80] All of these Reformed theologians argue that in some sense Christ died for all. So the question arises, how do Reformed theologians relate the satisfaction of Christ to the redemption of the elect?

The answer to this question is somewhat complex, as the variety of views defies a neat and tidy taxonomy. Nevertheless, Voetius offers a basic taxonomy of four chief views:

1. Universal satisfaction for every person, believer and unbeliever alike (the Remonstrants)
2. Those who affirm the universal sufficiency of Christ's satisfaction and argue that it is applied in some sense to all but only effectively for the elect
3. Those who admit the universal sufficiency of Christ's satisfaction but deny its application to all (the scholastics, e.g., Lombard, Aquinas, as well as Calvin, and others)
4. Those who hold that Christ died solely for the elect (William Ames, 1560–1609, and Franciscus Gomarus, 1563–1641)[81]

These four positions may be classified as universalism, hypothetical universalism, the classical sufficient-efficient position, and strict particularism. Among the latter two views, a number of Reformed theologians employ the sufficient-efficient distinction, including Calvin, Turretin, Zanchi, Ursinus, and Herman Witsius (1636–1708).[82] The strict particularists—those who reject the sufficiency-efficiency

[80] Davenant, *Dissertation on the Death of Christ*, 339; Girolamo Zanchi, *De Praedestinatione Sanctorum*, thesis 13, in *Miscellaneorum Libri Tres* (Heustadt: Excudebate Matthaeus Harnisius, 1592), 3:13–14.

[81] Gisbert Voetius, *Problematum de Merito Christi, Pars Secunda*, in *Selectarum Disputationum Theologicarum, Pars Secunda* (Utrecht: Johannem à Waesberge, 1654), 251–53; cf. P. L. Rouwendal, "Calvin's Forgotten Classical Position on the Extent of the Atonement: About Sufficiency, Efficiency, and Anachronism," *WTJ* 70(2008): 321–23.

[82] William Ames, *The Marrow of Theology*, trans. John Dykstra Eusden (1968; Grand Rapids: Baker, 1997), 1.24 (p. 150); Turretin, *Institutes*, 14.14.9; John Calvin, *The Gospel of St. John 11–21 and The First Epistle of John*, ed. David W. Torrance and T. F. Torrance, trans. T. H. L. Parker (Edinburgh: Oliver and Boyd, 1961), comm. 1 John 2:2 (p. 244); contra Torrance, *Scottish Theology: From John Knox to John McLeod Campbell* (Edinburgh: T&T Clark, 1996), 64; cf. Richard A. Muller, *Christ and the Decree: Predestination and Christology from Calvin to Perkins* (Grand Rapids: Baker, 1986), 34; Zanchi, *De Praedestinatione Sanctorum*, thesis 13, in *Miscellaneorum Libri Tres*, 3:13–14; Ursinus, *Commentary*, 222–24; Herman Witsius, *Economy of the Covenants between God and Man: Comprehending a Complete Body of Divinity*, 2 vols., trans. William Crookshank (1822; Escondido: The den Dulk Christian Foundation, 1990), 2.9.2, 6.

distinction and argue that Christ died strictly and exclusively for the elect—include Johannes Maccovius (1588–1644) and Wilhelmus à Brakel (1635–1711).[83] At first appearance, this taxonomy of views appears simple enough, but matters are complicated when the extent of Christ's satisfaction is coordinated with the lapsarian question. Modern assumptions connect supralapsarianism with strict particular satisfaction.[84] However, as we will see below, some supralapsarians advocate hypothetical universalism, and three of the four views were represented at the assembly (e.g., hypothetical universalism, sufficient-efficient, and strict particularism).

The minutes of the assembly contain some information about the debates over the extent of the satisfaction of Christ, though the record is at times spotty since the minutes fail to record entire speeches. Readers are left wondering what more was said. Nevertheless, on the morning of October 22, 1645, the assembly began to debate the subject of the "redemption of the elect only, by Christ."[85] Edmund Calamy was then recorded as stating:

> I am farre from universall Redemption in the Arminian sence, but that that [sic] I hould is in the sence of our devines in the sinod of Dort; that Christ did pay a price for all, absolute intention for the elect, conditional intention for the reprobate, in case they doe believe; that all men should be *salvibles, non obstante lapsu Adami* [saveable, in spite of the fall of Adam]; that Jesus Christ did not only dy sufficiently for all, but God did intend in giving of Christ & Christ in giving himselfe did intend to put all men in a state of salvation in case they doe believe.[86]

Calamy's statement is important because it fits within Voetius's taxonomy noted above, though important qualifications should be made.

First, Calamy rejects the "Arminian" position, which argues that Christ died sufficiently for all without exception. The Remonstrance,

---

[83] Maccovius, *Scholastic Discourse*, 11.17; Wilhelmus à Brakel, *The Christian's Reasonable Service*, trans. Bartel Elshout, 4 vols. (Morgan, PA: Soli Deo Gloria, 1992), 1:599–600.

[84] See, e.g., J. B. Torrance, "Strengths and Weaknesses of the Westminster Theology," in *The Westminster Confession in the Church Today*, ed. Alasdair I. C. Heron (Edinburgh: Saint Andrews, 1982), 47.

[85] *MPWA*, sess. 522, October 22, 1645 (3:692). For analysis of the debate, see Lee Gatiss, "'Shades of Opinion within a Generic Calvinism.' The Particular Redemption Debate at the Westminster Assembly," *RTR* 69, no. 2 (2010): 101–18.

[86] *MPWA*, sess. 522, October 22, 1645 (3:692).

or Arminian Articles (1610), for example, states, "Christ, the Savior of the world, died for all and for every individual, so that he has obtained for all, by his death on the cross, reconciliation and remission of sins." Second, Calamy connects his own position with "our devines in the sinod of Dort," which is a reference to the British delegation to the Synod of Dort (1618–1619). This is a crucial identification because Calamy specifically aligns his own form of hypothetical universalism with the British delegation at Dort, not with the later views of Cameron and Amyraut. This admission reveals that there were at least two different types of hypothetical universalist positions, which for the sake of simplicity I call hypothetical universalism (generally) and the particular form Amyraldianism.

In the assembly's debates Calamy defends a number of points that place his views within the hypothetical universalism advocated by the British delegation at Dort. The British delegation argued that the satisfaction of Christ was extended to "all adults," rendered human nature as potentially being redeemed, but in the end was only applied to the elect.[87] The Synod of Dort is infamously known for its codification of the dreaded "limited atonement," but such characterizations fail to acknowledge that the synod embraced a classical formula that Christ died sufficiently for all and efficiently only for the elect, a formula that goes back to the Middle Ages and Peter Lombard and even earlier to the Patristic period. Ursinus, for example, cites Ambrose (339–397), Augustine (354–430), Cyril of Alexandria (ca. 376–444), and Prosper of Aquitaine (ca. 390–ca. 455) as examples of those who employ the sufficient-efficient distinction.[88]

Caricatures of Dort also fail to mention that the British delegation included hypothetical universalists. The official position of the British delegates offers the following on the extent of Christ's satisfaction:

> In as much as that price was paid for all, and will certainly promote all beleevers unto eternall life, yet is not beneficial unto all; because all have not the gift of fulfilling this condition of the gracious covenant. Christ therefore so dyed for all, that all and every one by

[87] Ibid. (3:693); M. W. Dewar, "The British Delegation at the Synod of Dort—1618–19," EQ 46, no. 2 (1974): 105; Mark Shand, "The English Delegation to the Synod of Dort," BRJ 28 (1999): 37–39.
[88] Cf. Synod of Dort, Head 2.2, 8; Peter Lombard, Sentences, trans. Giulio Silano, 4 vols. (Toronto: PIMS, 2007–2010), 3.20.5; Ursinus, Commentary, 222–24.

the means of faith might obtain remission of sins, and eternal life by vertue of that ransome paide once for all mankinde. But Christ so dyed for the elect, that by the merit of his death in special manner destinated unto them according to the eternal good pleasure of God, they might infallibly obtain both faith and eternal life.[89]

Calamy's view, that "Christ did pay a price for all . . . conditionall intention for the reprobate," echoes what the British delegation states here, namely, that a "price was paid for all . . . that all and every one by the means of faith might obtain remission of sins." In other words, Christ has died for all upon the condition that they believe.

Davenant, one of the British delegates to Dort, gives a fuller explanation of this position:

For in this ordination of God, according to which the death of Christ is appointed and proposed as a cause of salvation to every living person, applicable by faith, there is contained less than in the real application, but there is contained something more than in the mere and bare sufficiency of the thing considered in itself, this conditional ordination being excluded, which regards every partaker of human nature.[90]

Here Davenant specifies that Christ's death is ordained to be sufficient for all, and that it extends to anyone and everyone who shares in human nature, a point that Calamy raised in the assembly's debates. Davenant also contrasts his own view of ordained sufficiency with what he calls "bare sufficiency." In other words, it is one thing to say that Christ's death is inherently sufficient to bring satisfaction for the sins of all and entirely another to say that God specifically ordained it as such.

A key element to Davenant's position, and presumably Calamy's as well, is the distinction between ordaining the death of Christ to be an applicable remedy for salvation to all people upon the condition of faith and the absolute decree to appoint and effectually produce faith and salvation in specific individuals. As Davenant explains:

---

[89] George Carleton, *The Collegiate Suffrage of the Divines of Great Britaine, concerning the Five Articles Controverted in the Low Countries* (London: Robert Milbourne, 1629), 2.3 (pp. 47–48).
[90] Davenant, *Dissertation on the Death of Christ*, 378.

For as if God should create any herb endued with such a virtue that it might heal any one who labors under any disease whatever, and moreover should promise, that any one who should use it should undoubtedly recover his former health, any one would rightly conclude from thence, that this herb was a remedy for any disease, applicable, by the ordination of God, to all sick persons individually; but would not rightly infer that every individual would be infallibly cured by means of this remedy, because it would not be given to some that they should find this remedy, and others perhaps would not be willing to make use of it when it was found.[91]

Calamy and the British delegation at Dort, then, affirmed a non-Amyraldian hypothetical universalism. But Calamy was not alone in the assembly; other divines also held this view.

While there is some question about the exact nature of his influence, most signs point to James Ussher as the origin of this form of hypothetical universalism.[92] Ussher was intent on cutting a middle path between the Remonstrants and strict particularists.[93] Like Calamy and Davenant, Ussher considers Christ's satisfaction absolutely and relatively, that is, in and of itself and in its application. For Ussher, Christ's satisfaction renders the sins of humanity fit for pardon, and God is made "placable unto our *nature*"; this is the language Calamy employed in the debate.[94] Elsewhere Ussher writes that Christ gave sufficient satisfaction to make humanity's nature "a fit subject for mercy, and to prepare a *medicine* for the sinnes of the whole world."[95]

Ussher's view was influential among a number of theologians of the period, including William Twisse (ca. 1577–1646), a supralapsarian, the first moderator of the assembly.[96] Twisse, like Calamy, argued for hypothetical universalism but also maintained that faith was nec-

[91] Ibid., 390–91.
[92] Jonathan D. Moore, *English Hypothetical Universalism: John Preston and the Softening of Reformed Theology* (Grand Rapids: Eerdmans, 2007), 173–213.
[93] James Ussher, *The Whole Works of the Most Rev. James Ussher*, 17 vols. (Dublin: Hodges and Smith, 1847–1864), 12:554, 559, 565.
[94] James Ussher, *The Judgement of the Late Archbishop of Armagh and Primate of Ireland* (London: John Crook, 1658), 3–5.
[95] Ussher, *Judgement*, 14.
[96] See Hans Boersma, *A Hot Pepper Corn: Richard Baxter's Doctrine of Justification in Its Seventeenth-Century Context* (Vancouver: Regent College, 2003), 195–200.

essary to enjoy the benefits of Christ's satisfaction. Twisse based his views upon a number of passages of Scripture, such as Romans 5:18, which speaks of Christ dying for all as well as the elect:

> We say that pardon of sinne and salvation of soules are benefites purchased by the deathe of Christ, to be enjoyed by men, but how? Not absolutely, but conditionally, to witt, in case they believe, and only in case they believe. . . . So that we willingly professe, that Christ had both a full intention of his owne, and commandment of his Father to make a propitiation for the sinnes of the whole world, so farre as thereby to procure both pardon of sinne and salvation of soule to all that doe believe. . . . Now as touching these benefites, we willingly professe, that Christ dyed not for all, that is, he dyed not to obtaine the grace of faith and repentance for all, but only for God's elect; In as much as these graces are bestowed by God, not conditionally, least so grace should be given according to mens workes, but absolutely, And if Christ dyed to obtyene these for all absolutely, it would follow here hence that all should believe & repent and consequently all shoulde be saved.[97]

Twisse intertwined his hypothetical universalism with his understanding of the decree, in that God ordained some things necessarily, others contingently, and others freely.[98] This is language that appears in the Confession: God ordains whatsoever comes to pass, yet in such a way that no violence is offered to the will of creatures, nor is the liberty or contingency of second causes taken away (3.1).

Twisse and Calamy believed that God ordained the universal sufficiency of Christ's satisfaction but that its application is predicated upon the condition of faith. Both Twisse and Calamy, as well as the British delegation to Dort, believed these formulations were in harmony with the Canons of Dort. Indeed, the British delegation's presence, participation, and submission of their views to the Synod in the composition of the Canons prove they were acceptable and within the bounds of orthodoxy. Other divines at the assembly, including John Arrowsmith (1602–1659), Jeremiah Burroughs (1599–1646), Thomas

---

[97] William Twisse, *The Doctrine of the Synod of Dort and Arles, Reduced to the Practise* (Amsterdam: Successors to G. Thorp, 1631), 16–17.
[98] Ibid., 19–20.

Gataker (1574–1657), Richard Vines (1599–1656), and Lazarus Seaman (d. 1675), held similar views.[99]

The view was likely prevalent not only because of the influence of Ussher, Davenant, and others, such as John Preston (1587–1628), but also because of the Thirty-Nine Articles, which state that Christ "truly suffered, was crucified, dead, and buried, to reconcile his Father to us, and to be a sacrifice, not only for original guilt, but also for all actual sins of men" (§ 2). In fact, Davenant appeals to this very portion of the Thirty-Nine Articles to affirm the universal extent of Christ's satisfaction.[100] Hence, a qualified universalism, that is, that Christ's satisfaction in some sense extended to all, was part of the confessional air that the Westminster divines breathed, found both in the Thirty-Nine Articles and in the Canons of Dort with its use of the sufficient-efficient distinction.

The presence of hypothetical universalists at the assembly, however, does not automatically mean that the view was immediately accepted or sanctioned. As one can imagine, considerable debate ensued after Calamy made his initial remarks in favor of hypothetical universalism. Some accused him of holding to the Remonstrant view of universal satisfaction, but he parried the charge and further explained his views. Two of the Scottish divines, George Gillespie (1613–1648) and Samuel Rutherford (1600–1661), along with Thomas Goodwin, engaged Calamy's arguments.[101] In what appears to be a debate tactic, Gillespie tried to associate Calamy's views with those of Amyraut and Cameron.[102] In truth, Amyraut's views were somewhat different than those of Ussher, Davenant, or Calamy. Richard Baxter (1615–1691) notes that Richard Vines, one of the divines mentioned above, "*openly owned* Davenant's *way of Universal Redemption*," not Amyraut's.[103] But the divines were not unfamiliar with Amyraut's views; Robert Baillie (1602–1662), one of the Scottish divines, commented that Amy-

---

[99] Alex F. Mitchell and John Struthers, eds., *Minutes of the Sessions of the Westminster Assembly of Divines* (London, 1874), lv.

[100] Davenant, *Dissertation on the Death of Christ*, 355.

[101] *MPWA*, sess. 523, October 23, 1645 (3:698). For Rutherford's engagement of hypothetical universalism, see Samuel Rutherford, *The Covenant of Life Opened; or, A Treatise on the Covenant of Grace* (Edinburgh: Robert Broun, 1654), 1.20 (pp. 181–92). Note that, in context, Rutherford's arguments are against Davenant, not Amyraut (ibid., 1.20 [p. 183]).

[102] *MPWA*, sess. 522, October 22, 1645 (3:693).

[103] Richard Baxter, *Certain Disputations of Right to Sacraments, and the True Nature of Visible Christianity* (London: Thomas Johnson, 1657), preface.

raut's work, perhaps his *Brief Treatise on Predestination* (1634), went around the assembly from "hand to hand."[104]

Amyraut, unlike Ussher, Davenant, and Calamy, defended a hypothetical decree of predestination, which is different from a hypothetical extent of Christ's satisfaction. Amyraut distinguishes between predestination to *salvation* and predestination to *faith*. The former is conditional, and the latter is absolute and the means by which the former is attained.[105] According to Amyraut, God decrees to predestine the whole human race equally but conditionally upon faith. But because the whole human race is incapable of fulfilling the required condition, owing to no defect in the decree but the hardness of heart and stubbornness of the human condition, God makes a second decree that is absolute—a decree to predestine the elect to faith.[106] This distinction among the decrees, predestination to salvation versus predestination to faith, allowed Amyraut to explain how Christ's satisfaction was universal in its extent but particular in its application.

This particular construction, namely, conditional predestination, drew significant criticism from within the early modern Reformed world. However, at no time was it ever deemed as heresy, as one scholar has incorrectly labeled it.[107] In fact, Amyraut was exonerated on three different occasions by three separate national French synods: Alençon (1637), Charenton (1644–1645), and Loudun (1659). Throughout the process Amyraut repeatedly swore his allegiance to the decisions of Dort and offered his defense within the sufficiency-efficiency framework, though the Synod of Alençon instructed Amyraut not to speak of a "conditional, frustratory, or revocable Decree."[108] Nevertheless,

---

[104] Baillie, as cited in Mitchell and Struthers, *Minutes*, xxvi n2.

[105] Moïse Amyraut, *Breif traitte de la predestination et de ses principales dependances* (Saumur: Jean Lesnier & Isaac Desobrdes, 1634), 13 (p. 163); Amyraut, *Brief Treatise on Predestination*, trans. Richard Lum (ThD diss., Dallas Theological Seminary, 1986), 81.

[106] Amyraut, *Breif traitte*, 13 (p. 163–64); Amyraut, *Brief Treatise*, 82; cf. G. Michael Thomas, *The Extent of the Atonement: A Dilemma for Reformed Theology from Calvin to the Consensus* (Carlisle: Paternoster, 1997), 190–91.

[107] Brian G. Armstrong, *Calvinism and the Amyraut Heresy: Protestant Scholasticism and Humanism in Seventeenth-Century France* (Madison: The University of Wisconsin Press, 1969); cf. Richard A. Muller, "Divine Covenants, Absolute and Conditional: John Cameron and the Early Orthodox Development of Reformed Covenant Theology," *MAJT* 17 (2006): 36.

[108] John Quick, *Synodicon in Gallia Reformata; or, The Acts, Decisions, Decrees, and Canons of Those Famous National Councils of the Reformed Churches in France*, 2 vols. (London: T. Parkhurst and J. Robinson, 1692), 2:355; Thomas, *Extent of the Atonement*, 188, 205. See also Quick, *Synodicon*, 2:352–57, 397–411.

Baxter noted that half of the divines of England were Amyraldians.[109] In summary, Amyraldianism is somewhat different from the hypothetical universalism of Ussher, Davenant, Calamy, and Twisse. All Amyraldians were hypothetical universalists, but not all hypothetical universalists were Amyraldians.

What were the exegetical reasons behind the advocacy of hypothetical universalism? While the assembly debated a number of texts, John 3:16 provides a window into the issues at stake. Calamy believed that John 3:16 was the exegetical ground for God's intention to give Christ to the world and offer it love and philanthropy; additionally, he argued that the universal promulgation of the gospel to all of the nations was founded upon universal redemption, and God's offering of the gospel to all had to be "serious & true."[110] Other divines, such as Rutherford, objected to the satisfaction-gospel connection, though Gillespie noted that Calamy's appeal to the term *world* in John 3:16, "For God so loved the world," rested on a highly controverted text even among the Reformed. Gillespie denied that the term *world* denoted a general philanthropy to all indiscriminately. He believed that Calamy's error rested in his failure to distinguish between the decreed and revealed will of God: that God reveals that anyone who believes shall be saved, but God's revealed will does not govern his decreed, or secret, will.[111]

Calamy countered that he understood that the term *world* was taken in different senses: sometimes for the elect, sometimes for the whole world. But he qualified his remarks by adding that there was a twofold love of God: his general love for the reprobate, which included the general offer and general grace to all, and his special love for the elect.[112] John Lightfoot (1602–1675) entered the fray by arguing that he understood *world* in a different sense, to indicate the Gentiles in contrast to the Jews.[113] Hypothetical universalist Richard Vines stated his belief that *world* refers not to the Gentiles, but to a group more extensive than the elect. It denotes God's intention in the gift of Christ and the extent of God's love for all, though it is a general love of mankind.[114]

---

[109] Baxter, *Certain Disputations*, preface.
[110] *MPWA*, sess. 522, October 22, 1645 (3:694).
[111] Ibid., sess. 523, October 23, 1645 (3:699).
[112] Ibid., sess. 522, October 22, 1645 (3:696).
[113] Ibid.
[114] Ibid., sess. 522, October 22, 1645 (3:697).

In one of the last recorded comments on the debate, Rutherford offered several reasons why John 3:16 does not refer to the general love of God for all. Rutherford identified three elements of the arguments offered by Calamy and others: (1) the word *loved* refers to a general love to the elect and reprobate alike; (2) the word *world* should be understood generally and distributively of the aforementioned love; and (3) this universal distribution of God's general love is grounded upon God's intention but conditioned upon the necessity of faith. Rutherford first argued that Christ's love in the Gospel of John is directed exclusively at the elect, which is paralleled in other passages, such as John 15:13, on Christ laying down his life for his friends. If the other parallels indicate anything, it is that God's love is commensurate with election, and there is "not one scripture in all the New Testament wher it can be expounded for the generall" love of God. Second, Rutherford argued that the love mentioned in John 3:16 is restricted to the church; he cited Romans 5:8 ; Galatians 2:20; and Ephesians 5:21. And third, John 3:16 is an actual saving love, and therefore not a general love for all.[115] The question now presses in, what room, if any, do the Standards have for hypothetical universalism?

A number of commentators, including B. B. Warfield (1851–1921), A. A. Hodge (1823–1886), and John Murray, have maintained that the Standards leave no room for Amyraldianism.[116] However, Warfield, Hodge, and Murray share in the idea that all hypothetical universalists were Amyraldians, rather than devotees of the earlier and different strand of universalism found in Ussher, Davenant, and the British delegation to Dort. On the one hand, it does seem difficult to square Amyraut's order of the decrees (first the decree of salvation for all dependent upon the condition of faith, followed by a second decree of predestina-

---

[115] Ibid., sess. 523, October 23, 1645 (3:699). The assembly's annotations on Scripture argue against the hypothetical universalist interpretation of John 3:16: "For Christ speaketh not here of that common love of God, whereby he willeth the good of conservation to the creature; so he loveth all the creatures; but of his special love, whereby he willeth man should be saved by Christ, and he is truly said to love the world, because they whom he loveth to eternal life are in the world, a part of the world, and gathered by his word; and holy Spirit into the body of the Church, out of all ages and parts of the world, God love all that he made" (*Annotations*, comm. John 3:16).

[116] Lee Gatiss, "A Deceptive Clarity? Particular Redemption in the Westminster Standards," *RTR* 69, no. 3 (2010): 181–82; B. B. Warfield, "The Making of the Westminster Confession, and Especially of Its Chapter on the Decree of God," in E. D. Warfield et al., *Works of Benjamin B. Warfield*, 6:142–44; A. A. Hodge, *The Confession of Faith: A Handbook of Christian Doctrine Expounding the Westminster Confession* (1869; Edinburgh: Banner of Truth, 1958), 73; John Murray, "The Theology of the Westminster Confession of Faith," in *Collected Writings of John Murray*, vol. 4, *Studies in Theology* (Edinburgh: Banner of Truth, 1982), 255–56.

tion to faith) with what the Confession states about God's decrees: "In his sight all things are open and manifest; his knowledge is infinite, infallible, independent upon the creature, so as nothing is to him contingent, or uncertain" (2.2).[117] So Amyraldianism does seem to be precluded by the language of the Standards. Gillespie specifically raised this issue in the debates: "Ther is a concatenation of the death of Christ with the decrees, therefore we must see what they hould concerning that which in order goes before & what in order followes after."[118] In the context of this statement Gillespie specifically names Cameron and Amyraut. What about the other form of hypothetical universalism?

A number of points in the Confession seemingly present challenges for anyone who would assert the universality of Christ's satisfaction. The initial idea under discussion when this debate surfaced in the assembly was the following: "Neither are any other redeemed by Christ, effectually called, justified, adopted, sanctified and saved; but the Elect only" (3.6). This does not present a challenge to the hypothetical universalists, however, because the Confession states that only the elect are "redeemed by Christ," which is a point they would affirm, given that they typically distinguish between making satisfaction and applying it in redemption.[119] Ussher, for example, writes:

> We must, in the matter of our redemption, carefully put a distinction betwixt the satisfaction of Christ absolutely considered, and the application thereof to every one in particular: the former was once done for all, the other is still in doing: the former brings with it sufficiency, abundant to discharge the whole debt; the other adds to its efficacy.[120]

Hence, a hypothetical universalist could agree with Confession 3.6, given the distinction between satisfaction made and its application.

The issue of Christ's satisfaction arises again in the Confession and Larger Catechism: "The Lord Jesus . . . fully satisfied the Justice of his Father; and purchased, not only reconciliation, but an everlasting inheritance in the Kingdom of Heaven, for all those whom the Father

---

[117] Gatiss, "Deceptive Clarity," 191; Muller, "Revising the Predestination Paradigm."
[118] *MPWA*, sess. 522, October 22, 1645 (3:693).
[119] Gatiss, "Deceptive Clarity," 184.
[120] Ussher, *Works*, 12:554.

hath given unto him" (8.5). The Larger Catechism similarly states, "Redemption is certainly applied, and effectually communicated to all those for whom Christ hath purchased it, who are in time by the Holy Ghost inabled to believe in Christ according to the Gospel" (q. 59). Given these statements, Murray and others have argued that the acquisition of Christ's satisfaction is coextensive with its application.[121]

However, as recent analysis has demonstrated, theologians employed a distinction between impetration (or redemption accomplished) and intercession that the Confession does not directly address.[122] Ussher explains that he connects Christ's impetration not to his satisfaction but to his intercession. In other words, for Ussher, Christ's completed work is part of his intercessory work as High Priest but not his satisfaction. Ussher appeals, for example, to John 17:9, "I pray not for the [reprobate] *World*," and argues:

> I must needs esteem it a great folly to imagine that he hath impetrated *Reconciliation* and Remission of sinnes for that world. I agree therefore thus farre with Mr. Aimes in his Dispute against *Grevinchovius*, That *application* and *impetration*, in this latter we have in hand, are *of equal extent*; and, That forgivenesse of sinnes is not by our Savior impetrated for any unto whom the merit of his death is not *applied* in particular.[123]

Hence, a hypothetical universalist like Ussher had no problem arguing that Christ's impetration and intercession were coextensive. Ussher bracketed out Christ's satisfaction, which was universal.

These points in the Confession do not specifically advocate hypothetical universalism. In fact, the Standards lean in the direction of strict particularism, given the absence of the sufficiency-efficiency distinction.[124] But neither are they written in such a manner as to preclude or proscribe hypothetical universalism.[125] Again, Baxter claims, "I have spoken with an eminent Divine, yet living, that was of the

---

[121] Gatiss, "Deceptive Clarity," 187; Murray, "The Theology of the Westminster Confession," 256.

[122] Gatiss, "Deceptive Clarity," 187; cf. Leigh, *Treatise of the Covenant of Grace*, 2.2 (p. 255); Leigh, *Body of Divinity*, 5.4 (p. 416).

[123] Ussher, *Judgement*, 19–20; Gatiss, "Deceptive Clarity," 187. Cf. William Ames, *Rescriptio Scholastica & Brevis ad Nic. Grevinchovii Responsum Illud Prolixum, Quod Opposuit Dissertationi de Redemptione Generali, & Electione ex Fide Praevisa* (Harderwijk: Nicolai à Wieringen, 1645).

[124] Contra Torrance, *Scottish Theology*, 146.

[125] Mitchell and Struthers, *Minutes*, lvi–lvii.

Assembly, who assured mee that they purposely avoided determining that Controversie, and some of them protest themselves for the middle way of Universal Redemption."[126] In other words, as a historical observation (if Baxter's report is credible), the Westminster Standards appear to be only somewhat more tightly drawn than the Canons of Dort regarding the extent of Christ's satisfaction.[127] This is to say nothing about the orthodoxy or heterodoxy of hypothetical universalism. Given the debate surrounding the extent of Christ's satisfaction, especially Amyraut's examination at the Synod of Charenton in 1644–1645, which was around the same time as the debates over these same matters in the assembly, it is likely that the divines completely avoided the sufficiency-efficiency language to mitigate debates over the subject.[128]

Confirmation that the Standards leave hypothetical universalism as an option appears when we compare the Confession with Turretin's Formula Consensus (1675), which was written specifically to refute Amyraut, though not necessarily the view of Davenant, Ussher, or Twisse. Turretin likely considered those three within the pale of orthodoxy, since Davenant and other hypothetical universalists were signatories to Dort, whereas Amyraut's views arose some fifteen years later. The Formula Consensus states:

We can not approve the contrary doctrine of those who affirm that of His own intention, by His own counsel and that of the Father who sent Him, Christ died for all and each upon the impossible condition, provided they believe; that He obtained for all a salvation, which, nevertheless, is not applied to all, and by His death merited salvation and faith for no one individually and certainly (*proprie et actu*), but only removed the obstacle of Divine justice, and acquired for the Father the liberty of entering into a new covenant of grace with all men. (§ 16)[129]

Nothing of this nature appears in the Westminster Standards. And even the Formula characterizes Amyraut's view as "contrary to the plain Scriptures and the glory of Christ" (§ 16), but not as heresy.

[126] Baxter, *Certain Disputations*, preface; Gatiss, "Deceptive Clarity," 194.
[127] *PRRD*, 1:76–77; Gatiss, "Deceptive Clarity," 194.
[128] Muller, "Revising the Predestination Paradigm."
[129] Formula Consensus Helvetica (1675), in A. A. Hodge, *Outlines of Theology* (1860; Grand Rapids: Banner of Truth, 1991), appendix (pp. 656–63).

Conclusion

The doctrine of Christ according to the Standards rests squarely upon the Scriptures but also extends its hands across the centuries to express its fellowship and agreement with the teachings of the ancient church in the ecumenical councils. Along with the Reformers, the divines wanted the world to know its agreement with the ancient church and the belief in the full deity and humanity of Christ, as well as other key teachings that fended off ancient and contemporary heresies such as Arianism, Eutychianism, Nestorianism, and Socinianism. The divines also seated Christ's work within the context of the dual covenants, works and grace. As covenant surety, Christ offered satisfaction and his obedience on behalf of the elect to save them, and them alone. This is a point that set apart Reformed theology from the Remonstrants, as well as others who advocated universal satisfaction. However, the debates surrounding the Standards' composition, works from the period, and the Standards themselves exhibit a certain sophistication that should be taken into consideration.

In a day when scholastic distinctions are scarcely employed, readers should take note of the careful arguments offered by the various members of the assembly, such as Edmund Calamy. One need not approve of or agree with them but should acknowledge that what may be clear-cut in our own day may not have been so easily decided in the past. Our own present theological sophistication has not exceeded the abilities of our forefathers, but Reformed churches have largely lost the theological ability to debate issues exegetically, theologically, and precisely, or scholastically. Reformed theology these days seems to be dominated more by bumper-sticker statements and slogans than by carefully reasoned argumentation. Moreover, present-day Reformed churches are largely unfamiliar with the very documents they purport to profess, such as the Canons of Dort. Few people are likely aware of the doctrinal diversity that marks the so-called doctrine of "limited atonement."

My hope is that this chapter has shed a little light on this subject to show that the divines, along with the broader early modern Reformed tradition, exercised a principled diversity on a number of subjects, such as the extent of Christ's satisfaction, while at the same time rejecting Remonstrant views. Such an ethos characterizes the question of the extent of Christ's satisfaction but does not mark issues to be treated in the next chapter on the doctrine of justification. The divines were insistent upon a number of key points regarding the doctrine upon which the church stands or falls.

7

Justification

The doctrine of justification has been called the material principle of the Reformation, a status made evident in one of the period's slogans, *sola fide*. In other words, we are justified by faith alone in Christ alone (*solus Christus*) by God's grace alone (*sola gratia*). Heinrich Bullinger (1504–1575) called justification the "well-spring of all good works."[1] Peter Martyr Vermigli (1489–1562) believed that justification is the "stay of our salvation."[2] Herman Rennecher (b. 1550) once wrote that justification is the "first and chiefest prop and foundation of our fayth and Salvation."[3] These sentiments were equally shared by a number of the Westminster divines. Anthony Burgess (d. 1644), one of the divines, noted that there were significant controversies over this issue, which arose from antinomianism—the view that the moral law is no longer binding upon Christians—as well as from Arminianism and Socinianism. But as Burgess believed, "Truth is a Depositum." In other words, justification was a truth that had been deposited with the church and entrusted into its care.

Citing an Aristotelian maxim, Burgess writes, "It is a greater injustice to deny a little thing deposited, then a great summe that we are indebted for, because he that depositeth any thing in our custody, trusteth in us as a faithful friend." To that end, he argues,

---

[1] Heinrich Bullinger, *The Decades of Henry Bullinger*, ed. Thomas Harding, 4 vols. (1849–1852; Grand Rapids: Reformation Heritage, 2004), 1:121.

[2] Peter Martyr Vermigli, *Most Learned and Fruitful Commentaries of D. Peter Martir Vermilius* (London: John Daye, 1558), fol. 108.

[3] Herman Rennecher, *The Golden Chayne of Salvation* (London: Thomas Man, 1604), § 27 (p. 202).

[Of] all points of Divinity, there is none that with more profit and comfort we may labour in, then in that of Justification, which is stiled by some *articulus stantis & cadentis ecclesiae*, the Church stands or fals, as the truth of this is asserted, and a modest, sober vindication of this point from contrary errors, will not hinder, but much advantage the affectionate part of a man, even as the Bee is helped by her sting to make honey.[4]

Burgess invoked Martin Luther (1483–1546), who according to Reformation lore, called justification the *articulus stantis aut cadentis ecclesiae*, "as if this were the *soul* and *pillar* of Christianity."[5] Burgess also summoned the testimony of Martin Chemnitz (1522–1586), the well-known second-generation Lutheran Reformer, who trembled at the thought of a speech Luther once gave saying that after his death the doctrine of justification would be corrupted.[6]

Later theologians shared Burgess's concerns. In his sermons upon the assembly's Shorter Catechism, Thomas Watson (1620–1686) echoed Burgess's sentiments. Watson believed that justification "is the very Hinge and Pillar of CHRISTIANITY; and an Errour about *Justification* is dangerous, like a Crake in the Foundation, or an Errour in the first Concoction." Watson contended that justification is a "Spring of the Water of Life," and to corrupt it with poison was a damnable error. Like Burgess, Watson invokes the saying of Luther that after his death the doctrine would be corrupted; and so he notes, "As it hath been in these latter Times, the *Arminians* and *Socinians* have cast a dead Fly into this Box of precious Oyntment."[7] Naturally, the Confession echoes a number of these concerns in its explanation of justification. Yet the assembly's initial deliberations over these matters were not a walk in the park.

---

[4]Anthony Burgess, *The True Doctrine of Justification Asserted and Vindicated* (London: Thomas Underhill, 1651), preface.

[5]Ibid., lect. 1 (p. 3).

[6]Ibid., lect. 1 (p. 4); cf. Martin Chemnitz, *Loci Theologici II*, vol. 8 of *Chemnitz's Works* (St. Louis: Concordia, 2008), loc. 13 (pp. 813–1050). A number of early modern works attribute the phrase *articulus stantis et cadentis ecclesiae* to Luther (see, e.g., Francis Turretin, *Institutes of Elenctic Theology*, ed. James T. Dennison Jr., trans. George Musgrave Giger [Phillipsburg, NJ: P&R, 1992–1997], 16.1.1). Luther did write something similar, but the precise phrase has been traced to Reformed theologian Johannes Heinrich Alsted (1588–1638) and his 1618 work *Theologia Scholastica Didacta* (Alister McGrath, *Iustitia Dei: A History of the Christian Doctrine of Justification*, 3rd ed. [Cambridge: CUP, 2005], vii n1).

[7]Thomas Watson, *A Body of Practical Divinity* (London: Thomas Parkhurst, 1692), q. 21 (p. 131).

On the contrary, the initial discussions over justification were marked by intense debates. Theologians are wont to contest the finer points of doctrine, and understanding the assembly's deliberations over justification is important to grasping what the divines finally concluded over the doctrine and related matters. This chapter surveys the assembly's debates over justification and then turns to explain what the Confession contains. As Watson and Burgess noted, crucial to a proper understanding of the Confession's doctrine of justification is the historical context in which the Confession was written. In particular, it was the clear and present danger of antinomianism, Arminianism, Socinianism, and Roman Catholicism that shaped the assembly's doctrine. This chapter also covers the relationship between justification and adoption, an often ignored but nevertheless important doctrine.

Historical Background

When the assembly was first called by Parliament, its initial task was to revise the Thirty-Nine Articles, which were at that time the doctrinal standards for the Church of England. Article 11 states: "We are accounted righteous before God, only for the merit of our Lord and Savior Jesus Christ by faith, and not for our own works or deservings: Wherefore that we are justified by faith only is a most wholesome doctrine, and very full of comfort, as more largely is expressed in the Homily on Justification." One might expect that the doctrine of justification would be a subject on which the divines would exercise great agreement and harmony, but this was far from the truth. In his personal journal on the assembly's proceedings, John Lightfoot (1602–1675) noted that the debate was "our great question" and "great scruple," and that a number of the divines expended "a great deal of time & pains" in arguing their points of view.[8] The assembly debated justification over thirteen sessions spanning a two-week period (September 5–19, 1643).[9] It would therefore far exceed the scope of this

---

[8] Chad Van Dixhoorn, "Reforming the Reformation: Theological Debate at the Westminster Assembly, 1643–52," 7 vols. (PhD diss., University of Cambridge, 2004), 1:271.
[9] Ibid., 2:lxxix; for coverage of these debates, see ibid., 1:270–344; Van Dixhoorn, "The Strange Silence of Prolocutor Twisse: Predestination and Politics in the Westminster Assembly's Debate over Justification," *SCJ* 40, no. 2 (2009): 395–418.

modest chapter to cover these debates in every detail. Nevertheless a summary of the debates, participants, and doctrinal issues is necessary for a full appreciation of what the Standards offer on the doctrine of justification.

In the debates over justification there were two chief parties, those who believed in the imputation of the active obedience of Christ (IAOC) and those who did not; the former included Charles Herle (1598–1659), Thomas Goodwin (1600–1680), William Price (d. 1666), Lazarus Seaman (d. 1675), Joshua Hoyle (bap. 1588, d. 1654), William Gouge (1575–1653), and Thomas Wilson (ca. 1601–1653); and the latter included Thomas Gataker (1574–1654), Richard Vines (1599–1656), William Twisse (1577–1646), and William Rayner (ca. 1595–1666). Though one should keep in mind that each of the two parties may have been united in its position, this does not necessarily mean they agreed in the exegetical or theological route in getting to that position.[10] And though this debate was waged within the assembly, it was in the wake of the heated debates on the Continent surrounding the controversial views of Johannes Piscator (1546–1625).[11]

Opponents of the Active Obedience

In his work on Christian doctrinal aphorisms, which was purportedly drawn from John Calvin's (1509–1664) *Institutes*, Piscator argued that justification is only the remission of sins.[12] In his death and crucifixion Christ was obedient and suffered the penalty of the law on behalf of believers, and his suffering is imputed by faith alone to believers.[13] In his exegesis of Romans 5:19, Piscator argued that Christ brought justification through his blood, that is, his suffering, not his obedience to the law. Piscator succinctly states, "We are therefore not just by the holy life of Christ."[14] In his exegesis

---

[10] Van Dixhoorn, "Reforming the Reformation," 1:315–16.

[11] Cf. Edward Leigh, *A Systeme or Body of Divinity: Consisting of Ten Books* (London: William Lee, 1654), 7.6 (pp. 513–14).

[12] Johannes Piscator, *Aphorismi Doctrinae Christianae, Maximam Partem ex Institutione Calvini Excerpti* (Herborn: Corvinus, 1592), 13.1 (p. 66); Piscator, *Aphorismes of Christian Religion; or, A Verie Compendious Abridgement of M. I. Calvins Institutions* (London: Richard Field and Robert Dexter, 1596).

[13] Piscator, *Aphorismi Doctrinae Christianae*, 13.4, 7 (pp. 67–68).

[14] Johannes Piscator, *Analysis Logica Epistolae Pauli ad Romanos: Una cum Scholiis et Observantionibus Locorum Doctrinae*, 4th ed. (Herbornae Nassoviorum: Chistophorus Corvinus, 1608), comm. Rom. 5:19 (pp. 105–6): "Ergo non sumus iusti effecti por sanctam vitam Christi" (p. 106).

of Romans 4, Piscator contended that when Paul writes of imputation, he does not say that God imputes Christ's righteousness (or
obedience), but rather it is the non-imputation of sin; hence justification is only the forgiveness of sins.[15] The German Reformed
theologian also believed that if Christ's satisfaction and obedience
were imputed to sinners, they would have no need to offer obedience to the law because Christ would already have performed it in
their place.[16] Piscator's views were challenged and went against the
grain of common interpretation not only of key scriptural texts but
also of the Heidelberg Catechism, which states that Christ imputes
"his righteousness and holiness as if I had never committed a single
sin or had ever been sinful, having fulfilled myself all the obedience
which Christ has carried out for me, if only I accept such favor with
a trusting heart" (q. 60).[17]

In the assembly's debates Gataker was one of the chief representatives for those who rejected the IAOC. In fact, he offered the most
speeches against the IAOC:[18]

Divine	Speeches against the IAOC
Thomas Gataker	25
Richard Vines	23
Thomas Temple	6
William Twisse	4
Francis Woodcock	4

[15] Johannes Piscator, *A Learned and Profitable Treatise on Mans Iustification. Two Bookes* (London: Thomas Creede for Robert Dexter, 1599), 1.6 (pp. 13–28).

[16] Johannes Piscator, "Pastoribus Ecclesiarum Gallicarum," in *Praestantium ac Eruditorum Virorum Epistolae Ecclesiasticae et Theologicae Varii Argumenti*, ed. Christian Hartsoeker and Philip van Limborch, 2nd ed. (Amsterdam: Henricum Dendrinum, 1660), 156–62; Piscator, "Letter of the French Synod," in *The Works of James Arminius*, ed. and trans. James Nichols and William Nichols, 3 vols. (1825–1875; Grand Rapids: Baker, 1996), 1:696–700, esp. 698; R. Scott Clark, "Do This and Live: Christ's Active Obedience as the Ground of Justification," in *Covenant, Justification, and Pastoral Ministry*, ed. R. Scott Clark (Phillipsburg, NJ: P&R, 2007), 232–33.

[17] Cf. John Calvin, *Institutes of the Christian Religion*, trans. John Allen (Grand Rapids: Eerdmans, 1949), 3.11.23; Zacharias Ursinus, *The Smaller Catechism*, q. 42, in *An Introduction to the Heidelberg Catechism: Sources, History, and Theology*, ed. Lyle D. Bierma et al. (Grand Rapids: Baker, 2005), 148; Ursinus, *The Commentary of Dr. Zacharias Ursinus on the Heidelberg Catechism*, trans. G. I. Williard (1852; Phillipsburg, NJ: P&R, n.d.), 327–28; Caspar Olevianus, *In Epistolam D. Pauli Apostoli ad Romanos Noatae* (Geneva: Eustathium Vignon, 1579), comm. Rom. 5:12 (pp. 196–97); Johannes Wollebius, *Compendium Theologiae Christianae*, 1.17.8; 1.30.15, in *Reformed Dogmatics*, ed. and trans. John W. Beardslee III (Oxford: OUP, 1965); Clark, "Do This and Live," 231–32.

[18] Van Dixhoorn, "Reforming the Reformation," 1:332.

Divine	Speeches against the IAOC
Stanley Gower	3
Francis Taylor	3
William Raynor	2

In a work published after the assembly Gataker spells out his position by rejecting what he believes are two erroneous positions, that of the Council of Trent, which confounds justification with sanctification, and Piscator's view that justification is only the remission of sins.[19] Gataker, in contrast to Piscator, believed that *pardon* is different from *remission*; the former removes guilt and the latter merely removes sin.[20] In his argument, Gataker appeals to Calvin, who cites Acts 13:38–39, and concludes, "After the remission of sins, this justification is mentioned." Within the same context Calvin also states that justification is "no other than an acquittal from guilt of him who was accused."[21] So for Gataker, justification is the pardon (or acquittal) of sin with a "full satisfaction intervening."[22] Gataker writes:

> *To justifie is no other, then to assoil the partie questioned from guilt, as approved innocent, or guiltless*, which is another matter then meerlie to pardon. Neither is this difference a slight matter or light weight, and unworthy much regard, since that herein *Socinus* states the Controversie between the Orthodox Divines, and himself with his adherents, in his *Theological Prelections, cap.* 15 thus speaking. . . . *The question is, whether in our justification by Christ, our sins are done away by some compensation or satisfaction, or by remission and condonation. The most say this is done by satisfaction intervening; but we by simple condonation.* And the former way *Calvine* expresslie takes to, where he delivers his mind more fullie.[23]

Gataker was interested in distancing himself not only from Piscator but also from Faustus Socinus (1539–1604), who had already

---

[19] Thomas Gataker, *An Antidote against Errour, concerning Justification* (London: Henry Brome, 1679), 7, 13, 16.
[20] Ibid., 16.
[21] Calvin, *Institutes*, 3.11.3.
[22] Gataker, *Antidote against Errour*, 15.
[23] Ibid., 16; cf. Faustus Socinus, *Praelectiones Theologicae Fustis Socini Senensis* (Racoviae: Sebastiani Sternacii, 1609), 15 (p. 86).

earned himself the reputation of being a heretic. Gataker's distancing himself from the former was likely an effort to identify himself with Calvin rather than the questionable views of Piscator (though both Gataker and Piscator appealed to Calvin in support of their views). And Gataker wanted to demonstrate his orthodoxy by exposing the errors of Socinianism; this was especially necessary because critics had leveled this charge against those who denied the IAOC.[24]

In contrast to the perceived differences between Piscator and Socinus on the one hand, and his own views on the other, Gataker believed that justification is the pardon of sin, which thereby produces the remission of sins.[25] He argues, *"Remission simplie and nakedlie considered in it self, is a work of mercie or favor onlie: whereas Justification, to speak properlie, is a work of Justice, Deut. 25.1."* Hence, *"Remission of sinne, tho it be not the same with Justification, yet is it a necessarie consequent of efficacious Justification grounded upon satisfaction tendred and accepted, made and admitted."*[26]

Proponents of the Active Obedience

On the other side of the debate the majority of the divines were in favor of including the active obedience of Christ in their revisions of article 11 of the Thirty-Nine Articles.[27] One proponent, Daniel Featley (1582–1645), offered five speeches in favor, which by no means classified him as the most prolific speaker, in that there were others who spoke far more often:[28]

---

[24] See Thomas Gataker, *Mr. Anthony Wotton's Defence against Mr. George Walker's Charge, Accusing Him of Socinian Heresie and Blasphemie* (Cambridge: Roger Daniel, 1641). In this work Gataker, recounts the views of Anthony Wotton (ca. 1561–1626), who denied the IAOC in justification; he places Wotton's views in parallel columns next to those of Socinus to prove Wotton's orthodoxy. Readers should also note that George Walker (bap. 1582, d. 1651) was a Westminster divine and noted heresiographer of the seventeenth century (cf. Anthony Wotton, *De Reconciliatione Peccatoris: Ad Regium Collegium Cantabrigiense, Libri Quator. In Quibus Doctrine Ecclesiae Anglicanae de Justificatione Impii Explicatur & Defenditur* [Basilae, 1624], 2.1 [pp. 30–33]; Gataker, *Antidote against Errour*, 11).
[25] Gataker, *Antidote against Errour*, 19, 23.
[26] Ibid., 23.
[27] Edward Leigh cites several works that argued in favor of the IAOC, including George Carleton, *Consensus Ecclesiae Catholicae contra Tridentinos* (Frankfurt: Rulandios, 1613), tertia controversia, § 3 (pp. 330–36); Daniel Featley, *Sacra Nemesis, The Levites Scourge* (Oxford: Leonard Lichfield, 1644), 12–49. Leigh also mentions an unidentifiable work by "L'Empereur," which is likely Constantine L'Empereur (1591–1648), a Dutch Hebraist, theologian, professor of Hebrew at the University of Leiden, and colleague of Lodewijk de Dieu (1590–1642), Daniel Heinsius (1580–1655), Johannes Buxtorf (1564–1629), and Johannes Buxtorf the younger (1599–1664). Featley was also a correspondent with Archbishop James Ussher (1581–1656) (Alexander Chalmers, "Empereur (Constantine)," in *The General Biographical Dictionary*, vol. 13 [London: J. Nichols, 1814], 203–4).
[28] Van Dixhoorn, "Reforming the Reformation," 1:332–34.

Divine	Speeches for the IAOC
Joshua Hoyle	25
George Walker	24
Herbert Palmer	18
Thomas Goodwin	17
Lazarus Seaman	16
William Gouge	13
13 others	63

It is noteworthy, however, that all five of Featley's speeches were re-corded and later published, which provides an excellent window into the debate.[29] In his speeches Featley was keen to highlight what he termed the "double obedience of Christ," or the general and special obedience, which, according to him, some called the active and pas-sive obedience. He argued that both were necessary for justification and that Piscator and Daniel Tilenius (1563–1633), a Remonstrant theologian, denied this, arguing only for the imputation of the passive obedience of Christ.[30]

In his second speech to the assembly, Featley set forth answers to five key objections to the IAOC.[31] The first objection was that Christ as a man was obligated to fulfill the law for himself so that he would be a blameless priest; his obedience was his own priestly qualification and seal of authenticity and purity for his sacrifice on behalf of sinners. Featley countered that by virtue of the hypostatic union of the two natures of Christ, he was bound to fulfill the law not only for himself but also for the people he represented; Christ was a "publike person."

The second objection was that Scripture attributes redemption and reconciliation to Christ's blood, not his obedience. Featley argued that when Scripture speaks of the blood of Christ, it does so by way of synecdoche for his entire obedience. The third objection was that the one who is freed from the guilt of sin is reputed as if he had ful-

[29] Daniel Featley, *The Dippers Dipt; or, The Anabaptists Duck'd and Plung'd over Head and Ears, at a Disputation in Southwark* (London: Richard Reyston, 1647), 192–211.
[30] Ibid., 195–96.
[31] Ibid., 196–97.

filled the law, whether regarding sins of omission or commission. But Featley instead believed that the one who is freed from the guilt of sin is merely innocent, not righteous. The innocent person is certainly freed from punishment, but because he has not actively fulfilled the law throughout the entirety of his life, he has no right to the title of eternal life; Featley cites Leviticus 18:5 in this respect: "Doe this and thou shalt live."

The fourth objection was that if Christ's active obedience is imputed to sinners then there is no need for the remission of sins because whoever has fulfilled the whole law does not require the forgiveness of sins. Featley opposed this point by arguing that Christ's active obedience could not be imputed before a person's sins were first forgiven: "For it is not righteous with god, to accompt him righteous, who hath no way satisfied for his sinnes, neither by himselfe nor other: the captive must first be freed, before he be advanced to honour." The fifth and ultimate objection was that believers are freed from eternal death and therefore attain eternal life by the imputation of Christ's passive obedience. Featley allowed for the "connexion of the causes of our salvation, that whosoever is freed from eternal death, is stated in eternal life," but he nevertheless countered that the causes for each were not the same. He illustrated the point in the following manner: if you open the shutters on a window, sunlight usually enters the room, but the fact that the window lies open does not mean that sun automatically enters the room.

Beyond these five answers to common objections Featley then offered five positive reasons for the IAOC. First, he argued that justification is distinct from redemption and satisfaction, and therefore the imputation of Christ's passive obedience is insufficient for justification (Dan. 9:24; 1 Cor. 1:30). Second, the Scriptures state that righteousness (*dikaiōma*, Romans 5) is imputed, not the mere passive obedience. Third, fulfilling the ceremonial law is different, according to Featley, from Christ's passive obedience. The elements of the ceremonial law were legal acts and "a kind of confession," and therefore given to believers. Fourth, Featley pointed out the irony that opponents of the IAOC argued for a partial imputation of Christ's active obedience. According to most Reformed theologians, Christ's suffering upon the cross was an act of both passive and active obedience; hence, if opponents of the IAOC were willing to give some part of the active obedience to believers, then why not the whole part? Fifth, and last, unless believers receive the IAOC, then they must be barred from eternal life, because such is the nature of the law: "Doe this and thou shalt live; and, if thou wilt enter into life, keep the Commandments" (Lev. 18:5; Matt. 19:17).[32]

Featley was concerned with other objections, as well as with refuting the errors of "miscreants" such as Papists, Arminians, antinomians, and Socinians. For example, antinomians commonly argued that if Christ fulfilled the law in the stead of believers, then what need for holiness was there? Featley acknowledged that since Christ's active obedience is imputed to believers, they are not obligated to fulfill the law "to justifie us before God, or procure us a title to the Kingdome of Heaven." Rather, their fulfillment of the law is to other ends, such as the glory of God, to demonstrate their faith by their works, to make one's calling and election sure, to adorn one's profession of faith with holy conversation, to avoid scandal, and to avert God's judgment.[33] An objection of the Papists was that if Christ's righteousness is imputed, then believers must receive all of it, which means they are as righteous as Christ. Featley appealed to Luther: "All believers, according to the speech of *Luther*, are *aque justi ratione justitiae imputatae*, equally just in respect of imputed justice, though not *inhaerentis*, of inherent; in respect of passive, not active righteousness."[34] In other words, Christ's righteousness was inherent whereas ours is imputed.

The Outcome of the Debate

The final outcome of 275 speeches and two weeks of debate appears in the revised article 11 (table 6).[35]

There are some striking differences, such as the warning against the impenitent, presumably a shot across the bow at antinomianism. But key for our contextual understanding of the Standards is the

---

[32] Ibid., 197–98.
[33] Ibid., 199–200.
[34] Ibid., 200.
[35] *The Proceedings of the Assembly of Divines upon the Thirty Nine Articles of the Church of England*, appended to *The humble Advice of the Assembly of Divines, Now by Authority of Parliament Sitting at Westminster, concerning a Confession of Faith* (London: Company of Stationers, 1647), 8–9.

phrase "his whole obedience and satisfaction being by God imputed unto us and Christ with his righteousness." It is the phrase "whole obedience" that was intended to denote the imputation of both the active and passive obedience of Christ. The proponents of the IAOC appear to have won this round in the assembly's debates with the inclusion of this phrase. And it is the notable absence of this phrase, as well as any mention of "active or passive obedience," from the Confession that has led some to the conclusion that the assembly later accommodated the minority views of Gataker, Twisse, and the other opponents of the IAOC.[36] The question of whether the divines accommodated the opponents of the IAOC will be treated in the next section, which examines justification according to the Standards. Briefly stated, the Standards do not accommodate the minority position but affirm the IAOC.

Table 6. Revision of article 11 of the Thirty-Nine Articles

Original Article 11	Revised Article 11
We are accounted righteous before God, only for the merit of our Lord and Savior Jesus Christ by faith, and not for our own works or deservings: Wherefore that we are justified by faith only is a most wholesome doctrine, and very full of comfort, as more largely is expressed in the Homily on Justification.	We are justified, that is, we are accounted righteous before God, and have remission of sins, nor for nor by our own works or deservings, but freely by his grace, onely for our Lord and Saviour Jesus Christs sake, his whole obedience and satisfaction being by God imputed unto us and Christ with his righteousness, being apprehended and rested on by faith onely. The Doctrine of Justification by Faith onely, is an wholsom Doctrine, and very full of comfort: notwithstanding God doth not forgive them that are impenitent, and go on still in their trespasses.

Justification according to the Standards

The opening paragraph of the Confession's chapter on justification does not identify the opponent, but a Roman Catholic view of justification is in the crosshairs:

[36] Van Dixhoorn, "Reforming the Reformation," 1:323–30. Based upon Van Dixhoorn's work others have offered the same argument, but for dogmatic reasons (J. R. Daniel Kirk, "The Sufficiency of the Cross (I): The Crucifixion as Jesus' Act of Obedience," *SBET* 24, no. 1 [2006]: 36–43).

> Those whom God effectually calleth, he also freely justifieth: not,
> by infusing righteousness into them, but by pardoning their sins,
> and by accounting and accepting their persons as righteous; not,
> for any thing wrought in them, or done by them, but for Christs
> sake alone; nor, by imputing faith it self, the act of believing, or any
> other evangelical obedience, to them, as their righteousnesse, but,
> by imputing the obedience and satisfaction of Christ unto them,
> they receiving, and resting on him and his righteousnesse by faith;
> which faith, they have, not of themselves, it is the gift of God. (11.1)

The divines contrast infused and imputed righteousness, which was
one of the chief dividing factors between the Reformation and Roman
Catholic formulations of justification. The sixth session of the Council
of Trent (1547), for example, argued in favor of justification through
union with Christ, though instead of righteousness being imputed
and hence an alien righteousness (the obedience of Christ accredited
to the sinner's account), Rome argued in favor of infused righteousness:

> In the process of justification, together with the forgiveness of sins
> a person receives, through Jesus Christ into whom he is grafted, all
> these infused at the same time: faith, hope, and charity. For faith,
> unless hope is added to it and charity too, neither unites him per-
> fectly with Christ nor makes him a living member of his body. (§ 7)

So the divines reject the infusion of righteousness, but they also
reject the Remonstrant position when they write that the act of believing, or faith, is not imputed for righteousness. Throughout his writings on justification Jacob Arminius (1560–1609) places an emphasis
upon the importance of faith. In his letter of April 5, 1608, to Hippolytus a Collibus (1561–1612), the ambassador from the Elector Palatine
to the States General, Arminius explains that the word *impute* means
"that faith is not righteousness itself, but is graciously accounted for
righteousness." Arminius further elaborates:

> Faith is imputed to us for righteousness, on account of Christ and
> his righteousness. In this enunciation, faith is the object of imputa-
> tion; but Christ and his obedience are the impetratory or merito-

rious cause of justification [*causa iustificationis impetratoria seu meritoria*]. Christ and his obedience are the object of our faith; but not the object of justification or divine imputation, as if God imputes Christ and his righteousness to us for righteousness.[37]

This is perhaps one of the clearest statements from Arminius on how he understands the role and function of faith in justification. For Arminius, strictly speaking, a person is not justified by the imputed righteousness of Christ; rather, God looks upon the sinner's *faith* as righteousness. God is willing to do this because of Christ's obedience. One can illustrate Arminius's position with the strict use of prepositions: justification occurs *on the basis* of faith and not *by* or *through* faith. For Arminius, faith is not purely instrumental. This explanation for the role of faith is not an isolated example, but is a repeated theme throughout Arminius's writings.[38]

Arminius was well aware that his interpretation was not common. In a letter to Johannes Utenbogaret (1557–1644), another fellow Remonstrant, he writes:

> But some one will reply, "Justification is attributed to faith, on account of the object which faith receives, and which is Christ, who is our righteousness." This is not repugnant to my meaning, but it renders a reason why God imputes our faith to us for justification. But I deny that this expression is figurative, *We are justified by faith*, that is, by the thing which faith apprehends.[39]

Arminius's explanation of his interpretation is key to understanding his exegesis of Romans 4:3 (cf. Gen. 15:6), the text cited in the quote above (cf. Rom. 4:5, 22–24). In his *Certain Articles* (ca. 1607) Arminius again explains the difference between the common interpretation and his own:

---

[37] Jacob Arminius, "Letter to Hippolytus a Collibus, 8 April 1608," § 5, in *Works*, 2:702; Arminius, *Epistola ad Hypolytum a Collibus . . . nec Non Articuli Diligenti Examine Perpendendi*, in *Opera Theologica* (Leiden: Godefridum Basson, 1629), 945.

[38] See, e.g., Jacob Arminius, "Arminius to Utenbogaert, 10 Apr 1599," in *Works*, 2:50n; Arminius, *Praestantium ac Eruditorum Virorum Epistolae Ecclesiasticae et Theologicae*, epist. 46 (p. 97); cf. Keith D. Stanglin and Richard A. Muller, "*Bibliographia Arminiana*: A Comprehensive, Annoted, Bibliography of the Works of Arminius," in *Arminius, Arminianism, and Europe: Jacobus Arminius (1559/60–1609)*, ed. Th. Marius van Leeuwen, Keith D. Stanglin, and Marijke Tolsma (Leiden: Brill, 2009), 269.

[39] "Arminius to Utenbogaert," in *Works*, 2:50n; Arminius, *Epistolae Ecclesiasticae*, epist. 46 (p. 97).

In this enunciation, "Faith is imputed to the believer for righteous-ness," is the word "faith" to be *properly* received as the instrumen-tal act by which Christ has been apprehended for righteousness? Or is it to be *improperly* received, that is, by a metonymy, for the very object which faith apprehends?[40]

This is the specific issue at stake: is faith foundational or instrumental for justification? Arminius embraces the former—faith is foundational for justification—and this is the view that the divines reject.

Prior to Arminius and the rise of Remonstrant theology, the specific role of faith had only been dealt with in terms of the Roman Catholic assertion that faith was defined not as trust, but as obedience, or "faith which worketh by love" (Gal. 5:6). In the sixth session of Trent, for example, the council specifically appealed to Galatians 5:6 in its declaration on justification: "Hence it is very truly said that faith with-out works is dead and barren, and in Christ Jesus neither circumci-sion is of any avail nor uncircumcision, but faith working through love" (§ 7). Reformed theologians viewed such a move as seeking to base justification upon faith rather than seeing faith as instrumen-tal.[41] Contemporaries of Arminius, and even dialogue partners, dif-fered from him on this crucial point.[42]

When Arminius's ideas began to spread, they were met with stiff resistance and concern because Reformed theologians believed that Arminius and other Remonstrant theologians were espousing Socin-

---

[40] Jacob Arminius, *Articuli Nonnulli Diligenti Examine Perpendendi, Eo Quod inter Ipsos Reformatae Religionis Professores de Iis Aliqua Incidit Controversia*, 23.16 (*Works*, 2:728), in *Opera Theologica* (Leiden: Godefridum Basson, 1629), 963; cf. Stanglin and Muller, "*Bibliographia Arminiana*," 277.
[41] Calvin, *Institutes*, 3.11.2; Girolamo Zanchi, *De Religione Christiana Fides—Confession of Chris-tian Religion*, ed. Luca Baschera and Christian Moser, 2 vols. (Leiden: Brill, 2007), 19.6 (1:342–43); Theodore Beza, *The Christian Faith*, trans. James Clark (Lewes: Focus Christian, 1992), 4.6 (p. 17); 4.7 (p. 18); Beza, *Confessio Christianae Fidei* (Geneva: Ioannis Crispini, 1570), 7; Robert Rollock, *Analysis Dialectica Roberti Rolloci Stoti, Ministri Iesu Christi in Ecclesia Edinburgensi, in Pauli Apostoli Epistolam ad Romanos* (Edinburgh: Robertus Walde-grave,1594), 52; Ursinus, *Commen-tary*, qq. 59–61 (pp. 328–29, 332); Jeremias Bastingius, *An Exposition or Commentarie upon the Cat-echisme of Christian Religion* (London: John Legat, 1595), q. 61 (fol. 125); Bastingius, *In Catechesin Religionis Christianae Quae in Ecclesiis et Scholis tum Belgii, tum Palatinatus Traditur, Exegemata, sive Commenarii* (Dordtrecht: Joahannes Caninius, 1588), 205.
[42] Lucas Trelcatius, *A Briefe Institution of the Common Places of Sacred Divinitie*, trans. John Gawen (London: T. P. for Francis Burton, 1610), 2.9 (pp. 256–57); Trelcatius, *Scholastica, et Methodica, Locorum Communium, s. Theologiae Institutio Didacticè, & Elencticè in Epitome Explicata* (London, 1604), 89; Francis Junius, *Opuscula Theologica Selecta*, ed. Abraham Kuyper (London: Williams and Norgate, 1882), 36.17 (p. 221); cf. Arminius, *Friendly Conference with Dr. F. Junius*, in *Works*, 3:1–248; Arminius, *Amica cum D. Francisco Iunio de Praedestinatione Collatio*, in *Opera Theologica*, 445–611; Wollebius, *Compendium Theologiae Christianae*, 30.8 (p. 165); Wollebius, *Compendium Theologiae Christianae* (Basil, 1633), 247; Johannes Polyander et al., *Synopsis Purioris Theologiae*, ed. Herman Bavinck (New York, 1881), 33.27 (p. 337).

ian formulations on the doctrines of justification and faith.[43] Sibrandus Lubbertus (ca. 1556–1625), one of the delegates to the Synod of Dort (1618–1619), wrote a letter to the church in Geneva warning them that Arminius's doctrine of justification was aligned not only with Socinus's views, but also with those of the antitrinitarian Michael Servetus (1511–1553).[44] Lubbertus also wrote to the cities of Heidelberg, Bern, and Paris to warn them about Arminius's views.[45]

The Synod of Dort was the first ecclesiastical body to deal with Arminius's understanding of faith. The Canons state:

> Having set forth the orthodox teaching, the synod rejects the errors of those who teach that what is involved in the new covenant of grace which God the Father made with men through the intervening of Christ's death is not that we are justified before God and saved through faith, insofar as it accepts Christ's merit, but rather that God, having withdrawn his demand for perfect obedience to the law, counts faith itself, and the imperfect obedience of faith, as perfect obedience to the law, and graciously looks upon this as worthy of reward of eternal life.[46]

The Reformed church saw the error and rejected it. Likewise, the closest predecessor to the Confession, the Irish Articles (1615), also identifies and rejects the error:

> When we say that we are justified by faith only, we do not mean that the said justifying faith is alone in man without true repentance, hope, charity, and the fear of God (for such a faith cannot justify); neither do we mean that this, our act, to believe in Christ,

[43] Aza Goudriaan, "Justification by Faith and the Early Arminian Controversy," in *Scholasticism Reformed: Essays in Honour of Willem J. van Asselt*, ed. Maarten Wisse, Marcel Sarot, and Willemien Otten (Leiden: Brill, 2010), 155–78.
[44] Ibid., 172; Goudriaan cites and translates, "Epistolica disceptatio de fide iustificante deque nostra coram Deo justificante, habita inter praestantissimum virum D. Sibrandum Lubbertis . . . et Petrum Berium Disceptatur autem An fides a Deo habeatur pro omni legis iustitia, quam nos praestare tenebamur, adeoque an ipse actus fide to credere, imputetur in iustitiam sensu proprio. Ait hic, negat ille." (Delft: I. Andreae, 1612), 168–69.
[45] Th. Marius van Leeuwen, "Introduction: Arminius, Arminianism, and Europe," in van Leeuwen, Stanglin, and Tolsma, *Arminius, Arminianism, and Europe*, xvii; Sibrandus Lubbertus, "Lubbertus to the Company of Pastors, *Registres de la Compagnie des pasteurs*, ed. G. Cahier, M. Campagnolo et al. (Geneva: Droz, 1991), 44–45, 208–9, 45, as cited in Nicholas Fornerod, "'The Canons of the Synod Had Shot Off the Advocate's Head': A Reappraisal of the Genevan Delegation at the Synod of Dort," in *Revisiting the Synod of Dort (1618–19)*, ed. Aza Goudriaan and Fred van Lieburg (Leiden: Brill, 2011), 188–89.
[46] Canons of Dort, second main point, art. 2, rej. of error 4.

or this, our faith in Christ, which is within us, does of itself justify us or deserve our justification unto us (for that were to account ourselves to be justified by the virtue or dignity of something that is within ourselves). (§ 36)

One of the chief contributors to the Irish Articles, James Ussher (1581–1656), who was also invited to participate in the assembly but declined because of his loyalties to the crown, was well aware of Arminius's views on faith and therefore sought to eradicate it.[47]

In fact, George Walker (1581–1651), one of the divines, targeted Arminius's views and categorized him among "heretics" such as Servetus and Socinus. Walker writes that Arminius:

did first secretly teach and instill it into the ears and hearts of many disciples; and afterwards did openly profess it, as we read in his Epistle *ad Hyppolytum de Collibus*, wherein he confesses that he held, faith to be imputed for righteousness to justification, not in a metonymical, but in a proper sense: And although this and other errors held by him are condemned in the late Synod of Dort: yet his disciples the Remonstrants do obstinately persist in this error, though some of that sect, would seem to decline and disclaim it.[48]

Other heresiographers, such as Thomas Edwards (1599–1647), made similar judgments about Arminius's understanding of faith.[49] Likewise, Francis Roberts (1609–1675) rejected Arminius's position.[50]

---

[47] Alan Ford, *James Ussher: Theology, History, and Politics in Early-Modern Ireland and England* (Oxford: OUP, 2007), 162. Note Ussher's explanation of faith: "But how is this great benefit of justification applied unto us, and apprehended by us? This is done on our part by faith alone: and that not considered as a virtue inherent in us, working by love; but only as an instrument or hand of the soul stretched forth, to lay hold on the Lord our Righteousness (Rom 5.1 & 10.10, Jer 23.6). So that faith justifies only relatively, in respect of the object which it fastens on; to wit, the righteousness of Christ" (James Ussher, *A Body of Divinity; or, The Sum and Substance of Christian Religion* [1648; Herndon: Solid Ground Christian Books, 2007], 17 (p. 175); "Letter XXXVI, Mr. Thomas Warren to Dr. James Ussher," in *The Whole Works of the Most Rev. James Ussher, D.D.*, ed. C. R. Elrington and J. H. Todd, 17 vols. (Dublin, 1829–1864), 15:141–42.

[48] George Walker, *Socinianisme in the Fundamental Point of Justification Discovered, and Confuted* (London: John Bartlet, 1641), 5–6. Cf. a similar work, though treating other subjects, written by Daniel Featley, *Pelagius Redivivus; or, Pelagius Raked Out of the Ashes by Arminius and His Schollers* (London: Robert Mylbourne, 1626).

[49] Thomas Edwards, *The Second Part of Gangraena; or, A Fresh and Further Discovery of the Errors, Heresies, Blasphemies, and Dangerous Proceedings of the Sectaries of This Time* (London: Ralph Smith, 1646), 69.

[50] Francis Roberts, *Mysterium et Medulla Bibliorum. The Mysterie and Marrow of the Bible* (London: George Calvert, 1657), 600.

That the divines reject justification based upon faith—whether because faith and obedience are conflated or because faith is itself accounted as righteousness—precludes Roman Catholic, Remonstrant,
and Socinian views. The Socinian Racovian Catechism (1609) explains
that to have faith means to "trust in God as at the same time to trust
in Christ," but it also includes obedience. Faith is "to obey God not only
in those things commanded in the law delivered by Moses, that are not
annulled by Christ, but also in all those which Christ has delivered
beyond and in addition to the law." The Racovian Catechism bases its
view upon James 2:26, which states that faith without works is dead, as
well as James 2:23: "Abraham believed God, and it was imputed unto
him for righteousness." Hence, "it is necessary that the faith to which
alone and in reality salvation is ascribed, or which alone is necessarily
followed by salvation, should comprehend obedience."[51] So, then, what
alternative do the divines offer in the place of these rejected views?

The divines state that God justifies sinners by "imputing the obedience and satisfaction of Christ unto them, they receiving, and resting
on him and his righteousness by faith." First, note how faith is characterized in a passive manner, in that faith most certainly works by love,
as Paul explains in Galatians 5:6. The divines recognize this fact in
their chapter "Saving Faith," which states that faith yields obedience
to God's commands, trembles at the threats of the law, and embraces
the promises of God in both this life and eternal life to come. However,
when it comes to justification, faith is passive: "But the principall Acts
of saving faith, are, Accepting, Receiving, and Resting upon Christ
alone for Justification, Sanctification, and Eternal life, by vertue of
the Covenant of Grace" (14.2). In other words, faith is in no way foundational for a person's justification. Stated differently, believers are
not justified upon the ground of faith—faith is purely instrumental.
The divines write: "Faith, thus receiving and resting on Christ and his
righteousness, is the alone instrument of Justification" (11.2). But the
question arises, if faith is the instrumental means by which sinners
lay hold of the imputed "obedience and satisfaction of Christ," does
this phrase denote Christ's passive *and* active obedience? In light of

---

51 *The Racovian Catechism*, trans. Thomas Rees (London: Longman, Hurst, Rees, Orme, and Brown,
1818), 5.9 (pp. 322–23).

the earlier debates over the revision of article 11, did the divines advocate the necessity of the IAOC?

In their original work of revising article 11 the divines added the word "whole" to the phrase "obedience of Christ" to indicate that both the active and passive obedience were imputed to the sinner in justification. Confession 11.1 merely says, "the obedience and satisfaction of Christ." A number of commentators have claimed this as evidence that the divines backed away from their original decision to require the IAOC. In other words, the majority of the divines accommodated the minority view; or the question of the IAOC was viewed as a debatable matter, an internecine debate but not a test of orthodoxy.[52] One of the chief pieces of evidence that has been brought forth in support of this contention is that when congregational churchman adopted a modified version of the Confession in the Savoy Declaration (1658) under the guidance of Thomas Goodwin, one of the original Westminster divines, and John Owen (1616–1683), they specifically modified this statement:

- *WCF.* "By imputing the obedience and satisfaction of Christ unto them"
- *Savoy.* "By imputing Christ's active obedience to the whole law, and passive obedience in his death"

The offered explanation is that the Savoy Declaration adds what was omitted by the Westminster divines.[53]

Yet others find this argumentation unpersuasive. Based upon a holistic reading of the Standards (Confession, Larger and Shorter Catechisms), a number of historians believe that the divines affirm the necessity of the IAOC, and their case is correct for several reasons.[54]

[52] Van Dixhoorn, "Reforming the Reformation," 1:323–30; Kirk, "The Sufficiency of the Cross," 36–43; Robert A. Letham, *The Westminster Assembly: Reading Its Theology in Historical Context* (Phillipsburg, NJ: P&R, 2009), 250–64; Alexander F. Mitchell and John Struthers, *Minutes of the Westminster Assembly (1644–49)* (1874; Edmonton: Still Waters Revival, n.d.), lxv–lxvii; William Barker, *Puritan Profiles: 54 Contemporaries of the Westminster Assembly* (1996; Fearn: Mentor, 1999), 176; cf. Alan D. Strange, "The Imputation of the Active Obedience of Christ at the Westminster Assembly," in *Drawn into Controversie: Reformed Theological Diversity and Debates within Seventeenth-Century British Puritanism*, ed. Michael A. G. Haykin and Mark Jones (Göttingen: Vandenhoeck & Ruprecht, 2011), 31–33.
[53] Van Dixhoorn, "Reforming the Reformation," 1:330.
[54] Strange, "Imputation of the Active Obedience," 50–51; Jeffrey K. Jue, "The Active Obedience of Christ and the Theology of the Westminster Standards: A Historical Investigation," in *Justified in Christ: God's Plan for Us in Justification*, ed. K. Scott Oliphint (Fearn: Christian Focus, 2007), 99–130; Carl R. Trueman, "The Harvest of Reformation Mythology? Patrick Gillespie and the Covenant of Redemption," in Wisse, Sarot, and Otten, *Scholasticism Reformed*, 212.

First, the following paragraph in chapter 11 states, "Christ by his obedience, and death, did fully discharge the debt of all those that are thus justified, and did make a proper, reall, and full satisfaction to his Fathers Justice in their behalf" (11.3). At first glance this might not seem all that significant, but subsequent editions of the Confession remove a crucial piece of grammar, thus obscuring the point the divines made. In the Scottish Free Presbyterian edition of the Standards, which is supposed to be a reprint of the original Critical Text produced by S. W. Carruthers, a comma has been removed:[55]

- *Scottish Free Presbyterian Carruthers's edition.* "Christ, by His *obedience and death*, did fully discharge the debt of all those that are thus justified."
- *Original 1647.* "Christ by his *obedience, and death*, did fully discharge the debt of all those that are thus justified."

The difference is barely noticeable but is significant because in the original, two separate aspects of Christ's work are distinguished by a comma, which in later editions has been removed. This combines what was once separate and reflected the passive *and* active obedience. This fact, which past historians, pro or con, have not previously noted, also demonstrates the necessity of employing original documents in historical research rather than retyped copies.

Second, in the broader context of the Standards, the series of Larger Catechism questions on the humiliation of Christ (qq. 46–50) explains that Christ perfectly fulfilled the law (q. 48), which is distinguished from his death (qq. 49–50). And when questions 70–71 on justification are held together with questions 46–50, taken as a whole they impress upon the reader the necessity of the active obedience of Christ. This is especially true against the backdrop of the dual-covenant structure of works and grace in which, as Featley pointed out in his appeal to Leviticus 18:5 in his speeches favoring the IAOC, the law demands obedience to obtain eternal life. Leviticus 18:5 was a common proof text for the covenant of works.[56]

---

[55] *Westminster Confession of Faith* (1646; Glasgow: Free Presbyterian Publications, 1995).
[56] See, e.g., WCF 7.1 (cites Rom. 10:5; Gal. 3:12); William Pemble, *Vindiciae Fidei; or, A Treatise of Justification by Faith* (1625; Oxford: John Adams, Edward and John Forrest, 1659), 2.1 (p. 159); John Preston, *The New Covenant; or, The Saints Portion* (London: Nicolas Bourne, 1639), 314;

Third, there are a number of indicators from Featley's speeches supporting the IAOC that few commentators take into account.[57] When the assembly was initially revising the Thirty-Nine Articles and its statement on justification, Featley saw two liabilities to the phrase "whole obedience" for three reasons—namely, "redundancie, deficiencie, and noveltie." He believed that the word *whole* was redundant because this would entail, in his mind, Christ's obedience to the ceremonial law, something for which believers were not responsible. He thought that the word *obedience* was deficient because it did not accurately convey what was imputed to believers; not even the terms *active* and *passive* obedience were accurate in Featley's mind. He believed that the sinner's malady and therefore remedy was threefold:[58]

Malady	Remedy
Original sin	Christ's original righteousness
Sins of omission	Christ's active obedience
Sins of commission	Christ's passive obedience

Featley, consequently, was aware of the possible weaknesses of the phrase "whole obedience." While this is circumstantial evidence, these weaknesses indicate why the phrase was not used in the later composition of the Confession and catechisms. It should be noted, however, that the phrase "whole obedience" is used by some Reformed theo-

---

Preston, *The Brest-Plate of Faith and Love* (London: Nicolas Bourne, 1630), 38; Thomas Hooker, *The Unbeleevers Preparing for Christ* (London: Andrew Crooke, 1638), 59; Edward Fisher, *The Marrow of Modern Divinity: Touching Both the Covenant of Works, and the Covenant of Grace* (London: G. Calvert, 1645), 48; Samuel Rutherford, *The Covenant of Life Opened; or, A Treatise of the Covenant of Grace* (Edinburgh: Robert Brown, 1654), 1.13 (p. 89); Robert Rollock, *A Treatise of Our Effectual Calling*, 3, in *Select Works of Robert Rollock*, ed. William M. Gunn, 2 vols. (1844–1849; Grand Rapids: Reformation Heritage, 2008), 1:34; Turretin, *Institutes*, 8.6.4; Wilhelmus à Brakel, *The Christian's Reasonable Service*, trans. Bartel Elshout, 4 vols. (Morgan, PA: Soli Deo Gloria, 1992), 12 (1:360); Benedict Pictet, *Christian Theology*, trans. Frederick Reyroux (London: R. B. Seeley and W. Burnside, 1834), 3.7 (p. 155); James Ussher, *A Body of Divinitie; or, The Summe and Substance of Christian Religion* (London: Thomas Downes and George Badger, 1645), 125; David Dickson, *Truths Victory over Error* (Edinburgh: John Reed, 1684), 19 (pp. 137–38); Patrick Gillespie, *The Ark of the Testament Opened* (London: R. C., 1681), 1.5 (pp. 180–81); Leigh, *Body of Divinity*, 4.1 (p. 306); Herman Witsius, *Conciliatory; or, Irenical Animadversions*, trans. Thomas Bell (Glasgow: W. Lang, 1807), 8.1–2 (pp. 86–87); Bastingius, *Exposition*, fol. 122; cf. William Whitaker, *An Answer to the Ten Reasons of Edmund Campian* (London: Felix Kyngston, 1606), 252–53; John Downame, *The Christian Warfare against the Devil World and Flesh* (London: William Stansby, 1634), 2.8 (p. 103).

[57] Cf. Van Dixhoorn, "Reforming the Reformation," 1:328.

[58] Featley, *Dippers Dipt*, 204–5. Fellow divine Edward Leigh also adopts this same threefold understanding of Christ's imputed righteousness and specifically cites Featley's speech from the assembly (*Body of Divinity*, 7.6 [p. 517]).

logians to refer to the active and passive obedience of Christ.[59] For example, John Davenant (1572–1641) explains:

> With respect to the explanation of the terms, when we speak of *the death of Christ*, we comprehend in it the whole obedience of Christ, active and passive, the completion of which, and as it were the last act, was effect in his death; on which account Divines are accustomed by synecdoche to attribute to his death what relates to his entire obedience.[60]

Fourth, one element that no one to date has explored is how the phrase "obedience and satisfaction" was used in the literature of the period. The bulk of the analysis regarding the Confession and the IAOC has centered upon the assembly's debate, the revisions of the Thirty-Nine Articles, chapter 11 of the Confession, and the missing word *whole*, from "whole obedience." No one, to my knowledge, has asked whether the phrase "obedience and satisfaction" means anything other than the active and passive obedience of Christ. In works that predate the assembly, such as John Downame's *Christian Warfare* (1634), the phrase is used to denote the active and passive obedience of Christ: "We obtained the remission of our sins, not for our workes or inherent righteousness, or any virtue that is in our selves, but by and for the alone merits, obedience, and full satisfaction of Christ," which in context is referred to as "the obedience and satisfaction of Christ."[61] This phrase also appears in George Walker's defense of the doctrine of justification;

---

[59] Cf. Thomas Cranmer, *An Answer to a Crafty and Sophistical Cavillation Devised by Stephen Gardineri* (1555; Cambridge: CUP, 1844), 86; Trelcatius, *Briefe Institution*, 2.9 (p. 261); Walker, *Socinianisme*, dedicatory epistle, 73, 139; Petrus de Witte, *Catechizing upon the Heidelbergh Catechisme, of the Reformed Christian Religion* (Amsterdam: Printed by Gillis Joosten Saeghman, 1664), q. 37 (p. 13); Roberts, *Mysterium et Medulla Bibliorum*, 2.1 (p. 31); Richard Baxter, *The Life of Faith*, 3.8, in *The Practical Works of the Late Reverend and Pious Mr. Richard Baxter*, 4 vols. (1660; London: Thomas Parkhurst, Jonathan Robinson, and John Lawrence, 1707), 3:598; John Owen, *The Doctrine of Justification by Faith through the Imputation of the Righteousness of Christ, Explained, Confirmed, & Vindicated* (London: R. Boulter, 1677), 295.

[60] John Davenant, *An Exposition of the Epistle of St. Paul to the Colossians*, trans. Josiah Allport (1627; London: Hamilton, Adams, and Co., 1831), 341. Thomas Watson, among others, divided Christ's satisfaction into two parts and did not refer to the "obedience of Christ." Watson writes: "His SATISFACTION, and this consists of two Branches: 1. *His Active Obedience* . . . 2. *His Passive Obedience*" (*Body of Practical Divinity*, q. 15 [p. 100]).

[61] Downame, *Christian Warfare*, 2.2 (p. 274); cf. William Perkins, *A Clowd of Faithfull Witnesses, Leading to the Heavenly Canaan; or, A Commentarie upon the 11. Chapter to the Hebrewes*, v. 2, in *The Workes of That Famous and Worthy Ministery of Christ, in the Universitie of Cambridge, Mr. William Perkins* (London: Cantrell Legge, 1618), 5; Francis Cheynell, *The Rise, Growth, and Danger of Socinianisme, Together with a Plaine Discovery of a Desperate Designe of Corrupting the Protestant Religion* (London: Samuel Gellibrand, 1643), 4 (p. 41).

this is significant because Walker offered twenty-four speeches, second only to Joshua Hoyle's twenty-five, in favor of the IAOC.[62]

Another appearance of the phrase occurs in James Ussher's *Body of Divinitie*, where he asks, "What then are the parts of Christ's Obedience and Satisfaction?" Ussher answers:

> His *Sufferings* and his *Righteousness, Phil.* 2.5, 6, 7, 8. *1 Pet.* 2.23; For it was requisite, that he should *first* pay all our Debt, and satisfy God's Justice, *(Esa.* 53.5, 6. *Job* 33.24) by a price of infinite Value. (1 *Tim.* 2.6) Secondly, Purchase and merit for us God's Favour, *(Ephes.* 1.6) and Kingdom, by a most absolute and perfect Obedience, *(Rom.* 5.19). By his suffering he was to merit unto us the Forgiveness of our sins; and by his fulfilling the Law he was to merit unto us Righteousness: Both which are necessarily required for our Justification.[63]

Ussher's work was published in 1645, which was well in advance of the assembly's debates over chapters 11 and 12 on justification and adoption in session 678 on July 23, 1646.[64] The employment of the phrase "obedience and satisfaction" before and during the assembly, therefore, indicates that it was reflective of both the active and the passive obedience of Christ. The same can also be said for works employing the phrase that were released after the publication of the Confession, or those interpreting the Standards' use of the phrase.[65] Hence, these four reasons (the grammar of the 1648 original, the broader context of the Standards, the perceived deficiencies of the term *whole obedience*, and the contextual meaning of "obedience and satisfaction" before, during, and after the assembly) indicate that the divines did not accommodate the minority views of Gataker, Twisse, and others. Given this evidence, it is safe to conclude that the Standards affirm the IAOC.

---

[62] Walker, *Socinianisme*, 139, 232.
[63] Ussher, *Body of Divinitie*, 171.
[64] Strange, "Imputation of the Active Obedience of Christ," 44; Mitchell and Struthers, *Minutes*, 258–59.
[65] Giovanni Diodati, *Pious and Learned Annotations upon the Holy Bible* (London: Nicholas Fussell, 1651), comm. 1 Cor. 6.11; Roberts, *Mysterium et Medulla Bibliorum*, 609; John Wallis, *A Brief and Easie Explanation of the Shorter Catechism* (London: Peter Parker, 1662), n.p.; Baxter, *Life of Faith*, 3.7 (p. 598); Samuel Annesley, *The Morning Exercises at Cripplegate*, vol. 6 (1675; London: Thomas Tegg, 1844), 558–59; Owen, *Doctrine of Justification*, 190, 339; John Brown, *The Life of Justification Opened* (Utrecht, 1695), 6 (p. 47).

Now, if the divines were concerned with affirming the IAOC, they were equally concerned about antinomianism, the teaching that Christians are in no way obligated to the moral law since they have been freed from its demands through their justification.[66] The antinomian controversies will be covered in the subsequent chapter on sanctification, but suffice it for now to recognize that one of the tenets of antinomianism was the doctrine of justification from eternity. Some Reformed theologians were jealous to guard the purity of justification from mixture with human effort, such as good works. Richard Baxter (1615–1691) identified justification from eternity— i.e., justification as an immanent act of the Trinity, not a transient act—as a chief pillar of antinomianism.[67] The common argument for justification from eternity runs as follows: God not only decrees justification but also justifies the elect in eternity; hence, when a person comes to faith, that awakening is not the moment of his justification but rather the discovery of his justified status. Reputed antinomian theologians employed the distinction between justification *in foro Dei* (in the court before God) and *in foro conscientiae* (in the court of conscience).[68]

The question of justification from eternity was not theoretical, since William Twisse, the assembly's first moderator, held to this doctrine. Twisse believed that justification was God's eternal will not to punish the sinner, which was an immanent act of God from eternity (*actus immanens in Deo, fuit ab aeterno*).[69] Since God decreed from eternity to justify sinners through Christ's work, justification *by faith* did not mean that a person was not justified until he exercised faith but that

---

[66] John Lightfoot notes a number of times in his personal journal that the assembly took up the subject of antinomianism in its deliberations (John Lightfoot, *The Journal of the Proceedings of the Assembly of Divines*, vol. 13 of *The Whole Works of the Rev. John Lightfoot* [London: J. V. Dove, 1824], 9, 12, 71, 85, 299, 304, 308).

[67] Richard Baxter, *Confession of His Faith* (London, 1654), 151–52.

[68] Perhaps one of the better-known advocates of justification from eternity was English theologian Tobias Crisp (1600–1643), whom Curt Daniels identifies as the one who popularized the *in foro Dei–in foro conscientiae* distinction (Curt Daniels, "Hyper-Calvinism and John Gill," [PhD diss., University of Edinburgh, 1983], 309). Cf. Tobias Crisp, *Christ Alone Exalted*, vol. 1 (London: John Bennett, 1832), 323–24. This distinction was employed by others, such as William Pemble (1591–1623), *Vindiciae Gratiae: A Plea for Grace. More Especially the Grace of Faith*, 2nd ed. (London, 1629), 2.1 (pp. 21–22); cf. Hans Boersma, *A Hot Pepper Corn: Richard Baxter's Doctrine of Justification in Its Seventeenth-Century Context of Controversy* (Vancouver: Regent College, 2004), 71–72.

[69] William Twisse, *Vindiciae Gratiae, Potestatis, ac Providentiae Dei Hoc Est, ad Examen Libelli Perkinsiani de Praedestinationis Modo et Ordine, Institutum a Iacobo Arminio, Responsio Scholastica, Tribus Libris Absoluta* (Amsterdam: Ioannem Ianssonium, 1632), 1.2.25 (p. 194, though erroneously paginated as 294); Boersma, *Hot Pepper Corn*, 84n129.

he was justified because of Christ.[70] To explain how this all coheres, Twisse employs the *in foro Dei–in foro conscientiae* distinction:

> And in this sense, justification takes place through faith, as someone's absolution is pronounced before the spectacle of a lawsuit and in front of a tribunal of the Judge. For God has set up his tribunal in our hearts, our own conscience prosecutes, terrifies, torments us as the accused according to the law of God. Finally, when at some time the mercy of God thus arises, the Spirit of God, through the voice of the Gospel, raises up, comforts, recreates, and pronounces that our sins have been discharged because of Christ. And the Holy Spirit does this by kindling faith in our hearts by which we come to rest in the mercy of God the Father and in the secure satisfaction of Christ the Son.[71]

Here Twisse writes of not only the tribunal of the Judge (*tribunali Iudicis*) but also the tribunal of the heart (*tribunali in cordibus*). These two courts play a role in the adjudication of the sinner's justification.

Twisse explains how the two relate: "But the external notification of this one will," that is, the decree and justification from eternity,

> by means of a kind of judicial and forensic absolution, which is through Word and Spirit in front of the tribunal of every man's conscience—is that imputation of the righteousness of Christ and also remission of sins and justification, and the absolution which follows faith; for and thereby the inward purpose of absolving, which was from eternity, is manifested.[72]

For Twisse, the sinner's justification took place in eternity past and eventually becomes manifest once the sinner comes to faith. Hence the sinner's justification has already taken place, but he later learns of his justified status through faith.

The divines rarely identify the specific institutions or theologians holding erroneous views, and they follow this trend when they affirm that justification is an act executed in history, thus rejecting justifica-

---

[70] Boersma, *Hot Pepper Corn*, 85; Twisse, *Vindiciae Gratiae*, 2, criminatio 4, sect. 4 (p. 79).

[71] Twisse, *Vindiciae Gratiae*, 2, criminatio 4, sect. 4 (p. 79), as translated by Boersma, *Hot Pepper Corn*, 85n135, in consultation with Twisse's original.

[72] Twisse, *Vindiciae Gratiae*, 1.2.25 (p. 197), as translated by Boersma, *Hot Pepper Corn*, 86n136, in consultation with Twisse's original.

tion from eternity: "God did, from all eternity, decree to justifie all the elect, and Christ did, in the fullnesse of time, die for their sins, and rise again for their justification: nevethelesse, they are not justified, until the holy Spirit doth, in due time, actually apply Christ unto them" (11.4). The divines specify that God has decreed to justify the elect, but the decision to justify the elect and the actual justification of a person in time are distinct though connected things.

This distinction was not unique to the assembly, nor to the period. Reformed theologians like John Davenant drew upon it from medieval works such as Aquinas's commentary on Peter Lombard's (ca. 1096–1164) *Sentences*, where Thomas distinguishes between God's purpose to communicate his goodness and the act of communication. Davenant argues that predestination is an immanent act of God from which flows his goodness to creatures. Other acts, such as calling, justification, reconciliation, and glorification, are external, or transient, acts of God. Davenant therefore concludes:

> We confess, therefore, the eternal will in God of justifying and reconciling to himself all the elect; but we deny that they ought to be said to have been justified or reconciled from eternity: In the same manner as we acknowledge that there was in God an eternal will of creating the world, and yet we deny that the world was created from eternity.[73]

Francis Roberts succinctly explains: "To say that a man is actually Pardoned and Justified from eternity; is To confound *Gods Decrees* with the *execution of his Decrees*, To destroy the use of Faith and Repentance prescribed in Scripture, And to make a man *actually Pardoned, before he actually was a Sinner*. Which are very absurd."[74] Roberts distinguishes between the immanent and transient acts of God. He maintains that immanent acts, such as God's decree, reside in him but "produce no real effect out of him," whereas transient acts are effects outside of God. Immanent acts are identical with God's essence and are eternal, and transient acts are the same as the effects brought about by the decree.[75]

---

[73] John Davenant, *Dissertation on the Death of Christ*, 5, in *Colossians*, 466.
[74] Roberts, *Mysterium et Medulla bibliorum*, 3, aphor. 1 (p. 1469).
[75] Ibid.

Anthony Burgess, one of the divines, likewise explains that the pardon of sin is a transient act, so therefore justification is in part also a transient act. He supports this point by explaining, among a number of arguments against justification from eternity, that Scripture speaks of Christians at one time being under a state of wrath and condemnation before they were justified. Hence a person's predestination unto salvation does not mean he has already been justified.[76] In this respect, Davenant, writing before the assembly, and Roberts, writing after it, serve as historical bookends to what we find in Burgess and the Confession, which was the majority report in the tradition.[77]

Nevertheless, some within the assembly, such as Thomas Goodwin, at first glance give the impression that they embraced justification from eternity. In fact, later theologians have argued that Goodwin, William Ames (1576–1633), Herman Witsius (1636–1708), and Johannes Maccovius (1588–1644) were proponents of this doctrine.[78] This is correct in one sense, as Ames, for example, places justification in the divine decree: "This judgment [adoption] progresses in the same steps as justification. It was first in God's predestination. . . . Afterward it was in Christ. . . . And then it was in the faithful themselves."[79] However, Ames also argues that a person is not justified until he exercises faith.[80] A similar pattern unfolds in the views of Goodwin, who embraces the *tria momenta* ("three moments") of justification, like Ames.[81] Furthermore, Maccovius expressly embraces the distinction

---

[76] Burgess, *True Doctrine of Justification*, lect. 20 (pp. 167–68); see also Thomas Blake, *Vindiciae Foederis; or, A Treatise of the Covenant of God Entered with Man-kinde*, 2nd ed. (London: Abel Roper, 1658), 22 (pp. 130–36). Blake interacts with Bartholomäus Keckerman, *Systema S. S. Theologiae, Tribus Libris Adornatum* (Hanau: Guilielmum Antonium, 1602), 1.6 (p. 122). Cf. Leigh, *Body of Divinity*, 3.1 (p. 216), 3.2 (p. 225).

[77] See, e.g., Turretin, *Institutes*, 16.9.3; J. H. Heidegger, *Corpus Theologiae Christianae*, 2 vols. (Zurich: J. H. Bodmer, 1732), 22.79 (2:303): "Neque illa proprie ab aeterno peragitur, quia Deus decretum justificandi aeternum non ante fidem exequitur, sed in tempore"; Petrus van Mastricht, *Theoretico-Practica Theologia* (Utrecht and Amsterdam, 1715), 6.6.18 (p. 707); Samuel Maresius, *Collegium Theologicum sive Systema Breve Universae Theologiae*, 6th ed. (Geneva, 1662), 11.58 (pp. 255–56). Leonard Rijssen, *Summa Theologiae Didactico-Elencticae* (Berne, 1703), 14.9 (p. 474); Peter Bulkeley, *The Gospel Covenant; or, The Covenant of Grace Opened* (London: Matthew Simmons, 1651), 4.6 (pp. 358–59); Witsius, *Irenical Animadversions*, 5.4–5 (pp. 62–63); Samuel Rutherford, *Exercitationes Apologeticae pro Divia Gratia* (Amsterdam: Henricum Laurentii Bibliopolam, 1636), 1.2.21 (pp. 44–47).

[78] E.g., John Gill, *A Complete Body of Doctrinal and Practical Divinity* (1839; Paris: The Baptist Standard Bearer, 2007), 2.5 (pp. 201–9).

[79] William Ames, *The Marrow of Theology*, ed. John Dykstra Eusden (1968; Grand Rapids: Baker, 1997), 1.28.3.

[80] Ibid., 1.17.16–17.

[81] Thomas Goodwin, *Justifying Faith*, in *The Works of Thomas Goodwin*, 12 vols. (1861–1866; Edinburgh: Banner of Truth, 1985), 8:134–39; cf. Mark Jones, *Why Heaven Kissed Earth: The Christology*

between justification in time and in the eternal decree.[82] Hence, a number of theologians were keen on connecting justification to the decree but were careful to distinguish between the decree and its execution in time.

The rest of Confession, chapter 11, on justification affirms two important elements. The first is that God continues to forgive the sins of justified believers, and that justified sinners never fall from their justified state (11.5). This affirmation directly contradicts the Roman Catholic position of Trent, which argued that a person can lose his justified status through mortal sin but reacquire it through penance, which was called the "second plank of justification."[83] The Confession characterizes the justified sinner's transgressions not in terms of losing one's status but in terms of incurring the fatherly displeasure of God. Justified sinners may for a season "not have the light of his countenance restored unto them, until they humble themselves, confesse their sins, beg pardon, and renew their faith and repentance" (11.5), but such persons never fall away from salvation, apostatize, or lose their justified status.

The second point, contra Anabaptist and Roman Catholic claims, is that believers in both Testaments, Old and New, lay hold of the same justification—one that looks by faith alone to Christ alone by God's grace alone (11.6). By way of contrast, early Anabaptist theologian Balthasar Hubmaier (ca. 1480–1528) claimed that Old Testament saints were not saved in the same manner as New Testament Christians. He writes:

> The patriarchs of old had the benefit of the promises of God as in Abraham's bosom; where they were preserved until the time of Christ's descent into hell. When the gospel was proclaimed to them there by the Spirit of Christ, only then did they really live in the Christ who had been given them and obtain redemption and

---

of the Puritan Reformed Orthodox Theologian, Thomas Goodwin (1600–80) [Göttingen: Vandenhoeck & Ruprecht, 2010], 232–38; Carl R. Trueman, The Claims of Truth: John Owen's Trinitarian Theology (Carlisle: Paternoster, 1998), 28.

[82] Johannes Maccovius, Loci Communes (Franequerae, 1650), 676: "Certe, si Christus, quatenus ille Mediator est, et quatenus causa meritoria, justificationis solus author est, ab aeterno no fuit, sed ut effet popositum: pariratione, non eramus justificati ab aeterno, etiamsi decretum fuisset apud Deum ab aeterno, de nobis iustificandis in tempore."

[83] Council of Trent, sess. 6, January 13, 1547, first decree, chap. 14.

eternal joy through the joyful message that he has vanquished Sin, death, devil, and hell. Only then were the holy fathers freed of their pains in hell which they (but not the soul of Christ) had suffered there for a long time.[84]

From the earliest days of the Reformation, Reformed theologians such as Bullinger and Calvin argued for the continuity between the Old and New Testaments in terms of their common doctrine of salvation.[85] Medieval theologians such as Lombard argued that Old Testament men were justified through circumcision and women were justified by their faith and good works.[86] But the Confession maintains that ever since the fall of Adam, salvation has been the same for all of the elect because they all participate in the one covenant of grace (7.5–6). This means that all believers, under both the Old and the New Testaments, are justified by grace alone through faith alone in Christ alone.

Justification and Adoption

One last thing to note regarding the Confession's doctrine of justification is its relationship to the doctrine of adoption. Historically, a number of Reformed theologians treated the doctrine of adoption as part of justification. For example, Heinrich Bullinger writes: "Paul putteth faith for an assured confidence in the merit of Christ; and he useth justification for absolution and remission of sins, for adoption into the number of the sons of God, and lastly for the imputing of Christ his righteousness unto us."[87] Echoing this pattern, Turretin makes the same point with his question, "What is the adoption which is given to us in justification," which he raises within his locus on justification. He answers, "The other part of justification is adoption or the bestowal of a right to life, flowing from Christ's righteousness, which acquired for us not only deliverance from death, but also a right to life by the

[84] Balthasar Hubmaier, A Christian Catechism (1526), q. 19.
[85] Heinrich Bullinger, De Testamento seu Foedere Dei Unico & Aeterno Heinrychi Bullingeri Expositio (Zürich: Christoffel Froschouer, 1534), fols. 8–10; Bullinger, A Brief Exposition of the One and Eternal Testament or Covenant of God (1534), in Fountainhead of Federalism: Heinrich Bullinger and the Covenantal Tradition, ed. and trans. Charles McCoy and J. Wayne Baker (Louisville: WJK, 1991), 107–8; Calvin, Institutes, 2.10.1–23.
[86] Peter Lombard, The Sentences, trans. Giulio Silano (Toronto: PIMS, 2007–2010), 4.1.7.
[87] Bullinger, Decades, 3.9 (2:338).

adoption with which he endows us."[88] Similar formulations appear in William Ames, William Perkins, John Davenant, Johannes Heidegger (1633–1698), and Franz Burman (1632–1679).[89] Theologians closer to the time of the assembly, such as James Ussher, also viewed adoption as a concomitant of justification.[90]

But treating adoption as a subset of justification was by no means standard. Other Reformed theologians, such as Juán de Valdes (ca. 1509–1541), Pierre Viret (1511–1571), John Owen, and John Downame, treated adoption separately in its own right.[91] Westminster divine Edward Leigh also followed this pattern. In contrast to most Reformed theologians of the period, Leigh treated adoption before the doctrine of justification in his explanation of the order of salvation. He placed adoption in a unique place in his exposition of union with Christ: effectual calling, conversion, faith, adoption, justification, and sanctification.[92] Leigh set forth this order because he believed that as soon as a person is united to Christ by faith, he or she is made a child of God through the sonship of Christ.[93] Leigh enumerates the manifold blessings of adoption by dividing them into two broad categories. First, sinners are cut off from their original familial bonds in the old Adam. Second, sinners are engrafted into God's family and have the rights and privileges of a natural son. This means that believers

1. receive the Spirit of sanctification (Rom. 8:15),
2. have the honor of sons (John 8:35),

---

[88] Turretin, *Institutes*, 16.6.1.

[89] Ames, *Marrow of Theology*, 1.18.5–8; William Perkins, *A Golden Chaine*, § 37, in *The Works of That Famous and Worthie Minister of Christ, in the Universitie of Cambridge, M. W. Perkins* (London: John Legat, 1603), 88; John Davenant, *A Treatise on Justification; or, the Disputatio de Justitia Habituali et Actuali*, trans. Josiah Allport, 2 vols. (London: Hamilton, Adams, and Co., 1844), 23.9 (1:175); Johannes Heidegger, *Corpus Theologiae Christianae*, vol. 2 (Tiguri: Ex Officina Heideggeriana, 1732), 22.62, 86 (pp. 296, 306); Franz Burman, *Synopseos Theologiae et Speciatim Oeconomiae Foederum Dei*, vol. 2 (Geneva: Johannes Picteti, 1675), 6.6.1 (p. 218); cf. Heinrich Heppe, *Reformed Dogmatics: Set Out and Illustrated from the Sources*, ed. Ernst Bizer, trans. G. T. Thomson (London: George Allen & Unwin, 1950), 552.

[90] Ussher, *Body of Divinity*, 200.

[91] Juán de Valdes, *Juán de Valdes' Commentary upon St. Paul's Epistle to the Romans*, trans. John T. Betts (London: Trübner and Co., 1883), comm. Rom. 8:14 (pp. 125–26); Pierre Viret, *A Verie Familiare & Fruiteful Exposition of the XII Articles of the Christian Faieth Conteined in the Commune Crede, Called the Apostles Crede* (London: John Day & Wyllyam Seres, 1548), fol. f1; John Owen, *Of Communion with God the Father, Son, and Holy Ghost*, 1.10, in *The Works of John Owen*, vol. 2 (1965; Edinburgh: Banner of Truth, 1997), 207–33; Downame, *The Christian's Warfare*, 2.21 (pp. 926–28).

[92] Leigh, *Body of Divinity*, 7.1–11 (pp. 485–534).

[93] Ibid., 7.5 (p. 510).

3. have the boldness of access and may cry out to God, "Abba, Father" (Eph. 3:12),
4. possess the inheritance of sons (Rom. 8:27) and therefore have a double right to heaven in terms of title and redemption.[94]

Leigh was unique in placing adoption before justification and in giving it a distinct place within the order of salvation.

Whether Leigh exerted any influence upon the assembly's deliberations remains a mystery, since the minutes mention little to nothing about its deliberations over justification and adoption. In some ways the Confession presents the same connections between justification and adoption as Bullinger and other Reformed theologians had argued: "All those that are justified, God vouchsafeth, in, and for his only Son Jesus Christ, to make partakers of the grace of adoption" (12). In other words, the Confession makes adoption a consequence of justification. However, the fact that adoption has its own separate chapter signals that the divines wished to identify it as a distinct element of the order of salvation in its own right. Some have argued that the Confession was the first symbol in church history to devote an entire chapter to the doctrine of adoption.[95] And so it is possible that in the wake of the publication of the Confession, theologians began to give the doctrine greater specific attention. This pattern is evident at least in works that exposit the Confession or catechisms, such as David Dickson's (ca. 1583–1663) *Truths Victory over Error* and Watson's *Body of Practical Divinity*.[96]

Issues related to the placement and separate treatment of the doctrine aside, the key point is that Reformed theologians viewed adoption as the consequence of justification; the one produces the other and its concomitants. In his catechism Samuel Rutherford asks the question, "Quhat ar the fruittis of our justificatioun?" He answers, "Adoptione to ceartainte of salvatione and Christian libertie."[97] Once a person is justified by faith in Christ, he or she is given right and

---

[94] Ibid., 7.5 (p. 511).
[95] Tim J. R. Trumper, "The Theological History of Adoption I: An Account," *SBET* 20, no. 1 (2002): 8.
[96] Dickson, *Truths Victory over Error*, 12.1 (pp. 85–87); Watson, *Body of Practical Divinity*, q. 21 (pp. 134–39).
[97] Samuel Rutherford, *The Soume of Christian Religion*, 23, in *Catechisms of the Second Reformation*, ed. Alexander F. Mitchell (London: James Nisbet & Co., 1886), 207.

title to eternal life and inheritance, something granted only to sons and heirs. The Confession offers a number of the benefits of adoption: "They," all those who are justified,

> are taken into the number, and enjoy the liberties and priviledges of the children of God, have his Name put upon them, receive the spirit of Adoption, have accesse to the Throne of Grace with bold-nesse, are inabled to cry, Abba, Father, are pitied, protected, pro-vided for, and chastened, by him, as by a Father; yet, never cast off, but sealed to the day of redemption, and inherit the promises, as heyres of everlasting salvation. (12.1)

Believers receive all of these benefits as a consequence of their justi-fication. In other words, because of the imputed obedience and satis-faction of Christ, received by faith alone, believers are designated as heirs of eternal life and possess numerous benefits only befitting of princes.

Conclusion

All in all, the Confession's chapter 11 sets forth the classic Reforma-tion doctrine of justification by grace alone through faith alone in Christ alone—*sola gratia*, *sola fidei*, and *solus Christus*. Justification, according to the divines, is a legal act by which sinners are pardoned of their sin and receive the imputed active and passive obedience of Christ, which gives them the status of righteous vis-à-vis the demands of the law, as well as constituting them royal heirs. Given the sur-rounding context of the antinomian controversies, along with political and theological pressure, the divines could have sought to create a role for the believer's good works in justification. This was certainly a genuine concern of some within the assembly, especially the divines who objected to the IAOC on the grounds that the active obedience negated the necessity of the believer's own observation of the law.

But with the real threat of encroaching Arminianism and Socini-anism, the assembly could just as easily have pushed the doctrine of justification back into eternity past to protect it from the perceived threat of the alchemy of divine and human cooperation in justification. Instead, the divines embraced neither antinomianism nor neonomian-

238   The Theology of the Westminster Standards

ism, but they occupied the middle ground of fidelity to the scriptural doctrine of justification. In the following chapter we will explore sanctification, a doctrine that was under attack from antinomian theologians. Like its doctrine of justification, the Confession's statements about sanctification were shaped not only by the biblical witness but also by the exigencies of the day.

8

Sanctification

Given the importance of the doctrine of justification, one of the chief flash points of the sixteenth-century Reformation, rigorous debates over the precise manner in which the doctrine should be expressed marked the assembly's activities. But the divines were also interested in other elements of soteriology. Since the divines believed that justification is one part of the unbreakable golden chain of salvation, they were equally interested in other doctrines of soteriology, such as sanctification. The divines feared the corruption of the doctrine of justification, but with the threat of Antinomianism they were similarly concerned about the integrity of the doctrine of sanctification. Hence, before we can survey what the Standards have to say about sanctification, it is important to situate this doctrine historically in the milieu of the antinomian controversies that raged prior to and during the assembly. We must also locate the doctrine in the broader context of the golden chain of salvation. These contextual issues will make up the larger portion of this chapter, as they are vital to understanding the Confession's doctrine of sanctification.

Historical Context

Historians have noted that the Westminster Assembly met in the midst of a civil war and that cannon fire could often be heard in the background over the assembly's sometimes-heated deliberations. However, there was another war being waged during the assembly's confession-writing labors, a war against antinomianism. In fact, during the assembly on a number of different occasions the names and works of reputed antinomian theologians were brought to the assembly's attention.[1] One petition addressed to the assembly complained of a number of individuals who, by preaching, printing, publishing, "& by other waies," were disseminating antinomian doctrine "in and about the citty of London" and perverting the "Doctrines of free grace, justification by faith in Christ & of sanctification." The petitioners were concerned that antinomians would "soone draw millions of soules to cast off the whole morall law of God."[2] The petition specifically mentioned four books:

> John Eaton, *The Honey-Combe of Free Justification by Christ Alone*
> Tobias Crisp, *Christ Alone Exalted*
> John Eaton, *The Discovery of the Most Dangerous Dead Faith*
> Anonymous, *A Sermon upon Rev. 3:18*[3]

But what were the characteristics and beliefs of antinomianism?

A basic definition of antinomianism is the idea that believers are completely free from the moral law because they are justified in Christ. However, within seventeenth-century theology a number of characteristics have been identified among those accused of this error:

1. Prime evidence of justification is the testimony of the Holy Spirit, not sanctification.
2. Faith is not the condition of justification but rather a consequence of it.
3. The sinner cannot prepare for salvation by his good works.
4. Christ does not merely renew the fallen sinner but completely overtakes him so that all is of Christ.
5. God in no sense sees any sin in his children.

---

[1] John Lightfoot, *The Journal of the Proceedings of the Assembly of Divines*, in *The Whole Works of the Rev. John Lightfoot*, vol. 13 (London: J. V. Dove, 1824), 9, 12, 71, 85, 299, 304, 308.

[2] John Lightfoot, "A Briefe Journal of Passages in the Assembly of Divines," August 10, 1643, in Chad Van Dixhoorn, "Reforming the Reformation: Theological Debate at the Westminster Assembly, 1643–52," 7 vols. (PhD diss., Cambridge University, 2004), 2:26.

[3] Ibid., 2:27; cf. John Eaton, *The Honey-Combe of Free Justification by Christ Alone* (London: Robert Lancaster, 1642); Eaton, *The Discovery of the Most Dangerous Dead Faith* (London: William Adderton, 1641); Tobias Crisp, *Christ Alone Exalted: Being the Compleat Works of Tobias Crisp, D.D.* (London: William Parkhurst, 1690); Anonymous, *Two Treatises. The First of Christs Counsell to the Angell of the Church of Laodicea . . . The Second of Holy Meditations, & Contemplations of Jesus Christ* (London: John Sweeting, 1642).

6. Christians can nevertheless live in sin.

7. The law of God is not necessary for one's conversion or for life after conversion.[4]

Edward Fisher (fl. 1627–1655) wrote in the preface of his *Marrow of Modern Divinity*, published in 1645, that antinomian controversies had begun some eighteen or twenty years earlier.[5] The antinomian movement in seventeenth-century England was no small event, though some scholars have described it as an "underground" phenomenon, given that it was forced to reside in the outer rim of English society.[6] Antinomianism was forced to the fringes and underground by the strict penalties that might be brought to bear against anyone preaching or publishing such views. But far from being monolithic, antinomianism took a number of different strands.

Samuel Rutherford (1600–1661), citing Romans 6:1 and 7:7, made the case that antinomianism first appeared in Paul's day, but that in recent years John Calvin (1509–1564) had opposed the Libertines, and Martin Luther (1483–1546) had debated Johannes Agricola (ca. 1492–1566) and the antinomians of Eisleben.[7] According to Rutherford, Anabaptist theologians were a significant fount of antinomian theology; he names Thomas Müntzer (ca. 1489–1525) as one reputed source.[8] Another strand originated when the pre-Reformation Luther edited and published a fourteenth-century mystical treatise, *Theologia Germanica*, which taught a form of perfectionism.[9] This treatise was influential upon Anabaptist figures such as Hans Denck (ca. 1495–1527), who some Westminster divines believed was another source of antinomian theology.[10]

[4] Barry Howson, *Erroneous and Schismatical Opinions: The Question of Orthodoxy Regarding the Theology of Hanserd Knowllys (c. 1599–1691)* (Leiden: Brill, 2001), 114.

[5] Edward Fisher, "To the Reader," in *The Marrow of Modern Divinity* (London: G. Calvert, 1645).

[6] David R. Como, *Blown by the Spirit: Puritanism and the Emergence of an Antinomian Underground in Pre-Civil-War England* (Stanford: Stanford University Press, 2004), 3.

[7] Samuel Rutherford, *A Survey of the Spiritual Antichrist* (London: Andrew Crooke, 1648), 1.1, 2; 1.10–11 (pp. 1, 2, 68–69); cf. John Calvin, *Treatises against the Anabaptist Libertines*, trans. and ed. Benjamin Wirt Farley (Grand Rapids: Baker, 1982); Calvin, *Contre la secte phantastique et furieuse des libertines, qui se nomment spirituelz* (Geneva, 1547); Martin Luther, *Against the Antinomians (1539)*, in *LW*, 47:99–120; Timothy J. Wengert, *Law and Gospel: Philip Melanchthon's Debate with John Agricola of Eisleben over Poenitentia* (Grand Rapids: Baker, 1997).

[8] Rutherford, *Spiritual Antichrist*, 1.3 (p. 6).

[9] Cf. Wolfgang von Hinten, *Der Franckforter (Theologia Deutsch): Kritische Textausgabe* (London: Artemis, 1982); Martin Luther, *The Theologia Germanica of Martin Luther*, trans. Susanna Winkworth (Mineola, NY: Dover, 2004).

[10] Rutherford, *Spiritual Antichrist*, 1.14; 2.84 (pp. 163, 193).

Antinomianism also originated from homegrown sources, such as the so-called Family of Love (aka Familists or *Familia Caritatis*), which had its genesis in the teachings of Hendrik Niclaes (aka Henry Nichols, ca. 1501–ca. 1580). The basic elements of Familist piety included a radical allegorical interpretation of scriptural narratives believed to be symbolic references to spiritual transformations that have taken place within the individual believer's soul. Familists also held that Christians have already been resurrected with Christ, which opponents took as a denial of the bodily resurrection. Familists also maintained that believers, by virtue of their union with Christ, have been returned to Adam's pre-fall state of perfection and are therefore free from the law and sin.[11]

Another form of antinomianism came from John Eaton (ca. 1574–ca. 1630), one of the leading English antinomians of the seventeenth century, among whom were John Saltmarsh (d. 1647), William Dell (ca. 1607–1669), Robert Towne (1592–1663), and Tobias Crisp (1600–1642).[12] Rutherford also identified Anne Hutchinson (1591–1643), a New England antinomian, whom he called the "American Jezebel," a reference to Revelation 2:20.[13] Eaton believed that God sees no sin whatsoever in the elect because they have been justified by faith.[14] Eaton, for example, writes:

> Papists, and all others that are ignorant of *Free Justification* (that is, how perfectly we are healed by the same in the sight of God) but are carried with a legall holinesse, doe pervert Sanctification and Repentance; that whereas they are not healing (for *by Christs stripes alone we are healed*) but are declarative, merely declaring to the eyes of men, that we are healed, beautified, and approved of in the sight of God, by being by Justification made *perfectly holy and righteous, from all spot of sinne, in the sight of God freely*; They confound them, and make Repentance, and Sanctification and holy

---

[11] Como, *Blown by the Spirit*, 38–39; Christopher W. Marsh, *The Family of Love in English Society, 1550–1630* (Cambridge: CUP, 1994), 1–34; Rutherford, *Spiritual Antichrist*, preface, 1.9 (p. 55ff.),
[12] Christopher Hill, "Antinomianism in 17th-century England," in *The Collected Essays of Christopher Hill*, vol. 2, *Religion and Politics in 17th Century England* (Sussex: Harvester, 1986), 164; cf. John Saltmarsh, *Sparkles of Glory; or, Some Beams of the Morning-Star* (London: Giles Calvert, 1647).
[13] Cf. Rutherford, *Spiritual Antichrist*, 1.7 (pp. 38ff.); Michael P. Winship, *Making Heretics: Militant Protestantism and Free Grace in Massachusetts, 1636–1641* (Princeton: Princeton University Press, 2002), 188–210.
[14] Como, *Blown by the Spirit*, 41.

walking, and such like to beautifie, heale, adorne, and approve us
to the sight of God; running hereby into a preposterious cark and
care to approve our selves to Godward, under the name of Sanctification and Repentance, by our own righteousnesse, wrought in
us by the spirit, as the Papists say, and by holy walking in all Gods
Commandments; confessing *free Justification* by the By, but flatly
preaching as if we were not made perfectly holy and righteous from
all spot of sinne in the sight of God, freely.[15]

For Eaton, the imputed righteousness of Christ eradicates any presence of sin in the believer. Eaton argued that Christ would never unite
himself to a "sow, or filthy swine," and hence God does not see any sin
in the elect.[16]

All of these sampled forms fall under the common label of antinomianism, but are somewhat different in nature. Those Anabaptists
indebted to *Theologia Germanica* held an optimistic anthropology, in
which believers are capable of perfection and therefore no longer in
need of the moral law. Familists had an exaggerated view of union
with Christ, one that virtually merges the believer with Christ, so
much so that they have been "Christed with Christ and Godded with
God."[17] And the likes of Eaton had an exaggerated doctrine of justification whereby the need for sanctification is virtually swallowed whole
by the imputation of Christ's righteousness.

One of the questions that naturally arises is, why was antinomianism so rampant in seventeenth-century England? There is no single
reason, but at least two factors account for its presence. First, in the
early seventeenth century some theologians had built an entire system
for the regulation of morality, which was extrapolated from the express
and implied meaning of the moral law as found in the Decalogue.[18]
Many preachers inveighed against traditional cultural practices long
in place since the Middle Ages, such as the casual use of oaths, fre-
quenting alehouses, or going to theaters.[19] An illustrative example of
this type of ethos comes from the title page of John Downame's (1571–

---

[15] Eaton, *Honey-Combe of Free Justification*, XIII (p. 379).
[16] Ibid., 65; Hill, "Antinomianism in 17th-century England," 165.
[17] Como, *Blown by the Spirit*, 39; Rutherford, *Spiritual Antichrist*, 1.25 (pp. 226–27); cf. Saltmarsh, *Sparkles of Glory*, 255–56.
[18] Como, *Blown by the Spirit*, 128–29.
[19] Ibid., 130.

1652) *Guide to Godlynesse*, where the image of a woman representing "repentance" stands over abandoned playing cards, a mirror, and a theater mask.[20]

A second reason lies in the rise of neonomianism, or works-righteousness vis-à-vis the doctrine of justification. If antinomians made justification swallow sanctification, then neonomians made sanctification consume justification. Theologians of the period rejected Roman Catholic, Arminian, and Socinian versions of justification, which argued that a person's justification hinges upon his own good works in addition to the works of Christ.[21] The impetus, then, was to eliminate any form of human cooperation in one's salvation so that it is entirely a work of God. However, other versions of neonomianism arose within congregations that were considered part of the broader Reformed church.

A high-profile version of this phenomenon occurred in the opposition to Archbishop William Laud (1573–1645). In previous generations the rise or decline of Reformed theology was largely tied either to the reforms of monarchs, such as Henry VIII (1491–1547) or Elizabeth I (1533–1603), or the deaths of Edward VI (1537–1553) and Mary I (1516–1558). But under the reign of Charles I (1600–1649) a number of the king's reforms were halted and reversed by his subjects.[22] In fact, under the Elizabethan and Jacobean reigns, Reformed doctrine flowed quite freely from the "official" pulpit of St. Paul's Cross, the London church where royalty and high ranking clergy, such as the archbishop of Canterbury, were regularly in attendance. However, after 1628 Reformed doctrine all but vanished from this highly visible pulpit.[23] Moreover, Reformed ministers were almost entirely passed over in appointments to bishoprics between 1625 and 1641, and Charles regularly appointed Arminians to Scottish bishoprics

[20] Ibid.; cf. John Downame, *A Guide to Godlynesse; or, A Treatise of a Christian Life* (London: Philemon Stephens, 1629).

[21] Council of Trent, sess. 6, January 13, 1547, first decree, chap. 7; Jacob Arminius, "Certain Articles to be Diligently Examined and Weighed," 22.16, in *The Works of James Arminius*, ed. and trans. James Nichols and William Nichols, 3 vols. (1825–1875; Grand Rapids: Baker, 1996), 2:728; Arminius, *Articuli Nonnulli Diligenti Examine Perpendendi, Eo Quod inter Ipsos Reformatae Religionis Professores de Iis Aliqua Incidit Controversia*, 23.16, in *Opera Theologica* (Leiden: Godefridum Basson, 1629), 963; *The Racovian Catechism*, trans. Thomas Rees (London: Longman, Hurst, Rees, Orme, and Brown, 1818), 5.9 (pp. 322–23).

[22] Peter Marshall, *Reformation England: 1480–1642* (New York: Bloomsbury Academic, 2003), 194.

[23] Ibid., 197; also Nicholas Tyacke, *Anti-Calvinists: The Rise of English Arminianism c. 1590–1640* (Oxford: OUP, 1991), 248–65.

through the 1630s.[24] While these actions undoubtedly produced political consequences, which culminated in civil war, there were definitely theological implications. That is, the perceived growth and spread of neonomianism produced an antinomian reaction. These two broader historical observations do not provide us with "silver bullet" answers as to why antinomianism arose so quickly, but they do give us context to see why the ideology grew.

The Place of Sanctification in the Golden Chain

In order to understand the place of sanctification, especially as it relates to justification and union with Christ, as these were two areas by which antinomians undermined the doctrine, it is necessary to set forth the common understanding of the golden chain, or *ordo salutis* (order of salvation)—the sequential manner in which theologians explain the benefits of redemption.[25] Recent analysis of the origins of the *ordo salutis* has claimed that it was a post-Reformation development foreign to early modern Reformed theology.[26] However, this analysis fails to examine the issue of the *ordo* from the vantage point of other terms, such as the *golden chain*.

First, it is true, *ordo salutis* became a technical term in post-Reformation theology, typically denoting the sequence of election, calling, faith, justification, sanctification, perseverance, and glorification, or some iteration thereof.[27] However, the term or its variants (*ordo salutis, salutis ordo, order of salvation*) were used by early modern Reformed theologians such as Heinrich Bullinger (1504–1575), Peter Martyr Vermigli (1499–1562), Girolamo Zanchi (1516–1590), and Augustin Marlorat (1506–1562) to denote the process of redemption.[28]

[24] Marshall, *Reformation England*, 197, 211.
[25] This section is based in part upon J. V. Fesko, "Romans 8:29–30 and the Question of the *Ordo Salutis*," *Journal of Reformed Theology* 8 (2014): 35–60.
[26] Richard B. Gaffin Jr., "Biblical Theology and the Westminster Standards," *WTJ* 65 (2003): 173; Gaffin, *By Faith, Not by Sight: Paul and the Order of Salvation* (Milton Keynes: Paternoster, 2006), 18; William B. Evans, *Imputation and Impartation: Union with Christ in American Reformed Theology* (Eugene, OR: Wipf & Stock, 2008), 265.
[27] Cf. Richard A. Muller, *Calvin and the Reformed Tradition: Studies on the Work of Christ and the Order of Salvation* (Grand Rapids: Baker, 2012), 202–43; Louis Berkhof, *Systematic Theology: New Combined Edition* (Grand Rapids: Eerdmans, 1996), 415–22; J. V. Fesko, *Union with Christ and Justification in Early Modern Reformed Theology (1517–1700)* (Göttingen: Vandenhoeck & Ruprecht, 2012), 53–102.
[28] Heinrich Bullinger, *In Divinum Iesu Christi Domini Nostri Evangelium Secundum Ioannem* (Zurich: Frosch, 1543), 4.8 (p. 103); Peter Martyr Vermigli, *In Primum Librum Mosis, Qui Vulgo*

Second, other terminology should be taken into account when examining the question of the *ordo salutis*, such as the *golden chain*. Robert Barclay (1648–1690), a seventeenth-century Quaker theologian, confirms the connection between the two terms. Concerning Romans 8:30, Barclay writes, "This is commonly called the *golden chain*, as being acknowledged to comprehend the method and order of Salvation."[29] The two terms, then, *ordo salutis* and *golden chain*, were used interchangeably. The common citation of Romans 8:30 for both terms (*ordo salutis* and *catena aurea*, or golden chain) opens another vista upon the *ordo* that has largely been ignored.

The first and perhaps best-known illustration of this point comes from William Perkins (1558–1602) and his *Golden Chaine* (1592). Perkins's work was erroneously characterized as a predestinarian system where every doctrine was deduced from the one doctrine of election, but more responsible scholarship has identified it as a schematized *ordo salutis*.[30] Given his *Golden Chaine*, people typically identify Perkins almost exclusively with the *ordo salutis*. But it may come as a surprise that, like his predecessors, Perkins also prominently affirmed the doctrine of union with Christ. In fact, Heinrich Heppe (1820–1879) explained that union with Christ is one of the chief themes of Perkins's theology.[31] A contemporary of Perkins, Herman Rennecher (b. 1550), also wrote a treatise by a similar name, *Aurea Salutis Catena* (1597).[32] The works of Rennecher and Perkins were anticipated by Theodore Beza's (1519–1605) *Summa Totius Christianismi*. Beza's intent was to show the order of causes of salvation and damnation, not to set forth an entire system of doctrine as some have alleged.[33] Beza's little work

Genesis Dicitur (1569; Zurich: Excudebat Christophorus Froschouerus, 1579), 31–32; Hieronymi Zanchii, *De Tribus Elohim, Aeterno Patre, Filio, et Spiritu Sancto, Uno Eodemque Iehova* (Neustadt an der Weinstrasse: Typis Matthaei Harnisii, 1589), 4.3.4 (p. 85); Augustin Marlorat, *A Catholike and Ecclesiasticall Exposition of the Holy Gospell after S. John*, trans. Thomas Timme Minister (London: Thomas Marshe, 1575), 559.

[29] William Barclay, *An Apology for the True Christian Divinity, as the Same Is Held Forth, and Preached by the People, Called, in Scorn, Quakers* (Aberdeen: John Forbes, 1678), 145.

[30] Richard A. Muller, "Perkins' *A Golden Chaine*: Predestinarian System or Schematized *Ordo salutis*?" *SCJ* 9, no. 1 (1978): 68–81.

[31] Heinrich Heppe, *Geschichte des Pietismus und der Mystik in der Reformierten Kirche* (Leiden: Brill, 1879), 24–26; also see Richard A. Muller, *Christ and the Decree: Christology and Predestination in Reformed Theology from Calvin to Perkins* (Grand Rapids: Baker, 1986), 131–32.

[32] Herman Rennecher, *Aurea Salutis Catena* (Lichae, 1597); Rennecher, *The Golden Chayne of Salvation* (London, 1604).

[33] For relevant literature, see Richard A. Muller, "The Use and Abuse of a Document: Beza's *Tabula Praedestinationis*, The Bolsec Controversy, and the Origins of Reformed Orthodoxy," in *Protestant*

includes a chart, much like the chart in Perkin's *Golden Chaine*, which was intended to be read from the bottom to the top; in other words, the reader is supposed to progress in the same way Paul proceeds in Romans:

> Unless something prevents them, they should begin at the lowest degrees and so ascend up to the highest (as Paul in his epistle to the Romans which is the right order and way to proceed in matters of theology, from the law to the remission of sins, and then by degrees as he gradually progresses to the highest degree) or else let them consist in that point which is most agreeable to Scripture or matter which they have in hand, rather than begin at the very top [and] descend to the bottom.[34]

In Beza's mind, he was following the order of degrees (or causes) found not simply in Romans 8:30, but also in the entirety of Romans. This is evidence that Beza was not merely proof texting. Some have accused theologians of basing the whole *ordo* upon one isolated text of Scripture.[35] However, when read in context, early modern Reformed appeals to Romans 8:29–30 were merely the tip of the exegetical iceberg; Reformed theologians appealed to a host of texts to establish the nature and characteristics of the golden chain.[36]

More evidence surfaces in the early seventeenth-century characterization of the work of another well-known early orthodox Scottish Reformed theologian, Robert Rollock (ca. 1555–1599). Rollock was known both in Scotland and abroad on the Continent, as is evidenced by Beza's hearty approval of Rollock's commentaries on Romans and Ephesians:

Scholasticism: Essays in Reassessment, ed. Carl R. Trueman and R. Scott Clark (Carlisle: Paternoster, 1999), 33–35.

[34] Theodore Beza, *Summa Totius Christianismi, sive Descriptio et Distributio Causarum Salutis Electorum, & Exitii Reproborum, ex Sacris Literis Collecta* (Geneva: Iohannis Crispini, 1570), § 7; Beza, *A Brief Declaration of the Chiefe Poyntes of Christian Religion Set Forth in a Table* (London, n.d.). Cf. Muller, "Use and Abuse," 52–53. Note that the old English translation has been compared and amended, based on the Latin original.

[35] G. C. Berkouwer, *Faith and Justification*, trans. Lewis B. Smeades, Studies in Dogmatics (Grand Rapids: Eerdmans, 1954), 31–32; Otto Weber, *Foundations for Dogmatics*, trans. Darrel Guder, 2 vols. (Grand Rapids: Eerdmans, 1983), 2:337; Richard B. Gaffin, *Resurrection and Redemption: A Study in Paul's Soteriology* (1978; Phillipsburg, NJ: P&R, 1987), 137.

[36] Cf. e.g., Robert Rollock, *A Treatise of Our Effectual Calling*, 34, in *Select Works of Robert Rollock*, ed. William M. Gunn, 2 vols. (1844–1849; Grand Rapids: Reformation Heritage, 2008), 1:245; Francis Roberts, *Mysterium et Medulla Bibliorum: The Mysterie and Marrow of the Bible* (London: George Calvert, 1657), 1488.

For why should not I esteem as a treasure, and that most previous, the Commentaries of my honorable brother, Master Rollock, upon the Epistle to the Romans and Ephesians, both of them being of special note among the writings apostolical? For so I judge them And I pray you, take it to be spoken without all flattery or partiality, that I never read or met with any thing in this kind of interpretation more pithily, elegantly, and judiciously written.[37]

If Beza read the commentaries, which is a likely scenario, he would have been exposed to Rollock's explanation of Romans 8:30, in which he describes this verse as that which contains a chain of gold that briefly elaborates the benefits of God. For Rollock, this text is a *locus classicus* ("classic place") or *sedes doctrinae* ("chair passage for a doctrine") for the golden chain. Rollock treats the foreknowledge and predestination of God, predestination to death, how the elect are called by the decree, effectual calling, sin, free will, the covenant of God, faith, hope, repentance, the sacraments, the church, justification and glorification, and good works. Rollock then moves on to exegete the verse that follows Romans 8:30.[38]

In addition to Perkins, Rennecher, Beza, and Rollock, a host of theologians employ the term *golden chain* in reference to the *ordo salutis*. The *ordo* is therefore a familiar doctrine well before the eighteenth century. Theologians who employ the term *golden chain* in its English or Latin forms, for example, include, but are not limited to, William Whitaker (1547–1595), Richard Turnbull (d. 1593), John Downame, William Pemble (1591–1623), Richard Sibbes (1577–1635), George Walker (1581–1651), Thomas Edwards (1599–1647), Edward Leigh (1602–1671), John Arrowsmith (1602–1659), Franciscus Gomarus (1563–1641), Samuel Annesley (1620–1696), Francis Turretin (1623–1687), Melchior Leydekker (1642–1712), and Leonard Rijssen (ca. 1636–1700).[39]

---

[37] Theodore Beza, "Master Beza's Epistle," in *Select Works of Robert Rollock*, ed. William M. Gunn, 2 vols. (repr.; Grand Rapids: Reformation Heritage, 2008), 1:10.

[38] Rollock, *Works*, 1:lxxii n2; cf. Rollock, *Analysis Dialectica . . . in Pauli Apolstoi Epistolam ad Romanos* (Edinburgi, 1594), 138–218.

[39] William Whitaker, *An Answere to the Ten Reasons of Edmund Campian* (London: Felix Kyngston, 1606), 234; Richard Turnbull, *An Exposition upon the Canonicall Epistle of Saint James* (London: John Windet, 1606), 122; John Downame, *The Christian Warfare against the Devil World and Flesh* (London: William Stansby, 1634), 158; Downame, *The Summe of Sacred Divinitie* (London: William Barret, 1620), 299–300, 453; William Pemble, *Vindiciae Fidei; or, A treatise of justification by faith* (Oxford: John Adams, Edward and John Forrest, 1659), 154; Richard Sibbes, *A Breathing after God* (London: R. M., 1639), 148; George Walker, *Socinianisme in the Fundamentall Point of Justification*

Nevertheless, some historians have criticized the Westminster Confession because it supposedly embraces the *ordo salutis* apart from the doctrine of union with Christ. T. F. Torrance (1913–2007), for example, has argued that the Confession embraces the medieval notion of the *ordo salutis*, which means that various stages of grace eventually lead to union with Christ.[40] Torrance argues that such a pattern is the polar opposite of John Calvin, who held that believers are first united to Christ and therefore, being united to him, share in all of his benefits. Torrance claims that because the Standards embrace federal theology, they produce a very legalistic and constitutional character, one marked by frigid logical precision.[41] Some historians contend, therefore, that the *ordo* is absent from early modern Reformed theology because that theology was more in favor of articulating soteriology in terms of union with Christ.[42] Torrance claims that union with Christ is absent from the Standards because it is set forth in terms of an *ordo salutis*. A better answer to this issue is to recognize the middle ground, namely, the Standards embrace both the *ordo salutis* and union with Christ.

The presence and compatibility of both ideas is evident first by the overall structure of the Confession. In its treatment of soteriology the Confession begins with effectual calling (10), which includes regeneration (10.2; cf. 13.1), and is followed by justification (11), adoption (12), and sanctification (13).[43] These elements of soteriology are discussed in a logical and orderly fashion within the broader context of chap-

---

Discovered, and Confuted (London: John Bartlet, 1641), 346; Thomas Edwards, *The Third Part of Gangraena: or, A New and Higher Discovery of the Errors, Heresies, Blasphemies, and Insolent Proceedings of the Sectaries of These Times* (London: Ralph Smith, 1646), 13; Edward Leigh, *A Treatise of Divinity Consisting of Three Bookes* (London: William Lee, 1646), 5; Franciscus Gomarus, *Selectorum Evangelii Iohannis locorum Illustratio*, in *Opera Theologica Omnia* (Amsterdam: Joannis Janssonii, 1644), 442; John Arrowsmith, *Armilla Catechetica: A Chain of Principles; or, An Orderly Concatenation of Theological Aphorismes and Exercitations* (Cambridge: John Field, 1659), 321; Samuel Annesley, ed., *The Morning Exercises at Cripplegate, St. Giles in the Field, and in Southwark*, vol. 5 (1652; London: Thomas Tegg, 1844), 270, 349, 532; Francis Turretin, *Institutes of Elenctic Theology*, ed. James T. Dennison Jr., trans. George Musgrave Giger (Phillipsburg, NJ: P&R, 1992–1997), 16.1.1; 9.4; 17.1.11; Turretin, *Institutio Theologiae Elencticae*, 3 vols. (Edinburgh: John D. Lowe, 1847); Melchior Leydekker, *Melchioris Leydeckeri S.S. Theol. Doctoris & Professoris de Veritate Religionis Reformatae seu Evangelicae* (Utrecht: Typis Rudolphi à Zyll, 1688), 579; Leonard Rijssen, *Compendium Theologiae Didactico-Elencticae* (Amsterdam: Georgium Gallet, 1695), 146, 159.

[40] Cf. similar criticisms of the *ordo*, see Gaffin, *Resurrection and Redemption*, 135–43.

[41] T. F. Torrance, *Scottish Theology: From John Knox to John McLeod Campbell* (Edinburgh: T&T Clark, 1996), 128–29.

[42] See, e.g., comments by Richard B. Gaffin Jr., "Union with Christ: Some Biblical and Theological Reflections," in *Always Reforming: Explorations in Systematic Theology*, ed. A. T. B. McGowan (Leicester: Apollos, 2006), 280–81.

[43] On the inclusion of regeneration with effectual calling, see Berkhof, *Systematic Theology*, 470–71.

ters 9–18 and materially embody the idea of the golden chain or *ordo salutis*. George Downame (ca. 1560–1634), for example, fleshes out this idea when he explains the *ordo salutis* (or sequence) in a manner similar to the order of benefits presented in the Confession:

> It hath beene the received opinion, and usuall practice of all *Orthodox* Divines, to hold and set downe in this order the degrees of salvation, which are wrought in this life, viz. Our vocation, justification, sanctification. And that in order of nature vocation, (wherein justifying faith is begotten) goeth before justification; and that justification, wherein we are made just before GOD by imputation of CHRISTS righteousnesse, goeth before sanctification: wherein we, being already justified from the guilt of sinne, and redeemed from the hand of our spirituall enimies, and reconciled unto God, receive grace to worship him in holinesse and righteousnesse before him.[44]

One of the common ways to refer to the various benefits of union with Christ was to discuss the "degrees of salvation."[45] This is the same language Beza employed in his *Summa Totius Christianismi* when he discussed the "degrees" of redemption until he progressed to the "highest degree."[46] In his abridgment of Calvin's *Institutes*, William Lawne, for example, writes, "For the Lord doth finish our salvation by these degrees of his mercy, when he calleth the elect unto himself, having called them doth justify them, having justified them doeth glorify them." The marginal note reads: "Degrees and steppes to salvation."[47]

The *ordo* is present not only in terms of the logical ordering of the Confession's treatment of soteriology but also in a number of key statements within those chapters. The elect are effectually called and are

---

[44] George Downame, "An Appendix to the Treatise of the Certainty of Salvation," in *The Covenant of Grace; or, An Exposition upon Luke 1.73, 74, 75* (London: Ralph Smith, 1647), 281–82.

[45] See, e.g., William Perkins, *A Golden Chaine*, § 15, in *The Workes of That Famous Minister of Christ, in the Universitie of Cambridge, Mr. William Perkins* (London: John Legat, 1616), 24; Peter Martyr Vermigli, *Loci Communes* (London: Thomas Vautrollerius, 1583), 1109; Vermigli, *The Common Places of the Most Famous and Renowned Divine Doctor Peter Martyr* (London, 1583), 105.

[46] Beza, *Summa Totius Christianismi*, 7; Beza, *Brief Declaration*, 52–53.

[47] William Lawne, *An Abridgement of the Institution of Christian Religion Written by M. John Calvin* (Edinburgh: Thomas Vaultrollier, 1585), 3.18.1 (p. 213). See also, Downame, *The Christian Warfare*, 2.6 (p. 98); Lucas Trelcatius, *A Briefe Institution of the Common Places of Sacred Divinity* (London: Francis Burton, 1610), 2.9 (p. 267).

entirely passive in this process and enabled to answer the call of God (10.1–2), and they answer this call by faith (14.1). And those whom God effectually calls, "he also freely justifieth . . . not, for any thing wrought in them, or done by them" (11.1), which excludes sanctification as any ground or reason for a person's justification. Consequent to justification, believers are made "partakers of the grace of Adoption" (12). The Confession then goes on to treat sanctification and good works as flowing consequently from, not leading antecedently to, a "true and lively faith" (16.2). In the explanation of these various benefits, good works, for example, do not precede faith or effectual calling. Likewise, sanctification is not foundational to justification but subsequent to it in the Confession's treatment of salvation.

But the fact that the divines do not explicitly invoke the doctrine of union with Christ at this point does not mean it is absent from the Confession. For example, the elect are chosen according to the "eternal and immutable purpose . . . in Christ" (3.5). The Confession speaks of the doctrine of perseverance as a benefit for those "whom God hath accepted in his Beloved" (17.1). The emphasis upon union with Christ is most explicit in the Larger Catechism. In the questions preceding its explanation of salvation, the catechism asks, "What special Benefits doe the members of the Invisible Church enjoy by Christ?" It responds, "The members of the Invisible Church, by Christ, enjoy Union and Communion with him, in Grace and Glory" (q. 65).[48] The catechism then proceeds to explain the nature of the union that Christ and believers share: "The Union which the Elect have with Christ, is the work of Gods grace, whereby they are spiritually and mystically, yet really and inseparably joined to Christ, as their head and husband, which is done in their effectual calling" (q. 66). Hence, contrary to Torrance's claims, the divines do not posit a series of steps leading to union with Christ but rather argue that believers are united to Christ immediately upon their effectual calling.

Then Larger Catechism question 69 explains the nature of the communion that believers and Christ share: "The Communion in

---

[48] Note that question numbers are absent from the original version of the Larger Catechism but are provided for ease of reference. Cf. James Ussher, *A Body of Divinitie; or, The Summe and Substance of Christian Religion* (London: Thomas Downes and George Badger, 1645), 193.

grace, which the members of the Invisible Church have with Christ, is, their partaking of the vertue of his Mediation, in their Justification, Adoption, Sanctification, and whatever else in this life manifests their Union with him." In other words, the various elements found within the Confession (effectual calling, justification, adoption, sanctification, perseverance, and glorification) all manifest the believer's union with Christ. These different elements of salvation are not steps that progressively lead to union but are instead the constituent elements both of their union and of the unbreakable golden chain of salvation.

The assembly's *Annotations* on the Bible and the formulations of Edward Leigh illustrate these conclusions. The *Annotations* comment on Romans 8 by noting: "Seeing that we being justified by faith in Christ, do obtain remission of sins, and imputation of righteousness, and are also sanctified by the Spirit: it followeth from hence that they that are engrafted into Christ by faith are out of all danger and condemnation." The *Annotations* show that a person is engrafted into Christ by faith and receives the double benefit of justification and sanctification. The *Annotations* also state, "The fruits of the Spirit, or effects of sanctification, which is begun in us, do not engrafte us into Christ, but declare that we are engrafted into him." This statement hints at the idea of a logical order between justification and sanctification, as works do not secure one's redemption but are the evidence of a person's redeemed state. But further into the divines' commentary, hints give way to express statements. The divines acknowledge the reality of the believer's union with Christ, but they also explain the significance of Romans 8:29, where Paul "proveth by a *sorites* or golden chaine, the glorification of Gods children, no link whereof can be unlincked, because the fastning thereof is the work of Gods omnipotence."[49]

In the early modern context a *sorites* was a series of causes and effects in a serial or logical argument. In his commentary on Romans, Johannes Piscator (1546–1625) characterizes Romans 8:29–30 as containing "that golden chaine, that is, the degrees of the sorites."[50] One

---

[49] *Annotations*, comm. Rom. 8:1–4.
[50] Johannes Piscator, *Analysis Logica Epistolae Pauli ad Romanos; Una cum Scholiis et Observationibus Locorum Doctrinae* (Herborn: Christophori Corvini, 1595), 169: "Aurea illa catena, id est, gradatione & sorite." In another context, the same phrase, "sorite & gradatione" is used to denote

...

possible source for the use of this language in the assembly's *Annotations* comes from Giovanni Diodati's (1576–1649) annotations on the Bible, where he makes the following comments on Romans 8:29–30:

> Certainty of glory, proved by a *Sorites*, wherein we have the golden chain of salvation: where are the—Linke of the chaine, our Predestination, set forth by its Cause, Gods foreknowledge: *Whom he did foreknow:* ch. 8.29. End, our conformity in being sons by adoption, for the honour of his natural son set forth. . . . The middle Linkes 1. *Vocation*. 2. *Justification*, ch. 8.30. 3. Last Linke: *viz. Glorification.*[51]

Therefore in the assembly's *Annotations* union and the golden chain reside together.

A similar pattern emerges in Edward Leigh's treatment of soteriology. Leigh begins his treatment with the subject of soteriology and elaborates its two chief elements, union and communion with Christ.[52] The union between Christ and believers is not merely a relative one, a likely reference to neonomian views such as those of Richard Baxter, but neither is it an essential one, a reference to antinomian views: "Some make our Union with Christ to be only a relative Union, others an essentiall personall Union, as if we were Godded with God, and Christed with Christ."[53] Leigh contends that such hyperbolic expressions (i.e., "Godded with God") originated with Gregory of Nazianzen (ca. 329–390), were repeated by Luther, and then were erroneously employed by others.[54] The believer's union with Christ is more than relative because certain passages of Scripture (John 15:1–2; 1 Cor. 6:17;

---

a series of necessary causes (Franciscus Gomarus, *Analysis & Explicatio Epistolae ad Romanos*, in *Opera Theological Omnia* [Amsterdam: Joannis Janssonii, 1644], 65). In the same Romans context where Gomarus defines *sorites*, Vermigli explains Rom. 10:17 in the same manner: "This is called a sorites argument, from what is piled together, that which is gathered from the causes of the effects" (*Appellatur hoc argumenti genus Sorites, à coacervando: Causae quippe aggregantur effectis*) (Peter Martyr Vermigli, *In Epistolam S. Pauli Apostolis ad Rom. D. Petri Martyris Vermilii Florentini* [Basel: Petrum Pernam, 1560], 1039).

[51] Giovanni Diodati, *Pious and Learned Annotations upon the Holy Bible* (London: Nicholas Fuzzell, 1651), comm. Rom. 8:29–30.

[52] Edward Leigh, *A Systeme or Body of Divinity: Consisting of Ten Books* (London: William Lee, 1654), 7.1 (p. 486).

[53] Richard Baxter held to a relative or political union (see Richard Baxter, *Aphormismes of Justification, with Their Explication Annexed* [Hague: Abraham Brown, 1655], thesis 54 [p. 133]).

[54] Rutherford also has a section in his nearly one-hundred-page defense of Luther against the charge of antinomianism where he explains the hyperbolic nature of Luther's statements regarding union with Christ (Rutherford, *Spiritual Antichrist*, 1.11 [pp. 123–25]).

12) reveal that it is a real union. Other passages of Scripture liken the union to the mystery of the Trinity (John 6:57; 14:20; 17:21–23). And the union is actually wrought by the Holy Spirit (1 Cor. 12:13). But on the other hand, the union is not an essential one because, though Christ's two natures are essentially united to form one person, believers are united to Christ to form one body, not one person. Moreover, the one body is mystical, not natural.[55]

Leigh elaborates upon the specific nature of the believer's union with Christ by giving six points. The union is:

1. *Real*. Though we are on earth and he is in heaven, the same Holy Spirit mutually indwells us.
2. *Mutual*. The whole God-man belongs to the believer because of the marital union.
3. *Spiritual*. Christ's Spirit is given to and abides in believers.
4. *Operative*. Where Christ dwells he casts out Satan, takes possession of the soul, furnishes his graces, restores his image, communicates life, and gives strength so believers can bear their crosses.
5. *Intimate*.
6. *Strong and inseparable*. Death dissolves marriage but not this union.[56]

Leigh opens his treatment of soteriology with an explanation of the doctrine of union, but does not therefore reject the idea of an *ordo salutis*. He notes, "Our union with Christ by the Spirit is wrought in our Effectuall Calling."[57] In a subsequent chapter, Leigh treats the benefits that believers enjoy as a result of their union with Christ. In contrast to the Standards, Leigh argues that as soon as a person is united to Christ, ostensibly in his effectual calling, "he is made the childe of God in the Sonship of Christ."[58] In other words, for Leigh, adoption follows effectual calling and precedes faith and justification. Nevertheless, he explains that once a person believes, his sins are imputed to Jesus, Christ's righteousness is imputed to the believer,

---

[55] Leigh, *Body of Divinity*, 7.1 (p. 487).
[56] Ibid., 7.1 (pp. 487–88).
[57] Ibid., 7.2 (p. 489).
[58] Ibid., 7.5 (p. 510).

and he is acquitted from sin and death and accepted as righteous unto eternal life.[59] Leigh establishes the relationship between justification and sanctification by arguing that the former causes the latter: "The immediate effect of it [justification] is Sanctification, and the healing of our nature, *Rom.* 8.1."[60] This was not an uncommon way of explaining the relationship of justification and sanctification. Rutherford similarly writes: "But take Sanctification for holy walking in the strength of the grace of justification, and grace inherent in us; so we say, Justification and Sanctification ought not to bee separated, but both concurre to make us Saints; the one as the cause, the other as the unseparable effect."[61]

The Reformed tradition commonly explains the relationship between justification and sanctification in terms of cause and effect to avoid the error of Roman Catholicism, which confounds justification and sanctification.[62] Leigh cites several sources to explain why sanctification follows justification. First is the maxim of Augustine (354–430), "Good works do not precede justification, but follow justification." Second is the saying of Bernard of Clairvaux (1090–1153), "Good works are the evidence of secret predestination, omens of future happiness." And third is the opinion of Luther, "Outside the state of justification no one's good works can truly be commended as excellent."[63] But Leigh's

[59] Ibid., 7.6 (p. 512).
[60] Ibid., 7.7 (p. 520).
[61] Rutherford, *Spiritual Antichrist*, 2.73 (p. 155). Note, pagination in section 2 of Rutherford's work restarts.
[62] Leigh, *Body of Divinity*, 7.6 (p. 512). Cf. Peter Martyr Vermigli, *Predestination and Justification*, ed. and trans. Frank A. James III, The Peter Martyr Library (Kirksville, MO: Truman State University Press, 2003), 144; Girolamo Zanchi, *De Religione Christiana Fides—Confession of Christian Religion*, ed. Luca Baschera and Christian Moser, 2 vols. (Leiden: Brill, 2007), 21.4 (pp. 362–63); Gulielmus Bucanus, *A Body of Divinity; or, Institutions of Christian Religion* (London: Daniel Pakeman, Abel Roper, and Richard Tomlins, 1659), loc. 31 (p. 381); Bucanus, *Institutiones Theologicae, seu Locorum Communium Christianae Religionis* (Geneva, 1625), 31.38 (p. 325); Johannes Heinrich Alsted, *Synopsis Theologiae* (1627), 36 (p. 83); William Ames, *The Marrow of Theology*, trans. John Dykstra Eusden (Grand Rapids: Baker, 1968), 29 (p. 167); Ames, *A Sketch of the Christian's Catechism*, trans. Todd M. Rester (Grand Rapids: Reformation Heritage, 2008), LD 24 (p. 121); Downame, *The Christian Warfare*, 2.52 (p. 275); Downame, *The Summe of Sacred Divinitie* (London: William Barret, 1620), 2.1 (p. 300); Joseph Hall, *No Peace with Rome. Wherein Is Proved, That (as Termes Now Stand) There Can Be No Reconciliation of the Reformed Religion with the Romish*, 7, in *The Works of Joseph Hall, B. of Norwich* (1617; London: Ed. Bruster, 1647), 615; Thomas Cartwright, *A Confutation of the Rhemists Translation, Glosses and Annotations on the New Testament* (Leiden: William Brewster, 1618), comm. Matt. 25 (p. 120); Rennecher, *Golden Chaine*, § 31 (p. 243); John Davenant, *A Treatise on Justification; or, the Disputatio de Justitia Habituali et Actuali*, trans. Josiah Allport, 2 vols. (London: Hamilton, Adams, and Co., 1846), 23 (1:170, 172); Turretin, *Institutes*, 17.2.12.
[63] Leigh, *Body of Divinity*, 7.6 (p. 516). Leigh does not provide citations for the Latin quotations, but Augustine's maxim appears in his exposition of Psalm 31 (see Augustine, *Exposition of the Psalms 1–32*, trans. Maria Boulding, *The Works of Saint Augustine*, vol. 15, pt. 3 [Hyde Park: New

belief that justification precedes sanctification does not mean that the two benefits of union with Christ can be separated. Leigh writes, "Although we distinguish between Justification and Sanctification, yet we acknowledge that they are inseparable, and that one doth necessarily follow the other."[64]

At the same time, Leigh does not totally compartmentalize the different elements of union with Christ or posit some sort of temporal unfolding of the golden chain. Leigh notes that all of the benefits are received simultaneously in union with Christ, but he stipulates, "Sanctification is of the same time with Justification, but Justification doth in order of nature go before it, for all the graces of Sanctification are bestowed on a man as in Christ (Eph. 1.3) so one." This type of statement is common. Davenant, for example, observes, "This renewal of the heart pertains to sanctification, and is not *the cause*, but the *companion* of obtained justification; coming together in point of *time*, but subsequent in the order of *causality*."[65] Davenant makes a similar observation regarding the causal priority of imputation when he writes regarding imputation and remission of sins, "Although they are simultaneous as to time, yet as to the causality, the imputation precedes the remission, and is a necessary pre-requisite, that this remission may be obtained."[66] Anthony Burgess (d. 1664), one of the divines, makes a similar observation regarding the simultaneity of the reception of justification and sanctification but nevertheless assigns the "priority of nature" to the former.[67] James Ussher (1581–1656) also notes that justification and sanctification differ "in the order, not of time, wherein they goe together, *Rom.* 8.30."[68]

Beyond the question of the priority of justification to sanctification, Leigh explains that there was a debate between George Downame and Leigh's tutor, William Pemble. Pemble believed that sanctification precedes justification and was criticized for this. The precise nature

City, 2000], 364–65). And note that the Augustine maxim, or a similar version, appears in Zanchi, Vermigli, Davenant, and Rutherford (Zanchi, *De Religione*, 21.4 [pp. 362–63]; Vermigli, *Justification*, 151–52; Davenant, *Treatise on Justification*, 25 [1:195]; Rutherford, *Spiritual Antichrist*, 2.47 [pp. 62–63]).
[64] Leigh, *Body of Divinity*, 7.11 (p. 530).
[65] Davenant, *Treatise on Justification*, 24 (1:192).
[66] Ibid., 24 (1:178).
[67] Anthony Burgess, *The True Doctrine of Justification Asserted and Vindicated* (London, 1647), lect. 20 (p. 172).
[68] Ussher, *Body of Divinitie*, 202.

of the debate involves categories somewhat removed from contemporary Reformed theology, namely, the concept of an infused habit of grace.[69] Pemble argued that in effectual calling the "universall or generall habite of grace, containing in it all sanctifying graces is infused" into the believer. Downame, on the other hand, believed that Pemble confused effectual calling (or vocation) with sanctification.[70] William Ames (1576–1633) and Robert Rollock likewise note that there was a common confusion of regeneration and sanctification.[71] But Leigh thought the dispute could be resolved by employing a distinction:

> As Sanctification is taken for the act of the holy Ghost working holinesse into us, so it goes before Faith and Justification, so the Apostle puts it before justifying, saying *1 Cor.* 16.21 [actually 6:11] *But ye are sanctified, justified*; but as it is taken for the exercise of holiness in regard of amendment of heart and life, so it follows Justification in nature, but it is joyned with it in time. The Apostle *Rom.* 8.30 placeth Vocation before Justification, which Vocation is the same thing with the first Sanctification or Regeneration. See *Act.* 26.18.[72]

Leigh's point is that sanctification, broadly considered as the infusion of the habit of holiness, is antecedent to justification because this infusion occurs in a person's effectual calling. However, if sanctification is narrowly considered as the exercise of holiness, or the ongoing process of sanctification, then it must follow justification. In technical terms, Leigh makes the distinction between sanctification as an *act* (i.e., the infusion of the habit of sanctification) and its *exercise*. A helpful explanation of this point comes from Johannes Maccovius (1588–1644): "Regeneration," which in this context refers to *sanctification*, "is perfect in its parts, not in degrees." In other words, in the act

---

[69] Contemporary Reformed theologians have erroneously argued that language in the Confession deals with *definitive* sanctification, a category that was developed by John Murray (1898–1975) but supposedly anticipated by Calvin (Richard B. Gaffin Jr., "A Response to John Fesko's Review," *Ordained Servant* 18 [2009]: 111; Ralph Cunnington, "Definitive Sanctification: A Response to John Fesko," *EQ* 84, no. 3 [2012]: 234–52, esp. 240–45). To be certain, I have yet to find a single early modern Reformed theologian, confession, or catechism that speaks of a forensic aspect of sanctification, something that Murray himself acknowledged (John Murray, "The Agency in Definitive Sanctification," in *Collected Writings of John Murray*, vol. 2, *Select Lectures in Systematic Theology* [Edinburgh: Banner of Truth, 1977], 286; cf. Muller, *Calvin and the Reformed Tradition*, 208–9n27).
[70] Downame, "Appendix," 281–82; cf. William Pemble, *Vindiciae Gratiae. A Plea for Grace. More Especially the Grace of Faith*, in *The Workes of That Late Learned Minister of God's Holy Word, Mr. William Pemble* (Oxford: John Adams, Edward and John Forrest, 1659), 15–29.
[71] Ames, *Marrow of Theology*, 1.29.6 (p. 168); Rollock, *Treatise of Our Effectual Calling*, 34 (1:244–45).
[72] Leigh, *Body of Divinity*, 7.10 (p. 530).

of sanctification the whole of man is sanctified; that is, the dominion of sin throughout the whole person is broken. But moving forward, sanctification is imperfect in terms of its degree.[73] Nevertheless, the point should not be missed: Leigh did not conceive of the golden chain as a series of temporal stages or degrees but rather employed it to make distinctions among the several benefits of union with Christ and to delineate the natural order or degrees of redemption.

Thus, in the exposition of the doctrine of sanctification one should keep in mind the agreement between union with Christ and the golden chain. Neither are they incompatible nor is the *ordo salutis* a late development in Reformed theology. Moreover, readers should keep in mind the doctrinally tumultuous context in which the divines expounded the doctrine of sanctification. On the one side was neonomianism and the danger of compromising the doctrine of justification, and on the other was antinomianism and the menace of injuring the integrity of sanctification.

The Standards on Sanctification

The first step to understanding the Standards on the doctrine of sanctification should begin with the definition offered by the Shorter Catechism: "Sanctification is the work of Gods free grace, whereby we are renewed in the whole man after the image of God, and are inabled more and more to dye unto sin and live unto righteousness" (q. 35). Sanctification is the moral and spiritual transformation of the elect sinner. The divines link sanctification to the first degree of the golden chain when they write, "They who are effectually called, and Regenerated, having a new heart, and a new spirit created in them; are further sanctified really and personally, through the vertue of Christs death and resurrection, by his Word, and Spirit dwelling in them" (13.1). As previously noted, there was some debate whether to designate effectual calling as part of sanctification or as a distinct element of the golden chain. But the Confession does seem to reflect the debate that

---

[73] Johannes Maccovius, *Scholastic Discourse: Johannes Maccovius (1588–1644) on Theological and Philosophical Distinctions and Rules*, ed. and trans. Willem J. van Asselt et al. (Apeldoorn: Instituut voor Reformatieonderzoek, 2009), 14 (p. 239).

Leigh mentions when it says that those who are "effectually called, and Regenerated . . . are further sanctified."

The Larger Catechism elaborates upon the relationship between effectual calling and sanctification when it states that "the seeds of Repentance unto life, and of all other saving graces" are "put into their hearts," that is, the hearts of elect believers (q. 75).[74] The Standards do not employ the term *infused habit*, likely because the divines purposefully omitted reference to scholastic and academic language, but this concept lies behind this statement from the Larger Catechism, particularly with the language of "seeds of Repentance . . . put into their hearts."[75] Rutherford explains that Christ has met the legal requirements that stand against elect sinners in his "satisfactory punishment," but also asks how the "physicall inherency and essence of sin" is removed. Rutherford responds, "The essence reall [*sic*] of sin is only removed, as every other contrair is removed, by the expelling of sin out of its subject, and by introducing the contrair form, to wit, inherent righteousness, and the perfect habit of Sanctification and holinesse."[76] To appreciate fully the point Rutherford makes requires a brief exposition of the concept of a *habit*.

Historically the term *habit* originates with Aristotle's *Nicomachean Ethics*.[77] Aristotle explains that there are two kinds of virtue: intellectual and moral. Intellectual virtue is increased by instruction and therefore requires personal experience and time. Moral or ethical virtue, on the other hand, is a product of habit (*ethos*). He argues that no one has moral virtue engendered in him by nature. Aristotle uses a stone to illustrate his point. A person can try to train a stone to go against nature by throwing it upward. One can throw the stone up in the air ten thousand times and not effect a change in the stone's nature. Instead, nature gives only the capacity to change, and this change can only be brought to maturity by habit.[78] In other words, a

---

[74] Cf. Gaffin, who disapproves of this type of language and configuration in the "traditional *ordo salutis*," and critically cites Hodge, Berkhof, Kuyper, and Bavinck (Gaffin, *Resurrection and Redemption*, 140).

[75] See comments made by Edward Reynolds against the inclusion of scholastic language in the confession (*MPWA*, sess. 520,, October 20, 1645 [3:690]).

[76] Samuel Rutherford, *The Covenant of Life Opened; or, A Treatise of the Covenant of Grace* (Edinburgh: Robert Brown, 1654), 2.9 (p. 323).

[77] Maarten Wisse, "*Habitus Fidei*: An Essay on the History of a Concept," *SJT* 56, no. 2 (2003): 174.

[78] Aristotle, *The Nicomachean Ethics*, trans. H. Rackham, Loeb Classical Library (1926; Cambridge: Harvard University Press, 1968), 2.1.1–4; cf. Peter Martyr Vermigli, *Commentary on Aristotle's*

person can train himself to acquire a new habit and thereby change his nature.[79] In the history of theology the term *habit* was applied in three ways: (1) as a separate term, (2) in relationship to justification, and (3) in relationship to sanctification. It should be noted that when Reformed theologians employed the term, it was no longer used to denote something developed by training but rather something given by God.[80]

As a general term, *habit* means the spiritual capacity or disposition that belongs to one or both of the faculties of the soul: the mind or will. Theologians from the Middle Ages through the early modern period assume a classic Aristotelian "faculty psychology," in which the soul is distinguished into two parts, the intellect and will.[81] The term has been historically applied to both justification and sanctification. A *habitus gratiae* ("habit or disposition of grace") was a divine gift of God's grace infused into the soul so that it would become a part of human nature. The habit of grace was called *gratia iustificans* ("justifying grace") or *gratia sanctificans* ("sanctifying grace"). Historically Reformed theologians rejected these concepts insofar as they related to a forensic doctrine of justification. Justification was not on the basis of an infused habit of righteousness but based upon the *iustitia aliena* (the alien righteousness) of Jesus Christ, imputed by grace alone through faith alone to believers. In terms of justification, a habit of grace implied an intrinsic righteousness, which could not be a suitable ground for justification; the righteousness of Christ was seen as extrinsic and alien to the believer.[82]

A habit of grace regarding sanctification was a different matter for Reformed theologians. In sanctification righteousness was viewed as inherent vis-à-vis the work of the Holy Spirit. And generally speaking, Reformed theologians viewed sanctification not in terms of an infused habit, but rather in terms of cleansing (or *renovatio*). But the language of infused habits was not completely absent from early modern

---

Nicomachean Ethics, ed. Emidio Campi and Joseph C. McLelland, The Peter Martyr Library (Kirksville, MO: Trueman State University Press, 2006), 2.1 (pp. 287–97).

[79] Wisse, *"Habitus Fidei,"* 175.

[80] *PRRD*, 1:211, 286; Turretin, *Institutes*, 1.6.4.

[81] Cf. Peter Lombard, *The Sentences*, trans. Guilio Silano (Toronto: PIMS, 2007–2010), 2.27.1; *DLGTT*, s.v. *habitus* (p. 134); cf. Richard A. Muller, *"Fides* and *Cognitio* in Relation to the Problem of Intellect and Will in the Theology of John Calvin," *CTJ* 25 (1990): 212; *PRRD*, 1:355–59.

[82] *DLGTT*, s.v. *habitus fidei* (p. 134).

Reformed theology. An example is Rutherford's language cited above, which was not uncommon.

Thomas Hooker (1586–1647), an American colonial Reformed theologian, explains the manner in which believers receive the double benefit of union with Christ. In his explanation of 1 Corinthians 1:30, "Who of God is made unto us wisedome, and righteousnesse, and sanctification, and redemption," Hooker writes:

> Christ conveyes his grace two wayes; partly by imputing, partly by imparting: they are the termes of Divines, and I know not how to expresse my selfe better; but this if you will, partly by imputation, partly by communication: This is that I would have you to take notice of in the generall; they are both reall, but one is habituall; both these, both imputation and communication expresse a reall work of God upon the soule, but the last onely leaves a frame and a spirituall abilitie and qualitie in the soule; the conveyance by imputation doth not, it leaves a thing morall (as we use to terme it). These two, imputation, communication, are both in the Text; Christ is made righteousnesse, or justice, that is, hee doth justifie a sinner by imputation, and hee doth sanctifie and redeeme a sinner by communication; hee conveyes and workes some Spiritual abilitie, and leaves a Physicall change; when the Apostle saith, *Christ is made Iustice*, that is, he doth justifie a sinner by imputation, when he saith, *Christ is made sanctification, and Redemption*, that is, by way of communication; hee delivers the soule from the pollution of sinne, that is, sanctification; hee delivers the soule from the power and dominion of sinne, that is, redemption; This communication it is a Spiritual habit, or a spiritual power, or a spirituall qualitie or abilitie; (take which you will) left upon the soule.[83]

Hooker does not use the language of *habit* in connection with justification, because that would inevitably lead him to say that justification rests upon a habit of faith and infused righteousness. But he does employ the term *habit* to describe sanctification as the communication of a power, quality, or ability.

---

[83] Thomas Hooker, *The Soules Exaltation. A Treatise Containing the Soules Union with Christ, on 1 Cor. 6:17, the Soules Benefit from Union with Christ, on 1 Cor. 1:30, the Soules Justification, on 2 Cor. 5:21* (London: Andrew Crooke, 1638), 113; also Hooker, *The Covenant of Grace Opened* (London: G. Dawson, 1649), 71.

The Standards echo this language and the pattern found in Hooker in the Larger Catechism's explanation of the differences between justification and sanctification: "Although Sanctification be inseparably joined with Justification; yet they differ, in that God in Justification imputeth the righteousnesse of Christ, in Sanctification his Spirit infuseth grace, and enableth to the exercise thereof; in the former sin is pardoned, in the other it is subdued" (q. 77).[84] The catechism's use of the language of infused grace echoes the concept of habit. Andrew Willet (1562–1621), for example, explains that certain "Popish . . . distinctions of grace" must first be qualified before they can be used. He notes the differences between *gratia gratis data* ("freely given grace") and *gratia gratum faciens* ("sanctifying grace"), the latter of which makes people acceptable to God. Willet then writes:

> The grace which maketh us acceptable to God, they hold to be a grace or habite infused, for the which we are acceptable: wherein they err, in ascribing that to a created or infused grace, which is only the work of the free grace and favour of God toward us: this word (*grace*) is either taken actively for the love, grace, and favour of God; or passively, for those several gifts and graces, which are wrought in us by the favour of God; The first grace is as the cause, the other graces are the effects: the first is without us, the other within us: the first is the original grace in God, the other are created graces. Now we hold that we are made acceptable unto God, only by the first grace of God towards us, which is grounded in Christ, the Romanists ascribe our acceptance with God to the other.[85]

Willet is willing to allow the Roman Catholic concept of infused grace, but only in its proper place: that is, in sanctification not justification. Equally noteworthy is how he interchangeably employs the terms *habit* and *infused grace*.

---

[84] Cf. *PRRD*, 1:358–39.

[85] Andrew Willet, *Hexapla: That Is, a Six-Fold Commentarie upon the Most Divine Epistle of the Holy Apostle S. Paul to the Romanes* (Cambridge: Leonard Greene, 1620), 283. Cf. William Whitaker, *An Answere to the Ten Reasons of Edmund Campian* (London: Felix Kyngston, 1606), 225; William Fulke, *A Defense of the Sincere and True Translation of the Holy Scriptures into the English Tongue* (London: Aug. Mathewes, 1633), 2 (p. 131); Amandus Polanus, *The Substance of Christian Religion* (London: John Oxenbridge, 1595), 94; Pemble, *Vindiciae Fidei*, 2.3 (p. 171); John Davenant, *An Exposition of the Epistle of St. Paul to the Colossians*, trans. Josiah Allport (1627; London: Hamilton, Adams, and Co., 1831), comm. Col. 1:19 (p. 231); Pemble, *Vindiciae Gratiae*, 21; Thomas Watson, *A Body of Practical Divinity* (London: Thomas Parkhurst, 1692), 139.

A similar pattern emerges in John Davenant's commentary on Colossians when he writes: "The act of mortification attributed to us is nothing else than the *energia*, or operation springing from infused grace, even that which we have called the *internal* or *habitual* mortification effected by the Holy Spirit."[86] The use of the term *habit* in connection with sanctification occurs in a number of theologians, including Heinrich Bullinger (1504–1575), John Calvin, John Downame, William Pemble, Edward Kellett (1583–1641), Samuel Annesley (1620–1696), and John Owen (1616–1683).[87]

Edward Leigh was not the only theologian to draw attention to the debate about the proper relationship between effectual calling and sanctification. Richard Baxter (1615–1690) also took notice. Baxter contended that *conversion, repentance, regeneration, sanctification*, and *vocation* are terms all used to express the same work of the Holy Spirit upon the soul, and they contain only minor differences; Leigh makes the same observation.[88] In terms of vocation, or effectual calling, Baxter argues that it is sometimes taken for the act of God (1 Thess. 2:12) and is taken in a twofold sense: (1) common, when sinners are brought to an outward profession; and (2) special, when people are savingly converted to Christ. Baxter claims that the latter sense refers to the "first Effect on the Soul, even the Act of Faith itself above all other Graces, and following Obedience."

Significant, however, is Baxter's observation about the debate over the proper use of these terms: "Some Divines conceive that *Vocation* is a work different from *Sanctification*, because they conceive that it is only the Spirit's causing the first Act of Faith in the Soul, and by that Act a Habit is effected, and therewith the Seed of all Graces, which

---

[86] Davenant, *Colossians*, comm. Col. 3:5 (p. 33).
[87] Heinrich Bullinger, *The Decades of Henry Bullinger*, ed. Thomas Harding, 4 vols. (1849–1852; Grand Rapids: Reformation Heritage, 2004), 4.2 (3:100–102); John Calvin, *The Bondage and Liberation of the Will: A Defence of the Orthodox Doctrine of Human Choice against Pighius*, ed. A. N. S. Lane, trans. G. I. Davies (Grand Rapids: Baker, 1996), xxiv–xxvi, 211–12; Calvin, *Defensio Sanae et Orthodoxae Doctrinae de Servitute & Liberatione Humani Arbitrii, adversus Calumnias Alberti Pighii Campensis* (Genevae: Ioannem Gerardum, 1543), 202–3. Downame, *The Christian Warfare*, 2.31 (p. 192); Pemble, *Vindiciae Gratiae*, 19; Edward Kellett, *Miscellanies of Divinitie Divided into Three Books* (Cambridge: Printers to the University, 1633), 1.8 (p. 192); Samuel Annesley, ed., *The Morning Exercises at Cripplegate, St. Giles in the Fields, and in Southwark*, vol. 2 (London: Thomas Tegg, 1844), serm. 19 (p. 407); John Owen, *Pneumatologia; or, A Discourse concerning the Holy Spirit* (London: Nathaniel Ponder, 1674), 4.6.2, 31, 35 (pp. 411, 432, 435).
[88] Leigh, *Body of Divinity*, 7.10 (p. 530).

they call the work of Sanctification."[89] Baxter's description echoes the language of the Standards, especially its phrase "Seed of all Graces," which parallels the Larger Catechism's language, "having the seeds of Repentance unto life, and of all other saving graces put into their hearts" (q. 75).[90] However, more direct confirmation of this connection comes from Thomas Vincent's (1634–1678) commentary on the Shorter Catechism: "Our Sanctification is begun in our regeneration, and effectual calling wherein our minds are first enlightened, and our wills renewed, and the habits of all graces are infused."[91]

To be clear, though *habit* language conceives of sanctification in terms of the infusion of grace and a disposition toward holiness, the Confession clearly establishes the source of sanctification as Christ and the Spirit, in that believers are "really and personally" sanctified "through the vertue of Christs death and resurrection, by his Word, and Spirit dwelling in them" (13.1). In other words, believers are not inhabited by an impersonal force but are indwelt by Christ and are in union with him. William Bridge (1600–1670), one of the divines, repeatedly refers to the habit of infused grace in sanctification, but makes the following distinction: "Now if Christ were in a believer only by the habit of grace, and Christ in the soul were nothing else but the habit of grace; here were yet a great distance from Christ: but now, if Jesus Christ be really united unto each believer by his Spirit, here is a close union indeed."[92] Bridge's link between infused habits and union with Christ is not unique to Reformed theologians but has ancient pedigree dating back at least to Peter Lombard (ca. 1095–1160), which drew the interest of a young Luther.[93] Nevertheless, through the infusion of grace, the "Dominion of the whole body of sin is destroyed"

---

[89] Richard Baxter, *A Treatise of Conversion, Preached and Now Published for the Use of Those That Are Strangers to a True Conversion, Especially the Grossly Ignorant and Ungodly* (London: Nevill Simmons, 1658), 1.3 (pp. 6–7).

[90] Cf. Pemble, *Vindiciae Gratiae*, 20–21.

[91] Thomas Vincent, *An Explicatory Catechism; or, An Explanation of the Assemblies Shorter Catechism* (London: Thomas Parkhurst, 1673), 35.6 (p. 106).

[92] William Bridge, "The Spiritual Life," in *The Works of the Rev. William Bridge*, 5 vols. (London: Thomas Tegg, 1845), serm. 4 (1:373).

[93] Cf. Peter Lombard, *The Sentences*, trans. Giulio Silano (Toronto: PIMS, 2007), 1.17; Martin Luther, *Luthers Randbemerkungen zu den Sentenzen des Petrus Lombardus (1509)*, in *Werke*, pt. 1, band 9 (1893; Berlin: Verlag Hermann Böhlaus Nachfolger Weimar, 2003), 43. I'm grateful to Sean McKinney, who drew my attention to these sources (see Sean McKinney, "Chosen to Choose: Election, Grace, and Free Will in the Sentences of Peter Lombard" (MA thesis, Westminster Seminary California, 2013), 45–46.

and the habit of grace leads to actual "practice of holinesse, without which no man shall see the Lord" (13.1). The dominion of sin is broken, that is, it no longer has the believer in its control and grip. If the dominion of sin is broken, then it naturally follows that "Sanctification is throughout, in the whole man." But the Confession stipulates that sanctification is imperfect: "Yet imperfect in this life, there abideth still some remnants of corruption in every part: whence ariseth a continual, and irreconcilable warre; the flesh lusting against the spirit, and the spirit against the flesh" (13.2).

Such an affirmation has a twofold target. First, it is a direct rejection of a chief antinomian tenet of perfectionism. A number of antinomian groups taught that Christians, either because of the all-encompassing nature of justification or because of the believer's union with Christ, were completely and totally free from sin. The justified sinner was considered perfect and free from sin. But on the other hand, the statement also has implications for neonomianism, whether in its Roman Catholic, Arminian, or Socinian form. A cardinal teaching of neonomianism was the idea that a person's good works were somehow requisite for his justification, which presupposed the acceptability of the believer's good works before the divine bar. However, if these good works, which were the fruit of a person's sanctified state, were nevertheless tainted because of the abiding remnants of corruption throughout the whole person, they would never be sufficient for the person's justification. This is why, according to the divines, justification has to rest upon the completed work of Christ and not the believer's good works (cf. WCF 11.2–3). These conclusions are found in a broad cross section of Reformed theologians.[94]

Nevertheless, a person's imperfect sanctification during his life does not mean that it will always remain unfinished. The Confession specifies that there will be an end to the "continuall, and irreconcileable warre." The Confession continues, "In which warre, although the remaining corruption, for a time, may much prevail;

---

[94] E.g., Ames, *Sketch of the Christian's Catechism*, LD 24 (pp. 121–22); Ames, *Marrow of Theology*, 1.29.34–35 (p. 169); Rennecher, *Golden Chaine*, § 31 (p. 243); Watson, *Body of Practical Divinity*, 140; Leigh, *Body of Divinity*, 7.11 (p. 533); David Dickson, *Truths Victory over Error* (Edinburgh: John Reed, 1684), 13.2 (pp. 89–90); cf. Heinrich Heppe, *Reformed Dogmatics: Set Out and Illustrated from the Sources*, ed. Ernst Bizer, trans. G. T. Thomson (London: George Allen & Unwin, 1950), 565–80.

yet, through the continuall supply of strength from the sanctifying Spirit of Christ, the regenerate part doth overcome: and so, the Saints grow in grace, perfecting holinesse in the fear of God" (13.3). In the common theological nomenclature of the period, sanctification gives way to glorification. Upon a person's death, his soul immediately returns to God and is "made perfect in holiness" (32.1), and on the last day, soul and body are reunited and "made conformable to his own," that is, Christ's "glorious Body" (32.3).

Conclusion

Exploring the Confession's statements about sanctification in the twin context of the antinomian controversies and the golden chain provides the necessary backdrop for understanding several things. First, the divines were equally concerned about the twofold benefit of union with Christ: justification and sanctification. They believed that these two benefits were vital to the broader doctrine of salvation and held off the threats of antinomianism and neonomianism. At the same time, we can also peer into the window of the past and appreciate how the divines held certain categories together that moderns find incompatible. In this case, the divines held union with Christ together with the golden chain, or the *ordo salutis*, the sequential understanding of the various degrees of redemption. The divines did not, as some have claimed, maintain a temporal administration of the different elements of redemption but rather granted the simultaneity of their reception. But the divines nevertheless logically arranged them to explain how each benefit relates to the other. In this respect Christians are perfectly righteous in Christ from the vantage point of their justification, because they are justified on the basis of the imputed righteousness of Christ. But on the other hand, believers are imperfectly holy, and though they may struggle in their daily Christian walk, they will eventually be glorified, and every last vestige of sin will be finally, completely, and indefectibly removed from them. As we proceed in our survey of the theology of the Standards, we now must turn our attention to several key doctrines that pertain to the function of the law in the believer's life.

9

The Law of God and the Christian Life

The Christian's relationship to the law of God has a central place in the process of salvation. The topic of the law of God does not exhaust the subject of Christian life, but it certainly entails many elements connected with it, such as: How does the law relate to a person before he is saved and then after he is saved? Also, how, if at all, does the law regulate the church's relationship to the broader culture, especially the government? These questions reflect issues considered in the discussions of the previous chapters on justification and sanctification but merit further consideration. Reformed theologians, with few exceptions, were clear that the law of God has one function prior to a person's conversion, what is called the *pedagogical* use of the law—that which shows the sinner his inability to meet the law's demands. This function drives the sinner to Christ. The sinner does not offer his own good works in obedience to the law in order to justify himself. The sinner instead looks to Christ by faith alone and trusts in the perfect law keeping of Christ to secure his justification.

Once a person is justified, the law still has a function in the Christian life. Post-conversion, the law has a normative function for the believer; that is, it shows the Christian what type of conduct pleases God. This has historically been called the *third*, or *normative*, use of the law. Hence, in the Christian life there are the seemingly contradictory functions of the law, but they nevertheless coalesce in the doctrine of the Westminster Standards under two categories—Christian liberty and the continuing moral obligation of the law in one's sanctification. A related question is how redeemed Christians regard the role of civil government in the Christian life. Hence this chapter will survey what the Standards have to say about Christian liberty, the normative use of the law, and the role of the moral law for civil government. These different aspects of the law will also provide us with the categories to examine one commandment in particular, the fourth, to see how all of these doctrinal categories relate together.[1]

Christian Liberty

In discussions about Reformed theology one usually hears about the doctrine of justification by faith alone. The Westminster divines devote a chapter of the Confession to this cardinal doctrine of the Reformation. Intimately connected to the doctrine of justification is the subject of Christian liberty, to which the divines also devote an entire chapter. The Confession states, "The Liberty which Christ hath purchased for Beleevers, under the Gospel, consists, in their freedome from the guilt of sin, the condemning Wrath of God, the Curse of the Moral Law" (20.1). All of these freedoms—freedom from guilt, wrath, and curse—are a result of the believer's justification. In his compendium of John Calvin's (1509–1564) *Institutes*, for example, William Lawne explains that Christian liberty is, "as it were an appurtenance," or a subordinate part or adjunct, "of justification."[2] These two doctrines go hand in hand because justification secures the sinner's pardon for sin as well as the imputation of Christ's righteousness (11.1).

The Confession follows a well-worn path on the connection between justification and Christian liberty. The Second Helvetic Confession (1566), for example, speaks of Christ imparting to believers through faith his fulfillment of the law by the imputation of his righteousness and obedience (12.3) and then immediately segues to the manner in

---

[1] For an older but nonetheless useful survey of these issues, see Ernest F. Kevan, *The Grace of Law: A Study in Puritan Theology* (1976; Morgan, PA: Soli Deo Gloria, 1999).

[2] William Lawne, *An Abridgement of the Institution of Christian Religion Written by M. John Calvin* (Edinburgh: Thomas Vaultrollier, 1585), 3.19 (p. 216).

which the law is no longer binding: "The law of God is therefore abrogated to the extent that it no longer condemns us, nor works wrath in us. For we are under grace and not under the law" (12.4). This means that since the law has no claim upon the justified sinner, the guilt of sin, wrath of God, and curse of the law are effectively neutralized.

If proof texts are any indication (e.g., Ps. 119:71; Rom 8:1, 28; 1 Cor. 15:54–57), justification is a prominent source of a person's freedom from the law (such as with the citation of Rom. 8:1), but sanctification also stands behind it. The divines write of believers

> being delivered from this present evil World, bondage to Satan, and Dominion of sin; from the evil of afflictions, the sting of death, the victory of the grave, and everlasting damnation; as also, their free access to God, and their yielding obedience unto him, not out of slavish fear, but a Childe-like love and willing minde. (20.1)

Since the believer has been freed from the curse of the law as well as the dominion of sin, he is now freed to serve Christ in obedience. The justified sinner has been delivered from the law as a covenant of works (19.1–2). The Larger Catechism helpfully illuminates this point when it states, "They that are regenerate, and believe in Christ, be delivered from the Morall Law as a covenant of workes, so as thereby they are neither justified nor condemned" (q. 97). On this point one of the common distinctions theologians of the period employ is the law as a *covenant* versus a *rule*.

Samuel Bolton (1606–1654), one of the divines, explains that believers are freed from the law as a covenant but not as a rule.[3] If a person were under the law as a covenant, then he would be subject to its condemnation for failing to fulfill its obligations and hence would be subject to its curses.[4] But in and through Christ, who has met the law's demands, believers are freed from the maledictions and curses: "But now those that are beleevers, they are freed from the law, as a covenant of life and death. And therefore are free from the *curses and maledictions* of the Law, the law hath nothing to *doe* with them, as

---

[3] Samuel Bolton, *The True Bounds of Christian Freedome; or, A Treatise Wherein the Rights of the Law Are Vindicated, the Liberties of Grace Maintained* (London: Austin Rice, 1656), 25.
[4] Ibid., 29.

touching their *eternall* state and condition."[5] The divines stipulate that these blessings are common to all believers, whether before or after Christ. However, believers who live after Christ's ministry enjoy a greater dispensation of freedom because they have been released from the "yoke of the Ceremonial Law, to which the Jewish Church was subjected; and in greater boldnesse to accesse to the Throne of Grace, and in fuller communications of the free Spirit of God, than Beleevers, under the Law, did ordinarily partake of" (20.1; cf. 19.6).

Hence it follows from these doctrinal conclusions that if the justified sinner is free from the curse of God's law because "Christ hath purchased for Beleevers" liberty, then "God alone is Lord of the Conscience, and hath left it free from the Doctrines and Commandments of men, which are, in any thing contrary to his Word, or beside it, if [sic] matters of Faith, or Worship" (20.2). As usual, the divines offer a statement that does not appear to have a specific theological opponent in view. Nevertheless, this particular idea goes back to the Reformed church's long-standing debate with the Roman Catholic Church over the extent of church authority, especially as it pertains to the Christian life. This is evident in how this passage echoes similar sentiments from Calvin's *Institutes* where he writes about monastic vows: "It is a thing truly to be deplored, that the Church, after its liberty has been purchased by the inestimable price of the blood of Christ, should have been so oppressed with a cruel tyranny, and almost overwhelmed with an immense mass of traditions."[6]

Calvin offers the same line of argumentation presented in the Confession; namely, Christ has purchased the church's freedom, hence it is free from both the curse of the law and the commandments of men. Calvin explains, "This was the consequence of their rivaling each other in the contrivance of vows to add a stronger and stricter obligation to the common bonds."[7] Calvin believed that the only obligation that could be laid upon believers is the law, and therefore obedience to the will of God is alone necessary.[8] Careful attention to the Confes-

---

[5] Ibid., 28–29.
[6] John Calvin, *Institutes of the Christian Religion*, trans. John Allen (Grand Rapids: Eerdmans, 1949), 4.13.1; cf. similar conclusions in Bolton, *True Bounds*, 54.
[7] Calvin, *Institutes*, 4.13.1.
[8] Ibid., 3.8.4–5.

sion's adjectives is vital to understanding the boundaries of Christian liberty, in that no one may impose an obligation upon the justified sinner if it is in any way *contrary* to the Word of God or *beside* it in matters of faith or worship. A likely target in view here was *evangelical counsels.*

Evangelical counsels were derived from Roman Catholic teaching that distinguished between a *precept* (or commandment) and *counsel* (pious advice). The former implies obligation and the latter is left to the discretion of the one to whom it is given. Thomas Aquinas (1225–1274), for example, argues that counsels are given in addition to the commandments of the "New Law," that is, the commandments of the New Testament, in order to elevate one's spiritual standing or more quickly attain the status of one who is worthy of eternal life. The typical three counsels include vows of poverty, celibacy, and obedience.[9] Protestant theologians rejected these evangelical counsels from the earliest days of the Reformation because they perceived them as ways that Christians might somehow make satisfaction for their sins, or as acts of supererogation above and beyond what the law required of them.[10] In other words, Roman Catholicism was placing things beside or, in some cases, against the law of God.[11]

Calvin's comments about one of the evangelical counsels, the vow of celibacy, provide a greater context for the subject of Christian liberty:

> Now, it is evident what great superstition has for some ages prevailed in the world on this subject. One person vowed that he would drink no wine; as though abstinence from wine were a service in itself acceptable to God. Another obliged himself to fast; another to abstain from meat on certain days, which he had falsely imagined to possess some peculiar sanctity beyond others. There were some vows far more puerile, though not made by children. For it was

[9] Thomas Aquinas, *Summa Theologica*, IaIIae, q. 108, art. 4.
[10] Philip Melanchthon, *Loci Communes Theologici*, in *Melanchthon and Bucer*, ed. Wilhelm Pauck, LCC (Philadelphia: Westminster, 1969), 59–61; Augsburg Confession, 27.3, 54, 61–62; Calvin, *Institutes*, 2.8.56.
[11] William Pemble, *Vindiciae Fidei; or, A Treatise of Justification by Faith* (Oxford: John Lichfield, 1629), 7.2 (p. 262); also Andrew Willet, *Hexapla: That Is, a Six-Fold Commentary upon the Most Divine Epistle of the Holy Apostle S. Paul to the Romans* (Cambridge: Leonard Greene, 1620), 180; Thomas Blake, *Vindiciae Foederis; or, A Treatise of the Covenant of God Entered with Man-Kinde* (London: Abel Roper, 1658), § 11 (p. 62). There is the dispute, for example, about whether Christ's command to love one's enemy (Matt. 5:43) was a counsel (Aquinas) or a command (e.g., Melanchthon, Calvin).

esteemed great wisdom to vow pilgrimages to places of more than common holiness, and to perform the journey either on foot, or with the body half naked, that the merit might be augmented by the fatigue. . . . For whatever may be the judgment of the flesh, God holds nothing in greater abomination than services of human invention.[12]

Calvin levels his criticism against the Roman Catholic idea that monks could take vows not specifically commanded in the Bible either to earn merit toward their final justification or to advance into a heightened spiritual status in the Christian life. In this regard, the Confession echoes the Reformed rejection of such ideas in its chapter on "lawfull Oathes and Vowes":

No man may Vow, to do any thing forbidden in the Word of God, or what would hinder any duty therin commanded; or which is not in his own power, and, for the performance whereof, he hath no promise of ability from God. In which respects, Popish Monastical Vows, of perpetual singl life, professed Poverty, and Regular Obedience, are so far from being degrees of higher Perfection, that they are superstitious and sinful snares, in which, no Christian may intangle himself. (22.7)

The Confession's chapter on Christian liberty, therefore, is also intimately connected with its chapter on lawful oaths and vows.

The Normative Use of the Law

In the early days of the Reformation theologians were accustomed to speaking of two uses of the law: a civil and pedagogical use. But it was Philip Melanchthon (1497–1560), a Lutheran theologian, who first formally codified the idea of a third use.[13] In the 1535/36 edition of his *Loci Communes*, in contrast to the initial 1521 edition, Melanchthon presents three uses of the law: the civil (which applies to all men), the pedagogical (which reveals man's sinfulness and drives him to Christ), and the normative use (which is for those who are justified by faith,

---

[12] Calvin, *Institutes*, 4.13.7.
[13] Cf. Edward Engelbrecht, *Friends of the Law: Luther's Use of the Law for the Christian Life* (St. Louis: Concordia, 2011). I am grateful to my colleague Dave VanDrunen for drawing my attention to this work.

teaching them about what good works are pleasing to God).[14] When Calvin set out to write his own *Institutes* (1536), he followed Melanchthon's pattern and explained the law in terms of three uses—Calvin copied Melanchthon.[15] Shortly after this the three uses of the law began to appear in other works by theologians such as John Hooper (ca. 1495–1555), the Bishop of Gloucester and a Protestant Reformer eventually executed by Mary I of England (1553–1558). Hooper notes that the first use of the law is civil and external, that which forbids and punishes transgressions of political and civil ordinances. The second use informs and instructs man concerning what sin is, accuses, and condemns unless the sinner flees to Christ. And the third use "is to show unto the Christians what works God requireth of them."[16] Similar explanations of the three uses of the law appear, for example, in Heinrich Bullinger (1504–1575), Jeremias Bastingius (1551–1595), and Jacob Arminius (1560–1609).[17]

In this vein the Confession is emphatic about the Christian's freedom from the law as it pertains to his justification, and specifically the guilt of sin, the wrath of God, and the curse of the law. But Christians are not free from the law in every sense. In Bolton's distinction between the law as a covenant and as a rule, believers are freed from being justified by obedience to the law as a covenant, but the law is still a rule for the Christian life.[18] In his *Marrow of Modern Divinity*, Edward Fisher (fl. 1627–1655) explains that the law as a covenant no longer has a place in the justified believer's life: "For it being the proper office of the law as it is the covenant of works not to excuse and justifie in the conscience, but to accuse and condemn, in that no man fulfilleth it: therefore as it is the covenant of works, it must not come

[14] Philip Melanchthon, *Loci Communes (1535–36)*, CR 21:405–6; Melanchthon, *Loci Communes Theologici*, 49–57; Richard A. Muller, *The Unaccommodated Calvin: Studies in the Foundation of a Theological Tradition* (Oxford: OUP, 2000), 129, 244n75.
[15] John Calvin, *Institutes of the Christian Religion: 1536 Edition*, trans. Ford Lewis Battles (Grand Rapids: Eerdmans, 1986), 1.33 (pp. 35–36); Calvin, *Institutio 1536*, CR 29 (CO 1): 49–50; Muller, *Unaccommodated Calvin*, 244n75.
[16] John Hooper, *A Declaration of the Ten Holy Commandments of Almighty God*, § 2, in *Early Writings of John Hooper, Lord Bishop of Gloucester and Worcester*, ed. Samuel Carr (1549; Cambridge: CUP, 1843), 282.
[17] Heinrich Bullinger, *Epitome Temporum et Rerum ab Orbe Condito*, in *Daniel Sapientissimus Dei Propheta* (1565; Zurich: Excudebat C. Froschouerus, 1576), fol. 20r; Jeremias Bastingius, *An Exposition or Commentarie upon the Catechisme of the Christian Religion* (Cambridge: John Legat, 1589), 168; Jacob Arminius, *Public Disputations*, 12.4–5, in *The Works of James Arminius*, ed. and trans. James Nichols and William Nichols, 3 vols. (1825–1875; Grand Rapids: Baker, 1996), 2:198–99.
[18] Bolton, *True Bounds*, 26.

into the conscience, nor into the case of justification." Fisher invokes Wolfgang Musculus (1497–1563) on this point and his contention that, in this sense, the Ten Commandments are abrogated in the life of the believer.[19]

But then Fisher turns his attention to the question of the law as a *rule* in the life of the believer. Here he appeals to Martin Luther (1483–1546), who explains in his Galatians commentary that there is ceremonial and civil righteousness, but in addition to this there is a righteousness of the law by which Moses shows believers their duties, "in which respect they are to be admonished and urged; wherefore such doctrines and admonishons ought to be among Christians, as it is certain there was among the Apostles, whereby every man may be admonished of his estate and office."[20] Again, Fisher cites Musculus on the point that though the law of Moses is formally abrogated in terms of its demands, such a conclusion should not be understood to undermine the substance of Moses. A Christian is not free to engage in wickedness and ungodly conduct.[21] Fisher concludes his explanation with an appeal to Calvin, who maintains that though Christians are elevated above the law in terms of their justification, it is not at all superfluous for the Christian life.[22]

---

[19] Edward Fisher, *The Marrow of Modern Divinity* (London: G. Calvert, 1645), 121; cf. Wolfgang Musculus, *Common Places of Christian Religion* (London, 1563), fols. 119–20.

[20] Fisher, *Marrow of Modern Divinity*, 122–23; cf. Martin Luther, *A Commentarie of M. Doctor Martin Luther upon the Epistle of S. Paule to the Galatians* (Thomas Vautroullier, 1588), fol. 5. Samuel Rutherford has a nearly one-hundred-page defense of Luther against the accusation that he taught antinomianism (Samuel Rutherford, *A Survey of the Spiritual Antichrist* [London: Andrew Crooke, 1648], 1.11–13 [pp. 69–163]). Rutherford quotes a letter from Luther where he writes: "And truly, I wonder exceedingly, how it came to be imputed to me, that I should reject the *Law* of ten *Commandments*, there being extant so many of my owne expositions (and those of several sorts) upon the Commandments, which also are daily expounded and used in our Churches, to say nothing of the *Confession* and *Apology*, and other bookes of ours" (Rutherford, *Spiritual Antichrist*, 1.11 [p. 71]; cf. Augsburg Confession, 20.1–37; *Apology of the Augsburg Confession*, 20, in *The Book of Concord: The Confessions of the Evangelical Lutheran Church*, ed. Robert Kolb and Timothy J. Wengert [Minneapolis: Fortress, 2000], 235–37). Rutherford also argues that Luther materially embraces the threefold use of the law: "The Law according to *Luther* hath three speciall uses. 1. *That it may reveale sinne and wrath, and by this be a pedagogue to lead the sinner to Christ.* 2. *To be a rule of a holy life.* 3. *To discipline and compesce, with the fury and feare of wrath, hypocrites and wicked men, that they may be discipline externall, and not goe with loose raines after their lusts*" (Rutherford, *Spiritual Antichrist*, 1.11 [p. 86]). What is implicit in Luther and explicit in Melanchthon later became explicit in confessional Lutheranism (see "Concerning Good Works," 4, and "Concerning the Third Use of the Law," 6, Formula of Concord, in *Book of Concord*, 497–500, 502–3). In particular, concerning the third use of the law, the Formula of Concord states: "The law has been given to people for three reasons: first, that through it external discipline may be maintained against the unruly and the disobedient; second, that people may be led through it to a recognition of their sins; third, after they have been reborn—since nevertheless the flesh still clings to them—that precisely because of the flesh they may have a sure guide, according to which they can orient and conduct their entire life."

[21] Fisher, *Marrow of Modern Divinity*, 123; Musculus, *Common Places*, fol. 119.

[22] Fisher, *Marrow of Modern Divinity*, 124.

Such patterns of argumentation were common in Reformed theology and explain why similar points appear in the Confession. The Confession explains that believers are not under the law as a covenant of works by which they might be justified or condemned, but it stipulates that the law is of "great use to them, as well as to others; in that, as a Rule of life informing them of the will of God, and their duty, it directs, and binds them to walk accordingly; discovering also the sinfull pollutions of their nature, hearts, and lives" (19.6). The Confession employs the distinction mentioned by Bolton, namely, the difference between the law as a covenant and as a rule. As a rule, the law restrains corruptions by forbidding sin, and it demonstrates what sin deserves and what afflictions people might expect from their sins even though believers are freed from its curse.

Under this aspect of the normative use of the law early modern Reformed theologians often wrote of God's discipline or fatherly chastisement of his children, in distinction from his curse, condemnation, or wrath. For example, Anthony Burgess (d. 1644), one of the divines, distinguished between two types of God's displeasure, the one of an enemy and the other of a father. The former invokes God's holy hatred, and the latter his fatherly frown.[23] Correlative to this is another category by which Reformed theologians distinguished between legal and evangelical obedience to the law. Legal obedience is performing what the law requires under one's own moral power; no one, save Christ, has fulfilled the law in this sense. Evangelical obedience comes only by faith in Christ, the only one who fulfilled the law on behalf of sinners. Only through faith in Christ can Christians seek to obey God's law.[24] Rutherford explained that evangelical obedience arose in respect of the authority of the Lawgiver, a "meditatory and Evangelike obligation, from the sweet attractions and drawing coards of the secrets of Christs love" and from "Evangelike faith that purifieth the heart."[25]

The law as a rule, however, also shows "Gods approbation of obedience, and what blessings they [the regenerate] may expect upon the

[23] Anthony Burgess, *The True Doctrine of Justification Asserted and Vindicated* (London: Thomas Underhill, 1651), lect. 5 (p. 35).
[24] William Perkins, *A Commentary on Galatians*, ed. Gerald T. Shepherd (1617; New York: Pilgrim, 1989), comm. Gal. 3:10 (p. 165).
[25] Rutherford, *Spiritual Antichrist*, 2.37 (p. 37).

performance thereof" (19.6). Such functions of the law, as part of the normative use, are not "contrary to the grace of the Gospel, but doe sweetly comply with it" (19.7). As Samuel Bolton observes:

> The Law as it is considered as a *rule* can no more be *abolished* or changed, then the nature of good and evil can be abolished and changed. The substance of the Law is the summe of Doctrine concerning *piety* towards God, and Charity towards our neighbours, *temperance* and *sobriety* towards our selves. And for the substance of it, it is Morall and Eternall, and cannot be abrogated.[26]

Recall that Fisher cited Musculus, who claimed that the Ten Commandments were abrogated for believers because of their justification, but in terms of the commandments' *substance* they are still binding, which is the same point that Bolton makes above. While Fisher and Musculus do not use the specific terms (the law as a *covenant* versus a *rule*), we can distinguish between the abrogation of the covenantal administration of the moral law (e.g., the covenant of works), and the non-abrogation of the substance of the law, which is perpetually binding. James Ussher (1581–1656) similarly explains that the law directs regenerate believers because in this dark world they are naturally blind, and therefore the Word acts as a lamp unto their path (Ps. 119:105). The law is also a "prick" that incites believers to obedience. And lastly, the law keeps believers humble because it constantly reminds them of how far they regularly fall short of fulfilling it.[27]

The Christian and the Magistrate

The Christian's responsibility to the law of God is not limited to soteriology alone. Given that they embraced the threefold division of the law (the civil, pedagogical, and normative uses), Reformed theologians therefore believed that all people, Christian and non-Christian alike, were subject to and under the authority of the law in some sense. But the divines also affirm what was by this point a long-standing

---

[26] Bolton, *True Bounds*, 74–75.
[27] James Ussher, *A Body of Divinitie; or, The Summe and Substance of Christian Religion* (London: Thomas Downes and George Badger, 1645), 205.

distinction regarding the law of God—the threefold division of the moral, ceremonial, and judicial laws. Recognition of these divisions goes back as far as Augustine (354–430). He distinguished between a moral precept, such as "Thou shalt not covet," and a "symbolical" precept, such as the requirement to circumcise male infants on the eighth day.[28] However, Aquinas is often credited with formalizing the threefold distinction: "We must therefore distinguish three kinds of precept in the Old Law; viz. 'moral' precepts, which are dictated by the natural law; 'ceremonial' precepts, which are determinations of the Divine worship; and 'judicial' precepts, which are determinations of the justice to be maintained among men."[29] The Confession, like earlier Reformed symbols, recognizes these distinctions (19.1–4).[30] The Confession, however, makes a number of important qualifications.

The moral law was given in the covenant of works and even after the fall continues as a perpetual perfect rule of righteousness. It was also republished in the Decalogue in the Mosaic covenant (19.1–2, 5). The ceremonial law is slightly different, as it was given specifically to Israel with definite redemptive-historical purposes in mind:

> Beside this Law, commonly called Moral, God was pleased to give to the people of Israel, as a Church under age, Ceremoniall Laws containing several typicall Ordinances, partly of worship, prefiguring Christ, his graces, actions, sufferings, and benefits; and partly holding forth divers instructions of moral duties. All which Ceremonial Laws are now abrogated, under the new Testament. (19.4)

The ceremonial law has a redemptive and revelatory function as it points to the person and work of Christ in shadows and types before Christ's earthly ministry. Upon Christ's incarnation and ministry, it is abrogated.[31] In the assembly's *Annotations*, the divines offer the following comment for one of their proof texts, Galatians 4:1–3:

---

[28] Augustine, *Repy to Faustus the Manichaean*, 6.2, in *NPNF*[1] 4:167.

[29] Aquinas, *Summa Theologica*, IaIIae, q. 99, art. 4. *Pace* Fergusson, who claims the divines were following Calvin and his use of this distinction; the distinction significantly antedates Calvin and is the common medieval inheritance of the Reformation (Sinclair B. Ferguson, "An Assembly of Theonomists? The Teaching of the Westminster Divines on the Law of God," in *Theonomy: A Reformed Critique*, ed. William S. Barker and W. Robert Godfrey [Grand Rapids: Zondervan, 1990], 320).

[30] Cf., e.g., Second Helvetic Confession, 12.1.

[31] Calvin, *Institutes*, 2.7.16; John Davenant, *An Exposition of the Epistle of Paul to the Colossians*, trans. Josiah Allport (1627; London: Hamilton, Adams, and Co., 1831), 465.

By the elements of the world he [Paul] understandeth the corporal types and carnal Ceremonies of the Law, which are called elements or rudiments; because that God by them instructed the Church as it were by rudiments, and afterwards poured out his holy Spirit most plentifully in the time of the Gospel.[32]

Samuel Bolton explains that the ceremonial law was an appendix to the first table of the law and was an ordinance that contained precepts for Israel's worship as the church in its infancy. The ceremonial law had three purposes: (1) to keep Israel under hope; (2) to preserve the nation from will worship; and (3) to be a wall of separation between Israel and the Gentiles.[33] Francis Roberts (1609–1675) holds a common opinion that the ceremonial laws were required by God and imposed on Israel only "till the time of Reformation," a reference to Hebrews 9:10, which Roberts explains referred to the time of the New Testament. The ceremonial law "consisted of many vanishing shadows, and Typical Ordinances *partly* Typifying or Prefiguring The Person, office and benefits of Jesus Christ our Redeemer, the Soul and Substance of those shadows."[34]

Concerning the judicial law, the divines delimit its scope and function to Israel as a nation—it was not intended to be universally applied to all nations. The Confession states, "To them also, as a Body Politique, he gave sundry Judicial Laws, which expired together with the State of that people; not obliging any other now, further than the general equity thereof may require" (19.4). Some have interpreted this statement to suggest that the judicial laws of the Old Testament are still binding upon the nations, but this conclusion fails to recognize that the divines employ a technical term when they write of "general equity."[35] In short, *general equity* is another term for *natural law*.[36] Calvin, for example, explains this connection in the following manner:

[32] *Annotations*, comm. Gal. 4:1–3.
[33] Bolton, *True Bounds*, 71–72.
[34] Francis Roberts, *Mysterium et Medulla Bibliorum: The Mysterie and Marrow of the Bible* (London: George Calvert, 1657), 3.4 (pp. 689–90).
[35] Greg L. Bahnsen, *Theonomy in Christian Ethics* (1977; Nacogdoches: Covenant Media, 2002), 41–91.
[36] David VanDrunen, *Natural Law and the Two Kingdoms: A Study in the Development of Reformed Social Thought* (Grand Rapids: Eerdmans, 2010), 169; A. Craig Troxel and Peter J. Wallace, "Men in Combat over the Civil Law: 'General Equity' in WCF 19.4," *WTJ* 64 (2002): 307–18; cf. Ferguson, "Assembly of Theonomists," 329–34.

It is certain that the law of God, which we call the moral law, is no other than a declaration of natural law, and of that conscience which has been engraven by God on the minds of men, the whole rule of this equity, of which we now speak, is prescribed in it. This equity, therefore, must alone be the scope, and rule, and end, of all laws.

General equity, according to Calvin, is "natural" and "is the same to all mankind."[37] Samuel Rutherford makes this same point when he writes: "But we conceive, of the whole judiciall Law, as judiciall, and as it concerned the Republick of the Jews only, is abolished, though the morall equity of all these be not abolished."[38]

So, then, what does it mean when the divines write that the judicial laws of Israel have expired together with the State of Israel, not obliging any other now further than natural law might require? What is moral equity? The idea behind Confession 19.4 is that a person or government may employ the judicial laws that were given to Israel, but only insofar as they occur in natural law. Calvin explains this principle when he writes:

> For the objection made by some, that it is an insult to the law of God given by Moses, when it is abrogated, and other laws are preferred to it, is without any foundation; for neither are other laws preferred to it, when they are more approved, not on a simple comparison, but on account of the circumstances of time, place, and nation; nor do we abrogate that which was never given to us. For the Lord gave not that law by the hand of Moses to be promulgated among all nations, and to be universally binding; but after having taken the Jewish nation into his special charge, patronage, and protection, he was pleased to become, in peculiar manner, their legislator, and, as became a wise legislator, in all the laws which he gave them, he had a special regard to their peculiar circumstances.[39]

Calvin's point is that there are unique circumstances for Israel's situation in the Promised Land, hence God gave them judicial laws that

---

[37] Calvin, *Institutes*, 4.20.16.
[38] Samuel Rutherford, *The Divine Right of Church-Government and Excommunication* (London: John Fibld, 1646), 22.17 (p. 493).
[39] Calvin, *Institutes*, 4.20.16.

were peculiar to them and not universally applicable to the nations. Paul Baynes (1560–1617), a Reformed theologian who followed William Perkins (1558–1602) at Cambridge as a professor of divinity, succinctly explains: "For the first, we are free from them," namely the judicial laws, "as ordinances political delivered; they bind us, 1, as the perpetual equity of God, agreeable to the law of nature and moral, is in them."[40]

Samuel Bolton argues that the judicial law was an appendix to the second table of the law and chiefly served three purposes. First, it gave the people a rule of common and public equity, or justice. Second, it distinguished Israel from the other nations. And, third, it foreshadowed (or typified) the kingdom and rule of Christ. That which typified Christ's kingdom has ceased with his advent, but that which was common and of general equity remains in force. On what grounds does it remain in force? Bolton cites a common maxim: "Those judgments which are common and naturall, are morall and perpetuall."[41] One thing to remember is that theologians of the period were quite comfortable in appealing to natural law as a theological category. In his explanation of the Confession, David Dickson (1583–1663) argues, "All the Precepts of the Moral Law, belong to the Law of Nature, naturally ingraven, upon the hearts of men perpetually, and necessarly [sic] from Natural reason it self; Rom. 2.15."[42] Recall the number of references in the Standards to the "light of nature" and its function outside matters pertaining to soteriology (cf. WCF 1.1, 6; 10.4; 11.1; LC qq. 2, 60, 121, 151).[43]

Francis Turretin (1623–1687) makes similar observations and gives a number of examples of laws that are not universally applicable:

Such as the laws concerning the right of primogeniture (Dt. 21:17), asylums (Dt. 19:2), the Jubilee, the not sowing of fields with dif-

---

[40] Paul Baynes, *An Entire Commentary upon the Whole Epistle of St Paul to the Ephesians* (Edinburgh: James Nichol, 1861), comm. Eph. 2:15 (p. 162); Ferguson, "Assembly of Theonomists," 332–33.

[41] Bolton, *True Bounds*, 72.

[42] David Dickson, *Truths Victory over Error* (Edinburgh: John Reed, 1684), 20.5 (p. 146).

[43] On how conscience according to the light of nature falls short of true grace, see Thomas Goodwin, *The Work of the Holy Ghost in Our Salvation*, 6.4, in *The Works of Thomas Goodwin*, 12 vols. (1861–1866; Eureka: Tanski, 1996), 6:252–62; cf. Mark Jones, *Why Heaven Kissed Earth: The Christology of the Puritan Reformed Orthodox Theologian, Thomas Goodwin (1600–80)* (Göttingen: Vandenhoeck & Ruprecht, 2010), 62–64.

ferent kinds of seed, the not wearing garments of wool and linen and the like. Although they might have had a political end also, they will (because they were typical) cease to bind on that very account.[44]

Turretin goes on to comment that the Mosaic law is better than human laws, generally speaking, "But not inasmuch as they are founded upon the natural law, whose source is God. Therefore, when the Roman laws are preferred to the Mosaic, they are not preferred simply as enacted by men, but as derived from natural and common right they can be more suitable to places, times, and persons."[45] Some theologians, such as Rutherford, believed not only that the Scriptures are useful as special revelation but also that the Old Testament narratives function as a natural law casebook.[46] These types of opinions and distinctions are common in the early modern period and can be found in various Reformed theologians, such as James Ussher (1581–1656), Edward Leigh (1602–1671), Francis Cheynell (1608–1665), and David Dickson—which explains why this understanding of the judicial law appears in the Confession.[47]

These theologians agreed about the legitimacy of the category of general equity and that Israel's judicial laws had expired. But there was much disagreement regarding specific points of how to exegete and apply various passages of Scripture. David Dickson notes that some of the "otherwise Orthodox" erred because they maintained "that the whole Judicial Law of the Jews is yet alive, and binding all of us, who are Christian Gentiles."[48] Others, like Edward Leigh, believed that though blasphemy was a sin, it was no longer punishable by death. Leigh looked to Theodore Beza (1519–1605) as an authority in this matter, and argued, "We are not obliged (saith Beza) to the

---

[44] Francis Turretin, *Institutes of Elenctic Theology*, ed. James T. Dennison Jr., trans. George Musgrave Giger (Phillipsburg, NJ: P&R, 1992–1997), 11.26.5.

[45] Ibid., 11.26.10.

[46] John Coffey, *Politics, Religion and the British Revolutions: The Mind of Samuel Rutherford* (Cambridge: CUP, 1997), 153.

[47] Ussher, *Body of Divinitie*, 204; Edward Leigh, *A Treatise of Divinity Consisting of Three Bookes* (London: William Lee, 1646), prolegomena; Francis Cheynell, *The Divine Trinunity of the Father, Son, and Holy Spirit* (London: Samuel Gellibrand, 1650), 473–74; Dickson, *Truths Victory over Error*, 19.4 (p. 144). On the function and role of natural law in the early modern Reformed tradition, see VanDrunen, *Natural Law and the Two Kingdoms*, 67–211; Stephen J. Grabill, *Rediscovering the Natural Law in Reformed Theological Ethics* (Grand Rapids: Eerdmans, 2006).

[48] Dickson, *Truths Victory over Error*, 19.4 (p. 144).

Judicial Laws, as they were given by Moses to one people, yet so far we are bound to observe them, as they comprehend that general equity which ought to prevaile every where."[49] Not all shared Leigh's opinion. For example, John Cotton (1585–1652), who was invited to participate in the Westminster Assembly by the Congregationalists (e.g., Thomas Goodwin and Jeremiah Burroughs), believed that heretics should be put to death.[50] Cotton reasoned that if treason against earthly princes was justly punished by death, then this principle should especially apply all the more to treason against the Lord of heaven.[51]

Cotton produces several reasons why heretics, particularly Roman Catholics, should be put to death. First, he cites Leviticus 24:16, "He that blasphemeth the name of God, shall surely be put to death."[52] Second, if blasphemers are heretics, then so are those heretics that seduce people to worship false gods.[53] Third, death is a suitable punishment for a "soul murther."[54] Fourth, Cotton appeals to natural law, the *iustitia Britanniae* ("justice of Britain"), in that it is a crime to commit conspiracy or treason against the state. Anyone who would lead people astray and encourage them to embrace Catholicism would be guilty of treason because he would be sowing seeds of rebellion, inculcating rebellion among the king's subjects through the promotion of a religion contrary to the one professed by the king.[55] For these and several other reasons, Cotton concludes:

> For the use of the point, it may first serve to justifie the holy and righteous equity of all those laws above mentioned, whether in *England* or *Holland*, for putting Popish Priests and Jesuites to death. . . . Besides, are not *Moses* Morall Lawes of perpetuall equity, and therefore to be observed in all Ages? Is blasphemy more tolerable in the New Testament, or thrusting men away from God? Is it not as odious now as then? Is not murther of soules as dam-

---

[49] Leigh, *Treatise of Divinity*, prolegomena.
[50] See John Winthrop, *Winthrop's Journal, "History of New England," 1630–1649*, ed. James Kendall Hosmer, vol. 2 (New York: Charles Scribner's Sons, 1908), 71; for an overview of Cotton's views on these matters, see VanDrunen, *Natural Law and the Two Kingdoms*, 216–34.
[51] John Cotton, *The Pouring Out of the Seven Vials; or, An Exposition, of the 16. Chapter of the Revelation, with an Application of It to Our Times* (London: R. S., 1642), vial 3 (p. 9).
[52] Ibid., vial 3 (p. 9).
[53] Ibid., vial 3 (p. 10).
[54] Ibid., vial 3 (p. 11).
[55] Ibid., vial 3 (p. 14).

nable now as then? Is not conspiracie and sedition as damnable and capital now as then? Is not the law of retaliation as just in the New Testament as in the old?[56]

In other words, Cotton appeals to general equity to arrive at his conclusions. Cotton's arguments demonstrate that Reformed theologians agreed concerning the legitimacy of the category of general equity and natural law, but there was significant disagreement about its application.[57]

The Law in Action: The Fourth Commandment

Given the gathered data—the three functions (civil, pedagogical, normative) and categories of the law (moral, judicial, ceremonial), and natural law (or general equity)—one might think that each of the Bible's laws neatly falls under one particular classification. But this is not so. Some commandments, such as the fourth, concerned complex matters and transgressed a number of these different classifications. A second issue relevant to the Standards and the law in the Christian life is the question of legalism. The accusation that the Confession embodies legalism is both recent and historical.[58] Thomas Rogers (d. 1616), an Anglican minister, for example, complained that Presbyterians "have introduced anew, & more then either Jewish, or Popish superstition into the land . . . that the Lords day (even as the old Sabbath of the Jewes) must necessarily bee kept, and solemnized of all, and every Christian, under the paine of eternal condemnation both of bodie, and soule."[59]

In other words, the Presbyterian doctrine of Sabbath observance was supposedly novel and legalistic because it required the observation of abrogated Old Testament laws. Given frequent citation of Old Testament texts and some of the longer answers in the Larger

---

[56] Ibid., vial 3 (pp. 15–16); also Cotton, "How Far Moses Judicialls Bind Mass[achusetts]," in *Proceedings of the Massachusetts Historical Society*, vol. 16 (Boston: Massachusetts Historical Society, 1903), 274–84, esp. 281, 284.

[57] Cf. VanDrunen, *Natural Law and the Two Kingdoms*, 230–34.

[58] See, e.g., T. F. Torrance, *Scottish Theology: From John Knox to John McLeod Campbell* (Edinburgh: T&T Clark, 1996), 127–29; Holmes Rolston III, *John Calvin versus the Westminster Confession: Holmes Rolston III Calls on the Reformer Himself to Refute the Oppressive Legalism of the Calvinists and to Free 20th Century Man for Responsible Life with a Gracious God* (Louisville: WJK, 1986).

[59] Thomas Rogers, *The Faith, Doctrine, and Religion, Professed, Protected in the Realme of England, and Dominions of the Same* (London: John Legat, 1625), preface, § 3r.

Catechism, some might be inclined to agree with such an accusation. For example, question 145 of the Larger Catechism employs 350 words in its list of ways people violate the ninth commandment. On the other hand, seldom do critics take into account the historical context in which the assembly's exposition of the law took place. Few note that in some respects the Larger Catechism's exposition of the law is a literary genre unto itself, a document that was intended both for theological instruction and for case law for the civil magistrate. The historical context is vital, therefore, to a proper understanding of how the fourth commandment functions in the Standards.

At first blush, there is a noticeable difference between the Heidelberg and Larger Catechisms chiefly in terms of the word count. The Heidelberg Catechism says, in question 103:

> What does God require in the fourth commandment?
>
> First, that the ministry of the gospel and Christian education be maintained, and that I diligently attend church, especially on the Lord's day, to hear the word of God, to participate in the holy sacraments, to call publicly upon the Lord, and to give Christian service to those in need. Second, that I cease from my evil works all the days of my life, allow the Lord to work in me through his Spirit, and thus begin in this life the eternal Sabbath.

By way of contrast, the Larger Catechism quotes the fourth commandment in full, and then exposits the commandment over a series of six questions in more than five hundred words. This alone is not evidence of legalism, since the catechisms have different aims. A better parallel to the Heidelberg Catechism's exposition of the law is the Shorter Catechism's treatment—it is far more concise. However, as others note, there is a looming shadow over the assembly's exposition of the fourth commandment.[60]

By the time of the assembly in the 1640s the fourth commandment had become the center of a pitched battle where politics and theology intersected in a bitter contest over how the "Christian Sabbath," the Lord's Day, or Sunday was supposed to be observed. In

---

[60] Carl R. Trueman, *Histories and Fallacies: Problems Faced in the Writing of History* (Wheaton: Crossway, 2010), 92–93.

early post-Reformation England, Sabbath observance was already a subject of controversy. This is evident in Nicholas Bownde's (d. 1603) *Doctrine of the Sabbath* (1595), where he complained that the Sabbath was profaned by interludes (secular plays), May poles (setting up a pole in a communal area around which a festival was held and bonfires were lit), Morris dances (dancing celebrations historically rooted in Spain's expulsion of the Moores), archery, bowling, and the like.[61] In the wake of such works, many parish ministers sought to encourage their congregations to observe the Sabbath. However, when King James I (1566–1625) returned from a trip in Scotland, he found great discontent among the citizens. James believed they were discontent because they had been deprived of Sunday recreational activities. James subsequently issued his notorious *Book of Sports* (1618) in which he outlined various activities permitted on Sunday.[62]

The very issues raised in Bownde's *Doctrine of the Sabbath* were taken up in the *Book of Sports*. The latter book encouraged people to attend church and even rebuked "Recusants," Roman Catholics who refused to attend Protestant worship services.[63] The book, however, detailed a number of permissible recreational activities:

> That after the end of Divine Service, Our good people be not disturbed, letted, or discouraged from any lawfull Recreation; Such as dauncing, either men or women, Archerie for men, leaping, vaulting, or any other harmlesse Recreation, nor from having of May-Games, Whitson Ales, and Morris-dances, and the setting up of May-poles and other sports therewith used, so as the same be had in due and convenient time, without impediment or neglect of

---

[61] Nicholas Bownde, *The Doctrine of the Sabbath, Planely Layde Forth, and Soundly Proved by Testimonies Both of Holy Scripture, and Also of Olde and New Ecclesiasticall Writers* (London: Thomas Man, 1595), 131–32. Other works from this period include, John Deacon, *A Treatise Intitled; Nobody Is My Name, Which Beareth Everi-Bodies Blame. Wherein Is Largely Laied Forth the Lawfull Bounds of All Buying and Selling, according to the Infallible Line of the Lawes of the Lord* (London: Robert Waldegrave, 1587); John Sprint, *Propositions Tending to Prove the Necessarie Use of the Christian Sabbaoth, or Lords Day; and That It Is Commanded unto Us in Gods Word* (London: Thomas Mann, 1607); John Prideaux, *The Doctrine of the Sabbath* (London: Henry Seile, 1634); William Twisse, *Of the Morality of the Fourth Commandment, as Still in Force to Binde Christians* (London: John Rothwell, 1641); Twisse, *The Christian Sabbath Defended* (London: Thomas Pierrepont, 1652); George Walker, *The Doctrine of the Sabbath* (Amsterdam, 1628); cf. Kenneth L. Parker, *The English Sabbath: A Study of the Doctrine and Discipline from the Reformation to the Civil War* (Cambridge: CUP, 1988), 15, 217.

[62] King James I, *The King's Majesties Declaration to His Subjects, concerning Lawful Sports to Be Used (1618)* (1618; Philadelphia: Benj. Ashworth, 1866), preface.

[63] Ibid., 9.

divine Service: And that women shall have leave to carry rushes to the Church for the decoring of it, according to their old custome.[64]

The list is not exhaustive, as an earlier proclamation from Queen Elizabeth (1533–1603), "Sunday Plays and Games" (1569), also mentions the following permissible Sunday activities:

The Shotinge with the Standerd, the Shotinge with the Brode Arrowe, the Shotinge at the twelve skore Prick, the Shotinge at the Turke, the Keppinge for Men, the Runninge for Men, the Wrastlinge, the Throwinge of the Sledge, and the Pytchinge of the Barre, with all such other games, as have at anye time heretofore or now be licensed, used or played.[65]

Hence many recreational activities were the subject of controversy long before the Westminster Assembly.

In fact, Sabbath-observance controversies and polemics date back to the Middle Ages and even earlier, most famously enshrined in the sixth-century "Epistle on Sunday." This was an apocryphal letter purportedly from Christ that contained instruction on how the Lord's Day should be observed and the consequences of its violation.[66] Also noteworthy is the fact that the *Book of Sports* gives a brief list of games that were forbidden on Sunday: "Beare and Bull-baitings, Interludes, and at all times in the meaner sort of People by the Law prohibited, Bowling."[67]

This already-heated controversy and list of permissible and impermissible Sunday sports provides important contextual information. The *Book of Sports* specifically complains about "Puritanes and precise people" who prohibited and unlawfully punished people for lawful recreation on "Sundayes and other Holy dayes, after the afternoone Sermon or Service."[68] Yet, for as much precision that supposedly attends the

---

[64] Ibid., 8–9.

[65] Ibid., 11–12.

[66] "Our Lord's Epistle on Sunday," 25, in John the Blind Audelay, *The Counsel of Conscience*, ed. Susanna Fein (Kalamazoo, MI: Medieval Institute, 2009); Parker, *English Sabbath*, 9–14; Oliver Pickering, "The Make-up of John Audelay's *Counsel of Conscience*," in *My Wyl and My Wrytying: Essays on John the Blind Audelay*, ed. Susanna Fein (Kalamazoo, MI: Medieval Institute, 2009), 128; R. Priebsch, "John Audelay's Poem on the Observance of Sunday and Its Sources," in *An English Miscellany: Presented to Dr. Furnivall in Honour of His Seventy-Fifth Birthday*, ed. William Paton Ker et al. (Oxford: Clarendon, 1901), 397–407.

[67] James, *Lawful Sports*, 9.

[68] Ibid., 5.

"Puritan" exposition of the law, the *Book of Sports* gives a similarly styled list of acceptable and unacceptable Sunday activities, though by its own admission the book was anything but "Puritan." The prolix style of the Larger Catechism, therefore, is attributable to its stated purpose as a lengthy exposition of Christian doctrine, but also to the literary conventions of the period. The divines were interested not merely in setting forth the basic principles of the fourth commandment, as they did in the Shorter Catechism, but also in engaging the specific issues under dispute, such as what was and was not lawful on the Lord's Day.

These matters were not idly debated. They were hotly contested, and each side believed that the fate of the nation was at stake. The *Book of Sports* attributed the spread of Roman Catholicism to the absence of Sunday recreational activities.[69] On the other side of the issue was Henry Burton's (1578–1648) *Divine Tragedie Lately Acted; or, A Collection of Sundrie Memorable Examples of Gods Judgements upon Sabbath-Breakers* (1641).[70] In his work Burton lists fifty-six examples of people who engaged in dancing, plays, ale drinking, sports, and the like and suffered grievous consequences, typically death. Example 3 is illustrative:

> A Maid at Enfield neer London, hearing of the libertie, which was given by the book, which was published for sports, would needs go daunce, with others on the Lords day, saying she would go daunce, so long as she could stand on her legs; she daunced so long, that thereof within two or three dayes she died.[71]

Another states that "where the Father drew ale upon the Lords day and so prophaned it: In the same place his son the next day drew his last breath: for that the punishment inflicted was stamped with the resemblance of the sin convicted."[72] Another incident is recorded in example 21: a bowler flung his bowling ball at his fellow bowler, hitting him on the ear, which caused blood to issue forth, and shortly thereafter the stricken man died.[73] All of these tragedies were occasioned,

---

[69] Ibid., 6.
[70] Henry Burton, *A Divine Tragedie Lately Acted; or, A Collection of Sundrie Memorable Examples of Gods Judgements upon Sabbath-Breakers* (London, 1641).
[71] Ibid., 4.
[72] Ibid., 12.
[73] Ibid.

in the mind of Burton and others, by the publication of the *Book of Sports*.[74] It is only natural, then, that the divines would want to be specific as to what was lawful and unlawful on the Sabbath.

Issues of historical context and genre aside, the Larger Catechism begins its explanation of the fourth commandment like its treatment of the other nine, with a quotation of the passage of Scripture (q. 115). That the divines quote Scripture demonstrates that the commandment is, of course, special revelation, though it is also natural revelation. Recall that the Confession states that the moral law was originally given to Adam and inscribed upon his heart, which is evidenced by the citation of Romans 2:14–15. The moral law was then subsequently "delivered by God upon Mount Sinai, in ten Commandments, and written in two Tables" (19.2, 3). Hence, there is a double attestation of the fourth commandment, in natural and special revelation. The Larger Catechism (q. 121) confirms this overlap with respect to the fourth commandment by appealing to equity to prove the reasonableness of the dedication of one day in seven for worship:

> Q. What are the Reasons annexed to the fourth Commandment, the more to enforce it?
> A. The Reasons annexed to the fourth Commandment, the more to enforce it, are taken from the equity of it, God allowing us six dayes of seven for our own affairs, and reserving but one for himself.[75]

The Confession further illuminates this point: "As it is of the Law of Nature, that, in general, a due proportion of time be set apart, for the Worship of God; so, in his word, by a positive, Moral, and perpetuall Commandment, binding all men, in all Ages, he hath particularly appointed One Day in Seven, for a Sabbath, to be kept holy unto him" (21.7). The divines do stipulate that there is "less light of nature" in the fourth commandment than in others (LC q. 122), and that the acceptable way this day is to be observed is only revealed in Scripture (21.1). General and special revelation, or the moral law and natural law, overlap in the fourth commandment.[76]

---

[74] Ibid., 16.
[75] See Dickson, *Truths Victory over Error*, 21.11 (pp. 188–89).
[76] Ibid., 20.5 (p. 146).

The same can be said regarding the overlap of the moral and ceremonial law in the fourth commandment, as is most evident in the Confession's contention that the day of worship has changed from the last day of the week to the first:

> [The day] from the beginning of the World to the Resurrection of Christ, was the last Day of the week; and, from the Resurrection of Christ, was changed into the First Day of the week, which, in Scripture, is called the Lords Day, and is to be continued to the end of the World, as the Christian Sabbath. (21.7)

Reformed theologians offer a number of explanations behind the change of the Sabbath from the last day of the week to the first. James Ussher, for example, explains that the change occurred to remind people of the resurrection of Christ, and God's initial creation rest, which Christ entered when he ceased from his own labors and afflictions: "As the one therefore was specially sanctified, in regard of the Creation of the World: so was the other, in respect of the restauration and redemption of the world, which is a greater worke then the Creation."[77] Ussher also recognizes that there was a ceremonial dimension to the commandment and hence a change of day. He rejects the idea that the entire commandment is ceremonial and therefore abolished by the death of Christ, which was the view of Luther and Calvin.[78] Because the commandment was placed in the midst of other perpetual moral commandments in the Decalogue, was written directly by the finger of God, was written in tables of stone, and appeared in the creation before any manifestation of the ceremonial

---

[77] Ussher, *Body of Divinitie*, 244.

[78] Parker, *English Sabbath*, 24–27; Robert Cox, ed., *The Whole Doctrine of Calvin about the Sabbath and the Lord's Day: Extracted from His Commentaries, Catechism, and Institutes of the Christian Religion* (Edinburgh: Maclachlan and Stewart, 1860). Calvin rejects the very common distinction between the ceremonial and moral aspects of the fourth commandment: "Thus vanish all the dreams of false prophets, who in past ages, have infected the people with a Jewish notion, affirming that nothing but the ceremonial part of this commandment, which, according to them, is the appointment of the seventh day, has been abrogated, but that the moral part of it, that is, the observance of one day in seven, still remains" (*Institutes*, 2.8.34). Calvin rejects the older medieval distinction (e.g., Aquinas's interpretation), but this is the interpretation that became commonplace in the Reformed tradition. Luther similarly makes this point when he argues that the fourth commandment is entirely ceremonial and has no parallel in natural law, hence it is excluded from the moral law and no longer binding: "But since one must now affirm the liberty given by God, let us tell them that Moses in no wise pertains to us in all his laws, but only to the Jews, except where he agrees with the natural law, which, as Paul teaches is written in the hearts of Gentiles (Rom. 2:15). Whatever is not written there we should include among the ceremonies that were necessary for the people of Moses but free for us, as also the Sabbath is, as Paul (Col. 2:16) and the last chapter of Isaiah (66:23) bear witness" (Martin Luther, *Lectures on Deuteronomy*, comm. Deut. 7:1–2, in *LW*, 9:81–82; cf. Luther, "How Christians Should Regard Moses," in *LW*, 35:161–80, esp. 164–66).

law, Ussher concludes it was part of the moral law.[79] However, he also argues that virtually every commandment has some ceremonial aspects connected to it. And regarding the Sabbath before Christ, the fourth commandment contains a "Ceremoniall representation of our eternall rest," but it is an "accessory and accidentall." Now that the time for the abrogation of the ceremonies has come, its ceremonial use "may well fall away, and yet the commandment remaine, it being out of the substance of the Commandment."[80]

One Continental Reformed theologian of the period, Petrus de Witte (1622–1669), gives one of the clearest explanations of the ceremonial aspects of the fourth commandment in his exposition of the Heidelberg Catechism, which reflects the Reformed consensus on the interpretation of the fourth commandment.[81] He rejects the notion

---

[79] Ussher, *Body of Divinitie*, 242–43.

[80] Ibid., 243. Similar types of distinctions between ceremonial and moral aspects of the fourth commandment were common among Reformed theologians (see Thomas Cranmer, *A Confutation of Unwritten Verities*, in *Miscellaneous Writings and Letters of Thomas Cranmer, 1556*, ed. John Edmund [1556; Cambridge: CUP, 1846], 61; Thomas Cartwright, *Christian Religion: Substantially, Methodicallie, Plainlie, and Profitablie Treatised* [London: Thomas Mann, 1611], 90; Roberts, *Mysterium et Medulla Bibliorum*, 696; John Mayer, *A Commentary upon All the Prophets Both Great and Small* [London: Abraham Miller and Ellen Cotes, 1652], 8).

[81] See, e.g., Heinrich Bullinger, *The Decades of Henry Bullinger*, ed. Thomas Harding, 4 vols. (1849–1852; Grand Rapids: Reformation Heritage, 2004), 2.4 (1:253–67); Zacharias Ursinus, *The Commentary of Dr. Zacharias Ursinus on the Heidelberg Catechism*, trans. G. W. Williard (1852; Phillipsburg, NJ: P&R, n.d.), LD 38, q. 103 (pp. 557–74); Thomas Becon, *The Catechism of Thomas Becon* (1560; Cambridge: CUP, 1844), 3 (p. 82); Theodore Beza, "Of the Fourth Commandment of Gods Lawe," in *Propositions and Principles of Divinity Propounded and Disputed in the Universitie of Geneva* (London, 1595), 39.5 (p. 124). Noteworthy is Sprint's citation of numerous theologians, Reformed and Lutheran, on this point, including Bullinger, Ursinus, Hyperius, Musculus, Calvin, Beza, Vermigli, Pezel, and Perkins, among other Reformed theologians; and Hemmingius and Chemnitz, among the Lutherans (Sprint, *Propositions*, B3r; cf., e.g., Ursinus, *Commentary*; Bullinger, *Decades*; Beza, "Fourth Commandment"; Niels Hemmingsen, *Syntagma Institutionum Christianrum* [Radaeus: Aegidium Radaeum, 1581], 360–65; Martin Chemnitz, *Examination of the Council of Trent*, trans. Fred Kramer, vol. 1, pt. 4, of *Chemnitz's Works* [1971; St. Louis: Concordia, 2007], 4.1.64 [p. 416]; William Perkins, *A Commentarie or Exposition, upon the Five First Chapters of the Epistles to the Galatians* [Cambridge: John Legat, 1604], comm. Gal. 4:10 [pp. 302–81, esp. 315–16]; Musculus, *Common Places*, fols. 60–70, esp. fols. 69–70; Peter Martyr Vermigli, *The Common Places of the Most Famous Divine Doctor Peter Martyr* [London, 1583], 2.3 [pp. 297–307]; Andreas Hyperius, *Commentarii D. Andreae Hyperii, Doctissimi ac Clarissimi Theologi*, comm. 1 Cor. 16:1–2, in *Omnes D. Paul Apostoli Epistolas* [Tiguri: Christophrum Froschoverum, 1584], 331; Edward Dering, *27 Lectures or Readings upon the Epistle to the Hebreues*, lect. 4.19, in *M. Derings Workes* [London: Paul Linely, 1597], n.p.; Gervase Babbington, *A Verie Fruitefull Exposition of the Commandments by Way of Questions and Answers* [London: Thomas Orwin, 1590], 168; William Fulke, *Praelections upon the Sacred and Holy Revelation of S. John* [London: Thomas Purfoote, 1573], comm. Rev. 1:10 [fol. 5]; Alexander Nowel, *A Catechisme; or, First Instruction and Learning of Christian Religion* [London: John Daye, 1577], fols. 12r–13v). Sprint cites Christoph Pezel's, *Argumentorum et Obiectionum*, but his citation appears to be incorrect. But similar comments appear in Pezel's commentary on Genesis (Christoph Pezel, *Argumentorum et Obiectionum, de Praecipuis Articulis Doctrinae Christianae* [Neustadt: Matthaei Harnisch, 1591]; Pezel, *In Primum Librum Mosis, Qui Inscribitur Genesis Commentarius* [Neustadt: Wilhelmi Harnisii, 1599], 30–31). Also noteworthy is that the Synod of Dort (1618–1619) interpreted the fourth commandment in the same way (H. H. Kuyper, ed., *De Post-Acta of Nahandelingen van de nationale Synode van Dordrecht in 1618 en 1619 gehouden een Historische Studie* [Amsterdam, 1899], 184–86; Parker, *English Sabbath*, 169). Note, though, that in Sprint's citation of Calvin (*Institutes*, 2.8.31–32), he does not cite those paragraphs where Calvin acknowledges that the Sabbath command was abrogated (2.8.28–29).

that the fourth commandment is merely ceremonial for many of the same reasons given by Ussher, such as its inclusion in the Decalogue. "But," he asks, "is there not for all this something Ceremonial?" to which he responds:

> Yes. Namely the strict keeping of the seventh, or last day of the week with the Circumstances exprest, Exod. 16:23. *Bake that which you will bake to day, and seeth that you will seeth*, and vers. 29. and 35:3. *Ye shall kindle no fire throughout your habitations on the Sabbath-day*; being a type as of the rest of the Messias [*sic*] in the grave, so of ours, after that the weeks of our life shall be ended, Isa. 66:23. And to the *Jews* a sign of their Deliverance out of *Egypt*, Exod. 12:17. Deut. 5:15. and to distinguish them from other Heathens, signifying their Sanctification, Exod. 31:13, 15. Ezek. 20:12. *Moreover also, I gave them my Sabbaths, to be a sign between me and them, that they might know that I am the Lord that Sanctify them.* So that that Ceremonial rest was an Appendix of the Commandment, and as a Sacrament of the Old Testament.[82]

De Witte, like Ussher, echoes an interpretive approach that dates back to the Middle Ages and Aquinas's explanation of the distinctive ceremonial aspects of the fourth commandment.[83] If it is not already evident, the explanation of the law is not straightforward or easily confined to one category of the law but is nuanced, theologically sophisticated, and exegetically attentive to various aspects of the text, not only as it rests in its original context, but also as it appears throughout the whole of Scripture, from creation, to Sinai, to the consummation.

To this point, I have said little about the specific instructions and prohibitions regarding this commandment. The Larger Catechism (q. 117) explains what is generally required and then gives direct guidance (q. 118):

> The Sabbath or Lords day is to be sanctified, by an holy resting all the day, not onely from such workes as are at all times sinfull, but even from such worldly imployments and recreations as are on

---

[82] Petrus de Witte, *Catechizing upon the Heidelbergh Catechisme, of the Reformed Christian Religion* (Amsterdame: Gillis Joosten Saeghman, 1664), LD 38, q. 103 (p. 702).
[83] Aquinas, *Summa Theologica*, IIaIIae, q. 122, art. 4; Parker, *English Sabbath*, 19–20.

other dayes lawfull; and making it our delight to spend the whole time (except so much of it as is to be taken up in works of necessity and mercy) in the publike and private exercises of Gods worship; and to that end we are to prepare our hearts, and with such fore-sight, diligence and moderation to dispose, and seasonably to dispatch our worldly business, that we may be the more free and fit for the duties of that day.

The Larger Catechism provides similar counsel in its list of prohibitions (q. 120):

The sins forbidden in the fourth Commandment, are, all omissions of the duties required, all carelesse, negligent, and unprofitable performing of them, and being weary of them, all profaning the day by idlenesse, and doing that which is in it selfe sinfull, and by all needlesse works, words, and thoughts about our worldly imployments and recreations.[84]

In light of the historical context and the specific enumeration of accepted and prohibited recreational activities, the Larger Catechism seems somewhat general in its treatment of the fourth commandment. Though many have accused the Standards of legalism, they mention no specific forbidden sports but only those "wordly imployments and recreation" that were lawful on other days. The Standards are not vague on these points, however. To discover what other activities were encouraged, one should naturally turn to the Confession's chapter 21, "Religious Worship, and the Sabbath Day," which mentions prayer (21.4), the reading and hearing of the preaching of the Word (21.5), and acts of mercy (21.8). All these activities naturally fall under the normative use of the law, since one of the chief purposes behind the fourth commandment was to remind the people of God that it was a day of blessing for them (LC q. 121).

The fourth commandment has pedagogical and civil aspects as well as normative. The necessity to remember the work of Christ on the Lord's Day falls under the pedagogical aspects of the law, especially

---

[84] John Lightfoot records in his journal the proceedings in November 1644, when the assembly debated matters pertaining to Sabbath observance (John Lightfoot, *Journal of the Proceedings of the Assembly of Divines*, in *The Whole Works of Rev. John Lightfoot*, vol. 13 [London: J. F. Dove, 1824], 327–30).

seeing that judgment might fall upon believers who failed to hallow the Sabbath. The Larger Catechism also includes issues related to the civil use of the law. It explains that the charge of keeping the Sabbath "is more specially directed to governors of families and other superiors" (q. 119), which would include anyone in a position of authority by God's ordinance, "whether in Family, Church, or Commonwealth" (q. 125). Ussher argues that the fourth commandment is specifically directed at "Householders and Magistrates."[85] Common opinion among theologians of the period was that magistrates, and hence superiors, were required to enforce both tables of the law, including the fourth commandment. Dickson explains: "The supream Magistrate is *Custos utriusque Tabulae*, a Keeper of both Tables of the Law of God. As well of the first Table, which relates to Religion, and our duty to God; as of the second which related to righteousness, and our duty to our neighbour."[86]

On this particular point Ussher explains that the head of household was responsible for seeing to his family's observance of the Sabbath in his own home, as well as for ensuring that his servants were free to observe it as well. The magistrate's duties vis-à-vis the fourth commandment included ensuring that "all within his gates kept the Lords day," including "strangers, though Turks and Infidels . . . causing them to cease from labour, and restraining them from all open and publick Idolatry, or false Worship of God; much more all his owne Subjects, whome he ought to force to heare the Word."[87] Others, such as Edward Leigh, were of the same view, and he cites Melanchthon and Beza in support.[88] In a telling statement, Rutherford explains why magistrates must enforce both tables of the law:

> Scripture and the Law of nature, and right reason, which is a deduction from Scripture, is able sufficiently in all Canons and Constitutions to regulate both Rulers and people, and to determine what is convenient in Circumstances; and the Lord here is an infallible Judge, speaking in his Word, as he is in all matters, which they call Fundamental; yea, the Scripture shall be imperfect in

---

[85] Ussher, *Body of Divinitie*, 249.
[86] Dickson, *Truths Victory over Error*, 23.2 (p. 210).
[87] Ussher, *Body of Divinitie*, 249.
[88] Leigh, *Body of Divinity*, prologue.

the duties of the second Table, if it do not determine what is active scandal, or soul-murther, as it doth determine what is Idolatry, what is lawful Worship.[89]

In other words, relying upon Scripture, natural law, and the reasoned examination of Scripture, magistrates must enforce both tables of the law. If the first table of the law were not enforced, that would lead to violations of the second table. Hence the Confession states that magistrates had the responsibility to "maintain Piety, Justice, and Peace, according to the wholesome Laws of each Commonwealth" (23.2). And though the magistrate was not to administer Word and sacraments or the keys of the kingdom of heaven, it was his duty

> to take order that Unity and Peace be preserved in the Church, that the Truth of God be kept pure, and intire; that all Blasphemies and Hereises be suppressed; all corruptions and abuses in Worship and Discipline prevented, or reformed; and all the Ordinances of God duly settled, administred, and observed. (23.3)

To that end the magistrate had the authority and power to call church synods and the responsibility to ensure that "whatsoever is transacted in them, be according to the minde of God" (23.3). Remember, the Westminster Assembly was convened not by any church but by Parliament. Reformed theologians in Scotland and England were committed to the idea that the magistrate had the responsibility to preserve the one true religion in all three kingdoms. This commitment is especially evident in the Scottish National Covenant (1638) and the Solemn League and Covenant (1643).[90]

---

[89] Rutherford, *Divine Right*, 656; cf. Coffey, *Politics*, 153.

[90] For the National Covenant and Solemn League and Covenant, see *Westminster Confession of Faith* (Glasgow: Free Presbyterian Publications, 1995), 345–60; cf. VanDrunen, *Natural Law and the Two Kingdoms*, 197–99. As common as this view was in the early modern period, it would later be revised by subsequent generations. Such changes are evident in the 1789 revisions to the Westminster Standards by the Presbyterian Church (USA) in its first general assembly. Old theology took a slightly different shape in the new world as the assembly adopted changes to WCF 23.3: "Yet, as nursing fathers, it is the duty of civil magistrates to protect the church of our common Lord, without giving the preference to any denomination of Christians above the rest, in such a manner that all ecclesiastical persons whatever shall enjoy the full, free, and unquestioned liberty of discharging every part of their sacred functions, without violence or danger. And, as Jesus Christ hath appointed a regular government and discipline in his church, no law of any commonwealth should interfere with, let, or hinder, the due exercise thereof, among the voluntary members of any denomination of Christians, according to their own profession and belief." The magistrate was no longer a *defensor fide* but a "nursing father," a phrase commonly employed among colonial writers, secular and sacred alike, drawn from Isaiah 49:23. Moreover, even infidels were to be protected by the magistrate: "It

The actions of Parliament provide evidence that the divines reflected the theology and practice of the day as that pertained to the magistrate's responsibility to enforce both tables of the law. On April 8, 1644, Parliament passed an ordinance "for the better observation of the Lords-Day." The ordinance recounts how good laws in the past had been enacted but ignored and that "divers ungodly Books have been published by the Prelatical Faction, against the morality of that day." The ordinance then goes on to state:

> The Lords and Commons for remedy thereof, do Order and Ordain, and be it Ordered and Ordained, That all the Lawes Enacted and in force, concerning the observation of the Lordsday, be carefully put in execution; and that all and singular person and persons whatsoever, shall on every Lords-day, apply themselves to the sanctification of the same, by exercising themselves thereon, in the duties of Piety and true Religion, publickly and privately: And that no person or persons whatsoever, shall publickly cry, shew forth or expose to sale, any Wares, Merchandizes, Fruit, Herbs, Goods or Chattels whatsoever, upon the Lords day, or any part thereof; upon pain, That every person so offending, shall forfeit the same Goods so cryed, shewed forth, or put to sale: And that no person or persons whatsoever shall, without reasonable cause for the same, travel, carry burthens, or do any worldly labours, or work whatsoever, on that day, or any part thereof; upon pain, That every one travelling

is the duty of civil magistrates to protect the person and good name of all their people, in such an effectual manner as that no person be suffered, either upon pretense of religion or of infidelity, to offer any indignity, violence, abuse, or injury to any other person whatsoever: and to take order, that all religious and ecclesiastical assemblies be held without molestation or disturbance" (23.3). Notably, American revisions deleted "tolerating false religions" as a violation of the second commandment in the Larger Catechism, q. 109; implied in this is the idea that Christian magistrates no longer have the responsibility to suppress heresy. According to the American revisions the magistrate no longer has the right to call synods or determine matters of doctrine (WCF 31.1). Though unstated, the implication is that, according to the American revisions, the magistrate is no longer the custodian of both tables of the law (cf. Leah Farish, "The First Amendment's Religion Clauses: The Calvinist Document That Interprets Them Both," *Journal of Religion & Society* 12 [2010]: 1–22; Guy Klett, ed., *Minutes of the Presbyterian Church in America: 1706–1788* [Philadelphia: Presbyterian Historical Society, 1976], minutes for September 19, 1729 and May 26, 1788 [pp. 103–4, 635–37]; VanDrunen, *Natural Law and the Two Kingdoms*, 245–47; D. G. Hart, "American Presbyterianism: Exceptional," *Journal of Presbyterian History* 84, no. 1 [2006]: 12–16). For a brief but useful survey of the historical context of this period in American colonial history and the events surrounding the formation of the national Presbyterian church, see D. G. Hart and John R. Muether, *Seeking a Better Country: 300 Years of American Presbyterianism* (Phillipsburg, NJ: P&R, 2007), 70–90). The first amendment of the US Constitution, therefore, should be read in tandem with the 1789 revisions to the Westminster Standards to see how American Presbyterians articulated the magistrate's role in matters pertaining to religion, e.g., "Congress shall make no law respecting an establishment of religion, or prohibiting the free exercise thereof" (accessed May 7, 2013, www.usconstitution.net).

contrary to the meaning of this Ordinance, shall forfeit for every
offence, ten shillings of lawfull money; and that every person car-
rying any burthen, or doing any worldly labour or work, contrary
to the meaning thereof, shall forfeit five shillings of like money for
every such offence.[91]

Beyond injunctions against labor and travel, the ordinance also prohibited recreation, including "wrastlings, Shooting, Bowling, ring-
ing of Bells for Pleasure or Pastime, Masque, Wake, called Feasts,
Church-Ale, Dancing, Games, Sport," upon pain of a five-shilling fine
against any person over the age of fourteen caught committing such
offenses. Such a fine was no small matter as a shilling was approximately a day's wage.[92]

Any parent or guardian of a child caught violating the Sabbath
was liable to a twelve-pence fine for every offence; a pence was roughly
equivalent to the present-day British pound in terms of buying power.
Local magistrates were also enjoined to enforce these prohibitions
and use the collected fines for the "Poor of the Parish." But like the
above-cited divines, Parliament did not enact these laws out of malice
or legalistic motives. Rather, they believed the welfare of the nation
was at stake because people profaned the Lord's Day "to the manifest
indangering of souls, prejudice of the true Religion, great dishonour
of Almighty God, and provocation of his just wrath and indignation
against this Land."

Conclusion

In this survey of the Standards on the Christian life and the law, there
is no patch of life where the divines do not find God's moral law as it
is inscribed upon the heart of man, written on the tables of stone at
Sinai, or rewritten in the hearts of the redeemed by Christ and the
Spirit. The law spans all of redemptive history under the categories
of the moral, ceremonial, and judicial laws, and though the latter two

---

[91] C. H. Firth and R. S. Rait, eds., *Acts and Ordinances of the Interregnum, 1642–1660* (London, 1911), 420–22, accessed September 12, 2012, http://www.british-history.ac.uk/report.aspx?compid= 55931. All subsequent quotations from this ordinance are cited from this source; cf. Parker, *English Sabbath*, 218.

[92] Francis Turner, "Money and Exchange Rates in 1632," accessed September 12, 2012, http://1632 .org/1632Slush/1632money.rtf.

have expired with the advent of Christ and the dissolution of Old Testament Israel, they still serve the church, whether as reminders of fulfilled christological types or as examples of scripturally embedded natural laws situated for Israel's tenure in the land but still applicable in the present day and binding upon Christians and non-Christians alike. Common opinion of the day was that the civil magistrate had the responsibility of enforcing both tables of the law. But the law was equally applicable to sinners, whether in its political, pedagogical, or normative uses. Though there was large agreement over these principal issues, Reformed theologians did not agree where the boundaries for these distinctions began and ended. Hence, the Standards reflect the broader consensus on these matters but not always specific application and exegesis of issues or Scripture.

10

The Church

With any historical subject, the original context of an idea is absolutely crucial to understanding the concepts under examination, and this is especially so with regard to the doctrine of the church. A number of issues swirl about the doctrine of the church for which the original historical context of early modernity provides invaluable information not only for issues such as the sacraments (baptism and the Lord's Supper), but also for matters pertaining to the relationship between the church and the civil magistrate. Though moderns are accustomed to ideas about the separation of church and state and even have such ideas codified in modified versions of the Westminster and Belgic Confessions, such was not the case in early modern Europe. In our own day debates rage about whether a political leader may or may not be a Christian. In other words, people want to know about the religious beliefs of their political leaders. But in the early modern period the question was whether the king was the head of the church or merely one of its members. Was ecclesiastical power in any way distinct, or even different, from civil power? Was the magistrate involved in the affairs of the church, and if so, to what extent?

Given that monarchial rule was the default mode of governments in sixteenth-century Europe, it is natural that a number of Reformed theologians would argue for the view that the magistrate had authority over the church in all matters, spiritual and doctrinal. The person most famously associated with such a view is Thomas Erastus

(1524–1583), a Swiss theologian and physician, who argued that the magistrate was responsible for church discipline.[1] Erastus received support from some of his peers, including Rudolf Gwalther (1519–1586), though there is debate about the extent to which Heinrich Bullinger (1504–1575) supported his views. Erastus was opposed by the likes of Theodore Beza (1519–1605).[2] In the seventeenth century Erastus's views were taken up by a number of others, including Lewis Du Moulin (1606–1680) and several Westminster divines, including John Selden (1584–1654), John Lightfoot (1602–1675), and Thomas Coleman (1598–1647).[3] The assembly's debates over church polity and the relationship between the respective powers of the church and the magistrate were some of its most famous.[4]

In spite of the intensity of the debate the assembly nevertheless did not embrace Erastianism but instead distinguished between civil and ecclesiastical powers. The divines did so by means of a common early modern doctrine of the two kingdoms. While theologians, at their best, decide matters of doctrine based upon the Scriptures, they are also children of their time. The long shadow of civil supremacy in churchly affairs hung over the assembly's deliberations, whether the claim of Henry VIII (1491–1547) that he was the head of the church or the civil war against Charles I (1600–1649), which was instigated, at least in part, by his "meddling" in church affairs.[5] Hence the divines were

---

[1] Thomas Erastus, *The Theses of Erastus Touching Excommunication* (Edinburgh: Myles MacPhail, 1844); cf. Charles D. Gunnoe Jr., *Thomas Erastus and the Palatinate: A Renaissance Physician in the Second Reformation* (Leiden: Brill, 2010); Robert S. Paul, *The Assembly of the Lord: Politics and Religion in the Westminster Assembly and the 'Grand Debate'* (Edinburgh: T&T Clark, 1985), 127–32, 492–515.

[2] Theodore Beza, *Tractatus Pius et Moderatus de Vera Excommunicatione, et Christiano Presbyterio, Jampridem Pacis Conciliandae Causa* (Genève: Jean Le Preux, 1590).

[3] Lewis Du Moulin, *Of the Right of Churches and of the Magistrates Power over Them* (London: R. D., 1658); Du Moulin (aka Irenaeus Philalethes), *Automachia; or, The Selfe-Contradition of Some That Contend about Church-Government* (London, 1643).

[4] Cf. Thomas Goodwin et al., *A Copy of the Remonstrance Lately Delivered into the Assembly by Thomas Goodwin, Jeremiah Burroughs, William Greenhill, William Bridge, Philip Nie, Sidrach Simson, and William Carter. Declaring the Grounds and Reasons of Their Declining to Bring into the Assembly, Their Modell of Church-Government* (London, 1645); *The Answer of the Assembly of Divines by Authority of Parliament Now Sitting at Westminster. Unto the Reasons Given by the Dissenting Brethren, of Their Not Bringing in a Model of Their Way* (London: John Field, 1645); Thomas Goodwin and Jeremiah Whitaker, *The Reasons Presented by the Dissenting Brethren against Certain Propositions concerning Presbyteriall Government* (London: Humphrey Harward, 1648); *The Reasons of the Dissenting Brethren against the Third Proposition, concerning Presbyteriall Government. Humbly Presented* (Edinburgh: Evan Tyler, 1648); Paul Joseph Smith, "The Debates on Church Government at the Westminster Assembly of Divines, 1643–1646" (PhD diss., Boston University Graduate School, 1975); Paul, *Assembly of the Lord*, 249–312, 522–46.

[5] See, e.g., Diana Newton, *Papists, Protestants and Puritans 1559–1714* (Cambridge: CUP, 1998), 37–49; Nicholas Tyacke, *Anti-Calvinists: The Rise of English Arminianism c. 1590–1640* (Oxford:

keen to delineate exactly where the magistrate's power ended and where the church's power began in theological and spiritual affairs, and they did so with the doctrine of the two kingdoms. This chapter will survey the Standards on the relationship between the church and the magistrate, and the doctrine of the sacraments—baptism and the Lord's Supper, the signs and seals of Christ's covenanted kingdom, the church.

The Church and the Magistrate

The previous chapter noted that according to a number of early modern Reformed theologians the civil magistrate was the custodian of both tables of the law and was responsible for suppressing heresy and ensuring that true religion was observed under his or her jurisdiction. John Lightfoot, who recorded the assembly's activities in a personal journal, notes how on one Monday morning (September 9, 1644) the assembly took time to reflect upon a recent defeat in battle. The divines enumerated the assembly's sins, such as neglect of service, failures to attend the assembly, leaving early, numerous divines absenting themselves from the assembly's prayers, neglect in the amount of time given to debate, some speaking too much and others speaking too little, irreverent behavior, anger in debate, partisanship, and not conducting ministerial examinations in a serious manner. Lightfoot also recounts the sins of the army, which included swearing, gaming, and drinking, as well as an overall lack of discipline. The list of the sins of Parliament, however, evidences in a concrete way how the civil magistrate was supposed to suppress false teaching. Parliament's sins included failing to uphold the Solemn League and Covenant; inattention to suppressing antinomians and Anabaptists; not seeking to promote religion; failing to suppress stage plays, taverns, profaneness, and the ridicule of ministers; and not selling church properties to see to the financial needs of ministers.[6] That these were genuine concerns for members of the assembly is

---

OUP, 1991), 181–244; Robert Bucholz and Newton Key, *Early Modern England 1485–1714* (West Sussex: Wiley-Blackwell, 2009), 212–49.

[6]John Lightfoot, *The Journal of the Proceedings of the Assembly of Divines*, vol. 13 of *The Whole Works of Rev. John Lightfoot* (London: J. F. Dove, 1824), 309–10. The assembly's reaction to this event appears in sess. 281, September 9, 1644, *MPWA*, 3:279–88.

evident in a sermon preached on the occasion by one of the Erastian divines, Thomas Coleman.[7]

The context of the relationship between the church and the magistrate is an important element to factor. Though the magistrate was the custodian of both tables of the law and was in some measure involved in determining the orthodoxy or heterodoxy of doctrine, the Westminster divines did not believe that there were no differences between the two powers. Contemporary readers of the Standards likely miss the finely nuanced distinctions present in the Confession, statements that reveal the differences between the church and magistrate and the scope of their respective authority and roles. The first of the distinctions appears in the Confession's definition of the church. The Confession embraces what was by now a standard distinction regarding the visible and invisible church, a distinction that goes back to Augustine (354–430) and was broadly confessed during the Reformation.[8] The invisible church "consists of the whole number of the Elect, that have been, are, or shall be gathered into One, under Christ the Head thereof, and is, the Spouse, the Body, the Fulness of Him that filleth all in all" (25.1).

By contrast, the visible church,

> which is also Catholique or Universal, under the Gospel (not confined to one Nation, as before, under the Law) consists of all those, throughout the World, that professe the true Religion; and of their Children: and is, the Kingdom of the Lord Jesus Christ, the House and Family of God, out of which, there is no ordinary possibility of Salvation. (25.2)

The last portion of this statement is key, one that reveals a difference when compared to what the Confession has to say about the nature of the civil magistrate. The Confession states, "God, the supreme Lord and King of all the World, hath Ordained Civil Magistrates, to be, under him, over the People, for his own Glory, and the

---

[7] Thomas Coleman, *Gods Unusual Answer to a Solemn Fast; or, Some Observations upon the Late Sad Successe in the West, upon the Day Immediately Following Our Publique Humiliation; in A Sermon before the Honorable Houses of Parliament, on a Fast Specially Set Apart upon That Occasion; in Margarets Westminster, Sept. 12 1644* (London: Christopher Meredith, 1644).

[8] Augustine, *On Christian Doctrine*, 3.32.45, in *NPNF*[1] 2:569; Augsburg Confession, 7–8; Tetrapolitan Confession, 15; Belgic Confession, 19; Second Helvetic Confession, 27.16; Thirty Nine Articles, 19.

Publique good" (23.1). At first glance, especially to modern readers, the differences between these statements might not be detected, but they are significant. The visible church is the "Kingdom of the Lord Jesus Christ," but "God, the supreme Lord and King of all the World," is over civil magistrates. The former identifies Jesus Christ as the King of the church but does not say the same vis-à-vis the civil magistrate. This distinction was specifically and deliberately inserted by George Gillespie (1613–1648) in the midst of the assembly's debates in order to distinguish the respective powers of church and the magistrate. Gillespie insisted that the word *Christ* be removed and replaced by the word *God* in the Confession's chapter 23, on the magistrate. The minutes state the following: "Upon a motion Mr Gilespy for an alteration in the chapt about the civill magistrate, and upon debate it was Resolved upon the Q.: that in the said chapter, for the word 'Christ', the word 'God' shall be put in 3 places."[9] These differences alone might not seem very significant, but they are merely the tips of two important icebergs when it comes to defining the nature and scope of the authority and the functions of the church and civil magistrate.[10]

The stated distinctions (Christ as King of the church and God as King of the world) reflect a common Protestant doctrine popularly associated with Martin Luther (1483–1526), namely, the doctrine of the two kingdoms.[11] Despite its popular association with Lutheran theology this doctrine was equally attested among early modern Reformed theologians. John Ball (1585–1640), who wrote an oft-cited work on the covenant of grace, offers a typical explanation of Christ's relationship to the church and civil magistrate. He succinctly states that Jesus, as the second person of the Trinity, rules over the *natural kingdom*: "Christ's natural kingdom does belong unto him as God co-essential and coeternal with the Father." By way of contrast, Christ rules over the church by virtue of his role as Mediator:

---

[9] *MPWA*, sess. 752, December 4, 1646 (4:356).
[10] David VanDrunen, *Natural Law and the Two Kingdoms: A Study in the Development of Reformed Social Thought* (Grand Rapids: Eerdmans, 2010), 179.
[11] Cf. Martin Luther, "An Open Letter on the Harsh Book against the Peasants," in *LW*, 46:63–85; Luther, "Temporal Authority: To What Extent It Should Be Obeyed," in *LW*, 45:75–130; William J. Wright, *Martin Luther's Understanding of God's Two Kingdoms: A Response to the Challenge of Skepticism* (Grand Rapids: Baker, 2010); Heinrich Bornkam, *Luther's Doctrine of the Two Kingdoms* (Philadelphia: Fortress, 1966); VanDrunen, *Natural Law and the Two Kingdoms*, 55–62.

Therefore to sit on the right hand of the Father does not note glory and dominion properly divine, which does belong to the son as coessential and coeternal with his Father, and is his by nature: but glory and dominion next unto that which is essentially divine, which belongs to Christ as Mediator, and which is his not by nature, but by donation and unction of his Father, being made the Head of his Church, a Prince of Peace, and King of Righteousness. This glory and dominion was given unto Christ.[12]

Ball distinguishes between the *natural* and *mediatorial* kingdoms. Of interest is that he draws upon the work of Zacharias Ursinus (1534–1583) to argue his point. This, as we will see, is just one example of the host of theologians invoked in the defense and articulation of the two-kingdoms doctrine. But what, precisely, does the distinction between the natural and mediatorial kingdoms entail?

Two of the most thorough treatments on the nature of church government come from Scottish divines at the assembly, George Gillespie and Samuel Rutherford (1600–1661). Of the two, the former's treatment of the two kingdoms is a bit more organized and succinct. Hence, we will focus our attention upon it with ancillary reference to Rutherford's work.[13] Gillespie begins the section of his treatise by defining the agreement and differences between civil and ecclesiastical powers, a distinction that rests upon the idea that there are two different kingdoms. Gillespie notes that the two kingdoms agree in ten points:

1. They are both from God.
2. Both are required to observe the law and commandments of God.
3. According to Luther, civil magistrates and church officers are considered "fathers" vis-à-vis the fifth commandment (Ex. 20:12).[14]
4. The magistrate and ministry are both appointed for the glory of God and the good of men.
5. Both are mutually beneficial to one another.

---

[12] John Ball, *A Treatise of the Covenant of Grace* (London: Edward Brewster, 1645), 2.3 (p. 306).
[13] Samuel Rutherford, *The Divine Right of Church-Government and Excommunication* (London: Christopher Meredith, 1646).
[14] Cf. Martin Luther, *The Small Catechism*, 4th comm., in *The Book of Concord: The Confessions of the Evangelical Lutheran Church*, ed. Robert Kolb and Timothy J. Wengert (Minneapolis: Fortress, 2000), 352; Luther, *The Large Catechism*, 4th comm., in *Book of Concord*, 400–410.

6. They are both governmental powers.
7. Each requires singular qualifications, gifts, and endowments.
8. They have degrees of censure and correction relative to the gravity of the offense.
9. They may only impose a penalty upon one who is guilty of offense.
10. Both have jurisdiction in "external matters" in that, even though churchly power is concerned chiefly with a person's internal spiritual state, church discipline manifests itself in the excommunication of people, as Andrè Rivet (1572–1651) has explained.[15]

On the other hand, Gillespie is equally interested in demonstrating how ecclesiastical and civil authorities differ. He offers ten points of disagreement:[16]

1. *Efficient cause.* The King of the nations has instituted the civil power; the King of saints has instituted the ecclesiastical power.
2. *Matter.* The civil magistrate employs the earthly scepter and temporal sword, and it is monarchial and legislative as well as punitive and coercive. Ecclesiastical power possesses and employs the keys of the kingdom of heaven.
3. *Forms.* The civil magistrate is an authority and dominion immediately subordinate to God, whereas ecclesiastical power is ministerial and is exercised in immediate subordination to Jesus Christ as King of the church.
4. *Ends.* The supreme end of the civil magistrate is the glory of God as King of the nations. The ends of ecclesiastical authority are twofold, proximate and remote. Proximately the end or goal is the glory of Jesus Christ; and remotely, the glory of God.
5. *Effects.* The civil power effects civil laws, punishments, and rewards. Ecclesiastical power determines controversies of faith,

---

[15] George Gillespie, *Aaron's Rod Blossoming; or, The Divine Ordinance of Church Government Vindicated* (1646; Edinburgh: Robert Ogle, and Oliver & Boyd, 1844), 2.4 (pp. 85–86). Cf. André Rivet, *Praelectiones in Cap. xx. Exodi. In quibus Ita Explicatur Decalogus, ut Casus Conscientiae, Quos Vocant ex Eo Suborientes, ac Pleraeque Controversiæ Magni Momenti, Quae circa Legem Moralem Solent Agitari, Fuse & Accurate Discutiantur* (Lugduni Batavorum: Franciscum Hegerum, 1637), 193–210.
[16] Gillespie, *Aaron's Rod Blosssoming*, 2.4 (pp. 86–90). Francis Turretin offers a similarly organized and terminologically defined explanation of the difference between the two kingdoms (Francis Turretin, *Institutes of Elenctic Theology*, ed. James T. Dennison Jr., trans. George Musgrave Giger [Phillipsburg, NJ: P&R, 1992–1997], 18.29.14–18).

the order and decency of the church, the ordination and disposition of church officers, and church discipline.

6. *Interests.* Civil power only has in view the things of this
   life—peace, war, justice, and issues related to the king and
   national interest—all things that are external to man. Ecclesiastical power deals with matters pertaining to God, things
   relevant to the inward man, as a number of theologians have
   argued, such as Francis Junius (1545–1602), Lambert Daneau
   (ca. 1530–1595), and Remonstrant theologian Daniel Tilenus
   (1563–1633).[17]

7. *Adjuncts.* Ecclesiastical power should not be exercised without
   prayer, but no such requirement exists for civil power. And in
   many cases civil power is given to one person, whereas ecclesiastical power is given to an assembly.

8. *Correlations.* Under civil authority people are gathered under
   a commonwealth or civil corporation, whereas the church is a
   spiritual corporation.[18]

9. *Ultimate termination.* The church can go no further than excommunication, whereas civil authorities can put criminals to
   death, as Walo Messalinus (aka Claudius Salmasius) (1588–
   1653) has argued.[19]

10. *Divided execution.* Sometimes the church must censure some-
    one whom the magistrate does not deem worthy of punishment
    and vice versa—that is, someone might suffer the penalty of the
    spiritual sword but not the temporal sword, and another might
    suffer under the temporal sword but not the spiritual sword, as
    David Pareus (1548–1622) has argued.[20]

---

[17] Francis Junius, *Ecclesiastici sive de Natura et Administrationibus Ecclesiae Dei, Libri Tres, Nunc Primum Conscripti, atque in Lucem Editi*, 3.4, in *Opera Theologica Francisci Iunii Biturigis* (Geneva: Samuelem Crispinum, 1613), 1586–87; Daniel Tilenus, *Syntagma Disputationum Theologicarum in Academia Sedanensi Habitarum: Auctore Daniele Tileno* (Christophori Corvini, 1607), 2.32.
[18] A number of early modern Reformed theologians affirm this point. Watson, for example, writes: "His *Kingdom is Spiritual*: he rules in the Hearts of Men. He sets up his Throne where no other King doth" (Thomas Watson, *A Body of Practical Divinity* [London: Thomas Parkhurst, 1692], 16 [p. 109]; cf. Edward Fisher, *The Marrow of Modern Divinity* [London: G. Calvert, 1645], 185; James Ussher, *A Body of Divinitie; or, The Summe and Substance of Christian Religion* [London: Thomas Downes and George Badger, 1645], 179).
[19] Walo Messalinus, *De Episcopis et Presbyteris contra D. Petavium Loiolitam Dissertatio Prima* (1641), 6.
[20] Gillespie's reference is to the commentary of Zacharias Ursinus, which was edited posthumously by his student David Pareus (David Pareus, *Explicationum Catecheticarum Absolutum Opus, Totiusque Theologiae Purioris quasi Novum Corpus, Davidis Parei Opera Extrema Recognigtum* (Geneva, 1603). Ursinus's lectures also appear in English translation: Zacharias Ursinus, *The Commentary of Dr. Zacharias Ursinus on the Heidelberg Catechism*, trans. G. W. Williard (1852; Phillipsburg, NJ: P&R, n.d.), q. 85, art. 4 (p. 450).

So despite the similarities between ecclesiastical and civil authority, there are some significant differences between them that warrant distinguishing them as two kingdoms.

As Gillespie distinguishes them, a *particular* kingdom is subject to the reign of Christ as Mediator, which consists of only the church; and a *general* kingdom is under Christ's authority as the eternal Son of God, by which he is Head over all principalities, powers, and all creatures.[21] Such a twofold kingdom, according to Gillespie, is necessary not only for the reasons elaborated above, but also because it is necessary to affirm Christ's full deity and hence authority over the creation. Socinians denied that "Christ only hath but one kingdom, which he exerciseth as Mediator over the church, and in some respect over all things; but by no means [did] they admit that Christ, as God, reigneth over all things."[22]

In other words, matters pertaining to the relationship between church and the magistrate also extended to issues related to the person and work of Christ, in this case his full divinity. Gillespie enlists Josuae Stegmanni (1588–1632), the *Leiden Synopsis*, Franciscus Gomarus (1563–1641), Willem Apollonius (1602–1657), and Amandus Polanus (1561–1610), to substantiate and corroborate this contention.[23] In these cited sources Gillespie appeals to the distinction between the temporal and spiritual reigns of Christ. The assembly's comments on 1 Corinthians 15:24, also referenced by Gillespie, are representative of the other cited theologians:

> Christ hath a double Kingdom; 1. Essential, as God, and this Christ possesseth with his Father and the Spirit for ever. 2 Oeconomical, as Mediatour betwixt God and Man; and this Kingdom which he received from his Father, he shall surrender up again to his Father after he hath subdued sin and death, and put all his enemies under his feet.[24]

---

[21] Gillespie, *Aaron's Rod Blossoming*, 2.5 (p. 90); cf. a similar distinction in Ussher, *Body of Divintie*, 360.

[22] Gillespie, *Aaron's Rod Blossoming*, 2.5 (p. 90).

[23] Josuae Stegmanni, *Iosuae Stegmanni Photinianismus: h.e. Succincta Refutatio Errorum Photinianorum* (1626), disp. 27, q. 6; Johannes Polyander, André Rivet, Antonius Walaeus, and Antonius Thysius, *Synopsis Purioris Theologiae* (Lugduni Batavorum: Didericum Donner, 1881), 26.53 (p. 261); Amandus Polanus, *Syntagma Theologiae Christianae* (Hanoviae: Johannis Aubrii, 1610), 6.29 (cols. 2860–71); Willem Apollonius, *Jus Maiestatis circa Sacra, sive Tractatus Theologicus, de Jure Magistratus circa Res Ecclesiasticas* (Medioburgi Zelandorum: Iacobum Fierensium, 1642), 1.2 (pp. 33–46).

[24] *Annotations*, comm. 1 Cor. 15:24.

Gillespie is not satisfied, however, with merely enumerating the agreement and disagreement between the general and particular kingdoms of Christ, but gives nine reasons that prove the "distinction of the twofold kingdom of Christ."[25] Gillespie offers the following arguments:[26]

1. The general kingdom of Christ naturally flows from his godhead, but the particular kingdom of Christ belongs to his office as Mediator, and if he were not Mediator, then he would not reign as Mediator.

2. These two kingdoms, one proper to Christ as the God-man and the other proper to him as well as to the Father and Spirit, "are most different and distinct kingdoms."[27]

3. One kingdom is eternal, since Christ is eternally God, but as 1 Corinthians 15:24–25 states, the other kingdom will not be forever, as is also argued in the *Leiden Synopsis* and by Zacharias Ursinus.[28]

4. Since Christ administers one kingdom by evangelical ordinances and the other by divine power, there are consequently two distinct and different kingdoms.[29]

5. In the one kingdom Christ is subordinate to his Father as his vicegerent, and in the other he is equal to the Father; consequently, there are two kingdoms.[30]

6. One kingdom is dispensed in time through Christ's anointing, and the other naturally accompanies his divine nature, which

---

[25] Gillespie, *Aaron's Rod Blossoming*, 2.5 (p. 91).

[26] Ibid., 2.5 (pp. 91–93); VanDrunen, *Natural Law and the Two Kingdoms*, 182–83.

[27] So also Rutherford, *Divine Right*, 23.19 (p. 510).

[28] *Synopsis Purioris*, 26.35 (pp. 256–57).

[29] So also Rutherford, *Divine Right*, 23.19 (pp. 528–29).

[30] Other Reformed theologians who distinguish between the two kingdoms include, e.g., Calvin, Rutherford, Girolamo Zanchi (1516–1590), Turretin, Samuel Maresius (1599–1673), Johannes Heinrich Alsted (1588–1638) (John Calvin, *Institutes of the Christian Religion*, trans. John Allen [Grand Rapids: Eerdmans, 1949], 2.15.3; Turretin, *Institutes*, 18.29.1–25; Rutherford, *Divine Right*, 22.19 [pp. 510–11]; Girolamo Zanchi, *De Religione Christiania Fides—Confession of Christian Religion*, ed. Luca Baschera and Christian Moser, 2 vols. [Leiden: Brill, 2007], 25.1 [1:425]; 26.1 [1:479]; Samuel Maresius, *Collegium Theologicum sive Systema Breve Universae Theologiae Comprehensum Octodecim Disputationibus* [Geneva: Johannes Antonii & Samuelis De Tournis, 1662], 10.59 [p. 222]; Johannes Henricus Alstedius, *Theologia Scholastica Didactica Exhibens Locos Communes Theologicos Methodo Scholastica* [Hanover, 1618], 587, as cited in Heinrich Heppe, *Reformed Dogmatics: Set Out and Illustrated from the Sources*, ed. Ernst Bizer, trans. G. T. Thomson [London: George Allen & Unwin, 1950], 481). I was unable to locate a copy of Alted's *Theologia Scholastica* to verify the statement in context, but Alsted makes a similar point in Johannes Henricus Alstedius, *Synopsis Theologiae Exhibens Oeconomiam Singulorum Locorum Communium Theologcorum* (Hanover: Conraid Eyfridi, 1627), 30.16 (p. 75). For a survey of these doctrines in the early modern period, see VanDrunen, *Natural Law and Two Kingdoms*, 67–211.

he has by eternal generation, which means they are two very different kingdoms.

7. The Scriptures hold forth two kingdoms, one over all creatures and the other only over the church (Ps. 115:3; Isa. 9:6–7; Dan. 4:34–35; Zech. 9:9; Matt. 2:6; Luke 1:32–33; Rom. 9:5; Heb. 3:6).

8. Ephesians 1:21–23 shows the twofold supremacy of Christ, the one kind over all things and the other over the church only.

9. Colossians 1:15–17 distinguishes between Christ's twofold pre-eminence, the one form universal and belonging to him as the eternal Son of God, and another economical, particular, and only over the church, as Calvin argues in his commentary.[31]

Once again, Gillespie enlists a number of other theologians in support of these arguments, including Christian Becmanus (1580–1648), Theodore Beza (1519–1605), Girolamo Zanchi (1516–1590), Bullinger, Daniel Tossanus (1541–1602), and Paul Baynes (ca. 1573–1617).[32] One of the chief points of contention in some of these works, such as Becmanus's analysis of Colossians 1, is an anti-Socinian polemic that sought to defend the deity of Christ while distinguishing this from his mediatorial work as the God-man.

Before we return to the text of the Confession, a few comments about Gillespie's arguments for the two kingdoms are in order. First, as previously stated, though the doctrine of the two kingdoms is commonly associated with Lutheran theology, it is equally characteristic of the Reformed. Present-day antipathies and Reformed-Lutheran denominational lines of division were not drawn as firmly then as they are now. For example, in the broader context of his two-kingdoms arguments Gillespie cites Lutheran theologian Johann Gerhard (1582–1637) on several points.[33] The diversity of names, largely of Continental Reformed theologians, demonstrates that the two-kingdoms doctrine was no minor phenomenon. This is not to say that there were no dissenting voices or variations on this theme. Both Gillespie and

[31] Cf. John Calvin, *Galatians, Ephesians, Philippians, and Colossians*, in *CNTC* (1965; Grand Rapids: Eerdmans, 1996), comm. Col. 1:18 (p. 310).
[32] E.g., Christian Becmanus, *Exercitationes Theologiae* (Amsterdam: Joannem Janssonium, 1643), exer. 8 (pp. 114–40).
[33] Cf. Gillespie, *Aaron's Rod Blossoming*, 2.5 (pp. 113); Johann Gerhard, *Locorum Theologicorum cum pro Adstruenda*, vol. 6 (Jena: Typis & Sumptibus Tobiae Steinmanni, 1619), 6.283–85, 294, 310–11 (pp. 459–60, 474, 498–99).

Rutherford take aim at the views of Johannes Maccovius (1588–1644) and Nicolaus Vedel (1596–1642), both of whom, according to Gillespie, "Ascribe a sort of papal power to the civil magistrate, to the great scandal of the reformed church."[34] And there were those, like Edward Leigh (1602–1671), who generally accepted the two-kingdoms arguments but argued for three kingdoms.

Leigh's *Body of Divinity* maintains the kingdom of Christ's power or excellence, by which he is the Lord of all things (Ps. 24:1); the kingdom of his grace, in which he has ruled in the hearts of his elect ever since the world began (Ps. 2:6; Jer. 23:5; Ezek. 37:22; Zech. 9:9; Luke 11:20; 17:21); and his kingdom of glory, in which Christ is presently in glory in perfect felicity and happiness and where all believers will one day join him (Luke 12:32; 13:29; 23:42; 1 Cor. 6:9; 2 Pet. 2:11).[35] On the third kingdom (glory), Leigh refers readers to the work of an Anglican minister, Robert Crakanthorpe (1567–1624), for further supporting argumentation.[36] And in the marginalia, Leigh notes that the twofold versus threefold kingdom of Christ was a matter of dispute among some of the Reformed.[37] Other disagreements included those who believed that the office of bishop, an office generally rejected by Continental Reformed theologians, stood between the church and magistrate and therefore possessed spiritual and political powers.[38]

Beyond the anti-Socinian polemic, which asserted Christ's deity and hence his universal lordship over the creation, the historical context included debates with the Erastians within the assembly. The divines were undoubtedly shaped by the recent historical past,

---

[34] Gillespie, *Aaron's Rod Blossoming*, 2.5 (p. 116); cf. Nicolaus Vedel, *De Episcopatu Constantini Magni, seu de Potestate Magistratuum Reformatorum, circa Res Ecclesiasticas* (Franekerae: Idsardum Alberti, 1642).

[35] Edward Leigh, *A Systeme or Body of Divinity: Consisting of Ten Books* (London: William Lee, 1654), 5.4 (p. 420).

[36] Richard Crakanthorpe, *The Defence of Constantine with a Treatise of the Popes Temporall Monarchie. Wherein, besides Divers Passages, Touching Other Counsels, Both Generall and Provinciall, the Second Roman Synod, under Silvester, Is Declared to Be a Mere Fiction and Forgery* (London: John Teague, 1621).

[37] Leigh, *Body of Divinity*, 5.4 (p. 420). It seems that the three-kingdom view appears in the catechisms. The Shorter Catechism says that the "Kingdom of Grace may be advanced our selves and others brought into it, and kept in it," which reflects the church in its present state as it awaits the consummation. But the catechism then states that "the Kingdom of Glory may be hastened" (q. 102). Correlatively, the Larger Catechism mentions people being brought into the church, "that Christ would rule in our hearts here," and that Christ "would be pleased so to exercise the kingdome of his power in all the world, as may best conduce to these ends" (q. 191). These are the three kingdoms that Leigh mentions, the kingdoms of power, grace, and glory. I am grateful to my colleague Dave VanDrunen, for drawing my attention to these portions of the catechisms.

[38] Cf. Zanchi, *De Religione*, 25.21 (1:449); Calvin, *Institutes*, 4.11.8.

when the Church of England was under the monarch. Gillespie notes that the magistrate in England was a member of the church not as a magistrate but as a Christian, and ministers of the church located in England were subject to the magistrate not as ministers but as citizens of the commonwealth of England.[39] Hence Gillespie writes:

> The civil magistrate is God's vicegerent, but not Christ's; that is, the magistrate's power hath its rise, origination, institution, and deputation, not from that special dominion that Christ exerciseth over the church as Mediator and Head thereof, but from that universal lordship and sovereignty which God exerciseth over all men by right of creation.[40]

Along similar lines Rutherford makes the case that there is mutual subordination between the church and magistrate, that the church submits to the magistrate in all civil matters, and the magistrate submits to the church in all spiritual matters. This is what he calls "independent supremacy." It is worth noting that Rutherford appeals to a number of Protestant theologians and confessions to confirm his point, including Antonius Waleaus (1573–1639), Jacobus Trigland (1583–1654), the Leiden professors and their famous *Synopsis*, Wilhelm Zepper (1550–1607), Calvin, Petrus Cabel Javius, John Cotton (1585–1652), and David Pareus, as well as the Second Helvetic Confession, the Anglican Confession, the Scottish Confession, and two Lutheran confessions, the Confessions of Suevica (Sweden) and Saxony.[41]

---

[39] Gillespie, *Aaron's Rod Blossoming*, 2.5 (p. 116); see also Rutherford, *Divine Right*, 24.20; 27.23 (pp. 543, 555, 600–601).

[40] Gillespie, *Aaron's Rod Blossoming*, 2.9 (p. 137).

[41] Rutherford, *Divine Right*, 24.20 (p. 560); Antonius Walaeus, *Tractatus de Munere Ministrorum Ecclesiae: Et Inspectione Magistratus circa Illud*, 2, in *Antonii Walaei Opera Omnia* (Leiden: Adriani Wyngaerden, 1647), 16–49; Jacobus Trigland, *Dissertatio Theologica de Cvili & Ecclesiastica Potestate* (Amsterdam: Iohannem Iansonium, 1642), 5 (pp. 103–14); *Synopsis Purioris*, 50.46 (pp. 620–21); Calvin, *Institutes*, 4.11.1–16; John Cotton, *A Model of Church and Civil Power*, 82–138, in Roger Williams, *The Bloudy Tenent of Persecution for Cause of Conscience Discussed* (1644; London: Hanserd Knollys Society, 1848), 190–364; Peter Martyr Vermigli, *Common Places* (London, 1583), 4.13.1–33 (pp. 226–45). Rutherford may be referencing Wilhelm Zepper, *Legem Mosaicarum Forensiu Explanatio, Ubi Quaestio, an et Quatenus Abolitaeillae Sint, Ventilatur* (Herborn: Corvinum, 1614). And I was unable to consult an original edition of Pareus's commentary on Hosea with the preface, as cited by Rutherford; cf. David Pareus, *Davidis Parei In Hoseam Prophetam Commentarius* (Frankfurt: Johannis Lancelloti, 1616), preface. The commentary also appears in *Davidis Parei Sacrarum Literarum. Operum Theologicorum Tomus Primus* (Geneva: Petri Chouët, 1642), 463ff. I was unable to locate any works or information for "Petr. Cabel Javius," though this might be a reference to Pieter Cabeljauw (ca. 1608–1668), and his *Apologetica Rescriptio pro Libertate Ecclesiae in Exercenda Disciplina Spirituali* (Amstelodami: J. Jassonium, 1642). Rutherford also cites the following confes-

Again, this is further evidence that the two-kingdoms doctrine was neither an isolated phenomenon nor inherited from one theologian but was broadly attested and professed by Lutheran and Reformed theologians alike. But what is also of interest is the list of theologians that Rutherford identifies as those who disagree with the two-kingdoms position: he includes Erastus, Remonstrant theologian Johannes Utenbogaeret (1557–1644), Vedel, Hugo Grotius (1583–1645), Bullinger, Gwalther, the Remonstrants in general, and some of the theologians under Henry VIII, a reference possibly including Thomas Cranmer (1489–1556).[42]

Against this historical backdrop and the Confession's affirmations that the visible church is the kingdom of Christ and that God is over the civil magistrate, the respective responsibilities and roles that the Confession defines naturally follow. The Confession maintains that Christians may accept and execute the office of magistrate to maintain piety, peace, and justice according to the wholesome laws of the commonwealth, as well as wage war upon just and necessary occasions (23.2). That Christians were equally subject to the magistrate and church, though in different ways, in no way mitigated their eligibility to serve as magistrates. This position contrasted with Anabaptist views, which maintained that Christians were not allowed to serve as magistrates or engage in war.[43] Given the magistrate's temporal and this-worldly authority, he was not allowed to administer Word and sacrament or hold the power of the keys of the kingdom, namely, church discipline.[44]

---

sions: Second Helvetic Confession, 18; Suevica Confession, 23; Confession of Saxony, 12; Scottish Confession, 24. Given Rutherford's confessional citations the distinct possibility is that he references, without mention, Beza's *Harmony of Confessions*, which contains all of the aforementioned confessions of faith (Theodore Beza, *An Harmony of the Confessions of the Faith of the Christian and Reformed Churches, Which Purely Profess the Holy Doctrine of the Gospel, in All the Chief Kingdoms, Nations, and Provinces of Europe* [Cambridge: Thomas Thomas, 1586]).

[42] Heinrich Bullinger, *The Decades of Henry Bullinger*, ed. Thomas Harding, 4 vols. (1849–1852; Grand Rapids: Reformation Heritage, 2004), 2.7 (1:323–44); Thomas Cranmer, "The Archbishop's Speech at the Coronation of Edward VI, 20 Feb 1547," and "Questions and Answers Concerning the Sacraments and the Appointment and Power of Bishops and Priests," in *Miscellaneous Writings and Letters of Thomas Cranmer, Archbishop of Canterbury, Martyr, 1556*, ed. John Edmund Cox (Cambridge: Parker Society, 1846), 116, 127.

[43] Cf. Schleitheim Confession, 6; Short Confession of Faith, 18, 37; Dordrecht Confession, 14; Balthasar Hubmaier, "On the Sword," in *Balthasar Hubmaier: Theologian of Anabaptism*, ed. H. Wayne Pipkin and John H. Yoder (Scottsdale: Herald, 1989), 492–523; William R. Estep, *The Anabaptist Story: An Introduction to Sixteenth-Century Anabaptism*, 3rd ed. (1975; Grand Rapids: Eerdmans, 1996), 237–306; Mark J. Larson, "John Calvin, the Geneva Reformation, and Godly Warfare: Church and State in the Calvinian Tradition" (PhD diss., Calvin Theological Seminary, 2005).

[44] See Rutherford, *Divine Right*, 27.22 (pp. 639–43); also Turretin, *Institutes*, 18.32.1–28.

Because the divines believed the magistrate was custodian of both tables of the law, however, he was still charged with maintaining the peace and unity of the church and suppressing blasphemy, as well as heresy. The magistrate was also responsible for maintaining the purity of worship by calling synods to decide doctrinal disputes and enforcing synodical decisions by the power of the sword (23.3; cf. 31.2).[45] Such a view differs from Remonstrant doctrine, which advocated religious freedom and tolerance. The Remonstrant Confession of 1621, primarily written by Simon Episcopius (1583–1643), maintains that the magistrate was to care for the church by guarding its outward order and rule and preserving public worship. Like the Westminster Confession, the Remonstrant Confession also affirms the power of the magistrate to call synods and preside over them. However,

> it is neither his right nor duty to command the execution of the decrees of synods by any secular power, and to coerce and repress those who hesitate to subscribe to them for conscience's sake, either with threats or fines, still less with exiles, imprisonments, chains and finally death or other such kinds of atrocious punishments.[46]

Among the likely reasons for this statement were the political consequences that fell upon the Remonstrants in the wake of the decisions of the Synod of Dort (1618–1619) and the condemnation of their doctrine.[47]

---

[45]As noted in the previous chapter, these portions of the Standards were later revised, in 1789, at the first general assembly of the Presbyterian Church (USA). Equally noteworthy is that the Belgic Confession has similar statements regarding the role of the civil magistrate, which were later revised in the twentieth century. The original article on the Belgic reads: "[God] has placed the sword in the hands of government, to punish evil people and protect the good. And the government's task is not limited to caring for and watching over the public domain but extends also to upholding the sacred ministry, with a view to removing and destroying all idolatry and false worship of the Antichrist; to promoting the kingdom of Jesus Christ; and to furthering the preaching of the gospel everywhere; to the end that God may be honored and served by everyone, as he requires in his word" (36). The revision of this article now reads: "For this purpose He [God] has invested the magistracy with the sword for the punishment of evil-doers and for the protection of them that do well. Their office is not only to have regard unto and watch for the welfare of the civil state, but also to protect the sacred ministry, that the kingdom of Christ may be thus promoted. They must therefore countenance the preaching of the Word of the gospel everywhere, that God may be honored and worshipped by every one, as He commands in his Word" (cf. *Psalter Hymnal* [n.p.: Publication Committee of the Christian Reformed Church, 1959]; *Acts of Synod 1938 of the Christian Reformed Church* [Grand Rapids: Office of the Stated Clerk, 1938], art. 34 [pp. 16–20]).
[46]Mark A. Ellis, ed., *The Arminian Confession of 1621* (Eugene, OR: Pickwick, 2005), 25.3–4 (pp. 134–35).
[47]Cf. Rutherford, *Divine Right*, 27.23 (pp. 606–7); Jonathan I. Israel, *The Dutch Republic: Its Rise, Greatness, and Fall 1477–1806* (Oxford: OUP, 1995), 450–505; Maarten Prak, *The Dutch Republic in the Seventeenth Century* (Cambridge: CUP, 2005), 201–21.

The Westminster divines recognize only one Head of the church, Jesus Christ. This counters the claims not only of Erastians but also of Roman Catholics, who claim that the pope is the head of the church on earth (25.6). In his exposition of the Confession, David Dickson (1583–1662) specifically mentions Erastians, Roman Catholics, and Arminians as erring in this point. He cites as counterevidence Beza's *Harmony of Protestant Confessions* to show that the Reformed have historically maintained that Christ alone is Head of the church.[48] The government of the church manifest in its synods and councils has the limited power "ministerially to determine Controversies of Faith, and cases of Conscience" and to ensure that worship and the government of the church are properly performed. Such determinations must be consonant with the Word of God (31.3). By "ministerially," the divines mean that synods and councils are not themselves invested with authority and therefore do not legislate, as only Christ as the supreme lawgiver can do this.[49] Rather, the authority of synods and councils is derivative of Christ's authority, and synodical or conciliar decisions have authority only insofar as they concur with the Word of God.

Recall what the divines have said regarding Christian liberty: "God alone is the Lord of the Conscience, and hath left it free from the Doctrines and Commandments of men, which are, in any thing contrary to his Word; or beside it, if [sic] matters of Faith, or Worship" (20.2). And synods and councils may only handle ecclesiastical matters and "are not to intermeddle with Civil Affairs which concern the Commonwealth; unless by way of humble Petition, in cases extraordinary; or, by way of Advice, for satisfaction of Conscience" (31.5). Along with the power to determine doctrinal matters consonant with the Word of God is the authority to preach the Word and administer the sacraments, something that only ministers "lawfully ordained" may perform (27.4; LC q. 158).

The Sacraments

The kingdom of Christ is the visible church, and this is a covenanted kingdom, one that has signs and seals of God's covenant with his

---

[48] David Dickson, *Truths Victory over Error* (Edinburgh: John Reed, 1684) 25.8 (pp. 253–55); cf. Beza, *Harmony of the Confessions*; also Rutherford, *Divine Right*, 24.20; 26.22 (pp. 556–57, 560, 578–79).
[49] See, e.g., Turretin, *Institutes*, 18.31.1–25.

people. Before we look specifically at the two signs and seals, baptism and the Lord's Supper, it is first necessary to examine what the Confession has to say about sacraments in general.

The Sacraments in General

The divines' explanation of the sacraments in general appears in chapter 27 of the Confession, which serves as the entry point for baptism and the Lord's Supper, in contrast to Roman Catholicism's seven sacraments. In many respects, one can find different antecedent streams of theological thought codified in this chapter. For example, like a number of Reformed witnesses before them, the divines explain that the sacraments are "holy Signes, and Seals of the Covenant of Grace" (27.1).[50] This reveals a difference between the typical Reformed understanding of the sacraments and the Roman Catholic idea, which sees the sacraments as instruments of divinely infused grace. According to the Council of Trent, divine grace, which carries various virtues, is infused into the soul—Trent speaks in terms of an infused thing or substance.[51] By contrast, the Confession states that the sacraments "represent Christ, and his benefits" (27.1). This Westminster conception of the sacraments correlates with its doctrine of the visible church: "Unto this Catholique Visible Church, Christ hath given the Ministry, Oracles, and Ordinances of God, for the gathering and perfecting of the Saints, in this life, to the end of the World: and doth, by his own presence and Spirit, according to his promise, make them effectual thereunto" (25.3).

There are two key things to note. First, the sacraments do not merely represent an invisible grace, which is a common aphoristic statement regarding the nature of the sacraments that can be traced to Augustine and that Ulrich Zwingli (1484–1531) and Calvin also employed, albeit critically in the case of the latter.[52] This Augustinian aphorism does not appear in the chapter on the sacraments or in

---

[50] Cf. Calvin, *Institutes*, 4.14.1, 5; Belgic Confession, 33; Heidelberg Catechism, q. 66; Ursinus, *Commentary*, 342.

[51] *The Catechism of the Council of Trent: Ordered by the Council of Trent*, ed. St. Charles Borromeo (1566; Rockford: Tan, 1982), 143, 188.

[52] Augustine, *Questions on the Pentateuch*, 3.84 (Patrologia Latina, ed. J.-P. Migne, 217 vols. [Paris, 1844–1864], 34:712); Augustine, *City of God*, 10.5, in *NPNF*[1] 2; Ulrich Zwingli, *Reckoning of the Faith*, in *Creeds and Confessions in the Christian Tradition*, ed., Jaroslav Pelikan and Valerie Hotchkiss, 3 vols. (New Haven, CT: Yale University Press, 2003), 2:262; Calvin, *Institutes*, 4.14.1.

the Larger or Shorter Catechisms. The closest the Standards come to the Augustinian definition is in the explanation of the parts of a sacrament: "The parts of a Sacrament are two; the one, an outward and sensible signe, used according to Christs own appointment; the other an inward and spirituall grace thereby signified" (LC q. 163).[53] This omission of Augustine's aphoristic definition is especially evident when the divines define a sacrament in the Shorter Catechism: "A Sacrament is an holy Ordinance instituted by Christ; wherein, by sensible Signs, Christ and the benefits of the New Covenant, are represented, sealed, and applied to Believers" (q. 92; cf. LC q. 162). For the Roman Catholic Church, the sacraments are visible forms of invisible grace, whereas in the Westminster Standards, the sacraments are visible signs that represent Christ first and foremost.[54] Despite criticisms that the Confession has no links between ecclesiology, christology, and soteriology, such affirmations show that the divines sought to emphasize that Christ's reign over the church involves his Word and his institution of the sacraments, which are signs and seals of the covenant of grace.[55] In short, the divines continue the thread of Christ and covenant throughout the Confession, and these ideas continue in their ecclesiology.

Second, the Standards explain that the sacraments are for the "gathering, and perfecting of the Saints" (25.3). Elsewhere, the Standards seem to embrace a sacramental efficacy that is closer to Rome than to Geneva: "The Sacraments become effectuall means of salvation, not by any power in themselves, or any vertue derived from the piety or intention of him by whom they are administered; but only by the working of the holy Ghost, and the blessing of Christ, by whom they are instituted" (LC q. 161). At first blush, this seems very similar to a Roman Catholic understanding of the sacraments. In fact, some have drawn the conclusion that the Confession teaches baptismal regeneration. David Wright claims, "The Westminster divines viewed baptism as the instrument and occasion of regeneration by the Spirit, of the remission of sins, of engrafting into Christ (cf. XXVIII.i). The

---

[53] Cf. Leigh, *Body of Divinity*, 8.7 (p. 656).
[54] Cf. *Catechism of the Council of Trent*, 143.
[55] For this criticism, see T. F. Torrance, *Scottish Theology: From John Knox to John McLeod Campbell* (Edinburgh: T&T Clark, 1996), 145.

Confession teaches baptismal regeneration."[56] However, this is a misreading of the Standards because such a conclusion fails to define properly baptismal regeneration or consider the broader statement regarding the sacraments being effectual means of salvation, not justification.

Nowhere do the Standards state that a person is regenerated by baptism. In fact, a key tenet of the Roman Catholic understanding of baptism is that the administration of the rite *ex opere operato* regenerates the adult and infant alike and cleanses each of original sin at the moment of administration.[57] This aspect of the Roman Catholic understanding is evident in that Rome denominates baptism as the instrument of justification.[58] The absence of baptismal regeneration in the Confession is apparent when one considers its documentary-source history. Recall, the divines were first called to amend the Thirty-Nine Articles (1571), and they also used James Ussher's (1581–1656) Irish Articles (1615) as a starting point for their own confession writing. The statements of both the Thirty-Nine Articles and the Irish Articles were clearly available and well known, yet the divines chose not to employ them (table 7).

The divines did not employ the term *instrument*, as do the Thirty-Nine Articles. Moreover, in contrast to the Irish Articles, the divines stipulated that baptism is an entrance into the visible church, and they did not mention justification, which further distances their view from anything resembling baptismal regeneration and the views of the Council of Trent.

It is one thing to say that baptism regenerates and justifies and entirely another to say that the sacraments are effectual means of salvation. The sacraments—note the plural (e.g., both baptism and the Lord's Supper, not just baptism)—and the preaching of the Word

---

[56] See David F. Wright, *What Has Infant Baptism Done to Baptism? An Enquiry at the End of Christendom* (Milton Keynes: Paternoster, 2005), 99; also, Wright, "Baptism at the Westminster Assembly," in *The Westminster Confession into the 21st Century*, ed. J. Ligon Duncan, 3 vols. (Fearn: Christian Focus, 2003–2009), 1:161–85, esp. 168–70.

[57] Regarding baptismal regeneration, some theologians of the period understood that the Thirty-Nine Articles allowed such a reading, whereas others, such as James Ussher, did not hold to such a view (cf. James Ussher, "Letter CCI: Ussher to Ward," and Samuel Ward, "Letter CLXX: Ward to Ussher," in *The Whole Works of the Most Rev. James Ussher*, 17 vols. [Dublin: Hodges and Smith, 1847–1864], 15:9, 505. For the bigger picture and the discussion among Ussher, Ward, George Downame, and William Bedell, see Ussher, *Works*, 15:46–47, 144–45, 480–83, 493, 499–507, 508–20, 538). I am grateful to Jay Collier for alerting me to this correspondence.

[58] Council of Trent, sess. 6, January 13, 1547, first decree, chap. 7.

and prayer are effectual means of *salvation* (LC q. 154). Salvation is a broad encompassing term that has in view the entire process of redemption but more specifically the believer's sanctification, as the sacraments are for the "perfecting of the Saints" (25.3). For example, the Word is tied to a person's regeneration, not baptism: "The Spirit of God maketh the Reading, but especially the Preaching of the Word, an effectual means of enlightening, convincing, and humbling sinners . . . and establishing their hearts in holinesse and comfort through faith unto salvation" (LC q. 155; cf. SC q. 89). In the same way, the Spirit takes the sacraments and uses them as he does the Word.

Table 7. The Thirty-Nine Articles, the Irish Articles, and the Confession on baptism

Thirty-Nine Articles (1571)	Irish Articles (1615)	Westminster Confession (1646)
Baptism is not only a sign of profession, and mark of difference, whereby Christian men are discerned from other that be not christened; but it is also a sign of regeneration or new birth, whereby, *as by an instrument, they that receive baptism rightly,* are grafted into the Church; the promises of the forgiveness of sin, and our adoption to be the sons of God by the Holy Ghost, are visibly signed and sealed; faith is confirmed, and grace increased by virtue of prayer unto God. (§ 27, emphasis added)	Baptism is not only an outward sign of our profession, and a note of difference, whereby Christians are discerned from such as are no Christians; *but much more a Sacrament of our admission into the Church, sealing unto us our new birth (and consequently our justification, adoption, and sanctification)* by the communion which we have with Jesus Christ. (§ 89, emphasis added)	Baptism is a Sacrament of the New Testament, ordained by Jesus Christ, not onely for the solemn Admission of the Party Baptized *into the Visible Church;* but also, to be unto him a sign, and seal of the Covenant of Grace, of his ingrafting into Christ, of Regeneration, of Remission of sins, and of his giving up unto God through Jesus Christ, to walk in newness of life. Which Sacrament is, by Christ's own appointment, to be continued in his Church until the end of the World. (27.1, emphasis added)

It seems difficult, if not impossible, to affirm that the Standards teach baptismal regeneration or anything close to approaching an *ex opere operato* view of the sacraments. The divines repeatedly explain that the sacraments are "signs and seals" of Christ and the benefits of the covenant of grace (LC qq. 165, 167; SC q. 94). The Confession, without naming the Roman Catholic view of sacramental efficacy, rejects it when it states:

> The Grace which is exhibited in, or by the Sacraments rightly used, is not conferred by any power in them: neither doth the efficacy of a Sacrament depend upon the Piety, or Intention of him that doth administer it: but, upon the work of the Spirit, and the word of Institution, which contains, together with a Precept authorizing the use thereof, a Promise of benefit to worthy Receivers. (27.3)

There are several points to note from this statement. We see a continuance of the rejection of Donatism, which taught that the efficacy of the sacrament depends upon the one who administers it.[59] Though this paragraph does not explicitly state it, the promise of God is what is central and made effectual by the Holy Spirit. One should also note that the sacraments are only effectual to "worthy Receivers," those who possess faith. Edward Leigh differentiates between the Roman Catholic and Reformed views when he explains that the former argues that the sacraments function like a pen in the hand of the writer, whereas the latter maintains "that except the receiver be thus and thus qualified, he loseth the benefit of the sacraments. See *Acts* 10.47."[60] In this regard Confession 28.6 is noteworthy, as baptism is only effective "to such (whether of age, or infants) as that Grace belongeth unto, according to the Councel of Gods own Will, in his appointed time." In other words, baptism is an effective means of grace only for the elect, not indiscriminately for anyone who receives the sacrament.

Two other things concerning the sacraments are noteworthy. First, the divines explain the nature of the sacramental union—the relationship between the sign and the thing signified. They explain that sometimes the names and effects of the one, the things signified, are attributed to the other, the sign, because of the sacramental union (27.2).[61] Second, like other past Reformed theologians, they also explain that the sacraments of the Old Testament, though different from those of the New Testament, signified and exhibited the same thing—

---

[59] See, e.g., Augustine, *The Letters of Petilian, the Donatist*, 3.15.18, in *NPNF*[1] 4:603.
[60] Leigh, *Body of Divinity*, 8.7 (p. 657).
[61] Cf. Ussher, *Body of Divintie*, 405–6.

the accidents were different but they were substantively the same, the substance being Christ (27.5; cf. 7.5).

Baptism

In chapter 28 the divines treat the subject of baptism and begin with an important distinction that stands in contrast to Anabaptist views on the sacraments.[62] Baptism is "the solemn admission of the party baptized into the visible church."[63] There is no way to know whether a person—adult or infant—is one of the elect and whether in the case of an adult the profession of faith is valid. When a person is baptized the rite admits him or her into the visible covenant community. Baptism is a sign and seal of the covenant of grace, union with Christ, regeneration, the remission of sins, surrender to God, and walking in the newness of life (28.1).

The Confession also affirms the practice of infant baptism, stating, "Not only those that do actually profess faith in and obedience unto Christ, but also the infants of one, or both, believing parents are to be baptized" (28.4). Infants born within the visible covenant community have a right to the sign of admission. If an infant is born outside the visible church, then such a one has to wait to make a valid profession of faith (LC q. 166; SC q. 95). We find a fuller statement of this theological principle in the Westminster Directory for Public Worship. Regarding the administration of baptism, the minister is instructed to show:

> That the Promise is made to Believers and their seed, and that the seed and posterity of the faithfull, born within the church, have by their birth, interest in the Covenant, and right to the Seal of it, and to the outward Privileges of the Church, under the Gospel, no lesse then the Children of Abraham, in the time of the Old Testament; the Covenant of Grace, for substance being the same; and the Grace of God, and the consolation of Believers, more plentiful

---

[62] Cf. Hans Denck, *Confession before the Nuremberg Council*, 2; Balthasar Hubmaier, *A Christian Catechism*, qq. 32–42; Hubmaier, "On the Christian Baptism of Believers," "Dialogue with Zwingli's Baptism Book," "Old and New Teachers on Believers Baptism," "Dialogue with Oecolampad on Infant Baptism," 95–149, 166–233, 245–95; Schleitheim Confession, 1; Concept of Cologne, 5; Short Confession of Faith, 31–32; Dordrecht Confession, 7; Estep, *Anabaptist Story*, 201–35.

[63] Leigh, *Body of Divinity*, 8.8 (p. 662); cf. William Gouge, *A Short Catechisme, Wherein Are Breifely Laid Down the Fundamentall Principles of Christian Religion* (London: John Beale, 1615).

than before: That the Son of God admitted little Children into his presence, embracing and blessing them, saying, For of such is the Kingdom of God: That children by Baptisme are solemnly received into the bosome of the visible Church, distinguished from the world, and them that are without, and united with Beleevers; and that all who are baptized in the Name of Christ, do renounce, and by their Baptisme are bound to fight against the Devil, the World and the Flesh: That they are Christians, and federally holy before Baptisme, and therefore are they baptized. That the inward Grace and virtue of Baptisme is not tyed to that very moment of time wherein it is administered, and that the fruit and power thereof reacheth to the whole course of our life.[64]

Two things demonstrate that the divines did not formulate their understanding of baptism to teach baptismal regeneration.

First, the Confession 28.5 explains that though it is a great sin to contemn or neglect baptism, grace and salvation are not so inseparably joined to it that a person cannot be regenerated or saved without it. The paragraph also states that baptism does not mean that all who receive the rite are undoubtedly regenerated. Second, the Confession rejects the Roman Catholic view of *ex opere operato* by explaining, "The efficacy of Baptism is not tied to that moment of time wherein it is administered." In other words, just because a person is baptized, he or she does not automatically receive the grace annexed to it. The person might receive it later in life, or not at all if he or she is not elect. The Confession explains: "By the right use of this Ordinance, the grace promised, is not only offered, but really exhibited, and conferred, by the Holy Ghost, to such (whether of age or infants) as that Grace belongeth unto, according to the Councel of Gods own Will, in his appointed time" (28.6). The divines wanted to ensure that God's sovereignty in salvation was not bound to a mechanical view of the sacraments, as in Roman Catholicism. The assembly did discuss and debate the way in which God's grace accompanies the sacrament of baptism, however.

---

[64] For a brief history of the Directory, see John H. Leith, *Introduction to the Reformed Tradition* (1977; Atlanta: John Knox, 1981), 190–92. For theological argumentation for the validity of infant baptism from a Westminster divine, see Samuel Rutherford, *The Covenant of Life Opened* (Edinburgh, 1655), 95–118.

The extant records are a bit sparse, and even then, what is recorded is at times somewhat cryptic. For example, Jeremiah Whitaker (1599–1654) is recorded as saying:

> That it does confer grace I do not find, but our divines do hold it. . . .
> When they oppose the Papists, they say it is more than a sign and
> seal. . . . Chamier says the grace that is signified is exhibited, so it
> is in the French Confession; it does *efficaciter donare*. . . . I conceive
> that it does not confer it *ex opere operato*.[65]

Now, it should be noted that the ellipses are part of the original minutes—they are gaps in the record, not editorial elisions.[66] There are several other things to note.

First, Whitaker appeals to French Reformed theologian Daniel Chamier (1565–1621), who was trained under Theodore Beza at Geneva.[67] Second, Whitaker also appeals to the French Confession (1559), which states: "We believe, as has been said, that in the Lord's supper, as well as in baptism, God gives us really and in fact that which he there sets forth to us; and that consequently with these signs is given the true possession and enjoyment of that which they present to us" (37). Third, further in Whitaker's statement, he says that benefits accrue "from the union of the sign and the thing signified which is in the analogy, . . . and in *conjuncta exhibitione* as Ursin[us] . . . when we lawfully receive it."[68] Here Whitaker appeals to Ursinus's commentary on the Heidelberg Catechism. Ursinus writes:

> The names and properties of the things signified are attributed to
> the signs; and, on the other hand, the names of the signs are attributed to the things signified, on account of their analogy, or on
> account of the signification of the things through the signs, and on
> account of the joint exhibition and reception of the things with the
> signs in their lawful use.[69]

---

[65] *MPWA*, sess. 566, January 5, 1645 (3:732–33). For biographical information on Jeremiah Whitaker, see James Reid, *Memoirs of the Westminster Divines*, 2 vols. (1811; Edinburgh: Banner of Truth, 1982), 2:216–446; William Barker, *Puritan Profiles: 54 Contemporaries of the Westminster Assembly* (1996; Fearn: Mentor, 1999), 136–40; cf. Leigh, *Body of Divinity*, 8.7 (p. 658).

[66] Wright, "Baptism at the Westminster Assembly," 163–66.

[67] Samuel MacCauly Jackson, *The New Schaff-Herzog Encyclopedia of Religious Knowledge*, vol. 3 (New York: Funk and Wagnalls, 1909), 1.

[68] *MPWA*, sess. 566, January 5, 1645 (3:733).

[69] Ursinus, *Commentary*, 355.

Though the information is sparse, this small window into the inner
workings of the assembly indicates that multiple streams of Reformed
theology fed into the discussion on baptism.

Whitaker's one statement appeals to the French Confession, which
was heavily influenced by Calvin. He also invokes the opinions of
Chamier, another French Reformed theologian trained in Geneva by
Calvin's successor. But in addition to this he also quotes Ursinus's
commentary on the Heidelberg Catechism.[70] Hence, we can clearly
see the different influences. One can only imagine how many other
sources were cited and quoted that fed into the final product. If the
references in Edward Leigh's treatment of baptism in his *Body of Divinity* are any indication of the reading habits and wealth of theological resources available to the assembly, then one can say that the
divines embraced not the views of one man but rather a constellation
of testimony on the subject.

In his treatment of baptism Leigh references the work of Westminster divines William Gouge (1575–1653), Daniel Featley (1582–
1645), Cornelius Burgess (ca. 1589–1665), George Gillespie, and
Thomas Goodwin (1600–1680). Beyond the assembly Leigh engages
Andrè Rivet, William Ames (1576–1633), Peter Ramus (1515–1572),
Martin Luther, Zanchi, William Perkins (1558–1602), Thomas Aquinas (ca. 1225–1274), Peter Lombard (ca. 1100–1160), Gerhard Johann Vossius (1577–1649), Tertullian (ca. 160–220), Origen (ca.
185–254), Richard Baxter (1615–1691), Calvin, and Johannes Crocius (1590–1659).[71] These names represent just a fraction of those
that appear in the text and marginalia, but they nevertheless demonstrate that the divines engaged, were aware of, employed, and
learned from Patristic, medieval, Reformation, and contemporary
theologians. What little information we possess from the assembly's
deliberations demonstrates not only the breadth of the knowledge of

---

[70] For Ursinus's influence upon the assembly, see R. Scott Clark and Joel Beeke, "Ursinus, Oxford, and the Westminster Divines," in Duncan, *The Westminster Confession into the 21st Century*, 2:1–32.

[71] See, e.g., Daniel Featley, *The Dippers Dipt; or, The Anabaptists Duck'd and Plung'd over Head and Ears at a Disputation in Southwark* (London: N. B. and Richard Royston, 1647); Gouge, *Brief Catechism*; Peter Ramus, *Commentariorum de Religione Christiana Libri Quatuor* (Francofurti: Andreas Wechel, 1594), 4.5 (pp. 271–76); Gerhardi Joannis Vossii, *De Baptismo Disputationes XX, & Una de Sacramentorum Vi, atque Efficacia* (Amsterdam: Ludovicum Elzevirium, 1648); Johannes Crocius, *Anti-Weigelius, Id Est, Theologiae, Quam Valentinus Weigelius, ex Paracelsi Potissimum & Veterum Haereticorum Lacunis Haustam*, vol. 2 (Cassellis: Jacobus Genschins, 1651), 7.1 (pp. 117–19).

the divines but also the variegated nature of the sources they employed. They did not appeal to one narrow strand of the tradition, but drew upon the whole of it.

The question remains, however, in what way is baptism a benefit to a person who cannot remember being baptized? The Directory for Worship affirms that God's grace in baptism "reaches to the whole course of our life," and therefore those who have been baptized are "To look back to their Baptisme . . . to stirre up their faith; to improve and make right use of their Baptisme, and of the Covenant sealed thereby betwixt God and their souls." But receiving baptism is no guarantee of a person's salvation. As Leigh explains: "Baptism is not thus effectual to all but onely to the elect, Mark 16.16. These great benefits of union with Christ, regeneration & pardon of sin are not alwaies bestowed at Baptism, Act. 19.3,4."[72]

The Standards make several liturgical observations concerning baptism. It is to be administered to a person only once (28.7). Since the divines believed that baptism is chiefly a sign and seal of the covenant of grace, baptism is first and foremost the promise of God and second the promise of the one baptized (LC q. 166). Stated simply, the promise depends not upon the fidelity of the person baptized, as it would in an Anabaptist voluntarist soteriology, but upon God.[73] This emphasis is no surprise, given the divines' view of God's sovereignty and the covenant, and the dangers they saw from the abuse or diminution of baptism. Robert Baillie (1602–1662), one of the Scottish divines, comments in a letter, "At our sitting down this day, a great many of our brethren did complain of the great increase and insolencie, in diverse places, of the Antinomian and Anbaptisicall conventicles."[74] Recall Lightfoot's record that the assembly's sins included a lack of zeal in challenging antinomians and Anabaptists.

Like the nascent Reformed tradition before them, the divines ex-

---

[72] Leigh, *Body of Divinity*, 8.8 (p. 663).
[73] See, e.g., Conrad Grebel, "Letters to Thomas Müntzer by Conrad Grebel and Friends," in *Spiritual and Anabaptist Writers*, ed. George Hunston Williams, LCC (Philadelphia: Westminster, 1957), 80; Hughes Oliphant Old, *The Shaping of the Reformed Baptismal Rite in the Sixteenth Century* (Grand Rapids: Eerdmans, 1992), 90; David Steinmetz, *Reformers in the Wings* (Grand Rapids: Baker, 1981), 210, 216; Steinmetz, "Scholasticism and Radical Reform: Nominalist Motifs in the Theology of Balthasar Hubmaier, *MQR* 45 (1971): 123–44, esp. 130.
[74] Robert Baillie, *The Letters and Journals of Robert Baillie*, ed. David Laing, 2 vols. (Edinburgh: Robert Ogle, 1841), 2:215.

press a moderate degree of ambivalence regarding the proper mode of baptism: "Dipping of the person into the water is not necessary; but baptism is rightly administered by pouring, or sprinkling water upon the person" (28.3).[75] This statement allows all three modes of baptism, though the divines express a preference for sprinkling.[76] This conclusion is evident from the proof text the divines cite, namely, Hebrews 9:10. The Directory for Worship offers helpful comments: "That the water, in baptism, represents and signifies . . . the blood of Christ . . . That baptizing, or sprinkling and washing with water, signifies the cleansing from sin by the blood and for the merit of Christ."[77]

Even though the three modes of baptism are mentioned, this small statement in the Confession took some three days of theological discussion and debate to compose. John Lightfoot comments in his personal journal, "We fell upon a large and long discourse, whether dipping were essential or used in the first institution, or in the Jews' custom."[78] The initial vote on the matter was 25–24 to exclude dipping, or immersion, in the Directory, though it should be noted that the debate was not over dipping versus the other modes, but whether dipping should be placed on the same level as sprinkling and pouring. The divines returned to the issue and later agreed to the statement that we find in the Directory. Lightfoot comments, "But as for the dispute itself about dipping, it was thought fit and most safe to let it alone. . . . But this cost a great deal of time about the wording."[79] The debate over this subject was likely fueled because Particular Baptists (Baptists who held to a Reformed view of soteriology) were working on their own confession of faith during the same timeframe.[80]

---

[75] Indifference on the mode of baptism was characteristic of medieval, Lutheran, and Reformed authors of the early modern period (cf. Thomas Aquinas, *Summa Theologica*, IIIa, q. 66, arts. 7–8; Philip Melanchthon, *Loci Communes [1543]*, trans. J. A. O. Preus [St. Louis: Concordia, 1992], 13 [p. 143]; Leonard Hutter, *Compend of Lutheran Theology*, trans. H. E. Jacobs and G. F. Spieker [Philadelphia: The Lutheran Bookstore, 1868], 21.17 [p. 177]; Calvin, *Institutes*, 4.15.19; Johannes Wollebius, *Compendium Theologiae Christiane*, 23.1.89, in *Reformed Dogmatics*, ed. John W. Beardslee [New York: OUP, 1965]; Turretin, *Institutes*, 19.11.11–12; Ussher, *Body of Divinitie*, 413). This indifference is likely for the first time rejected in the Second London Confession (1689), 19.4.
[76] Cf. Martin Luther, *The Holy Sacrament of Baptism*, in *LW*, 35:29; Calvin, *Institutes*, 4.15.19.
[77] Directory for Public Worship, in *Westminster Confession*, 382.
[78] Lightfoot, *Journal*, 299; cf. Wright, "Baptism at the Westminster Assembly," 177–79.
[79] Lightfoot, *Journal*, 301; see also Richard A. Muller and Rowland S. Ward, *Scripture and Worship: Biblical Interpretation and the Directory for Worship* (Phillipsburg, NJ: P&R, 2007), 129–30.
[80] See the First London Confession (1644), 40; cf. Leigh, *Body of Divinity*, 8.8 (p. 665).

The Lord's Supper

When examining the doctrine of the Lord's Supper, we should be mindful that this subject was one of the most hotly contested doctrines during the Reformation. Whatever hopes there might have been for a unified Protestant Reformation were dashed upon the rocks of diverse opinions on this matter.[81] Two issues splintered Protestantism. First, was the Lord's Supper a means of grace? This issue did not divide Roman from Reformed views but did reveal fissures among the Reformed vis-à-vis the views of Zwingli. Second, in what manner was Christ present in the supper? Opinions on this question were sharply divided, and therefore the Confession's treatment of the supper is a veritable minefield of unnamed opponents whose theological views it dismisses.

Chapter 29 begins with a rehearsal of the broad contours of the doctrine of the Lord's Supper: it was instituted by Christ, is observed in the church until the end of the world, seals the benefits of his work upon "true Beleevers" as a perpetual remembrance of Christ's sacrifice, and is for their "Spiritual nourishment & growth in him" (29.1). The second paragraph engages Roman Catholic views when it rejects the idea that the supper is a sacrifice:

> In this Sacrament Christ is not offered up to his Father; nor, any real Sacrifice made at all, for remission of sias [*sic*] of the quick or dead; but only a Commemoration of that one offering up of himself, by himself, upon the Cross, once for all: and, a spiritual Oblation of all possible praise unto God, for the same: So that, the Popesh Sacrifice of the Mass (as they call it) is most abominably injurius to Christs one, only Sacrifice, the alone Propitiation for all the sins of his elect. (29.2)

The Confession specifically rejects the views of the Council of Trent, which characterizes the supper as a "divine sacrifice" because "the very same Christ is contained and offered in bloodless manner who made a bloody sacrifice of himself once for all on the cross." According to Trent

---

[81] See, e.g., Jill Raitt, *The Colloquy of Montbéliard: Religion and Politics in the Sixteenth Century* (Oxford: OUP, 1993), 73–109; Alister E. McGrath, *Reformation Thought: An Introduction* (1988; Oxford: Blackwell, 1993), 159–87; Robert Kolb, *Confessing the Faith: Reformers Define the Church, 1530–80* (St. Louis: Concordia, 1991), 115–20; Martin Luther, *The Marburg Colloquy and the Marburg Articles (1529)*, in *LW*, 38:3–90.

this "sacrifice" is propitiatory and therefore suitable "for the sins, penalties, satisfactions, and other needs of the faithful who are living, but also for those who have died in Christ but are not yet fully cleansed."[82]

Rome's assertion that the supper is a sacrifice sets Trent upon a very different trajectory from what one commonly finds in Reformed views. Trent teaches that Christ "offered his body and blood to God the Father under the forms of bread and wine" and gave this to his disciples, thereby constituting them as priests.[83] But according to Trent, with the priestly consecration of the bread and wine, Christ is "truly, really, and substantially contained in the propitious sacrament of the holy eucharist under the appearance of those things which are perceptible to the senses."[84] The council does not employ the terms, but what lies behind such a statement is the Thomist distinction between the substance (what a thing actually is) and the accidents (what a thing looks like, its external appearance) of the Lord's Supper. This means that the elements may look, taste, feel, and smell like bread and wine, but in reality are the actual body and blood of Christ.[85] The council affirms transubstantiation, namely, that the bread and wine are transformed into the body and blood of Christ. Transubstantiation necessitates the worship of the elements.[86] The Confession is very pointed in its rejection of these two ideas, but reserves its harshest criticism for transubstantiation:

> That Doctrine which maintains a change of the substance of Bread and Wine, into the substance of Christs Body and Blood (commonly called Transubstantiation) by Consecration of a Priest, or by any other way, is repugnant, not to Scripture alone, but even to common Sense and Reason; overthroweth the nature of the Sacrament, and hath been, and is, the cause of manifold Superstitions; yes, of gross Idolatries. (29.6; cf. 29.4)

These are some of the strongest words of rejection in the Confession, and that should come as no surprise, given the heated debates over the years on this particular subject.

---

82 Council of Trent, sess. 22, September 17, 1562, first decree, chap. 2.
83 Ibid., sess. 22, § 1.
84 Ibid., sess. 13, § 1, October 11, 1551.
85 Aquinas, *Summa Theologica*, IIIa, q. 75.
86 Council of Trent, sess. 13, October 11, 1551, first decree, chap. 5.

328   The Theology of the Westminster Standards

In his treatment of the Lord's Supper, Edward Leigh provides ten reasons for rejecting transubstantiation:[87]

1. Christ would have to hold himself in his own hands and eat and drink his own flesh because, according to the Gospel accounts, he ate the supper with his disciples.
2. Christ would need two bodies, one broken and having the blood separated from the cup, and the other whole and having the blood in the body that holds the cup.
3. Christ's blood would have been shed before his crucifixion.
4. His one body would have to be in a thousand places at once in order to facilitate the celebration of the supper in different locations.
5. A true body is finite and cannot be in multiple places at once.
6. Accidents would be without a subject, but Aristotle maintains that accidents are the very substance of a thing (cf. Aquinas, *Summa Theologica*, IaIIae, q. 90, art. 2).
7. The same thing would be and not be at the same time.
8. It is inhumane because no one but cannibals eats human flesh.
9. Our senses would be deceived because the sacrament looks like bread and wine but is not.
10. There is no change of the water in baptism, yet it too is a sign like the supper.

In addition to these reasons for rejecting transubstantiation, Leigh cites a host of literature that polemically engages this particular subject. He notes the work of William Attersoll (d. 1640), who gives twenty-six reasons for rejecting transubstantiation; in fact, Leigh's own list echoes Attersoll's at a number of points.[88] Leigh also cites Gilbert Primrose (ca. 1580–1642), Joseph Hall (1574–1656), Daniel Featley, Edward Chaloner (1590–1625), Thomas Morton (bap. 1564, d. 1659), Moïses Amyraut (1596–1664), and William Ames.[89]

---

[87] Leigh, *Body of Divinity*, 8.9 (p. 698); see also Dickson, *Truths Victory over Error*, 29.4 (pp. 293–98); Ussher, *Body of Divintie*, 424–25.

[88] William Attersoll, *The New Covenant; or, A Treatise of the Sacraments: Whereby the Last Testament of Our Lord and Saviour Jesus Christ, through the Shedding of His Pure and Precious Blood, Is Ratified and Applied unto the Conscience of Every True Beleever* (London: W. Iaggard, 1614), 3.5 (pp. 354–69).

[89] Gilbert Primrose, *The Table of the Lord* (London: Nicholas Bourne, 1626), 127–58; Joseph Hall, *No Peace with Rome. Wherein Is Proved, That, as Terms Now Stand, There Can Be No Reconciliation of the Reformed Religion with the Romish* (London: William Pickering, 1852), 4 (p. 95–104);

Even though the Confession reserves its sharpest criticism for Roman Catholic views of the supper, it has mild words of rejection for other Protestant views, whether of Zwingli or of the Lutheran church. Ulrich Zwingli, for example, rejected the idea that the sacraments are means of grace and instead contended that they are merely signs and pledges of the believer's faith: "A channel or vehicle is not necessary to the Spirit, for he himself is the virtue and energy whereby all things are born, and has no need of being borne."[90] For Zwingli, the sacraments, therefore, were only man's pledge of fidelity to God; they were not seals of God's promises to the church.[91] This understanding of the Lord's Supper is especially evident in Zwingli's characterization of it:

> The deliverance and exodus from Egypt was a type of his [Christ's] redemption, and in that deliverance a lamb was slain and eaten as a sign of the Passover and the blood was sprinkled on the side posts and the upper door posts, all which expressly typified and represented the Lord Jesus Christ. In the same way he himself instituted a remembrance of that deliverance by which he redeemed the whole world, that we might never forget that for our sakes he exposed his body to the ignominy of death, and not merely that we might not forget it in our hearts, but that we might publicly attest it with praise and thanksgiving, joining together for the greater magnifying of the sacrament of his sacred passion, which is a representation of Christ's giving of his body and shedding of his blood for our sakes.[92]

For the divines and the broader Reformed tradition, the sacraments were most certainly the means by which Christians can "con-

---

Daniel Featley, *The Romish Fisher Caught and Held in His Owne Net* (London: Robert Milbourne, 1624), appendix, 52–112; Thomas Morton, *The Lords Supper; or, A Vindication of the Sacrament of the Blessed Body & Blood of Christ according to Its Primitive Institution* (London: R. M., 1652), 5.3 (pp. 331–32); Moïse Amyraut, *De l'élévation de la foy et de l'abaissement de la raison en la créance des mystères de la religion* (Saumur: Jean Lesnier, 1641), 3, 4, 8–10 (pp. 76–124, 257–305); Moïse Amyraut, *Syntagma Thesium Theologicarum in Academica Salmuriensi Disputatarum*, 2nd ed., 2 vols. (Saumur: Jean Lesnier, 1664), vol. 2, part 3, 150–95; William Ames, *Bellarminus Enervatus a Guililelmo Amesio S. S. Theologiae Doctore in Academia Franekerana*, vol. 3 (Amsterdam: Johannem Jansonium, 1629), 4.3 (pp. 135–45); cf. John Bede, *The Masse Displayed* (Oxford: John Lichfield, 1619), 10 (pp. 61–98).

[90] Ulrich Zwingli, *Reckoning of the Faith*, 7; cf. W. P. Stephens, "Zwingli's Sacramental Views," in *Prophet, Pastor, Protestant: The Work of Huldrych Zwingli after Five Hundred Years*, ed. E. J. Furcha and H. Wayne Pipkin (Allison Park, PA: Pickwick, 1984), 161; Stephens, *The Theology of Huldrych Zwingli* (Oxford: Clarendon, 1986), 187–88.

[91] Ulrich Zwingli, *Of Baptism*, in *Zwingli and Bullinger*, ed. G. W. Bromiley (Philadelphia: Westminster, 1953), 131. Cf. Stephens, "Sacramental Views," 155, 165; Stephens, *Theology*, 180, 192.

[92] Ulrich Zwingli, *On the Lord's Supper*, in Bromiely, *Zwingli and Bullinger*, 234.

firm our interest in him [Christ]." But they were also "holy Signes, and Seals of the covenant of Grace . . . to represent Christ, and his benefits" (27.1). In this vein, and in contrast to Zwingli's views, the Confession explains: "Worthy receivers outwardly partaking of the visible Elements, in this Sacrament, do then also, inwardly by faith, really and indeed, yet not carnally and corporally, but Spiritually, receive, and feed upon Christ crucified, and all benefits of his death" (29.7). Christ is spiritually received in the Lord's Supper.

But the divines also reject the Lutheran understanding of the supper when they say: "The Body and Blood of Christ being then, not corpo[r]ally or carnally, in, with, or under the Bread and Wine; yet, as really, but Spiritually, present to the Faith of Believers in that Ordinance, as the Elements themselves are to their outward senses" (29.7).[93] The Confession neither mentions the group that holds this view nor names this position, as it does with the Roman Catholic view of transubstantiation (29.6), nevertheless the Lutheran doctrine of *consubstantiation* is in view. It teaches that the body and blood of Christ are with (*con-*) the bread and wine: "We believe, teach, and confess that in the Lord's Supper the body and blood of Christ are truly and substantially present, and that they are truly distributed and taken together *with* the bread and wine."[94] Like the Reformed, the Lutherans affirm that Christ's presence in the supper is spiritual, and they reject transubstantiation: "We believe, teach, and confess that the body and blood of Christ are taken with the bread and wine, not only spiritually through faith, but also by the mouth, nevertheless not Capernaitically [carnally], but after the spiritual and heavenly manner, by reason of the sacramental union."[95]

At first glance one might think there is little difference between the Lutheran and Reformed views, and from a certain vantage point this is

---

[93] Cf. William Ames, *The Marrow of Theology*, trans. John Dykstra Eusden (Grand Rapids: Baker, 1968), 1.40.22–31; Wollebius, *Compendium Theologiae Christianae*, 1.24.13; Dickson, *Truths Victory over Error*, 29.5 (pp. 298–301).

[94] Formula of Concord, art. 7, affirm. 1, emphasis added. Cf. Augsburg Confession, 10; Martin Luther, Small Catechism, "The Sacrament of the Altar," in *Book of Concord*, 362–63; Luther, Large Catechism, 5, in *Book of Concord*, 467–76, esp. 467; Luther, Smalcald Articles, 3.6, in *Book of Concord*, 320–21. For a collection of quotations on the Lutheran doctrine of the Lord's Supper, see Heinrich Schmid, *The Doctrinal Theology of the Evangelical Lutheran Church* (Philadelphia: Lutheran Publication Society, 1899), 555–82.

[95] Formula of Concord, art. 7, affirm. 6; cf. Hutter, *Compend*, 21.11 (pp. 181–82); Martin Chemnitz, *The Lord's Supper*, trans. Luther Poellot, vol. 5 of *Chemnitz's Works* (St. Louis: Concordia, 2007), 3 (pp. 37–44).

true. Both churches affirm the spiritual consumption of the body and blood of Christ and reject transubstantiation. Yet the significant differences lie in the mode of Christ's presence in the supper. The Lutherans locate Christ's presence *with* the elements, whereas historically the Reformed have argued that Christ's human nature is finite and therefore localized at the right hand of the Father. The Lutherans argue for an earthly presence of Christ, and the Reformed for a heavenly presence; for the Lutherans Christ descends to be present in the elements, but for many of the Reformed the Spirit lifts human souls to heaven to feed upon Christ.[96] According to the Reformed, Lutheran views encounter the obstacle of the finitude of Christ's human nature. How can a finite human nature be distributed to multiple locations when the supper is celebrated around the globe? This is why Lutherans have historically argued for the ubiquity of Christ's human nature through the *communicatio idiomatum* ("sharing of attributes").[97] In the Lutheran understanding of the phrase, Christ's human nature takes on the divine attribute of omnipresence, which then allows for the ubiquitous presence of the body of Christ in the celebration of the supper.

---

[96] Peter Martyr Vermigli, *Dialogue on the Two Natures in Christ*, trans. John Patrick Donnelly (Kirksville, MO: Sixteenth Century, 1995), 5–6 (pp. 111–64); Vermigli, *Dialogus de Utraque in Christo Natura* (Tiguri, 1561); Calvin, *Institutes*, 4.17.15, 18, 31–32; Zacharias Ursinus, *Smaller Catechism*, q. 65, *Larger Catechism*, qq. 300–301, in *An Introduction to the Heidelberg Catechism: Sources, History, and Theology*, ed. Lyle D. Bierma et al. (Grand Rapids: Baker, 2005), 153, 218–19; Dickson, *Truths Victory over Error*, 29.6 (pp. 301–3); Gallican Confession, 36; Belgic Confession, 35; Polanus, *Syntagma*, 6.56 (p. 500); Heppe, *Reformed Dogmatics*, 642–46. Cf. First Helvetic Confession, 20; Second Helvetic Confession, 21; Consensus Tigurinus, 22–25; John Calvin, *Mutual Consent as to the Sacraments*, in *John Calvin: Tracts and Letters*, ed. Henry Beveridge, 7 vols. (Edinburgh: Banner of Truth, 2009), 2:199–244; Heinrich Bullinger, *Common Places of Christian Religion* (London: Thomas East and H. Middleton, 1572), 8.6–10 (pp. 199–212). Given the cleavage between Zurich and Geneva, it appears that the Confession is written to accommodate both positions and follows patterns found in the Consensus Tigurinus; this point is especially evident when one compares Consensus Tigurinus 20 with Westminster Confession 18.6 regarding the efficacy of baptism.

[97] See, e.g., Martin Chemnitz, *The Two Natures of Christ*, trans. J. A. O. Preus, vol. 6 of *Chemnitz's Works* (1578; St. Louis: Concordia, 2007), 19–21 (pp. 233–66); Chemnitz, *De Duabus Naturis in Christo* (Lipsiae, 1580); Chemnitz, *The Lord's Supper*, 12 (pp. 198–99); Formula of Concord, Solid Declaration, 8 (pp. 616–34); Nicolaus Hunnius, *Diaskepsis Theologica: A Theological Examinatinon of the Fundamental Difference between Evangelical Lutheran Doctrine and Calvinist or Reformed Thinking* (Malone, TX: Repristination, 2001), 3.4, §§ 490–513 (pp. 218–43); *Diaskepsis Theologica de Fundamentali Dissensu Doctrinae Evangelicae-Lutheranae, & Calvinianae, seu Reformatae* (1626). One point worth noting is that Lutheran theologians rejected the term *consubstantiation*, because they did not conceive of Christ's bodily presence in the sacrament as a "local inclusion of the body and blood of Christ in the bread or wine." Rather, they affirmed, like the Reformed, a sacramental union, which is brought about by Christ's promise, "so that when the bread is distributed, the body of Christ is also at the same time truly present and distributed, the blood of Christ is also truly present and distributed at the same time" (Hutter, *Compend*, 21.15 [p. 184]). Hutter explains that the sacramental union is "supernatural and inexpressible" and that the use of the words *in*, *with*, and *under* vis-à-vis the Lord's Supper are intended to reject transubstantiation and draw attention to the supernatural manner in which the body of Christ is received, i.e., the sacramental union (ibid., 21.16–17 [pp. 184–85]). Cf. Formula of Concord, Solid Declaration, 7, in *Book of Concord*, 592–615.

Edward Leigh offers two reasons why the Lutheran view should be rejected. First, it overthrows human reason; a human body can only be present in one place at any one time. Second, it contradicts sound theology; at the conclusion of his earthly ministry Christ ascended to heaven at the right hand of the Father.[98] Leigh positively cites Luther, Philip Melanchthon (1497–1560), and other Lutheran theologians, such as Martin Chemnitz (1522–1586) and Johann Gerhard. But Leigh does register his disagreement with these Lutheran luminaries. He cites the work of John Rainolds (1549–1607), who argued that Luther rejected the seven sacraments of Rome, but that the German reformer still endorsed more than two. It should be noted, though, that in Luther's Large Catechism he advocates only two sacraments, baptism and the Lord's Supper. With regard to the presence of Christ, noted Rainolds, shortly before his death Luther supposedly admitted to Melanchthon that he had overstated his views in the Lord's Supper controversies.[99] Rainolds may have had in view Luther's brief confession about the supper written shortly before he died. In this work Luther does not concede anything but in fact reiterates his commitment to his earlier views on the supper.[100]

Leigh also cites Nicolaus Vedel (1596–1642), who argues sympathetically against the Lutheran position. Vedel maintains with the Lutherans that the church's only consolation in the supper is the presentation of the body of Christ, but claims that the Reformed deny that Christ's body is present in, with, or under the bread, unless such expressions are accepted merely as figures of speech. Such an approach to the supper, at least according to Leigh's citation of Vedel, can foster a modicum of peace between the two communions if the Reformed can condescend to speak in such terminology.[101] Evidence of sympathies toward Lutheran views surface in Reformation history, for example, in Calvin's willingness to sign the modified Augsburg

---

[98] Leigh, *Body of Divinity*, 8.9 (p. 696).

[99] Ibid.; John Rainolds, *Censura Librorum Apocryphorum Veteris Testamenti, adversum Pontificios, Inprimis Robertum Bellarminum*, 2 vols. (Oppenheim: Heironymi Galleri, 1611), vol. 1, praelect. 4 (cols. 53–54).

[100] Martin Luther, *Brief Confession concerning the Holy Sacrament*, in *LW*, 38:287–319; cf. Solid Declaration, 7, in *Book of Concord*, 598.

[101] Leigh, Body of Divinity, 8.9 (p. 696); also Nicolaus Vedel, *Rationale Theologicum seu de Necessitate et Vero Usu Principiorum Rationis ac Philosophiae in Controversiis Theologicis Libri Tres* (Geneva: Jacobum Chouët, 1628), 3.20 (pp. 779–80).

Confession (i.e., *Confessio Augustana Variata*, 1540) and Beza's inclusion of a number of Lutheran confessions in his *Harmony of Protestant Confessions*, as well as the silence found about Lutheran views on the supper in some works, such as Ussher's *Body of Divinitie*.[102] The Confession's mild rejection of the Lutheran view, therefore, indicates a certain degree of agreement and sympathy with it.

Nonetheless, whatever sympathies may have existed for the Lutheran view on the supper, other implications separated the two churches, and the Confession addresses them. One of the driving factors behind the Lord's Supper controversy was the proper interpretation of Christ's statement "This *is* my body" (Matt. 26:26; Mark 14:22; Luke 22:19; 1 Cor. 11:24, emphasis added). Is the verb "is" literal or figurative? Lutherans and Roman Catholics opted for a literal referent, and hence argued that Christ's body and blood were given in the supper, whereas the Reformed generally opted for a figurative referent.[103] The assembly's *Annotations* explain that when Christ says, "This is my blood," he employs a *synechdoche*; that is, one part is named for the whole. The cup was filled not with blood but with wine, which was "a sign and seal" of Christ's work upon the cross.[104]

These exegetical trajectories led Roman Catholics to venerate the elements of the supper, since, for them, the elements literally became the body and blood of Christ, which is something the Confession rejects (29.4).[105] Christ's presence in the elements, according to Lutheran views, meant that everyone and anyone, believer and unbeliever alike, who consumed the supper received Christ. For the Confession, only "worthy receivers outwardly partaking of the visible Elements, in this Sacrament, do then also, inwardly by faith, really and indeed, yet not carnally and corporally, but Spiritually, receive,

---

[102] Philip Schaff, *The Creeds of Christendom*, 3 vols. (1930; Grand Rapids: Baker, 1991), 1:240–42; John Calvin, "Last Admonition of John Calvin to Joachim Westphal," in Beveridge, *Tracts and Letters*, 2:355; Ussher, *Body of Divinitie*, 424–26; Ussher, "Calvinus ad Schallingio," *CO* 16:430, epist. 2607; R. Scott Clark, "Calvin: A Negative Boundary Marker in American Lutheran Self-Identity, 1871–1934," in *Sober, Strict, and Scriptural: Collective Memories of John Calvin, 1800–2000*, ed. Johan de Niet et al. (Leiden: Brill, 2009), 245n2.

[103] Cf., e.g., Hutter, *Compend*, 21.3–4 (pp. 178–79); Chemnitz, *Lord's Supper*, 6–7 (pp. 65–90); Leigh, *Body of Divinity*, 8.9 (pp. 698–99); Turretin, *Institutes*, 19.26.1–39.

[104] *Annotations*, comm. 1 Cor. 11:25. Readers should note, however, that the rhetorical device is more properly a *metonymy*, where one thing is used to talk about another.

[105] Cf. Council of Trent, sess. 13, October 11, 1551, first decree, chap. 5; sess. 22, September 17, 1562, first decree, chap. 5; sess. 22, canons on the mass, 3; Leigh, *Body of Divinity*, 8.9 (pp. 696–97).

and feed upon Christ crucified, and all the benefits of his death" (29.7).[106] The next sentence indicates that the divines have Lutheran views in the crosshairs: "The Body and Blood of Christ being then, not corporally or carnally, *in, with, or under* the Bread and Wine; yet, as really but Spiritually, present to the Faith of Believers in that Ordinance, as the Elements themselves are to their outward senses" (29.7, emphasis added). At this point the Confession repeats the standard Lutheran confessional language ("in, with, or under") and rejects it. According to the Confession, only the elect receive Christ in the supper because he is received through the Spirit by faith and not orally, that is, merely through the consumption of bread and wine.

Conclusion

To say the least, the doctrine of the church is a thicket of controversy on a number of different fronts even among Protestants, whether in the church's relationship to the magistrate or in the nature and administration of the sacraments. When reading the Confession on these matters one must pay careful attention to the absence or presence of words, such as the affirmation that *Christ's* kingdom is the church but that *God* is over the civil magistrate, or repetition of phrases that were commonly known to the framers of the confession, but perhaps not as well known to modern-day readers. The absence of language critiquing other positions, such as Zwinglian and Lutheran views on the sacraments, also reveals a degree of sympathy for these groups when compared to the strongly worded polemical characterization of the Roman Catholic views on church and sacraments, especially transubstantiation. So if the Confession's doctrine of the church establishes the theological structure by defining orthodoxy and fencing off heterodoxy and heresy, what type of worship should characterize this theological architecture? The next chapter addresses this question.

---

[106] Cf. Chemnitz, *Lord's Supper*, 3 (pp. 38–39), Hutter, *Compend*, 21.27 (pp. 190–91); Formula of Concord, Solid Declaration, 7, in *Book of Concord*, 605–6.

11

Worship

One of the hallmarks of Reformed theology is the doctrine of the regulative principle of worship (RPW). Briefly stated, the RPW is the teaching that only those things commanded in Scripture may be performed in the worship of God. In recent years many have misunderstood the RPW because they have divorced it from its historical context, which is vital to understanding this doctrine.[1] The fundamental question at stake in the RPW is, who decides what should and should not be done in public worship? Depending upon their ecclesiastical affiliation, theologians give different answers to this question. For Roman Catholic and a number of Anglican theologians, the church has the authority to institute ceremonies in worship. For Protestant theologians, with some differences between the Reformed and Lutherans, only God through his Word may prescribe worship.[2]

Contemporary readers should recognize that these two answers arise from a number of different theological presuppositions about the authority of Scripture, the authority of the church, the doctrine of justification, which is connected to the doctrine of Christian liberty, and

---

[1] See, e.g., John Frame, "Some Questions about the Regulative Principle," *WTJ* 54 (1992): 357–66; cf. T. David Gordon, "Some Answers about the Regulative Principle," *WTJ* 55 (1993): 321–29.

[2] For an overview of early modern Reformed views on worship, see Horton Davies, *The Worship of the English Puritans* (1948; Morgan, PA: Soli Deo Gloria, 1997). For differences between Luther and Calvin on the use of images, see Heiko A. Oberman, "The Controversy over Images at the Time of the Reformation," in *The Two Reformations: The Journey from the Last Days to the New World*, ed. Donald Weinstein (New Haven, CT: Yale University Press, 2003), 86–96; Helmar Junghans, "Luther on the Reform of Worship," in *Harvesting Martin Luther's Reflections on Theology, Ethics, and the Church*, ed. Timothy J. Wengert (Grand Rapids: Eerdmans, 2004), 207–25.

the doctrine of the two kingdoms. All of these doctrines collectively shape the worship of the Reformed churches, which we find codified in the Westminster Standards. But though common principles drove and established Reformed worship as presented in the Standards, the Westminster divines did not all agree precisely on how they were to be put into practice. There was some diversity of opinion and practice on a number of issues related to worship and the RPW. Hence this chapter will survey the historical and theological backgrounds to the RPW, explore what the Standards have to say about worship, and briefly survey areas of disagreement on worship practices among the divines.

Historical Background

As some commentators have noted, the Westminster Assembly was a decidedly English affair, which inextricably connects the events, debates, decisions, and final product of the assembly to the antecedent English history.[3] The political context of the assembly is decisive. In the ebb and flow of Protestant versus Roman Catholic rule, the respective reigns of Henry VIII (1509–1547), Edward VI (1547–1553), Mary I (1553–1558), and Elizabeth I (1558–1603) brought a series of sometimes violent shifts in the theology and worship of the Church of England. Under Edward VI, worship was relatively uniform under the auspices of the Book of Common Prayer (BCP) but for a time was disrupted by Mary I's brief reign after Edward's death. Elizabeth I sought permanently to formalize worship practices throughout the Church of England by the Act of Uniformity of 1559. The Act of Uniformity prescribed that the whole church was bound to use the "Matins," a common morning prayer liturgy that originated in the Roman Catholic Church. The act also mandated the use of Evensong, a standard evening prayer liturgy, the celebration of the Lord's Supper, the use of the BCP, and specific "lessons" for every Sunday of the year.[4] Failure

---

[3] Robert S. Paul, *The Assembly of the Lord: Politics and Religion in the Westminster Assembly and the 'Grand Debate'* (Edinburgh: T&T Clark, 1985), 2; Robert Letham, *The Westminster Assembly: Reading Its Theology in Historical Context* (Phillipsburg, NJ: P&R, 2009), 11–26. On the historical context of the Standards regarding worship, see Letham, *Westminster Assembly*, 300–304.

[4] "Elizabeth's Act of Uniformity (1559)," in *Documents Illustrative of English Church History: Compiled from Original Sources* (London: Macmillan, 1896), 80 (pp. 458–59).

to follow the queen's act resulted in steep penalties. If any minister, parson, or vicar refused to follow the worship practices outlined in the Act of Uniformity and BCP, then he would forfeit promotion for an entire year if convicted. For a second offense, the minister would be imprisoned for one whole year and be deprived of all promotions. For a third offense, the minister was required to surrender all promotions and suffer life imprisonment.[5]

Ministers were not the only ones liable to criminal penalty, for anyone who disrupted a minister while performing duties prescribed in the BCP was subject to one year in prison "without bail or mainprize." For a second offense, a person was liable to life in prison. Like their ministerial counterparts, if anyone spoke against the BCP in any manner, through "interludes, plays, songs, rhymes, or by other open words," he was liable to a fine of 100 marks. For a second offense there was a fine of 400 marks, and a third offense required the confiscation of all the person's "goods and chattels," and life in prison.[6] In the sixteenth century 100 marks was worth approximately £50, which in that day was a hefty fine since a household servant would ordinarily make only £2–5 per year.[7] The drafters of the Act of Uniformity were well aware that this fine was stiff and therefore had a provision for those who failed to pay; convicts were given six weeks from the time of their conviction to pay their fine, and if they failed to do so, they were imprisoned for six months for the first offense without possibility of "bail or mainprize."[8] Failure to pay the fine for a second offense meant imprisonment for twelve months without possibility of bail.[9] But penalties could be levied not merely for undermining the BCP but also for failure to attend church on Sundays or holy days. The idea behind this provision was to prevent dissenters from absenting themselves from worship. Such dissenters would suffer not only church discipline but also a fine of 12 pence, which was approximately a week's wage for a household servant.[10]

The Act of Uniformity enjoined the enforcement of these rules and

---

[5] Ibid., 80 (pp. 460–61).
[6] Ibid., 80 (p. 462).
[7] http://www.elizabethan.org/compendium/6.html, accessed October 9, 2012.
[8] "Act of Uniformity (1559)," in *English Church History*, 80 (p. 462).
[9] Ibid., 80 (pp. 462–63).
[10] Ibid., 80 (p. 463).

penalties upon the church and the civil magistrate.[11] As noted, the Act of Uniformity was a decree or proclamation not of the church but of the queen, and was enforced by mayors, bailiffs, and other local government officials, a move that would later encourage the divines to incorporate the doctrine of the two kingdoms in the Confession, limiting the power of the magistrate in the spiritual and theological oversight of churchly affairs (cf. WCF 23.2; 31.2–3).[12] To ensure that everyone in the realm was aware of the requirements, rites, and ceremonies of the BCP, parishioners were required to purchase, at their own expense, a copy of the book for their personal use.[13] Though the events of the Act of Uniformity dated back to 1559, they were no distant memory for the Westminster divines but a present reality. Westminster divine Samuel Rutherford (1600–1661) wrote in 1637 from an Aberdeen prison that he was charged with treason for preaching against the king. Rutherford was removed from his ministry because he refused to submit to the altered BCP that was imposed upon the churches of Scotland by Archbishop William Laud (1573–1645) and Bishop Matthew Wren (1585–1667).[14]

When they wrote the Confession's statements on worship, the divines also had in view the doctrine of the Roman Catholic Church. According to the Council of Trent (1546), Christ gave the apostles, and hence the church, authority to decide matters in doctrine and worship. Trent states:

> The council clearly perceives that this truth and rule are contained in written books and in unwritten traditions which were received by the apostles from the mouth of Christ himself, or else have come down to us, handed on as it were from the apostles themselves by the inspiration of the Holy Spirit.[15]

This proclamation places church tradition and Scripture on equal footing, which meant that the church can impose ceremonies and rites not found in Scripture. Given the Church of England's theologi-

---

[11] Ibid., 80 (pp. 463–64).
[12] Ibid., 80 (p. 465).
[13] Ibid., 80 (pp. 464–65).
[14] Samuel Rutherford, "Letter to John Stuart," in *Letters of Samuel Rutherford* (1664; Edinburgh: Banner of Truth, 1984), no. 161 (pp. 298–301).
[15] Council of Trent, sess. 4, April 8, 1546, first decree.

cal heritage and its initial incremental steps toward reformation, it had a similar view of church authority and tradition. The Thirty-Nine Articles state: "The church hath power to decree rites or ceremonies and authority in controversies of faith. And yet it is not lawful for the church to ordain any thing that is contrary to God's word written, neither may it so expound one place of Scripture, that it be repugnant to another" (20).

Theological Background

The immediate historical background is important to understanding the Confession on worship, but the underlying theological issues are equally important. Disagreements about worship had been ongoing ever since the start of the Reformation, and this is something of which early modern Reformed theologians were acutely aware. In his massive treatise on worship, William Ames (1576–1633) draws upon Martin Luther's (1483–1546) criticisms of Roman Catholic worship. According to Luther, Rome did not keep what God commanded—it created all sorts of ceremonies and ignored what the Word says about baptism, the Eucharist, absolution, and calling. The original context of Luther's criticisms was his commentary on Genesis, particularly Abraham's sacrifice of Isaac in Genesis 22, about which he writes, "Abraham adds nothing over and above his calling." In other words, Abraham did not add to or take away from God's command but instead rested in the fear and command of God, ready to obey. Luther says:

> But in the church one must consider who is giving the command, what kind of person he is, and how important he is. If this is not done, the devil very easily changes "Who is giving the command, what kind of person is he, and how important is he?" into "What is being commanded, what is its nature, and how important is it?"[16]

Though Luther's comments arose later in his career, in 1539, his observations were still in the early days of the Reformation and illustrate the early polemic against Roman Catholic worship. Luther offers a number of observations on the regulatory nature of the Word of God

---

[16] William Ames, *A Fresh Suit against Human Ceremonies in God's Worship* (London: n.p., 1633), 1.5 (p. 65); Martin Luther, *Lectures on Genesis: Chapters 21–25*, comm. Gen. 22:19, in *LW*, 4:179–80.

in worship in his comments on Genesis 22.[17] For example: "The papists reproach us severely because we do not accept their self-chosen works and forms of worship. This, however, is a theological issue for us, lest we enter upon a kind of life or work concerning which we do not have God's express command."[18] The chief issue between Rome and the Protestant Reformers was whether people were bound to Scripture and tradition or only to Scripture in matters of doctrine—in this case, specifically worship.

Similar doctrinal beliefs were common in the Church of England, most notably from the pen of Anglican theologian Richard Hooker (1554–1600). Hooker believed that worship was supposed to be defined and determined by God's Word. However, he did not believe that every matter in worship was defined and established by God:

> God hath foreprized things of greatest weight, and hath therein precisely defined, as well that which every man must perform, as that which no man may attempt, leaving all sorts of men in the rest, either to be guided by their own good discretion, if they be free from subjection to others, or else to be ordered by such commandments and laws as proceed from those superiors under whom they live.[19]

For Hooker, some matters were firmly established by the Word, but in areas undefined, the church was at liberty to act according to its discretion. Hooker pithily states his principle: "Those things which the law of God leaveth arbitrary and at liberty, are all such subject to the positive laws of men."[20]

In contrast, the Reformed stood upon the principle that only things specifically commanded in Scripture could be performed in worship. In his work on worship, Westminster divine George Gillespie (1613–1648) cited a number of Reformed theologians on this point, including Peter Martyr Vermigli (1499–1562), Girolamo Zanchi (1516–1590), John Calvin (1509–1564), and John Knox (ca. 1514–1572).[21] Gillespie's

---

[17] See, e.g., Luther, *Lectures on Genesis*, comm. Gen. 22:3, 13, in *LW*, 4:103, 135.
[18] Ames, *Fresh Suit*, 1.12 (p. 140); Luther, *Lectures on Genesis*, comm. Gen. 21:4, in *LW*, 4:8.
[19] Richard Hooker, *The Works of Mr. Richard Hooker in Eight Books of the Laws of Ecclesiastical Polity*, 3 vols. (London: W. Baynes and Son, 1821), 5 (2:291).
[20] Ibid.
[21] John Calvin, *Institutes of the Christian Religion*, trans. John Allen (Grand Rapids: Eerdmans, 1949), 4.10.17; John Knox, "A Letter to the Queen Dowager, Regent of Scotland, 1556," in *The Works of John Knox*, ed. David Laing, vol. 4 (Edinburgh: James Thing, 1845), 69–84, esp. 80–81; Peter

citations and quotations from this cluster of theologians include a series of commonly cited scriptural texts to support the claim that only
what is commanded in worship may be performed. Zanchi's comments
arise from his exposition of the second commandment, which prohibits
the creation of graven images (Ex. 20:4), and among other texts Knox
refers to Leviticus 10:1 and Deuteronomy 4, two commonly cited passages included among the Confession's proof texts in its chapter on
religious worship (21.1).

Concerning Leviticus 10:1 the assembly's *Annotations* state, "In
Gods worship Gods command, not mans wit, or will, must be our rule."
Such a statement rules out what early modern theologians called "will
worship"—worship governed by human will rather than the divine
will.[22] Both Exodus 20:4 and Deuteronomy 4 deal with images. Citing Amadus Polanus (1561–1610) and the *Leiden Synopsis*, Gillespie
argues that these texts concern the regulation of worship.[23] Polanus
explains that the second commandment is different from the first commandment in that the first determines the proper substance or subject
of religious worship, which was a common way other early modern
Reformed theologians treated this commandment.[24] That is, the first
commandment treats the question of whom we should worship, and
the second commandment explains the manner in which God should
be worshipped.

This understanding of the second commandment is a theological
thread that appears in the assembly's catechisms. The Shorter Catechism states, "The second Commandment requireth, the receiving,

Martyr Vermigli, *Melachim, Id Est, Regum Libri Duo Posteriors cum Commentariis Petri Martyris
Vermilii* (Heidelberg: Andreas Cambierus, 1599), comm. 1 Kings 8:65; Girolamo Zanchi, *De Lege
Dei*, 1.14, in *Operum Theologicorum D. Hieronymi Zanchi*, vol. 2, pt. 4 (n.p., 1619), cols. 362–63;
George Gillespie, *A Dispute against the English-Popish Ceremonies, Obtruded upon the Church of
Scotland* (n.p., 1660). I have consulted both an original and a contemporary critical edition of Gil-
lespie's work and will cite the following edition in subsequent references: George Gillespie, *A Dispute
against the English Popish Ceremonies*, ed. Chris Coldwell (Dallas: Naphtali, 2013), 3.7.11, 13, 14
(pp. 266–67, 269, 270).

[22] William Ames, *The Marrow of Theology*, trans. John Eusden Dystrka (1968; Grand Rapids: Baker,
1997), 2.13.1, 13 (pp. 278–79).

[23] Gillespie, *Dispute*, 3.5.6 (p. 230); cf. Johannes Polyander, André Rivet, Antonius Walaeus, and Antonius Thysius, *Synopsis Purioris Theologiae*, ed. Herman Bavinck (Lugduni Batavorum: Didericum
Donner, 1881), 19.4 (p. 163).

[24] Amandus Polanus, *Syntagma Theologiae Christianae* (Hanoviae: Johannis Aubrii, 1615), 6.10
(p. 353); cf. Ames, *Marrow of Theology*, 2.13.11–12, 33 (pp. 279, 281); Edward Leigh, *A Systeme or
Body of Divinity: Consisting of Ten Books* (London: William Lee, 1654), 9.3 (pp. 767–88); Johannes
Wollebius, *Compendium Theologiae Christianae*, 2.5, in *Reformed Dogmatics*, ed. John W. Beardslee
(Oxford: OUP, 1965), 202–3; James Ussher, *A Body of Divinitie; or, The Summe and Substance of
Christian Religion* (London: Thomas Downes and George Badger, 1645), 222–36.

observing, and keeping pure and intire all such religious Worship and Ordinances, as God hath appointed in his Word" (q. 50). Alternatively, the second commandment also "forbiddeth the worshipping of God by Images, or any other way not appointed in his word" (q. 51). The Larger Catechism naturally provides a fuller answer:

> The duties required in the second Commandment, are, the receiving, observing, and keeping pure and entire, all such religious worship and Ordinances as God hath instituted in his word: particularly, Prayer and Thanksgiving in the name of Christ, the reading, preaching, and hearing of the Word; the administration and receiving of the Sacraments; Church-government and Discipline; the Ministery [sic], and maintenance thereof; religious fasting, swearing by the name of God, and vowing unto him: As also the disapproving, detesting, opposing all false worship; and, according to each ones place and calling, removing it, and all monuments of Idolatry. (q. 108)

While contemporary readers might be doubtful that the second commandment entails everything listed in the Larger Catechism's answer, the divines did not crassly proof text. Rather, as with any doctrinal point, they argued according to the analogy of Scripture and saw each text as interconnected to a web of others. This is evident in the proof texts to this question in the catechism.[25]

The numerous proof texts to question 108 show that Reformed theologians insisted upon the sole authority of Scripture in matters of worship because, in their minds, this protected the church from the arbitrary rules and laws that human beings might try to impose, such as with the Act of Uniformity. In this respect the doctrine of justification and its concomitant doctrine of Christian liberty form part of the core concerns behind the RPW. Gillespie, citing a number of other Reformed theologians—including Martin Bucer (1491–1551), David Pareus (1548–1622), Polanus, Calvin, Remonstrant theologian Daniel Tilenus (1563–1633), and Patristic theologian John Chrysostom (ca. 347–407)—believed that he was standing in defense of Christian

---

[25] The divines cite Deut. 6:13; 7:15; 17:18–19; 32:46–47; Pss. 16:4; 76:11; Isa. 19:21; 30:22; Joel 2:12–13; Matt. 16:19; 18:15–17; 28:19, 20; Acts 2:42; 10:33; 15:21; 17:16–17; 1 Corinthians 5; 7:5; 9:7–15; 11:21–30; 12:28; Eph. 4:11–12; 5:20; Phil. 4:6; 1 Tim. 5:16–17; 6:13–14; 2 Tim. 4:2; James 1:21–22.

liberty: "Shall we bear the name of Christians, and yet make no great account of the liberty which has been bought to us by the dearest drops of the precious blood of the Son of God?"[26] The only person who can ultimately enjoin duties upon redeemed man for the worship of God is God himself, and for other matters, known as *adiaphora* ("things indifferent"), people are free to do or not do. To allow someone or an institution, such as the Roman Catholic Church, to command things beyond the Word of God and then have people submit to them is tantamount to becoming a slave to that person or institution.[27] The implication of the Confession's doctrine of worship is that on the authority of the Word of God the church has the unique function of overseeing the worship and theology of the church. Regulating the worship of the church is not a function, per se, of the civil magistrate. Regarding matters of indifference, churches are largely free to choose the time, meeting location, and venue for worship. The Scriptures are silent on such matters.

Despite the differences between the Reformed and Lutheran approaches to worship, some divines, such as Gillespie, nevertheless appealed to Lutheran theologians such as Martin Chemnitz (1522–1586). Gillespie sought to demonstrate commonly shared convictions concerning worship. Chemnitz cited, for example, the practices of the ancient church when he said:[28]

> Because now all ceremonies, also those which are not the most ancient, are laid upon consciences as necessary under threat of anathema, although one clearly sees into what said misuse very many such things have degenerated, many things must be very diligently considered in this dispute about the ceremonies which are reported to have been instituted and used by the ancients in the administration of the sacraments.[29]

Chemnitz enumerates eight reasons why human-instituted ceremonies have no place in worship:

---

[26] Gillespie, *Dispute*, 1.3.1–2 (pp. 26–27).
[27] Ibid., 1.3.2 (p. 28); 1.4.2 (p. 31).
[28] Ibid., 1.3.2 (p. 28).
[29] Martin Chemnitz, *Examination of the Council of Trent*, trans. Fred Kramer, vol. 2, pt. 2, of *Chemnitz's Works* (1971; St. Louis: Concordia, 2007), 10.7 (p. 113).

1. The ceremonies have no institution from God.
2. The Son of God instituted the sacraments in such a way that the church is not permitted to add other ceremonies in addition to them.
3. Ceremonies of human origin are said to add beauty to the ceremonies prescribed by God, hence the simplicity of God's instituted ceremonies is deemed insufficient, which is an unacceptable conclusion.
4. The pomp and splendor of the human ceremonies obscures the ceremonies that have been prescribed by God.
5. The ceremonies of Rome supposedly impart blessings apart from any specific word or promise from God.
6. In the eyes of common people, the humanly devised ceremonies are deemed as important as those instituted by God, which is an unacceptable conclusion.
7. Numerous rites that were practiced in the ancient church were not required but were optional.
8. People in the church often confuse divinely commanded ceremonies with those of human origin, thus undermining the authority of the Word of God.[30]

Though Chemnitz was a Lutheran theologian, Gillespie nonetheless had a great deal of agreement with him on the impropriety of human-originated ceremonies in worship. Both theologians agreed that the Reformation was an attempt to return to the simplicity of the worship of the early church.

John Cameron (1579–1625), a Scottish Presbyterian theologian who taught at the Academy in Saumur, France, illustrated this point by tracing worship through redemptive history. He observed that the Old Testament church had many ceremonies because it was in its infancy, but with the advent of Christ, the shadows gave way to the reality—obscurity and imperfection gave way to clarity and perfection. Cameron appealed to Colossians 2:16–23 and argued that Rome has piled human ceremony upon ceremony, in marked contrast to the early church. The early church had three ceremonies: baptism, the supper, and perhaps the miraculous healing of the sick. Cameron

---

[30] Ibid., 10.7 (pp. 113–16).

remarks, "Their [*sic*] will not be found any other ceremony in those primitive times, so admirable was their simplicity. But the number of them was multiplied afterwards, not by divine but by humane institution."[31] Cameron then closes his argument with a stinging remark: "We tell them [Roman Catholics] this multitude of rites, and traditions is more suteable to the superstition of Turkes, Jewes, and infidels, amongst whome all these vanities have beene, and are still in use."[32]

But not all proponents of extra-scriptural worship ceremonies believed that these rites originated by human innovation and invention. Rather, some believed that natural law is a source of divine revelation, and as such, is a fount of legitimate extra-scriptural ceremonies. For example, Hooker writes:

> We must not think but that there is some ground of Reason even in Nature, whereby it cometh to pass that no nation under heaven either doth or ever did suffer some public actions which are of weight, whether there they be civil and temporal, or else spiritual and sacred, to pass without some visible solemnity: the very strangeness whereof and difference from that which is common, doth cause popular eyes to observe and to mark the same.[33]

Hooker believed that certain things such as holidays (i.e., holy days) or kneeling at communion could be supported from natural law and therefore practiced.[34] In response to this claim Gillespie offers four points of counterargument:[35]

1. The law of nature cannot direct us unto a supernatural end; it only directs us to do good and only reveals the law.
2. Ceremonies, given their sacred, spiritual, and mystical significance, direct us to a supernatural end, hence they provide guidance far beyond what the light of nature could possibly do.
3. According to numerous witnesses—Francis Junius (1545–1602), the Leiden professors, Thomas Aquinas (1225–1274), Zanchi,

---

[31] John Cameron, *An Examination of Those Plausible Appearances Which Seeme Most to Commend the Romish Church, and to Prejudice the Reformed* (Oxford: Edward Forrest, 1626), 10 (p. 36).
[32] Ibid., 10 (p. 40).
[33] Hooker, *Ecclesiastical Polity*, 14.1 (1:434–35); Gillespie, *Dispute*, 3.9.1 (p. 359).
[34] Hooker, *Ecclesiastical Polity*, 5.69 (2:358–60).
[35] Gillespie, *Dispute*, 3.9.6–9 (pp. 363–65).

Diego Estella (Roman Catholic theologian, 1524–1578), Pareus, and Augustine (354–430)—natural law is universal and demonstrated by the common consent of all people. As Paul writes, the law of nature is manifest in the Gentiles (Rom. 1:19). If certain ceremonies are warranted by natural law, then all people should practice and acknowledge said ceremonies.[36]

4. Whatever is derived from natural law for the purpose of worship should only be that which promotes order and decency in all actions.

Based upon these reasons, natural law is insufficient to guide the church in matters of worship.

Another exegetical field of battle was the proper interpretation of Colossians 2:16 and questions about the celebration of holy days and the prohibition of eating meat: "Let no man therefore judge you in meat, or in drink, or in respect of an holyday, or of the new moon, or of the sabbath days." Roman Catholic theologian Cardinal Robert Bellarmine (1542–1621) argued that in this verse Paul's subject of consideration was the abrogation of Old Testament Jewish festivals, not New Testament Christian holy days such as Advent, Christmas, Epiphany, Lent, and Easter. Bellarmine believed that Paul only had in view the abrogation of the Sabbath, a Jewish ceremony that ceased with the advent of Christ.[37] Reformed interpreters, such as John Davenant (1572–1641), readily acknowledged that there were numerous Jewish Old Testament festivals (e.g., Exodus 23; Leviticus 23). Davenant argues:

Christians are not to be condemned as though they were transgressors of the Divine law, or guilty of the violation of conscience, because from henceforth they did not abstain from meat or drink forbidden by the ceremonial law, or because they did not observe

---

[36] Francis Junius, "De Legibus Mosis Iudicialibus et Earum Observatione," in *D. Francisci Junius Opuscula Theologica Selecta*, ed. Abraham Kuyper (Amsterdam: Fredericum Muller, 1882), 1.1–5 (pp. 343–48); *Synopsis Purioris*, 18.26 (p. 157); Zanchi, *De Lege Dei*, 1.9, in *Opera*, vol. 2, pt. 4, col. 193; Diego Estella, *In Sanctum Iesu Christi Evangelium Secundum Lucam Doctissima Pariter & Piissima Commentaria*, vol. 1 (Antuerpiae: Hieronymum & Ioan. Bapt. Verdussen, 1655), comm. Luke 6:31 (p. 298); Aquinas, *Summa Theologica*, IaIIae, q. 94, art. 4; Augustine, *Confessions*, 10.6; David Pareus, *In Divinam ad Romanos S. Pauli Apostoli Epistolam Commentarius* (Francofurti, 1608), comm. Rom. 1:19 (cols. 91–94).

[37] Robert Bellarmine, *Controversiarum de Ecclesia Triumphante. Liber Tertius. De Iis Ribus*, 3.10, in *Opera Omnia*, ed. Justinus Fèvre, vol. 3 (Paris: Lucovicum Vivès, 1870), 302.

the feasts enjoined by the same law, whatever false apostles had superstitiously determined to the contrary.[38]

Here Davenant contends that Christians were not obligated to observe abrogated Old Testament elements of the ceremonial law, but neither were they required to observe the superstitious teachings of false apostles, those who likely imposed the necessity of these Old Testament ceremonies upon the church at Colossae. Davenant therefore draws a parallel between the false teachers at Colossae and the false teaching of the Roman Catholic Church and its attempt to impose false worship upon the church.[39]

Davenant makes three consequent observations based upon his understanding of this verse. First, "seducers" always try to load the consciences of people in the church with ceremonies and condemn them if they fail to observe them. Second, it is the duty of all Christians to reject any ceremony imposed upon them under the plea of necessity or merit or righteousness (Gal. 5:1). Third, the prohibition against certain foods or the practice of hallowing certain days should not be retained (Rom. 14:17; 1 Cor. 10:25; Gal. 4:9–10). Based on these three reasons Davenant charges Roman Catholics with two errors:

1. They err because they forbid certain meats at certain times.
2. They attribute "extraordinary perfection" to abstinence from meat.[40]

Davenant's chief criticism, then, is that the Roman Catholic Church, apart from the authority of Scripture, requires Christians to abstain from meat, a requirement that Paul specifically rejects.[41]

Davenant takes a softer stance toward Christian festival days, with which Paul also deals in this text. Without question some Re-

---

[38] John Davenant, *An Exposition of the Epistle of St. Paul to the Colossians*, trans. Josiah Allport, vol. 1 (1627; London: Hamilton, Adams, and Co., 1831), comm. Col. 2:16 (p. 479).

[39] Ibid., 479–80.

[40] Ibid., 480–81.

[41] The practice of abstinence from meat began when the early church encouraged Christians to fast on the fourth and sixth days of the week (Wednesday and Friday), particularly to remember the sufferings of Christ on Good Friday. Meat, therefore, was prohibited, but not fish, since many believed it was not meat (cf. *Didache*, 8.1, in *The Apostolic Fathers*, ed. Michael W. Holmes [Grand Rapids: Baker, 2007], 355; Clement of Alexandria, *Stromata, or Miscellanies*, 7.12, in *ANF* 2:544; *Shepherd of Hermas*, "Parable," 5.1, in Holmes, *Apostolic Fathers*, 569; Tertullian, *On Fasting*, X, XIV, in *ANF* 4:103, 109, 112; Aquinas, *Summa Theologica*, IIaIIae, q. 147, art. 8).

formed theologians, such as George Gillespie, argued against such a conclusion not only because of its affinity to the Roman Catholic view but also because they believed that to embrace festival days was to return to the shadows of the Old Testament laws even though Christ, the substance (Col. 2:17), had already come.[42] Another Scottish theologian, Robert Rollock (ca. 1555–1599), argues:

> O as the Papists here are busie about meates, holy dayes of their owne making, and such like, from the which the Lord hath freed us: To impose lawes necessarie to be kept (as they speake) under the paine of salvation and damnation; as the eating of flesh on Friday: O vaine foole! As for things necessarie to salvation and the worship of God, Papists passe over them as frivolous.[43]

Rollock's contention is that the Roman Catholic Church was apparently more concerned about people not eating meat on Fridays than about reforming their understanding of the gospel. He goes on to argue that there are two types of holy days: those commanded by God and those commanded by men. In the Old Testament, God commanded numerous holy days before the advent of Christ, which is evident by a cursory reading of the Pentateuch, for example. But as far as the holy days enjoined upon the church after the advent of Christ, Rollock comments, "Reade the Scripture from the beginning to the end, and yet thou shalt finde but one day onely injoyned thee to be kept, and that by the law Morall, and this day is the Lords Sabboth."[44]

Davenant counters that the Old Testament laws were partly moral and partly ceremonial and that with Christ's advent only the ceremonial aspect of the law has been abrogated. Hence, the moral obligation to observe certain holy days is still required by New Testament Christians: "Those great benefits of the Incarnation, the Passion, the Resurrection, and Ascension of the Son of God, and the Descent of the Holy Spirit, should be celebrated annually in the church."[45] To this end the church and the magistrate, argues Davenant, could prescribe

---

[42] Gillespie, *Dispute*, 1.8.4 (pp. 57–58).
[43] Robert Rollock, *Lectures upon the Epistle of Paul to the Colossians* (London: Felix Kyngston, 1603), lect. 19 (p. 201).
[44] Ibid., lect. 19 (p. 202).
[45] Davenant, *Colossians*, comm. Col. 2:16 (p. 485).

appointed days beyond the Lord's Day on which the church would gather to worship God.[46] Davenant's view reflects what was typical of Continental Reformed views regarding holy days. The church order written by the Synod of Dort, for example, states:

> The congregations shall observe, in addition to Sunday, also Christmas, Easter and Pentecost, with the following days. Since in most cities and Provinces of the Netherlands, besides these the days of the Circumcision and Ascension of Christ are also observed, all ministers, wherever this is still the custom, shall put forth effort with the authorities that they may conform with the others. (§ 67)[47]

The church order of Dort therefore required ministers to celebrate extra-dominical holy days, as is evident by its use of the phrase "shall observe" (*zullen onderhouden*). From one vantage point the agreement between Davenant, Gillespie, and Robert Rollock, over and against the claims of the Roman Catholic exegesis of Colossians 2:16, is evident. But there are also different opinions, with Davenant and Dort opposing Rollock and Gillespie regarding the propriety of certain holy days.

The Confession and the Directory for Public Worship

Given these contours in the debates over worship between Roman Catholic, Anglican, and Reformed theologians, we find the broader context for appreciating the Confession's opening statement on religious worship, with its acknowledgment of natural law: "The light of Nature sheweth that there is a God, who hath Lordship and Soveraignty over all, is good, and doth good unto all, and is therefore to bee feared, loved, praised, called upon, trusted in, and served, with all the heart, and with all the soule, and with all the might" (21.1). However, the Confession limits how natural law functions, dictating only matters related to decency and order, such as the principle that some time should be set apart to worship God, as Gillespie argued: "It is of the

---

[46] Ibid., 486.
[47] Richard R. DeRidder, ed., *The Church Orders of the Sixteenth Century Reformed Churches of the Netherlands Together with Their Social, Political, and Ecclesiastical Context*, trans. Richard R. DeRidder et al. (Grand Rapids: Calvin Theological Seminary, 1987), 554–55; cf. C. Hooijer, ed., *Oude Kerkordeningen der Nederlandsche Hervormde Gemeenten (1563–1638)* (Zalt-Bommel: Joh. Noman en Zoon, 1865), 457. My thanks to Mark Van der Pol for drawing my attention to this passage.

Law of Nature, that, in general, a due proportion of time be set apart, for the Worship of God" (21.7).

A similar statement appears in the opening chapter of the Confession, which says that natural law is the means to govern some circumstances, not elements, of worship: "There are some circumstances concerning the Worship of God, and the Government of the Church, common to human actions and Societies, which are to be ordered by the Light of Nature and Christian Prudence, according to the generall Rules of the Word, which are always to be observed" (1.6). Beyond such principles, the Confession argues:

> But, the acceptable way of Worshipping the true God, is instituted by himselfe, and so limited by his own revealed Will, that he may not bee Worshipped according to the imaginations and devices of men, or the suggestions of Satan, under any visible representation, or any other way not prescribed in the holy Scripture. (21.1)

The last clause of this statement alludes to the second commandment's prohibition against images of God and reflects the broader Reformed appeal to this commandment as a chief *locus classicus* for the RPW.

The rest of the Confession's statements naturally flow from the foundation that Scripture governs worship. For example, it insists that religious worship is given only to the triune God, and not to "Angels, Saints, or any other Creature: and, since the Fall, not without a Mediator; nor in the mediation of any other, but of Christ alone" (21.2). This statement stands in opposition to the Roman Catholic teaching of the veneration of the saints. Rome believed that saints intercede on behalf of believers and should be invoked in prayer and worship, and with the use of relics and images. Trent states that the bishop of the church "must also teach that images of Christ, the Virgin Mother of God, and the other saints should be set up and kept, particularly in churches, and that due honor and reverence is owed them." Likewise Trent also promotes prayers for the dead, something that the Confession naturally rejects (21.4–5).[48]

The Confession's chapter on worship does not merely reject unlawful worship practices but sets forth a series of scripturally mandated

---

[48] Council of Trent, sess. 25, December 3–4, 1563, on the veneration of saints and images.

elements of worship, which can be subdivided into two categories, ordinary and extraordinary (table 8).[49]

Table 8. Ordinary versus extraordinary elements of worship

Ordinary	Extraordinary
• Reading the Scriptures • Preaching the Word • Hearing the Word • Singing of Psalms • Due administration and worthy reception of the sacraments	• Religious oaths • Vows • Solemn fastings • Thanksgivings upon special occasions

Whatever the Confession has to say about the mandated elements of worship should be read along with the catechisms, but especially with the Directory for Public Worship (DPW). The divines wrote the directory as something distinct from the BCP. They note in the preface to the DPW the "long and sad experience" with the Church of England's liturgy, which contained "many unprofitable and burdensome Ceremonies" that were "disquieting the Consciences of many Godly Ministers and people who could not yield unto them."

Hence the divines "resolved to lay aside the former Leiturgy [sic], with the many Rites and Ceremonies formerly used in the Worship of God." Rather than set forth specific required forms, the divines offered "generall heads" which "contain the substance of the Service and Worship of God." In other words, the DPW offers general *direction*, not binding forms. Whatever it prescribes, it does so because such ceremonies or elements are mandated by Scripture, not human invention. Nonetheless, Thomas Edwards (1599–1647), the well-known heresiographer, noted that some Independents were nonetheless opposed to the creation of the DPW because they believed it violated the second commandment.[50] John Turner (fl. 1645), an Independent, writes about the DPW: "May not the Directory-Booke be read and obeyed in the Church of Christ? A. The Directory-Booke may not, because Christ

---

[49] For the use of the ordinary-extraordinary categories to define the elements of worship, see, e.g., Leigh, *Body of Divinity*, 8.11–13 (pp. 735–47); 9.3 (p. 772).
[50] Thomas Edwards, *The First and Second Part of Gangraena; or, A Catalogue and Discovery of Many of the Errors, Heresies, Blasphemies and Pernicious Practices of the Sectaries of This Time* (London: Ralph Smith, 1646), 31.

hath made a better, wise, more ancient, and more infallible booke of direction, for to direct his Church in his written word."[51]

Disputed Worship Practices

Wedding Ceremonies and Rings

Though there was great agreement among the Reformed about the principles of worship, they were not of one mind on every particular subject. The assembly illustrates the maxim that when you have three Presbyterians, you get five opinions. The minutes of the assembly record a number of issues that divided the divines in their deliberations, such as the propriety of ministers conducting marriage ceremonies and funeral services. To contemporary readers such questions seem oddly out of place, given how such practices are virtually an unquestioned norm. However, for the divines the long shadow of the Roman Catholic Church hung over the assembly's deliberations.

In particular, the divines were concerned that if ministers performed marriage ceremonies, that might lend credence to the idea that marriage is a sacrament, as Rome maintained.[52] In their deliberations over the creation of the DPW some divines argued that marriage is merely a "civil contract," but others, such as Rutherford, believed there is something divine about marriage, but did not regard it as formally part of worship. Thomas Goodwin (1600–1680) made a similar observation, acknowledging that marriage is a type of Christ and the church.[53] Jeremiah Burroughs (ca. 1600–1646) adamantly opined that the DPW should not include anything about marriage because people in the church might believe that it is therefore part of divine worship. Debate on this matter also centered upon the degree to which marriage was considered a vow and therefore a part of worship as an extraordinary element. In other words, is marriage a vow merely between two parties, or is it a vow to God?[54]

The final outcome appears in the DPW, which characterizes the

---

[51] John Turner, *A Heavenly Conference for Sions Saints, to Enlighten Themselves and Teach Their Children. Together with Saints Beliefe* (London, 1645), 64.

[52] Council of Trent, sess. 7, March 3, 1547, canons on the sacraments, 1; sess. 24, November 11, 1563.

[53] Cf. Thomas Goodwin, *Exposition of Various Portions of the Epistle to the Ephesians*, comm. Eph. 5:30, in *The Works of Thomas Goodwin*, 12 vols. (1861–1866; Eureka: Tanski, 1996), 2:423–25.

[54] *MPWA*, sess. 327, November 21, 1644 (3:463–66).

minister's role as one fitting to *solemnize* marriage even though it is not a sacrament and is "common to mankinde." The DPW offers other counsel regarding the place and time that marriage ceremonies should be performed, namely, "in the place appointed by Authority for publique Worship, before a competent number of credible witnesses, at some convenient hour of the day, at any time of the year, except on a day of Publique Humiliation. And we advise that it be not on the Lords day." Such counsel was meant to protect the importance of marriage but also advised against, though did not prohibit, performing the ceremony on a Sunday, likely because the divines wanted to ensure that people in the church did not mistake marriage as part of worship or a sacrament.

A further consideration that distances the DPW from Roman Catholic practice is that it instructs the minister to give a solemn charge to the couple, not a sermon. Once the couple exchanged vows (the DPW calls them "words" perhaps as a result of debate over the matter), the minister, "then, without any further Ceremony," was to face the congregation and pronounce them "Husband and Wife."[55] The stipulation "without any further Ceremony" was a reference to and rejection of the exchange of wedding rings, a Roman Catholic practice.[56]

The Lord's Prayer

Other disputes arose concerning the nature of the Lord's Prayer (Matt. 6:9–13). Is it a scripturally mandated form and therefore required or merely a pattern for prayer? Despite the differences of opinion over this question, Robert Baillie (1599–1662), one of the Scottish divines, notes that the Independents in the assembly did not object to the inclusion of the Lord's Prayer in the DPW.[57] But even then, the Lord's Prayer is not imposed upon ministers: "And because the Prayer which Christ taught his Disciples, is not only a Patern of Prayer, but it self a most comprehensive Prayer, we recommend it also to be used in the Prayers of the Church."[58]

---

[55] *Directory for the Publique Worship of God*, 30.

[56] Richard A. Muller and Rowland S. Ward, *Scripture and Worship: Biblical Interpretation and the Directory for Worship* (Phillipsburg, NJ: P&R, 2007), 134.

[57] Robert Baillie, *A Dissuasive from the Errours of the Time: Wherein the Tenets of the Principall Sects, Especially of the Independents, Are Drawn Together in One Map* (London: Samuel Gellisbrand, 1645), 148.

[58] Cf., e.g., William Gouge, *A Guide to Goe to God; or, An Explanation of the Perfect Patterne of Prayer, the Lords Prayer* (London: Edward Brewster, 1626).

Preaching Methodology

Early modern Reformed preaching was not monolithic, which means that there were diversified opinions about how a sermon should be executed.[59] Given the differences, the DPW contains general counsel that sermons should be based upon Scripture, have a brief introduction, not be burdened by too many points of organizational division, be expressed in plain terms so that common people can understand, be simply illustrated, and confute false doctrine. Also, sermons need not address every doctrine in a particular text. The DPW does not enjoin these requirements upon ministers but rather recommends them: "This Method is not prescribed as necessary for every man, or upon every Text; but only recommended, as being found by experience to be very much blessed of God, and very helpful for the peoples understandings and memories."

The DPW is likely worded in this manner because of the advisory nature of the directory and also because some of the divines disagreed with some common preaching methodologies. Anthony Tuckney (1599–1670) voiced his concern over the "prescription of preaching by doctrine, reason, and use, as too strait for the variety of gifts, and occasion doth claim liberty."[60] Tuckney's concern was also shared by William Gouge (1575–1653) and Thomas Gattaker (1574–1654). These concerns were taken into account in the final wording of the DPW, as quoted above, though according to John Lightfoot's (1602–1675) journal, "it cost a great deal of time, before we could find terms for it."[61]

The Public Reading of Scripture

On a related topic, there was also debate concerning the public reading of Scripture in the vernacular language of the people, which Reformed theologians promoted from the earliest days of the Reforma-

---

[59] See, e.g., Hughes Oliphant Old, *The Reading and Preaching of the Scriptures in the Worship of the Christian Church*, vol. 4, *The Age of the Reformation* (Grand Rapids: Eerdmans, 2002), 43–157, 251–329, 409–48.
[60] Thomas Watson's (1620–1686) *Body of Divinity* is an example of the type of preaching to which Tuckney objected (Thomas Watson, *A Body of Practical Divinity* [London: Thomas Parkhurst, 1692]).
[61] John Lightfoot, *The Journal of the Proceedings of the Assembly of Divines*, vol. 13 in *The Whole Works of the Rev. John Lightfoot* (London: J. F. Dove, 1824), 278. No significant information appears in the minutes regarding this debate (*MPWA*, sess. 232, June 5, 1644 [3:131]).

tion.[62] Some, such as Herbert Palmer (1601–1647) and Charles Herle (1597–1659), were of the opinion that only ordained ministers should be allowed to read the Scriptures in worship, but Lightfoot records that "many spake against them."[63] This did not immediately resolve the debate, for Lightfoot notes that this question "was canvassed 'pro et contra' exceedingly."[64] Palmer "stood exceedingly" upon the idea that the public reading of Scripture in worship was the sole right of the minister, because "the word read is the mouth of God to the people, and who is to be so but a minister? and where do we find any pattern in the Scripture to the contrary?"[65]

Advocates of the other side raised a number of counterpoints. For example, they feared that the burden would be too heavy upon the minister if he alone were required to read all of the Scripture in a worship service. Such an argument might seem weak to contemporary readers because, by comparison, very little Scripture is read in public worship these days. The DPW, however, leaves the specific amount of Scripture readings to the wisdom of the minister, but suggests that ordinarily one chapter from each Testament should be read, and sometimes more, depending upon the length of the chapters. This reading of Scripture was in addition to the sermon text, for the DPW suggests that the public reading of Scripture should ordinarily be *lectio continua*, that is, a sequential chapter-by-chapter reading of Scripture on each Lord's Day.

Other arguments included the permission for "probationers" or "expectants" (candidates for the ministry who were not yet ordained) to read the Scriptures publicly as part of their preparation and testing to determine their suitability for ordained ministry. Lightfoot also mentions several scriptural arguments. In the New Testament there was a reading of the law before it was preached (Luke 4; Acts 13). Among the Jews the "Karraim," a Jewish sect extant about thirty years before Christ's ministry, also made provision for "readers of the law," while the Pharisees were the "expositors," or preachers. Lightfoot notes that

---

[62] See, e.g., William Whitaker, *Disputations on Holy Scripture against the Papists, Especially Bellarmine and Stapleton* (1588; Orlando. FL: Soli Deo Gloria, n.d.), 1.2.15 (p. 238).
[63] Lightfoot, *Journal*, 282.
[64] Ibid., 283.
[65] Ibid.

this issue occupied the assembly "all the morning," and was eventually referred to committee.[66] The DPW does not side with Herle and his minister-only position on the public reading of Scripture. The DPW explains that since the reading of the Word is a means of grace, it should be performed by pastors and teachers, and those "who intend the Ministery [sic], may occasionally both reade the Word, and exercise their gift in Preaching in the Congregation, if allowed by the Presbytery thereunto."

Holy Days

There was universal rejection of Roman Catholic imposition of worship ceremonies, but there was some difference among the Reformed regarding the legitimacy of some holy days. Given the slim presence of Anglicans (Episcopalians) at the assembly, it is only natural that the Standards reflect the views of the Independents and Presbyterians on the illegitimacy of extra-dominical days of worship. The Confession recognizes only one day of worship—the Lord's Day, or the Sabbath (21.7–8). The DPW specifically addresses the subject of holy days, which was something several of the divines wanted to treat in order to refute the Roman Catholic and Anglican views. The minutes state:

> Ordered: That in the Directory for the sabbath day something be expressed against parish feasts commonly called by the name of Rushbearings, whittsunales, wakes, as prophane and superstitious.

> Ordered: [The Lord's Day] being the standing holy day under the New Testament to be kept by all the churches of Christ, consider of something concerning holy dayes and holy places & what course may be thought upon for the reliefe of servants.[67]

Even though the assembly ordered such considerations, not all the divines shared these concerns. The minutes indicate that the assembly was embroiled in lengthy debate over this issue.[68] Nevertheless, the outcome of their deliberations appears in an appendix to the DPW.

[66] Ibid.; David Jennings, *Jewish Antiquities; or, A Course of Lectures on the Three First Books of Godwin's Moses and Aaron* (London: William Baynes and Son, 1823), 1.9 (p. 298).
[67] *MPWA*, sess. 325, November 19, 1644 (3:458–59).
[68] Ibid., sess. 329 , November 25, 1644; sess. 339, December 11, 1644; sess. 348, December 27, 1644; sess. 349, December 30, 1644 (3:468, 479, 489–91).

The divines write: "There is no Day commanded in Scripture to be kept holy under the Gospel, but the Lords-day, which is the Christian Sabbath. Festival dayes, vulgarly called Holy dayes, having no Warrant in the Word of God, are not to be continued." But the divines were not entirely opposed to all extra-dominical worship. They also acknowledged special occasions when a separate day of public fasting or thanksgiving was appropriate, and hence they gave counsel concerning the observation of such days in the DPW. Edward Leigh (1602–1671) notes: "An holy Feast is an extraordinary Thanksgiving for some notable deliverance out of some desperate danger, testified with feasting before God with joy and gladnesse, sending Presents to our friends, and Portions to the needy."[69] In other words, on scriptural grounds the divines allowed celebration and thanksgiving for special occasions but not the regular observance of holy days, such as Christmas and Easter.

Psalmody

In the seventeenth century the singing of psalms was hardly an innovation in Presbyterian worship, as the practice was a long-standing one that stretched back to the early church, most notably documented by John Cassian (ca. 360–435). It was Cassian's views on the importance of singing psalms in worship that found their way to the desks of Thomas Cranmer (1489–1556) and Martin Bucer. Cranmer played a crucial role in the composition of the BCP, which employed the chanting of psalms in worship, and Bucer created the Strasbourg Psalter, which showcased metrical psalms for singing in worship. Bucer's Psalter helped inspire the creation of the Genevan Psalter, which influenced others in England and Scotland. English and Scottish exiles who had sought refuge in Geneva during the Marian persecution brought back their Genevan Psalters to the British Isles, which led to the creation of other Psalters.[70] So from a historical standpoint, psalm singing was not unique to the Reformed church. In fact, the Synod of

---

[69] Leigh, *Body of Divinity*, 8.12 (p. 739).
[70] Hughes Oliphant Old and Robert Cathcart, "From Cassian to Cranmer: Singing the Psams from Ancient Times until the Dawning of the Reformation," in *Sing a New Song: Recovering Psalm Singing for the Twenty-First Century*, ed. Anthony T. Selvaggio and Joel R. Beeke (Grand Rapids: Reformation Heritage, 2010), 1–13.

Laodicea (AD 350) and the Council of Bracatara (AD 563) banned the singing of nonscriptural hymns.[71]

By the time of the Westminster Assembly, however, not all agreed about the necessity of psalm singing. Leigh rehearses the history of psalm singing, noting its practice in the Old Testament and how the Reformed churches would begin and end their worship services with a psalm in order to acquaint the congregation with this vital part of God's word.[72] He notes that Reformed theologians agreed that psalms could be sung lawfully, but also states that a number of theologians believed that "Songs and Psalms of our own inditing (say some) agreeable to Scripture, *Sing unto the Lord a new Song*, framed on a fresh occasion, therefore *1 Cor.* 14.26," were permissible.[73] Leigh, like Calvin and Ames before him, points out that a psalm is "but a musical prayer for the most part, therefore we may make Songs for our selves agreeable to the Word of God as well as prayers."[74] Leigh then appeals to Paul's statement that the church is to use "Psalms, Hymns, and spiritual Songs, *Ephs.* 5.19. & *Col.* 3.16." Based upon this observation, Leigh asks: "Who can shew any reason to limit his speech to Scripture-psalms? Why may not one praise God in a Song for our deliverance in 88, or the Gun pouder treason?"[75] Leigh's reference is to England's victory over the Spanish Armada in 1588 and the notorious but nonetheless failed "Gunpowder Plot" (1605), when Roman Catholics sought to blow up Parliament during its opening session and install a monarch who was sympathetic to the Roman Catholic Church.[76]

Other Reformed theologians, such as Scottish Presbyterian theologian David Dickson (1583–1663), however, did not share Leigh's opinions. Dickson noted that some were entirely opposed to psalm singing in worship, such as the Quakers. Nevertheless, he offers five reasons why psalms should be sung in worship:

---

[71] Joel R. Beeke, "Psalm Singing in Calvin and the Puritans," in Selvaggio and Beeke, *Sing a New Song*, 16.
[72] Leigh, *Body of Divinity*, 8.3 (p. 609).
[73] Ibid., 8.3 (p. 610).
[74] Ibid.; John Calvin, *1 Corinthians*, in *CNTC* (1960; Grand Rapids: Eerdmans, 1996), 292–93; Calvin, *Institutes*, 3.20.32; Ames, *Marrow of Theology*, 2.9.44–48 (pp. 262–63).
[75] Leigh, *Body of Divinity*, 8.3 (p. 610).
[76] Barry Coward, *The Stuart Age: England 1603–1714*, 3rd ed. (1980; London: Longman, 1994), 79–81.

1. The precedent of Christ and the apostles (Matt. 26:30), Paul and Silas (Acts 16:25), and Moses and the Israelites (Exodus 15).
2. The fact that God commanded the singing of psalms in the Old Testament, which was neither a type nor a part of the ceremonial law; hence it is not abrogated under the New Testament (Ps. 30:4; 149:1).
3. The general and universal commands in the New Testament (1 Cor. 14:15; Eph. 5:19; Col. 3:16).
4. James's words: "Is any among you afflicted? let him pray. Is any merry? let him sing psalms" (James 5:13).
5. The fact that when the church sings psalms, God is glorified.[77]

Dickson's and Leigh's views represent two competing understandings of what Scripture commanded regarding what should be sung in worship. Leigh believed that psalms and scriptural songs should be sung, and Dickson believed only psalms were commanded.

At first glance the Confession appears to support the views of exclusive psalmody (Dickson), not the inclusive view (Leigh), because the Confession states that the "singing of Psalms with grace in the heart" is an acceptable practice in worship, and the divines cite Colossians 3:16: "Let the word of Christ dwell in you richly in all wisdom; teaching and admonishing one another in psalms and hymns and spiritual songs, singing with grace in your hearts to the Lord." However, when one digs a bit deeper, the evidence points in the opposite direction for a number of reasons. First, Leigh and Dickson both appeal to Colossians 3:16, which shows that there were at least two divergent readings of this verse. The former argues that psalms are included but that "hymns and spiritual songs" refer to non-inspired musical compositions; and the latter contends that the verse refers only to psalms.[78] The assembly's *Annotations* embrace Leigh's understanding of the verse in question and explain that *psalms* are the psalms of David, *hymns* are certain "ditties" composed on special occasions, and *spiritual songs* were not composed before hand but were "prick't before them with musical notes, but such as men endited by an

[77] David Dickson, *Truths Victory over Error* (Edinburgh: John Reed, 1684), 21.9 (pp. 184–86).
[78] Cf. Rollock, *Colossians*, comm. Col. 3:16 (p. 337); Davenant, *Colossians*, comm. Col. 3:16 (pp. 140–41).

extraordinary gift."[79] In other words, spiritual songs were composed extemporaneously.

Second, the DPW endorses the propriety of psalmody in worship and states that it is the duty of Christians to praise God publicly and corporately, as well as privately in the home.[80] However, the DPW states only that the psalms should be sung, not that they should be sung exclusively. The DPW is silent regarding the use of non-inspired songs in worship. Third, when one considers how the word *psalm* was used by seventeenth-century exegetes, the evidence shows that the term encompassed both the Psalms of David and uninspired scriptural songs. Recent research surveying the views of a number of sixteenth- and seventeenth-century theologians, such as John Daillie (1584–1670), Matthew Poole (ca. 1624–1679), and Thomas Manton (1620–1677), confirms the broad use of the term *psalm* to denote scriptural and extra-scriptural religious musical compositions.[81] Poole notes that even though the Septuagint uses the three terms that Paul employs in Colossians 3:16 to denote different types of songs within the Psalter, other places in Scripture, such as Luke 24:44, use the term translated "psalms" more generically.[82]

Given these three reasons—the different interpretations of Colossians 3:16, the absence of a prohibition against non-inspired scriptural songs in worship, and the varied definition of the term *psalm*—the most likely scenario is that the Standards promote the inclusive use of psalmody in worship as a necessary element but are silent regarding the use of non-inspired scriptural songs in worship.[83] This conclusion appears sound when one compares the DPW with the Church Order approved by the Synod of Dort, which states, "In the churches only the 150 Psalms of David, the Ten Commandments, the Lord's Prayer,

[79] *Annotations*, comm. Eph. 5:19.
[80] *Directory for the Publique Worship of God*, 40.
[81] Nick Needham, "Westminster and Worship: Psalms, Hymns? And Musical Instruments?," in *The Westminster Confession into the 21st Century*, ed. J. Ligon Duncan, 3 vols. (Fearn: Christian Focus, 2003–2009), 2:223–306.
[82] Matthew Poole, *Annotations upon the Holy Bible: Wherein the Sacred Text Is Inserted, and Various Readings Annexed, Together with the Parallel Scriptures*, vol. 3 (New York: Robert Carter & Brothers,), comm. Col. 3:16 (p. 725), comm. Eph. 5:19 (p. 676); cf. John Daillie, *XLIX Sermons upon the Whole Epistle of the Apostle St. Paul to the Colossians* (London: Thomas Parkhurst, 1672), serm. 41, Col. 3:16 (pp. 95–96); Thomas Manton, *A Practical Commentary; or, An Exposition with Notes on the Epistle of James* (London: Luke Fawne, 1658), comm. James 5:13 (pp. 568–69, esp. 572). Needham, "Westminster and Worship," 249–50, 258, 269.
[83] Needham, "Westminster and Worship," 281.

the 12 Articles of Faith, the Songs of Mary, Zacharias, and Simeon shall be sung."[84] Dort's position is basically one of exclusive psalmody, whereas the DPW is inclusive and silent regarding the use of other songs in worship.

One related area regarding singing in worship that the Standards apparently avoid altogether is the question of whether congregations could or should be accompanied by musical instruments, such as the organ. This is an interesting omission because Parliament decreed on May 9, 1644, that ecclesiastical organs should be destroyed along with images and all superstitious monuments.[85] Leigh notes that Robert Bellarmine was in favor of the use of musical instruments while a number of other theologians were opposed, such as Aquinas, Ames, Andrè Rivet (1572–1651), Zanchi, and Wilhelm Zepper (1550–1607).[86]

Conclusion

The RPW is at the same time rigorous and flexible. According to the Standards and the DPW, worship had to be conducted in accordance with the commands of Scripture, which precluded a number of Roman Catholic and Anglican ceremonies. The differences between the Reformed and their Roman Catholic and Anglican counterparts stemmed largely from the differing views of church authority. For the former the church was under the authority of God's Word and for the latter the church was on equal footing with it. This meant that Roman Catholics, and Anglicans to a certain extent, believed they could create human-originated ceremonies for worship. For the Reformed, much of the ceremonial pomp and circumstance of the Old Testament had given way to a beautiful simplicity because of the advent of Christ, so to go back to such ornamental worship was, in effect, to turn back the clock on redemptive history and return to the practices of the Jewish

---

[84] DeRidder, *Church Orders of the Sixteenth Century*, § 69 (p. 555).

[85] Needham, "Westminster and Worship," 291.

[86] Leigh, *Body of Divinity*, 8.3 (p. 610); Robert Bellarmine, *De Bonis Operibus Particulari*, 1.16–17, in *Opera Omnia*, vol. 4 (Naples: Josephum Giulian, 1858), 665–69, Aquinas, *Summa Theologica*, IIaIIae, q. 91, art. 2, ad 4; Ames, *Marrow of Theology*, 2.9 (pp. 262–63); André Rivet, *Catholicus Orthodoxus, Oppositus Catholico Papistae* (Leiden: Abrahamum Commelinum, 1630), 2.36.9–10 (pp. 561–64); Girolamo Zanchi, *Commentarius in Epistolam Sancti Pauli ad Ephesios*, Pars Altera, ed. A. H. Hertog (Amsterdam: Joannem Adamum Wormser, 1889), comm. Eph. 5:19 (p. 235). Wilhelm Zepper, *De Politia Ecclesiastica sive Forma, ac Ratio Administrandi, et Gubernandi Regni Christi, Quod Est Ecclesia in His Terres* (Herbornae: Christophori Corvini, 1595), 1.13 (pp. 106–7).

church. This was an unacceptable move that restricted the Christ-bought freedom of Christians. The RPW was all about freedom from arbitrary practices in worship—the freedom to obey God's commands.

At the same time, though the Reformed contended for freedom from will-worship and human-originated ceremonies—a freedom granted by the Word of God—this did not mean that worship practices or convictions were monolithic. The brief survey of debated issues certainly demonstrates the variegated nature of Reformed worship under the aegis of the RPW. In this respect the Standards and DPW function as a series of documents that reflect a consensus on fundamental principles and a diversity in the manner of the implementation of commonly held doctrinal convictions.

12

Eschatology

Whenever people approach the Westminster Standards to investigate matters of eschatology, or last things, they invariably want to know what the Standards have to say about the millennial question. Are the Standards a-, pre-, or postmillennial? Another question that frequently arises regarding the original version of the Confession is, why would the divines identify the pope as the antichrist (25.6)? In the minds of many critics, such a claim represents an embarrassing gaffe that had to be corrected by later generations, most notably in the 1789 American revisions of the Standards. Once again it is important to take the time to understand both the historical context and the theology of the early modern period. What many do not realize is that the divines were quite sober in their confessional proclamations about last things. And as strange as it might seem today to conclude that the pope is the antichrist, given the tumult of their period, many of the divines believed they were living in the terminal generation before the return of Christ. In light of these broad observations, it is necessary to examine the Standards on the subject of eschatology from within the milieu of early modernity so that the contemporary reader may better grasp what the Standards claim and teach.

Historical Background

Ever since the apostolic era and the numerous passages of Scripture warning people of the imminent return of Christ, every age has had people who thought they were living in the terminal generation, and the seventeenth century is no exception.[1] King James I (1566–1625) believed that the general neglect for the laws of England, not only among citizens but especially among the clergy, and a contempt for the church were signs that the "latter dayes" were "drawing on."[2] James did not base this conviction solely on what he observed in his kingdom but based it also upon his understanding of Scripture. James published a pamphlet expositing Revelation 20:7–10, which he believed was a prophecy of the latter time, "our last age."[3] He was hardly alone in his convictions that he was living in the latter days. Ever since the beginning of the Reformation theologians such as Martin Luther (1483–1546) anticipated the imminent return of Christ. Luther drew attention to numerous cosmic perturbations and therefore thought that "the greater part of them have bene already sene, and that many others not here are to bee looked for"—signs such as falling stars, "many Sunnes at one time," rainbows, sky-borne signs in the shapes of darts and swords, and the like. Luther, as King James would later opine, also believed that church officials were more interested in preserving their own honor than in furthering the cause of the gospel.[4]

John Calvin (1509–1564) likewise argued that the last days were upon the world because, according to his exegesis of a number of key texts in 1 and 2 Thessalonians, Daniel, and the Olivet Discourse in Matthew's Gospel, he believed that the last days would bring a great apostasy within the church. The time of apostasy was now upon him because a number of antichrists, such as the papacy and the rise of Islam throughout Europe, had appeared.[5] Calvin was somewhat unusual in his identification of antichrist, in that he did not strictly identify him with the pope, as other theologians of the sixteenth century had done, though he did believe the pope was the leader of

---

[1] For a survey of English early modern eschatology, see Bryan W. Ball, *A Great Expectation: Eschatological Thought in English Protestantism to 1660* (Leiden: Brill, 1975).

[2] James I, "A Speech in the Starre-Chamber, the 20 June 1616," in *The Workes of the Most High and Mightie Prince James* (London: Robert Baker and John Bill, 1616), 554.

[3] James I, *Ane Fruitfull Meditatioun Contening ane Plane and Facill Expositioun of Ye 7.8.9 and 10 Veris of the 20 Chap. of the Revelatoun* (Edinburgh: Henri Charteris, 1588), fol. A3r.

[4] Martin Luther, *A Very Comfortable, and Necessary Sermon in These Our Dayes, Made by the Right Reverend Father, and Faithful Servaunt of Jesus Christ Martin Luther, concerning the Coming of our Savior Christ to Judgement, and the Signes That Go Before the Last Day* (n.p., 1570), fols. 255, 258, 266.

[5] John Calvin, *Romans and Thessalonians*, in *CNTC* (1960; Grand Rapids: Eerdmans, 1996), comm. 2 Thess. 2:1–3 (pp. 396–400).

antichrist's kingdom; Calvin instead argued that antichrist was manifest in a number of ways, including the papacy.[6] Many other theologians, such as Heinrich Bullinger (1504–1575) and Andreas Osiander
(1498–1552), contributed to the conviction that the return of Christ
was imminent. In Osiander's *Conjectures of the Ende of the Worlde*,
the German Lutheran theologian claimed that the Scriptures were
correct when Jesus said that no man knows the day or hour of his
return. But Osiander nevertheless contended that Christians could
make legitimate conjectures in order to discern the general time frame
of when Christ would return.[7] Osiander believed that one of the signs
of Christ's return was the "fall of the Antichriste of Rome."[8]

Bullinger, in his published sermons on Revelation, identified the
pope as the antichrist.[9] Augustine Marlorat's (1506–1562) commentary on Revelation was a compilation of comments drawn from several
Reformed theologians, including Bullinger, Pierre Viret (1511–1571),
Sebastian Meyer (1465–1545), Antoine du Pinet (ca. 1510–1584), François Lambert (ca. 1486–1530), Wolfgang Musculus (1497–1563), Caspar Megander (1495–1545), Johannes Oecolampadius (1482–1531),
Konrad Pellikan (1478–1556), and Lutheran theologian Justus Jonas
(1493–1555).[10] In his commentary, Marlorat argues that antichrist is
not any one man but a kingdom, one that sets itself against Christ's
kingdom.[11] Reflecting the fact that his commentary is a compilation,
Marlorat draws the antichrist-papacy and antichrist-Islam connection,
since a number of the aforementioned theologians held these views.[12]

When one combines these exegetical-theological opinions with the
events of the period, such as the "Protestant" victory of England over

---

[6] Cf. John Calvin, *Institutes of the Christian Religion*, trans. John Allen (Grand Rapids: Eerdmans, 1949), 4.7.25; Calvin, *Thessalonians*, comm. 2 Thess. 2:7–8 (pp. 403–4); Katherine R. Firth, *The Apocalyptic Tradition in Reformation Britain 1530–1645* (Oxford: OUP, 1979), 34–35.
[7] Andreas Osiander, *The Conjectures of the Ende of the Worlde*, trans. George Joye (n.p., 1548), A4r–A5v.
[8] Ibid., A3v; Firth, *Apocalyptic Tradition*, 62.
[9] Heinrich Bullinger, *A Hundred Sermons upon the Apocalips of Jesu Christe* (n.p., 1561), serm. 58 (pp. 385–91).
[10] Cf., e.g., Sebastian Meyer, *In Apocalypsim Iohannis Apostoli D. Sebastiani Meyer Ecclesiastae Bernesis Commentarius* (Tiguri: Ex Officina Froschovianna, 1539); Antoine du Pinet, *Exposition de l'Apocalypse de Sainct* (Geneva, 1557); François Lambert, *Exegeseos in Sanctam Divi Ioannis Apocalypsim* (Marburg: Franz Rhode, 1528); Irena Backus, *Reformation Readings of the Apocalypse: Geneva, Zurich, and Wittenberg* (Oxford: OUP, 2000), 63.
[11] Augustine Marlorat, *A Catholike Exposition upon the Revelation of Sainct John* (London: H. Binnerman, 1574), fol. 184.
[12] Ibid., fols. 183–86.

the "Roman Catholic" Spanish Armada in 1588, the failed Gunpowder Plot by Roman Catholics in 1605, the ongoing Thirty Years War (1618–1648) with its many of battles between Protestant and Catholic armies, and the perceived threat of encroaching Catholicism through the influence of Archbishop William Laud (1573–1645), it should be no surprise that many of the Westminster divines thought they were on the precipice of the consummation of the world and the second advent of Christ. Divines believing in the imminence of Christ's return included Jeremiah Burroughs (ca. 1600–1646), Thomas Goodwin (1600–1680), and Edmund Calamy (1600–1666). In a sermon preached in 1645 Burroughs told his congregation that mighty stirrings were occurring in the world and that the expectation of Christ's return was greater than ever before. Just as with the Samaritan woman's expectations of the Messiah's advent (John 4), so the godly saints of Burroughs's day were all the more expectant of Christ's return, and Burroughs exhorted his congregation to pray fervently for it.[13]

Independent divine Thomas Goodwin calculated that the world would end by 1666.[14] His exegesis was part of a much larger exegetical conversation among a number of commentators. An abbreviated version of his argument runs as follows: First, Revelation 13:18 mentions the number of the beast, which is 666. Goodwin explains that the Greeks and Hebrews seldom mentioned the number 1,000. In this particular case, he inferred that 666 was actually 1666. Hence, he believed that 666 referred to 1,666 years after the birth of Christ. Second, Revelation 11:3 states that the two witnesses would prophesy for 1,260 days, which Goodwin took not for days but for years. This means that the rise of antichrist, the pope, had to begin around AD 406 (1,666 − 1,260 = 406). As Paul indicates in 2 Thessalonians 2:7–8, the man of lawlessness would assume power and begin to appear in the world. According to Goodwin, Pope Innocent I (AD 401–417) began to usurp authority over all churches around 406.[15] Despite his mathematically precise exegesis, Goodwin was flexible on the exact date of Christ's

---

[13] Jeremiah Burroughs, *Jerusalems Glory Breaking Forth into the World, Being a Scripture-Discovery of the New Testament Church, in the Latter Days Immediately Before the Second Coming of Christ* (London: Giles Calvert, 1675), 111–12; Ball, *Great Expectation,* 5.
[14] Ball, *Great Expectation,* 119–20.
[15] Thomas Goodwin, *An Exposition of the Revelation,* in *The Works of Thomas Goodwin,* 12 vols. (1861–1866; Eureka: Tanski, 1996), 3:73–75.

return, and like other theologians of the period he was convinced it would occur before the end of the seventeenth century. Burroughs, for example, writes:

> Now the breaking of the Roman Empire was at the raising up of those ten several sort of governments called in Revelations *ten Kings*, and the raising up of those Kings was 400 yeares and something more after Christ, as Chronologers tell us, between the 400 and 500 yeares. It is hard to reckon to a yeare, there is so much difference in Chronologers computations; after that time there must be 1260 dayes, that is 1260 yeares. Make this computation, and compare all these Scripture one with another, it cannot be long, but in this century that is now currant, these *latter dayes* are here meant, when the people of God and the Jews shall *returne to Jehovah, and David their King, and feare the Lord and his goodnesse.*[16]

Burroughs, much like Goodwin, believed that the demise of the Roman Empire led to the rise of the ten kings (Rev. 17:12), which also brought about the rise of the antichrist, the pope, around AD 400.[17]

Edmund Calamy also expected that Christ would soon return and warned of it in a sermon that he preached from Jeremiah 18:7–10 before the House of Commons during a solemn fast on December 22, 1641. Calamy told his audience that the only way to avert God's wrath upon England was to bring about a reformation, both personal and national. This did not mean that every person in England would have to turn to Christ for reformation to occur; a nation could repent of its sins generally. This repentance needed to take place at multiple levels—court, country, city, church, and state—and hence produce general reformation. But how was such a reformation to be accomplished?

Calamy believed it would occur in two ways. First, the House of Commons, as the representative governing body of England, should seek and implement reformation. Second, just as in the prophet Nehemiah's day, the nation's governing body could promote reformation as magistrates in a lawful manner. Calamy encouraged the House of Commons to call a synod to unify worship and doctrine in England.

---

[16] Jeremiah Burroughs, *An Exposition of the Prophesie of Hosea* (London: R. Dawlman, 1643); lect. 3, Hos. 3:5 (p. 749); Ball, *Great Expectation*, 120.

[17] Goodwin, *Revelation*, 74.

This would mean excluding Roman Catholics, whom Luther likened to foxes covered with dust entering a house to sweep it with their tails, but instead raising more dirt and creating chaos in the church.[18]

This brief historical sketch provides the requisite contextual data to understand the Standards and what they have to say about eschatology, or last things. Given the wars and rumors of wars, the perceived rise of antichrist, and the eager anticipation of the end of the world with the recent onset of the Reformation, the Westminster divines were set on edge. They expected the imminent return of Christ within a matter of decades.

Personal Eschatology

We can begin with a survey of personal eschatology. What happens to individuals upon their death and when they appear before the judgment seat at the consummation? How does a person's justification bear upon his or her necessary appearance before the judgment seat of Christ on the last day?

Soul Sleep

The Confession's initial statements about eschatology deal with what happens to people after they die. Without naming the doctrine of soul sleep, the Confession rejects the teaching that upon death a person enters an unconscious state and there awaits the return of Christ and the general resurrection, at which time the person is awakened from this unconscious state. Such a teaching featured prominently among Anabaptists in the sixteenth century. One of the Reformation's initial negative responses to this doctrine came from Ulrich Zwingli (1484–1531), who in 1531 penned his *Exposition of the Faith*, in which he rejected the doctrine of soul sleep.[19]

Around the same period Heinrich Bullinger also rejected the doctrine, and Calvin followed suit with his own work *Psychopannychia*.[20]

---

[18] Edmund Calamy, *Englands Looking-Glasse, Presented in a Sermon, Preached before the Honorable House of Commons, at Their Late Solemne Fast, December 22. 1644* (London: Christopher Meredith, 1642), 45–48; Ball, *Great Expectation*, 103.

[19] Ulrich Zwingli, *An Exposition of the Faith*, in *Zwingli and Bullinger*, ed. G. W. Bromiley (Philadelphia: Westminster, 1953), 273–76.

[20] Heinrich Bullinger, *The Decades of Henry Bullinger*, ed. Thomas Harding, 4 vols. (Grand Rapids: Reformation Heritage, 2004), 4.10 (2:390).

This work was written in 1534, two years before his famous 1536 first edition of the *Institutes of the Christian Religion*. But fellow Reformer Wolfgang Capito (1478–1541) advised Calvin that he should not publish the work, and Calvin followed his counsel. Calvin later revised and eventually published it in 1542.[21] His overall argument is that once saints die, they immediately go to dwell in the presence of the Lord. Their souls do not sleep—there is no unconscious state for those who die. Hence, the title of Calvin's work reflects his thesis; *psychopannychia* literally means staying awake all night.[22] Lutheran and Reformed theologians would later repeatedly cite Calvin's work.[23] The Roman Catholics also rejected the doctrine at the Fifth Lateran Council (1513).[24]

Though Anabaptists affirmed soul sleep, so did a number of mainstream Protestants. Martin Luther believed that when people die, they rest and sleep in peace, though the postmortem sleep is deeper than any sleep known to living man: "Thus after death," writes Luther, "the soul enters its chamber and is at peace; and while it sleeps, it is not aware of its sleep."[25] And though subsequent Lutheran theologians did not embrace Luther's opinion, his views did, for a time, spread throughout England, as is evident not only in William Tyndale's (ca. 1492–1536) promotion of the doctrine but also in the teaching of the Church of England.[26] Tyndale likely followed the teaching of Luther. And the Forty-Two Articles (1553), written under the guidance

---

[21] John Calvin, *Psychopannychia; or, The Souls Imaginary Sleep between Death and Judgment*, in *John Calvin: Tracts and Letters*, ed. Henry Beveridge, vol. 3 (Edinburgh: Banner of Truth, 2009), 413–90.

[22] Wulfert de Greef, *The Writings of John Calvin: An Introductory Guide*, trans. Lyle D. Bierma (Grand Rapids: Baker, 1993), 165–67.

[23] See, e.g., William Ames, *Bellarminus Enervatus* (Oxford: Excudebat Guilielmus Truner, 1629), 2.2.25 (p. 110); André Rivet, *Catholicus Orthodoxus, Appositus Catholico Papistae* (Leiden: Abrahamum Commelinum, 1630), 2.42 (p. 594); Johannes Cloppenburg, *Gangraena Theologiae Anabaptisticae* (Amsterdam: Gerardus Borstius, 1684), disp. 27.9–10 (pp. 186–87); Richard Baxter, *The Saints Everlasting Rest*, 2nd ed. (London: Thomas Underhill, 1651), 2.10 (p. 302).

[24] Fifth Lateran Council, sess. 8, December 19, 1513, in *Decrees of the Ecumenical Councils*, ed. Norman P. Tanner, 2 vols. (Washington, DC: Georgetown University Press, 1990), 1:605.

[25] Martin Luther, *Lectures on Genesis Chapters 21–25*, comm. Gen. 25:7–10, in *LW*, 4:313; cf. Paul Althaus, *The Theology of Martin Luther*, trans. Robert C. Schultz (Philadelphia: Fortress, 1975), 414–16.

[26] Cf. Leonard Hutter, *Compend of Lutheran Theology*, trans. H. E. Jacobs and G. F. Spieker (Philadelphia: Lutheran Bookstore, 1868), 29.7 (pp. 226–27); Heinrich Schmid, *The Doctrinal Theology of the Evangelical Lutheran Church* (Philadelphia: Lutheran Publication Society, 1889), 632–34; Johann Andreas Quenstedt, *Theologia Didactico-Polemica, sive Systema Theologicum* (Lipsiae: Fritsch, 1702), 4.17.16 (pp. 538–39); William Tyndale, *An Answere unto Sir Thomas Mores Dialoge*, ed. Anne M. O'Donnell and Jared Wicks (Washington, DC: Catholic University of America Press, 2000), 2.8 (p. 118; see also 345–46).

of Thomas Cranmer (1489–1556), confessed the doctrine of soul sleep, arguing that all who die sleep until the day of judgment.[27]

The divines were undoubtedly aware of the advocacy of soul sleep, given its presence in the Forty-Two Articles, but they rejected it nonetheless. The Confession states, "The Bodies of men, after death, return to dust, and see corruption: but, their Souls (which neither dye, nor sleep) having an immortal subsistence, immediately return to God who gave them" (32.1). One of the proof texts cited is Luke 23:43, which is about Christ's interaction with the repentant thief on the cross, to whom Jesus said, "Verily I say unto thee, To day shalt thou be with me in paradise." For the divines, the rejection of soul sleep was not simply a speculative question about what happened after death. Rather, it involved a proleptic anticipation of the respective destinies of the elect and non-elect. Immediately upon death the souls of the righteous "are received into the highest heavens, where they behold the face of God, in light and glory, waiting for the full Redemption of their Bodies." That is, upon death believers immediately enjoy the beatific vision (e.g., Matt. 5:8).[28] Conversely, the "Souls of the wicked are cast into hell, where they remain in torments and utter darkeness, reserved to the Judgment of the great Day." The Confession also stipulates, "Beside these two Places, for Souls separated from their bodies, the Scripture acknowledgeth none" (32.1).

Thus, without mentioning the doctrine, the Confession also rejects the Roman Catholic doctrine of purgatory, a doctrine that separated Roman Catholics from Protestants generally, and especially the Reformed. The doctrine of purgatory was appended to the intermediate state, the period of time between a person's death and glorification. What contemporary readers might not realize is that the intermediate state and the rejection of purgatory as an unscriptural doctrine are connected to the respective Reformed and Roman Catholic doctrines of justification. Given the animus between the Reformed and Roman Catholics over justification, it should be no surprise that the

---

[27] W. F. Wilkinson, ed., *The Articles of the Church of England*, 2nd ed. (London: John W. Parker, 1850), § 40 (p. 104).

[28] See, e.g., John Davenant, *An Exposition of the Epistle of St. Paul to the Colossians*, trans. Josiah Allport (1627; London: Hamilton, Adams, and Co., 1831), comm. Col. 1:15 (p. 183); cf. Thomas Aquinas, *Summa Theologica*, IaIIae, qq. 2–5.

doctrine of purgatory was one of the more frequently disputed doctrines between the two parties.[29]

Briefly, Roman Catholics taught that justification is a lifelong process in which a person is initially justified through baptism, and then through the use of the sacraments is strengthened and equipped to cooperate with the grace of God in order to become more just. Then, at the consummation and final judgment, the person is finally declared righteous in a second, or final, justification. The Roman Catholic Church teaches that upon death purgatory awaits those who have not yet acquired the necessary righteousness by faith working through love. The Council of Trent (1563) officially declared about purgatory, "The souls detained there are helped by the prayers of the faithful and most of all by the acceptable sacrifice of the altar."[30]

Trent reiterated what was codified in the Middle Ages at the First Council of Lyon (1245) and by theologians such as Thomas Aquinas (1225–1274).[31] Aquinas based his doctrine of purgatory upon 2 Maccabees 12:44: "For if he had not hoped that they that were slain should have risen again, it had been superfluous and vain to pray for the dead." Aquinas argued that if prayers for the dead are legitimate, and it would be unnecessary to pray for those saints who were already in heaven, then "some kind of cleansing remains after this life."[32]

---

[29] See, e.g., John Frith, *A Disputation of Purgatorye* (London, 1533); Rudolf Gwalther, *Antichrist* (Emden: Christophor Trutheall, 1556), serm. 3 (fol. 96); Thomas Cranmer, *An Homily or Sermon of Good Works Annexed unto Faith*, in *Miscellaneous Writings and Letters of Thomas Cranmer*, ed. John Edmund (1556; Cambridge: CUP, 1846), 148; Marlorat, *A Catholike Exposition upon the Revelation of Sanct John*, fol. 11r; William Perkins, *An Exposition of the Symbole or Creed of the Apostles*, in *The Workes of That Famous and Worthy Minister of Christ, in the Universitie of Cambridge, Mr. William Perkins* (London: John Legat, 1616), 322; Francis Junius, *Animadversiones ad Controversiam Sextam Christianae Fidei, Quae et Secunda Tomi, de Purgatrio*, in *Opera Theological Francisi Iunii Biturigis*, vol. 2 (Geneva: Samuelem Crispinum, 1613); Pierre Du Moulin, *The Buckler of the Faith* (London: Nathaniel Newbery, 1631), A4r; John Davenant, *Colossians*, comm. Col. 2:8 (p. 396); John Preston, *The New Covenant; or, The Saints Portion* (London: Nicolas Bourne, 1639), 487; Edward Leigh, *A Systeme or Body of Divinity: Consisting of Ten Books* (London: William Lee, 1654), 10.3 (pp. 866–67); cf. Martinus Becanus, *Disputatio de Purgatorio Calvinistarum* (Moguntiae: Joannis Albini, 1609); Franciso Suarez, *Summa Commentariorum ac Disputationum: De sacramentis, indulgentiis, suffragiis, Puragorio, Clavibus Ecclesiae, Sacrificio Missae, Censuris, ac Irregularitate, Tum Generatim cum Speciatim*, ed. Jacques Cardon et al. (Lugduni: Iacobi Cardon & Petris Cavellat, 1627).

[30] Council of Trent, sess. 25, December 3–4, 1563, first decree.

[31] Council of Lyon I (1245), in *The Sources of Catholic Dogma*, ed. Henry Denzinger, trans. Roy J. DeFerrari (London: B. Herder, 1954), § 456 (pp. 180–81); Thomas Aquinas, *Two Articles on Purgatory*, in *Summa Theologica*, 5 vols. (Allen: Christian Classics, 1948), appendix 2 (5:3010–11).

[32] Aquinas, *Two Articles on Purgatory*, 3010.

Justification and the Final Judgment

Tied to the question of purgatory in reference to the doctrine of justification is the question, how do the divines relate justification to the final judgment, if at all? First, contemporary readers must account for the backdrop of Roman Catholic views regarding justification and the final judgment. As noted above, the Council of Trent implied that at the final judgment believers receive their second, or final, justification. This conclusion was based upon the idea that once a person is justified in his baptism, he has the responsibility of increasing in that righteousness to obtain justification in the end.[33] Roman Catholic theologians such as Robert Bellarmine (1542–1621) and Benedictus Pererius (1535–1610) were noted advocates of this twofold justification.[34]

A number of early modern Reformed theologians were aware of this formulation and rejected it. Richard Hooker (1554–1600), for example, noted that the Reformed agreed with Rome on the necessity of the application of Christ's merit to the sinner. However, when explaining the disagreements between the Reformed and Rome, he highlighted the issue of infused versus imputed righteousness. Hooker explains that Roman Catholics believe that the

> first receipt of grace in their divinity is the first justification; the increase thereof, the second justification. . . . Unto such as have attained the first justification, that is to say, the first receipt of grace, it is applied farther by good works to the increase of former grace, which is the second justification. If they work more and more, grace doth more increase, and they are more and more justified.[35]

Other Reformed theologians who noted and rejected the Roman Catholic twofold justification included Jeremias Bastingius (1551–1595), William Perkins (1558–1602), Robert Rollock (1555–1598), Andrew Willet (1562–1621), Thomas Cartwright (ca. 1535–1603), Pierre Du

---

[33] Council of Trent, sess. 6, January 13, 1547, first decree, chap. 10.

[34] Benedictus Pererius, *Commentariorum et Disputationum in Genesim*, vol. 3 (Lugduni: Horatii Cardon, 1601), comm. Gen. 15, disp. 4, §§ 48–51 (pp. 249–53); Robert Bellarmine, *De Iustificatione Impii Libri Quinque*, 4.18, in *Disputationum Roberti Bellarmini* (Neapoli: Josephhum Giuliano, 1858), 593–97.

[35] Richard Hooker, *A Learned Discourse of Justification, Works, and How the Foundation of Faith Is Overthrown*, §§ 4–5, in *The Works of Mr. Richard Hooker in Eight Books of The Laws of Ecclesiastical Polity*, 3 vols. (London: W. Baynes and Son, 1821), 3:339–41.

Moulin (1568–1658), Samuel Rutherford (1600–1661), and Francis Roberts (1609–1675).[36]

On the other hand, some Reformed theologians argued for a twofold justification of a different nature. Anthony Burgess (d. 1664), one of the divines, writes, "But there are some learned and Orthodox Writers, that do admit of a first and second Justification, but not in the Popish sense, they utterly abhorre that, yet they affirm a first and second Justification."[37] Burgess explains the nature of this twofold justification:

> The *first Justification* is that acknowledged by the Orthodox, whereby, though sinners in our selves, yet believing are justified before God. The *second*, whereby thus justified out of our selves, we are justified before God in our selves. The first Justification is the cause of the second, and the second is the effect and demonstration of the first. The first is by faith, the second by works, and both are necessary.[38]

Burgess's description of this "orthodox" variant of a twofold justification differs from Roman Catholic versions, most notably by its use of causal language connecting the first and second justifications. This causal relationship would be rejected by Roman Catholics because Rome held that the believer's works—energized by the grace of the sacraments and not the initial justification in baptism—were the cause of one's final justification. According to Roman Catholic theologians, believers cooperate with God's sacramental grace to contribute toward their further justification. Burgess notes four Reformed theologians

---

[36] Jeremias Bastingius, *An Exposition or Commentarie upon the Catechisme of Christian Religion* (Cambridge: John Legat, 1589), q. 60 (fol. 85); William Perkins, *A Golden Chaine*, § 51, in *The Workes of That Famous and Worthy Minister of Christ, in the Universitie of Cambridge, Mr. William Perkins* (London: John Legat, 1616), 96; Robert Rollock, *A Treatise of Our Effectual Calling*, chap. 5, in *Select Works of Robert Rollock*, ed. William Gunn, 2 vols. (1844–1849; Grand Rapids: Reformation Heritage, 2008), 1:60–61; Andrew Willet, *Hexapla in Genesin, That Is, a Sixfold Commentary upon Genesis* (London: Thomas Creede, 1608), comm. Genesis 15 (p. 179); Thomas Cartwright, *A Confutation of the Rhemists Translation, Glosses and Annotations on the New Testament* (Leiden: William Brewster, 1618), comm. Rom. 4:6 (p. 341); Pierre Du Moulin, *The Buckler of the Faith* (London: Nathaniel Newbery, 1631) 158–59; Samuel Rutherford, *The Covenant of Life Opened* (Edinburgh: Robert Broun, 1655), 1.19 (p. 158); Francis Roberts, *Mysterium et Medulla Bibliorum: The Mysterie and Marrow of the Bible* (London: Goerge Calvert, 1657), 3.3, aphor. 5, q. 4 (p. 622).

[37] Anthony Burgess, *The True Doctrine of Justification Asserted and Vindicated*, 2nd ed. (London: Thomas Underhill, 1654), serm. 16 (p. 151); Joel R. Beeke and Mark Jones, *A Puritan Theology: Doctrine for Life* (Grand Rapids: Reformation Heritage, 2012), 49.

[38] Burgess, *Doctrine of Justification*, 151.

who were reputed to articulate such an "orthodox" twofold justification: Lodewijk de Dieu (1590–1642), Martin Bucer (1491–1551), John Calvin (1509–1564), and Girolamo Zanchi (1516–1590).[39]

In his *Institutes*, for example, Calvin argues that a person is justified by faith alone, "independently of all works." But he nuances his interaction with Roman Catholic critics to make the point that it is one thing to discuss the intrinsic value of works vis-à-vis justification and another thing to note the place of works "after the establishment of the righteousness of faith." Calvin explains that once a sinner is admitted into communion with Christ by God's grace and is reconciled to God, he obtains the remission of sins and is clothed in the righteousness of Christ, as if it were his own, when he stands before the divine bar. "Where remission of sins has been previously received," writes Calvin, "the good works which succeed are estimated far beyond their intrinsic merit; for all their imperfections are covered by the perfection of Christ, and all their blemishes are removed by his purity, that they may not be scrutinized by the Divine judgment." With the cloak of Christ's righteousness covering the imperfection of the believer's works, therefore, "works are accounted righteous, or, which is the same thing, are imputed for righteousness."[40]

Along these lines, de Dieu also appeals to Calvin's comments on Acts 10:35, "But in every nation he that feareth him, and worketh righteousness, is accepted with him."[41] Calvin explains that this verse may give the impression that salvation rests upon the merit of a person's works. Calvin dismisses this idea and points out that the verse does not deal with justification. But he does raise the question as to whether works can in any way gain God's favor for the believer. Calvin maintains that when God calls, regenerates, and recreates his own image in sinners whom he redeems, he does not encounter a mere man, one destitute of grace, but recognizes his own work in him. "Therefore," writes Calvin, "God regards the faithful as accepted

[39] Lodewijk de Dieu, *Animadversiones in D. Pauli Apostoli Epistolam ad Romans* (Lugduni Batavorum: Elzeviriorum, 1646), comm. Rom. 8:4 (pp. 105–10); Calvin, *Institutes*, 3.17.8; Martin Bucer, Metaphrasis *et Enarratio in Epist. D. Pauli Apostoli ad Romanos* (Basilae: Petrum Pernam, 1562), comm. Romans 2 (p. 119); cf. Girolamo Zanchi, *De Religione Christiana Fides—Confession of Christian Religion*, ed. Luca Baschera and Christian Moser, 2 vols. (Leiden: Brill, 2007), 19.11 (1:347).
[40] Calvin, *Institutes*, 3.17.8.
[41] De Dieu, *Animadversiones*, 110. De Dieu also cites Calvin, *Institutes*, 3.17.5 to the same effect.

because they lead godly and righteous lives." But these works, in Calvin's judgment, are not inherently worthy of divine approbation; they are only acceptable through faith, which "borrows from Christ what works lack."[42]

What is immediately apparent, whether in de Dieu's or Burgess's citation of these passages, is that Calvin does not denominate his position as a second justification, though he does address the question as to how the believer's good works are accepted before the divine bar. Moreover, others, such as Zanchi, offer similar explanations for this so-called second justification. Zanchi argues that a person is never justified by his works, but always by faith alone. However, his faith "is declared by his works whether he bee just or no."[43] In other words, this so-called "orthodox" double justification is not the same type of double justification advocated by Roman Catholic theologians. Moreover, it is different from the formulations of Richard Baxter (1615–1691), who later came under significant criticism by two respected Westminster divines, Anthony Burgess and Richard Vines (1599–1656), as well as by John Owen (1616–1683), for his advocacy of a final justification based upon the believer's good works.[44]

The "orthodox" double justification is also different from the views of Jacob Arminius (1560–1609), who held, unlike his peers, that justification is not complete until the final judgment.[45] Arminius speaks of the beginning of justification at a person's conversion, and its completion at the final judgment:

> But the end and completion of justification will be near the close
> of life, when God will grant, to those who end their days in the
> faith of Christ, to find his mercy absolving them from all the sins

[42] John Calvin, *Acts 1–13*, in *CNTC* (1968; Grand Rapids: Eerdmans, 1996), comm. Acts 10:35 (pp. 308–9).

[43] Zanchi, *De Religione*, 19.11 (pp. 347–49).

[44] Hans Boersma, *A Hot Pepper Corn: Richard Baxter's Doctrine of Justification in Its Seventeenth-Century Context of Controversy* (Vancouver: Regent College, 2004), 33; cf. Richard Baxter, *Aphorismes of Justification* (1649; Hague: Abraham Brown, 1655); Burgess, *Doctrine of Justification*, serm. 23 (p. 220); John Owen, *The Doctrine of Justification*, in *The Works of John Owen*, 24 vols. (1850–1853; Edinburgh: Banner of Truth, 1993), 5:284–85, 137–40.

[45] Several of the divines identified that Arminius was heterodox on justification (William Twisse, *The Riches of God's Love unto the Vessells of Mercy*, vol. 1 [Oxford: Thomas Robinson, 1653], 80; Robert Baillie, "Sermon on Zechariah 3:1–2, 28 February 1644," in *Sermons Preached before the English Houses of Parliament by the Scottish Commissioners to the Westminster Assembly of Divines 1643–1645*, ed. Chris Coldwell [Dallas: Naphtali, 2011], 208–9; George Walker, *Socinianisme in the Fundamental Point of Justification Discovered, and Confuted* [London: John Bartlet, 1641], 66–69).

which had been perpetrated through the whole of their lives. The declaration and manifestation of justification will be in the future general judgment.[46]

Since Arminius held that believers can fall away, their justification, though supported by the grace of God, also hinges upon their faithfulness. Justification, therefore, cannot be completed until it is certain that the believer will not fall away.[47]

Burgess addresses these issues—the unorthodox and orthodox double justifications—by noting that many criticized the uncommon view of the orthodox double justification. He draws attention, for example, to David Pareus's (1548–1622) criticism of Bucer's view, which the former characterized as a facile attempt to appease Roman Catholics.[48] Burgess grants that the Reformed certainly recognize that, subsequent to a person's justification, his good works are acceptable in Christ before the divine tribunal, but he stipulates:

> Yet that this should be called a second Justification, and that before God, there seemeth to be no ground from the Scripture; for (as you heard) *Abraham* and *David* after their first Justification are still said in some manner to be *justified*, viz. *By faith, not by works*. Its true, God doeth accept of beleevers as sincere, that they are not hypocrites, but they are not justified by this; for *David* crieth out, *Psal.* 19 *Who can understand the errours of his heart?* so that there is hypocrise in the heart of the most upright man for which God might justly condemn him.[49]

Burgess desires to purge the doctrine of justification of too much subtlety, especially as it relates to the final judgment: "Oh let not any

---

[46] Jacob Arminius, *Private Disputation*, 48.12, in *The Works of James Arminius*, ed. and trans. James Nichols and William Nichols, 3 vols. (1825–1875; Grand Rapids: Baker, 1996), 2:407; cf. Heidelberg Catechism, qq. 56, 59–60; Belgic Confession, 22–23; Zacharias Ursinus, *The Commentary of Dr. Zacharias Ursinus on the Heidelberg Catechism*, trans. G. W. Williard (Phillipsburg, NJ: P&R, n.d.), 324–40; Caspar Olevianus, *A Firm Foundation: An Aid to Interpreting the Heidelberg Catechism*, trans. and ed. Lyle D. Bierma (Grand Rapids: Baker, 1995), 324–42; William Perkins, *A Golden Chaine; or, The Description of Theologie, Containing the Order of the Causes of Salvation and Damnation, according to God's Word* (London: Edward Alde, 1592), 49.3–4; Johannes Polyander, André Rivet, Antonius Thysius, and Antonius Waleaeus, *Synopsis Purioris Theologiae*, ed. Herman Bavinck (Lugduni Batavorum: Didericum Donner, 1881), 33.8 (p. 332).

[47] Jacob Arminius, *A Letter to Hippolytus a Collibus*, in *Works*, 2:725; also Arminius, *Apology or Defence*, § 2, in *Works*, 1:741–42.

[48] Cf. Brian Lugioyo, *Martin Bucer's Doctrine of Justification: Reformation Theology and Early Modern Irenicism* (Oxford: OUP, 2010).

[49] Burgess, *Doctrine of Justification*, serm. 16 (p. 152).

subtil distinctions poison thee!"[50] He notes that Turks (i.e., Muslims), Jews, Papists, and formal Protestants (presumably the likes of Baxter and Arminius) were all agreed that some personal righteousness had to be established in order to stand before the divine bar, but about such righteousness Burgess writes that works "can no more stand before Gods judgement then stubble before the fire: such a righteous-nesse may have greater applause in the world, but bring it to God it is abominable. As the eye can endure to look upon a Candle or the stars, but is not able to endure the glorious beams of the Sun."[51] So the question remains, given the parameters of the expressed views, where do the Westminster Standards fall? Do they advocate an "orthodox" double justification?

The first thing readers should observe is the Confession's state-ment that after death believers are immediately "received into the highest Heavnes, where they behold the face of God, in light and glory waiting for the full Redemption of their Bodies," whereas unbelievers "are cast into Hell" (32.1). These two diverse ends for believers and un-believers occur before the final judgment. When they address the issue of the final judgment, the divines write that all persons "shall appear before the Tribunal of Christ, to give an account of their Thoughts, Words, and Deeds; and, to receive according to what they have done in the Body, whether good or evil" (33.1). Of interest is the series of proof texts the divines cite, which includes Ecclesiastes 12:14; Matthew 12:36–37; Romans 2:16; 14:10, 12; 1 Corinthians 6:3; 2 Corinthians 5:10; 2 Peter 2:4; and Jude 6. Noteworthy is the fact that none of these texts are cited in the Confession's chapter on justification. Hence, thus far, the Confession states that believers will have to give an account of their actions before the tribunal of Christ but mentions nothing of a second or final justification.

The closest the divines get to addressing the question of justifica-tion and the final judgment appears in the Shorter Catechism: "What benefits do Believers receive from Christ at the resurrection?" The catechism responds, "At the Resurrection, Believers being raised up in glory, shall be openly acknowledged and acquitted in the day of

---

[50] Ibid., serm. 16 (pp. 152–53).
[51] Ibid., serm. 16 (p. 153).

Judgement, and made perfectly blessed in full injoying of God to all eternity" (q. 38; cf. LC q. 90). What do the divines mean by "openly acknowledged and acquitted," and is this language intended to convey the idea of a second justification? The most likely answer is no. It is telling that when the divines chose their terms, they specifically did not employ the word *justify* or any variant thereof. Their choice of words likely reflects Burgess's above-cited comments about the impropriety of speaking of a second justification.

Other theologians of the period, such as Edward Leigh (1602–1671), follow a similar pattern when explaining the reasons for the final judgment:

1. That God's decree might be fulfilled (Acts 17:31).
2. That God's honor may be vindicated (Eccles. 3:16).
3. That God's justice may be cleared (Eccles. 9:1; Isa. 30:33; Rom. 2:15; 2 Tim. 4:8), and that he would call all people to account for their actions.
4. In respect of the saints, that their innocence may be made manifest, and their good works rewarded, and all things set straight.
5. That the wicked might be fully punished.

In this respect, Leigh notes how the day of judgment for believers is nothing to be feared but eagerly anticipated:

> It is comfortable to the godly, the Scripture seldome speaks of the day of Judgement, but it cals on them to rejoyce, *Lift up your heads*, Luke 21.28. It is a phrase implying the comfort, hope and boldnesse that the people of God have, or ought to have: *comfort your selves with these words*. It is compared to a day of refreshing, to the meeting of the Bridegroom, all which imply, that that time is [a] matter of joy and consolation to the godly, it is their marriage and coronation day.[52]

Leigh places emphasis upon the final judgment as comfort and vindication, not a second justification. A similar emphasis appears in Jo-

---

[52] Leigh, *Body of Divinity*, 10.2 (pp. 860–61).

hannes Maccovius (1588–1644), who explains that the final judgment is all about condemnation or acquittal, not a second justification.[53]

Further evidence appears when we explore what several Reformed theologians of the period have to say about passages of Scripture that relate to the final judgment and the consummation.[54] One such passage is Revelation 19:8, which speaks of the marriage feast of the lamb at the consummation: "And to her was granted that she should be arrayed in fine linen, clean and white: for the fine linen is the righteousness of saints." Franciso Ribera (1537–1591), one Roman Catholic interpreter among others, claimed that the "righteousness of the saints" is their good works, their merit.[55] Reformed interpreters commonly pointed to the doctrine of justification in the explanation of this passage. David Pareus (1548–1622), for example, counters Ribera's exegesis and argues that the righteousness of the saints "was given" (ἐδόθη) to them, which contradicts the idea that their fine linen was their own good works. He argues that the works of believers could never be "righteousness" (δικαιώματα) because their works are like menstrual cloths (Isa. 64:6). Pareus points out that in Christ's parable of the wedding feast (Matt. 22:12) some guests possessed good works—they obeyed the call and attended the wedding. But these guests were nonetheless thrown out because they were not appropriately clothed—they were not dressed in fine linen. What, ultimately, does the fine linen represent? Pareus argues: "Therefore this *fine linen* or *wedding garment* is Christ himself with his righteousnesse, with which we being clothed are acceptable to God: For *Iehovah is our righteousnesse*, that is, he is made righteousnesse unto us" (cf. Rev. 7:14–15). The fine linen worn by the saints is "called the *righteousnesses* or *justifications of the saints*, because they are imputed to the Saints by Christ the bridegroome."[56] This was a common explanation of this passage.[57]

---

[53] Johannes Maccovius, *Scholastic Discourse: Johannes Maccovius (1588–1644) on Theological and Philosophical Rules*, trans. Willem J. van Asselt et al. (Apeldoorn: Instituut voor Reformatieonderzoek, 2009), 20.5 (p. 277).

[54] Ball, *Great Expectation*, 224–25.

[55] Francisco Ribera, *In Sacram Beati Ioannis Apostoli, & Evangelistae Apocalypsin Commentarii* (Lugduni: Ex Officina Iuntarum, 1593), comm. Rev. 19:8 (p. 358).

[56] David Pareus, *A Commentary upon the Divine Revelation of the Apostle and Evangelist John* (Amsterdam: C. P., 1644), comm. Rev. 19:8 (pp. 482–83).

[57] So Marlorat, *A Catholike Exposition upon the Revelation of Sainct John*, fol. 265; Bullinger, *Apocalips*, serm. 82 (pp. 564–65); *Dutch Annotations*, comm. Rev. 19:8; cf. *Annotations*, comm. Rev. 19:8.

Richard Sibbes (ca. 1577–1635) offers similar observations. He explains that the doctrine of justification provides believers with great assurance that they have been clothed with the righteousness of Christ: "If wee be cloathed with the Garments of Christs righteousnesse, wee may goe through the wrath of God: for, that alone is wrathproofe; that will pacifie God, and pacifie the Conscience too. It is a righteousnesse of Gods owne providing, and accepting."[58] In a sermon preached before the House of Lords, on Zephaniah 2:3, "Seek ye the Lord, all ye meek of the earth, which have wrought his judgment; seek righteousness, seek meekness: it may be ye shall be hid in the day of the Lord's anger," one of the divines, William Bridge (ca. 1600–1671), told his audience to find shelter in Christ: "In the day of Gods Anger Seek Righteousnesse."[59] For Bridge, this righteousness is Christ. He told his audience, "Do not come unto Christ that you may live wickedly; nor think to be first holy, that you may come unto Christ; but come unto Christ that you may be holy. Seek the Lord and his righteousness in this respect."[60]

Another consideration appears in how the Standards and theologians of the period explain how God executes the judgment. James Ussher explains the differences between the believer and the nonbeliever at the final judgment, and the disparate experiences each will have. God will bring all people to judgment, that is, he will pronounce an irrevocable sentence of either absolution or condemnation. There are two moments of judgment, according to Ussher: the first at a person's death, when he is immediately sent either to heaven or to hell, and the second at the general resurrection on the last day.[61] Ussher lists four differences between the treatment of the elect and the non-elect:

1. The elect are raised as members of the body of Christ by virtue of the power of his resurrection, whereas the non-elect, as malefactors, will be brought forth from the grave by the judicial power of Christ and the power of the curse of the law.

---

[58] Richard Sibbes, *The Brides Longing for Her Bride-Groomes Second Comming* (London: R. Harford, 1638), 82–83.
[59] William Bridge, *The Saints Hiding-Place In the Time of Gods Anger* (London: Peter Cole, 1646), 24.
[60] Ibid., 25.
[61] James Ussher, *A Body of Divinitie; or, The Summe and Substance of Christian Religion* (London: Thomas Downes and George Badger, 1645), 445–46.

2. The elect are raised unto eternal life, which is called resurrection to life, whereas the non-elect are raised to condemnation, hence it is called the resurrection of condemnation.

3. The bodies of the elect will be glorified, powerful, nimble, and impassible, whereas the non-elect will have bodies suited for the punishment of hell.

4. The elect will be placed at the right hand of Christ, and the non-elect at his left hand.[62]

Immediately evident is that *before* the final judgment there is already a difference in how the elect and non-elect are treated.

But when Ussher turns to discuss the specifics of the final judgment, he makes no recourse to a second justification; he instead employs the language of acquittal. For Ussher, once the elect and non-elect are placed at the right and left hands of Christ respectively, Christ will open the "book of record, by which the dead shall be judged" (see Rev. 20:12). At this point, Christ will cause all to remember whatever good or evil they have done in their lives, "the secrets of all hearts then revealed." Christ will then open the book of life, "the eternal decree of God to save his Elect by Christ, which decree shall then at length be made known to all." Then the act of judgment follows "wherein the Elect shal first be acquitted, that they may after as assistants joyne with Christ in the judgement of the reprobate men and Angels." The evidence brought forth in the judgment will be each man's conscience, which will reveal all of his actions, whether good or evil.

Even then, the elect and the non-elect are treated differently. Ussher writes:

1. The Elect shall not have their sinnes, for which Christ satisfied, but onely their good works remembered. 2. Being in Christ, they and their works shall not undergoe the strict triall of the Law simply in itself, but as the obedience thereof doth prove them to be true partakers of the grace of the Gospel.[63]

What, according to Ussher, makes the works of the elect acceptable before the divine tribunal? The works of the wicked will be condemned

[62] Ibid., 447.
[63] Ibid., 448.

strictly in accordance with the law, and as such, their wages will be damnation. But the works of the elect will be pronounced just, because their works, "though imperfect, doe prove their faith (whereby they lay hold on Christ and his meritorious righteousnesse) to be a true faith, as working by love in all parts of obedience."[64] Ussher calls this evaluation of the believer's works an *acquittal*, not a second justification.

Another resource on this question of acquittal (not justification) at the final judgment comes from Thomas Watson's (1620–1686) sermons on the Shorter Catechism. Watson explains that the day of judgment will be terrible for the wicked but a day of comfort to the righteous. Christ will own the elect by name, those whom the world rejected and scorned, and will openly acknowledge them to be precious in his eyes before the unbelieving world. Christ as Judge will plead for his people even though it is odd, notes Watson, to have the Judge also serve as an advocate. Christ will plead his own blood for his people and vindicate them from all unjust censures. Christ will absolve his people before men and angels and profess to the world all the good deeds the saints have done. Christ will call his saints to join him at the divine bar, from which they will judge the world with Christ (cf. LC q. 90). In all of these descriptions of the final judgment Watson repeatedly invokes the word *acquittal*, not justification.[65]

The idea that works demonstrate or are evidence of genuine faith is a common theme in early modern Reformed literature and frequently appears in the context of explanations of the final judgment. William Ames (1576–1633), for example, maintains that the end of the world brings the "declaration of justification and redemption which is shown in their effects," namely, the resurrection unto life, and the wicked have a resurrection unto condemnation.[66] Likewise, the sins of the faithful do not come into judgment because, according to Ames, "They are covered and taken away by the sentence of justification; the last judgment will be a confirmation and manifestation of that sentence. It would not be right that they should again be brought to light."[67] Others, such as

---

[64] Ibid., 449.
[65] Thomas Watson, *A Body of Practical Divinity* (London: Thomas Parkhurst, 1692), 239–41.
[66] William Ames, *The Marrow of Theology*, trans. John Dykstra Eusden (1968; Grand Rapids: Baker, 1997), 1.41.3, 19 (pp. 214–15).
[67] Ibid., 1.41.22 (p. 216).

Johannes Wollebius (1589–1629), argue along similar lines, and they also speak of the *acquittal* of believers, not a second or final justification.[68] On this note, it is interesting to observe that Baxter, who advocated a final or second justification, writes of both justification and acquittal at the final judgment.[69] The idea of a second or final justification was common among Roman Catholic and neonomian theologians and consequently a target for Reformed anti-Roman polemics. Hence the language of a second (or final) justification does not appear in the Westminster Standards or in any other major Reformed Confession.[70]

Millennialism

When we move beyond the issue of personal eschatology and proceed to matters of general eschatology, questions inevitably arise concerning the millennium: what, for example, is the nature of the thousand-year reign of Christ mentioned in Revelation 20:4? The millennial question is inseparable from matters that pertain to the end of the world. During the early modern period there were largely two competing understandings of the millennium: premillennialism, which is the idea that Christ will return and usher in a literal thousand-year reign on earth, and postmillennialism, which teaches that Christ will return to the earth after the thousand-year reign; opinions were divided, though, on whether this reign is a literal or figurative thousand years.[71] Today, although some people zealously promote their

---

[68] William Perkins, *An Exposition of the Symbole of the Apostles*, in *The Workes of That Famous and Worthy Minister of Christ, in the Universitie of Cambridge, Mr. William Perkins* (London: John Legat, 1616), 264; Johannes Wollebius, *Compendium Theologiae Christianae*, 1.35.6–12, in *Reformed Dogmatics*, ed. John W. Beardslee (Oxford: OUP, 1965), 184; Gulielmus Bucanus, *Body of Divinity; or, Institutions of Christian Religion* (London: Daniel Pakeman, Abel Roper, and Richard Tomlins, 1659), 38 (pp. 494–95); Benedict Pictet, *Christian Theology*, trans. Frederick Reyroux (London: R. B. Seeley and W. Burnside, 1834), 9.4 (p. 418); John Flavel, *An Exposition of the Assembly's Shorter Catechism*, in *The Works of John Flavel*, 6 vols. (1820; Edinburgh: Banner of Truth, 1997), 6:214; John Edwards, *Theologia Reformata; or, The Body and Substance of the Christian Religion* (London: John Lawerence, 1713), 456; Thomas Adams, *A Commentary or, Exposition upon the Divine Second Epistle General Written by the Blessed Apostle St. Peter* (London: Jacob Bloome, 1633), comm. 2 Pet. 3:7 (p. 1239); Francis Junius, *The Apocalyps, or Revelation of S. John the Apostle* (Cambridge: John Legat, 1596), comm. Rev. 19:8 (p. 248); Francis Turretin, *Institutes of Elenctic Theology*, ed. James T. Dennison Jr., trans. George Musgrave Giger (Phillipsburg, NJ: P&R, 1992–1997), 16.9.11. See also the appendix at the end of this chapter.

[69] Richard Baxter, *The Saints Everlasting Rest* (London: Thomas Underhill, 1651), 1.5.1 (p. 49).

[70] Cf. Heidelberg Catechism, qq. 52, 62; Belgic Confession, 37; Second Helvetic Confession, 16.10; Thirty-Nine Articles, 18, 22.

[71] Generally on the question of millennialism, see Derek Thomas, "The Eschatology of the Westminster Confession and Assembly," in *The Westminster Confession into the 21st Century*, ed. J. Ligon Duncan, 3 vols. (Fearn: Christian Focus, 2003–2009), 2:351–71.

millennial views, charges of heresy are rare. Historic pre-, a-, and postmillennialists typically accept one another as orthodox, despite their disagreements. But such doctrinal latitude was not the case in the early modern period.

During the later days of the Reformation common opinions about premillennialism (chiliasm or millenarianism) were quite negative. The idea of an earthly reign of Christ smacked of crass literalism, which had more in common with Jewish exegesis of the Scriptures than with responsible interpretation. The Augsburg Confession (1530), written by Philip Melanchthon (1497–1560), connected premillennialism with the doctrine of the Anabaptists and condemned them for "spreading Jewish opinions to the effect that before the resurrection of the dead the godly will take possession of the kingdom of the world, the ungodly being suppressed everywhere."[72] Calvin was unimpressed with the "millenarians, who limited the reign of Christ to a thousand years." Calvin writes: "Their fiction is too puerile to require or deserve refutation. . . . Those who assign the children of God a thousand years to enjoy the inheritance of the future life, little think what dishonor they cast on Christ and his kingdom." Calvin believed that the premillennial appeal to the book of Revelation misunderstood its nature, namely, that it is about the history of the church before the return of Christ, not a thousand-year reign after his return.[73]

First-generation Reformer and leader of the Zurich churches Heinrich Bullinger also rejected premillennialism and codified this rejection in the Second Helvetic Confession (1566). In its chapter on the person and work of Christ, under its rejection of the teaching of various sects, the confession states:

> We further condemn Jewish dreams that there will be a golden age on earth before the day of judgment, and that the pious, having subdued all their godless enemies, will possess all the kingdoms of the earth. For evangelical truth in Matthew, chapters 24 and 25, and Luke 18, and apostolic teaching in 2 Thessalonians 2, and 2 Timothy, chapters 3 and 4, present something quite different.[74]

---

[72] Augsburg Confession, 18; cf., e.g., Thomas Müntzer, "Sermon before the Princes: An Exposition of the Second Chapter of Daniel, 13 July 1524," in *Spiritual and Anabaptist Writers*, ed. George Hunston Williams, LCC (Philadelphia: Westminster, 1952), 49–70.

[73] Calvin, *Institutes*, 3.25.5.

[74] Second Helvetic Confession, 11.14.

Perhaps owing to Bullinger's influence upon the English Reformation, the same type of rejection appears in the Forty-Two Articles (1552), which were written under the supervision of Thomas Cranmer. Article 41 states that the millenarians promote a fable contrary to the Scriptures and embrace Jewish ravings with their teaching of a thousand-year reign.[75]

Despite these negative estimations of premillennialism, a few Reformed voices advocated this view in the late sixteenth and early seventeenth centuries. Three Reformed theologians, Johannes Piscator (1546–1625) of Strasbourg, Joseph Mede (1586–1638) in England, and Johannes Heinrich Alsted (1588–1638) in Herborn, were well-known advocates of premillennialism.[76] These theologians were able to influence a number of divines present at the Westminster Assembly, including Thomas Goodwin and the moderator William Twisse (1578–1646). In fact, Twisse wrote the preface to the English translation of Mede's *Key of the Revelation*.[77] Not only did Twisse find Mede's exegesis convincing, but some of the historical events unfolding around him led him to believe that the millennium would be soon upon them. In correspondence between Twisse and Mede, for example, Twisse opined that the English colonies in the Americas could likely be the location of the New Jerusalem:

> Now, I beseech you, let me know what your opinion is of our *English* Plantations in the New world. Heretofore I have wondered in my thoughts at the Providence of God concerning that world, not discovered till this world of ours is almost at an end; and then no footsteps found of the knowledge of the true God, much less of Christ. And then considering our English Plantations of late, and the opinion of many grave Divines concerning the Gospel's fleeting Westward; sometimes I have had such thoughts, Why may not that be the place of New Jerusalem?[78]

---

[75] Wilkinson, *Articles of the Church of England*, 99.

[76] Johannes Heinrich Alsted, *The Beloved City; or, The Saints Reign on Earth a Thousand Years; Asserted and Illustrated from LXV Places of Holy Scripture* (London, 1643); Johannes Piscator, *In Apocalypsin Johannis Commentarius* (Herborn: Christoph Corvini, 1613); Joseph Mede, *The Key of Revelation, Searched and Demonstrated out of the Naturall and Proper Charecters of the Visions* (London: Phil Stephens, 1643).

[77] Mede, *Key of the Revelation*, fols. A3r–B4v.

[78] William Twisse to Joseph Mede, "Epistle XLII, 2 March 1634," in *The Works of the Pious and Profoundly-Learned Joseph Mede* (London: Richard Royston, 1672), 799; Jeffrey K. Jue, *Heaven upon Earth: Joseph Mede (1586–1638) and the Legacy of Millenarianism* (Dordrecht: Springer, 2006), 184.

Mede was not convinced of Twisse's speculations, but this nonetheless helps provide the context of what some of the Westminster divines believed about such matters.[79]

Mede exercised a degree of influence over Goodwin, whom he tutored at Cambridge.[80] In his exposition of Ephesians, Goodwin explains that Christ himself will not reign on earth for one thousand years, but that heaven itself will descend and thereby extend the reign of Christ upon earth. Goodwin writes:

> He hath appointed a special world on purpose for him, between this world and the end of the day of judgment,—and the day of judgment itself is part of it, if not the whole of it,—wherein our Lord and Savior Jesus Christ shall reign; which the Scripture eminently calleth the "world to come;" Christ's world, as I may so call it: that as this present world was ordained for the first Adam, and God hath given it unto the sons of men, so there is a world to come appointed for the second Adam, as the time after the day of judgment is God the Father's in a more eminent manner, who then shall be all in all.[81]

Goodwin speaks of this reign of Christ occurring "between this world and the end of the day of judgment," that is, in the middle of history, not at its end.

Despite the growing popularity of premillennialism (or chiliasm), there was a strong backlash against the position. Mede stayed in contact with many of his former Cambridge colleagues, among whom was William Ames. In correspondence with Mede, Ames intimated that the former's work on the book of Revelation was not getting a positive reception in the Netherlands. One Dutch scholar, Daniel van Laren, believed that Mede had fallen into the errors of the Jews with an overly literalistic reading of the Apocalypse.[82] Other opponents to Mede's view included Lodewijk de Dieu and Ames, both of whom were not convinced of Mede's exegesis of Revelation 20:4 and the contention

---

[79] Jue, *Heaven upon Earth*, 184.

[80] Ibid., 177–78.

[81] Thomas Goodwin, *An Exposition of the Epistle to the Ephesians*, serm. 33, in *The Works of Thomas Goodwin*, 12 vols. (1861–1866; Eureka: Tanski, 1996), 1:506; Jue, *Heaven upon Earth*, 178.

[82] William Ames to Joseph Mede, "Epistle XXVII, 11 October," in *Works*, 782; Jue, *Heaven upon Earth*, 215; cf. Daniel Van Laren (pseudo. Theocritus Justus), *In Apocalypsin Beati Johannis Theologi* (1627).

that the first resurrection from the dead is physical.[83] Other opponents
included Johannes Maccovius (1588–1644), who believed that

> the general resurrection will take place at the same time, so that
> we might tightly hold this against those who state that a thousand
> years before the general resurrection the martyrs will be raised
> and reign with Christ on earth. For the Holy Spirit shows us only
> two visible comings of Christ: one in the flesh when He became
> man, and another in the flesh, when He shall come to judge the
> quick and the dead: He immediately connects the resurrection of
> the dead with this coming, Mt. 24.30–31.[84]

Other Reformed Continental opponents of premillennialism included
Antonius Walaeus (1573–1639), Gisbert Voetius (1589–1676), and
Moïse Amyraut (1596–1664).[85]

Opposition to premillennialism also appeared within the assembly
itself. The most notable dissatisfaction and opposition among the assembly arose from one of the Scottish advisors, Robert Baillie (1602–
1662). Baillie wrote in a letter that he had been enjoying reading a
recent publication by John Forbes (1593–1648), a theology professor
at the University of Aberdeen, but that he could not find anything
in its index against "the Millenaries." Baillie was surprised because
Forbes's work covered doctrinal errors and controversies from the
time of the apostles down to the seventeenth century, and he found
nothing in it against premillennialism.[86] Baillie lamented, "I cannot
dream why he should have omitted ane errour so famous in antiquitie,
and so troublesome among us." Baillie noted that a number of independents, including Goodwin and Jeremiah Burroughs, and others

[83] Jue, *Heaven upon Earth*, 217–28; William Ames to Joseph Mede, "Epistle XXVIII, 27 May" in *Works*, 782–83.
[84] Johannes Maccovius, *Scholastic Discourse: Johannes Maccovius (1588–1644) on Theological and Philosophical Distinctions and Rules*, trans. Willem J. van Asselt et al. (Apeldoorn: Instituut voor Reformatieonderzoek, 2009), 19.6 (p. 273).
[85] Antonius Walaeus, *De Chiliastarum Opinione*, in *Opera Omnia*, 2 vols. (Lugduni Batavorum: Ex Officina F. Hackii, 1643), 1:537–58; Gisbert Voetius, *De Regno Millenario*, in *Selectarum Disputationum Theologicarum*, pt. 2 (Utrecht: Johannem à Waesberge, 1654), 1249–66; Moïse Amyraut, *Du regne de mille anes ov de la prosperite de l'eglise* (Saumur: Isaac Desbordes, 1654); Jue, *Heaven upon Earth*, 228–33.
[86] Robert Baillie, "Letter to Mr. Spang, 4 Sept 1645," in *The Letters and Journals of Robert Baillie*, vol. 2 (Edinburgh: Robert Ogle, 1841), 313; cf. John Forbes, *Instructiones Historico-Theologiae: De Doctrina Christiana & vario Rerum Statu, Ortisque Erroribus & Controversiis, Jam Inde a Temporibus Apostlicis, ad Tempora Usque Seculi Decimi-Septimi Priora* (Amsterdam: Ludovicum Elzevirium, 1645).

such as Twisse, Stephen Marshall (ca. 1594–1655), Herbert Palmer (1601–1647), "and many more, are express Chiliasts."[87]

Baillie was convinced that premillennialism was problematic, and he even labeled it heresy. He wrote a work on the errors of the Independents (i.e., Congregationalists) and in the final chapter argued that the literal thousand-year reign of Christ on earth is contrary to Scripture.[88] Baillie begins the chapter by calling premillennialism "sparckles of new light" that originated with the "Hereticke *Cerinthus*" (ca. AD 100), whom Irenaeus (130–202) opposed in his *Against Heresies*.[89] Premillennialism was advocated by some of the Greek and Latin fathers, but "it was quickly declared, both by the Greek and Latine Church, to be a great error, if not an heresie." From the time of Augustine (354–430), claims Baillie, no one embraced the teaching until the Anabaptists exhumed it from the grave. After that, Alsted and Piscator promoted the doctrine, as did Mede at Cambridge. Baillie also mentions John Archer (fl. 1640s) and Robert Maton (1607–1653) as contemporary advocates.[90]

Among other arguments, Baillie enumerates nine reasons why premillennialism is an error:

1. From the point of Christ's ascension until the final judgment, he abides in heaven. Orthodox divines hold that Christ has two advents (his incarnation and the consummation), not three (including also a millennial reign).
2. Christ sits at the right hand of the Father until the final judgment.
3. The resurrection at the consummation includes both the wicked and the righteous and occurs on the last day, not before.
4. Christ's kingdom is spiritual, not earthly, and the Scriptures do not know of another type of kingdom.

---

[87] Baillie, "Letter to Mr. Spang," 313.

[88] Robert Baillie, *A Dissuasive from the Errours of the Time: Wherein the Tenets of the Principall Sects, Especially of the Independents, Are Drawn Together in One Map* (London: Samuel Gellibrand, 1645), 11 (pp. 224–52).

[89] Cf. Irenaeus, *Against Heresies*, 1.26.1–2, in *ANF* 1:351–52.

[90] Baillie, *Errours of the Time*, 224; cf. Robert Maton, *Christs Personall Reigne on Earth, One Thousand Yeares with His Saints the Manner, Beginning, and Continuation of His Reigne Cearly Proved* (London: John Hancock, 1652); John Archer, *The Personal Reign of Christ upon Earth in a Treatise Wherein Is Fully and Largely Laid Open and Proved That Jesus Christ, Together with the Saints, Shall Visibly Possess a Monarchiacal State and Kingdom in This World* (London: Benjamin Allen, 1642).

5. As long as the church is upon the earth, it is a mixed body, consisting of elect and reprobate, good and bad, as a corporate company under the cross and subject to various temptations—one that always requires Word and sacrament, prayer and ordinances. Hence, the idea that the earthly church would have glorified saints ruling over the rest of the world in a temporal kingdom is incorrect.
6. Christ's return is not supposed to be predictable, but if his millennial reign begins in 1650 or 1695, as some have alleged, then this would tell us that the return of Christ would occur in 2651 or 2696.
7. The reward of the martyrs is eternal life in the heavens, not a temporal reign upon the earth for one thousand years.
8. An earthly kingdom of Christ requires the restoration of Jerusalem and the Jewish kingdom after its destruction by the Romans, but Scripture denies this according to Ezekiel 16:53, 55.
9. Antichrist is supposed to be destroyed before the millennial reign according to chiliasts, but Scripture is clear that antichrist will continue until the day of judgment.[91]

Baillie also discerns other exegetical problems with premillennialism. Concerning Revelation 20:4 and the first resurrection, he argues that premillennialists take this passage literally and fail to understand that "most of this Booke," the book of Revelation, "is Mysticall and Allegorical." He also, in line with Reformation heremeneutical principles, contends that Revelation 20:4 is a difficult and obscure passage of Scripture, and that there are other places in the Bible that speak of the resurrection more clearly and with less obscure and nonmystical terms.[92] As the Confession states: "The infallible Rule of Interpretation of Scripture is the Scripture it selfe: and therefore, when there is a Question about the true and full sense of any Scripture . . . it must be searched and known by other places that speak more clearly" (1.9). Baillie also believes that premillennialism weakens the nature of Christ's reign because it limits it to one thousand years. But when we speak of the reign of Christ, we must

[91] Baillie, *Errours of the Time*, 225–33.
[92] Ibid., 234.

do so according to the nature of his person, which is eternal; hence his reign must be much longer than one thousand years.[93] While today's readers might think that Baillie's opinions were extreme, his views were quite common; a number of Reformed theologians of the period, to lesser and greater degrees, identified chiliasm as error, or even heresy.[94]

But the million-dollar question is, how do the Standards handle this subject? Compared with some of the speculations about the timing of the end of the world, the Confession is marked by a discernable sobriety—there is no attempt to discuss, hint, or allude to any possible date for the end of the world. Nor does the Confession address the nature of the millennium. It simply discusses what happens to a person upon his death and the general resurrection from the dead (32.1–3). In the following chapter the Confession discusses the general events surrounding the day of judgment and then remarks:

> As Christ would have us to be certainly perswaded, That there shall be a Day of Judgment both to deter all men from sin, and for the greater consolation of the Godly in their Adversity: so, will he have that Day unknown to men, that they may shake off all carnal Security, and be always watchful, because they know not at what hour the Lord will come; and, may be ever prepared to say, Come Lord Jesus, come quickly, Amen. (33.3)

At first glance one might be led to the conclusion that the divines left all issues of the timing and nature of the millennial reign off to the margins, but upon closer examination important details in the Larger Catechism should be considered.

In their often discreet manner, the divines quietly reject premillennialism in the Larger Catechism. The catechism explains that at the

---

[93] Ibid., 237.

[94] William Whitaker, *An Answere to the Ten Reasons of Edmund Campian* (London: Felix Kyngston, 1606), 126; John Rainolds, *The Summe of the Conference between John Rainoldes and John Hart: Touching the Head and the Faith of the Church* (London: George Bishop, 1598), 8.2 (p. 406); Cartwright, *A Confutation of the Rhemists Translation*, comm. Rev. 20:6 (p. 756); Thomas Edwards, *The First and Second Part of Gangraena; or, A Catalogue and Discovery of Many of the Errors, Heresies, Blasphemies and Pernicious Practices of the Sectaries of This Time* (London: Ralph Smith, 1646), 15; Roberts, *Mysterium et Medulla Bibliorum*, 4.1, aphor. 1 (pp. 1242–43); Richard Baxter, *The Life of Faith* (London: R. W., 1670), 28 (pp. 594–607); Giovanni Diodati, *Pious and Learned Annotations upon the Holy Bible* (London: Nicolas Fussell, 1651), comm. Rev. 20:3.

last day there will be a general resurrection of the dead, both the just and the unjust (q. 87). In the following question they ask (q. 88):

Q. What shall immediately follow after the resurrection?

A. Immediately after the resurrection shall follow the generall and finall judgement of Angels and men, the day and hour whereof no man knoweth, that all may watch and pray, and be ever ready for the coming of the Lord.

The Catechism speaks of only *one* resurrection, and then the final judgment follows that event *immediately*; there is no room for a millennial reign between the resurrection and final judgment. So the Standards reject premillennialism but do so silently; the view is not mentioned by name, nor do any statements indicate that other views are erroneous or heretical. In other words, the Standards neither embrace nor condemn the view, which stands in marked contrast to the stronger and explicit rejections in the Augsburg Confession, the Forty-Two Articles, and the Second Helvetic Confession. So whatever invective some members of the assembly might have had for premillennialism, the rest of the divines were more circumspect in their treatment of it.

Conclusion

We find very circumspect and prudent treatments of matters pertaining to eschatology in the Westminster Standards. The divines reject soul sleep, purgatory, and premillennialism. Given their historical context, it seems only natural that they would identify the pope as the antichrist, however out of place such judgments may seem to modern readers. And despite the belief among a number of the divines that theirs was the terminal generation, all such speculations were left out of the Standards. What is interesting, however, is that, despite the belief in the imminent return of Christ, the divines thought one of the most urgent things they could do was write a confession of faith.

This historical-theological context sheds new light upon the confessional-writing activity of the divines. Were contemporary Christians to believe that the world would end in the next ten to twenty years, what activities might they carry out? Would they retreat from the rest of the world, build a fortress, and stockpile weapons, food, and supplies, or would they naturally and without question engage in the reformation of the church? Would they write a confession of faith and two catechisms? This is precisely what the Westminster divines did, which demonstrates how important they believed orthodox theology and practice to be in the life of the church and its corporate and individual eschatology.

Appendix: Twofold Justification and the Reformed Tradition

Some, such as G. K. Beale, have recently claimed that "it is not uncommon in the Reformed tradition to speak of what has been called variously a 'twofold justification,' or a past justification by faith and a subsequent justification by works, or a 'first justification' and a 'second justification.'"[95] Beale cites Heinrich Heppe's *Reformed Dogmatics* and Turretin as examples.

However, these citations are misleading and, in the case of Turretin, erroneous. Heppe cites Johannes Heidegger and Franz Burman,[96] and though Burman does speak of a first and second justification, Heidegger seems to be addressing the question of how to harmonize James and Paul. In the section prior to the passage cited by Heppe (and Beale), Heidegger states that justification is perfect and indivisible, which mitigates Beale's appeal to Heidegger.[97] Then, concerning the so-called "second justification," Heidegger states specifically that one may ascend from the effect to the cause. The justification of the sinner is first, and the justification of the righteous is the effect, sign, or manifestation of the first. In other words, the second is the evidence that the first is present and valid.[98]

This second justification is highly qualified. The imprecision of Beale's citation of Turretin is especially evident in that he states:

> Turretin sees multiple temporal phases of justification: (1) the justified state of the believer at the inception of faith; (2) the pardon

---

[95] G. K. Beale, *A New Testament Biblical Theology: The Unfolding of the Old Testament in the New* (Grand Rapids: Baker, 2011), 506.
[96] Heinrich Heppe, *Reformed Dogmatics*, trans. G. T. Thomson, ed. Ernst Bizer (London: George Allen & Unwin, 1950), 562–63; Beale, *Biblical Theology*, 506n91.
[97] Johannes Heidegger, *Corpus Theologiae Christianae*, vol. 2 (Tiguri, 1732), 22.79 (p. 303).
[98] Ibid., 22.80 (p. 303).

of particular sins during the course of the saint's life, based on the prior and ongoing justified condition; (3) the declaration of this justification made immediately after death; and (4) publicly later on the last day—"an adjudication of the reward, in accordance with the preceding justification."[99]

The problem with this quotation is that Beale fails to quote the words immediately preceding the public "justification" on the last day. Turretin states that justification is made "publicly on the last day (*which is not so much justification, as a solemn declaration of the justification once made*, and an adjudication of the reward, in accordance with the preceding justification."[100]

Thus there is reason to question whether Beale has accurately summarized what Turretin has stated concerning these phases, especially when Beale claims precedence for a twofold justification, a first and a second, in the Reformed tradition; Turretin specifically steers clear from this conclusion. Beale fails to quote Turretin's key rejection, isolating instead the phrase "an adjudication of the reward, in accordance with the preceding justification." In fact, in several places in the broader context Turretin states that the "*declaration* of justification is falsely confounded with justification itself," and "the final judgment is nothing else than a public and solemn manifestation of preceding judgments."[101] Or again, justification

is finished in one judicial act and brings to the believer the remission of all sins. Hence the Romanists (from their fictitious hypothesis concerning physical justification by an infusion of righteousness) falsely make it twofold: the first, that by which a man from being unjust is made just by an infusion of righteousness; the second, that which from being just he is made more just by the increase of righteousness.[102]

Turretin goes to great lengths to reject a twofold justification and to affirm that whatever works are brought forth at the final judgment are "sign and proof"; and "still falsely would anyone maintain from

---

[99] Beale, *Biblical Theology*, 506n91.
[100] Turretin, *Institutes*, 16.9.11, emphasis added.
[101] Ibid., 16.9.7, emphasis added.
[102] Ibid., 16.10.5.

this a twofold gospel justification—one from faith in this life (which is the first); the other (and second) from works on the day of judgment (as some hold, agreeing too much with Romanists on this point)."[103] This is the point that Heidegger, Turretin's colleague, makes above. Hence, *pace* Beale, it is uncommon to talk of a twofold justification in early modern Reformed theology.[104]

---

[103] Ibid., 16.10.8.
[104] Cf. Beeke and Jones, *Puritan Theology*, 796–99, 801–2.

13

Conclusion

Historical context is all-determinative for understanding the theology contained in the Westminster Standards. As helpful and necessary as popular commentaries on the Standards are, a contextually sensitive reading of the documents must first be established. What political and theological concerns did the divines have, and how do these concerns appear in the Confession and catechisms? Who were the dialogue partners of the divines, whether positively or negatively?

I once had a ministerial colleague tell me that he had no use whatsoever for anything written by a Roman Catholic: "I only read Reformed authors." This same colleague also loved to read so-called Puritan authors and professed to love the Westminster Standards. The more I have investigated the Confession and catechisms, the more I am struck that yesterday's Reformed minister is theologically worlds apart from today's Reformed minister. The divines would have likely branded my colleague a sectarian, given his overly narrow views on the importance of broad reading. The Westminster divines were not only profoundly learned men, but also Reformed Catholics. They culled insights from a broad spectrum of sources, including Patristic, medieval, Roman Catholic, Remonstrant, Rabbinic, philosophical, and Reformed authors. Divines such as William Twisse, the assembly's first moderator, were quite knowledgeable of the writings of Aquinas, Duns Scotus, and a host of other medieval theologians.

396   The Theology of the Westminster Standards

This broad cornucopia of knowledge, evident in the multiplicity of sources cited from seventeenth-century Reformed works, also demonstrates, and hopefully destroys, the facile characterization that the Westminster divines were *Calvinists*, either somehow indebted to Calvin for certain ideas apart from specific primary-source citations, or working from Calvinistic premises from which they sometimes departed. In past years the attempt to establish a broad Reformed cross-section of sample views on a particular doctrine has been hampered by the unavailability of primary sources. Most people reached for what they had on hand—Calvin's *Institutes*. But now with the wide-open access through scanned books readily available on the Internet, students of the Westminster Standards are no longer limited to the books to which they have physical access. Using a word like *unprecedented* risks exaggeration, but with unprecedented resources like the PRDL, we can now easily investigate the theology of the Westminster Standards from an abundance of primary sources.

Such primary-source-anchored research will undoubtedly be filled with rich insights and confirm many people's long-cherished beliefs about the Reformed faith. By reading the works of the men associated with the Standards or of those who actually participated in their composition, we theological Hobbits, like Zacchaeus in his sycamore tree, can stand on the shoulders of giants in order to catch a glimpse of the glory of God. At the same time, we will undoubtedly be challenged. While many profess the theology of the Westminster Standards, there are often subtle but substantive differences between seventeenth- and twenty-first-century Reformed doctrine for which we must account. The Standards affirm things like natural law, divine sovereignty, contingency, the covenant of works, the imputation of the satisfaction and obedience of Christ, free will, *sola fide*, infused grace in sanctification, the law as a covenant versus a rule, Christian liberty, the regulative principle of worship, the doctrine of the two kingdoms, sacraments as signs and seals of the covenant of grace, and many other teachings. These doctrines are often missed, misunderstood, or misstated, even within the Reformed community. There is much to learn from the great theological minds that wrote the Westminster Standards.

Once we have competently grasped the theological content of the Standards, we are better equipped to understand the Scriptures and enter into theological dialogue with our forebearers. Hopefully this book on the theology of the Westminster Standards represents one small step in this general direction. *SDG*.

Select Annotated Bibliography

In an effort to encourage others to study the history and theology of the Westminster Standards, I offer the following select annotated bibliography divided according to essential primary and secondary sources. With historic primary sources I indicate whether a work is available in a reprint edition or through the Post-Reformation Digital Library (www.prdl.org), Early English Books Online (EEBO), or Google Books. What might no longer be in print and therefore costly to obtain as such is often now available free of charge through the Internet. What used to cost thousands of dollars, either in travel to libraries scattered throughout Europe or in purchases from antiquarian book dealers, is now relatively inexpensive as you can download PDFs and read them on your computer or tablet. Never before has researching the theology of the Westminster Standards been so accessible. Many primary sources are now a few mouse clicks away.

There are undoubtedly many other books that could be listed. In fact, entire books are devoted to the bibliography of the Westminster Assembly. The following are books that I have found useful and recommend to those who want to know more. For those who want more, as I tell my students, "bird-dog the footnotes," both in this book and in those listed below.

Primary Sources

Ames, William. *A Fresh Suit against Human Ceremonies in God's Worship*. London: n.p., 1633.

This is one of the key Reformed works on the regulative principle of worship. It is exhaustive and cited by Reformed works of the period. This edition is available through the PRDL.

———. *The Marrow of Theology*. Translated by John Dykstra Eusden. 1968; Grand Rapids: Baker, 1997.

William Ames was one of the seventeenth century's most respected theologians. He was the assistant to the moderator of the Synod of Dort (1618–1619) and participated in the synod's activities, as well as in behind-the-scenes negotiations. The *Marrow* is an excellent example of a complete handbook on doctrine divided into doctrine and practice, or ethics. Latin and English seventeenth-century editions of the *Marrow* are available through the PRDL.

Arminius, Jacob. *The Works of James Arminius*. Edited and translated by James Nichols and William Nichols. 3 vols. 1828–1875; Grand Rapids: Baker, 1996.

Crucial to identifying a number of the Confession's rejections of doctrines is locating the persons who held the views. In this case, the works of Arminius are important for understanding the broader context of the theology of the Standards. The Confession, for example, has key rejections in its chapters on the decree and justification that address Arminius's formulations. Used editions of Arminius's works can be found, though seventeenth-century editions of his treatises and letters in various languages appear on the PRDL, in addition to this cited nineteenth-century edition.

Bolton, Samuel. *The True Bounds of Christian Freedome; or, A Treatise Wherein the Rights of the Law Are Vindicated, the Liberties of Grace Maintained*. London: Austin Rice, 1656.

Bolton's work is vital to a proper understanding of the law in the Standards not only because he was one of the Westminster divines, but also because his taxonomy of the different views on the Mosaic covenant helps contemporary readers witness from a primary source the diversity of views present in and about the assembly. Bolton's work has been popularized by its publication by Banner of Truth in a Puritan Paperback edition, but note that Bolton's appendix is not included in this popular reprint. Bolton was promoting John Cameron's threefold (subservient) view through the translation and publication of this appendix. For scholarly research, Bolton's original edition should be consulted and is available through the PRDL.

Bullinger, Heinrich. *The Decades of Henry Bullinger.* Edited by Thomas Harding. 4 vols. 1849–1852; Grand Rapids: Reformation Heritage, 2004.

Underappreciated in our own day, Bullinger was a giant in the sixteenth and seventeenth centuries. His *Decades* was one of the first comprehensive treatments of doctrine from one of the Reformation's first-generation Reformers. A series of fifty sermons, it was translated into many different languages and greatly esteemed in the British Isles and the European continent. The nineteenth-century Parker edition is available at the PRDL, as well as other original-language editions.

Burgess, Anthony. *The True Doctrine of Justification Asserted and Vindicated, from the Errours of Papists, Arminians, Socinians, and More Especially Antinomians.* London: Thomas Underhill, 1651.

This is an important exhibit of how one of the Westminster divines explains and defends the doctrine of justification. A number of seventeenth-century editions of this work are available through the PRDL.

———. *Vindiciae Legis; or, A Vindication of the Morall Law and the Covenants.* London: Thomas Underhill, 1647.

For any attempt to understand the Confession's treatment of the law, especially as it relates to the covenants of works and grace and the Mosaic covenant, Burgess's work is a standard representative treatment and also one of the more frequently cited during the latter seventeenth century. This edition is available at the PRDL.

Burroughs, Jeremiah. *Jerusalems Glory Breaking Forth into the World, Being a Scripture Discovery of the New Testament Church, in the Latter Days Immediately Before the Second Coming of Christ.* London: Giles Calvert, 1675.

This is a premillennial work by one of the assembly's Independent divines and one who believed that the end of the world was imminent. This work is available through EEBO.

Calvin, John. *Institutes of the Christian Religion*. Translated by John Allen. Grand Rapids: Eerdmans, 1949.

Calvin's work should be used carefully for the following reasons. First, Calvin's esteem and perceived influence has been exaggerated in the present day. While Calvin was certainly influential, the extent of citations and correspondence between Calvin and other Reformers shows that in his own day Calvin was one theologian among many others. Second, Richard Muller has documented that the common Battles translation of Calvin's *Institutes* has been edited in such a manner that Calvin's finer points and technical language are often obscured, and editorial insertion of proof texts have clouded Calvin's original presentation and arguments. Hence, older editions of the *Institutes* are preferred, though citations should be cross-checked against original Latin editions. In earlier years the critical edition of Calvin's works was the only way to access original editions, but now through the PRDL, one can investigate Calvin's *Institutes* in all of its editions. Older translations, such as the Beveridge edition, can be found on the Internet. Third, claims about Calvin's supposed influence over the rest of the tradition should be governed not by contemporary estimation of Calvin's theology but by historical primary-source evidence.

The Catechism of the Council of Trent: Ordered by the Council of Trent. Edited by St. Charles Borromeo. 1566; Rockford: Tan, 1982.

Any engagement with sixteenth-century Roman Catholicism should reference primary sources, such as Trent's catechism. A Google search should turn up a number of free electronic versions of this catechism. This work should be read in tandem with the Dogmatic Decrees of the Council of Trent, available in Schaff's *Creeds of Christendom* or Pelikan and Hotchkiss's *Creeds and Confessions of Faith in the Christian Tradition*.

Coldwell, Chris, ed. *Sermons Preached before the English Houses of Parliament by the Scottish Commissioners to the Westminster Assembly of Divines 1643–45*. Dallas: Naphtali, 2011.

This is a tremendously helpful primary source in that it is a handsomely bound edition of sermons preached by the Scottish advisors to the Westminster Assembly. It therefore not only showcases preaching from the period but also enables readers to see what theological concerns the Scottish divines had, especially as they preached these sermons to Parliament.

Davenant, John. *A Dissertation on the Death of Christ*. In *An Exposition of the Epistle of St. Paul to the Colossians*. Translated by Josiah Allport. Vol. 1. London: Hamilton, Adams, and Company, 1831.

Written by one of the English delegates to the Synod of Dort, Davenant's work is important as an example of an orthodox hypothetical universalism. Davenant's explanation demonstrates one way the sufficiency of Christ's satisfaction was explained, and it was embraced by a number of the Westminster divines. This nineteenth-century edition is available through the PRDL.

Dickson, David. *Truths Victory over Error*. Edinburgh: John Reed, 1684.

This is one of the earliest commentaries on the Confession and is available in a nice reprint edition through Banner of Truth. An eighteenth-century edition is available on PRDL.

Erastus, Thomas. *The Theses of Erastus Touching Excommunication*. Edinburgh: Myles MacPhail, 1844.

The Erastians at the assembly provoked some of the more heated debates over the responsibilities of the civil magistrate vis-à-vis excommunication. Therefore, a firsthand knowledge of Erastus's views is necessary to understand precisely what some members of the assembly were promoting. This edition is available through the PRDL.

Featley, Daniel. *The Dippers Dipt; or, The Anabaptists Duck'd and Plung'd over Head and Ears, at a Disputation in Southwark*. London: Richard Reyston, 1647.

Featley was one of the vociferous advocates for the IAOC during the assembly's debates, and a number of his speeches in favor of the IAOC are included in this work. Hence, for both sides of the debate, one should read Featley along with Gataker's *An Antidote against Errour*. Featley's work is available through the PRDL.

Fisher, Edward. *The Marrow of Modern Divinity: Touching Both the Covenant of Works, and the Covenant of Grace*. London: G. Calvert, 1645.

Fisher's work is one of the more important of the seventeenth century, as Fisher avoided both antinomianism and neonomianism. The work was commended by one of the Westminster divines and published in the midst of the assembly's labors. One should note that nineteenth-century editions and reprints of Fisher's work with Thomas Boston's explanatory notes are significantly different from the original edition. Boston's version should be characterized as his own work and not Fisher's. Sometimes Boston adds additional words, phrases, and sentences not found in the original to elaborate Fisher's meaning. Hence, Fisher's original work, not later editions, should be used for scholarly research. There are various nineteenth-century editions of Fisher's volume available through the PRDL.

Gataker, Thomas. *An Antidote against Errour, concerning Justification.* London: Henry Brome, 1679.

Gataker's work is important because he was one of the divines who argued against the IAOC. This volume is available through EEBO, a service to which many schools of theology and seminaries subscribe.

Gillespie, George. *Aaron's Rod Blossoming; or, The Divine Ordinance of Church Government Vindicated.* 1646; Edinburgh: Robert Ogle, and Oliver & Boyd, 1844.

This book, along with Rutherford's *Divine Right of Church-Government*, is the counterargument to views presented in Erastus's *Theses on Excommunication*. Gillespie's book presents his case for the doctrine of the two kingdoms. This reprint edition, as well as the seventeenth-century original in two editions, is available through the PRDL.

———. *A Dispute against the English Popish Ceremonies.* Edited by Chris Coldwell. Dallas: Naphtali, 2013.

This critical edition of Gillespie's work on worship should be read and owned by anyone who wants a primary-source treatment of the regulative principle of worship by one of the Scottish divines at the Westminster Assembly. Various editions of this work are available through the PRDL.

Goodwin, Thomas. *The Works of Thomas Goodwin*. 12 vols. Eureka: Tanski, 1996.

Goodwin was one of the Independent divines and the assembly's regular contributors to debate. His twelve-volume collected works provide readers with a broad cross-section of labors, from sermons, to exegesis, to theology, such as his work on christology or on the doctrine of justification. If you scour the Internet, you can find these books for free, or you can purchase them in reprint editions, either new or used.

An Harmony of the Confessions of the Faith of the Christian and Reformed Churches, Which Purely Profess the Holy Doctrine of the Gospel, in All the Chief Kingdoms, Nations, and Provinces in Europe. Cambridge, 1586.

This is one of the more important sixteenth-century confessional documents for several reasons. First, it was intended to be the Reformed counterpart to the Lutheran Formula of Concord (1577). It was compiled under the supervision of Theodore Beza and was intended to show both the unity among the Reformed and the Reformed agreement with the Lutherans. Second, this harmony was cited by theologians such as Edward Leigh as evidence of the uniformity of opinion among the Reformed. While perhaps many Reformed in the present day are unaware of the document, it was commonly cited in the early modern period and was also adopted by numerous Reformed cities on the Continent. Reprint editions are available, and digital copies of both seventeenth- and nineteenth-century editions are available through the PRDL.

Leigh, Edward. *A Systeme or Body of Divinity: Consisting of Ten Books*. London: William Lee, 1654.

Leigh's work is perhaps one of the more important resources that one can obtain to understand the theology of the Westminster Standards. An exhaustive treatment of theology, it covers all of the major loci and is thoroughly annotated. This allows the reader to see not only what works Leigh regarded as crucial, but also the broad scope of who might be cited for a particular doctrine. Leigh's volume is also essential because, though he was not a formal member of the assembly, as a member of Parliament during the composition of the Standards, Leigh undoubtedly had contact and interaction with a number of the divines. This particular edition is available through PRDL.

Lightfoot, John. *The Journal of the Proceedings of the Assembly of Divines.* In *The Whole Works of the Rev. John Lightfoot.* Vol. 13. London: J. V. Dove, 1824.

Much that is left out of the assembly's minutes is captured in other works, such as Lightfoot's *Journal.* A free PDF of Lightfoot's work can be obtained through Google Books.

Mede, Joseph. *The Key of Revelation, Searched and Demonstrated out of the Naturall and Proper Charecters of the Visions.* London: Phil Stephens, 1643.

This was one of the key sources for premillennialism (or chiliasm) in seventeenth-century England. Mede's work contains a preface written by the first moderator of the assembly, William Twisse. This edition is available through the PRDL.

Mitchell, Alexander, and John Struthers, eds. *Minutes of the Sessions of the Westminster Assembly of Divines.* Edinburgh: William Blackwood and Sons, 1874.

For those not able to obtain the Oxford edition of the minutes, the nineteenth-century Mitchell and Struther's edition is an accessible alternative. It obviously leaves out a lot of material but still gives the reader a good sense of the nature of the debates, labors, and conduct of the assembly on a host of issues. There are various reprint editions available on the new- and used-book market, and it is also available on PRDL.

Piscator, Johannes. *A Learned and Profitable Treatise on Mans Justification: Two Bookes.* London: Thomas Creede for Robert Dexter, 1599.

Much controversy surrounds Piscator's denial of the IAOC, and therefore one should read firsthand what he has to say and how he makes his case exegetically and theologically. This book can be obtained through EEBO, to which many schools of theology and seminaries subscribe.

Rees, Thomas, ed. *The Racovian Catechism.* London: Longman, Hurst, Rees, Orme, and Brown, 1818.

In the seventeenth century one of the greatest perceived threats to the church was Socinianism, the theological movement founded largely by Faustus Socinus. His beliefs were codified in the *Racovian Catechism*. Hence, in order to study seventeenth-century heresy, one should consult this work. This nineteenth-century edition is available through the PRDL.

Rutherford, Samuel. *The Covenant of Life Opened; or, A Treatise on the Covenant of Grace*. Edinburgh: Robert Brown, 1654.

Rutherford was highly respected in his own day for his acumen, skill, and learning, and his treatment of the covenant of grace is a window into the soteriology of the Westminster Standards. Additionally, he defends and expounds the covenant of redemption in this work. The 1655 edition is available through the PRDL.

———. *The Divine Right of Church-Government and Excommunication*. London: Christopher Meredith, 1646.

Rutherford's work is one of the chief counterarguments to the Erastian claim that the civil magistrate was responsible for excommunication. One should begin by reading Erastus's *Theses on Excommunication* and then read Rutherford, along with Gillespie's *Aaron's Rod Blossoming*. This edition of Rutherford's work is available through the PRDL.

———. *A Survey of the Spiritual Antichrist*. London: Andrew Crooke, 1648.

This is an in-depth examination of the origins and spread of antinomianism in seventeenth-century England and Scotland. Unlike some Reformed theologians today who characterize Martin Luther's theology as antinomian, Rutherford spends nearly a hundred pages defending Luther's orthodoxy. Rutherford's work is essential reading for anyone who wants to understand how one of the Westminster divines refuted antinomianism. This edition is available through the PRDL.

Ussher, James. *A Body of Divinitie, or The Summe and Substance of Christian Religion*. London: Thomas Downes and George Badger, 1645.

Ussher's work should be consulted for a number of reasons. First, though Ussher denied that he was the author of this work, it offers the investigator a complete system of theology published in the midst of the assembly's confession-writing activity and is thus reflective of Reformed theology of the period. Second, Ussher reportedly edited the work by gathering statements from other documents and works for his own personal use. Hence, it is valuable because it is broadly informed. Third, Ussher was initially nominated to serve at the assembly but declined, given his loyalty to the king. However, his nomination is indicative of the respect he earned from his peers. Ussher's influence, however, was present through the use of the Irish Articles (1615), a confession that he played a key role in composing, as a source document for the Confession. Ussher's work can be purchased in a reprint edition, and original editions are digitally available at the PRDL.

Van Dixhoorn, Chad, ed. *The Minutes and Papers of the Westminster Assembly 1643–62*. 5 vols. Oxford: Oxford University Press.

Any serious scholarly study of the Standards must consult the minutes and papers of the assembly. Van Dixhoorn's work is massive and exhaustive, fully annotated, and indexed. But as usual with most Oxford titles, this five-volume set is not cheap, listing right around $1,000.

Watson, Thomas. *A Body of Practical Divinity*. London: Thomas Parkhurst, 1692.

An early commentary on the Shorter Catechism, this particular volume is interesting and helpful not only in how it explains the catechism, but also as an example of early modern Reformed preaching. Banner of Truth has a nice reprint edition of this work, and there are a number of editions available on the PRDL.

Whitaker, William. *A Disputation on Holy Scripture against the Papists Especially Bellarmine and Stapleton*. Translated by William Fitzgerald. 1849; Orlando, FL: Soli Deo Gloria, 2005.

Whitaker's disputations on Scripture were among the sixteenth century's standard works on the doctrine. Reformed theologians regularly cited it as the authoritative treatment of the subject in the seventeenth century. Digital copies of the nineteenth-century edition are available at the PRDL.

Secondary Sources

Ball, Bryan W. *A Great Expectation: Eschatological Thought in English Protestantism to 1660*. Leiden: Brill, 1975.

Ball offers a useful survey of the various eschatological views during early modernity.

Barker, William. *Puritan Profiles: 54 Contemporaries of the Westminster Assembly*. 1996; Fearn: Christian Focus, 1999.

This is a contemporary version of James Reid's much larger *Memoirs of the Westminster Divines*. Barker's work is very readable and helpful, not only in the profiles he gives for significant Westminster divines, but also for a number of key theological figures who lived around the time of the assembly.

Benedict, Philip. *Christ's Churches Purely Reformed: A Social History of Calvinism*. New Haven, CT: Yale University Press, 2002.

A fascinating in-depth exploration of the sixteenth-century Reformation, this book offers a thorough treatment of many different facets of the event, such as theology, politics, and life in early modern Europe. It also documents how widespread the Reformation was and does not fall into the "John Calvin did it all" mythological narrative. This is a must-read for any serious student of the Reformation.

Como, David R. *Blown by the Spirit: Puritanism and the Emergence of an Antinomian Underground in Pre-Civil-War England*. Stanford: Stanford University Press, 2004.

Very few commentators take note of the historical context of the assembly—in particular, the threat of antinomianism. Hence, a thorough knowledge of the different doctrines, groups, and beliefs that swirled about the creation of the Standards is vital. Como's work is excellent, as it amply documents the different strands of antinomianism that were extant in seventeenth-century England right before the outbreak of the civil war.

Ford, Alan. *James Ussher: Theology, History, and Politics in Early-Modern Ireland and England*. Oxford: Oxford University Press, 2007.

Though Ussher was never a divine, he was nominated to serve. His influence was considerable, however, not only through the Irish Articles (1615), a source document for a number of passages in the Confession, but also through his *Body of Divinitie*, which was published in 1645. Ford's intellectual biography, therefore, is quite helpful in providing a frame of reference for one of the assembly's "ghost" members, if you will.

Fraser, Antonia. *Faith and Treason: The Story of the Gunpowder Plot*. New York: Anchor, 1996.

This is an engaging, well-researched, and well-written book about the notorious Gunpowder Plot, in which Roman Catholics sought to blow up Parliament—and the king—in its opening session so that a pro–Roman Catholic monarch could be installed upon England's throne. Understanding an event such as this helps the reader grasp the ethos, beliefs, and passions of the day and gives greater historical texture to the Westminster Standards.

Gatiss, Lee. "A Deceptive Clarity? Particular Redemption in the Westminster Standards," *Reformed Theological Review* 69, no. 3 (2010): 180–96.

———. "'Shades of Opinion within a Generic Calvinism': The Particular Redemption Debate at the Westminster Assembly," *Reformed Theological Review* 69, no. 2 (2010): 101–18.

These two essays are helpful analyses, based upon the minutes of the assembly, that outline and explore the debates regarding the extent of Christ's satisfaction.

Heppe, Heinrich. *Reformed Dogmatics: Set Out and Illustrated from the Sources*. Translated by G. T. Thomson. Edited by Ernst Bizer. London: George Allen and Unwin, 1950.

With many of early modernity's best Reformed theological works written in Latin, few readers have the ability to delve into this vast wealth of theological knowledge. Filled with primary-source quotations from early modern Reformed theologians, this work is therefore quite useful in surveying the larger body of early modern Reformed theology. On this count, a benefit of Heppe's work is that one can place Calvin in context; his name and quotes appear along with many others from the tradition. But there are two important caveats when one uses this work. First, Heppe has sometimes reorganized subjects and placed quotes in ways that change the significance of a theologian's intended meaning. Second, while the numerous quotations are illustrative and helpful, if they are pressed to make a certain point, they should be verified and checked within the broader context of the original source.

Jue, Jeffrey K. *Heaven upon Earth: Joseph Mede (1586–1638) and the Legacy of Millenarianism.* Dordrecht: Springer, 2006.

This work treats the origin, development, and dissemination of Mede's premillennialism; it also investigates the premillennial connections to some of the Westminster divines, such as William Twisse.

Marsh, Christopher W. *The Family of Love in English Society, 1550–1630.* Cambridge: Cambridge University Press, 1994.

Familism is one of the more frequently mentioned antinomian sects in seventeenth-century Reformed theological works. Samuel Rutherford discusses Familism at some length in his *Survey of the Spiritual Antichrist.* Marsh's work is one of the few in-depth analyses of this sect and should therefore be read.

Marshall, Peter. *Reformation England 1480–1642.* London: Bloomsbury, 2003.

This is a helpful survey of early modern English history, covering the impact of the Reformation and its development on English soil.

Muller, Richard A. *Dictionary of Latin and Greek Theological Terms: Drawn Principally from Protestant Scholastic Theology.* Grand Rapids: Baker, 1986.

This is the best dictionary for understanding early modern theological works. As the subtitle indicates, the definitions are drawn from Protestant scholastic works, which means that many of the technical terms found in theological works, often mistranslated when rendered into English, appear in this book. My recommendation to students is that they not only consult this reference work, but also read it cover to cover.

———. *God, Creation, and Providence in the Thought of Jacob Arminius.* Grand Rapids: Baker, 1991.

Here is an important study, one of the few, on aspects of Arminius's doctrine. It is a tremendous resource, thoroughly researched and even-handed in its analysis. Unfortunately, this book is out of print, so if you can obtain a copy on the used-book market, do so.

————. *Post-Reformation Reformed Dogmatics: The Rise and Development of Reformed Orthodoxy, ca. 1520 to ca. 1725*. 4 vols. Grand Rapids: Baker, 2003.

For anyone interested in early modern Reformed theology, anything bearing Muller's name is required reading. That is especially the case with *Post-Reformation Reformed Dogmatics*. What makes Muller's works vital is that his research is thoroughly entrenched in the primary sources. Volume 1 treats prolegomena; volume 2, Scripture; volume 3, the doctrine of God; and volume 4, the doctrine of the Trinity.

Muller, Richard A., and Rowland S. Ward. *Scripture and Worship: Biblical Interpretation and the Directory for Worship*. Phillipsburg, NJ: P&R, 2007.

Muller wrote the first part of the book on Scripture, and Ward the second part on the Directory for Public Worship. Both portions are required reading for understanding the doctrines of Scripture and worship in the Westminster Standards.

Pearse, Meic. *The Age of Reason: From the Wars of Religion to the French Revolution 1570–1789*. The Baker History of the Church 5. Grand Rapids: Baker, 2006.

This helpful overview of the sixteenth through eighteenth centuries helps the reader situate the Westminster Assembly in the broader context of early modernity. It also highlights the complexities of politics and theology, as they were thoroughly intertwined in this period.

Reid, James. *Memoirs of the Westminster Divines*. 2 vols. 1811; Edinburgh: Banner of Truth, 1982.

This work is a compilation of brief profiles on most of the Westminster divines. It is helpful for historical research to be able to read biographical synopses as well as notable works or accomplishments by the divines. The original 1811 edition is available through Google Books.

Schaff, Philip. *The Creeds of Christendom*. 3 vols. 1930; Grand Rapids: Baker, 1991.

The Westminster Standards should be compared against other early modern Reformed symbols, and Schaff's *Creeds of Christendom* is a useful resource in this respect. Various editions can be found through Google.

Strange, Alan D. "The Imputation of the Active Obedience of Christ at the Westminster Assembly." In *Drawn into Controversie: Reformed Theological Diversity and Debates within Seventeenth-Century British Puritanism*, edited by Michael A. G. Haykin and Mark Jones, 31–51. Göttingen: Vandenhoeck & Ruprecht, 2011.

This is a helpful analysis of the debates over the IAOC. Strange makes a credible case, based upon the minutes of the assembly, that the divines intended to advocate the IAOC.

VanDrunen, David. *Natural Law and the Two Kingdoms: A Study in the Development of Reformed Social Thought*. Grand Rapids: Eerdmans, 2010.

The doctrines of natural law and the two kingdoms have long been thought to be alien to early modern Reformed theology. While VanDrunen's work covers the Patristic period to the present day, his treatment of the sixteenth and seventeenth centuries is necessary reading for understanding how these doctrines functioned in the Reformed tradition.

Warfield, B. B. *The Westminster Assembly and Its Work*. Vol. 6 of *The Works of Benjamin B. Warfield*. 1931; Grand Rapids: Baker, 1981.

The sixth volume in Warfield's collected works contains a series of essays that the lion of Princeton Seminary wrote on various aspects of the work and theology of the Westminster Assembly. It is quite helpful, is historically nuanced, and does not suffer from many of the foibles of more recent works, such as the idea that Calvin was the key theologian of the Reformed tradition. You can purchase this work in a reprint edition or in a ninety-nine-cent Kindle edition from Amazon. This book is a must-read for serious students of the Westminster Assembly.

Wedgwood, Cicely Veronica. *The Thirty Years War*. 1938; New York: New York Review Book, 2005.

This is a standard treatment of the Thirty Years War and one that gives the broader theological, political, and military context of the timewhen the divines were writing the Westminster Standards. This book helps the reader understand that Roman Catholicism was no idle threat in the minds of many, but a clear and present danger to the security of the nation and the souls of its citizens.

General Index

Abraham Ibn Ezra, 92
absolute necessity, 105–6
absolute-relative distinction, 101
acquittal, 377–78, 381–82
Act of Uniformity (1559), 336–38, 342
Adam, as federal representative, 141, 143
Adamic administration, 126
adiaphora, 343
Adolphus, Gustavus, 48
adoption, 234–37, 254
Agricola, Johannes, 241
alien righteousness, of Jesus Christ, 260
allegorical sense of Scripture, 85
Alsted, Johannes Heinrich, 308n30, 385, 388
ambiguity, in Westminster Standards, 28
Ambrose, on sufficient-efficient distinction, 193
American colonies, 385
Ames, William, 125, 328, 399–400
   on adoption, 235
   on contingency, 108
   on day of judgment, 382
   on decree, 102
   on justification, 232
   on musical instruments, 361
   on necessity, 106
   on premillennialism, 386
   on psalms, 358
   on sanctification, 257

   on Scripture, 69
   on worship, 339
Amyraldianism, 193, 195, 199–203
Amyraut, Moïse, 142n67, 190, 193, 197–98, 201, 203, 328, 387
Anabaptists, 55, 90, 129, 233, 301, 320, 324
   antinomianism of, 241, 243
   premillennialism of, 384
   on soul sleep, 369
anagogical sense of Scripture, 85
analogy of Scripture, 84, 86–87, 89, 93
Anglican Confession, 311
Annesley, Samuel
   on golden chain of salvation, 248
   on sanctification, 263
Annotations, of Westminster Assembly, 72, 117, 141, 142–43, 200n115, 252–53, 277, 333, 341, 359
Anselm, satisfaction theory of the atonement, 188
anthropomorphites, 55
antichrist, 363, 368, 389
   Islam as, 364, 365
   pope as, 36, 43, 63, 363–67, 391
   and Roman Catholicism, 37, 54,
antinomianism, 55, 63, 130, 209, 216, 229, 237, 258, 266, 301, 324
   perfectionism of, 265
   rise of, 240–45
antitrinitarianism, 87, 170, 171, 175
apocryphal books, 76
Apollonius, Willem, 307

apostasy, 364
Apostles' Creed, 84, 85, 173
Archer, John, 388
archetypal and ectypal theology,
81–83, 100, 138
Aretius, Benedict, 190
Arianism, 87, 172, 204
Aristotle, 58, 61, 259–60
Arminianism, 55, 87, 192–93, 209,
237, 244, 314
Arminius, Jacob, 400
on faith and justification, 218–22
on infra- and supralapsarianism,
116n63
on justification, 375–76
on predestination, 112–13, 114
rejection of *autotheos*, 182–83
on three uses of the law, 273
twofold covenant scheme, 135
Arrowsmith, John
eclectic use of sources, 123
on golden chain of salvation, 248
on preterition, 120
on satisfaction of Christ, 196
aseity of the Son, 180–82
assurance, 380
Athanasian Creed, 173
Atherton, John, 26
atonement, 27, 189
Attersol, William, 328
Augsburg Confession, 330n94,
332–33, 384, 391
Augustine, 58, 388
on authority of Scripture, 77
on covenant, 128
on fourfold state, 110
on justification and good works,
255
on law, 277
on natural law, 346
on necessity and contingency, 109
on preterition, 119
on sacraments, 315
on senses of Scripture, 85
on sufficient-efficient distinction,
193
on testimony of the church, 78

on visible and invisible church, 302
autotheos, 173–74, 181

Baillie, Robert, 26, 53, 197–98
on baptism, 324
on good and necessary consequence, 89
on Lord's Prayer, 353
on premillennialism, 387–90
Ball, Bryan W., 409
Ball, John, 66, 125, 152, 189
on covenant of works, 138–40
on Mosaic covenant, 152, 153
on two kingdoms, 303–4
baptism, 320–25
and justification, 317
mode of, 325
baptismal regeneration, 316–18, 321
Barclay, Robert, 246
Barker, William, 409
Barth, Karl, 24, 126
Basel, 36
Bastingius, Jeremias, 180, 273, 372
Baxter, Richard, 42n67, 202–3
on baptism, 323
hypothetical universalism of, 197
on infra- and supralapsarianism,
116n63, 117
on justification from eternity, 229
on twofold justification, 375
on union with Christ, 253
Baynes, Paul, 280
Beale, G. K., 392–94
Becmanus, Christian, 309
Belgic Confession, 68, 177, 299,
313n45
Bellarmine, Robert, 59, 76, 146, 186,
346, 361, 372
Benedict, Philip, 409
Bernard of Clairvaux, 255
Beza, Theodore, 58, 67, 96, 174, 322,
405
on blasphemy, 281–82
on church and state, 300
on fourth commandment, 293
on *ordo salutis*, 246–47
on two kingdoms, 309

extent of Christ's satisfaction, 170,
187–203, 204–5

faculty psychology, 260
faith, as instrument, 219, 223–24
Familists (Family of Love), 55, 242,
243
fatalism, 106
Fawkes, Guy, 44–45
Featley, Daniel, 173, 174, 176, 328,
403
on baptism, 323
on justification, 213–16, 225
federal theology, 125
as architectonic principle of Westminster Confession, 167
as legalistic, 249
Fenner, Dudley, 133–34
Ferdinand of Styria, 47
Ferguson, Sinclair B., 277n29
Fifth Lateran Council (1513), 369
final judgment, 372–83, 391–92
First Helvetic Confession (1536), 67,
68, 71
first use of the law. See law, civil use
of
Fisher, Edward, 125, 241, 403–4
on law as covenant and rule,
273–74
on moral law, 144, 146, 147
threefold covenant view, 150
Forbes, John, 387
Ford, Alan, 409–10
foreknowledge, 112–15
Form of Government, 54
Formula Consensus Helvetica, 158,
203
Formula of Concord, 274n20,
330nn94–95, 405
Forty-Two Articles (1552), 36,
369–70, 385, 391
fourth commandment, 283–96
Foxe, John, 37, 43
France, 40, 60
Francis, Robert, 222
Fraser, Antonia, 410
free choice, 110–11

freedom of the will, 110–11, 396
French Confession, 68, 177, 322–23

Gaffin, Richard B., Jr., 259n74
Gataker, Thomas, 46, 354, 404
on justification, 210, 211–13
on satisfaction of Christ, 196–97
Gatiss, Lee, 410
Geddes, Jenny, 50
general equity, 278–83
general kingdom, 307–9
Geneva Bible, 37, 159
Geneva Catechism (1541), 62
Genevan Psalter, 357
Gerhard, Johann, 58, 87–88, 309,
332
Germany, 60
Gillespie, George, 28, 197, 199, 201,
404
on baptism, 323
on church and civil magistrate, 303
on eternal generation, 178–79
on good and necessary consequence, 87–89
on holy days, 348, 349
on natural law, 349–50
on two kingdoms, 304–11
on worship, 340–46
God
attributes of, 99–101
condescension of, 138–39, 140
freedom of, 99, 101, 110
hidden and revealed will of, 100
necessary and free knowledge, 100
not author of sin, 108–9
sovereignty of, 95, 110, 396
twofold love of, 199–200
"Godded with God," 253
"God of God," 173–74
golden chain of salvation, 239,
245–58, 266
Gomarus, Franciscus, 248, 307
good and necessary consequence,
86–90, 93
Goodman, Godfrey, 46
Goodwin, Thomas, 62, 142n67, 224,
282, 405

imputation of active obedience of
Christ (IAOC), 210–17, 224, 226,
237, 396
opponents of, 210–13
proponents of, 213–16
imputed righteousness, 215, 218,
243
Independents, 351
"independent supremacy" of the
church, 311
infant baptism, 129, 320
infidels, protected by civil magistrate, 294n90
infralapsarians, 116
infused habit, 257, 259, 262, 264,
396
infused righteousness, 218
Innocent I, Pope, 366
instrument
baptism as, 317
faith as, 219–20, 223
intercession, 202
Irenaeus, 128, 388
Irish Articles (1615), 60, 174, 177,
221–22, 317, 408
on baptism, 318
on contingency, 104
on Scripture, 67, 68
Islam, 364–65

James I, King of England, 38, 44,
48–49, 285, 364
Javius, Petrus Cabel, 311
Jerome, 91, 128, 137
Jesus Christ
active obedience. See imputation
of active obedience of Christ
deity of, 170–84, 307, 309, 310
as head of the church, 314
intercession of, 202
person of, 170–84
as public person, 214
reign of, 386
return of, 363–68, 389
satisfaction and obedience of, 204
as scope of Scripture, 71–72
as second Adam, 155, 167

as substance of covenant, 154, 159
as surety of covenant, 160, 167,
185, 204
threefold office of, 169–70, 185–87
work of, 185–87
Jewel, John, 37, 62
Jonas, Justus, 365
Josephus, 59
judicial law, 277, 278–83, 296
Jue, Jeffrey, 411
Junius, Francis, 59, 142n67
on archetypal-ectypal distinction,
81–82
on infra- and supralapsarianism,
117
on natural law, 345
justice, marks covenant of works,
139
justification, 207–29
and adoption, 234–37
and baptism, 317
and Christian liberty, 268–69
and Christian life, 273, 274
and covenant of works, 167
from eternity, 229–33, 237
and final judgment, 372–83
as lifelong process, 371
and sanctification, 255–58, 262
as transient act of God, 231–32

Karraim, 355
Kellett, Edward, 263
Kimchi, David, 92
kingdom of Christ, visible church as,
312, 334
King James Bible, 159
Knox, John, 36, 340–41

Lactantius, 128
Lambert, François, 365
Lambeth Articles (1595), 116
Lapide, Cornelius à, 128, 187
Laren, David van, 386
Lasco, Johannes à, 35, 185
Latimer, Hugh, 36
Laud, William, 26, 49, 50, 52, 244,
338, 366

politics, and religion, 37–39, 63
Poole, Matthew, 360
pope, as antichrist, 36, 63, 363–67,
    391
Pope, James, 149–50
positive reprobation, 121
Post-Reformation Digital Library,
    396, 399
potentia absoluta, 100
potentia ordinata, 100
prayer, 353
preaching, 354
precept vs. counsel, 271
predestination, 95, 111–16, 198
    to faith, 198
    as immanent act of God, 231
    object of, 116–19
    to salvation, 198
premillennialism, 384–91
Preston, John, 61, 125, 143–44
preterition, 120–22
primary sources, 396
Primrose, Gilbert, 328
prohibition of eating meat, 346–48
Prosper of Aquitaine, 120, 193
Protestant Union, 47
providence, 106, 114
psalmody, 357–61
public fasting, 357
punishment, vs. satisfaction, 188
purgatory, 370–71, 391

quadriga, 85–86
Quakers, 55, 90, 358

Racovian Catechism, 80–81, 171–72,
    223, 406–7
Rainolds, John, 59, 332
Ramus, Peter, 323
rationalism, 68–69, 78, 81
Rayner, William, 210
"readers of the law," 356
recreation, 285–86, 296
Rees, Thomas, 406–7
Reformation
    formal cause of, 65
    as *reform* movement, 95

and teaching of early church, 169
reformed Catholicity, 29, 395
regeneration, 257, 258–59, 264
regulative principle of worship,
    335–36, 361–62
Reid, James, 412
religion and politics, 63
remission, 212
Remonstrant Confession (1621), 313
Remonstrants, 170, 190, 191, 192–
    93, 195, 204, 205, 218, 220, 312
Rennecher, Herman, 207, 246
reprobate, 119–22
republication, of covenant of works,
    126, 151, 167
resurrection, 380–81, 391
revelation, 69–75
Reymond, Robert, 172–73, 174
Reynolds, Edward, 259n75
Ribera, Francisco, 379
Ridley, Nicholas, 36
Rijssen, Andreas, 142n67
Rijssen, Leonard, 248
Rivet, Andre, 323, 361
Roberts, Francis, 232
    on ceremonial law, 278
    on justification, 231
    on twofold justification, 373
Rogers, Ezekiel, 66
Rogers, Thomas, 283
Rohls, Jan, 97
Rollock, Robert, 125
    on covenant, 166
    on golden chain of salvation,
        247–48
    on holy days, 348, 349
    on sanctification, 257
    twofold covenant scheme, 135–36
    on twofold justification, 372
Rolston, Holmes, 125–26, 127
Roman Catholic Church, 209
    on church authority, 65, 270
    on church creating the Word,
        73–74
    on church interpreting Scripture,
        83
    on doctrine and tradition, 90

Scripture Index

Acts

2:23	102
2:42	342n25
3:25	160
4:28	102, 109
7:8	160
10:33	342n25
10:35	374, 375n42
10:47	319
13	355
13:33–34	88
13:38	146
13:38–39	212
15:21	342n25
16:25	359
16:31	147
17:16–17	342n25
17:26	117n65
17:31	378
19:3	324
19:4	324
26:18	257

Romans

1:17	143n69
1:19	346, 346n36
1:19–20	69n19, 70n21
1:32	69n19
2	374n39
2:1	69n19
2:14	144, 145n75
2:14–15	69n19, 145, 145n75, 153, 288
2:15	280, 289n78, 378
2:16	377
3:20	146
3:21–22	163
3:27	146
3:28	146
4	211
4:3	219
4:5	219
4:6	373n36
4:22–24	219
5	215
5:1	222n47
5:8	200

5:12	145, 211n17
5:12–20	142, 143, 143n68
5:17	134n35
5:18	196
5:19	145, 210, 210n14, 228
6:1	241
7:7	241
8:1	255, 269
8:15	235
8:27	236
8:28	269
8:29	252, 253
8:29–30	245, 247, 253
8:30	135n40, 246, 247, 248, 253, 256, 257
9	132
9:5	309
9:21	117n65
10:5	126, 133n34, 134, 142, 142n67, 145, 146, 147, 153, 225n56
10:10	222n47
10:17	253n50
11:27	160
13:8	145n75
14:10	377
14:12	377
14:17	347

1 Corinthians

1:30	215, 261
2:6	67
5	342n25
6:3	377
6:9	310
6:11	257
6:17	253
7:5	342n25
9:7–15	342n25
10:25	347
11:21–30	342n25
11:24	333
11:25	159, 333n104
12	253–54
12:13	254

Index of the Westminster Standards